POWER MOVES BIBLE

365 Days of Discipline, Healing, Wealth & Identity Transformation.

By ***Sashette McPherson***

Rebuild Your Identity. Redefine Your Wealth.

A transformational daily guide created to help ambitious individuals strengthen their mindset, emotional discipline, confidence, financial habits, and future through intentional daily reflection and growth.

Powered by **Power Moves Global**

COPYRIGHT PAGE

Power Moves Bible: 365 Days of Discipline, Healing, Wealth & Identity Transformation

This publication is intended for educational, informational, motivational, and inspirational purposes only. It is not intended to provide financial, legal, tax, medical, psychological, or mental health advice. Readers should consult qualified professionals regarding their individual circumstances.

First Edition
ISBN (Hardback): 979-8-9968495-0-5
Published by **Power Moves Global LLC**
Website: www.powermovesglobal.com
Instagram: @powermovesglobal
Instagram: @therealsashette
Printed in the United States of America.

DEDICATION

To every person who ever felt emotionally exhausted while trying to build a better future.

To the dreamers rebuilding quietly behind the scenes.

To the disciplined people nobody clapped for yet.

To the individuals carrying invisible emotional battles while still showing up every day.

This book is for the people who refused to permanently surrender to pain, fear, failure, or survival mode.

May these words remind you that healing and ambition can exist together.

May you rebuild your identity intentionally.

May you protect your peace fiercely.

May you create wealth with wisdom.

May you become disciplined enough to sustain the life you are praying for.

And may you never forget:

Success is not a destination.

It is a disciplined identity practiced consistently.

— Sashette McPherson

INTRODUCTION

Eventually, every ambitious person reaches a moment where motivation stops being enough.

A moment where you realize that success is not simply about:

- money,
- status,
- achievement or external appearance.

It is about identity.

Because behind many financial struggles are deeper emotional battles that people rarely talk about openly.

Fear.

Self-doubt.

Inconsistency.

Emotional exhaustion.

Survival mode.

Generational habits.

Unhealed pain.

Scarcity thinking.

And invisible internal battles that quietly shape the way people:

- think,
- spend,
- build,
- love,
- lead, and ultimately live.

That realization became the foundation of Power Moves.

I created this book because I believe many people do not simply have financial problems.

They have a financial identity problem.

The way people see themselves affects the way they:

- manage money,
- respond to pressure,
- handle discipline,
- pursue opportunities,
- recover from failure,
- and build their future.

You cannot continuously think from survival mode while expecting to peacefully build abundance.

You cannot repeatedly operate from fear, chaos, and emotional instability while expecting long-term peace, wealth, and fulfillment.

Eventually, something deeper must change.

Identity.

Because success is not sustained by motivation alone.

It is sustained by:

- emotional discipline,

- self-awareness,
- consistency,
- healing,
- intentional thinking, and the ability to become someone capable of sustaining the life you desire.

This is why Power Moves Bible was created.

Not as another motivational book filled with temporary inspiration.

But as a daily transformational system designed to help you:

- rebuild your mindset,
- strengthen your discipline,
- heal emotionally,
- improve your financial thinking,
- develop consistency,
- protect your peace,
- and intentionally reconstruct the identity shaping your future.

This book exists at the intersection of:

- discipline,
- emotional healing,
- wealth consciousness,
- behavioral transformation,
- resilience,
- self-awareness,
- and intentional living.

Every page was written to challenge you to think deeper.

To reflect honestly.

To recognize patterns that may be silently limiting your growth emotionally, financially, and mentally.

Some days will encourage you.

Some days will confront you.

Some days will force you to examine the habits, fears, and emotional patterns you have spent years avoiding.

But every page was written with one purpose:

To help you become stronger internally so you can build differently externally.

Because real transformation is not built through temporary motivation.

It is built through repeated intentional choices practiced consistently over time.

One disciplined decision.

One healed response.

One courageous action.

One intentional habit at a time.

This book is not about perfection.

It is about reconstruction.

It is about becoming someone who:

- thinks intentionally,

• heals intentionally,

• spends intentionally,

• protects their peace intentionally,

• and builds their future intentionally.

Because your future changes when your identity changes.

And if you continue choosing:

• discipline over excuses,

• healing over self-destruction,

• peace over chaos,

• and growth over fear, your life may eventually become greater than anything your current limitations once convinced you was possible.

This book was designed to be used daily.

Not rushed.

Not skimmed.

Not consumed only during moments of motivation.

But revisited repeatedly during:

• difficult seasons,

• rebuilding seasons,

• healing seasons,

• disciplined seasons,

• and transformational seasons.

Some days you may read one page and immediately feel understood.

Other days, you may return to certain sections repeatedly because they speak directly to the season of life you are currently navigating.

That is intentional.

The Power Moves Bible was created to become:

• a daily reset,

• a discipline guide,

• an emotional mirror,

• a mindset rebuilder,

• and a reminder that your current circumstances do not have to become your permanent identity.

You are allowed to rebuild.

You are allowed to evolve.

You are allowed to heal.

You are allowed to become someone stronger than your fear, past, and survival patterns.

And every day you choose intentional growth; you are already changing your future.

Welcome to Power Moves Bible.

Let the rebuilding begin.

— Sashette McPherson

HOW TO USE THIS BOOK

The Power Moves Bible was intentionally designed to become part of your daily life.

This is not a book meant to be rushed through in one sitting.

It is a daily discipline and identity transformation experience.

Each day includes:

POWER QUOTE

A core statement designed to shift your mindset and perspective.

REFLECTION

A deeper message created to help you emotionally process, reflect, and strengthen your thinking and self-awareness.

WEALTH LESSON

A practical insight connecting emotional behavior, discipline, and long-term success.

AFFIRMATION

A daily declaration to help reinforce healthier beliefs, confidence, and intentional identity development.

TODAY'S POWER MOVE

A simple intentional action step designed to help you apply the lesson to your real life.

Recommended Ways To Use This Book

Morning Routine

Start your day by reading one entry every morning before social media or distractions.

Journaling Practice

Write down:

- thoughts,
- emotional reactions,
- goals,
- and reflections after each reading.

Emotional Reset

Use the Emotional Navigation Index whenever you feel:

- discouraged,
- fearful,
- emotionally exhausted,
- financially stressed,
- unmotivated or mentally overwhelmed.

Personal Growth Tool

Revisit specific days repeatedly during difficult seasons or periods where you need emotional clarity and discipline.

Family & Group Discussions

Use selected days for:

- discussions,
- coaching sessions,

- accountability groups,
- or personal development conversations.

This book is not about reading perfectly.

It is about practicing intentional growth consistently.

One healthy thought.

One disciplined decision.

One healed response at a time.

AUTHOR NOTE

To everyone reading this,

Thank you for trusting these words enough to allow them into your daily life.

Power Moves Bible was created during a vision much bigger than motivation alone.

I wanted to create something people could return to repeatedly during:

- difficult seasons,
- rebuilding seasons,
- healing seasons,
- and growth seasons.

Something that reminded people that success is not only external.

It is emotional.

Mental.

Behavioral.

Spiritual.

Financial.

This book is about becoming someone strong enough internally to sustain the life you desire externally.

I hope these pages help you:

- think differently,
- heal intentionally,
- discipline yourself consistently,
- and build your future with wisdom and peace.

Most importantly, I hope this book reminds you that your current circumstances do not have to become your permanent identity.

You are allowed to evolve.

You are allowed to rebuild.

You are allowed to heal.

You are allowed to become greater than your fears, past, and limitations.

Keep building.

Keep healing.

Keep making power moves.

— Sashette McPherson

TABLE OF CONTENTS

BOOK STRUCTURE FOR ALL 365 DAYS

PHASE 1 — RECONSTRUCTION (Days 1–90)

Themes:

Identity

Healing

Discipline

Awareness

Self-control

Breaking old cycles

PHASE 2 — EXECUTION (Days 91–180)

Themes:

Consistency

Wealth habits

Confidence

Financial discipline

Emotional control

Productivity

PHASE 3 — EXPANSION (Days 181–270)

Themes:

Leadership

Entrepreneurship

Building legacy

Investing

Ownership

Vision

PHASE 4 — POWER (Days 271–365)

Themes:

Mastery

Influence

Freedom

Purpose

Legacy

Transformation

EMOTIONAL NAVIGATION INDEX

What Is the Emotional Navigation Index?

The Emotional Navigation Index was intentionally created to help you navigate this book based on your current emotional state, mindset, or life season.

Instead of reading randomly, you can use this section as a guide whenever you feel emotionally overwhelmed, financially discouraged, unmotivated, fearful, stuck, anxious, inconsistent, heartbroken, or mentally exhausted.

Every section below was designed to connect specific emotions, struggles, behaviors, and thought patterns with the most relevant days inside this book.

This allows Power Moves Bible to become more than a motivational book.

It becomes:

• a daily emotional reset,

• a discipline guide,

• a mindset rebuilding system,

• and a transformational tool for healing, growth, peace, confidence, and wealth-building.

No matter what season of life you are currently in, there is a section designed to help guide you back toward clarity, discipline, emotional strength, and intentional living.

SECTION 1 — WHEN YOU FEEL LOST OR STUCK

Topics

Identity confusion • Feeling behind • Lack of direction • Reinvention • Starting over • Survival mode

Recommended Days

Day 9, Day 25, Day 45, Day 65, Day 88, Day 119, Day 156, Day 185, Day 214, Day 221, Day 241, Day 268, Day 304, Day 338

SECTION 2 — WHEN YOU LACK DISCIPLINE OR CONSISTENCY

Topics

Procrastination • Laziness • Weak habits • Comfort addiction • Excuses • Inconsistency • Delayed gratification

Recommended Days

Day 3, Day 8, Day 17, Day 23, Day 24, Day 37, Day 40, Day 44, Day 51, Day 63, Day 74, Day 82, Day 89, Day 101, Day 104, Day 117, Day 132, Day 144, Day 166, Day 171, Day 195, Day 222, Day 259, Day 310, Day 340, Day 348

SECTION 3 — WHEN YOU FEEL BROKE OR FINANCIALLY STRESSED

Topics

Scarcity mindset • Financial stress • Feeling behind financially • Wealth fear • Survival thinking • Financial instability

Recommended Days

Day 2, Day 7, Day 12, Day 19, Day 34, Day 41, Day 55, Day 68, Day 84, Day 93, Day 126, Day 149, Day 188, Day 205, Day 214, Day 241, Day 278, Day 283, Day 309, Day 312, Day 321, Day 342

SECTION 4 — WHEN YOU FEEL DEMOTIVATED OR EMOTIONALLY EXHAUSTED

Topics

Burnout • Emotional exhaustion • Giving up • Feeling unsupported • Feeling invisible • Hopelessness

Recommended Days

Day 5, Day 14, Day 20, Day 32, Day 46, Day 57, Day 72, Day 92, Day 97, Day 111, Day 143, Day 176, Day 198, Day 213, Day 245, Day 260, Day 285, Day 298, Day 341

SECTION 5 — WHEN YOU STRUGGLE WITH CONFIDENCE OR SELF-WORTH

Topics

Fear of judgment • Comparison • Low self-esteem • Feeling small • Imposter syndrome • Self-doubt

Recommended Days

Day 1, Day 10, Day 18, Day 27, Day 39, Day 58, Day 70, Day 85, Day 91, Day 96, Day 113, Day 134, Day 169, Day 207, Day 233, Day 243, Day 271, Day 286, Day 315, Day 328, Day 345

SECTION 6 — WHEN YOU NEED HEALING OR EMOTIONAL PEACE

Topics

Trauma • Emotional pain • Rejection • Shame • Fear • Heartbreak • Anxiety • Emotional overwhelm

Recommended Days

Day 6, Day 21, Day 36, Day 50, Day 71, Day 92, Day 110, Day 121, Day 127, Day 137, Day 173, Day 203, Day 225, Day 246, Day 255, Day 266, Day 292, Day 319, Day 344, Day 347, Day 362

SECTION 7 — WHEN YOU KEEP SELF-SABOTAGING

Topics

Avoidance • Toxic cycles • Emotional spending • Quitting early • Fear-based decisions • Self-destruction

Recommended Days

Day 15, Day 16, Day 28, Day 30, Day 43, Day 48, Day 61, Day 66, Day 77, Day 81, Day 99, Day 116, Day 118, Day 146, Day 151, Day 179, Day 191, Day 208, Day 216, Day 248, Day 261, Day 296, Day 305, Day 351

SECTION 8 — WHEN YOU NEED PURPOSE, WEALTH & POWER MOVES

Topics

Wealth building • Entrepreneurship • Ownership • Legacy • Leadership • Financial freedom • Purpose-driven success

Recommended Days

Day 4, Day 13, Day 22, Day 31, Day 49, Day 67, Day 86, Day 100, Day 125, Day 152, Day 174, Day 200, Day 216, Day 230, Day 250, Day 280, Day 287, Day 302, Day 308, Day 330, Day 356, Day 365

DAY 1

Become The Person First

POWER QUOTE

"Your future is waiting on the version of you that finally becomes disciplined."

REFLECTION

Most people are trying to change their bank account before they change their habits.

But wealth does not respond to wishful thinking. It responds to structure. To emotional maturity. To consistency.

You cannot build a millionaire life with a distracted identity.

Every successful person you admire became someone internally before they became successful externally.

The discipline you avoid today is connected to the life you keep praying for tomorrow.

Your future is not asking you to be perfect. It is asking you to become intentional.

Long-term peace and wealth are usually built by people who learned how to stay emotionally grounded during difficult seasons.

True growth begins the moment people stop avoiding themselves and start becoming intentional about who they are becoming.

Discipline becomes powerful when it continues existing even after excitement disappears.

A better future is usually created through small intentional decisions repeated consistently over time.

WEALTH LESSON

Your habits reveal your identity. If your habits are weak, your foundation will collapse under pressure. Build routines that align with the future you claim you want.

AFFIRMATION

"I am becoming the kind of person that can hold wealth, responsibility, and greatness."

TODAY'S POWER MOVE

Remove one distraction that keeps you inconsistent.

DAY 2

Scarcity Is Exhausting

POWER QUOTE

"Survival mode will keep you alive, but it will never allow you to build wealth."

REFLECTION

There are people making money every month who still feel poor emotionally.

Why? Because scarcity is not always about income. Sometimes scarcity is psychological.

Scarcity says:

Spend now.

Panic quickly.

Fear the future.

Doubt yourself.

Avoid planning.

But wealth requires emotional stability.

Long-term wealth requires patience. Structure. Vision. Clarity.

A wealthy mindset is not loud. It is calm.

Growth rarely happens inside comfort. It happens when people become honest about the habits, emotions, and decisions shaping their future.

Many individuals underestimate how deeply mindset, emotional discipline, and consistency influence the quality of their life over time.

Real transformation is not created through one powerful moment. It is created through repeated intentional choices practiced daily.

Scarcity convinces people to think only about today.

A wealthy mindset thinks beyond the present moment.

It understands that today's choices become tomorrow's reality.

Every intentional decision creates another opportunity to build stability instead of simply surviving.

That is why awareness matters so much.

The moment you recognize that scarcity is influencing your thinking, you regain the ability to choose differently.

You are no longer forced to react from fear.

You can respond with wisdom.

And over time, those wiser decisions become the foundation of lasting peace, confidence, and financial freedom.

WEALTH LESSON

Financial freedom is impossible without emotional control. Impulsive decisions destroy long-term wealth.

AFFIRMATION

"I no longer make decisions from fear, panic, or scarcity."

TODAY'S POWER MOVE

Track every dollar you spend today. Awareness creates transformation.

DAY 3

Discipline Is Self-Respect

POWER QUOTE

"Every promise you break to yourself weakens your confidence."

REFLECTION

Discipline is deeper than productivity.

It is self-respect.

Every time you make a promise to yourself and follow through, you strengthen the relationship you have with yourself. Every time you abandon your commitments, delay important responsibilities, or repeatedly choose comfort overgrowth, that relationship weakens.

Many people assume confidence comes from positive thinking. Confidence is often built through personal proof. You trust yourself when you consistently do what you said you would do.

The reason some individuals struggle to move forward is not because they lack intelligence, talent, or potential. It is because they have accumulated too many experiences of disappointing themselves. After enough broken promises, self-doubt begins to feel justified.

Discipline repairs that damage.

Each workout completed, each task finished, each boundary honored, and each responsibility handled becomes evidence that you are capable of leading your own life.

The small choices matter more than most people realize. Character is developed through ordinary moments when nobody is watching. The decision to follow through when excuses are available creates a level of self-respect that motivation alone can never provide.

When people learn to trust themselves again, they stop depending on temporary inspiration and start building a foundation that can withstand challenges, setbacks, and uncertainty.

The strongest confidence is not loud. It is the quiet certainty that comes from knowing you can rely on yourself.

WEALTH LESSON

Your future income is directly connected to your ability to stay consistent when emotions change.

AFFIRMATION

"I trust myself because I follow through."

TODAY'S POWER MOVE

Complete one task you have been procrastinating.

DAY 4

Wealth Loves Structure

POWER QUOTE

"Money flows toward people who can manage responsibility."

REFLECTION

A lot of people say they want financial freedom, but very few people want the habits that create it.

They want the outcome without the process.

They want peace without planning. They want wealth without tracking. They want stability without responsibility.

But money tends to reveal what already exists beneath the surface.

If your life is disorganized, your finances will often become disorganized. If your decisions are reactive, your money will eventually become reactive too.

This is why structure matters.

A budget is not a restriction. It is a roadmap. A financial plan is not a punishment. It is preparation.

The individuals who build lasting wealth rarely rely on luck. They rely on systems that help them make good decisions consistently.

Structure removes unnecessary guesswork. It creates clarity. It helps people recognize where their money is going, where it is being wasted, and where it can be used more intentionally.

Many financial struggles are not caused by a lack of income. They are caused by a lack of organization.

The truth is that freedom and structure are not opposites. They work together.

The more intentional you become with your time, money, and decisions, the more control you gain over your future.

Wealth is not built by hoping things work out. It is built by creating systems that allow success to happen repeatedly.

WEALTH LESSON

Financial clarity reduces stress. Confusion creates financial leakage.

AFFIRMATION

"I create systems that support the life I want to build."

TODAY'S POWER MOVE

Create a simple weekly financial plan.

DAY 5

Keep Going Quietly

POWER QUOTE

"Not every season of growth will be applauded."

REFLECTION

Some seasons of growth will feel invisible.

You will be making sacrifices that nobody notices, having conversations nobody hears, and fighting battles nobody fully understands.

That can be frustrating because people naturally want reassurance that their efforts are producing results.

But not every meaningful change comes with immediate evidence.

A tree does not become strong because of what people see above the surface. Its strength comes from what develops underground long before anyone notices its growth.

Life often works the same way.

There will be periods when your work receives little recognition. Your goals may seem far away. Your progress may feel slower than expected.

Do not mistake a lack of recognition for a lack of progress.

The habits you are building today are strengthening your future. The discipline you practice today is preparing you for responsibilities you have not yet received.

Many people quit because they expect encouragement at every stage of the journey. But some of the most important breakthroughs happen after long periods of unseen effort.

Keep showing up.

Keep learning.

Keep improving.

One day the results will become visible, but until then, allow your commitment to be stronger than your need for validation.

The people who accomplish extraordinary things are often the ones who kept working when nobody was paying attention.

WEALTH LESSON

Long-term success requires emotional independence.

AFFIRMATION

"I stay committed to my future even when validation is absent."

TODAY'S POWER MOVE

Spend one hour working on your future without posting it online.

DAY 6

Heal Before You Build

POWER QUOTE

"Unhealed pain will make you sabotage the very life you prayed for."

REFLECTION

Some people spend years trying to fix their finances without realizing the real battle is happening beneath the surface.

Money is often used as a tool to manage emotions.

Some people shop when they feel stressed. Some avoid their bank accounts when they feel anxious. Some stay busy because slowing down would force them to face what they have been carrying for years.

The behavior looks financial, but the root is emotional.

Unresolved pain has a way of showing up in unexpected places. It can influence the relationships you choose, the opportunities you avoid, the boundaries you struggle to enforce, and the decisions you make when life becomes difficult.

That is why healing is not separate from success.

A person can learn every financial strategy in the world and still struggle if fear, shame, guilt, or self-doubt are controlling their decisions.

True healing begins when people stop judging their wounds and start understanding them.

The goal is not to become someone who never struggles. The goal is to become someone who responds to struggle in a healthier way.

When emotional burdens begin to lighten, clarity increases. Decisions become more intentional. Confidence becomes more stable. Peace becomes easier to protect.

The life you are trying to build deserves a healthier version of you.

Sometimes the most productive thing a person can do is pause long enough to heal what has been silently influencing them for years.

WEALTH LESSON

Emotional awareness is a financial skill.

AFFIRMATION

"I release the habits that were created from pain, fear, and survival mode."

TODAY'S POWER MOVE

Write down three emotional habits that affect your finances.

DAY 7

Stop Waiting To Feel Ready

POWER QUOTE

"Confidence is built through movement, not overthinking."

REFLECTION

Countless opportunities are missed because people believe they need to feel ready before they begin.

They wait for more confidence.

More knowledge.

More certainty.

A better time.

But readiness is often created through action, not before it.

Very few successful people started with complete clarity. Business owners launch before they know everything. Leaders step forward before they feel fully prepared. Investors make decisions without being able to predict every outcome.

Progress has always required a certain level of uncertainty.

The problem is that fear convinces people they need guarantees. It tells them to wait until the risk disappears, the doubts fade, and the path becomes obvious.

Life rarely works that way.

Many of the opportunities that shape a person's future require a decision before all the answers are available.

The first step is often the hardest because it forces you to trust yourself instead of your comfort zone.

Waiting may feel safer in the moment, but waiting too long can become its own form of risk.

Every year people postpone goals, conversations, businesses, investments, and dreams because they are searching for certainty that does not exist.

At some point, the question is no longer whether you are ready.

The question becomes whether you are willing.

Because courage is not the absence of fear. It is the decision to move forward while fear is still present.

The future belongs to people who are willing to begin before they feel completely prepared.

WEALTH LESSON

Overthinking delays opportunities. Execution creates momentum.

AFFIRMATION

"I move forward even when I do not feel completely ready."

TODAY'S POWER MOVE

Take one action toward a goal you have been delaying.

DAY 8

Comfort Is Expensive

POWER QUOTE

"The cost of comfort is often a life of regret."

REFLECTION

Comfort feels safe because it asks very little from you.

It allows you to postpone difficult conversations, delay important decisions, avoid healthy risks, and continue living inside familiar routines. In the moment, choosing comfort often feels easier than choosing growth.

But comfort is not always free.

Sometimes it quietly costs you opportunities you never pursued, relationships you never repaired, businesses you never started, confidence you never developed, and dreams you slowly convinced yourself to forget.

The greatest danger of comfort is that it rarely feels dangerous while you are living inside it. Days become months. Months become years. Without realizing it, people can become experts at maintaining the life they secretly wish they had outgrown.

Growth almost always asks something from you.

It asks you to become uncomfortable long enough to develop new habits. It asks you to face uncertainty, accept temporary failure, and continue learning even when progress feels slow.

Discomfort is not always a sign that something is wrong. Often, it is evidence that something is changing.

The strongest people are rarely those who avoided discomfort. They are the ones who learned how to walk through it without allowing fear to determine the direction of their lives.

Every meaningful life requires moments where courage becomes more important than convenience.

The comfort you protect today may become the limitation you regret tomorrow.

Choose the temporary discomfort that creates long-term freedom rather than the temporary comfort that creates long-term regret.

WEALTH LESSON

Every level of wealth requires a new level of discipline.

AFFIRMATION

"I embrace temporary discomfort for long-term freedom."

TODAY'S POWER MOVE

Do something difficult that your future self will thank you for.

DAY 9

Reinvent Yourself

POWER QUOTE

"You are allowed to become someone completely different from who pain created."

REFLECTION

Many people spend years carrying an outdated version of themselves.

Not because they want to, but because the familiar feels safer than change.

They continue introducing themselves through old mistakes, old limitations, old fears, and old stories that no longer reflect who they are becoming.

But growth requires honesty.

At some point, you must decide whether you are going to keep living from your history or start building from your potential.

The person you were five years ago should not be responsible for making every decision today.

You have learned.

You have experienced more.

You have survived things that once felt impossible.

Why should your identity remain frozen while your life continues moving forward?

Reinvention is not about pretending your past never happened. It is about refusing to let your past have the final say over your future.

Every season of life teaches something different. Some seasons teach resilience. Some teach wisdom. Some teach boundaries. Some teach self-respect.

The lessons are meant to shape you, not trap you.

Many people remain stuck because they are waiting for permission to change.

You do not need permission.

You are allowed to outgrow old habits.

You are allowed to change your mind.

You are allowed to pursue a different path.

You are allowed to become someone your past would not recognize.

The strongest version of yourself is not found by holding on to who you used to be.

It is discovered by having the courage to become who you were always capable of becoming.

WEALTH LESSON

New results require a new identity.

AFFIRMATION

"I give myself permission to evolve."

TODAY'S POWER MOVE

Write down the qualities of the person you are becoming.

DAY 10

You Were Never Small

POWER QUOTE

"Do not confuse your current situation with your true potential."

REFLECTION

Life has a way of making people question themselves.

Disappointment can make a capable person feel inadequate. Rejection can make a talented person feel invisible.

Failure can make a strong person forget their strength.

Over time, difficult experiences can create a false narrative that says you are less capable, less valuable, or less important than you truly are.

But hardship is not a measurement of your worth.

Just because life has challenged you does not mean you were created for struggle alone.

Some of the most successful, impactful, and influential people once experienced seasons where they felt uncertain, overlooked, and discouraged. The difference is that they refused to allow those seasons to define them permanently.

Your current situation is a chapter, not the entire story.

The mistakes you made are not your identity.

The setbacks you experienced are not your identity.

The opinions others formed about you are not your identity.

There is often a gap between where a person is and who they are capable of becoming.

Do not confuse the gap with a limitation.

Inside every person is potential that has not yet been fully developed, confidence that has not yet been fully expressed, and opportunities that have not yet been fully discovered.

The goal is not to become someone else.

The goal is to stop doubting the greatness that already exists within you.

You were never created to spend your life shrinking, settling, or questioning your value.

You were created to grow into everything you are capable of becoming.

WEALTH LESSON

Confidence affects opportunities. People invest in certainty.

AFFIRMATION

"I stop shrinking myself to fit environments that were never meant for my growth."

TODAY'S POWER MOVE

Speak about yourself with confidence today.

DAY 11

Small Habits Create Big Futures

POWER QUOTE

"Your future is hidden inside your daily routines."

REFLECTION

People often wait for a major breakthrough to change their lives.

They imagine success arriving through one opportunity, one connection, one decision, or one lucky moment.

But most meaningful progress happens much differently.

It is usually built through small actions repeated over long periods of time.

A person becomes financially stable by making hundreds of responsible decisions. A healthy body is created through countless workouts, meals, and choices. A successful career is often the result of years of learning, improving, and showing up consistently.

The challenge is that small actions rarely feel significant in the moment.

Saving ten dollars may not feel life-changing.

Reading ten pages may not feel life-changing.

Waking up thirty minutes earlier may not feel life-changing.

But the accumulation of those actions creates results that eventually become impossible to ignore.

Many people abandon good habits because they focus only on immediate outcomes. They fail to recognize that every positive action is a deposit into their future.

The same principle works in reverse.

Small acts of procrastination, neglect, and avoidance may seem harmless today, but repeated often enough, they create consequences that are difficult to escape.

Life is constantly responding to what we repeatedly practice.

The future is not determined by what you do once.

It is influenced by what you choose to do consistently.

Never underestimate the power of a small habit maintained long enough to become part of who you are.

WEALTH LESSON

Compound discipline creates compound results.

AFFIRMATION

"I respect the power of small consistent actions."

TODAY'S POWER MOVE

Improve one daily habit by one percent today.

DAY 12

Wealth Begins In The Mind

POWER QUOTE

"You cannot maintain wealth with a survival mindset."

REFLECTION

Money does not simply reveal what you have.

It often reveals how you think.

Two people can earn the same income and experience completely different financial outcomes because their relationship with money is different.

One person approaches money with patience, planning, and confidence.

The other approaches money with fear.

Fear rushes decisions.

Fear reacts emotionally.

Fear focuses on immediate relief instead of long-term stability.

When people are afraid, they often spend to feel better, avoid difficult financial conversations, ignore important responsibilities, or make decisions based on panic instead of strategy.

The challenge is that fear rarely announces itself openly.

Sometimes it disguises itself as urgency.

Sometimes it appears as avoidance.

Sometimes it sounds like, "I'll deal with it later."

But financial growth requires a different mindset.

It requires the ability to pause before reacting.

To think before spending.

To plan before deciding.

The goal is not to become obsessed with money.

The goal is to become emotionally steady enough that money no longer controls your thoughts, decisions, or sense of security.

Financial wisdom grows when emotional stability becomes stronger than emotional urgency.

The more peacefully you think about money, the more intentionally you begin using it.

Wise financial decisions rarely happen by accident.

They are the result of a mind that has learned to pause, plan, and think beyond today's emotions.

Long before wealth appears in a bank account, it begins developing in the mindset that consistently chooses wisdom over fear.

WEALTH LESSON

Financial maturity matters more than temporary income spikes.

AFFIRMATION

"I think long-term, move strategically, and protect my future."

TODAY'S POWER MOVE

Review your financial goals for the next 12 months.

DAY 13

Build Something Bigger Than You

POWER QUOTE

"Wealth becomes more meaningful when it creates impact beyond yourself."

REFLECTION

Many people spend years chasing success without ever asking themselves why they want it.

They pursue more money, more recognition, and more achievements, hoping those things will finally make them feel fulfilled.

Sometimes they do.

Often, they discover that accomplishment without purpose still leaves something missing.

Money is a powerful tool, but it becomes far more meaningful when it is connected to something larger than personal gain.

True wealth creates opportunities not only for yourself, but for the people around you.

It allows you to help others.

To create jobs.

To support causes you believe in.

To provide security for your family.

To leave something valuable behind long after you are gone.

The most impactful people understand that success is not only measured by what they accumulate.

It is also measured by what they contribute.

Every person has the ability to influence lives in some way.

For some, it will be through leadership.

For others, it will be through service, mentorship, generosity, innovation, or creating opportunities for future generations.

The question is not whether you will leave a legacy.

The question is what kind of legacy you will leave.

Will people remember what you owned, or will they remember how you helped them?

Will your success stop with you, or will it continue creating value long after your journey is complete?

A life driven by purpose creates a different kind of motivation.

Because when your vision becomes bigger than yourself, your commitment becomes stronger than temporary obstacles.

Build a future that benefits more than just you.

That is where lasting impact begins.

WEALTH LESSON

Legacy thinking changes spending behavior.

AFFIRMATION

"I build with purpose, intention, and vision."

TODAY'S POWER MOVE

Write down what kind of legacy you want to leave behind.

DAY 14

Your Pace Is Still Progress

POWER QUOTE

"Slow progress is still progress."

REFLECTION

One of the fastest ways to lose joy is to spend your life measuring it against someone else's.

Comparison has a way of making people overlook how far they have come.

Instead of recognizing their own progress, they become consumed with what someone else achieved, purchased, accomplished, or experienced.

What they often forget is that every person's journey is different.

Some people find success early.

Some people discover their purpose later.

Some people need extra time to heal, learn, recover, and grow before they are ready for the next chapter of their lives.

There is nothing wrong with that.

Life is not a race with a universal finish line.

The pressure to constantly keep up with others causes many people to make decisions that are not aligned with their values, goals, or circumstances.

They rush relationships.

They rush careers.

They rush financial decisions.

They rush personal growth.

And in the process, they lose sight of what truly matters.

Your path was never meant to look exactly like anyone else's.

The lessons you need to learn, the challenges you need to overcome, and the experiences shaping your character are uniquely yours.

Progress is still progress, even when it feels slower than expected.

A step forward still counts.

A lesson learned still matters.

A difficult season survived is still evidence of growth.

Do not allow someone else's timeline to make you question your own.

The goal is not to arrive first.

The goal is to become the person you were created to be while making the journey.

Trust your pace.

Your story is unfolding exactly one chapter at a time.

WEALTH LESSON

Rushed decisions often create financial mistakes.

AFFIRMATION

"I trust my process and remain committed to growth."

TODAY'S POWER MOVE

Celebrate one area where you have improved.

DAY 15

Stop Betraying Yourself

POWER QUOTE

"Self-sabotage is often a lack of self-worth disguised as behavior."

REFLECTION

One of the most painful realities about self-sabotage is that it often happens without people realizing it.

They tell themselves they want success.

They want the healthier relationship.

The better finances.

The business.

The opportunity.

The peace.

Yet when those things begin moving closer, they hesitate.

They delay important decisions.

They avoid responsibilities.

They overthink simple actions.

They find reasons to quit when progress starts becoming real.

From the outside, it looks confusing.

But underneath the behavior is often a deeper belief:

"What if I am not ready?"

"What if I fail?"

"What if I lose it?"

"What if I do not deserve it?"

Many acts of self-sabotage begin long before the behavior appears.

They begin with quiet beliefs such as:

"I'm not enough."

"I always mess things up."

"People like me never succeed."

When those beliefs remain unchallenged, they quietly influence everyday decisions. People procrastinate, settle for less than they deserve, or abandon opportunities—not because they lack ability, but because they struggle to imagine themselves succeeding.

Lasting change begins when you stop arguing against your own potential and start allowing your actions to agree with the future you are trying to build.

You cannot spend years praying for opportunities while simultaneously convincing yourself you are unworthy of them.

At some point, you must stop fighting against your own future.

You must stop talking yourself out of possibilities.

You must stop shrinking your goals to match your fears.

The person standing between you and your next level may not be another individual.

It may simply be the version of yourself that is still learning to believe you deserve more.

The moment you begin supporting your own growth instead of resisting it, everything starts to change.

WEALTH LESSON

Your subconscious beliefs influence your financial behavior.

AFFIRMATION

"I stop sabotaging the future I prayed for."

TODAY'S POWER MOVE

Identify one behavior that repeatedly delays your progress.

DAY 16

Visibility Requires Courage

POWER QUOTE

"Your fear of being seen may be blocking your next level."

REFLECTION

There are countless people living far below their potential, not because they lack ability, but because they are afraid of being seen.

They fear criticism.

They fear rejection.

They fear making mistakes in public.

They fear what others might think if they pursue something bigger.

So they stay quiet.

They postpone opportunities.

They keep their ideas to themselves.

They wait for perfect confidence before taking action.

The problem is that confidence rarely arrives before action.

It usually develops because of action.

Every successful leader, entrepreneur, creator, and innovator had moments where they felt uncertain. The difference is that they chose to move forward despite those feelings.

Visibility requires vulnerability.

The moment you decide to share your voice, your work, your goals, or your vision, you accept that not everyone will understand or support you.

That is part of the process.

Trying to avoid all criticism often results in something far worse: a life filled with unrealized potential.

The world cannot benefit from gifts that remain hidden.

Your ideas cannot create impact if they are never shared.

Your talents cannot open doors if they are never displayed.

Your purpose cannot reach people if you constantly keep it behind fear.

You were not created to spend your life hiding from opportunities that were meant for you.

You were created to contribute, lead, build, and grow.

The people who make the greatest impact are not always the most fearless.

They are often the people who decided that their purpose was more important than their fear.

Do not allow fear of being seen to prevent the world from experiencing what you have to offer.

WEALTH LESSON

Opportunities increase when people can see your value.

AFFIRMATION

"I allow myself to be visible, confident, and impactful."

TODAY'S POWER MOVE

Post, speak, or share something that reflects your purpose.

DAY 17

Discipline Outlasts Motivation

POWER QUOTE

"Motivation changes daily. Discipline stays."

REFLECTION

Motivation feels powerful, but it is unreliable.

Some days you will feel energized, focused, and excited about your goals.

Other days you will feel tired, discouraged, distracted, or uninspired.

If your progress depends entirely on how you feel, your results will always be inconsistent.

That is why discipline matters.

Discipline is not about feeling motivated every day.

It is about honoring your commitments even when motivation is absent.

Anyone can pursue a goal when they feel inspired. The true test comes when the excitement fades and the work still needs to be done.

The people who create meaningful results understand that emotions change constantly. Some mornings they feel confident. Other mornings they feel uncertain.

Yet they continue moving forward.

They continue saving.

They continue learning.

They continue exercising.

They continue building.

Not because they always want to, but because they understand that long-term success is built through commitment rather than emotion.

Feelings are temporary.

Purpose lasts longer.

The ability to follow through during difficult days often separates those who achieve their goals from those who repeatedly start over.

There will always be reasons to quit, delay, or make excuses.

There will also always be reasons to keep going.

The future you are building deserves more than occasional effort.

It deserves consistency.

The strongest habits are not created when everything feels easy.

They are created when you choose to continue despite resistance.

That is where discipline becomes transformational.

AFFIRMATION

"I remain consistent regardless of my emotions."

TODAY'S POWER MOVE

Complete your responsibilities before entertainment today.

DAY 18

You Belong In Bigger Rooms

POWER QUOTE

"Do not let insecurity make you abandon your potential."

REFLECTION

Many capable people spend years playing smaller than they need to.

They stay quiet when they have something valuable to contribute.

They second-guess their ideas.

They downplay their achievements.

They hesitate to pursue opportunities because they assume someone else is more qualified.

The truth is that talent alone is rarely enough.

People must also believe they belong in the rooms they enter.

Confidence is not arrogance.

Arrogance believes it has nothing left to learn.

Confidence understands its value while remaining open to growth.

Too many individuals spend their lives waiting for permission to believe in themselves.

They wait for recognition.

They wait for validation.

They wait for someone else to confirm what they are capable of.

But self-belief cannot be outsourced.

At some point, you must decide that your voice matters.

You must decide that your experiences, ideas, skills, and perspective deserve to be expressed.

The world is filled with opportunities lost because talented people convinced themselves they were not ready.

Meanwhile, less qualified people stepped forward simply because they were willing to try.

Do not allow self-doubt to become the reason you remain invisible.

You do not need to know everything before you contribute.

You do not need to be perfect before you begin.

You do not need universal approval before you pursue your goals.

The next level of your life may require you to stop shrinking and start showing up fully.

Walk into the room.

Speak with confidence.

Share your ideas.

Own your value.

Your gifts cannot create impact while they remain unseen.

WEALTH LESSON

Networking and visibility create opportunities.

AFFIRMATION

"I belong in spaces that challenge me to grow."

TODAY'S POWER MOVE

Introduce yourself confidently in one new environment.

DAY 19

Financial Freedom Requires Responsibility

POWER QUOTE

"Freedom without discipline becomes chaos."

REFLECTION

Almost everyone wants freedom.

Financial freedom.

Time freedom.

Emotional freedom.

The freedom to make choices without constantly feeling restricted by circumstances.

What many people fail to realize is that freedom and responsibility are deeply connected.

The life you want cannot be separated from the responsibilities required to maintain it.

A person who cannot manage their money will struggle to create financial freedom.

A person who cannot manage their emotions will struggle to maintain healthy relationships.

A person who cannot manage their time will often find themselves overwhelmed, distracted, and frustrated.

Responsibility is not a burden.

It is preparation.

Every responsibility you learn to handle increases your capacity for greater opportunities.

The problem is that many people want the rewards without developing the habits necessary to sustain them.

They want success without discipline.

Freedom without accountability.

Results without ownership.

But life rarely works that way.

The ability to manage yourself is one of the most valuable skills you can develop.

When you learn to manage your finances, you gain options.

When you learn to manage your emotions, you gain stability.

When you learn to manage your time, you gain control.

These small forms of stewardship eventually create larger forms of freedom.

The most empowered people are not those with the fewest responsibilities.

They are often the people who learned how to handle their responsibilities well.

Freedom is not found by avoiding responsibility.

Freedom is created by becoming the kind of person who can be trusted with more.

WEALTH LESSON

Budgeting creates awareness, not restriction.

AFFIRMATION

"I become more responsible with my money and decisions."

TODAY'S POWER MOVE

Review your subscriptions and unnecessary expenses.

DAY 20

Keep Building Anyway

POWER QUOTE

"Do not stop building just because the results are taking time."

REFLECTION

One of the hardest parts of growth is continuing when there is little evidence that your efforts are working.

People naturally want results.

They want proof that the sacrifices matter.

They want confirmation that the work is paying off.

They want visible signs that they are moving in the right direction.

But many of life's greatest rewards take time.

A seed does not become a tree overnight.

A business does not become successful overnight.

A strong relationship, a healthy body, a stable financial future, and a meaningful life are all built through a process that requires patience.

The challenge is that patience often feels uncomfortable.

It can feel like standing still when progress is actually happening beneath the surface.

Many people quit too soon because they mistake delayed results for failure.

They assume that because they cannot see immediate change, nothing is changing.

That assumption has ended countless dreams.

What you do consistently today may not show visible results tomorrow.

But that does not mean your efforts are being wasted.

Every lesson learned, every responsibility handled, every healthy choice made, and every commitment honored is contributing to a future that is still being developed.

Progress is not always obvious.

Sometimes growth is happening in your mindset.

Sometimes it is happening in your character.

Sometimes it is preparing you for opportunities that have not arrived yet.

Trust the process enough to keep going.

Do not allow temporary frustration to convince you to abandon long-term goals.

The people who achieve meaningful success are often those who remained committed long enough to see the results of their patience.

Keep building.

Keep believing.

Keep showing up.

Your future may be developing in ways you cannot see yet.

WEALTH LESSON

Long-term thinking separates builders from dreamers.

AFFIRMATION

"I stay committed even when progress feels slow."

TODAY'S POWER MOVE

Spend one focused hour investing into your future.

DAY 21

Pain Is Not The End

POWER QUOTE

"Some of the strongest people were rebuilt by the very pain that almost destroyed them."

REFLECTION

Pain has the power to change people.

The question is whether it will make them smaller or stronger.

Every person eventually experiences moments that challenge who they are. A loss. A disappointment. A betrayal. A setback they never expected.

Those experiences often create a crossroads.

One path leads to bitterness, fear, and resignation.

The other leads to growth, wisdom, and resilience.

The difference is not the pain itself.

The difference is what a person chooses to do with it.

Many people unknowingly allow difficult experiences to become part of their identity. They begin defining themselves by what happened to them instead of who they are.

A failed business becomes proof they are incapable.

A broken relationship becomes proof they are unlovable.

A financial struggle becomes proof they will always be behind.

But pain was never meant to become a permanent label.

It was meant to teach, reveal, strengthen, and refine.

Some of life's greatest lessons are learned during seasons we would never voluntarily choose.

Those seasons reveal courage we did not know we possessed. They expose weaknesses that need attention. They develop patience, perspective, and strength that comfort could never create.

Healing does not mean pretending the pain never happened.

It means refusing to allow the pain to control the rest of your story.

You are more than what hurt you.

You are more than what you lost.

You are more than the difficult season you survived.

The strongest people are often not those who avoided hardship.

They are the ones who faced it, learned from it, and continued moving forward anyway.

Let your pain become part of your growth, not part of your identity.

WEALTH LESSON

Emotionally resilient people recover faster financially because they do not allow temporary setbacks to permanently define their future.

AFFIRMATION

"I refuse to let pain define the rest of my life. I allow it to refine me instead."

TODAY'S POWER MOVE

Write down one painful experience that taught you strength, wisdom, or resilience.

DAY 22

Think Bigger

POWER QUOTE

"Your current environment should not limit your future vision."

REFLECTION

Many of the limits people live with were never intentionally chosen.

They were inherited.

Inherited from environments where survival was the primary focus.

Inherited from conversations that emphasized what could go wrong instead of what was possible.

Inherited from generations that did the best they could with the information, resources, and opportunities they had available.

Over time, those limitations can begin to feel normal.

People stop dreaming bigger because nobody around them ever did.

They stop pursuing ambitious goals because they have never seen someone like themselves accomplish them.

Eventually, they begin treating possibility as if it belongs to other people.

But every breakthrough in history began with someone refusing to accept the limits placed on them.

Someone became the first entrepreneur in their family.

Someone became the first homeowner.

Someone became the first college graduate.

Someone became the first investor.

Someone became the first person to create a different future.

Why not you?

Your background may explain where you started, but it does not determine where you finish.

The environment around you influences your thinking, but it does not have to control it.

Sometimes growth requires expanding your vision before your circumstances expand.

You must learn to see opportunities before they become visible.

You must learn to believe in possibilities before they become reality.

Do not allow familiar surroundings to convince you that a bigger life is unavailable to you.

There is more available than what you have seen.

There is more possible than what you have experienced.

The future belongs to people who are willing to think beyond the limitations they inherited and build a reality their past could never have imagined.

WEALTH LESSON

Expanded thinking creates expanded behavior. People who think long-term make different decisions than people trapped in survival mode.

AFFIRMATION

"I allow myself to envision a greater future without guilt, fear, or limitation."

TODAY'S POWER MOVE

Write down three goals that scare you because they are bigger than your current circumstances.

DAY 23

Discipline Builds Freedom

POWER QUOTE

"The things you avoid today become the struggles you face tomorrow."

REFLECTION

Many people view discipline as something restrictive.

They imagine rules, routines, schedules, and responsibilities taking away their freedom.

What they fail to realize is that the absence of discipline often creates far greater limitations.

A person who never manages their finances eventually loses financial options.

A person who never manages their health eventually loses physical freedom.

A person who never manages their time often feels overwhelmed, reactive, and constantly behind.

The short-term comfort of avoiding responsibility frequently produces long-term frustration.

Discipline works differently.

It asks for effort today so that life becomes easier tomorrow.

It requires planning before problems appear.

It requires preparation before emergencies happen.

It requires consistency before results become visible.

This is why disciplined people often appear calmer during difficult seasons.

They are not immune to challenges.

They have simply spent years building systems that help them navigate those challenges more effectively.

The goal of discipline is not perfection.

The goal is creating a life with fewer preventable problems.

Every budget creates more financial clarity.

Every healthy habit strengthens future health.

Every productive routine reduces unnecessary stress.

The small choices you make today are either increasing your future freedom or reducing it.

That is why discipline should never be viewed as punishment.

It is one of the greatest forms of self-respect.

Because every responsible decision you make today becomes a gift to the person you will become tomorrow.

WEALTH LESSON

Financial freedom is not built through random motivation. It is built through repeated responsible decisions over long periods of time.

AFFIRMATION

"I choose discipline because I deeply value my future, my peace, and my potential."

TODAY'S POWER MOVE

Wake up one hour earlier and use that time intentionally toward your future.

DAY 24

Excuses Delay Greatness

POWER QUOTE

"Excuses feel comfortable until they become your lifestyle."

REFLECTION

Life is not always fair.

Some people begin with advantages others never receive.

Some face obstacles, setbacks, disappointments, and hardships that they did not choose.

Acknowledging those realities is important.

But there comes a point when focusing only on what happened begins to steal energy from what is still possible.

Many people remain stuck because they spend more time explaining their circumstances than improving them.

They become experts at identifying obstacles but never develop a plan for overcoming them.

The problem is not that challenges exist.

The problem is allowing those challenges to become permanent excuses.

Excuses provide temporary relief because they remove responsibility.

If someone else is always responsible for your situation, then you never have to confront the difficult work of changing it.

But relief and progress are not the same thing.

Progress begins when a person takes ownership of the parts of their life they can control.

Their attitude.

Their habits.

Their decisions.

Their effort.

Their response to adversity.

Ownership is powerful because it shifts your focus away from blame and toward action.

Instead of asking, "Who caused this?"

You begin asking, "What can I do next?"

Instead of dwelling on what cannot be changed, you focus on what can.

That mindset creates momentum.

You may not be responsible for everything that happened to you.

But you are responsible for what you choose to do moving forward.

The moment you accept responsibility for your future, you stop waiting for someone else to rescue you.

And that is often the moment real change begins.

WEALTH LESSON

Ownership creates transformation because accountability forces better decisions, stronger habits, and greater emotional maturity.

AFFIRMATION

"I stop making excuses and start making intentional adjustments that improve my future."

TODAY'S POWER MOVE

Identify one excuse that repeatedly appears in your life and replace it with one action step.

DAY 25

Start Again

POWER QUOTE

"You are never too late to rebuild your life."

REFLECTION

One of the most dangerous beliefs a person can carry is the belief that they are too late.

Too late to change.

Too late to start over.

Too late to pursue a dream.

Too late to repair the damage caused by past mistakes.

That belief has convinced countless people to abandon futures that were still possible.

The truth is that life rarely unfolds according to the timelines we create for ourselves.

Most people experience detours.

Plans fail.

Relationships end.

Careers change.

Unexpected challenges force them to begin again in ways they never anticipated.

That does not mean the opportunity is gone.

It simply means the path looks different than expected.

Many of the most inspiring success stories begin with a restart.

People have rebuilt businesses after bankruptcy.

Found purpose after years of confusion.

Returned to school later in life.

Changed careers after decades.

Found love after heartbreak.

Created extraordinary lives after seasons that once seemed hopeless.

What makes those stories powerful is not that they avoided failure.

It is that they refused to let failure become the final chapter.

Your past may contain mistakes, but it does not contain your entire future.

Regret can teach valuable lessons, but it should never become a permanent residence.

There is still time to learn.

Still time to grow.

Still time to heal.

Still time to build something meaningful.

Every day you choose to move forward becomes evidence that your story is still being written.

The question is not whether you wish things had happened differently.

The question is whether you are willing to begin again with the wisdom you have now.

Because it is never too late to become the person you were meant to be.

WEALTH LESSON

Recovery is possible when discipline returns. One intentional decision repeated consistently can completely change the direction of your life.

AFFIRMATION

"I give myself permission to begin again with wisdom, clarity, and courage."

TODAY'S POWER MOVE

Restart one goal you abandoned because of fear, discouragement, or delay.

DAY 26

Protect Your Energy

POWER QUOTE

"Your environment influences your discipline."

REFLECTION

Many people focus on changing their goals without ever examining their environment.

They want better habits.

Better results.

Better relationships.

A better future.

Yet they remain surrounded by influences that constantly pull them in the opposite direction.

Environment matters more than most people realize.

The conversations you listen to, the people you spend time with, the content you consume, and the standards you tolerate all have an impact on who you become.

Nobody remains unaffected by their surroundings.

Spend enough time around negativity, and it becomes easier to think negatively.

Spend enough time around complacency, and ambition begins to fade.

Spend enough time around chaos, and peace becomes difficult to maintain.

This is why boundaries are necessary.

Not because you believe you are better than anyone else.

But because you understand that your future deserves protection.

Every garden requires maintenance.

Healthy growth requires removing weeds that compete for resources.

Life is no different.

Some relationships inspire growth.

Others drain energy.

Some environments encourage accountability.

Others reward excuses.

Wisdom is learning the difference.

You cannot control every circumstance around you, but you can become intentional about what you repeatedly allow into your mind and life.

Protect your peace.

Protect your focus.

Protect your standards.

Protect your vision.

Because the environment you consistently tolerate will often become the environment that shapes your future.

Choose surroundings that support the person you are working to become.

WEALTH LESSON

Successful people intentionally protect their focus because attention is one of the most valuable forms of currency.

AFFIRMATION

"I protect my peace, focus, energy, and future intentionally."

TODAY'S POWER MOVE

Reduce time spent around unnecessary negativity or distractions today.

DAY 27

Confidence Is Built

POWER QUOTE

"Confidence grows every time you keep your word to yourself."

REFLECTION

Many people spend years searching for confidence without realizing where it comes from.

They believe confidence appears after success.

After recognition.

After achieving a goal.

But confidence is usually built long before those things happen.

It is created through repeated experiences of keeping your word to yourself.

Every time you follow through on a commitment, you send yourself a message:

"I can be trusted."

That message matters.

Because the relationship you have with yourself influences every area of your life.

When you consistently honor your commitments, your self-respect grows.

When you repeatedly abandon your goals, ignore your responsibilities, or make promises you never keep, doubt begins to take its place.

This is why confidence cannot be borrowed from other people.

Compliments may feel good.

Achievements may help.

But lasting confidence is built internally.

It comes from knowing that when challenges appear, you will respond.

When responsibilities arise, you will handle them.

When opportunities arrive, you will be prepared to step forward.

Confidence is not the belief that everything will go perfectly.

It is the belief that you can adapt, learn, recover, and continue moving forward even when things do not go according to plan.

The most confident people are rarely the people who never failed.

They are often the people who proved to themselves that failure would not stop them.

Trust is earned in relationships.

Self-trust is earned the same way.

One promise kept at a time.

WEALTH LESSON

Reliable people attract greater opportunities because consistency builds credibility, leadership, and trust.

AFFIRMATION

"I build confidence through action, consistency, and self-respect."

TODAY'S POWER MOVE

Finish every task you start today without abandoning it halfway through.

DAY 28

Stop Hiding Your Potential

POWER QUOTE

"Playing small will never create a powerful life."

REFLECTION

Fear has a unique way of convincing people to underestimate themselves.

It whispers that they are not ready.

Not qualified enough.

Not experienced enough.

Not talented enough.

So they hesitate.

They keep their ideas to themselves.

They avoid opportunities that could change their lives.

They watch others pursue goals they secretly desire while convincing themselves that someday they will be ready.

But someday often becomes years.

And years become regret.

The truth is that many people are not held back by a lack of ability.

They are held back by a lack of permission.

They are waiting for someone to tell them they are capable.

Someone to confirm they belong.

Someone to validate what they already know deep down.

That permission may never come.

You have to give it to yourself.

Potential grows through expression, not perfection.

The more you use your gifts, the more they develop.

Confidence is often the result of participation, not preparation.

Every conversation, opportunity, and challenge becomes part of the process that strengthens your abilities.

Your responsibility is not to wait until you feel extraordinary.

It is to faithfully use what you already have and allow growth to happen along the way.

Every time you choose visibility over hiding, action over hesitation, and belief over doubt, you expand what becomes possible.

The life you want requires your participation.

Your voice matters.

Your gifts matter.

Your ideas matter.

Stop making yourself smaller to accommodate fear.

The world needs the version of you that is willing to show up fully.

WEALTH LESSON

Visibility creates opportunities because people can only support, invest in, or believe in what they are able to see.

AFFIRMATION

"I stop shrinking myself out of fear and allow my gifts to take up space."

TODAY'S POWER MOVE

Share one idea, project, or goal publicly without overthinking it.

DAY 29

Your Habits Are Creating Your Future

POWER QUOTE

"Your life changes when your routines change."

REFLECTION

Every day, you are becoming someone.

Whether you realize it or not, your daily actions are shaping the person you will be tomorrow.

Most people focus heavily on goals.

They think about the outcome they want to achieve, the income they want to earn, the body they want to build, or the life they want to create.

Goals are important.

But habits are what determine whether those goals become reality.

A person's future is often hidden inside their routines.

The choices that seem insignificant today eventually become patterns.

Patterns become behaviors.

Behaviors become character.

And character influences the direction of an entire life.

This is why seemingly small decisions matter.

The books you read.

The conversations you entertain.

The way you spend your free time.

The standards you maintain when nobody is watching.

These choices may not appear significant in a single day, but their influence becomes powerful over months and years.

Many people want a different future while continuing to repeat the same routines that created their current reality.

Change rarely begins with a dramatic breakthrough.

It often begins with one better decision repeated consistently.

Your habits are constantly casting votes for the person you are becoming.

Every action is reinforcing an identity.

The question is whether your daily behaviors are supporting the future you desire.

The life you want is not built all at once.

It is built one choice, one routine, and one habit at a time.

WEALTH LESSON

Financial discipline is not only about large investments. It is about daily behaviors repeated long enough to create stability and growth.

AFFIRMATION

"I build routines that align with the future I desire to create."

TODAY'S POWER MOVE

Create or improve one daily routine that supports your long-term goals.

DAY 30

Stop Self-Sabotaging

POWER QUOTE

"You cannot heal in the same patterns that keep destroying you."

REFLECTION

Countless individuals believe their biggest obstacle is outside of them.

They blame circumstances.

They blame a lack of opportunity.

They blame other people.

Sometimes those factors play a role.

But often the greatest barrier to growth is hidden within the behaviors a person repeats every day.

Self-sabotage rarely announces itself clearly.

It often disguises itself as procrastination.

As perfectionism.

As avoidance.

As constantly starting over.

As making decisions that provide temporary comfort while creating long-term consequences.

The frustrating part is that many people genuinely want a better life.

They want stability.

They want success.

They want healthy relationships.

They want financial peace.

Yet their habits continue pulling them away from the very things they desire.

Why?

Because unresolved fears often create self-defeating behaviors.

People avoid opportunities because they fear failure.

They avoid commitment because they fear disappointment.

They delay action because they fear responsibility.

Without realizing it, they become trapped in cycles that repeatedly produce the same outcomes.

This is why awareness is so powerful.

You cannot change a pattern you refuse to acknowledge.

The moment you recognize a destructive cycle, you create an opportunity to interrupt it.

That awareness gives you a choice.

A choice to respond differently.

A choice to make a healthier decision.

A choice to stop repeating behaviors that no longer serve the future you want.

Real change begins when you stop asking, "Why does this keep happening?"

And start asking, "What pattern do I need to break?"

Because the cycle that created your current reality does not have to create your future.

WEALTH LESSON

Emotional patterns influence financial behavior more than most people realize. Healing unhealthy patterns improves decision-making.

AFFIRMATION

"I stop sabotaging the future I worked so hard to build."

TODAY'S POWER MOVE

Identify one repeated behavior that continuously delays your growth.

DAY 31

Wealth Requires Patience

POWER QUOTE

"Fast money often disappears quickly."

REFLECTION

Modern culture has convinced many people that success should happen quickly.

They see viral stories, overnight breakthroughs, and highlight reels that make achievement appear effortless.

What they rarely see are the years of preparation behind the scenes.

The sacrifices.

The setbacks.

The lessons learned through failure.

The countless days when progress felt almost invisible.

As a result, many people become discouraged when their journey takes longer than expected.

They compare their beginning to someone else's peak.

They assume slow progress means they are doing something wrong.

But lasting success is rarely built overnight.

The strongest foundations take time.

A healthy relationship takes time.

A meaningful career takes time.

Financial stability takes time.

Personal growth takes time.

Anything worth building usually requires patience.

The danger of chasing quick results is that it often encourages shortcuts.

People become focused on speed instead of sustainability.

They want immediate rewards without considering long-term consequences.

Yet the individuals who create lasting success understand something different.

They think in years, not days.

They value consistency over excitement.

They are willing to make small investments today that may not produce visible rewards until much later.

Patience is not passive.

It is the willingness to continue doing the right things even when immediate results are absent.

Do not allow someone else's timeline to make you question your own progress.

A slow and steady path that leads to stability is far more valuable than a rapid rise that cannot be sustained.

Success does not have to happen quickly to be meaningful.

It only needs to keep moving forward.

WEALTH LESSON

Patience protects people from impulsive decisions that destroy long-term wealth.

AFFIRMATION

"I remain patient, disciplined, and committed while building my future."

TODAY'S POWER MOVE

Review one long-term financial or personal goal and recommit yourself to it.

DAY 32

Rest But Do Not Quit

POWER QUOTE

"Exhaustion is not failure."

REFLECTION

There are seasons where life feels heavy.

Where motivation disappears. Where pressure increases. Where responsibilities become overwhelming.

And during those moments, many people begin questioning themselves.

But being tired does not mean you are weak.

It means you are human.

Rest is necessary. Healing is necessary. Recovery is necessary.

The danger is not resting. The danger is quitting completely because the process became uncomfortable.

Some breakthroughs happen right after the season where you almost gave up.

Do not abandon your future simply because you are emotionally exhausted today.

Pause if necessary. Recover if necessary. But continue moving forward.

Rest should never be confused with surrender.

Recovery gives your mind the opportunity to regain clarity, your body the chance to regain strength, and your spirit the space to regain hope.

Some of the most resilient people are not those who never became exhausted.

They are the ones who learned when to pause, recover with intention, and continue building the life they refused to give up on.

WEALTH LESSON

Burnout reduces clarity, discipline, and emotional control. Sustainable success requires intentional recovery.

AFFIRMATION

"I allow myself to rest without abandoning my future."

TODAY'S POWER MOVE

Take intentional rest today, then complete one important responsibility.

DAY 33

Focus Changes Everything

POWER QUOTE

"Distraction destroys more dreams than failure."

REFLECTION

One of the most valuable resources you possess is not money.

It is attention.

Where your attention goes, your energy follows.

Where your energy goes, results eventually appear.

That is why distraction has become one of the greatest obstacles to meaningful progress.

Modern life is filled with things competing for your focus.

Notifications.

Social media.

Entertainment.

Comparison.

Unnecessary drama.

Endless opinions.

Each one pulls a small piece of your attention away from what matters most.

Individually, these distractions may seem harmless.

Collectively, they can quietly consume years of potential.

Many people are not lacking talent.

They are lacking concentration.

They start projects but never finish them.

They create goals but rarely follow through.

They spend more time-consuming information than applying it.

As a result, they remain busy without becoming productive.

Focus changes that.

Focus allows you to direct your energy toward a single objective long enough for progress to occur.

It creates momentum.

It increases effectiveness.

It transforms effort into results.

The people who accomplish extraordinary things are not always the most gifted.

They are often the people who learned how to eliminate distractions and commit their attention to what matters most.

Your future deserves more than fragmented effort.

It deserves intentional focus.

Protect your attention.

Protect your priorities.

Protect your peace.

Because what consistently receives your focus will eventually influence the direction of your life.

WEALTH LESSON

Focused execution creates faster progress because energy is no longer being wasted on distractions.

AFFIRMATION

"I protect my attention and direct my energy toward purposeful growth."

TODAY'S POWER MOVE

Spend one full uninterrupted hour working on your future.

DAY 34

You Are Not Behind

POWER QUOTE

"Your journey is not invalid because it took longer."

REFLECTION

Comparison has a way of stealing joy from accomplishments that should be celebrated.

A person can make meaningful progress, achieve an important goal, or overcome a difficult obstacle, yet still feel dissatisfied because someone else appears to be further ahead.

That is the danger of comparison.

It shifts your attention away from your own journey and places it on someone else's.

Today, it is easier than ever to compare yourself to others.

You can open an app and instantly see promotions, engagements, vacations, new businesses, luxury purchases, and major life milestones.

What you rarely see are the struggles behind those moments.

The failures.

The sacrifices.

The doubts.

The setbacks.

The years of effort that existed before the visible success.

As a result, many people compare their behind-the-scenes reality to someone else's highlight reel.

That comparison is rarely fair.

Everyone's path unfolds differently.

Some people achieve certain goals early in life.

Others take a longer route and arrive later with greater wisdom, perspective, and maturity.

Neither path is wrong.

Life is not a competition to see who arrives first.

It is a journey of becoming the person you were created to be.

Do not measure your worth by someone else's progress.

Do not allow another person's success to make you overlook your own growth.

The fact that someone else is succeeding does not mean you are failing.

There is enough opportunity for more than one person to win.

Keep focusing on your development.

Keep honoring your process.

Keep taking the next step in front of you.

Your timeline does not need to look like anyone else's to be valuable.

Trust your journey.

Your story is still unfolding.

WEALTH LESSON

Rushed decisions often create long-term financial and emotional problems. Patience allows wiser choices.

AFFIRMATION

"I trust my timing and remain committed to my growth."

TODAY'S POWER MOVE

Celebrate one area where you have grown instead of comparing yourself to others.

DAY 35

Become Hard To Break

POWER QUOTE

"Resilience is one of the greatest forms of wealth."

REFLECTION

Life has a way of testing every person.

No one moves through life without experiencing disappointment, loss, rejection, uncertainty, or failure.

The difference is not whether challenges appear.

The difference is how people respond when they do.

Some people allow setbacks to convince them that the journey is over.

Others view setbacks as temporary obstacles rather than permanent endings.

That perspective changes everything.

Resilience is not pretending that pain does not exist.

It is acknowledging the difficulty while refusing to let it define your future.

Resilient people understand that progress is rarely a straight line.

There will be mistakes.

Unexpected delays.

Missed opportunities.

Moments when things fall apart despite your best efforts.

But those moments do not have the power to determine the rest of your story unless you allow them to.

The people who accomplish meaningful things are often not the people who avoided hardship.

They are the people who learned how to recover from it.

They learned how to stand back up after being knocked down.

How to adjust after failure.

How to continue after disappointment.

How to find hope after difficult seasons.

Every challenge you survive teaches something valuable.

It develops perspective.

It builds character.

It reveals strengths you may not have discovered otherwise.

The goal is not to become someone who never struggles.

The goal is to become someone who can endure struggles without losing sight of who they are.

Strength is not measured by how many times life knocks you down.

It is measured by your willingness to rise again.

Keep moving.

Keep rebuilding.

Keep believing.

Because resilience has a way of turning setbacks into stepping stones.

WEALTH LESSON

Resilient people adapt faster during difficult seasons because they refuse to let temporary setbacks destroy long-term vision.

AFFIRMATION

"I become stronger, wiser, and more resilient through every challenge."

TODAY'S POWER MOVE

Handle one difficult responsibility today without avoidance.

DAY 36

Healing Creates Clarity

POWER QUOTE

"A peaceful mind makes better decisions."

REFLECTION

Many of the decisions that shape a person's life are not made during calm moments.

They are made during stressful ones.

When pressure increases, emotions intensify.

When uncertainty appears, fear becomes louder.

When life feels overwhelming, it becomes easier to react instead of think.

That is why emotional health matters so much.

A person who is constantly overwhelmed often struggles to make clear decisions.

Stress can create impulsive choices.

Anxiety can create avoidance.

Anger can create reactions that damage relationships, opportunities, and progress.

When the mind is carrying too much, even simple decisions can feel difficult.

This is why protecting your peace is not a luxury.

It is a responsibility.

Peace creates space to think clearly.

It allows you to respond instead of react.

To evaluate situations more accurately.

To make decisions that align with your long-term goals rather than your temporary emotions.

Many people focus heavily on external success while neglecting their internal well-being.

But it is difficult to build a healthy life while carrying constant emotional chaos.

Your mental and emotional health influences your relationships.

Your finances.

Your confidence.

Your productivity.

Your ability to lead yourself through difficult seasons.

Taking care of yourself is not selfish.

It is necessary.

The clearer your mind becomes, the wiser your decisions become.

And wise decisions, repeated over time, have the power to change the direction of an entire life.

Protect your peace.

Protect your mind.

Protect your emotional well-being.

Because the quality of your decisions is often connected to the quality of the environment you create within yourself.

WEALTH LESSON

Stress impacts financial behavior. Emotional stability improves planning, patience, and long-term thinking.

AFFIRMATION

"I create peace within myself so I can build wisely."

TODAY'S POWER MOVE

Spend quiet time reflecting, journaling, or disconnecting from unnecessary noise.

DAY 37

Consistency Beats Talent

POWER QUOTE

"Small consistent actions outperform inconsistent bursts of motivation."

REFLECTION

Talent can open doors.

But talent alone rarely determines who succeeds.

History is filled with gifted individuals who never reached their potential because they lacked the discipline to remain committed when the work became difficult.

At the same time, there are countless people with average abilities who achieved extraordinary results because they refused to quit.

They kept showing up.

When progress was slow, they showed up.

When motivation disappeared, they showed up.

When setbacks occurred, they showed up.

That commitment created momentum.

Many people overestimate what can be accomplished in a few days and underestimate what can be accomplished over several years of consistent effort.

The challenge is that consistency is rarely exciting.

It often looks repetitive.

Ordinary.

Unremarkable.

Yet it is one of the most powerful forces in personal growth.

A single workout may not transform your health.

A single deposit may not create financial freedom.

A single productive day may not change your future.

But repeated often enough, those actions become powerful.

Success is frequently the result of doing simple things well for a very long time.

The people who achieve meaningful goals are not always the smartest, most talented, or most connected.

They are often the people who remained committed long enough for their efforts to compound.

Do not underestimate the value of showing up.

Even when you feel discouraged.

Even when results are not immediate.

Even when nobody notices.

Every day you continue is another step toward the future you are building.

Keep showing up.

Because consistency has a way of accomplishing what talent alone never can.

WEALTH LESSON

Financial and personal growth compound through consistency, not temporary emotional excitement.

AFFIRMATION

"I remain committed even when motivation changes."

TODAY'S POWER MOVE

Repeat one positive habit today even if you do not feel motivated.

DAY 38

Build Quietly

POWER QUOTE

"Not every move needs validation."

REFLECTION

Not every goal needs an audience.

Not every dream requires validation.

And not every step of your journey needs to be shared before it happens.

In a world where people constantly feel pressured to announce their plans, there is tremendous value in learning how to build quietly.

Many people become addicted to talking about what they are going to do.

They discuss their ideas.

Their goals.

Their future plans.

Their next moves.

But conversation alone does not create results.

Execution does.

There is a difference between appearing productive and actually making progress.

Real growth often happens away from public attention.

It happens during early mornings when nobody is watching.

During difficult decisions nobody applauds.

During moments of discipline that never receive recognition.

These are the moments that create lasting change.

Silence can be powerful because it protects your energy.

It allows you to focus on the work instead of managing other people's opinions about the work.

Not everyone will understand your vision.

Not everyone needs to.

The responsibility is not to convince people.

The responsibility is to continue building.

Some of the most important seasons of your life may look quiet from the outside.

But beneath the surface, foundations are being created.

Skills are being developed.

Character is being strengthened.

Goals are moving closer to reality.

Let your results speak louder than your announcements.

Let your progress speak louder than your promises.

And let your future be shaped by execution rather than explanation.

Because the strongest transformations are often built in private long before they become visible to the world.

WEALTH LESSON

Focused people protect their energy instead of constantly seeking external validation.

AFFIRMATION

"I allow my discipline to speak louder than my words."

TODAY'S POWER MOVE

Work on one important goal today without posting or announcing it online.

DAY 39

Stop Doubting Yourself

POWER QUOTE

"You were not created to live beneath your potential."

REFLECTION

Self-doubt has prevented countless people from pursuing opportunities that could have changed their lives.

Not because they lacked talent.

Not because they lacked intelligence.

Not because they lacked potential.

But because they convinced themselves they were not ready.

They waited for more confidence.

More certainty.

More experience.

More proof that they could succeed.

The problem is that confidence is rarely a prerequisite for action.

More often, confidence is a result of action.

Think about any skill you have developed in life.

You were not confident the first time you tried it.

You became confident because you practiced it.

You learned.

You improved.

You gained experience.

The same principle applies to nearly every goal worth pursuing.

Many people assume successful individuals were fearless from the beginning.

They were not.

They simply chose to act before they felt fully prepared.

They understood that growth requires movement.

Waiting until every fear disappears often means waiting forever.

There will always be unknowns.

There will always be risks.

There will always be reasons to hesitate.

But there will also always be opportunities available to those willing to take the first step.

Do not allow self-doubt to make decisions for you.

Do not allow fear to become the author of your future.

You do not need complete certainty to begin.

You only need enough courage to take the next step.

Because the person you are capable of becoming is often waiting on the other side of the action you have been postponing.

Start before you feel ready.

Learn as you go.

Grow through the process.

And trust that confidence will follow.

WEALTH LESSON

Confidence influences leadership, communication, opportunities, and long-term growth.

AFFIRMATION

"I stop underestimating the potential inside of me."

TODAY'S POWER MOVE

Speak positively about your future and abilities today.

DAY 40

Structure Creates Stability

POWER QUOTE

"Chaos drains energy. Structure creates peace."

REFLECTION

Many people spend their lives reacting to problems instead of preparing for them.

They wait until bills become overwhelming before creating a budget.

They wait until deadlines are approaching before creating a plan.

They wait until stress becomes unbearable before establishing routines.

As a result, life often feels chaotic and unpredictable.

The issue is not always a lack of effort.

Often, it is a lack of structure.

Structure creates stability because it reduces unnecessary decision-making.

When important areas of your life have systems in place, you spend less energy reacting and more energy executing.

A budget gives your money direction.

A schedule gives your time purpose.

A routine reduces uncertainty.

A plan creates clarity.

These tools are not designed to limit freedom.

They are designed to support it.

Many people view organization as restrictive when it is actually liberating.

Without structure, small problems often become large ones.

Tasks pile up.

Responsibilities get delayed.

Stress increases.

Mental energy becomes consumed by things that could have been prevented.

The most effective people are not necessarily those who work the hardest.

They are often the people who create systems that allow them to work more intentionally.

Structure provides a foundation during difficult seasons.

When emotions fluctuate, systems create consistency.

When motivation fades, routines provide direction.

When life becomes uncertain, preparation creates stability.

A well-organized life is not about controlling every detail.

It is about creating an environment where your goals have a greater chance of succeeding.

Build systems that support your future.

Because stability is rarely accidental.

It is usually the result of intentional structure.

WEALTH LESSON

Financial structure reduces emotional stress because preparation creates greater control and awareness.

AFFIRMATION

"I create systems that support peace, discipline, and long-term growth."

TODAY'S POWER MOVE

Organize one important area of your life that has been creating unnecessary stress.

DAY 41

Scarcity Will Drain You

POWER QUOTE

"Living in constant financial fear will eventually exhaust your spirit."

REFLECTION

Many people spend years living in survival mode without realizing it.

They wake up worried.

They make decisions from fear.

They constantly expect something to go wrong.

Even when life improves, their mind remains trapped in a state of scarcity.

Survival mode is exhausting because it teaches people to focus only on immediate threats.

It becomes difficult to think long-term.

Difficult to trust.

Difficult to plan.

Difficult to feel secure.

As a result, many people continue making reactive decisions even after their circumstances begin to change.

More income does not automatically create peace.

A bigger paycheck does not automatically eliminate fear.

If the mindset remains unchanged, the emotional burden often remains as well.

This is why wealth is about more than money.

True wealth includes stability.

Clarity.

Patience.

The ability to make decisions without panic controlling the outcome.

People who build strong futures develop the habit of slowing down before making important decisions.

Instead of allowing urgency to dictate their next move, they create thoughtful plans, evaluate their options, and choose actions that support the future they want to build.

Over time, that simple shift—from reacting to responding—creates greater stability, confidence, and peace.

The goal is not to ignore challenges.

The goal is to stop allowing fear to sit in the driver's seat of your life.

You are not meant to spend every day preparing for disaster.

You are meant to build.

To create.

To grow.

To move forward with intention.

There comes a point when healing requires leaving survival mode behind.

Because the future you want cannot be built by a mind that is constantly expecting the worst.

Peace begins when fear no longer controls your decisions.

And that peace creates space for strategy, wisdom, and lasting success.

WEALTH LESSON

Financial peace comes from preparation, planning, and emotional maturity — not avoidance or panic.

AFFIRMATION

"I replace fear, panic, and scarcity with discipline, clarity, and stability."

TODAY'S POWER MOVE

Review one financial area you have been avoiding and create a simple improvement plan.

DAY 42

Discipline Is Love

POWER QUOTE

"Discipline is one of the deepest forms of self-respect."

REFLECTION

Many people misunderstand discipline because they focus only on what it requires.

They see the sacrifice.

The effort.

The responsibility.

The discomfort.

What they often fail to see are the benefits discipline provides in return.

Discipline is not about restricting your life.

It is about improving it.

At its core, discipline is an expression of self-respect.

It is the decision to act in a way that honors your future, even when your present emotions are asking for something easier.

Every healthy choice sends a message.

Every responsible decision sends a message.

Every commitment you keep sends a message.

The message is simple:

"My future matters."

When you save money instead of spending impulsively, you are protecting your future.

When you establish boundaries, you are protecting your peace.

When you take care of your health, you are protecting your quality of life.

When you stay committed to your goals, you are protecting your potential.

These actions may seem small individually, but together they create a powerful foundation.

People often associate self-love with comfort.

But sometimes self-love looks like accountability.

Sometimes it looks like saying no.

Sometimes it looks like doing what is necessary rather than what is convenient.

The most caring thing you can do for your future self is prepare for the life you hope to create.

That preparation requires discipline.

Not because you are punishing yourself.

Because you value yourself.

Discipline is not evidence that you are being hard on yourself.

It is evidence that you believe your future is worth protecting.

And every time you follow through on what you know is right, you strengthen the relationship you have with yourself.

WEALTH LESSON

Self-control protects long-term wealth because emotional decisions often create unnecessary setbacks.

AFFIRMATION

"I choose disciplined decisions because I deeply value myself and my future."

TODAY'S POWER MOVE

Say no to one unhealthy habit or distraction today.

DAY 43

Fear Cannot Lead Your Life

POWER QUOTE

"Your future will suffer if fear becomes your decision-maker."

REFLECTION

Fear is a natural part of life.

Every person experiences it.

The fear of failure.

The fear of rejection.

The fear of embarrassment.

The fear of making the wrong decision.

The fear of stepping into something unfamiliar.

Fear itself is not the problem.

The problem begins when fear becomes the decision-maker.

Many people spend years trapped in situations they have outgrown because fear convinces them it is safer to stay where they are.

They remain in jobs they dislike.

They avoid opportunities that could help them grow.

They silence ideas that deserve to be shared.

They postpone dreams that continue calling them forward.

Not because they lack ability.

Because fear convinced them the risk was too great.

The truth is that every meaningful opportunity carries some level of uncertainty.

There are no guarantees.

No perfect timing.

No moment where all fear completely disappears.

That is why courage matters.

Courage is not fearlessness.

Courage is choosing to move forward even when fear is present.

It is having difficult conversations.

Taking the first step.

Submitting the application.

Starting the business.

Sharing the idea.

Making the decision.

The people who create extraordinary lives are not always the people with the least fear.

They are often the people who stopped allowing fear to control their choices.

Every time you choose courage, you expand your world.

You discover new opportunities.

You build confidence.

You prove to yourself that fear does not have the final say.

Do not wait for perfect certainty.

Do not wait until fear disappears.

Move anyway.

Because many of the opportunities that change your life exist on the other side of the fear you are currently facing.

WEALTH LESSON

Expansion requires calculated risk. Most opportunities exist outside of comfort zones.

AFFIRMATION

"I move forward with courage even when uncertainty exists."

TODAY'S POWER MOVE

Take one action today that fear has been delaying.

DAY 44

Laziness Is Often Emotional

POWER QUOTE

"Sometimes exhaustion is not physical. It is emotional."

REFLECTION

A lot of people call themselves lazy when they are actually emotionally overwhelmed.

Burned out. Discouraged. Mentally drained. Disconnected from purpose.

Not all exhaustion comes from doing too much. Sometimes it comes from carrying too much emotionally.

Unhealed stress, constant anxiety, and emotional pressure can slowly destroy motivation.

This is why self-awareness matters.

You cannot heal what you refuse to acknowledge.

Sometimes the solution is not harsher self-criticism. Sometimes the solution is restoration, clarity, and rebuilding structure slowly.

Meaningful growth begins when comfort stops controlling your choices and honesty starts guiding your habits, emotions, and decisions.

Mindset, emotional control, and consistency quietly shape the quality of a life long before the results become visible.

Lasting transformation is rarely built in one dramatic moment; it is formed through choices practiced with intention every day.

The version of you that keeps rebuilding, learning, healing, and growing is the version that eventually changes everything.

WEALTH LESSON

Mental and emotional health directly impact productivity, consistency, and financial growth.

AFFIRMATION

"I rebuild my energy, focus, and discipline with patience and compassion."

TODAY'S POWER MOVE

Rest intentionally today, then complete one meaningful responsibility.

DAY 45

Reinvention Requires Courage

POWER QUOTE

"You cannot evolve while staying attached to your old identity."

REFLECTION

Many people want a different life, but very few people consider what that new life might require from them.

A different future often requires a different version of you.

Not a fake version.

Not a perfect version.

A developed version.

A wiser version.

A stronger version.

Growth is not simply about adding new habits.

It is also about releasing old ones.

Old beliefs that no longer serve you.

Old excuses that keep you comfortable.

Old patterns that repeatedly create the same outcomes.

Old identities that were built during seasons you have already outgrown.

This is where many people struggle.

They want change, but they remain emotionally attached to the familiarity of who they have always been.

Even unhealthy patterns can feel comfortable when they are familiar.

The unknown can feel intimidating.

Yet every meaningful transformation requires stepping into unfamiliar territory.

The person who wants financial freedom may need to become more disciplined with money.

The person who wants healthier relationships may need to develop stronger boundaries.

The person who wants greater success may need to think differently, act differently, and make different decisions than they have in the past.

Growth requires change.

And change requires courage.

You cannot carry every old habit, mindset, and behavior into your next chapter.

Some things must be released so something better can be built.

Do not fear becoming unfamiliar with the person you used to be.

That discomfort is often evidence that growth is taking place.

You are not meant to remain the same forever.

You are meant to learn.

To evolve.

To mature.

To become.

The future you desire may be waiting for the version of you that is willing to grow into it.

WEALTH LESSON

Transformation happens when behavior begins aligning with long-term vision.

AFFIRMATION

"I release outdated habits and step fully into the person I am becoming."

TODAY'S POWER MOVE

Identify one habit or mindset that no longer aligns with your future.

DAY 46

Do Not Let One Bad Season Define You

POWER QUOTE

"A difficult season is not proof of a failed life."

REFLECTION

Every person experiences seasons they did not plan for.

Seasons filled with uncertainty.

Seasons marked by disappointment.

Seasons where progress seems slower than expected and the future feels difficult to see clearly.

During those moments, it is easy to make a dangerous assumption:

"This is how my life will always be."

But difficult seasons have a way of distorting perspective.

When you are standing in the middle of a storm, it can feel endless.

When you are carrying financial pressure, emotional pain, loss, or uncertainty, it can become difficult to imagine anything different.

Yet history is filled with people who once stood exactly where you stand today.

People who experienced setbacks.

People who lost opportunities.

People who faced rejection.

People who questioned themselves and wondered whether things would ever improve.

What made the difference was not that their circumstances changed overnight.

It was that they refused to stop believing in the possibility of a better future.

A difficult chapter does not determine the ending of a book.

It is simply one part of the story.

The same is true for your life.

Your current circumstances may be challenging, but they are not permanent.

Your disappointment is not your identity.

Your setback is not your identity.

Your struggle is not your identity.

There is still more to be written.

More to learn.

More to experience.

More to build.

More to become.

Do not allow today's pain to convince you that tomorrow holds no possibility.

Keep moving forward.

Keep believing.

Keep showing up.

Because some of life's most meaningful breakthroughs begin in seasons that once felt impossible to survive.

This season may be difficult.

But it is not the final chapter of your story.

WEALTH LESSON

Resilient people recover faster because they refuse to allow temporary setbacks to destroy long-term vision.

AFFIRMATION

"I refuse to define my future by temporary hardship."

TODAY'S POWER MOVE

Speak encouragement over yourself instead of criticism today.

DAY 47

Protect Your Vision

POWER QUOTE

"Not everyone deserves access to your dreams."

REFLECTION

Not everyone will understand the vision you carry.

Not because the vision lacks value.

But because people can only interpret life through the limits of their own experiences.

Someone who has never pursued a dream may struggle to understand ambition.

Someone who has never taken a risk may struggle to understand courage.

Someone who has settled for less may struggle to understand why you refuse to.

That is why you must be careful whose opinions you allow to influence your thinking.

Not every voice deserves equal weight.

Some advice is valuable.

Some criticism is helpful.

But some opinions are simply projections of another person's fears, limitations, and insecurities.

If you are not careful, those projections can become distractions.

You begin explaining instead of executing.

Defending instead of building.

Seeking approval instead of pursuing purpose.

The result is a loss of focus.

Every meaningful goal requires concentration.

Energy spent convincing others is often energy that could have been invested in creating results.

This does not mean ignoring wisdom or refusing feedback.

It means learning the difference between constructive guidance and unnecessary noise.

The people who accomplish extraordinary things are often those who remain committed to their vision even when others cannot fully see it yet.

Protect your mind from negativity.

Protect your confidence from unnecessary doubt.

Protect your purpose from constant explanation.

Your responsibility is not to make everyone understand your journey.

Your responsibility is to remain faithful to it.

Stay focused.

Stay committed.

Stay aligned with the future you are building.

Because the vision was given to you for a reason, and it deserves the attention required to bring it to life.

WEALTH LESSON

Focused people waste less energy defending themselves and spend more energy building.

AFFIRMATION

"I protect my vision and remain focused on my purpose."

TODAY'S POWER MOVE

Spend less time explaining your goals and more time executing them.

DAY 48

Stop Escaping Responsibility

POWER QUOTE

"Avoidance delays freedom."

REFLECTION

Avoidance often feels easier in the moment.

Ignoring the problem feels less uncomfortable than confronting it.

Postponing the conversation feels safer than having it.

Looking away from responsibilities feels easier than dealing with them.

But avoidance has a hidden cost.

The problems we refuse to face rarely disappear on their own.

More often, they grow.

A missed payment becomes a financial burden.

An unresolved conflict becomes a broken relationship.

A neglected responsibility becomes a source of stress and anxiety.

The longer something is ignored, the more power it often gains over your peace of mind.

This is why courage is not only about pursuing big dreams.

Sometimes courage is opening the bill you have been avoiding.

Making the phone call you have been postponing.

Having the difficult conversation.

Looking honestly at the habits that are holding you back.

Growth requires truth.

Not the truth we wish existed.

The truth that actually exists.

Real progress begins when you stop negotiating with reality and start responding to it.

Responsibility can feel heavy at first.

But responsibility also creates freedom.

Each responsibility you face lifts a little more weight from your shoulders.

Difficult conversations create clarity that avoidance never can.

As you consistently handle what once intimidated you, you begin trusting yourself to navigate life's challenges with greater confidence and maturity.

Avoidance creates temporary relief.

Responsibility creates lasting peace.

The life you want is not built by running from difficult things.

It is built by facing them.

One decision.

One conversation.

One responsibility at a time.

The moment you stop avoiding what matters is often the moment your life begins moving forward again.

WEALTH LESSON

Financial awareness creates empowerment because clarity allows intentional decision-making.

AFFIRMATION

"I face my responsibilities with honesty, maturity, and courage."

TODAY'S POWER MOVE

Handle one responsibility today that you have been procrastinating.

DAY 49

Wealth Is Built Slowly

POWER QUOTE

"Most lasting success is built quietly over time."

REFLECTION

People often celebrate success after it becomes visible.

They applaud the achievement.

The promotion.

The thriving business.

The financial freedom.

The breakthrough.

What they rarely see are the years that came before it.

The sacrifices made when nobody was paying attention.

The responsibilities handled when no rewards were guaranteed.

The countless moments when giving up would have been easier than continuing.

Every meaningful accomplishment has a story that most people never witness.

A story of persistence.

Of patience.

Of choosing long-term rewards over short-term comfort.

This is especially true when building wealth.

Many people are attracted to quick results.

Fast money.

Instant success.

Overnight transformations.

But sustainable wealth is rarely built that way.

Strong financial foundations are usually created through thoughtful decisions made consistently over long periods of time.

Saving when spending would have been easier.

Investing when immediate gratification felt more appealing.

Planning when others were reacting.

Remaining patient while others were searching for shortcuts.

The challenge is that progress often feels slow while it is happening.

That is why so many people quit too early.

They fail to recognize that meaningful results are often developing beneath the surface long before they become visible.

Do not become discouraged because your progress seems gradual.

The strongest foundations are rarely built in a hurry.

A tree that grows steadily develops deeper roots.

A house built carefully develops greater strength.

The same principle applies to your future.

Trust the process.

Respect the journey.

Respect the discipline required to keep going.

Because lasting success is not usually created by dramatic moments.

It is created by years of intentional decisions that eventually compound into extraordinary results.

WEALTH LESSON

Compounding works financially and personally. Small consistent actions eventually create major transformation.

AFFIRMATION

"I remain patient and disciplined while building long-term success."

TODAY'S POWER MOVE

Invest time, money, or energy into one long-term goal today.

DAY 50

Healing Is Productive

POWER QUOTE

"Healing is not wasting time. It is preparing for stability."

REFLECTION

Many people were taught to keep moving no matter how they felt.

Push through the stress.

Ignore the pain.

Suppress the emotions.

Keep performing.

Keep producing.

Keep surviving.

While resilience is valuable, constantly ignoring your emotional health comes with consequences.

What is unresolved internally eventually appears externally.

It influences relationships.

It affects confidence.

It shapes decision-making.

It impacts leadership.

It can even influence the way people earn, spend, save, and manage money.

This is why healing is not a distraction from success.

It is part of success.

Many people focus on building careers, businesses, and financial security while neglecting the condition of the person doing the building.

But no structure can remain healthy if the foundation is unstable.

The same principle applies to life.

Emotional health creates stability.

It improves self-awareness.

It strengthens relationships.

It helps people respond thoughtfully instead of reacting impulsively.

It creates the clarity necessary to make better long-term decisions.

Taking care of yourself mentally, emotionally, and spiritually is not a sign of weakness.

It is a form of preparation.

Preparation for greater responsibility.

Preparation for healthier relationships.

Preparation for stronger leadership.

Preparation for opportunities that require emotional maturity.

Healing is not about becoming perfect.

It is about becoming healthier.

It is about creating a life where past wounds no longer dictate present decisions.

The stronger your internal foundation becomes, the stronger everything built upon it can become.

Invest in your healing.

Invest in your peace.

Invest in your well-being.

Because the healthiest future is usually built by people who first took the time to become whole.

WEALTH LESSON

Peace improves clarity. Clear minds make wiser long-term decisions.

AFFIRMATION

"I allow myself to heal, recover, and grow into a healthier version of myself."

TODAY'S POWER MOVE

Spend intentional time doing something that restores your peace.

DAY 51

Discipline Creates Identity

POWER QUOTE

"Your routines eventually become your identity."

REFLECTION

Every person is becoming someone.

Not someday.

Right now.

The person you are becoming is being shaped by the choices you make every day.

The habits you practice.

The standards you maintain.

The responsibilities you honor.

The decisions you repeat.

Many people view success as a single event.

A destination they eventually arrive at.

But success is often the natural result of becoming a certain type of person over time.

A person who values preparation.

A person who follows through.

A person who honors commitments.

A person who remains consistent even when nobody is watching.

These qualities are not developed overnight.

They are built through repetition.

Every time you choose responsibility over avoidance, you strengthen your character.

Every time you keep a promise to yourself, you strengthen self-trust.

Every time you do what is necessary instead of what is convenient, you reinforce the identity you are creating.

At first, these choices may feel uncomfortable.

They may require conscious effort.

They may feel unnatural.

But repetition has a powerful effect.

Eventually, what once required discipline becomes routine.

What once required effort becomes automatic.

What once felt difficult becomes part of who you are.

This is how identity is formed.

Not through intentions.

Not through wishes.

Through repeated action.

The goal is not simply to perform disciplined behaviors.

The goal is to become a disciplined person.

Because once a behavior becomes part of your identity, consistency becomes far easier to maintain.

You stop acting disciplined.

You become disciplined.

And that shift has the power to change every area of your life.

WEALTH LESSON

Strong habits create stronger financial and emotional outcomes over time.

AFFIRMATION

"I build habits that align with the future I want to create."

TODAY'S POWER MOVE

Repeat one positive routine today regardless of your emotions.

DAY 52

You Deserve Better

POWER QUOTE

"Stop settling for environments that shrink your potential."

REFLECTION

The quality of your life is often connected to the standards you are willing to maintain.

Every person establishes standards, whether intentionally or unintentionally.

The relationships they tolerate.

The environments they remain in.

The behaviors they excuse.

The habits they allow to continue.

Over time, these standards begin shaping their reality.

Many people desire peace, confidence, and growth while remaining connected to situations that constantly undermine those very things.

Disrespect becomes acceptable.

Negativity becomes familiar.

Chaos begins to feel normal.

Over time, environments that drain your energy can quietly become environments you stop questioning.

What people repeatedly accept often becomes the standard they unconsciously expect from life.

Eventually, what they tolerate becomes what they experience regularly.

This is why healthy standards matter.

Standards are not about believing you are better than other people.

They are about recognizing what supports your well-being and what consistently damages it.

Every environment influences you.

Every relationship influences you.

Every repeated experience leaves an impact.

The question is whether those influences are helping you become the person you want to be.

Sometimes growth requires difficult decisions.

Sometimes it requires creating boundaries.

Sometimes it requires walking away from what is familiar.

Not because it is easy.

Because it is necessary.

You cannot consistently expose yourself to negativity and expect to maintain positivity.

You cannot remain surrounded by confusion and expect clarity.

You cannot continuously lower your standards while hoping for a higher-quality life.

Elevation often begins when standards rise.

When you decide that peace matters.

That growth matters.

That your future matters.

Choose environments that challenge you to improve.

Choose relationships that encourage your development.

Choose standards that align with the life you are working to build.

Because what you consistently accept will eventually shape who you become.

WEALTH LESSON

Healthy environments improve focus, emotional stability, and long-term productivity.

AFFIRMATION

"I choose environments that align with my healing, growth, and future."

TODAY'S POWER MOVE

Distance yourself from one unnecessary source of negativity today.

DAY 53

Focus On Becoming

POWER QUOTE

"Success begins internally before it becomes visible externally."

REFLECTION

Many people spend years chasing visible success.

They chase titles.

Recognition.

Status.

Money.

Influence.

None of those things are inherently wrong.

The problem arises when people become so focused on achieving success that they neglect the process of becoming the type of person capable of sustaining it.

External results are often easy to see.

Internal development is not.

Nobody applauds the private decisions that build character.

Nobody sees the discipline required to keep promises to yourself.

Nobody sees the emotional growth that occurs when you learn to respond wisely instead of reacting impulsively.

Nobody sees the quiet moments where integrity is strengthened and maturity is developed.

Yet those invisible moments often matter most.

Every lasting achievement is supported by qualities that were developed long before the achievement arrived.

Patience.

Discipline.

Resilience.

Self-awareness.

Responsibility.

These traits are the foundation beneath the visible results.

Without them, success can become difficult to maintain.

Many people want the rewards of growth without embracing the process that creates it.

They focus on appearing successful instead of becoming successful.

But appearances can only carry a person so far.

Character determines what happens next.

The strongest transformations begin internally.

They begin when a person commits to becoming wiser, stronger, healthier, and more disciplined than they were yesterday.

As that internal growth continues, external results often follow.

Focus less on impressing people.

Focus more on developing yourself.

Because the person you become is ultimately more important than any achievement you accomplish.

And when the right identity is built, success becomes a natural extension of who you are.

WEALTH LESSON

Inner growth affects external performance because identity influences behavior.

AFFIRMATION

"I focus on becoming the person capable of sustaining success."

TODAY'S POWER MOVE

Spend intentional time developing your mindset today.

DAY 54

Emotional Spending Is Expensive

POWER QUOTE

"Some purchases are emotional reactions, not financial decisions."

REFLECTION

Many financial mistakes have very little to do with a lack of knowledge.

They are often emotional decisions disguised as financial ones.

People spend when they are stressed.

They spend when they are bored.

They spend when they feel lonely.

They spend when they want approval.

They spend when they are trying to create a temporary feeling of happiness.

In those moments, money becomes more than a tool.

It becomes a coping mechanism.

The problem is that emotional relief purchased through spending rarely lasts.

The excitement fades.

The emotion passes.

But the financial consequences often remain.

This is why building wealth requires more than understanding numbers.

It requires understanding yourself.

You must learn to recognize the emotions influencing your decisions.

You must learn to pause before reacting.

To ask why you want something before buying it.

To determine whether a purchase is serving a genuine need or simply responding to a temporary feeling.

Awareness creates choice.

Without awareness, emotions often make decisions automatically.

With awareness, you gain the ability to respond intentionally.

Financial discipline is not about depriving yourself of everything you enjoy.

It is about making decisions that align with your long-term goals rather than your short-term emotions.

Every dollar has a purpose.

Every decision carries consequences.

The more intentional you become, the more control you gain over your financial future.

Money is a powerful tool.

But the person using the tool matters just as much as the tool itself.

Learn to master your emotions, and your financial decisions often become stronger as a result.

Because lasting financial success is not only built through knowledge.

It is built through awareness, intention, and self-control.

WEALTH LESSON

Emotional awareness improves financial discipline because controlled emotions create wiser decisions.

AFFIRMATION

"I make intentional financial decisions that align with my future."

TODAY'S POWER MOVE

Pause and reflect before every unnecessary purchase today.

DAY 55

Your Future Needs Stability

POWER QUOTE

"Financial freedom requires emotional maturity."

REFLECTION

Life will constantly present situations that test your emotions.

Unexpected expenses.

Disappointments.

Conflict.

Delays.

Stress.

Uncertainty.

The challenge is not whether these moments will happen.

The challenge is how you choose to respond when they do.

Many people live reactively.

They make decisions based on temporary emotions.

They speak before thinking.

Spend before planning.

Quit before evaluating.

React before understanding.

As a result, their lives often feel unpredictable and unstable.

Emotional maturity creates a different outcome.

Mature individuals understand that feelings are important, but feelings should not always be in control.

They learn how to pause.

To think before responding.

To evaluate situations from a long-term perspective rather than a temporary emotional one.

That moment of pause is where wisdom often begins.

It creates space for wisdom.

Space for perspective.

Space for better decisions.

The strongest leaders, healthiest relationships, and most stable lives are rarely built through impulsive reactions.

They are built through thoughtful responses.

A peaceful life is not something that happens by accident.

It is created intentionally.

Through preparation.

Through self-awareness.

Through learning how to remain grounded when circumstances become difficult.

Every situation presents a choice.

You can react immediately and allow emotions to lead.

Or you can pause, reflect, and respond with intention.

That choice shapes far more of your future than most people realize.

Stability is built one decision at a time.

Peace is built one response at a time.

And emotional maturity grows every time you choose wisdom over impulse.

Your future will be influenced not only by what happens to you, but by how you choose to respond when it does.

WEALTH LESSON

Long-term planning creates greater financial and emotional security.

AFFIRMATION

"I become more stable emotionally, mentally, and financially."

TODAY'S POWER MOVE

Review your long-term goals and identify one area needing more structure.

DAY 56

Stay Focused On Your Assignment

POWER QUOTE

"Distraction often arrives when purpose is near."

REFLECTION

Every meaningful goal requires attention.

Not occasional attention.

Not attention when it is convenient.

Sustained attention.

The problem is that attention has become one of the most contested resources in modern life.

Every day, countless distractions compete for it.

Notifications.

Entertainment.

Drama.

Comparison.

Other people's opinions.

Temporary pleasures that offer immediate satisfaction but little long-term value.

None of these things may seem dangerous on their own.

But together, they can slowly pull a person away from the future they are trying to create.

This is why focus matters.

Focus is not simply the ability to concentrate.

It is the ability to decide what deserves your energy and what does not.

Every time you say yes to something, you are also saying no to something else.

Every commitment consumes time.

Every distraction consumes attention.

Every unnecessary obligation reduces the energy available for what matters most.

Focused people understand this.

They become selective about what they allow into their lives.

Not because they are selfish.

Because they understand the cost of distraction.

The future they are building is too important to be constantly interrupted.

There will always be opportunities to waste time.

There will always be invitations to become distracted.

There will always be noise competing for your attention.

Your responsibility is to remain aligned with your purpose.

To protect your priorities.

To guard your peace.

To stay committed to the work that truly matters.

Because many dreams are not destroyed by failure.

They are destroyed by distraction.

And the ability to remain focused may be one of the greatest advantages you can develop.

Protect your attention.

Protect your purpose.

Protect your future.

The life you want deserves your full focus.

WEALTH LESSON

Focused execution creates momentum because energy is directed intentionally.

AFFIRMATION

"I protect my attention and remain committed to my purpose."

TODAY'S POWER MOVE

Remove one unnecessary distraction from your routine today.

DAY 57

Keep Showing Up

POWER QUOTE

"Consistency during difficult seasons creates powerful futures."

REFLECTION

It is easy to feel committed when everything is going well.

When progress is visible.

When opportunities are appearing.

When energy is high and confidence feels strong.

The real test comes when those conditions change.

What happens when results are delayed?

What happens when the work becomes repetitive?

What happens when support is limited and nobody seems to notice your effort?

Those are the moments that reveal character.

Many people begin with enthusiasm.

Few people learn how to continue when enthusiasm fades.

Yet the ability to continue is often what separates those who achieve their goals from those who abandon them.

Success is rarely determined by a single day of effort.

It is usually determined by what a person does during the days when quitting feels easier.

The days when progress feels invisible.

The days when discouragement appears.

The days when doubt tries to convince them that the effort is not worth it.

Those moments matter.

Because every time you continue despite difficulty, you strengthen something within yourself.

You develop endurance.

You build resilience.

You gain confidence from knowing that temporary emotions do not control your actions.

The strongest people are not those who never face hardship.

They are the ones who refuse to let hardship stop them.

Choose consistency again today.

Honor the commitments you made to yourself, even when progress feels slow.

The effort you invest during difficult seasons is often preparing you for opportunities you cannot see yet.

Your future is worth continuing to build.

There will be seasons when progress feels slow.

There will be seasons when the path feels difficult.

But if you continue long enough, those seasons will eventually pass.

And when they do, you will be grateful that you chose persistence over surrender.

Sometimes the most powerful thing you can do is simply keep going anyway.

WEALTH LESSON

Long-term success is built through repeated effort during emotionally difficult moments.

AFFIRMATION

"I continue building even when the process feels difficult."

TODAY'S POWER MOVE

Complete today's responsibilities regardless of your emotions.

DAY 58

Confidence Changes Energy

POWER QUOTE

"People feel the energy of someone who truly believes in themselves."

REFLECTION

Confidence is more powerful than many people realize.

It influences how you communicate.

How you make decisions.

How you handle challenges.

How you pursue opportunities.

And how you recover from setbacks.

Many people assume confidence comes from having all the answers.

It doesn't.

True confidence is not certainty that everything will go perfectly.

It is trust in your ability to handle whatever happens next.

Confident people do not believe they are incapable of failing.

They believe they are capable of learning.

Capable of adapting.

Capable of improving.

Capable of recovering.

That belief changes everything.

When people trust themselves, they become more willing to take healthy risks.

They speak up when opportunities appear.

They pursue goals that once felt intimidating.

They stop allowing fear to dominate every decision.

The opposite is also true.

When people constantly doubt themselves, they often hesitate.

They second-guess opportunities.

They remain silent when their voice matters.

They underestimate their potential before life even has the chance to test it.

This is why self-perception matters.

The way you view yourself influences the way you show up in the world.

If you see yourself as capable, resilient, and adaptable, your actions begin reflecting that belief.

Confidence is not arrogance.

Arrogance refuses growth because it believes it already knows enough.

Confidence remains teachable while still believing in its ability to grow.

The goal is not to become perfect.

The goal is to develop enough trust in yourself that uncertainty no longer controls your future.

Because when you believe you can learn, adapt, and recover, challenges become less intimidating and opportunities become easier to pursue.

And that confidence has the power to change the direction of an entire life.

WEALTH LESSON

Confidence improves communication, leadership, visibility, and opportunities.

AFFIRMATION

"I move through life with confidence, self-respect, and purpose."

TODAY'S POWER MOVE

Speak with certainty and confidence today.

DAY 59

Growth Requires Separation

POWER QUOTE

"Some seasons require distance from what no longer aligns."

REFLECTION

Growth has a way of changing what matters to you.

The things that once felt important may no longer hold the same value.

The environments that once felt comfortable may begin feeling restrictive.

The habits that once served you may start limiting your potential.

This is a natural part of personal development.

As people evolve, their priorities evolve as well.

The challenge is that growth often requires letting go.

And letting go is rarely easy.

People become attached to familiar routines.

Familiar relationships.

Familiar identities.

Even when those things are no longer helping them move forward.

Sometimes the discomfort of change is not caused by the future itself.

It is caused by the difficulty of releasing the past.

Yet every new chapter requires space.

A gardener cannot expect healthy growth while refusing to remove what is no longer thriving.

The same principle applies to life.

There are seasons when certain habits must be replaced.

Certain mindsets must be challenged.

Certain relationships must be reevaluated.

Not because those things were always bad.

But because they may no longer align with the person you are becoming.

This does not mean abandoning people carelessly or constantly chasing change.

It means having the wisdom to recognize when something has fulfilled its purpose in your life.

Growth often requires courage.

The courage to move forward without carrying everything from the past with you.

The courage to trust that releasing something familiar can create room for something healthier.

Do not fear outgrowing old versions of yourself.

Do not fear closing chapters that no longer support your future.

Every season teaches something valuable.

But not every season is meant to last forever.

Sometimes growth begins with addition.

And sometimes growth begins with release.

The key is knowing the difference.

WEALTH LESSON

Protecting your environment protects your progress because energy influences behavior.

AFFIRMATION

"I release what no longer aligns with my future."

TODAY'S POWER MOVE

Identify one thing that has been draining your peace or focus.

DAY 60

Discipline Creates Peace

POWER QUOTE

"A disciplined life creates less chaos."

REFLECTION

Many people spend their lives searching for peace.

They hope to find it in a vacation.

A different job.

More money.

A change in circumstances.

While those things can be helpful, lasting peace is often built long before circumstances improve.

It is built through preparation.

Preparation reduces uncertainty.

Preparation creates confidence.

Preparation helps people respond to challenges instead of constantly reacting to them.

Think about the person who maintains a budget.

They may still encounter financial difficulties, but they are often better equipped to navigate them.

Think about the person who plans their schedule.

They may still experience busy seasons, but they usually operate with greater clarity and direction.

Think about the person who establishes healthy boundaries.

They may still face difficult relationships, but they are less likely to be consumed by unnecessary chaos.

Structure creates stability.

And stability creates peace.

Many people resist systems because they view them as restrictive.

In reality, healthy systems create freedom.

They remove confusion.

They reduce stress.

They help protect what matters most.

Without preparation, small problems often become larger ones.

Without planning, important priorities can be neglected.

Without boundaries, unnecessary demands can consume valuable time and energy.

Peace is not always the absence of responsibility.

Often, peace is the result of managing responsibility well.

It is the confidence that comes from knowing you have prepared for what you can control.

The goal is not to create a perfect life.

The goal is to create a stable foundation.

A foundation strong enough to support your goals, relationships, finances, and well-being.

Peace rarely arrives by accident.

More often, it is built intentionally through the choices you make every day.

And one of the greatest gifts you can give your future self is the peace that comes from being prepared.

WEALTH LESSON

Structure creates emotional and financial stability because preparation reduces uncertainty.

AFFIRMATION

"I create a peaceful and disciplined life through intentional structure."

TODAY'S POWER MOVE

Plan your next seven days intentionally instead of reacting emotionally to life.

DAY 61

Stop Fear From Shrinking Your Life

POWER QUOTE

"Fear becomes dangerous when it starts making your decisions for you."

REFLECTION

Fear has prevented countless people from becoming who they were capable of becoming.

Not because they lacked talent.

Not because they lacked intelligence.

Not because they lacked opportunity.

But because fear convinced them to stay small.

It whispered that they were not ready.

Not qualified enough.

Not experienced enough.

Not good enough.

And over time, those thoughts became barriers that existed only in their minds.

Fear is persuasive.

It often disguises itself as caution.

As procrastination.

As overthinking.

As waiting for the perfect moment.

But perfect moments rarely exist.

The longer people wait for complete certainty, the more opportunities pass them by.

Fear has accompanied nearly every meaningful achievement throughout history.

The difference has never been the absence of fear.

The difference has been the willingness to move despite it.

Courage is rarely the feeling of confidence before action.

More often, it is the decision to take the next step while uncertainty still exists.

The difference is not that they were fearless.

The difference is that they chose not to let fear make their decisions for them.

Every meaningful achievement requires courage.

The courage to take action before you feel completely prepared.

The courage to risk rejection.

The courage to fail, learn, and try again.

The courage to believe that your future can be greater than your current circumstances.

Fear will always offer reasons to stay where you are.

Vision will always invite you forward.

The question is which voice you will follow.

Do not wait until fear disappears.

Move anyway.

Take the step.

Have the conversation.

Pursue the opportunity.

Trust yourself enough to begin.

Because every time you choose courage over fear, you expand what is possible for your life.

And the future you desire is often waiting on the other side of the risk you are afraid to take.

WEALTH LESSON

People who continuously avoid risk often avoid growth. Calculated courage creates expansion.

AFFIRMATION

"I refuse to allow fear to shrink the life I am capable of building."

TODAY'S POWER MOVE

Do one thing today that fear has been convincing you to avoid.

DAY 62

Your Environment Matters

POWER QUOTE

"Your environment can either strengthen your discipline or destroy it."

REFLECTION

Whether people realize it or not, their environment is influencing them every day.

The conversations they hear.

The expectations placed around them.

The habits that are normalized.

The attitudes that are constantly reinforced.

These influences may seem small in the moment, but over time they help shape beliefs, behaviors, and decisions.

Human beings naturally adapt to their surroundings.

Spend enough time around negativity, and negativity can begin to feel normal.

Spend enough time around excuses, and accountability can become uncomfortable.

Spend enough time around people with limited vision, and it becomes easier to lower your own expectations.

This is why environment matters so much.

Your surroundings either support your growth or compete against it.

They either strengthen your focus or weaken it.

They either encourage your development or pull you back toward old patterns.

That does not mean every environment must be perfect.

No environment is.

But it does mean you should pay attention to what consistently influences your thinking.

Ask yourself:

Are the people around me encouraging growth or reinforcing limitation?

Do my daily environments support the future I want to create?

Am I spending most of my time in places that challenge me to improve or places that keep me comfortable?

Sometimes growth requires changing what surrounds you.

Not because you are rejecting others.

Because you are protecting your future.

A healthy environment can accelerate progress.

It can inspire better habits.

Create greater focus.

Strengthen belief.

And make difficult goals feel more achievable.

Choose environments that align with the life you want to build.

Choose conversations that elevate your thinking.

Choose influences that strengthen your character.

Because over time, your environment becomes one of the architects of your future.

And your future deserves to be built in a place that helps you thrive.

WEALTH LESSON

Strong environments create stronger habits, clearer thinking, and healthier financial and emotional decisions.

AFFIRMATION

"I place myself in environments that support growth, peace, and discipline."

TODAY'S POWER MOVE

Evaluate whether your current environment is helping or hurting your growth.

DAY 63

Discipline Will Save You

POWER QUOTE

"Discipline will take you places motivation never could."

REFLECTION

Motivation is powerful, but it is unreliable.

Some mornings you wake up energized, excited, and ready to pursue your goals.

Other mornings feel completely different.

You feel tired.

Discouraged.

Distracted.

Uncertain.

That is the nature of emotion.

It changes.

It rises and falls.

It responds to circumstances, stress, and life experiences.

The mistake many people make is building their future around a feeling that was never designed to remain constant.

When motivation disappears, their progress disappears with it.

Their routines stop.

Their goals get delayed.

Their commitments become optional.

Over time, inconsistency creates frustration because their actions are controlled by how they feel in the moment.

Discipline operates differently.

Discipline is a decision.

It allows people to continue moving forward even when enthusiasm is absent.

It creates stability during seasons when emotions are unpredictable.

The person who builds a strong future is rarely the person who feels motivated every day.

It is usually the person who remains committed on the days when motivation is nowhere to be found.

The individual who continues exercising when they would rather rest.

Who continues saving when spending feels easier.

Who continues learning when progress feels slow.

Who continues showing up when nobody is watching.

These actions may appear small, but their impact becomes enormous over time.

A meaningful life is not usually built through occasional bursts of inspiration.

It is built through commitments honored repeatedly.

Day after day.

Month after month.

Year after year.

The routines that seem ordinary today often become the foundation of extraordinary results tomorrow.

Do not build your future on a feeling.

Build it on a commitment.

Because motivation may start the journey, but discipline is what carries people across the finish line.

WEALTH LESSON

Financial freedom is usually built through disciplined consistency, not emotional excitement.

AFFIRMATION

"I remain disciplined even when motivation disappears."

TODAY'S POWER MOVE

Complete an important task today without waiting to feel motivated first.

DAY 64

Stability Is Attractive

POWER QUOTE

"Peaceful lives are usually built intentionally."

REFLECTION

Many people spend years chasing excitement.

The next opportunity.

The next purchase.

The next achievement.

The next experience that promises to make them feel fulfilled.

Yet beneath that pursuit, many are searching for something much deeper.

Stability.

The ability to sleep peacefully at night.

The confidence that responsibilities are being handled.

The comfort of knowing their finances are under control.

The security that comes from having healthy routines and dependable habits.

Stability may not always appear exciting, but it provides something far more valuable: peace of mind.

There is strength in becoming dependable.

A dependable person follows through on commitments.

They manage their responsibilities consistently.

They make decisions with the future in mind rather than chasing temporary satisfaction.

Over time, that dependability becomes a source of confidence.

People trust them.

They trust themselves.

And that trust creates freedom.

Many individuals believe freedom comes from having no responsibilities.

In reality, freedom is often the result of managing responsibilities well.

Financial stability creates options.

Emotional stability creates healthier relationships.

Personal stability creates confidence during uncertain seasons.

These qualities are built gradually.

One responsible decision at a time.

One healthy habit at a time.

One commitment honored at a time.

The world often celebrates excitement.

But sustainable success is usually built on stability.

The strongest foundations are not dramatic.

They are reliable.

Consistent.

Steady.

Do not underestimate the value of becoming a person who can be counted on.

Because a stable life creates room for growth, opportunity, and fulfillment.

And in many ways, peace is one of the greatest forms of wealth a person can possess.

.

WEALTH LESSON

Financial stability creates emotional relief because preparation reduces chaos and uncertainty.

AFFIRMATION

"I build a stable life rooted in discipline, clarity, and peace."

TODAY'S POWER MOVE

Create one system today that reduces stress in your life.

DAY 65

You Are Allowed To Reinvent Yourself

POWER QUOTE

"You do not have to stay loyal to the version of yourself created by survival mode."

REFLECTION

One of the greatest barriers to personal growth is the belief that you must remain who you have always been.

People often become attached to old identities.

The version of themselves that was hurt.

The version that operated from fear.

The version shaped by insecurity, rejection, disappointment, or survival.

Over time, these identities can begin to feel familiar.

Comfortable, even.

Not because they are healthy, but because they are known.

The challenge is that what once protected you may eventually begin limiting you.

A mindset that helped you survive a difficult season may prevent you from thriving in a healthier one.

A behavior that once felt necessary may no longer serve the future you are trying to build.

Growth requires the courage to examine who you have become and ask whether that version still aligns with where you are going.

This is not about pretending the past never happened.

It is about refusing to let the past permanently define your future.

You are allowed to change.

You are allowed to develop new habits.

You are allowed to think differently.

You are allowed to set higher standards for yourself and your life.

Reinvention is not dishonesty.

It is development.

It is the decision to become more aligned with your potential than your limitations.

Every meaningful chapter of life requires growth.

And growth often requires becoming unfamiliar with the person you used to be.

That process can feel uncomfortable.

But discomfort is not always a sign that something is wrong.

Sometimes it is evidence that something is changing.

The future may require a stronger version of you.

A wiser version.

A more disciplined version.

A more confident version.

Do not be afraid to become that person.

Because some of the greatest opportunities in your life may be waiting for the version of you that is willing to evolve.

WEALTH LESSON

New financial and personal results usually require a new identity and new behaviors.

AFFIRMATION

"I allow myself to evolve into the person my future requires."

TODAY'S POWER MOVE

Write down three qualities the future version of you possesses.

DAY 66

Stop Escaping Your Potential

POWER QUOTE

"Self-sabotage is often fear disguised as behavior."

REFLECTION

Not all self-destruction looks dramatic.

Sometimes it appears in small decisions repeated over time.

The opportunity you never apply for.

The responsibility you continue postponing.

The conversation you avoid.

The habit you promise to change but never address.

These choices may seem insignificant in isolation, but together they can quietly shape the direction of an entire life.

This is how self-sabotage often works.

It rarely announces itself openly.

Instead, it disguises itself as procrastination.

Perfectionism.

Distraction.

Avoidance.

Excuses that sound reasonable in the moment.

Some people believe they are protecting themselves when they engage in these behaviors.

In reality, they are often protecting themselves from discomfort while simultaneously preventing growth.

Fear is frequently at the center of the cycle.

Fear of failure.

Fear of rejection.

Fear of responsibility.

Fear of success.

Fear of being fully seen.

Rather than risk disappointment, some people unconsciously limit themselves before life has the opportunity to test them.

The result is a life filled with unrealized potential.

This is why self-awareness is so important.

You cannot change patterns you refuse to acknowledge.

You cannot overcome behaviors you continue to justify.

Growth begins with honesty.

Honesty about what you are doing.

Honesty about what you are avoiding.

Honesty about the habits that are keeping you from the future you want.

Awareness creates choice.

And choice creates change.

The goal is not to criticize yourself for past mistakes.

The goal is to recognize what is no longer serving you and make a different decision moving forward.

Your future deserves more than fear-driven habits.

It deserves intentional action.

It deserves commitment.

It deserves a version of you that no longer abandons opportunities out of fear.

The moment you become aware of the cycle is the moment you gain the power to break it.

WEALTH LESSON

Financial growth becomes easier when unhealthy emotional patterns are addressed honestly.

AFFIRMATION

"I stop escaping my potential and begin honoring it fully."

TODAY'S POWER MOVE

Notice one self-sabotaging behavior and intentionally interrupt it today.

DAY 67

Wealth Requires Vision

POWER QUOTE

"You cannot build a powerful future while only thinking about surviving today."

REFLECTION

Many people spend their lives focused on what is directly in front of them.

Today's bills.

Today's problems.

Today's frustrations.

Today's emotions.

While these things deserve attention, a life built entirely around immediate concerns often struggles to create lasting progress.

Long-term success requires vision.

The ability to see beyond the current moment.

To make decisions based not only on what feels good today, but on what will serve you tomorrow.

This is one of the biggest differences between survival and strategy.

Survival asks, "What do I need right now?"

Vision asks, "What am I building for the future?"

That shift changes the way a person approaches nearly every decision they make.

When people develop a long-term perspective, they begin making different choices.

They become more intentional with money.

More thoughtful with time.

More selective with opportunities.

More patient with results.

They understand that every decision carries consequences beyond the present moment.

A single purchase may affect future financial freedom.

A daily habit may influence future health.

A repeated choice may determine future opportunities.

People with vision recognize that today's actions are connected to tomorrow's reality.

This does not mean ignoring present responsibilities.

It means handling present responsibilities while keeping future goals in mind.

The strongest builders think in years, not just days.

They understand that meaningful success is rarely created through impulsive decisions or temporary emotions.

It is built through intentional actions repeated consistently over time.

The future you want will not appear by accident.

It will be shaped by the decisions you make today.

So ask yourself:

Are your current choices supporting the future you desire?

Or are they only satisfying the present moment?

Because every day is an opportunity to build something greater than what exists right now.

And the people who think beyond today are often the ones who create the strongest tomorrows.

WEALTH LESSON

Vision creates stronger financial behavior because long-term thinking changes short-term choices.

AFFIRMATION

"I think beyond survival and build intentionally for my future."

TODAY'S POWER MOVE

Write down where you want your life financially and emotionally in five years.

DAY 68

You Are More Than Your Current Circumstances

POWER QUOTE

"Temporary struggle does not define permanent identity."

REFLECTION

Difficult seasons have a way of distorting perspective.

When financial pressure increases, it can feel like stability will never return.

When rejection happens repeatedly, it can feel like opportunities have disappeared.

When progress is delayed, it can feel like success belongs to everyone except you.

Over time, people can begin making a dangerous mistake.

They stop viewing hardship as something they are experiencing and start viewing it as who they are.

A temporary struggle becomes a permanent identity.

A setback becomes a label.

A difficult chapter becomes the entire story.

But circumstances and identity are not the same thing.

A person can experience financial hardship without being a failure.

A person can experience rejection without being unworthy.

A person can experience uncertainty without being lost forever.

Life moves through seasons.

Some seasons bring growth.

Some bring challenges.

Some bring lessons that can only be learned through adversity.

The key is remembering that no season lasts forever.

Many of the people you admire today once stood in places filled with doubt and uncertainty.

They faced setbacks.

Made mistakes.

Questioned themselves.

Wondered whether things would ever improve.

What separated them was not the absence of struggle.

It was their refusal to let struggle become their identity.

They continued believing.

Continued learning.

Continued taking small steps forward.

Even when the future was difficult to see.

Your current circumstances may be real, but they are not the final definition of your life.

There is more ahead.

More growth.

More opportunities.

More healing.

More victories.

Do not allow a temporary season to convince you that your future has been decided.

You are not the hardship you are facing.

You are not the setback you experienced.

You are not the disappointment you survived.

You are a person still becoming.

And your story is still being written.

WEALTH LESSON

Confidence and emotional resilience influence long-term success more than temporary setbacks.

AFFIRMATION

"I refuse to let temporary struggle define my future."

TODAY'S POWER MOVE

Speak about your future with belief instead of defeat today.

DAY 69

Protect Your Peace Aggressively

POWER QUOTE

"Peace is too expensive to constantly sacrifice for chaos."

REFLECTION

Peace is one of the most valuable things a person can possess.

Yet many people sacrifice it without realizing the cost.

They remain connected to environments that constantly create stress.

They entertain relationships that continuously drain their energy.

They tolerate patterns that leave them feeling exhausted, distracted, and emotionally overwhelmed.

Over time, that chaos begins affecting everything.

Focus becomes harder.

Decision-making becomes harder.

Discipline becomes harder.

Even simple responsibilities can feel heavier when the mind is carrying unnecessary emotional weight.

This is why protecting your peace matters.

Not because life should be free of challenges.

Challenges are part of growth.

But there is a difference between facing necessary challenges and continuously exposing yourself to avoidable chaos.

A peaceful mind functions differently.

It thinks more clearly.

Responds more wisely.

Creates more effectively.

Leads more confidently.

When peace is present, people are often able to focus their energy on building rather than simply surviving.

Many people worry that setting boundaries will disappoint others.

What they fail to realize is that constantly abandoning their own well-being creates even greater consequences.

Not everyone deserves unlimited access to your time.

Your attention.

Your emotions.

Your energy.

Access should be earned through respect, trust, and healthy behavior.

Protecting your peace is not selfish.

It is stewardship.

It is recognizing that your mind, emotions, and future deserve care.

Sometimes growth requires opening new doors.

Other times it requires closing old ones.

Not out of bitterness.

Not out of pride.

But because some environments are no longer compatible with the life you are trying to build.

Guard your peace carefully.

Because the quality of your inner world often determines the quality of the life you create around it.

And your future deserves an environment where growth can flourish.

WEALTH LESSON

Mental peace improves emotional control, productivity, and decision-making.

AFFIRMATION

"I aggressively protect my peace, focus, and emotional health."

TODAY'S POWER MOVE

Distance yourself from one unnecessary source of stress today.

DAY 70

Confidence Is Built Through Action

POWER QUOTE

"Every time you follow through, you strengthen your belief in yourself."

REFLECTION

Many people are waiting to feel confident before they take action.

They believe confidence comes first.

That one day they will suddenly feel ready, certain, and fearless enough to pursue their goals.

But confidence rarely works that way.

Confidence is usually the result of action, not the prerequisite for it.

It is built through experience.

Through effort.

Through keeping promises to yourself.

Every time you do something difficult, you create evidence.

Each difficult step creates evidence.

Evidence that you are capable of learning.

Evidence that you can adapt when life changes.

Evidence that setbacks are something you can survive rather than fear.

That evidence becomes self-trust.

And self-trust is the foundation of confidence.

The opposite is also true.

When people constantly abandon commitments, avoid responsibilities, or quit whenever things become uncomfortable, they slowly weaken trust in themselves.

Over time, doubt begins replacing confidence.

Not because they lack ability.

Because their actions are teaching them that their words cannot be relied upon.

This is why follow-through matters.

Every commitment you honor strengthens the relationship you have with yourself.

Every responsibility you complete reinforces your belief that you are capable.

Every difficult task you finish reminds you that discomfort is not something to fear.

Confidence is not created through positive thinking alone.

It is built through evidence gathered over time.

Small victories matter.

Keeping your routine matters.

Doing what you said you would do matters.

These actions may appear insignificant, but together they create something powerful.

A person who trusts themselves.

The strongest people are not always the most talented.

They are often the people who have developed enough self-trust to keep moving forward even when the outcome is uncertain.

Build that trust.

Honor your commitments.

Keep showing up.

Because confidence is not something you wait for.

It is something you earn through consistent action.

WEALTH LESSON

Confidence influences opportunities, leadership, communication, and long-term growth.

AFFIRMATION

"I strengthen my confidence every time I follow through on my commitments."

TODAY'S POWER MOVE

Complete one important task today that you have been avoiding.

DAY 71

Healing Is Not Weakness

POWER QUOTE

"Some of the strongest people are the ones who chose to heal instead of harden."

REFLECTION

Pain has the power to change people.

The question is whether that change leads to healing or protection.

Many people experience heartbreak, disappointment, betrayal, rejection, or loss and begin building walls around themselves.

Walls meant to prevent future pain.

Walls meant to create safety.

Over time, those walls can become prisons.

Some people stop trusting.

Some stop opening up.

Some become emotionally distant.

Some become controlled by fear, anger, or resentment.

These reactions are understandable.

They are often attempts to avoid being hurt again.

The problem is that what protects people from pain can also disconnect them from peace.

A person cannot fully experience healthy relationships while refusing vulnerability.

They cannot experience freedom while remaining chained to old wounds.

They cannot build the future they desire while constantly operating from unresolved pain.

This is why healing requires courage.

Not physical courage.

Emotional courage.

The courage to be honest about what hurt.

The courage to confront emotions instead of burying them.

The courage to stop pretending everything is fine when it is not.

Healing is difficult because it asks people to face what they would rather avoid.

But avoidance rarely creates freedom.

Awareness creates freedom.

Understanding creates freedom.

Growth creates freedom.

A healed person approaches life differently.

They respond rather than react.

They create healthier boundaries.

They make decisions from wisdom instead of fear.

They build relationships from trust instead of insecurity.

Healing does not erase the past.

It changes the way the past influences the present.

You do not have to remain the person your pain created.

You can become the person your healing reveals.

Because survival may help you endure difficult seasons.

But healing helps you truly live again.

And there is a difference between existing and being free.

WEALTH LESSON

Unhealed emotions often create unhealthy financial habits, avoidance patterns, and impulsive decisions.

AFFIRMATION

"I choose healing, growth, and emotional freedom over emotional survival."

TODAY'S POWER MOVE

Spend time reflecting on one emotional wound that still affects your behavior today.

DAY 72

Do Not Give Up During The Middle

POWER QUOTE

"Most people quit during the part where growth still looks invisible."

REFLECTION

There is a season in every journey where progress feels slow.

Where results are not obvious.

Where motivation feels low.

Where sacrifices feel unnoticed.

And it is usually during that middle season that many people give up.

But growth often happens quietly before it becomes visible publicly.

Seeds grow underground before anyone sees the results above the surface.

Do not confuse invisibility with failure.

Some of your greatest transformations are happening in moments where nobody is clapping for you yet.

The future belongs to people who continue building even when immediate rewards are absent.

The middle of the journey often feels ordinary, but it is where character is developed.

Every quiet day of discipline is strengthening something that future success will depend on.

Keep planting.

Keep building.

Keep believing.

The harvest almost always arrives after the season that tempted you to quit.

WEALTH LESSON

Long-term success requires patience and emotional endurance during slow seasons.

AFFIRMATION

"I remain committed even when progress feels invisible."

TODAY'S POWER MOVE

Continue working on one goal today even if results feel slow.

DAY 73

Protect Your Mind

POWER QUOTE

"What you constantly consume eventually shapes how you think."

REFLECTION

Every day, your mind is being shaped by something.

The content you consume.

The conversations you participate in.

The people you spend time with.

The environments you repeatedly enter.

Whether you realize it or not, these influences are helping form your beliefs, expectations, and decisions.

That is why protecting your mind is one of the most important responsibilities you have.

Many people are careful about what they eat.

Careful about what they spend.

Careful about where they go.

Yet they give little attention to what they allow into their thoughts.

Over time, repeated exposure becomes powerful.

Negative messages repeated often enough can become beliefs.

Fear repeated often enough can become hesitation.

Doubt repeated often enough can become identity.

This is why mental discipline matters.

Not because you can control every thought that enters your mind.

But because you can become intentional about which thoughts you continue feeding.

You can choose what voices receive your attention.

You can choose what influences deserve space in your life.

You can choose whether your mind is constantly being filled with fear or possibility.

The strongest mindset is not one that never faces negativity.

It is one that refuses to allow negativity to become the dominant voice.

Hope must be protected.

Vision must be protected.

Confidence must be protected.

The future you create will be influenced by the thoughts you repeatedly entertain today.

Your decisions begin in your mind long before they appear in your actions.

This is why every healthy life starts with healthy thinking.

Guard what you consume.

Guard what you believe.

Guard what you repeatedly tell yourself.

Because your mind is one of the most valuable assets you possess.

And what you allow to shape it will eventually help shape your future.

WEALTH LESSON

Healthy thinking improves emotional discipline and long-term decision-making.

AFFIRMATION

"I intentionally feed my mind thoughts that strengthen my future."

TODAY'S POWER MOVE

Reduce exposure to unnecessary negativity today.

DAY 74

Small Discipline Creates Big Change

POWER QUOTE

"Tiny disciplined actions repeated daily can completely transform a life."

REFLECTION

Countless individuals delay change because they believe transformation must happen dramatically.

But most life changes happen gradually.

One better decision.

One healthier habit.

One productive morning.

One disciplined choice at a time.

Consistency creates momentum.

The problem is that many people underestimate small actions because they do not produce immediate results.

But repeated behaviors eventually compound.

And over time, the person who stayed disciplined quietly becomes unrecognizable from who they used to be.

Never underestimate the power of daily discipline.

Most people overestimate what can happen in a single day and underestimate what can happen in a single year of disciplined living.

Small decisions rarely feel significant in the moment.

Yet repeated long enough, they quietly reshape identity, habits, finances, relationships, and the future itself.

Never underestimate what consistency can accomplish.

WEALTH LESSON

Financial growth compounds through repeated responsible behavior over time.

AFFIRMATION

"I respect the power of small disciplined decisions."

TODAY'S POWER MOVE

Improve one habit today by even a small percentage.

DAY 75

Stop Waiting For Perfect Timing

POWER QUOTE

"Perfect timing is often fear wearing a more acceptable disguise."

REFLECTION

Many people postpone change because they believe transformation must be dramatic.

They imagine a single breakthrough.

A life-changing opportunity.

A powerful moment that suddenly fixes everything.

While those moments can happen, most lasting transformation follows a different path.

It happens gradually.

Quietly.

One choice at a time.

A healthier meal.

A completed workout.

A saved dollar.

A productive morning.

A difficult conversation handled well.

A commitment honored when nobody else is watching.

These actions may appear insignificant on their own.

That is exactly why people often overlook them.

They want immediate results.

Immediate evidence.

Immediate rewards.

When those rewards fail to appear quickly, many abandon the process.

What they fail to realize is that small actions are powerful because they compound.

A single disciplined decision may not seem life-changing.

But hundreds of disciplined decisions create a completely different life.

The same principle applies in the opposite direction.

Small acts of neglect repeated over time can quietly create frustration, stress, and regret.

Life is often shaped less by major events and more by daily habits.

The future you experience tomorrow is being built by the choices you make today.

This should be encouraging.

Because it means transformation is accessible.

You do not need to change everything overnight.

You do not need to become perfect immediately.

You simply need to make the next right choice.

Then another.

Then another.

Progress is not always dramatic.

Sometimes it looks like consistency.

Sometimes it looks like patience.

Sometimes it looks like continuing when the results are not yet visible.

Trust the process.

Respect the small decisions.

Because one day you may look back and realize that the habits which once seemed insignificant were quietly transforming your life the entire time.

Great futures are rarely built through one massive decision.

They are built through thousands of small ones.

WEALTH LESSON

Action creates momentum faster than overthinking ever will.

AFFIRMATION

"I stop delaying my future waiting for perfect conditions."

TODAY'S POWER MOVE

Take one bold action today that you have been postponing.

DAY 76

Your Standards Shape Your Life

POWER QUOTE

"What you tolerate repeatedly eventually becomes your lifestyle."

REFLECTION

Every person is teaching others—and themselves—what is acceptable.

Through what they allow.

Through what they ignore.

Through what they repeatedly tolerate.

Over time, tolerance becomes reality.

A person who tolerates unhealthy habits eventually experiences the consequences of those habits.

A person who tolerates financial irresponsibility eventually experiences financial instability.

A person who tolerates disrespect eventually finds themselves surrounded by relationships that lack trust and honor.

Life often reflects the standards we consistently enforce.

This is why growth requires honest evaluation.

Not of what you want.

But of what you allow.

Many people dream of a better future while continuing to tolerate behaviors that keep them attached to their current reality.

They accept distractions that steal their focus.

They entertain excuses that weaken accountability.

They remain connected to patterns they know are preventing progress.

Then they wonder why nothing changes.

Change begins when standards become stronger than comfort.

When protecting your future becomes more important than maintaining familiar habits.

People with high standards are not necessarily more talented than everyone else.

They simply make different decisions.

They guard their time carefully.

They treat commitments seriously.

They become intentional about what they consume, who they listen to, and where they invest their energy.

These choices may appear small, but they create powerful results over time.

A strong life is rarely built by accident.

It is built by people who decide that certain things will no longer be acceptable.

Certain excuses.

Certain behaviors.

Certain patterns.

The moment you stop tolerating what is damaging your future is often the moment your future begins changing.

Because everything in life eventually grows to the level of what you are willing to accept.

Choose your standards carefully.

Your future is being shaped by them every day.

WEALTH LESSON

Higher standards improve financial discipline, emotional maturity, and decision-making.

AFFIRMATION

"I raise my standards because my future deserves better."

TODAY'S POWER MOVE

Identify one area where you need stronger boundaries or standards.

DAY 77

Stop Being Afraid Of Success

POWER QUOTE

"Some people fear success because they fear responsibility."

REFLECTION

Most people recognize the fear of failure.

Fewer people recognize the fear of success.

Failure feels obvious.

Success is often more complicated.

Success changes things.

It increases visibility.

It creates responsibility.

It raises expectations.

It requires growth.

For that reason, some people unconsciously resist the very opportunities they claim to want.

They say they want more influence, but avoid being seen.

They say they want more income, but resist the discipline required to manage it.

They say they want leadership, but avoid the responsibility that leadership demands.

The problem is not a lack of desire.

The problem is that part of them is still uncomfortable with expansion.

Growth asks people to become larger than their current comfort zone.

It asks them to develop new skills.

New habits.

New levels of maturity.

New levels of responsibility.

That process can feel intimidating.

Because every new level of life requires a new level of stewardship.

The opportunities you desire will eventually ask something from you.

Greater discipline.

Greater wisdom.

Greater emotional stability.

Greater accountability.

This is why preparation matters.

Do not focus only on receiving the opportunity.

Focus on becoming the person capable of carrying it well.

Success is not merely about obtaining more.

It is about becoming more.

More responsible.

More intentional.

More disciplined.

More prepared.

The future you are praying for may require growth before it arrives.

Not because you are incapable.

But because life is preparing you to sustain what you are asking for.

Do not fear becoming a larger version of yourself.

Do not fear the responsibility attached to growth.

Welcome it.

Because the next chapter of your life may depend less on your desire for success and more on your willingness to grow into it.

The opportunities ahead are not asking you to be perfect.

They are asking you to be prepared.

WEALTH LESSON

Greater opportunities require greater emotional discipline and responsibility.

AFFIRMATION

"I welcome growth, responsibility, and expansion into my life."

TODAY'S POWER MOVE

Act today like the future version of you already exists.

DAY 78

You Cannot Heal Through Avoidance

POWER QUOTE

"What you avoid emotionally eventually controls you."

REFLECTION

Most people do not realize how much power avoidance can have over their lives.

What begins as a temporary escape often becomes a long-term burden.

A difficult conversation gets postponed.

An emotion remains unaddressed.

A responsibility gets pushed aside.

A problem is ignored in the hope that it will eventually disappear on its own.

For a moment, avoidance feels like relief.

The discomfort fades.

The pressure seems smaller.

The situation feels easier to manage.

But the relief is usually temporary.

What is avoided rarely loses power.

More often, it grows in the background.

The conversation becomes harder.

The emotion becomes heavier.

The problem becomes larger.

And eventually, the very thing being avoided begins influencing decisions, emotions, and behavior.

This is why avoidance can be so deceptive.

It promises comfort while quietly creating captivity.

Freedom requires a different approach.

It requires honesty.

Honesty about what needs attention.

Honesty about what has been ignored.

Honesty about the fears, wounds, habits, or responsibilities that continue demanding energy because they have never been fully addressed.

This process is not always comfortable.

Growth rarely is.

But discomfort is often the price of freedom.

The moment you face what you have been avoiding, you begin taking back power.

You stop running.

You stop hiding.

You stop allowing unresolved issues to dictate your choices.

Healing begins with acknowledgment.

Progress begins with responsibility.

Change begins with awareness.

The strongest people are not those who avoid difficult realities.

They are those who learn how to face them with courage.

There is freedom waiting on the other side of honesty.

There is peace waiting on the other side of responsibility.

And there is growth waiting on the other side of the things you have been afraid to confront.

Because what you are willing to face can no longer control you.

WEALTH LESSON

Avoidance creates financial and emotional instability because ignored problems usually grow over time.

AFFIRMATION

"I face my emotions and responsibilities with honesty and courage."

TODAY'S POWER MOVE

Address one situation today that you have been emotionally avoiding.

DAY 79

Build A Life You Respect

POWER QUOTE

"Self-respect is built through disciplined living."

REFLECTION

Many people spend years searching for confidence.

They look for it in achievements.

Recognition.

Money.

Status.

Approval from others.

While those things may provide temporary validation, genuine confidence is usually built somewhere deeper.

It is built through self-respect.

Self-respect grows when your actions align with your values.

When you do what you said you would do.

When you honor your commitments.

When you make choices that support the life you want instead of sabotaging it.

Every time you follow through, you strengthen trust in yourself.

And trust is the foundation of confidence.

Think about the person who consistently keeps promises to themselves.

They wake up when they said they would.

They handle responsibilities instead of avoiding them.

They manage their finances with intention.

They protect their peace instead of constantly sacrificing it.

These actions may seem ordinary, but they create something powerful.

They create evidence.

Evidence that the person can rely on themselves.

Confidence is not built by convincing yourself that you are capable.

It is built by proving it to yourself repeatedly.

This is why integrity matters.

Not only integrity with others, but integrity with yourself.

When your words and actions consistently match, your self-respect grows.

When your self-respect grows, confidence follows naturally.

The goal is not perfection.

No one gets everything right.

The goal is alignment.

To live in a way that reflects your values.

To make decisions you can be proud of.

To create a life that feels authentic when nobody else is watching.

Because the strongest confidence is not based on applause.

It is based on knowing who you are.

Trusting who you are.

And respecting the person you are becoming.

That kind of confidence cannot be taken away by circumstances.

Because it was built from within.

WEALTH LESSON

Financial discipline increases self-trust and long-term stability.

AFFIRMATION

"I build a life that reflects discipline, integrity, and self-respect."

TODAY'S POWER MOVE

Do something today that your future self would deeply respect.

DAY 80

The Future Is Watching Your Habits

POWER QUOTE

"The person you become tomorrow is being shaped by what you repeat today."

REFLECTION

Most people focus on major decisions.

The new job.

The big purchase.

The relationship.

The investment.

The opportunity.

While those decisions certainly matter, life is often shaped more by what happens between the major moments.

The small choices.

The repeated behaviors.

The routines practiced every day.

These are the things that quietly build a future.

A habit may seem insignificant in a single moment.

One workout.

One budget review.

One productive morning.

One difficult conversation handled well.

On their own, these actions may appear ordinary.

But repeated over months and years, they become powerful.

This is because habits are not merely actions.

They are votes for the person you are becoming.

Every repeated behavior strengthens an identity.

The way you spend your time shapes your discipline.

The way you manage money shapes your financial future.

The way you respond to setbacks shapes your resilience.

The way you handle pressure shapes your character.

Whether intentional or not, your habits are constantly creating momentum.

They are either moving you toward the life you want or away from it.

Many people wait for motivation before changing their behavior.

But lasting change rarely begins with a feeling.

It begins with a decision.

A decision repeated often enough that it becomes a pattern.

A pattern repeated long enough that it becomes part of who you are.

This is why daily habits deserve attention.

They may seem small today, but they are building something larger than themselves.

The future is not created in a single dramatic moment.

It is created through thousands of ordinary moments that most people overlook.

Choose those moments carefully.

Choose your habits carefully.

Because one day, you will look at your life and discover that your routines have been shaping your reality all along.

And the habits you practice today are helping determine the person you become tomorrow.

WEALTH LESSON

Daily habits create long-term financial and emotional outcomes.

AFFIRMATION

"I build habits today that create freedom tomorrow."

TODAY'S POWER MOVE

Choose one habit today that aligns with the future you want to build.

DAY 81

Stop Abandoning Yourself

POWER QUOTE

"Every time you betray your own goals, you weaken your trust in yourself."

REFLECTION

One of the most damaging patterns a person can develop is repeatedly abandoning themselves.

Not through one major mistake.

But through small betrayals repeated over time.

Ignoring responsibilities.

Avoiding important goals.

Making promises and failing to keep them.

Choosing temporary comfort while sacrificing long-term growth.

At first, these decisions may seem insignificant.

But eventually they begin affecting something deeper than results.

They affect trust.

Specifically, the trust you have in yourself.

Every time you tell yourself you will do something and fail to follow through, your mind takes notice.

Every abandoned commitment becomes evidence.

Evidence that your words cannot be relied upon.

Evidence that your intentions and actions are disconnected.

Over time, this weakens confidence.

Not because you lack ability.

Because you have stopped proving reliability to yourself.

This is why self-sabotage can be so destructive.

It quietly damages the relationship you have with yourself.

The good news is that self-trust can be rebuilt.

Not through grand declarations.

Not through temporary motivation.

Through consistency.

Through keeping small promises.

Through honoring commitments even when nobody else is watching.

Through following through when excuses would be easier.

You do not need perfection to rebuild trust.

You need reliability.

The willingness to repeatedly do what you said you would do.

One promise at a time.

One responsibility at a time.

One disciplined choice at a time.

As those actions accumulate, something powerful begins to happen.

Your confidence grows.

Not because someone encouraged you.

Not because circumstances improved.

Because you have gathered evidence.

Evidence that you can depend on yourself.

Evidence that you can handle responsibility.

Evidence that you can continue moving forward even when emotions fluctuate.

The strongest confidence is built on self-trust.

And self-trust is earned through repeated acts of integrity.

Become someone you can rely on.

Because when you trust yourself, you become far more capable of creating the life you desire.

WEALTH LESSON

Long-term financial and emotional stability require self-trust. Consistency strengthens self-belief.

AFFIRMATION

"I stop abandoning myself and begin honoring the future I desire."

TODAY'S POWER MOVE

Follow through on one commitment today without making excuses.

DAY 82

Structure Protects Your Future

POWER QUOTE

"People who create structure experience less chaos."

REFLECTION

Many people desire peace, but few people realize how often peace is created by structure.

They imagine peace as the absence of responsibility.

The absence of pressure.

The absence of challenges.

But in reality, peace is often the result of being prepared for life's challenges rather than avoiding them.

This is where systems become powerful.

A budget creates financial awareness.

A schedule creates direction.

Boundaries protect energy.

Routines reduce unnecessary decision-making.

Planning creates clarity.

These tools may seem ordinary, but their impact is extraordinary.

Without structure, life often becomes reactive.

Important responsibilities are forgotten.

Deadlines are missed.

Money is spent impulsively.

Stress increases because everything feels urgent.

Small problems become larger because there is no system in place to manage them.

Over time, the lack of structure creates unnecessary chaos.

People begin feeling overwhelmed not because life is impossible, but because life is unsupported.

Structure changes that.

It creates order where confusion once existed.

It creates clarity where uncertainty once existed.

It creates confidence because people know what needs to be done and when it needs to be done.

This does not mean life suddenly becomes easy.

Unexpected challenges will still arise.

Difficult seasons will still come.

But prepared people navigate those seasons differently.

Their systems help keep them grounded when emotions become unpredictable.

Their routines help maintain momentum when motivation fades.

Their plans provide direction when circumstances become uncertain.

The strongest lives are rarely built by accident.

They are built intentionally.

One system at a time.

One routine at a time.

One prepared decision at a time.

Freedom is not usually found in avoiding structure.

More often, freedom is created because of it.

And the habits that create order today often become the foundation for peace tomorrow.

WEALTH LESSON

Financial organization reduces stress because awareness creates control.

AFFIRMATION

"I create systems that support peace, discipline, and stability."

TODAY'S POWER MOVE

Organize one area of your life that has been creating stress or confusion.

DAY 83

You Are Capable Of More

POWER QUOTE

"Do not let fear convince you to live beneath your potential."

REFLECTION

Many people spend years carrying a version of themselves that is far smaller than who they are capable of becoming.

Not because they lack talent.

Not because they lack intelligence.

Not because they lack potential.

But because somewhere along the way, they started believing the wrong story about themselves.

Sometimes those beliefs were formed by rejection.

Sometimes by failure.

Sometimes by criticism from people whose opinions were never meant to define your future.

Yet those experiences do not have the authority to determine what you are capable of becoming.

Maybe it came from painful experiences that slowly convinced them they were less capable than they truly are.

Over time, those experiences can become internal narratives.

"I am not good enough."

"I am not qualified enough."

"I am not capable enough."

The problem is that these stories often continue long after the circumstances that created them have passed.

People begin defining themselves by moments that were never meant to define them.

A setback becomes an identity.

A mistake becomes a label.

A difficult season becomes a permanent belief.

But your experiences are not the same as your potential.

A person can fail and still be capable.

A person can struggle and still be gifted.

A person can feel uncertain and still be destined for growth.

The greatest danger is not failure.

It is believing that failure revealed your limits.

Most limits are not discovered.

They are assumed.

This is why action matters.

Confidence rarely appears before movement.

It usually develops because of movement.

You take the step.

Learn the lesson.

Survive the challenge.

Build the skill.

Then confidence begins growing from the evidence you created.

The people you admire were not born believing they could accomplish everything they eventually achieved.

They became confident by continuing despite uncertainty.

You do not need to have every answer.

You do not need perfect confidence.

You do not need complete certainty.

You simply need the willingness to stop treating yourself as smaller than your potential.

Your future may be waiting on the other side of a belief you have not yet given yourself permission to hold.

Believe bigger.

Act bigger.

Grow bigger.

Because there is often far more inside you than you currently see.

WEALTH LESSON

People who believe in their ability to grow are more willing to pursue opportunities and long-term success.

AFFIRMATION

"I stop minimizing my potential and allow myself to grow fully."

TODAY'S POWER MOVE

Speak about your goals today with belief instead of hesitation.

DAY 84

Scarcity Changes Behavior

POWER QUOTE

"People who constantly fear losing often struggle to build peacefully."

REFLECTION

Many people believe scarcity is only a financial problem.

But scarcity often begins in the mind long before it appears in a bank account.

It is the constant feeling that there is never enough.

Not enough money.

Not enough time.

Not enough opportunity.

Not enough security.

When people live in scarcity for extended periods, it affects more than finances.

It affects how they think.

How they plan.

How they make decisions.

How they relate to others.

And how they view themselves.

Scarcity creates urgency.

Everything feels immediate.

Everything feels threatening.

Everything feels like it must be solved right now.

As a result, many people begin living reactively.

They make decisions from fear rather than wisdom.

They focus only on short-term relief rather than long-term solutions.

They struggle to plan because survival feels more urgent than strategy.

This mindset is exhausting.

It keeps people trapped in cycles of stress, worry, and emotional fatigue.

The challenge is that survival mode may help a person endure difficult seasons, but it is not designed to build a meaningful future.

A strong future requires something different.

Perspective.

Patience.

Emotional stability.

The ability to pause before reacting.

The ability to think beyond today's fear and consider tomorrow's possibilities.

This does not mean ignoring real challenges.

It means refusing to allow those challenges to control every decision.

The most successful builders are often people who learned how to remain steady when circumstances felt uncertain.

They developed the ability to think clearly under pressure.

To make decisions based on principles rather than panic.

To focus on possibilities rather than limitations.

Freedom begins when fear stops making every decision.

Wealth begins when strategy becomes stronger than survival instincts.

And peace begins when you realize that not every problem requires panic.

Sometimes it requires patience.

Sometimes it requires planning.

Sometimes it requires trust.

Move beyond survival.

Move toward intention.

Because the life you want cannot be built through constant fear.

It must be built through stability, wisdom, and vision.

WEALTH LESSON

Financial peace begins when emotional reactions are replaced with intentional planning and discipline.

AFFIRMATION

"I release scarcity thinking and build from clarity, stability, and vision."

TODAY'S POWER MOVE

Notice one fear-based financial habit and replace it with a healthier decision today.

DAY 85

Protect Your Focus

POWER QUOTE

"Every distraction steals energy from your future."

REFLECTION

Attention is one of the most powerful resources you possess.

Unlike money, time, or opportunities, attention determines how effectively you use all the other resources available to you.

Whatever consistently captures your attention eventually influences your thoughts.

Your habits.

Your priorities.

And ultimately, your future.

This is why distraction can be so costly.

Most distractions do not appear dangerous at first.

They seem harmless.

A few minutes scrolling.

A little unnecessary drama.

Constant comparison.

Endless entertainment.

Small interruptions throughout the day.

Individually, these things may seem insignificant.

But collectively, they can quietly consume the energy needed to build a meaningful life.

A distracted person often struggles to gain momentum.

Not because they lack talent.

Not because they lack ambition.

But because their focus is constantly divided.

Their energy is scattered across too many directions.

Progress requires concentration.

Growth requires attention.

Achievement requires sustained effort applied toward a clear purpose.

Extraordinary results are not always created by the most gifted people.

Often, they are the people who learned how to protect their focus.

They understand that every unnecessary distraction carries a hidden cost.

A cost paid in time.

A cost paid in energy.

A cost paid in missed opportunities.

This does not mean eliminating every form of enjoyment.

It means becoming intentional.

Intentional about what deserves your attention and what does not.

Intentional about where your energy is invested.

Intentional about protecting the focus required to build the future you want.

Attention is like sunlight.

When scattered, it warms many places but changes very little.

When concentrated, it becomes powerful enough to create transformation.

Guard your attention carefully.

Protect it from unnecessary noise.

Protect it from constant comparison.

Protect it from distractions that lead nowhere.

Because where your attention goes, your life often follows.

And the future you desire deserves your full focus.

WEALTH LESSON

Focused people execute faster because they waste less emotional and mental energy.

AFFIRMATION

"I protect my attention and direct my energy toward meaningful growth."

TODAY'S POWER MOVE

Spend one uninterrupted hour working toward your future today.

DAY 86

Wealth Requires Responsibility

POWER QUOTE

"Freedom without responsibility eventually becomes chaos."

REFLECTION

Almost everyone desires freedom.

Freedom from financial stress.

Freedom to choose how they spend their time.

Freedom from constant worry.

Freedom to build a life that aligns with their values and goals.

Yet many people misunderstand how freedom is created.

They see freedom as the absence of responsibility.

In reality, freedom is often the reward of responsibility.

The person who manages money wisely experiences greater financial freedom.

The person who develops emotional control experiences greater peace.

The person who plans intentionally experiences greater flexibility and stability.

Responsibility creates options.

Irresponsibility often creates limitations.

This is why maturity matters.

Maturity is not simply about age.

It is the ability to manage what has been entrusted to you.

Your time.

Your finances.

Your emotions.

Your relationships.

Your opportunities.

Many people focus on obtaining more while overlooking the responsibility required to sustain it.

They want greater income but avoid financial discipline.

They want greater influence but avoid accountability.

They want greater opportunities but resist the preparation necessary to handle them well.

The challenge is that receiving something and sustaining something are not the same skill.

A person can receive success and still lose it.

Receive money and still waste it.

Receive opportunities and still fail to maximize them.

Sustainable success requires stewardship.

The ability to handle responsibility consistently, even when nobody is watching.

The ability to remain steady when pressure increases.

The ability to make wise decisions when emotions are pulling in different directions.

This is what creates lasting freedom.

Not luck.

Not temporary motivation.

Not occasional effort.

Responsibility.

The future you desire will likely require more from you than the present version of yourself is currently carrying.

That is not a punishment.

It is an invitation to grow.

To become stronger.

Wiser.

More disciplined.

More prepared.

Because freedom is not something that simply arrives.

It is something that is built, protected, and sustained through responsibility.

And the people who handle responsibility well are often the people who experience the greatest freedom in the long run.

WEALTH LESSON

Long-term wealth requires emotional discipline, structure, and responsible decision-making.

AFFIRMATION

"I become more responsible, disciplined, and prepared for the future I desire."

TODAY'S POWER MOVE

Handle one responsibility today without procrastination or avoidance.

DAY 87

Keep Building Quietly

POWER QUOTE

"Not every season of growth needs an audience."

REFLECTION

Not every season of growth is meant to be public.

Some of the most important work you will ever do happens where few people can see it.

The early mornings.

The difficult decisions.

The sacrifices.

The healing.

The rebuilding.

The discipline required to keep moving forward when there is no audience applauding your effort.

Modern culture often celebrates visibility.

People are encouraged to document every achievement, announce every goal, and share every step of the process.

While there is nothing wrong with celebrating progress, there is also value in privacy.

Some things grow stronger when they are protected.

Some goals develop better when they are not constantly exposed to outside opinions.

Some seasons require focus more than attention.

This is why quiet growth is so powerful.

When your commitment is not dependent on recognition, it becomes more authentic.

When your discipline is not dependent on applause, it becomes more durable.

When your motivation is not dependent on validation, it becomes more sustainable.

The strongest foundations are often built in silence.

Athletes train long before competition.

Businesses are developed long before the public sees success.

Character is formed long before anyone recognizes its impact.

The same principle applies to personal growth.

You do not need to broadcast every improvement.

You do not need approval for every goal.

You do not need an audience to justify your progress.

Sometimes the greatest gift you can give yourself is the freedom to grow privately.

To learn privately.

To heal privately.

To build privately.

Not because you are hiding.

Because you are protecting what matters.

There will be a time for results.

A time for recognition.

A time for visible success.

Until then, stay committed to the process.

Continue doing the work.

Continue honoring your responsibilities.

Continue becoming the person your future requires.

Because what is built quietly is often built strongly.

And one day, the results will speak for themselves.

WEALTH LESSON

Focused execution becomes easier when energy is not constantly spent seeking external validation.

AFFIRMATION

"I remain committed to my growth even when nobody sees the process."

TODAY'S POWER MOVE

Work toward one important goal today without posting or announcing it publicly.

DAY 88

Feeling Lost Does Not Mean You Have No Purpose

POWER QUOTE

"Confusion is sometimes the beginning of transformation."

REFLECTION

Almost everyone experiences seasons where they feel uncertain about their direction.

Seasons where the future seems unclear.

Where motivation feels low.

Where confidence feels distant.

Where the next step is difficult to see.

During these moments, many people begin questioning themselves.

They wonder whether they are falling behind.

Whether they have missed their purpose.

Whether they are capable of becoming who they hoped to be.

The danger is not uncertainty itself.

The danger is believing that uncertainty means something is wrong with you.

Often, it does not.

Many seasons of confusion are actually seasons of transition.

You are no longer the person you used to be.

But you have not fully become the person you are growing into.

The old chapter is ending.

The new chapter is still being written.

That space between the two can feel uncomfortable.

It can feel lonely.

It can feel frustrating.

But it is often where some of the most important growth takes place.

A seed underground does not look impressive.

From the outside, it appears as though nothing is happening.

Yet beneath the surface, development is taking place.

Roots are forming.

Strength is developing.

Preparation is occurring.

The same is often true in life.

Not every season is meant for visible results.

Some seasons are meant for learning.

For healing.

For rebuilding.

For discovering new parts of yourself.

Which is why movement matters.

Many people wait for complete clarity before taking action.

But clarity often develops because of action.

You learn by trying.

You grow by moving.

You discover direction by taking steps forward.

Keep learning.

Keep exploring.

Keep showing up.

Even when every answer is not available yet.

You do not need to have your entire future figured out.

You simply need the courage to continue moving forward.

Because feeling lost does not mean you are broken.

It may simply mean you are growing into someone new.

And sometimes the most meaningful transformations happen in seasons when you cannot yet see the full picture.

WEALTH LESSON

Periods of uncertainty can become powerful seasons of growth when people remain disciplined and open to learning.

AFFIRMATION

"I trust that clarity will continue growing as I continue moving forward."

TODAY'S POWER MOVE

Spend time reflecting on what kind of life genuinely brings you peace and purpose.

DAY 89

Discipline Is A Daily Decision

POWER QUOTE

"Success is rarely one giant decision. It is repeated discipline."

REFLECTION

Many people imagine success as a dramatic event.

A breakthrough.

A major opportunity.

A single moment that changes everything.

While those moments can happen, they are rarely the full story.

Most successful lives are built long before anyone notices the results.

They are built through ordinary decisions repeated consistently over time.

Getting up when you planned to.

Handling responsibilities when you would rather avoid them.

Managing money with intention.

Protecting your health.

Working toward goals when motivation is absent.

These actions are not exciting.

They rarely attract attention.

Most people overlook them because they appear too small to matter.

But that is exactly where their power exists.

Success is often the result of doing simple things well for a long period of time.

The challenge is that discipline rarely provides immediate rewards.

The workout does not instantly transform your body.

The budget does not instantly create wealth.

The healthy decision does not instantly change your future.

Because growth operates differently.

It compounds.

Just as interest grows over time, disciplined actions accumulate quietly beneath the surface.

At first, progress feels invisible.

The effort seems disconnected from the outcome.

This is where many people quit.

They mistake delayed results for a lack of progress.

But the most powerful changes are often happening before they become visible.

While results may still be invisible, something important is already happening.

Character is strengthening.

Habits are taking root.

Confidence is becoming steadier.

Momentum is quietly building beneath the surface.

Then one day, what appeared ordinary begins producing extraordinary results.

People call it success.

They call it talent.

They call it luck.

What they often fail to see are the thousands of small decisions that made that success possible.

Never underestimate the power of ordinary discipline.

The future is rarely shaped by one giant decision.

More often, it is shaped by the choices you make every day when nobody is watching.

Keep showing up.

Keep doing the small things well.

Keep trusting the process.

Because the ordinary actions you repeat today may become the foundation of an extraordinary future tomorrow.

WEALTH LESSON

Consistency compounds financially, emotionally, and mentally over time.

AFFIRMATION

"I commit myself daily to discipline, growth, and intentional living."

TODAY'S POWER MOVE

Repeat one disciplined behavior today even if you do not feel motivated.

DAY 90

You Are Rebuilding More Than Money

POWER QUOTE

"Wealth is not only about finances. It is about rebuilding identity."

REFLECTION

A lot of people believe the solution to their problems is simply more money.

More income.

A larger savings account.

A better-paying opportunity.

And while money can certainly solve some challenges, it cannot automatically create peace.

It cannot create confidence.

It cannot create discipline.

It cannot create emotional stability.

The reality is some people experience financial growth while still feeling stuck internally.

Their circumstances improve, but their thinking remains unchanged.

Their income increases, but their stress remains.

Their opportunities expand, but their habits stay the same.

The issue is not always financial.

Sometimes it is foundational.

Because every external result is supported by an internal identity.

The way you think influences the way you act.

The way you act influences the habits you build.

The habits you build influence the life you create.

Ultimately lasting transformation must begin beneath the surface.

Not just in your bank account.

In your mindset.

In your discipline.

In your emotional maturity.

In your ability to handle pressure, uncertainty, and responsibility.

A person who develops these qualities becomes capable of sustaining greater success.

Without them, even valuable opportunities can be wasted.

Ultimately personal growth matters so much.

You are not simply building wealth.

You are building the person who will manage that wealth.

You are not simply pursuing opportunities.

You are becoming the person capable of maximizing those opportunities.

The goal is not only to have more.

The goal is to become more.

More disciplined.

More intentional.

More emotionally grounded.

More prepared for the future you desire.

Because lasting success is rarely created by external changes alone.

It is created when internal growth and external opportunity begin working together.

Never underestimate the power of becoming.

The strongest foundations are built from the inside out.

And the person you are becoming today will determine what you are able to sustain tomorrow.

WEALTH LESSON

Lasting financial transformation requires emotional growth, disciplined habits, and identity reconstruction.

AFFIRMATION

"I rebuild my identity, my discipline, and my future intentionally."

TODAY'S POWER MOVE

Reflect on how much you have grown emotionally, mentally, and financially over the past year.

DAY 91

Your Future Is Watching Your Discipline

POWER QUOTE

"The life you desire is being built through the choices you repeat daily."

REFLECTION

Whether you realize it or not, you are becoming someone every single day.

The question is not whether change is happening.

The question is what direction that change is taking.

Every decision contributes to an identity.

Every habit reinforces a pattern.

Every routine shapes a future.

For this reason daily choices matter far more than most people realize.

Many individuals think transformation happens through dramatic breakthroughs.

A life-changing event.

A major opportunity.

A single powerful decision.

While those moments can be important, they rarely create lasting change on their own.

Real transformation is usually much quieter.

It happens in ordinary moments.

The morning you get out of bed when you would rather stay comfortable.

The decision to save money instead of spending impulsively.

The choice to keep working when motivation disappears.

The willingness to remain committed when results are not yet visible.

These moments may seem insignificant.

Yet they are shaping who you are becoming.

Identity is not built through intentions alone.

It is built through repeated actions.

The way you manage your time shapes your discipline.

The way you manage money shapes your stewardship.

The way you respond to pressure shapes your character.

The way you handle setbacks shapes your resilience.

Day by day, these choices accumulate.

Growth is often so gradual that people fail to notice it until they suddenly realize they are responding, thinking, and living differently than they once did. It develops quietly.

Then one day, the person in the mirror thinks differently.

Acts differently.

Responds differently.

Lives differently.

Not because of one extraordinary moment.

Because of thousands of ordinary moments handled intentionally.

For this reason discipline matters.

Not because discipline is the goal.

Because discipline helps create the person capable of achieving the goal.

The future you desire is connected to the person you are becoming.

So pay attention to your habits.

Pay attention to your routines.

Pay attention to your repeated choices.

Because they are writing the story of your future long before the results become visible.

And every day, whether intentionally or unintentionally, you are becoming someone.

Make sure it is someone your future will thank you for becoming.

WEALTH LESSON

Daily discipline compounds over time and eventually creates emotional stability, stronger finances, and greater confidence.

AFFIRMATION

"I build my future intentionally through disciplined daily decisions."

TODAY'S POWER MOVE

Choose one repeated habit today that aligns with the future you want to create.

DAY 92

Healing Requires Honesty

POWER QUOTE

"You cannot heal what you continuously pretend does not hurt."

REFLECTION

Many people become skilled at hiding pain.

They smile when they are exhausted.

They stay busy when they are overwhelmed.

They continue performing while silently carrying burdens nobody else can see.

From the outside, everything appears normal.

But pain that is ignored does not simply disappear.

It often finds another way to express itself.

Sometimes through anger.

Sometimes through anxiety.

Sometimes through unhealthy relationships.

Sometimes through avoidance, self-sabotage, or destructive habits.

What remains unaddressed eventually demands attention.

Therefore emotional honesty is so important.

Not because honesty instantly removes pain.

But because honesty creates the possibility for healing.

Many people fear acknowledging what hurt them.

They worry that admitting pain makes them weak.

That recognizing wounds means they are broken.

The opposite is often true.

There is strength in telling the truth.

Strength in saying:

"That experience affected me."

"That disappointment hurt."

"That loss changed me."

"I am struggling."

"I need to heal."

These admissions are not signs of weakness.

They are signs of courage.

Because healing begins where denial ends.

You cannot repair what you refuse to acknowledge.

You cannot grow beyond wounds you pretend do not exist.

Awareness creates choice.

Choice creates action.

And action creates change.

This does not mean becoming trapped in the past.

It means understanding it honestly enough that it no longer controls the future.

The goal of healing is not to become someone who has never experienced pain.

The goal is to become someone who is no longer ruled by it.

A person who understands their wounds.

Learns from them.

Grows through them.

And continues moving forward with greater wisdom and freedom.

There is power in emotional honesty.

Because the moment you stop pretending everything is fine is often the moment true healing can begin.

And healing does not make you weaker.

It makes you freer.

WEALTH LESSON

Emotional healing improves decision-making because unhealed emotions often influence financial and personal behavior.

AFFIRMATION

"I allow myself to heal honestly, peacefully, and intentionally."

TODAY'S POWER MOVE

Journal honestly today about one emotion you have been suppressing.

DAY 93

Stop Operating From Panic

POWER QUOTE

"Fear-based decisions often create unstable outcomes."

REFLECTION

Fear is a normal part of life.

Every person experiences it.

Fear of failure.

Fear of rejection.

Fear of uncertainty.

Fear of losing something valuable.

The problem is not that fear exists.

The problem is when fear becomes the primary decision-maker.

Many people spend years operating from panic.

Every challenge feels like a crisis.

Every setback feels permanent.

Every uncertainty feels threatening.

As a result, they begin making emotional decisions instead of intentional ones.

They react instead of reflect.

They rush instead of prepare.

They seek immediate relief instead of long-term solutions.

Over time, this creates instability.

Financial instability.

Emotional instability.

Relational instability.

Not because life is impossible, but because fear has taken control of the steering wheel.

Because of this emotional regulation is such a valuable skill.

Emotional regulation does not mean suppressing feelings.

It means learning how to experience emotions without allowing them to control every action.

It is the ability to pause before responding.

To think before reacting.

To evaluate before deciding.

A calm mind sees possibilities that panic cannot see.

A calm mind plans more effectively.

Communicates more clearly.

Handles pressure more wisely.

Builds more intentionally.

This is one reason emotional stability is closely connected to long-term success.

People often focus on strategies, opportunities, and resources.

Yet many of the most important outcomes in life are shaped by how people respond when circumstances become difficult.

The person who remains grounded during uncertainty often makes better decisions than the person who panics.

Not because they know more.

Because they can think clearly.

The goal is not to eliminate fear.

The goal is to become stronger than it.

To develop the ability to acknowledge fear without surrendering to it.

To choose wisdom over panic.

Preparation over impulse.

Patience over reaction.

Because a calm mind builds differently.

It builds stronger foundations.

Stronger relationships.

Stronger finances.

Stronger futures.

And many of the most successful lives are not built by people who never felt fear.

They are built by people who learned how to stay steady when fear appeared.

WEALTH LESSON

Financial peace increases when emotional reactions are replaced with intentional planning and long-term thinking.

AFFIRMATION

"I refuse to let fear and panic control my decisions."

TODAY'S POWER MOVE

Pause before making emotional decisions today and ask yourself if they align with your long-term future.

DAY 94

Your Standards Determine Your Future

POWER QUOTE

"The quality of your life often reflects the standards you continuously tolerate."

REFLECTION

Every person has standards.

Some are intentional.

Others are invisible.

But whether you realize it or not, your standards are shaping your life every day.

They determine what you tolerate.

What you allow.

What you excuse.

And what you refuse to accept.

Which is why standards matter so much.

Many people dream about a better future while continuing to accept behaviors that keep them attached to their current reality.

They tolerate habits they know are hurting them.

They remain in environments that drain their energy.

They postpone responsibilities that would improve their life.

They normalize chaos and then wonder why peace feels so difficult to find.

Over time, what is tolerated becomes familiar.

And what becomes familiar often becomes permanent.

That is why raising your standards is one of the most powerful decisions you can make.

Higher standards change behavior.

The person who values peace protects their environment differently.

The person who values growth uses time differently.

The person who values freedom handles money differently.

The person who values health treats their body differently.

Standards influence choices.

Choices influence habits.

Habits influence outcomes.

Many people think transformation begins with motivation.

More often, transformation begins with a decision.

A decision that says:

"This is no longer acceptable."

No longer acceptable to ignore responsibilities.

No longer acceptable to tolerate unhealthy patterns.

No longer acceptable to settle for less than what aligns with your future.

This does not mean becoming perfect.

It means becoming intentional.

It means recognizing that every standard you raise creates a new level of accountability.

And every level of accountability creates the opportunity for growth.

Your future will be shaped by what you repeatedly allow into your life.

The conversations.

The habits.

The relationships.

The routines.

The environments.

Choose carefully.

Because what you tolerate today may become the reality you live tomorrow.

And the life you desire often begins the moment your standards become stronger than your excuses.

WEALTH LESSON

Strong standards improve financial discipline, emotional maturity, and long-term stability.

AFFIRMATION

"I raise my standards because my future deserves excellence."

TODAY'S POWER MOVE

Identify one area of your life where your standards need to increase.

DAY 95

Stop Comparing Your Journey

POWER QUOTE

"Comparison turns progress into discouragement."

REFLECTION

Comparison has become one of the most common sources of unnecessary frustration.

Every day, people are exposed to carefully selected highlights of other people's lives.

Promotions.

Vacations.

Relationships.

Business wins.

Financial milestones.

Major accomplishments.

What often goes unseen are the struggles behind those moments.

The setbacks.

The sacrifices.

The failures.

The healing.

The years of work that rarely make it onto a screen.

As a result, many people begin measuring their everyday reality against someone else's edited highlights.

Slowly, gratitude starts disappearing.

Progress feels smaller.

Success feels further away.

Life begins feeling like a competition it was never meant to be.

The problem with comparison is not that it motivates improvement.

The problem is that it often ignores context.

Every person is carrying a different story.

Different experiences.

Different challenges.

Different opportunities.

Different timelines.

Some people reach certain goals early.

Others arrive later.

Some people spend years healing from wounds nobody else can see.

Some spend years rebuilding after setbacks.

Some are laying foundations that will not produce visible results until much later.

None of these journeys are invalid.

Growth does not become less meaningful simply because it happens on a different schedule.

A delayed season is not a denied future.

A slower path is not a failed path.

Life is not a race against the people around you.

It is a commitment to becoming the best version of yourself.

The healthiest comparison is not between you and someone else.

It is between who you are today and who you were yesterday.

Are you growing?

Learning?

Healing?

Improving?

Moving forward?

If the answer is yes, then progress is happening.

Trust your process.

Respect your timeline.

Stay committed to your growth.

Because your journey was never designed to look exactly like anyone else's.

And some of the most meaningful successes arrive precisely when they are supposed to.

Focus on your path.

Your purpose.

Your progress.

The future belongs to those who continue building, even when their timeline looks different from everyone else's.

WEALTH LESSON

Comparison often creates emotional pressure that leads to unhealthy financial and personal decisions.

AFFIRMATION

"I honor my journey and trust my timing."

TODAY'S POWER MOVE

Celebrate one area where you have personally grown instead of comparing yourself to others.

DAY 96

Confidence Comes From Consistency

POWER QUOTE

"Confidence grows when your actions repeatedly prove you can trust yourself."

REFLECTION

Many people spend years waiting for confidence.

They tell themselves they will start when they feel ready.

When they feel certain.

When fear disappears.

When self-doubt finally goes away.

The problem is that confidence rarely arrives that way.

Confidence is usually not the starting point.

It is the result.

It is something that grows through action.

Through effort.

Through experience.

Through repeatedly proving to yourself that you are capable of handling challenges.

Every time you keep a promise to yourself, you create evidence.

Every time you follow through when it would be easier to quit, you create evidence.

Every time you act despite uncertainty, you create evidence.

And evidence creates self-trust.

That is why confidence and self-trust are so closely connected.

People who consistently honor their commitments begin believing in themselves more.

Not because they are pretending to be confident.

Because they have repeatedly demonstrated reliability.

The opposite is also true.

When people constantly abandon goals, avoid responsibilities, or break promises to themselves, they slowly weaken trust in their own abilities.

Over time, doubt grows stronger.

Not because they are incapable.

Because their actions have taught them not to rely on themselves.

The solution is not waiting for confidence to magically appear.

The solution is building it.

One decision at a time.

One promise at a time.

One act of discipline at a time.

You do not need to be fearless to move forward.

You do not need complete certainty.

You do not need perfect conditions.

You simply need the willingness to take the next step.

Then the next one.

Then the next one after that.

Eventually, those small acts of courage become evidence.

That evidence becomes self-trust.

And self-trust becomes confidence.

The strongest people are not always those who feel the least fear.

They are often the people who learned how to keep moving despite it.

Because confidence is not created by waiting.

It is created by doing.

And every disciplined action you take today is teaching you that you are more capable than you once believed.

WEALTH LESSON

Consistency builds credibility, leadership, emotional stability, and financial discipline.

AFFIRMATION

"I strengthen my confidence through consistency and disciplined action."

TODAY'S POWER MOVE

Complete one difficult responsibility today without procrastinating.

DAY 97

Keep Going Even When It Feels Slow

POWER QUOTE

"Slow progress is still progress."

REFLECTION

One of the greatest tests of discipline is continuing when there is little visible evidence that your effort is working.

Anyone can stay motivated when results are obvious.

When progress is fast.

When recognition is frequent.

When success feels close.

The challenge comes during the quieter seasons.

The seasons where you are working hard but seeing little return.

The seasons where growth feels invisible.

The seasons where doubt begins asking difficult questions.

"Is this worth it?"

"Am I making progress?"

"Does any of this actually matter?"

These moments test more than your patience.

They test your belief.

Your consistency.

Your commitment to a future you cannot yet see.

Many people quit during this stage.

Not because they lack potential.

But because they confuse delayed results with failure.

What they fail to recognize is that some of the most important forms of growth happen beneath the surface.

Skills are developing.

Character is strengthening.

Discipline is deepening.

Confidence is being earned.

Foundations are being built.

None of these things may be immediately visible.

Yet they are preparing you for what comes next.

Nature offers a valuable reminder.

A seed spends significant time growing beneath the ground before anyone sees evidence above the surface.

Roots develop first.

Strength develops first.

Preparation happens first.

Only later does visible growth appear.

Life often works the same way.

The most meaningful transformations usually begin internally.

Long before anyone notices externally.

Therefore delayed results should not automatically discourage you.

Sometimes they are evidence that a foundation is being built.

A foundation strong enough to support what is coming.

Stay committed.

Stay consistent.

Continue doing the work.

Continue honoring your responsibilities.

Continue becoming the person your future requires.

Because not all progress is visible.

And some of the most important growth in your life may be happening right now, even if you cannot fully see it yet.

Trust the process.

Trust the preparation.

Trust the invisible progress.

Because one day, what feels hidden today may become the very thing that changes your life.

WEALTH LESSON

Long-term growth requires patience because meaningful success compounds slowly over time.

AFFIRMATION

"I remain committed even when progress feels slow."

TODAY'S POWER MOVE

Continue working toward one long-term goal today even if motivation feels low.

DAY 98

Protect Your Identity

POWER QUOTE

"Your identity influences every decision you make."

REFLECTION

Every person carries a story about who they believe they are.

Some of these stories are empowering.

Others are limiting.

The challenge is that many people never stop to examine whether the stories they believe about themselves are actually true.

Instead, they accept them.

They repeat them.

They reinforce them.

And eventually, those beliefs begin shaping behavior.

A person who believes they are capable tends to approach opportunities differently.

A person who believes they are resilient tends to recover from setbacks differently.

A person who believes they can grow tends to respond to challenges differently.

The same principle works in reverse.

Someone who secretly believes they are incapable may hesitate before trying.

Someone who sees themselves as a failure may abandon goals prematurely.

Someone who believes they will never change may stop attempting to improve altogether.

This is why identity matters so much.

People often focus on changing their circumstances while ignoring the beliefs influencing their behavior.

Yet every action begins with a thought.

Every habit begins with a belief.

Every decision is influenced by how a person sees themselves.

Your self-perception affects how you manage money.

How you handle responsibilities.

How you pursue goals.

How you respond to pressure.

How you recover from mistakes.

The identity you reinforce internally eventually becomes visible externally.

This does not mean pretending to be someone you are not.

It means becoming intentional about the beliefs you repeatedly strengthen.

Pay attention to the words you use when speaking about yourself.

Pay attention to the labels you accept.

Pay attention to the stories you continue telling.

Because repeated thoughts become beliefs.

Repeated beliefs become behaviors.

Repeated behaviors become outcomes.

The goal is not perfection.

The goal is growth.

To build an identity that supports the future you want rather than limiting it.

To see yourself not only as who you have been, but as who you are capable of becoming.

Because your future is influenced by the identity you reinforce today.

And the person you consistently believe yourself to be is often the person you eventually become.

WEALTH LESSON

Healthy self-identity improves discipline, confidence, and long-term decision-making.

AFFIRMATION

"I build an identity rooted in discipline, confidence, peace, and growth."

TODAY'S POWER MOVE

Replace one negative thought about yourself with a stronger truth today.

DAY 99

Success Requires Emotional Maturity

POWER QUOTE

"Greater opportunities require greater emotional control."

REFLECTION

Many people focus on what success can provide.

More income.

More opportunities.

More influence.

More freedom.

What they often overlook is what success requires.

Greater responsibility.

Greater accountability.

Greater emotional stability.

Every new level of life introduces new challenges.

More decisions.

More pressure.

More expectations.

More situations that test your patience, character, and judgment.

Which is why emotional maturity matters so much.

A person may have talent but struggle with criticism.

They may have ambition but avoid accountability.

They may receive opportunities but lack the emotional discipline required to manage them effectively.

In these situations, success becomes difficult to sustain.

Because achievement is not only about reaching a destination.

It is about handling the responsibilities that come with it.

Emotionally mature people approach life differently.

They do not allow every emotion to dictate their actions.

They pause before reacting.

They take ownership of mistakes.

They remain teachable.

They learn how to navigate disappointment without giving up and success without becoming careless.

This does not mean they never experience frustration, fear, or stress.

It means they learn how to manage those emotions rather than becoming controlled by them.

That ability becomes increasingly valuable as life grows more demanding.

Many opportunities are lost not because people lack ability, but because they lack the emotional capacity to handle pressure effectively.

For that reason, personal growth is about more than acquiring skills.

It is also about developing emotional strength.

The ability to remain steady during uncertainty.

Focused during distractions.

Responsible during success.

Resilient during setbacks.

The life you desire may require a level of maturity you are still developing today.

That is not a weakness.

It is part of the process.

Growth is not simply about receiving more.

It is about becoming more.

More disciplined.

More grounded.

More self-aware.

More capable of carrying what you have been given.

Because success is rarely sustained by talent alone.

It is sustained by the character, wisdom, and emotional maturity behind it.

WEALTH LESSON

Emotional control protects long-term opportunities and financial stability.

AFFIRMATION

"I grow emotionally stronger, wiser, and more disciplined every day."

TODAY'S POWER MOVE

Respond calmly today in a situation where you would normally react emotionally.

DAY 100

You Are Building Legacy

POWER QUOTE

"The decisions you make today can change generations after you."

REFLECTION

Many people spend years focused only on immediate needs.

The next bill.

The next problem.

The next stressful situation.

The next obstacle that must be overcome.

And while survival is sometimes necessary, there comes a point where growth requires a bigger perspective.

A legacy perspective.

Legacy thinking changes the questions people ask.

Instead of asking, "How do I get through today?"

They begin asking, "What am I building for tomorrow?"

Instead of focusing only on temporary comfort, they begin considering long-term impact.

The impact of their decisions.

Their habits.

Their mindset.

Their character.

Their example.

Because every person leaves something behind.

Not only money.

Not only possessions.

But patterns.

Beliefs.

Values.

Standards.

And ways of thinking.

Future generations often inherit more than financial resources.

They inherit emotional patterns.

Relationship habits.

Mindsets about money.

Attitudes toward discipline.

Approaches to adversity.

Which is why personal growth matters so much.

The work you do on yourself today may influence people you never meet.

The healing you pursue may stop cycles that have existed for generations.

The discipline you develop may create opportunities that did not previously exist for your family.

The courage you demonstrate may inspire someone else to pursue a different future.

Never underestimate the power of one person deciding to change.

Throughout history, countless families have been transformed because one individual chose a different path.

One person chose responsibility over excuses.

One person chose healing over denial.

One person chose growth over comfort.

One person chose to think beyond themselves.

Legacy is not built in a single moment.

It is built through daily decisions repeated over time.

The choices you make today are helping shape the future that follows you.

For that reason, do not think only about what your decisions provide in the present.

Think about what they create in the future.

Think about the example they establish.

Think about the doors they may open.

Because your life is bigger than the current season you are experiencing.

And sometimes the most powerful thing a person can do is become the turning point that changes a family, a community, or a future generation forever.

WEALTH LESSON

Long-term wealth is built through intentional decisions repeated consistently across time.

AFFIRMATION

"I build wealth, discipline, healing, and legacy intentionally."

TODAY'S POWER MOVE

Make one decision today that benefits your long-term future instead of temporary comfort.

DAY 101

Discipline Will Carry You Further Than Talent

POWER QUOTE

"Talent may open doors, but discipline keeps them open."

REFLECTION

Many people spend years focused only on immediate needs.

The next bill.

The next problem.

The next stressful situation.

The next obstacle that must be overcome.

And while survival is sometimes necessary, there comes a point where growth requires a bigger perspective.

A legacy perspective.

Legacy thinking changes the questions people ask.

Instead of asking, "How do I get through today?"

They begin asking, "What am I building for tomorrow?"

Instead of focusing only on temporary comfort, they begin considering long-term impact.

The impact of their decisions.

Their habits.

Their mindset.

Their character.

Their example.

Because every person leaves something behind.

Not only money.

Not only possessions.

But patterns.

Beliefs.

Values.

Standards.

And ways of thinking.

Future generations often inherit more than financial resources.

They inherit emotional patterns.

Relationship habits.

Mindsets about money.

Attitudes toward discipline.

Approaches to adversity.

That is why personal growth matters so much.

The work you do on yourself today may influence people you never meet.

The healing you pursue may stop cycles that have existed for generations.

The discipline you develop may create opportunities that did not previously exist for your family.

The courage you demonstrate may inspire someone else to pursue a different future.

Never underestimate the power of one person deciding to change.

Throughout history, countless families have been transformed because one individual chose a different path.

One person chose responsibility over excuses.

One person chose healing over denial.

One person chose growth over comfort.

One person chose to think beyond themselves.

Legacy is not built in a single moment.

It is built through daily decisions repeated over time.

The choices you make today are helping shape the future that follows you.

For that reason, do not think only about what your decisions provide in the present.

Think about what they create in the future.

Think about the example they establish.

Think about the doors they may open.

Because your life is bigger than the current season you are experiencing.

And sometimes the most powerful thing a person can do is become the turning point that changes a family, a community, or a future generation forever.

WEALTH LESSON

Consistency compounds over time and often outperforms temporary talent or emotional motivation.

AFFIRMATION

"I remain disciplined even when emotions fluctuate."

TODAY'S POWER MOVE

Finish one important responsibility today without waiting to feel inspired first.

DAY 102

Stop Letting Temporary Emotions Control Permanent Decisions

POWER QUOTE

"A temporary emotion should never destroy a long-term future."

REFLECTION

Every person experiences emotions.

Anger.

Fear.

Disappointment.

Anxiety.

Frustration.

Excitement.

Emotions are a normal part of being human.

They provide valuable information about what is happening within us and around us.

The problem begins when emotions become the primary driver of our decisions.

Many of the most costly mistakes people make happen during highly emotional moments.

A person becomes angry and damages a relationship.

A person becomes discouraged and abandons a goal.

A person becomes anxious and makes a financial decision they later regret.

A person becomes fearful and walks away from an opportunity that could have changed their future.

The issue is not the emotion itself.

The issue is allowing temporary feelings to determine permanent decisions.

Emotionally mature people understand an important truth:

Feelings change.

A difficult emotion that feels overwhelming today may feel completely different tomorrow.

That is why creating space between emotion and action is so valuable.

Instead of reacting immediately, they pause.

They reflect.

They evaluate.

They ask questions.

They allow wisdom to participate in the decision-making process.

This does not mean ignoring emotions.

It means learning how to manage them.

Emotions should be acknowledged.

Respected.

Understood.

But they should not always be obeyed.

There is a difference between feeling fear and allowing fear to make every decision.

There is a difference between feeling anger and allowing anger to control behavior.

There is a difference between feeling anxiety and allowing anxiety to determine the future.

One of the greatest forms of strength is emotional discipline.

The ability to remain steady when circumstances become difficult.

The ability to think clearly when pressure increases.

The ability to respond intentionally rather than react impulsively.

This skill protects relationships.

Protects opportunities.

Protects finances.

Protects peace.

Most importantly, it protects your future.

Because many of life's biggest breakthroughs come from people who learned how to stay calm long enough to make wise decisions.

Feel your emotions.

Learn from your emotions.

But do not surrender control of your life to them.

A calm mind often sees what a reactive mind cannot.

And the future you desire deserves decisions made from wisdom, not impulse.

WEALTH LESSON

Emotional control improves financial stability because intentional decisions usually outperform impulsive reactions.

AFFIRMATION

"I pause, reflect, and respond wisely instead of reacting emotionally."

TODAY'S POWER MOVE

Before making decisions today, ask yourself whether they align with your long-term peace.

DAY 103

You Deserve To Experience Peace

POWER QUOTE

"Peace is not laziness. Peace is emotional stability."

REFLECTION

Not everyone grows up experiencing stability.

Some people become familiar with stress before they ever experience peace.

They learn how to survive uncertainty.

How to navigate chaos.

How to function while carrying emotional pressure.

Over time, survival becomes normal.

The constant tension.

The constant worry.

The constant feeling that something could go wrong at any moment.

When this becomes a person's normal experience, peace can feel unfamiliar.

Even uncomfortable.

Not because peace is bad.

Because it is different.

Many people spend years preparing for problems but never learn how to enjoy stability when it finally arrives.

They remain emotionally on guard.

Waiting for the next disappointment.

The next setback.

The next crisis.

Without realizing it, they continue living as if danger is always present.

But survival mode was never meant to become a permanent lifestyle.

It was designed to help people endure difficult seasons.

Not define the rest of their lives.

There is a difference between surviving and living.

Survival focuses on making it through the day.

Living focuses on building a meaningful future.

Survival reacts.

Living creates.

Survival protects.

Living grows.

This is why healing is so important.

Healing helps people recognize that peace is not something they must earn through suffering.

It is something they can intentionally build.

A peaceful life is not a perfect life.

Problems will still appear.

Challenges will still exist.

Unexpected situations will still happen.

The difference is that peace allows people to face those situations from a place of stability rather than panic.

A peaceful mind thinks clearly.

Makes wiser decisions.

Builds healthier relationships.

Pursues goals with greater consistency.

And creates a foundation strong enough to support long-term growth.

You deserve that kind of life.

A life where every day is not a crisis.

A life where your future is not controlled by fear.

A life where success is measured not only by what you achieve, but by how healthy and whole you feel while achieving it.

Do not become so comfortable with chaos that you forget peace is possible.

Do not become so accustomed to surviving that you forget how to live.

Because one of the greatest forms of growth is realizing that your future deserves more than survival.

It deserves stability.

It deserves healing.

It deserves peace.

WEALTH LESSON

Emotional peace improves decision-making, focus, and long-term financial discipline.

AFFIRMATION

"I allow peace, stability, and emotional balance into my life."

TODAY'S POWER MOVE

Create one healthy boundary today that protects your peace.

DAY 104

Structure Creates Freedom

POWER QUOTE

"People who prepare intentionally experience less chaos later."

REFLECTION

It is easy to believe freedom and structure are opposite.

They imagine structure as restrictive.

Rigid.

Limiting.

Something that takes away spontaneity and flexibility.

But in reality, the opposite is often true.

Structure is what makes freedom possible.

A budget creates financial awareness.

A schedule creates focus.

Boundaries protect energy.

Routines create stability.

Systems reduce unnecessary stress.

Without structure, life often becomes reactive.

People spend their days responding to problems instead of preparing for them.

Important responsibilities are forgotten.

Deadlines are missed.

Money is spent impulsively.

Priorities become unclear.

Everything begins feeling urgent because nothing has been organized intentionally.

Which is why so many people feel overwhelmed.

Not because they lack ability.

But because they lack systems that support their goals.

Structure creates clarity.

And clarity creates confidence.

When you know where your money is going, financial decisions become easier.

When you know how your time is being used, priorities become clearer.

When you establish healthy boundaries, relationships become healthier.

When routines become consistent, progress becomes more predictable.

None of these systems remove freedom.

They create it.

The person with a financial plan experiences greater financial freedom.

The person with healthy routines experiences greater flexibility.

The person with strong boundaries experiences greater peace.

The strongest individuals are rarely the ones relying on motivation every day.

They are often the ones who created systems that continue working even when motivation disappears.

Because motivation fluctuates.

Systems remain.

That is why preparation matters.

Good intentions are valuable.

But intentions without structure often produce inconsistent results.

The future you desire requires more than wishing.

More than hoping.

More than waiting.

It requires preparation.

The habits.

The routines.

The systems.

The daily practices that support the life you are trying to build.

Do not view structure as a limitation.

View it as a foundation.

Because the freedom you desire is often built upon the structure you are willing to create today.

And the strongest futures are rarely built accidentally.

They are built intentionally, one system at a time.

WEALTH LESSON

Financial organization creates confidence because awareness improves control and decision-making.

AFFIRMATION

"I create structure that supports my peace, discipline, and future."

TODAY'S POWER MOVE

Organize one financial or personal system today that has been creating stress.

DAY 105

You Are Allowed To Grow Beyond People's Expectations

POWER QUOTE

"You do not need permission to evolve."

REFLECTION

Growth changes people.

It changes priorities.

It changes habits.

It changes standards.

It changes the way people think, respond, and move through life.

While growth is often celebrated in theory, it is not always welcomed in practice.

Especially by people who became comfortable with an older version of you.

The version that thought smaller.

The version that tolerated more.

The version that lacked boundaries.

The version that doubted themselves.

The version that stayed predictable.

When you begin changing, some people may struggle to understand it.

Not because your growth is wrong.

Because your growth challenges the image they became accustomed to.

People often feel comfortable when others remain the same.

Change forces adjustment.

And not everyone is willing to adjust.

Which is why growth sometimes feels lonely.

You begin outgrowing habits that once felt normal.

Conversations that once felt meaningful.

Environments that once felt familiar.

Ways of thinking that once defined you.

The process can feel uncomfortable because growth often requires leaving something behind.

Old patterns.

Old limitations.

Old identities.

But this discomfort is not a sign that you should stop.

It is often a sign that transformation is taking place.

You are not required to remain small so others can remain comfortable.

You are not required to stay stuck in order to meet someone else's expectations.

You are allowed to heal.

Allowed to mature.

Allowed to become more disciplined.

Allowed to become more focused.

Allowed to pursue a bigger vision for your life.

Growth is not betrayal.

It is development.

It is the natural result of learning, healing, and becoming more intentional.

The future version of you is depending on the choices you make today.

The boundaries you establish.

The habits you build.

The standards you raise.

The courage you demonstrate.

Do not apologize for becoming the person you are capable of becoming.

Do not shrink to fit spaces you have outgrown.

Do not abandon your progress to maintain familiarity.

Keep growing.

Keep evolving.

Keep becoming.

Because the life you desire may require a version of you that does not yet fully exist.

And the courage to become that person is one of the greatest gifts you can give yourself.

WEALTH LESSON

Growth often requires emotional independence and the courage to outgrow limiting environments.

AFFIRMATION

"I allow myself to evolve fully without guilt or fear."

TODAY'S POWER MOVE

Make one decision today that aligns with the person you are becoming instead of the person you used to be.

DAY 106

Stop Feeding Self-Doubt

POWER QUOTE

"The way you speak to yourself affects the way you build your life."

REFLECTION

Every person has a voice they hear more than anyone else's.

Their own.

From the moment they wake up until the moment they fall asleep, they are engaged in an ongoing conversation with themselves.

The question is:

What is that conversation creating?

For many people, the internal dialogue is far harsher than any criticism they receive from others.

They focus on mistakes.

Magnify weaknesses.

Question their abilities.

And replay failures repeatedly.

Over time, these thoughts begin shaping identity.

Not because they are true.

Because they are repeated.

The mind tends to believe what it hears consistently.

That is why self-talk matters so much.

A person who constantly tells themselves they are incapable will often begin acting that way.

A person who repeatedly focuses on limitations may stop pursuing opportunities.

A person who continuously criticizes themselves may struggle to build confidence, even when evidence suggests they are capable.

This does not mean ignoring reality.

Healthy self-talk is not pretending everything is perfect.

It is speaking truthfully while remaining compassionate.

It is acknowledging mistakes without turning them into identity.

It is recognizing weaknesses without allowing them to define the future.

It is treating yourself with the same patience you would offer someone you genuinely care about.

Many people would never speak to a loved one the way they speak to themselves.

Yet they accept that harshness as normal.

The truth is that growth becomes much harder when your mind feels like a hostile environment.

Confidence grows more easily in an environment of encouragement.

Resilience grows more easily in an environment of belief.

Discipline grows more easily in an environment where mistakes become lessons rather than permanent labels.

Pay attention to the words you repeat.

Pay attention to the labels you accept.

Pay attention to the stories you continue telling yourself.

Because your thoughts influence your actions.

Your actions influence your habits.

And your habits influence your future.

The goal is not perfection.

The goal is creating an internal environment that supports growth.

One where honesty and compassion can exist together.

One where accountability and encouragement work side by side.

One where the voice you listen to most becomes a source of strength rather than limitation.

Because the way you speak to yourself today is helping shape the person you become tomorrow.

WEALTH LESSON

Healthy self-perception improves discipline, confidence, and long-term emotional stability.

AFFIRMATION

"I speak to myself with strength, belief, and emotional wisdom."

TODAY'S POWER MOVE

Replace one negative self-belief today with a stronger truth.

DAY 107

Your Healing Will Change Your Future

POWER QUOTE

"Healing changes the way people build their lives."

REFLECTION

Many people think healing is only about emotions.

They think it is simply about feeling better.

Feeling happier.

Feeling less stressed.

Feeling more at peace.

While healing certainly affects emotions, its impact reaches much deeper.

Healing changes how people see themselves.

How they communicate.

How they handle conflict.

How they manage money.

How they build relationships.

How they respond to pressure.

How they make decisions.

Unhealed pain often influences behavior in ways people do not immediately recognize.

A person may struggle to trust because of past betrayal.

They may avoid opportunities because of previous failures.

They may overspend because spending temporarily relieves emotional discomfort.

They may react defensively because old wounds still feel present.

Without realizing it, unresolved pain can become a silent architect of daily decisions.

Which is why healing matters so much.

Healing creates freedom.

Freedom from patterns that no longer serve you.

Freedom from reactions rooted in old experiences.

Freedom from emotional burdens that continue influencing the present.

A healed person is not someone who has never been hurt.

A healed person is someone who no longer allows old pain to control their future.

They learn how to respond instead of react.

How to communicate instead of withdraw.

How to build instead of merely survive.

Healing creates space.

Space for better choices.

Healthier relationships.

Greater self-respect.

Stronger boundaries.

Clearer thinking.

More intentional living.

The transformation often happens gradually.

One conversation.

One realization.

One healthy decision at a time.

At first, the changes may seem small.

But over time they compound.

The way a person thinks changes.

The way they act changes.

The way they lead changes.

The way they live changes.

As a result, healing should never be viewed as a distraction from success.

It is often a foundation for success.

Because the strongest lives are not built only through achievement.

They are built through wholeness.

Through self-awareness.

Through growth.

Through the courage to confront what needs attention and the commitment to keep moving forward.

Never underestimate the power of healing.

A single season of intentional healing can alter the direction of relationships, finances, opportunities, and decisions for years to come.

And sometimes the most important thing you build is not a business, a career, or a bank account.

Sometimes the most important thing you build is a healthier version of yourself.

WEALTH LESSON

Emotional healing improves financial behavior because regulated emotions create wiser decisions.

AFFIRMATION

"I allow healing to transform the way I live, think, and build."

TODAY'S POWER MOVE

Spend intentional time today caring for your emotional health.

DAY 108

Stop Waiting To Feel Perfect

POWER QUOTE

"Growth begins when excuses end."

REFLECTION

A lot of people delay their future because they believe they need to become perfect before taking action.

Perfect confidence.

Perfect timing.

Perfect preparation.

But perfection is often procrastination wearing a more acceptable disguise.

The people who change their lives usually begin while still nervous, uncertain, and imperfect.

Because growth happens through movement.

Not endless waiting.

You learn through doing.

You improve through repetition.

You strengthen through experience.

Do not allow perfectionism to become the reason your future stays delayed.

Transformation often begins in the uncomfortable moment when you finally tell the truth about what your habits are creating.

The way a person thinks, responds emotionally, and follows through eventually affects every area of their future.

A life changes when intentional decisions become consistent enough to reshape behavior, identity, and direction.

The version of you willing to keep learning, healing, adjusting, and rebuilding is the version that eventually changes the story.

WEALTH LESSON

Execution creates progress faster than overthinking ever will.

AFFIRMATION

"I stop waiting for perfection and begin moving with courage."

TODAY'S POWER MOVE

Take one imperfect but intentional step toward your future today.

DAY 109

Emotional Strength Is Powerful

POWER QUOTE

"People who control themselves well often build stronger lives."

REFLECTION

Many people misunderstand emotional strength.

They assume strong people do not feel fear.

Do not feel sadness.

Do not feel frustration.

Do not feel stress.

But emotional strength is not the absence of emotion.

It is the ability to manage emotion wisely.

Every person experiences difficult feelings.

The difference is how they respond to them.

Some people react immediately.

They speak before thinking.

Spend before planning.

Quit before evaluating.

Allow temporary emotions to determine permanent decisions.

Others learn a different approach.

They pause.

They breathe.

They reflect.

They create space between what they feel and what they do.

This space is where emotional discipline is developed.

It is where better decisions are made.

It is where relationships are protected.

It is where opportunities are preserved.

Life will always contain pressure.

Unexpected problems will arise.

Disappointments will happen.

Stressful seasons will come and go.

No amount of preparation can completely remove these realities.

What preparation can do is help you respond more effectively when they arrive.

Emotionally disciplined people understand that every feeling does not require an immediate reaction.

Not every frustration requires an argument.

Not every fear requires retreat.

Not every setback requires surrender.

Sometimes the strongest response is patience.

Sometimes it is perspective.

Sometimes it is choosing not to react until emotions have settled.

This type of self-control creates stability.

It protects relationships from unnecessary damage.

Protects finances from impulsive decisions.

Protects goals from temporary discouragement.

Protects opportunities from emotional overreactions.

Some people believe success is primarily about talent or intelligence.

But countless opportunities are lost because people lack emotional stability during difficult moments.

Success often places people under greater pressure, not less.

Which is why emotional strength becomes increasingly valuable as life expands.

The goal is not to suppress emotions.

The goal is to understand them without becoming controlled by them.

To feel deeply while still thinking clearly.

To remain human while also remaining intentional.

Because true strength is not found in pretending emotions do not exist.

True strength is found in learning how to lead yourself through them.

And the person who can remain grounded during difficult seasons often gains an advantage that lasts far beyond the temporary challenge itself.

WEALTH LESSON

Emotional discipline improves financial stability because calm thinking creates stronger long-term decisions.

AFFIRMATION

"I become emotionally stronger, calmer, and wiser every day."

TODAY'S POWER MOVE

Respond intentionally instead of emotionally in one situation today.

DAY 110

Your Future Deserves Your Best Effort

POWER QUOTE

"The life you want requires a version of you that stays committed."

REFLECTION

Almost everyone enjoys the beginning.

The excitement of a new goal.

The energy of a fresh start.

The motivation that comes from imagining a better future.

Beginnings are inspiring.

The challenge comes later.

When the excitement fades.

When progress feels slower than expected.

When distractions appear.

When obstacles emerge.

When results are not immediately visible.

This is where many people drift away from the very future they once wanted.

Not because they stopped caring.

Because commitment became harder than they expected.

The truth is that meaningful transformation requires more than enthusiasm.

It requires consistency.

Anyone can work hard for a few days.

Anyone can stay motivated for a short season.

The people who change their lives are often the people who learn how to continue long after motivation fades.

They understand that discipline is not about how you feel on your best days.

It is about what you do on ordinary days.

The days when energy is low.

The days when progress feels invisible.

The days when no one is encouraging you.

The days when quitting would feel easier.

These are the moments that shape the future.

Because commitment is proven when circumstances become difficult.

A person who stays committed develops something powerful.

Trust in themselves.

Every time they continue despite discomfort, they reinforce the belief that they can be relied upon.

Every time they honor their responsibilities, they strengthen their character.

Every time they keep moving forward, they build momentum.

The future you desire deserves that level of commitment.

It deserves preparation.

It deserves discipline.

It deserves focus.

It deserves the willingness to keep building even when immediate rewards are absent.

Do not confuse slow progress with failure.

Do not mistake difficulty for a sign to quit.

Do not allow temporary emotions to determine permanent outcomes.

Stay committed.

Stay focused.

Stay in the process.

Because most extraordinary results are not created by extraordinary effort once.

They are created by ordinary effort repeated consistently over time.

And one day, the work that felt unnoticed will become the foundation of the life you worked so hard to build.

The future belongs to those who remain committed long enough to meet it.

WEALTH LESSON

Long-term success requires emotional endurance and repeated disciplined action.

AFFIRMATION

"I remain committed to building the future I deserve."

TODAY'S POWER MOVE

Dedicate focused time today toward one long-term goal or responsibility.

DAY 111

Do Not Let Discouragement Make You Quit

POWER QUOTE

"Some of the most powerful breakthroughs happen after the season where people almost gave up."

REFLECTION

Discouragement rarely arrives all at once.

It often appears gradually.

A setback here.

A disappointment there.

A season where progress feels slower than expected.

A period where effort seems disconnected from results.

Over time, discouragement begins asking questions.

"Is this worth it?"

"Am I making any real progress?"

"Should I just give up?"

These questions are common.

Almost every person pursuing meaningful growth encounters them at some point.

The danger is not experiencing discouragement.

The danger is allowing discouragement to become a decision-maker.

Feelings are powerful, but they are not always accurate indicators of reality.

A difficult season does not automatically mean you are failing.

A slow season does not automatically mean you are stuck.

A challenging season does not automatically mean your effort is wasted.

Many of the most important transformations happen before visible results appear.

Skills develop before opportunities arrive.

Character strengthens before success becomes visible.

Discipline deepens before momentum accelerates.

Foundations are often built long before anyone sees the structure standing above them.

This is why emotional endurance matters.

Endurance is the ability to continue when emotions become unreliable.

To keep showing up when enthusiasm fades.

To keep building when recognition is absent.

To keep believing when outcomes remain uncertain.

The people who eventually change their lives are not always the most talented.

They are often the people who stayed in the process longer than others.

They learned how to continue through seasons that tempted them to quit.

They understood that temporary frustration should not be allowed to destroy long-term potential.

Every meaningful goal will encounter resistance.

Every worthwhile dream will experience moments of doubt.

Every journey of growth will include periods where progress feels slower than expected.

These moments are not signs that you should stop.

They are opportunities to strengthen the commitment that brought you this far.

Do not allow a temporary emotion to make a permanent decision.

Do not allow one difficult season to define the entire story.

Keep building.

Keep learning.

Keep showing up.

Because the future you are working toward may be closer than you realize.

And many of life's greatest breakthroughs belong to people who simply refused to quit during the seasons when quitting seemed most reasonable.

Sometimes the most courageous thing you can do is continue.

And often, that decision changes everything.

WEALTH LESSON

Long-term success requires emotional endurance because meaningful growth rarely happens instantly.

AFFIRMATION

"I continue building even when emotions try to convince me to stop."

TODAY'S POWER MOVE

Complete one important task today even if motivation feels low.

DAY 112

Your Habits Reveal Your Priorities

POWER QUOTE

"The way you repeatedly spend your time reveals what truly matters to you."

REFLECTION

People often judge their lives by intentions.

The goals they set.

The dreams they talk about.

The future they hope to create.

But intentions tell only part of the story.

Habits tell the rest.

What you repeatedly do reveals where your life is actually headed.

Not what you wish for.

Not what you plan to do someday.

What you consistently practice.

Every day, your habits are casting votes for the person you are becoming.

The way you spend your mornings.

The way you manage your money.

The way you use your attention.

The way you respond to pressure.

The way you invest your time.

These actions may seem small in isolation.

Yet together, they create direction.

Many people desire peace while maintaining habits that create stress.

They desire financial freedom while practicing financial inconsistency.

They desire growth while repeatedly choosing distraction.

The challenge is that outcomes often follow patterns.

A distracted lifestyle usually produces distracted results.

A reactive lifestyle often produces unnecessary instability.

A disciplined lifestyle creates a different future.

Not instantly.

Gradually.

The power of habits is not found in what they accomplish in a single day.

It is found in what they accomplish over months and years.

Small behaviors repeated long enough become character.

Character influences decisions.

Decisions influence outcomes.

That is why lasting transformation often begins with routine rather than motivation.

Motivation can inspire action.

But habits sustain it.

Motivation comes and goes.

Habits remain.

The most successful people are not always the most motivated.

They are often the people who built systems of behavior that support the life they want to create.

Their routines work for them instead of against them.

Their daily actions align with their long-term vision.

Take an honest look at your habits.

Not with judgment.

With awareness.

Ask yourself what your routines are producing.

Ask yourself whether your behaviors align with the future you say you want.

Because your habits are telling a story.

They are quietly shaping your identity.

Quietly influencing your future.

And whether intentionally or unintentionally, they are creating the life you will eventually experience.

Choose them carefully.

Because the future is often hidden inside the routines you repeat today.

WEALTH LESSON

Daily habits compound financially, emotionally, and mentally over time.

AFFIRMATION

"I build habits that align with the future I desire."

TODAY'S POWER MOVE

Evaluate whether your daily habits match the life you claim you want.

DAY 113

Confidence Requires Self-Respect

POWER QUOTE

"Confidence grows when your actions begin matching your standards."

REFLECTION

Countless people look for confidence in achievements, approval, or perfect timing.

They believe confidence comes from achievements.

Recognition.

Success.

Validation from other people.

While those things may influence confidence temporarily, lasting confidence is usually built on something deeper.

Self-respect.

Self-respect is the belief that your life has value.

That your future matters.

That your well-being deserves protection.

That your goals deserve effort.

That your peace deserves preservation.

This belief quietly influences behavior.

People who respect themselves make different decisions.

They become more intentional about where they spend their time.

More careful about the environments they remain in.

More protective of their energy.

More disciplined with their finances.

More committed to habits that support growth.

Not because they think they are better than anyone else.

Because they recognize their future is worth protecting.

This is where many people misunderstand confidence.

Confidence is not arrogance.

It is not superiority.

It is not believing you are more important than others.

True confidence is often much quieter.

It is the calm certainty that comes from consistently honoring yourself.

Keeping promises to yourself.

Following through on responsibilities.

Making decisions that align with your values.

Protecting your standards even when it would be easier not to.

Every time you do these things, you strengthen self-respect.

And self-respect becomes the foundation of confidence.

The opposite is also true.

When people repeatedly ignore their own boundaries, abandon their goals, or tolerate things that damage their well-being, self-respect begins to weaken.

Over time, confidence becomes difficult to maintain because the foundation beneath it has been neglected.

Which is why daily choices matter.

Every healthy boundary.

Every disciplined decision.

Every responsibility honored.

Every act of self-care.

Every moment of integrity.

These actions communicate a message to yourself:

"My future matters."

That message, repeated often enough, changes identity.

It changes standards.

It changes behavior.

And eventually, it changes the way a person moves through life.

If you want greater confidence, start by strengthening self-respect.

Treat yourself like someone whose future is worth protecting.

Honor your commitments.

Protect your peace.

Raise your standards.

Invest in your growth.

Because confidence is not something you pretend to have.

It is something you build through the way you consistently treat yourself.

And the person who respects themselves deeply often develops a confidence that no outside circumstance can easily take away.

WEALTH LESSON

People who value themselves often make stronger financial and emotional decisions long-term.

AFFIRMATION

“I respect myself enough to protect my peace, discipline, and future.”

TODAY’S POWER MOVE

Make one decision today that reflects higher self-respect.

DAY 114

Stop Running From Responsibility

POWER QUOTE

"Freedom grows when responsibility is handled consistently."

REFLECTION

Many people dream about freedom.

Financial freedom.

Emotional freedom.

Freedom over their time.

Freedom from stress.

Freedom to live life on their own terms.

Yet few people stop to consider what creates that freedom in the first place.

Responsibility.

The freedom people admire is often built upon responsibilities others were willing to accept.

The person with financial freedom usually learned how to manage money responsibly.

The person with emotional peace usually learned how to address difficult emotions honestly.

The person with greater flexibility often learned how to prepare before circumstances forced them to.

This is why responsibility should not be viewed as punishment.

Responsibility is preparation.

It is the process of becoming capable.

Capable of handling greater opportunities.

Greater resources.

Greater influence.

Greater freedom.

Avoidance may provide temporary comfort.

But it often creates long-term consequences.

The conversation avoided today may become a larger conflict tomorrow.

The budget ignored today may become financial stress later.

The responsibility postponed today may become a heavier burden in the future.

Problems rarely disappear because they are ignored.

More often, they grow.

Which is why maturity matters.

Mature people learn how to face reality honestly.

They do not run from responsibilities simply because they are uncomfortable.

They understand that discomfort is often part of growth.

Instead of constantly escaping pressure, they learn how to manage it.

Instead of panicking, they prepare.

Instead of avoiding difficult truths, they confront them with courage.

This mindset changes everything.

Because every responsibility handled today creates a stronger foundation for tomorrow.

Every challenge faced develops resilience.

Every difficult conversation builds confidence.

Every act of preparation creates greater stability.

Freedom is rarely the result of luck.

It is often the result of consistent responsibility practiced over time.

The future you desire will likely require more from you than your current situation demands.

More discipline.

More planning.

More accountability.

More ownership.

That is not something to fear.

It is an invitation to grow into the person capable of sustaining the life you want.

Do not run from responsibility.

Learn from it.

Grow through it.

Because the responsibilities you embrace today may become the freedoms you enjoy tomorrow.

And many of the most stable, successful, and peaceful lives are built by people who chose responsibility long before they saw the rewards.

WEALTH LESSON

Financial freedom increases when people consistently manage responsibilities instead of avoiding them.

AFFIRMATION

"I handle my responsibilities with maturity, discipline, and courage."

TODAY'S POWER MOVE

Address one responsibility today that you have been delaying emotionally.

DAY 115

Your Future Requires Emotional Stability

POWER QUOTE

"A peaceful future cannot be built through constant emotional chaos."

REFLECTION

Many people spend years pursuing external success.

A better career.

More income.

Greater influence.

Bigger opportunities.

While these goals can be valuable, they are often difficult to sustain without something equally important:

Emotional stability.

A person can achieve impressive results externally while struggling internally.

They can appear successful while feeling overwhelmed.

Accomplished while feeling exhausted.

Productive while feeling emotionally fragile.

The challenge is that internal instability eventually affects external outcomes.

It influences decision-making.

Relationships.

Discipline.

Confidence.

Leadership.

Financial behavior.

And countless other areas of life.

That is why emotional regulation matters so much.

Not because life will always be easy.

Because life will not.

Challenges are inevitable.

Pressure is unavoidable.

Unexpected setbacks will occur.

The goal is not to eliminate stress completely.

The goal is to develop the ability to remain grounded while experiencing it.

A calm mind operates differently than an overwhelmed one.

It sees situations more clearly.

It evaluates options more thoughtfully.

It communicates more effectively.

It responds with greater intention.

This creates a powerful advantage.

People often believe success is built primarily through effort.

Effort certainly matters.

But effort without stability can become unsustainable.

A person constantly operating from anxiety, panic, or emotional exhaustion will eventually struggle to maintain consistent progress.

Peace creates endurance.

Peace creates clarity.

Peace creates the space necessary for wise decisions.

This is why emotional stability should be viewed as an investment rather than a luxury.

It supports every other area of growth.

The person who develops inner stability becomes better equipped to handle opportunity.

Better equipped to manage pressure.

Better equipped to navigate uncertainty.

Better equipped to build a meaningful future.

Your goal should not be a life without challenges.

Your goal should be becoming the kind of person who can face challenges without losing themselves in the process.

Because growth needs a foundation.

Success needs a foundation.

And one of the strongest foundations a person can build is peace.

Not perfection.

Not constant happiness.

Peace.

The ability to remain steady when circumstances are not.

The ability to stay grounded when life becomes demanding.

The ability to continue building without allowing stress to control your direction.

Because peace does not slow growth.

Peace protects it.

WEALTH LESSON

Emotional regulation improves financial and personal decision-making because clear thinking creates stronger outcomes.

AFFIRMATION

“I build emotional stability, peace, and inner strength daily.”

TODAY’S POWER MOVE

Practice remaining calm today during a stressful moment instead of reacting impulsively.

DAY 116

Stop Destroying What You Pray For

POWER QUOTE

"Some people pray for growth while maintaining habits that destroy it."

REFLECTION

Many people genuinely desire a better future.

They want peace.

They want financial stability.

They want healthier relationships.

They want greater confidence.

They want meaningful growth.

The desire is real.

The challenge is that desire alone is not enough.

A person can sincerely want a different life while continuing habits that create the same outcomes.

They can hope for peace while constantly feeding chaos.

Hope for financial freedom while avoiding financial responsibility.

Hope for growth while resisting the changes growth requires.

This is where many people become frustrated.

They focus on what they want but rarely examine what their daily actions are producing.

The truth is that goals and habits must eventually work together.

Vision provides direction.

Behavior creates movement.

Without both, progress becomes difficult.

Imagine a person trying to travel north while walking south.

No matter how badly they want the destination, their actions are carrying them somewhere else.

The same principle applies to life.

Your routines are always moving you toward something.

Your habits are creating outcomes.

Your decisions are shaping a future.

Whether intentionally or unintentionally.

That is why self-awareness is so important.

It requires honesty.

The willingness to ask difficult questions.

Are my daily choices supporting the future I claim to want?

Are my habits creating the life I hope for?

Are my routines aligned with my values?

These questions are not meant to create shame.

They are meant to create clarity.

Because awareness creates opportunity.

The moment you recognize a pattern, you gain the ability to change it.

The moment you identify a contradiction, you gain the ability to correct it.

Transformation often begins when people stop blaming circumstances and start examining alignment.

When they realize that lasting change requires more than wishing.

It requires participation.

The future you desire deserves more than good intentions.

It deserves behaviors that support it.

Habits that reinforce it.

Decisions that move it forward.

The goal is not perfection.

The goal is alignment.

To make your actions reflect your vision.

Your routines reflect your values.

And your daily life reflect the future you are working to create.

Because real transformation begins when what you do finally matches what you say you want.

And when alignment is established, progress becomes much more difficult to stop.

WEALTH LESSON

Long-term success requires disciplined behavior that supports long-term goals consistently.

AFFIRMATION

"I align my habits, decisions, and mindset with the future I desire."

TODAY'S POWER MOVE

Notice one behavior today that contradicts your future goals and intentionally change it.

DAY 117

Discipline Is A Form Of Self-Love

POWER QUOTE

"Every disciplined decision says, 'My future matters.'"

REFLECTION

When people hear the phrase "self-love," they often think about comfort.

Rest.

Relaxation.

Kindness toward themselves.

These things are important.

But self-love is much bigger than comfort alone.

Real self-love includes responsibility.

It includes discipline.

It includes making decisions today that protect your future tomorrow.

A person who genuinely cares about their future understands that love is not only about feeling good in the moment.

It is also about doing what is necessary for long-term well-being.

Which is why discipline can be one of the highest forms of self-respect.

The disciplined person protects their health by making choices that support their body.

They protect their finances by managing money wisely.

They protect their peace by establishing healthy boundaries.

They protect their opportunities by preparing instead of procrastinating.

These actions may not always feel exciting.

Sometimes they require sacrifice.

Sometimes they require saying no.

Sometimes they require choosing what is beneficial over what is immediately comfortable.

But that is exactly what makes them powerful.

Discipline is not punishment.

It is protection.

It is the decision to care enough about your future that you are willing to prepare for it.

Many people mistakenly view discipline as restriction.

In reality, discipline often creates freedom.

The freedom that comes from good health.

The freedom that comes from financial stability.

The freedom that comes from emotional peace.

The freedom that comes from knowing you can trust yourself to follow through.

Every time you keep a promise to yourself, you strengthen that trust.

Every time you honor a healthy routine, you reinforce the belief that your future matters.

Every time you choose growth over temporary comfort, you invest in the life you are trying to create.

Therefore self-love cannot be measured only by how gently you treat yourself during difficult moments.

It must also be measured by how consistently you prepare for the future you say you want.

True self-love comforts when necessary.

But it also challenges.

It encourages growth.

It encourages responsibility.

It encourages better choices.

Because a person who truly values themselves does not only focus on today's feelings.

They also consider tomorrow's consequences.

And one of the greatest acts of love you can offer yourself is becoming disciplined enough to build a future you will one day be grateful for.

Because discipline is not the opposite of self-love.

Discipline is often self-love in action.

WEALTH LESSON

Self-discipline improves long-term stability because intentional habits create stronger outcomes over time.

AFFIRMATION

"I discipline myself because I deeply care about my future."

TODAY'S POWER MOVE

Choose one disciplined behavior today that supports long-term peace instead of short-term comfort.

DAY 118

Stop Hiding Your Gifts

POWER QUOTE

"The world cannot benefit from gifts you constantly hide."

REFLECTION

Many people assume that lack of success is caused by lack of talent.

Lack of intelligence.

Lack of opportunity.

Lack of ability.

While those challenges can exist, another obstacle often goes unnoticed:

Fear.

Fear has a remarkable ability to make capable people shrink.

It convinces them to stay quiet when they have something valuable to say.

It convinces them to remain hidden when they have gifts that could help others.

It convinces them to delay opportunities because visibility feels uncomfortable.

The challenge is that potential cannot create impact while it remains hidden.

A gift that is never used cannot serve anyone.

A voice that is never shared cannot influence anyone.

A vision that is never pursued cannot become reality.

Which is why courage matters.

Not because fear disappears.

Because it usually does not.

Courage is learning how to move forward while fear is still present.

Many people spend years waiting to feel completely confident before they step into bigger opportunities.

But confidence often develops after action, not before it.

The speaker becomes confident by speaking.

The leader becomes confident by leading.

The entrepreneur becomes confident by building.

The creator becomes confident by creating.

Growth requires participation.

It requires visibility.

It requires the willingness to be seen before you feel completely ready.

This can feel uncomfortable.

Visibility creates exposure.

Exposure creates vulnerability.

And vulnerability often creates fear.

But hiding has a cost as well.

Every opportunity avoided.

Every idea left unshared.

Every dream continuously postponed.

These costs quietly accumulate over time.

The world does not benefit from the gifts you never express.

And your future cannot fully develop if fear continues making your decisions.

You were not created to spend your life shrinking.

You were not created to silence your potential.

You were not created to hide your purpose because discomfort convinced you to stay small.

Your growth may require visibility.

It may require leadership.

It may require showing up before you feel fully prepared.

And that is okay.

Because every time you choose courage over fear, you create space for new possibilities.

New opportunities.

New relationships.

New impact.

New growth.

Do not wait until fear disappears.

Take the step anyway.

Share the idea anyway.

Use the gift anyway.

Because some of the greatest opportunities in your life may be waiting on the other side of the courage to finally stop hiding.

WEALTH LESSON

Visibility increases opportunities because people cannot support what they never see.

AFFIRMATION

"I stop hiding my gifts and allow myself to take up space confidently."

TODAY'S POWER MOVE

Share one idea, talent, or vision publicly today without overthinking it.

DAY 119

Feeling Lost Does Not Mean You Are Failing

POWER QUOTE

"Sometimes confusion is part of transformation, not proof of failure."

REFLECTION

Not every season of life comes with clear answers.

There are seasons where direction feels obvious.

Goals feel exciting.

Progress feels measurable.

The path ahead feels visible.

Then there are seasons that feel very different.

Seasons filled with uncertainty.

Questions.

Waiting.

Transition.

Moments where clarity seems distant and the future feels difficult to understand.

These seasons can be frustrating.

Many people begin assuming something is wrong with them simply because they feel uncertain.

They interpret confusion as failure.

Lack of clarity as lack of purpose.

Discomfort as evidence that they are moving in the wrong direction.

But that is not always true.

Sometimes confusion is not destruction.

Sometimes it is transition.

Think about every major transformation in life.

Before a new chapter begins, the old chapter usually ends first.

Before a new identity develops, the previous identity often starts fading away.

Before greater clarity arrives, there is often a period where familiar answers no longer seem sufficient.

This space between who you were and who you are becoming can feel uncomfortable.

The old version of your life no longer fits.

The new version has not fully arrived.

You find yourself standing in between.

And "in between" seasons are rarely comfortable.

Yet they are often necessary.

Growth frequently happens beneath the surface before it becomes visible.

New perspectives are forming.

Old patterns are being challenged.

Lessons are being learned.

Strength is being developed.

Even when progress is difficult to measure.

As a result uncertainty should not automatically be viewed as a problem.

Sometimes uncertainty is evidence that you are stretching beyond old limitations.

Sometimes it is evidence that growth is taking place internally before it becomes visible externally.

The key is to keep moving.

Keep learning.

Keep exploring.

Keep showing up.

You do not need to have every answer today.

You do not need to understand every detail of the future before taking the next step.

Clarity often arrives through movement rather than endless analysis.

One decision at a time.

One lesson at a time.

One day at a time.

Trust that growth is still happening.

Trust that not every important transformation is immediately visible.

Trust that periods of uncertainty do not last forever.

Because some of the most meaningful chapters of life begin during seasons that initially felt confusing.

And one day, what feels unclear now may become the very season that prepared you for everything that comes next.

Your future is still unfolding.

Give it time.

WEALTH LESSON

Periods of uncertainty can become powerful seasons of growth when people remain disciplined and open to learning.

AFFIRMATION

"I trust that clarity will continue growing as I continue moving forward."

TODAY'S POWER MOVE

Spend quiet time today reflecting on the life you genuinely want to create.

DAY 120

You Are Becoming Stronger

POWER QUOTE

"Every difficult season is teaching you something your future will need."

REFLECTION

When people are living through difficult seasons, it is often hard to see anything beyond the struggle.

They see the setbacks.

The delays.

The disappointments.

The uncertainty.

The emotional weight of carrying responsibilities while wondering when things will finally improve.

In those moments, it can feel like life is only taking from them.

Only testing them.

Only exhausting them.

But difficult seasons are not always taking something away.

Sometimes they are building something within you.

The challenge is that growth is often difficult to recognize while it is happening.

A person living through financial pressure may be developing resourcefulness.

A person navigating uncertainty may be developing patience.

A person recovering from disappointment may be developing resilience.

A person facing repeated obstacles may be developing perseverance.

These qualities rarely develop during easy seasons.

They are usually forged during difficult ones.

As a result some of the strongest people you will ever meet are not people who avoided hardship.

They are people who endured it.

People who kept moving forward when circumstances invited them to quit.

People who continued rebuilding when life seemed determined to tear things apart.

People who learned how to remain standing when everything felt unstable.

Over time, those experiences changed them.

Not just externally.

Internally.

They became calmer.

Wiser.

More disciplined.

More emotionally grounded.

More capable of handling challenges that once would have overwhelmed them.

This does not mean pain should be celebrated.

Difficult seasons are still difficult.

Loss still hurts.

Disappointment still hurts.

Waiting still hurts.

But pain and purpose can sometimes exist in the same season.

A season can be uncomfortable while still being valuable.

A season can be difficult while still preparing you for something greater.

This is why perspective matters.

Instead of asking only, "Why is this happening to me?"

Sometimes it is helpful to ask, "What is this season teaching me?"

"What strength is being developed?"

"What qualities am I building?"

Because one day you may discover that the season you wanted to escape became the season that prepared you.

Prepared you to lead.

Prepared you to endure.

Prepared you to succeed.

Prepared you to help someone else.

Do not underestimate the work being done within you right now.

Even if progress feels slow.

Even if the lessons feel difficult.

Even if the future remains unclear.

Some of the greatest strengths a person possesses are built during seasons they never would have chosen for themselves.

And the resilience you are developing today may become one of the greatest assets you carry into tomorrow.

WEALTH LESSON

Resilience strengthens long-term growth because emotionally strong people recover faster from setbacks.

AFFIRMATION

"I become wiser, stronger, and more disciplined through every season."

TODAY'S POWER MOVE

Reflect on one difficult season that helped strengthen who you are becoming.

DAY 121

Your Mind Needs Discipline Too

POWER QUOTE

"A disciplined life begins with disciplined thinking."

REFLECTION

Most people understand the importance of managing their actions.

They focus on behavior.

Habits.

Routines.

Decisions.

All of these things matter.

But many people overlook something that influences every one of those areas:

Their thinking.

Every day, thoughts are shaping behavior.

The way you view yourself affects your confidence.

The way you view money affects your financial decisions.

The way you view challenges affects your resilience.

The way you view the future affects your willingness to keep moving forward.

Thoughts are powerful because they often become the lens through which life is interpreted.

A person who constantly expects failure may begin avoiding opportunities.

A person who believes they are incapable may stop trying before they have given themselves a fair chance.

A person who continually focuses on limitations may struggle to recognize possibilities.

Over time, these patterns influence behavior.

And behavior influences outcomes.

That is why mental discipline matters.

Mental discipline is not pretending negative thoughts never exist.

It is learning how to evaluate them rather than automatically believing them.

Not every thought deserves your trust.

Not every fear deserves your attention.

Not every internal criticism deserves a permanent place in your identity.

Many thoughts appear automatically.

But what you repeatedly focus on becomes far more influential.

The mind grows in the direction of consistent attention.

Feed fear constantly, and fear becomes stronger.

Feed hopelessness constantly, and hope becomes weaker.

Feed possibility, growth, and constructive thinking, and those patterns begin strengthening as well.

This does not mean ignoring reality.

Healthy thinking is not blind optimism.

It is choosing perspectives that help you move forward rather than remain trapped.

It is acknowledging challenges without becoming consumed by them.

It is recognizing weaknesses while still believing growth is possible.

It is speaking to yourself with honesty without constantly reinforcing defeat.

Pay attention to what you repeatedly tell yourself.

Pay attention to the narratives you continue feeding.

Pay attention to the assumptions shaping your decisions.

Because your mind is one of the most important environments you will ever live in.

And just as unhealthy environments can limit growth, unhealthy thinking can do the same.

Protect your mind.

Challenge limiting beliefs.

Strengthen empowering ones.

Become intentional about the thoughts you cultivate daily.

Because the future you build externally is often influenced by the conversations happening internally.

And one of the most powerful forms of discipline is learning how to direct your mind toward growth instead of allowing it to drift toward limitation.

WEALTH LESSON

Strong mental habits improve emotional stability, confidence, and long-term decision-making.

AFFIRMATION

"I discipline my mind to think with clarity, belief, and purpose."

TODAY'S POWER MOVE

Catch and replace one negative thought pattern today with a healthier truth.

DAY 122

Peace Requires Boundaries

POWER QUOTE

"People who constantly sacrifice their peace eventually lose themselves emotionally."

REFLECTION

Many people struggle with boundaries because they confuse them with rejection.

They worry that saying no will disappoint someone.

They worry that creating distance will appear selfish.

They worry that protecting their own needs will make them seem uncaring.

As a result, they continue giving long after they are exhausted.

They overextend themselves.

Ignore their own limits.

Stay in unhealthy situations longer than they should.

And slowly, the cost begins to accumulate.

Their energy decreases.

Their peace weakens.

Their focus becomes scattered.

Their emotional well-being suffers.

What began as a desire to avoid disappointing others eventually becomes a pattern of disappointing themselves.

Which is why boundaries matter.

Boundaries are not walls designed to keep everyone out.

They are guidelines that protect what is valuable.

They protect your time.

Your energy.

Your attention.

Your healing.

Your emotional stability.

Healthy boundaries allow relationships to exist without destroying your well-being.

They create clarity.

They create respect.

They create sustainability.

Without boundaries, people often become overwhelmed by responsibilities that were never theirs to carry.

They begin solving problems that do not belong to them.

Managing emotions that are not theirs to manage.

Sacrificing their peace in an attempt to keep everyone else comfortable.

But peace requires protection.

And protection requires limits.

Not everyone deserves unlimited access to your time.

Not everyone deserves unlimited access to your energy.

Not everyone deserves unlimited access to your emotions.

Access should be earned through trust, respect, and healthy behavior.

This does not make you selfish.

It makes you wise.

Because the quality of your environment influences the quality of your life.

Relationships influence mindset.

Mindset influences decisions.

Decisions influence the future.

The people who build healthy lives understand that boundaries are not an act of rejection.

They are an act of stewardship.

They are taking responsibility for the well-being they have been entrusted with.

Protecting your peace is not selfish.

Protecting your healing is not selfish.

Protecting your future is not selfish.

It is necessary.

You cannot continuously pour into everything around you while neglecting yourself.

Eventually, something will suffer.

And too often, it becomes your own growth.

Create boundaries that support the life you are building.

Honor the limits that preserve your well-being.

Protect the peace that allows you to grow.

Because some of the most important things in your life will only thrive when they are properly protected.

And boundaries are one of the ways that protection is created.

WEALTH LESSON

Healthy emotional boundaries improve focus, emotional discipline, and long-term stability.

AFFIRMATION

"I create healthy boundaries that protect my peace and future."

TODAY'S POWER MOVE

Say no to one thing today that continuously drains your energy unnecessarily.

DAY 123

Stop Romanticizing Struggle

POWER QUOTE

"You were not created to suffer forever in survival mode."

REFLECTION

Some people spend so much time surviving that they forget there is another way to live.

They become accustomed to pressure.

Accustomed to stress.

Accustomed to constantly solving problems.

Accustomed to carrying emotional weight every day.

Over time, struggle becomes familiar.

And what is familiar often begins to feel normal.

This is why many people unintentionally build an identity around survival.

They become the person who always endures.

Always pushes through.

Always carries the burden.

Always prepares for the next challenge.

While resilience is valuable, survival was never meant to become a permanent destination.

It was meant to be a season.

A temporary response to difficult circumstances.

Not a lifelong identity.

There is a difference between surviving and living.

Survival focuses on making it through.

Living focuses on building something meaningful.

Survival reacts to problems.

Living creates possibilities.

Survival protects against loss.

Living creates space for growth.

Many people work hard for years but never stop to ask an important question:

"What am I working toward?"

If the answer is only more struggle, then something has been misunderstood.

Yes, discipline matters.

Yes, sacrifice matters.

Yes, hard work matters.

But those things should eventually contribute to something greater.

Peace.

Stability.

Clarity.

Freedom.

Well-being.

A healthy life is not a life without effort.

It is a life where effort is connected to purpose rather than constant panic.

A life where growth is supported by stability.

A life where success does not come at the cost of your emotional health.

That is why healing is so important.

Healing teaches people that peace is not weakness.

Rest is not laziness.

Stability is not something to feel guilty about.

You do not need to create chaos in order to feel productive.

You do not need to remain exhausted in order to feel worthy.

You do not need to live in permanent survival mode to prove your strength.

Strength is not only found in enduring hardship.

It is also found in building a life where hardship no longer controls every decision.

You deserve more than endless survival.

You deserve mornings with peace.

Goals pursued with clarity.

Relationships built on stability.

A future supported by intention rather than fear.

Keep building.

Keep growing.

Keep healing.

But remember why you started.

The goal is not merely to survive life.

The goal is to create a life worth enjoying.

Because true success is not only measured by what you achieve.

It is also measured by the peace you experience while achieving it.

WEALTH LESSON

Financial freedom becomes meaningful when it creates stability, peace, and healthier living.

AFFIRMATION

"I release survival mode and build intentionally toward peace and stability."

TODAY'S POWER MOVE

Notice one unhealthy struggle pattern you have normalized and challenge it today.

DAY 124

The Small Decisions Matter

POWER QUOTE

"Your future is quietly being shaped by your smallest repeated choices."

REFLECTION

Many people underestimate the power of small decisions.

They focus on dramatic breakthroughs.

Major opportunities.

Life-changing moments.

Big accomplishments.

Because of this, they often overlook the daily choices that quietly shape the future.

A single disciplined morning may not seem significant.

One healthy financial decision may not appear life-changing.

One focused hour of work may not feel extraordinary.

One completed responsibility may not seem remarkable.

Yet life is rarely transformed by one decision alone.

Life is transformed by what those decisions become when repeated consistently.

This is the principle of compounding.

Small actions accumulate.

Small disciplines build momentum.

Small improvements create larger outcomes over time.

The challenge is that compounding often works invisibly at first.

Results arrive slowly.

Progress feels gradual.

Growth can seem difficult to measure.

Because people do not see immediate change, they sometimes assume their efforts are not working.

But growth is often happening beneath the surface long before it becomes obvious.

Consider the person who saves a small amount consistently.

The person who reads every day.

The person who exercises regularly.

The person who improves one skill at a time.

The daily effort may appear insignificant in the moment.

Yet years later, the difference becomes undeniable.

What once seemed small becomes substantial.

As a result consistency matters more than occasional bursts of motivation.

Motivation may help you start.

Consistency helps you continue.

And continuation is what creates results.

Most people overestimate what can be accomplished in a day and underestimate what can be accomplished in a year.

The future is rarely built through one giant moment.

It is built through repeated choices that gradually create a different reality.

Every decision is casting a vote for the life you are creating.

Every habit is moving you in a direction.

Every routine is shaping who you become.

The question is not whether your daily choices matter.

The question is what they are building.

Do not dismiss small acts of discipline because they seem insignificant.

Do not abandon good habits because results are delayed.

Do not confuse gradual progress with lack of progress.

Keep showing up.

Keep improving.

Keep making the next right decision.

Because compounding is one of the most powerful forces in personal growth.

And often, the life people admire publicly was built through thousands of small choices nobody noticed privately.

The future you want is not created all at once.

It is created one decision at a time.

And those decisions, repeated consistently, have the power to change everything.

WEALTH LESSON

Small disciplined financial habits compound over time into larger stability and long-term growth.

AFFIRMATION

"I respect the power of small disciplined choices."

TODAY'S POWER MOVE

Make one small decision today that your future self will benefit from long-term.

DAY 125

Wealth Requires Emotional Control

POWER QUOTE

"Financial discipline becomes difficult when emotions constantly control decisions."

REFLECTION

Some are of the view that financial success is primarily an income problem.

They assume that once they earn more money, their financial stress will disappear.

While income certainly matters, money alone does not automatically create stability.

It does not automatically create discipline.

It does not automatically create peace.

And it does not automatically create wise decision-making.

As a result people with similar incomes can experience completely different financial outcomes.

The difference is often found in behavior.

And behavior is frequently influenced by emotion.

People do not only spend with their wallets.

They spend with their emotions.

Some people spend to celebrate.

Others spend to cope.

Some spend because they are anxious.

Others spend because they are seeking validation.

The transaction may look financial on the surface, but the root is often emotional.

The same principle applies to many financial decisions.

Fear causes people to panic during uncertainty.

Impatience causes people to abandon long-term plans.

Stress causes people to avoid budgets and financial conversations.

Impulsiveness causes people to prioritize immediate relief over long-term stability.

Which is why emotional maturity is such an important part of wealth-building.

A calm person approaches money differently than a fearful person.

They think long-term.

They prepare before problems arise.

They evaluate decisions carefully.

They understand that temporary emotions should not dictate permanent financial outcomes.

This does not mean emotionally mature people never feel fear.

It means they do not allow fear to make every decision.

They create plans instead of panicking.

They seek solutions instead of avoiding reality.

They learn how to delay gratification in pursuit of something greater.

Over time, these behaviors create stability.

And stability creates opportunity.

Many people focus exclusively on increasing income while ignoring the emotional habits influencing their finances.

Yet true financial growth often requires both.

Better earning.

And better decision-making.

The goal is not simply to make more money.

The goal is to become the type of person who can manage money wisely.

Because wealth is not only about acquiring resources.

It is about sustaining them.

Protecting them.

Growing them.

Using them intentionally.

And those abilities are often rooted in emotional discipline.

The person who learns how to manage emotions effectively gains an advantage that extends far beyond finances.

They become better at planning.

Better at patience.

Better at consistency.

Better at making decisions aligned with their future rather than their temporary feelings.

And over time, that emotional stability becomes one of the most valuable assets they possess.

Because wealth is not built only through what you earn.

It is also built through how wisely you think, choose, and respond.

WEALTH LESSON

Emotional regulation improves financial decision-making because calm thinking protects long-term goals.

AFFIRMATION

"I make financial decisions from wisdom instead of emotional pressure."

TODAY'S POWER MOVE

Pause before every unnecessary purchase today and ask yourself if it aligns with your future goals.

DAY 126

Your Future Is Bigger Than This Season

POWER QUOTE

"Temporary pain should never become permanent identity."

REFLECTION

When people are walking through difficult seasons, it is easy to believe the pain will last forever.

The stress feels constant.

The uncertainty feels endless.

The disappointment feels heavy.

The future feels distant.

And because the emotions are so present, many people begin assuming their current reality is permanent.

But life rarely stays the same forever.

Seasons change.

Circumstances change.

People change.

Growth happens.

Healing happens.

Opportunities appear.

New chapters begin.

The challenge is that when you are inside a difficult season, it can be hard to imagine life feeling different.

Your perspective becomes shaped by what is immediately in front of you.

You focus on the pressure.

The waiting.

The setbacks.

The unanswered questions.

Yet some of the strongest people you will ever meet once stood in seasons that felt impossible too.

They experienced loss.

Rejection.

Financial hardship.

Heartbreak.

Confusion.

Moments where they questioned whether things would ever improve.

What separated them was not the absence of difficulty.

It was their refusal to let temporary hardship become a permanent identity.

They continued moving forward.

Continued learning.

Continued rebuilding.

Continued believing that life could become better even when they could not yet see how.

This is one of the most important lessons difficult seasons can teach.

Your current circumstances are a chapter.

Not the entire story.

A chapter may be painful without defining the ending.

A chapter may be difficult without determining the future.

A chapter may be exhausting without lasting forever.

Life has a way of evolving in ways people cannot always predict.

The breakthrough you need may not have arrived yet.

The lesson may still be unfolding.

The growth may still be happening beneath the surface.

This is why hope matters.

Hope is not denying reality.

Hope is believing reality can change.

It is believing that today's struggle does not automatically determine tomorrow's possibilities.

Keep moving.

Keep learning.

Keep taking care of yourself.

Keep making the next right decision.

Even if progress feels small.

Even if clarity feels distant.

Even if the season feels longer than expected.

Because what feels overwhelming today may one day become the season that strengthened you.

The season that matured you.

The season that prepared you.

The season that helped create the future you are now grateful for.

Do not allow a temporary chapter to convince you that the story is over.

Your life is still unfolding.

And some of the most powerful chapters may still be ahead of you.

WEALTH LESSON

Resilience creates long-term success because emotionally strong people continue rebuilding after setbacks.

AFFIRMATION

"I trust that my future is greater than my current struggle."

TODAY'S POWER MOVE

Encourage yourself today instead of speaking negatively about your circumstances.

DAY 127

Healing Requires Patience

POWER QUOTE

"Not every wound heals overnight."

REFLECTION

Many people show patience toward others while refusing to show patience toward themselves.

They understand that learning takes time.

That recovery takes time.

That growth takes time.

Yet when it comes to their own healing, they expect immediate results.

They become frustrated when old emotions resurface.

Discouraged when progress feels slow.

Disappointed when they are not yet the person they hope to become.

But healing rarely follows a perfect timeline.

It is not a straight line from pain to peace.

There are good days.

Difficult days.

Breakthroughs.

Setbacks.

Moments of clarity.

Moments of confusion.

All of these experiences can exist within the same journey.

This is what makes healing challenging.

And this is also what makes healing human.

Many of the patterns people are trying to change did not develop overnight.

Years of disappointment.

Years of fear.

Years of unhealthy coping mechanisms.

Years of survival-based thinking.

These experiences often shape habits, beliefs, and emotional responses that become deeply rooted.

It should not be surprising that rebuilding takes time.

You are not simply changing behavior.

You are changing patterns.

Changing beliefs.

Changing ways of thinking.

Changing the relationship you have with yourself.

That kind of transformation deserves patience.

Too many people measure their healing by perfection.

But healing is not measured by never struggling again.

It is measured by progress.

By greater awareness.

By healthier responses.

By stronger boundaries.

By increased self-understanding.

By choosing growth even when it feels difficult.

Sometimes healing looks dramatic.

More often, it looks quiet.

A healthier decision.

A calmer response.

A boundary that was once impossible to set.

A difficult conversation handled differently.

A moment where you choose self-respect over self-abandonment.

These changes may seem small.

But they are evidence that growth is happening.

Be careful not to insult your progress simply because you are still growing.

Do not overlook how far you have come because you have not yet arrived where you want to be.

Growth is still growth.

Healing is still healing.

Progress is still progress.

The person you are becoming is being shaped through every lesson, every adjustment, and every intentional choice.

Give yourself permission to be a work in progress.

Give yourself permission to learn.

Give yourself permission to heal at a healthy pace.

Because the goal is not to become perfect overnight.

The goal is to become healthier over time.

And sometimes one of the most powerful forms of growth is learning how to offer yourself the same compassion you would freely give to someone else.

Be patient.

The rebuilding is working, even when it feels slower than you hoped.

WEALTH LESSON

Emotional healing strengthens long-term discipline because peace improves consistency and decision-making.

AFFIRMATION

"I allow myself to heal patiently and intentionally."

TODAY'S POWER MOVE

Speak to yourself with compassion today instead of harsh criticism.

DAY 128

Protect Your Attention

POWER QUOTE

"Your attention is too valuable to waste carelessly."

REFLECTION

Every person is given a limited amount of attention each day.

The question is:

Where is it going?

Many people think their future is primarily shaped by major decisions.

While important decisions certainly matter, daily attention often matters just as much.

Because attention directs energy.

And energy influences results.

Whatever consistently captures your attention eventually begins shaping your life.

If your attention is constantly consumed by negativity, your mindset is affected.

If your attention is constantly consumed by comparison, your confidence is affected.

If your attention is constantly consumed by distractions, your progress is affected.

Attention is powerful because it influences what grows.

What you focus on expands in your awareness.

What you repeatedly engage with begins influencing your thoughts, emotions, and behavior.

Which is why focus has become such a valuable skill.

Modern life is filled with distractions.

Notifications.

Social media.

Opinions.

Drama.

Comparison.

Endless streams of information competing for attention.

Many people spend so much time reacting to everything happening around them that they have little energy left for what truly matters.

Their goals receive leftovers.

Their growth receives leftovers.

Their healing receives leftovers.

Their purpose receives leftovers.

Meanwhile, distractions receive the best of their energy.

Focused people operate differently.

They become intentional about what enters their mind.

They understand that every "yes" to one thing is a "no" to something else.

Every hour spent feeding distraction is an hour unavailable for growth.

Every moment spent consumed by comparison is a moment unavailable for progress.

This does not mean living in isolation.

It means living intentionally.

Choosing what deserves your attention.

Choosing what deserves your energy.

Choosing what deserves a place in your mind.

Because not everything deserves access to your focus.

Some things deserve to be ignored.

Some things deserve to be released.

Some things deserve less attention than you have been giving them.

Protecting your attention is not about becoming disconnected from life.

It is about becoming connected to what matters most.

Your goals.

Your healing.

Your learning.

Your relationships.

Your purpose.

Your future.

Attention is one of the most valuable forms of currency you possess.

Spend it wisely.

Because the quality of your focus today is helping determine the quality of your future tomorrow.

And people who learn how to direct their attention intentionally often discover that focus is not merely a productivity skill.

It is a life-changing one.

WEALTH LESSON

Focused energy creates faster progress because less emotional energy is wasted unnecessarily.

AFFIRMATION

"I protect my attention and direct it toward meaningful growth."

TODAY'S POWER MOVE

Remove one major distraction from your environment today.

DAY 129

Stop Waiting For Validation

POWER QUOTE

"Not everybody will understand your vision before the results appear."

REFLECTION

Many people spend years waiting.

Waiting for confidence.

Waiting for certainty.

Waiting for the perfect opportunity.

And often, waiting for approval.

Approval from family.

Approval from friends.

Approval from society.

Approval from people who may not even understand the vision they carry inside them.

The problem with waiting for universal validation is that it rarely arrives.

Every meaningful goal will have critics.

Every ambitious vision will have doubters.

Every person pursuing growth will encounter individuals who cannot yet see what they see.

This is not because the vision lacks value.

It is because people can only understand life through the lens of their own experiences.

Someone who has never pursued your dream may struggle to understand it.

Someone who has never taken your path may question it.

Someone who has never imagined your future may underestimate it.

That is normal.

The mistake is allowing their uncertainty to become your limitation.

Too many people abandon goals because they mistake a lack of approval for a lack of potential.

They assume that if others do not immediately understand their vision, the vision must be wrong.

But history is filled with people who were misunderstood before they were celebrated.

People who continued building before anyone else believed.

People who kept working while others doubted.

People who remained committed when external validation was absent.

The truth is that not everyone needs to understand your purpose.

Not everyone needs to agree with your direction.

Not everyone needs to see what you see.

Your responsibility is not convincing everyone else.

Your responsibility is remaining faithful to the work required to build the future you desire.

That requires courage.

The courage to move forward without constant reassurance.

The courage to trust your growth before it becomes visible.

The courage to continue building when results are still developing.

Many people will only understand your vision after they see the outcome.

After the business succeeds.

After the goal is accomplished.

After the transformation becomes visible.

By then, what once seemed unrealistic suddenly appears obvious.

But the work was happening long before anyone noticed.

Do not allow the absence of approval to become the reason you stop.

Do not wait for permission to become who you are capable of becoming.

Do not place your future in the hands of people who cannot fully see what is possible for your life.

Trust the process.

Stay committed.

Keep building.

Because some of the most important decisions you will ever make require enough belief to continue before the applause arrives.

And often, the people who create extraordinary lives are simply the people who stopped waiting for permission and started taking responsibility for their future.

WEALTH LESSON

Emotional independence strengthens focus because less energy is spent seeking external validation.

AFFIRMATION

"I remain committed to my future even when others do not fully understand it yet."

TODAY'S POWER MOVE

Take one step toward your future today without seeking approval first.

DAY 130

Keep Becoming

POWER QUOTE

"You are allowed to continuously evolve."

REFLECTION

Growth is not a destination.

It is a process.

A lifelong journey of becoming.

Becoming wiser through experience.

Becoming stronger through challenges.

Becoming more disciplined through practice.

Becoming more self-aware through reflection.

The mistake many people make is believing growth has a finish line.

They imagine that one day they will finally arrive.

Finally have everything figured out.

Finally become the perfect version of themselves.

But life does not work that way.

Every season teaches new lessons.

Every level introduces new responsibilities.

Every chapter invites new growth.

The people who continue thriving are usually the people who remain teachable.

They remain willing to learn.

Willing to adapt.

Willing to evolve.

Unfortunately, many individuals become trapped by old versions of themselves.

Not because they cannot grow.

Because they become attached to familiar identities.

The identity they have always known.

The habits they have always practiced.

The beliefs they have always carried.

Even when those things no longer serve them.

Change can feel uncomfortable because it creates uncertainty.

It requires releasing what is familiar before fully becoming what is next.

That transition can feel awkward.

You may outgrow conversations you once enjoyed.

Habits you once defended.

Mindsets you once believed.

Versions of yourself that once felt permanent.

This is not failure.

This is development.

The person you needed to be in one season may not be the person you need to be in the next.

Growth often requires updating your thinking.

Raising your standards.

Strengthening your discipline.

Expanding your perspective.

Learning new skills.

Developing greater emotional maturity.

The goal is not to remain the same forever.

The goal is to become better over time.

To become more aligned with your values.

More intentional with your decisions.

More capable of handling the responsibilities connected to your future.

Give yourself permission to evolve.

Give yourself permission to release habits that no longer serve you.

Give yourself permission to think differently than you once did.

Growth does not require loyalty to outdated versions of yourself.

It requires honesty about what needs to change.

The strongest people are not those who resist evolution.

They are those who embrace it.

Those who continue learning.

Continue rebuilding.

Continue adapting.

Continue becoming.

Because every meaningful future requires growth.

And every season of growth asks the same question:

Are you willing to become who your future requires?

Keep saying yes.

Because the process of becoming may be one of the most important journeys of your life.

WEALTH LESSON

Long-term success requires continuous growth, learning, and emotional evolution.

AFFIRMATION

"I continue evolving into the strongest version of myself."

TODAY'S POWER MOVE

Identify one area where you know growth is currently required in your life.

DAY 131

Your Future Needs Consistency

POWER QUOTE

"Small consistent effort changes lives more than occasional intense motivation."

REFLECTION

Most people enjoy the beginning.

The excitement of a new goal.

The energy of a fresh start.

The optimism that comes from imagining a better future.

In the beginning, discipline feels easy because motivation is high.

The challenge comes later.

When the excitement fades.

When progress slows.

When obstacles appear.

When life becomes demanding.

When emotions become inconsistent.

This is where many people stop.

Not because they no longer want the goal.

Because they expected motivation to carry them further than it was designed to.

Motivation is valuable.

It helps people start.

But motivation was never meant to be the foundation of transformation.

Consistency is.

The people who create meaningful change understand that progress cannot depend entirely on how they feel.

There will be days when energy is high.

There will also be days when energy is low.

Days when confidence is strong.

Days when doubt is louder.

Days when the vision feels exciting.

Days when the work feels repetitive.

The difference between those who grow and those who remain stuck is often found in what happens during those ordinary moments.

Some people stop.

Others continue.

They continue when results are delayed.

Continue when recognition is absent.

Continue when progress feels slower than expected.

Continue when emotions are unreliable.

This ability creates something powerful.

Momentum.

Momentum is rarely created through dramatic effort.

It is created through repeated effort.

Small actions performed consistently.

Promises kept repeatedly.

Responsibilities handled regularly.

Over time, those actions begin stacking on top of one another.

The results may not appear immediately.

But eventually they become impossible to ignore.

A person who continues learning gains knowledge.

A person who continues saving builds stability.

A person who continues practicing develops mastery.

A person who continues showing up develops character.

This is the power of consistency.

It transforms ordinary actions into extraordinary outcomes.

Many people overestimate what they can accomplish in a week and underestimate what they can accomplish in a few years of disciplined effort.

The future is often shaped by the actions nobody applauds.

The habits nobody notices.

The work nobody sees.

The decisions made quietly behind the scenes.

So when motivation fades, do not panic.

When progress feels slow, do not quit.

When the process becomes repetitive, do not assume it has stopped working.

Continue anyway.

Because the life you desire will likely be built by what you do repeatedly, not occasionally.

And one day, the consistency that felt ordinary will become the reason your transformation looks extraordinary.

The people who change their lives are not always the people who start the strongest.

Often, they are simply the people who refused to stop.

WEALTH LESSON

Consistency compounds financially, emotionally, and mentally over time.

AFFIRMATION

"I stay consistent even when motivation changes."

TODAY'S POWER MOVE

Repeat one healthy habit today even if you do not feel emotionally inspired.

DAY 132

Laziness Is Sometimes Emotional Exhaustion

POWER QUOTE

"Not every unproductive season is caused by lack of ambition."

REFLECTION

Many people are far harder on themselves than they would ever be on someone else.

The moment their energy drops, they call themselves lazy.

The moment motivation disappears; they assume something is wrong with them.

The moment discipline feels difficult; they begin criticizing themselves.

But not every struggle with productivity is a discipline problem.

Sometimes it is an exhaustion problem.

Sometimes it is burnout.

Sometimes it is emotional overload.

Sometimes it is the result of carrying stress for far too long without recovery.

Human beings are not machines.

They are not designed to operate at maximum capacity every hour of every day.

Life places demands on people.

Responsibilities.

Relationships.

Financial pressure.

Disappointments.

Unexpected challenges.

Emotional burdens that are often invisible to everyone else.

When those pressures accumulate without relief, they begin affecting energy.

Focus.

Motivation.

Decision-making.

Eventually, a person who was once highly productive may struggle to complete even simple tasks.

Not because they suddenly became lazy.

Because they became depleted.

That is why self-awareness is so important.

Before criticizing yourself, it is worth asking a different question:

"What am I carrying right now?"

What stress has gone unaddressed?

What pressure has remained unresolved?

What emotional weight has been ignored?

Sometimes the issue is not a lack of discipline.

Sometimes the issue is that your mind and body are asking for recovery.

Recovery is not weakness.

Rest is not failure.

Pausing to rebuild does not mean abandoning your future.

In fact, sustainable growth often requires periods of restoration.

The strongest athletes recover.

The strongest leaders recover.

The strongest builders recover.

Because they understand that constantly operating from exhaustion eventually becomes unsustainable.

At the same time, recovery should not become avoidance.

The goal is not to stop moving forward.

The goal is to rebuild your capacity so you can continue moving forward effectively.

Healing and discipline are not enemies.

They work together.

Rest restores energy.

Discipline provides direction.

Healing restores clarity.

Discipline creates progress.

Both are necessary.

Learn to recognize the difference between laziness and depletion.

Between avoidance and exhaustion.

Between quitting and recovering.

Treat yourself with honesty.

But also with wisdom.

Because sometimes what appears to be a lack of motivation is actually a signal that something deeper needs attention.

And when that attention is given, energy often returns.

Focus often returns.

Hope often returns.

The goal is not to force yourself through every season at full speed.

The goal is to build a life where growth can continue without being carried entirely by exhaustion.

Because a future built through constant burnout is difficult to sustain.

But a future built through both discipline and restoration has the strength to last.

WEALTH LESSON

Mental and emotional wellness directly affect productivity, discipline, and financial growth.

AFFIRMATION

"I restore my energy, peace, and focus intentionally."

TODAY'S POWER MOVE

Give yourself intentional recovery today while still completing one meaningful responsibility.

DAY 133

Structure Reduces Stress

POWER QUOTE

"Preparation creates peace."

REFLECTION

Many people spend their lives trying to reduce stress without addressing one of its most common causes:

A lack of structure.

When life has no systems, everything begins feeling urgent.

Responsibilities pile up.

Deadlines are forgotten.

Bills become stressful.

Priorities become unclear.

Decisions become reactive.

Instead of directing life intentionally, people find themselves constantly responding to whatever problem appears next.

Over time, this creates exhaustion.

Not because life is impossible.

Because life is unsupported.

Structure changes that.

Structure creates order.

And order creates stability.

A budget creates awareness.

A schedule creates direction.

A routine creates consistency.

Healthy boundaries create emotional protection.

None of these systems remove every challenge.

But they reduce unnecessary chaos.

Many people assume discipline limits freedom.

They imagine routines as restrictive.

Budgets as limiting.

Planning as burdensome.

Yet the opposite is often true.

The person with a budget experiences less financial confusion.

The person with a schedule wastes less time deciding what to do next.

The person with healthy boundaries experiences less emotional overwhelm.

The person with routines spends less energy constantly starting over.

Structure reduces decision fatigue.

It reduces uncertainty.

It reduces the pressure of trying to remember everything at once.

Most importantly, it creates a foundation.

Because success becomes difficult to sustain when everything depends on memory, motivation, or emotional energy alone.

Systems provide support when motivation disappears.

Preparation provides stability when circumstances become stressful.

Which is why the strongest lives are rarely built accidentally.

They are built intentionally.

One system at a time.

One habit at a time.

One routine at a time.

Not because life becomes perfect.

Because life becomes more manageable.

Preparation is one of the greatest gifts you can give your future self.

The budget you create today may prevent stress months from now.

The routine you establish today may create stability years from now.

The boundary you enforce today may protect your peace far into the future.

You do not need perfect systems.

You simply need systems that support the life you are trying to build.

Small improvements create meaningful stability over time.

And often, the difference between feeling overwhelmed and feeling grounded is not talent, intelligence, or luck.

It is structure.

Because when life is supported by intentional systems, energy can be directed toward growth instead of constant recovery from chaos.

And that is where real progress begins.

WEALTH LESSON

Financial organization reduces anxiety because clarity creates greater emotional control and confidence.

AFFIRMATION

"I create systems that support peace, discipline, and emotional stability."

TODAY'S POWER MOVE

Organize one area of your life that has been creating unnecessary stress.

DAY 134

Stop Shrinking Yourself

POWER QUOTE

"You were not created to constantly make yourself smaller for acceptance."

REFLECTION

Many people spend years becoming less than they truly are.

Not because they lack ability.

Not because they lack intelligence.

Not because they lack potential.

But because somewhere along the way, they learned that standing out felt unsafe.

Perhaps they were criticized for being ambitious.

Mocked for thinking differently.

Rejected for wanting more.

Ignored when they expressed their ideas.

Over time, these experiences can quietly shape identity.

People begin shrinking themselves without realizing it.

They stop sharing their thoughts.

Stop pursuing bigger opportunities.

Stop believing in their own potential.

They lower their standards to fit the expectations of others.

Hide their gifts to avoid attention.

Downplay their strengths to avoid criticism.

The problem is that a life built around shrinking eventually becomes exhausting.

Because deep down, people know they were created for more than constant self-suppression.

Growth requires expansion.

Expansion in confidence.

Expansion in thinking.

Expansion in courage.

Expansion in the willingness to take up space in rooms where you once felt invisible.

This does not mean becoming arrogant.

Arrogance is believing you are above others.

Growth is simply becoming more fully yourself.

There is a difference.

Healthy confidence allows people to acknowledge their strengths without apology.

To use their gifts without guilt.

To pursue opportunities without constantly questioning whether they deserve them.

Many people wait for permission before they allow themselves to grow.

Permission from family.

Friends.

Coworkers.

Society.

But growth rarely works that way.

The people who build meaningful lives eventually realize that they cannot allow the opinions of others to become the ceiling for their future.

They must decide for themselves that their potential deserves expression.

This can feel uncomfortable.

Especially if you have spent years making yourself smaller.

But discomfort is often part of expansion.

The athlete grows stronger by challenging limits.

The leader grows by accepting responsibility.

The individual grows by stepping beyond familiar fears.

Your future may require a version of you that is more visible than the current version.

More confident.

More disciplined.

More courageous.

More willing to trust what has been placed inside you.

Do not confuse humility with self-rejection.

Do not mistake shrinking for kindness.

Do not assume that hiding your gifts serves anyone.

The world benefits when people use their strengths.

When they share their ideas.

When they pursue meaningful goals.

When they stop apologizing for becoming who they are capable of becoming.

You were not created to spend your life minimizing yourself.

You were created to grow.

To develop.

To contribute.

To become.

And there is nothing selfish, arrogant, or wrong about fully stepping into the person you were meant to be.

Because some of the greatest opportunities in your life will only appear once you stop shrinking and start showing up as your full self.

WEALTH LESSON

Confidence improves visibility, leadership, opportunities, and long-term growth.

AFFIRMATION

"I stop shrinking myself and allow my gifts to take up space."

TODAY'S POWER MOVE

Speak confidently about yourself and your goals today.

DAY 135

Your Pain Can Become Power

POWER QUOTE

"Some people break from pain. Others rebuild through it."

REFLECTION

Pain changes people.

The only question is how.

Some people allow pain to convince them that life will never improve.

They become trapped in bitterness.

Fear.

Distrust.

Hopelessness.

They carry old wounds into new seasons and unknowingly allow past experiences to shape future decisions.

Others choose a different path.

Not because the pain hurt less.

Not because the journey was easier.

But because they refused to let their suffering become the final chapter of their story.

The truth is that pain is one of life's greatest teachers.

Not because pain itself is desirable.

But because difficult seasons often reveal lessons comfort never could.

Pain teaches patience.

It teaches resilience.

It teaches humility.

It teaches self-awareness.

It teaches people what truly matters.

Many of the strongest individuals you will ever meet did not become strong during easy seasons.

They became strong because they survived difficult ones.

They learned how to keep moving when circumstances were heavy.

How to rebuild when things fell apart.

How to believe when outcomes were uncertain.

How to continue growing even while carrying emotional scars.

This does not mean pain should be glorified.

Some experiences should never have happened.

Some losses are deeply unfair.

Some wounds take years to fully heal.

Acknowledging this reality is important.

Healing is not pretending the pain was acceptable.

Healing is deciding the pain will not permanently control your future.

That decision changes everything.

Because once healing begins, pain starts transforming.

Lessons emerge.

Wisdom develops.

Perspective grows.

Strength increases.

The experience that once felt only destructive begins producing something valuable.

Not because the pain was good.

Because growth occurred in response to it.

Many people discover that their greatest ability to help others comes from what they survived themselves.

The struggle that nearly broke them becomes the story that encourages someone else.

The lesson learned through hardship becomes guidance for another person.

The healing they fought for becomes proof that healing is possible.

This is one of the most powerful transformations a person can experience.

When wounds stop being prisons and begin becoming sources of wisdom.

When suffering stops defining identity and starts contributing to purpose.

When pain loses its power to control the future.

You are not responsible for every wound you experienced.

But you are responsible for deciding what happens next.

Will the pain become a permanent limitation?

Or will it become part of the foundation that helps build a stronger future?

The choice is not always easy.

But it is powerful.

Because some of the most inspiring people in the world are not those who avoided pain.

They are those who learned how to heal from it.

And in doing so, transformed their suffering into strength, their wounds into wisdom, and their story into hope.

WEALTH LESSON

Emotionally resilient people recover faster from setbacks because they continue rebuilding instead of permanently surrendering.

AFFIRMATION

"I allow pain to strengthen me instead of destroy me."

TODAY'S POWER MOVE

Reflect on one difficult season that helped shape your strength.

DAY 136

Stop Escaping Your Life

POWER QUOTE

"Distractions often become emotional escape routes."

REFLECTION

Most people assume their greatest obstacle is what happened to them.

The disappointment.

The rejection.

The heartbreak.

The failure.

Sometimes those experiences are painful.

But often, the deeper obstacle is not the event itself.

It is the avoidance that follows.

Rather than facing difficult emotions, people search for distractions.

They stay busy.

Stay entertained.

Stay occupied.

Anything to avoid sitting alone with thoughts they do not want to confront.

Some people over-scroll.

Some overwork.

Some overspend.

Some overeat.

Some constantly seek noise because silence feels uncomfortable.

The distraction may look different, but the purpose is often the same:

Escape.

The problem is that avoidance provides relief without resolution.

It temporarily numbs discomfort without addressing its cause.

The emotions remain.

The wounds remain.

The patterns remain.

Waiting quietly beneath the surface.

Which is why the things people repeatedly avoid often become the things that quietly influence their lives.

Unaddressed fear affects decisions.

Unresolved pain affects relationships.

Unexamined beliefs affect confidence.

Ignored emotions affect behavior.

Whether acknowledged or not, what remains unresolved often continues shaping the future.

This is why honesty is so important.

Not harsh self-judgment.

Not shame.

Honesty.

The willingness to sit with yourself long enough to recognize what needs attention.

To admit what hurts.

To acknowledge what is broken.

To recognize what is no longer working.

This process can feel uncomfortable.

Growth often does.

But discomfort is not always something to escape.

Sometimes it is something to learn from.

Sometimes it is pointing toward an area that needs healing.

An area that needs understanding.

An area that needs change.

Freedom begins when avoidance ends.

When people stop running from difficult truths and start engaging with them honestly.

When they stop distracting themselves from reality and begin rebuilding intentionally.

This does not mean every problem is solved immediately.

Healing rarely works that way.

But awareness creates possibility.

What is acknowledged can be addressed.

What is understood can be changed.

What is faced can be healed.

The goal is not to live a life without struggle.

The goal is to become someone willing to face those struggles honestly.

To sit with discomfort without being controlled by it.

To confront reality without running from it.

To rebuild rather than escape.

Because true transformation requires more than movement.

It requires awareness.

And sometimes the most courageous thing a person can do is stop running long enough to meet themselves honestly.

That is often where healing begins.

And it is often where a completely different future starts to take shape.

WEALTH LESSON

Emotional avoidance often creates unhealthy financial habits and inconsistent decision-making.

AFFIRMATION

"I stop escaping my emotions and begin confronting my life honestly."

TODAY'S POWER MOVE

Spend intentional quiet time today without distractions or emotional escape.

DAY 137

You Are Stronger Than This Season

POWER QUOTE

"Temporary hardship should never convince you that your future has disappeared."

REFLECTION

Difficult seasons have a way of distorting perspective.

When life becomes heavy, people often stop seeing themselves clearly.

They focus on what is not working.

What has been delayed.

What has been lost.

What feels uncertain.

And gradually, they begin questioning things they once believed about themselves.

Their abilities.

Their purpose.

Their value.

Their future.

Their strength.

This is one of the most deceptive effects of hardship.

It convinces people that their current struggle is the full story.

That because they feel overwhelmed, they must be weak.

Because they feel uncertain, they must be incapable.

Because they are facing challenges, they must be failing.

But feelings are not always facts.

And difficult seasons are not always accurate reflection of who you are.

Often, they are simply chapters that demand more from you than previous seasons required.

The strongest people are rarely individuals who never struggled.

They are people who survived experiences they once thought would break them.

People who endured heartbreak and kept loving.

People who experienced setbacks and kept building.

People who faced disappointment and kept believing.

People who carried heavy burdens and still found the strength to continue moving forward.

What made them strong was not the absence of hardship.

It was their decision not to surrender their identity to it.

Hard seasons can reveal weakness.

But they can also reveal strength that was previously hidden.

Patience you did not know you possessed.

Courage you did not know existed.

Resilience you never had a reason to discover until life demanded it.

Which is why perspective matters during difficult times.

Instead of asking only, "Why is this happening?"

Sometimes it is worth asking, "What is this season revealing about me?"

"What strength am I developing?"
"What wisdom am I gaining?"
"What capacity am I building?"
Because many of the qualities that create a meaningful life are developed during seasons that initially feel unbearable.
The version of you that emerges from this chapter may be stronger than the version that entered it.
Wiser.
More grounded.
More resilient.
More prepared for what lies ahead.
Do not allow temporary struggle to permanently reduce your belief in yourself.
Do not allow one difficult chapter to convince you that the story is finished.
You have survived challenges before.
You have overcome obstacles before.
You have rebuilt before.
And those experiences are evidence that there is more strength within you than you may currently realize.
This season may be difficult.
It may be uncomfortable.
It may test you in ways you never expected.
But it is not your identity.
It is a season.
And seasons change.
Keep moving forward.
Keep believing.
Keep rebuilding.
Because this chapter is not here to destroy you.
It is shaping you into someone stronger than you were before.

WEALTH LESSON

Resilience strengthens long-term success because emotionally strong people continue rebuilding after setbacks.

AFFIRMATION

"I remain strong, resilient, and hopeful even during difficult seasons."

TODAY'S POWER MOVE

Encourage yourself today instead of speaking negatively about your current situation.

DAY 138

Protect Your Vision From Negativity

POWER QUOTE

"Not everybody deserves emotional access to your future."

REFLECTION

Not every opinion deserves influence over your life.

This is an important lesson because many people unknowingly allow the voices around them to shape the size of their future.

A person shares a dream.

Someone responds with doubt.

A person takes a risk.

Someone responds with fear.

A person pursues growth.

Someone responds with criticism.

Over time, repeated exposure to negativity can begin affecting confidence.

Not because the criticism is true.

Because people hear it often enough to start questioning themselves.

The reality is that many opinions are **REFLECTION**s of the person giving them.

People often speak from their own experiences.

Their own fears.

Their own limitations.

Their own disappointments.

Someone who stopped believing in their own dreams may struggle to believe in yours.

Someone who fears failure may discourage risk.

Someone who settled for less may feel uncomfortable watching others pursue more.

This does not make them bad people.

It simply means their perspective may be shaped by experiences that are not your own.

That is why discernment matters.

You should listen to wisdom.

You should remain teachable.

You should welcome constructive feedback.

But wisdom and negativity are not the same thing.

Constructive feedback helps you improve.

Negativity often tries to convince you not to try at all.

One strengthens growth.

The other weakens it.

Protecting your vision does not mean ignoring everyone.

It means learning which voices deserve influence.

The strongest builders understand this.

They carefully protect their environment.

They pay attention to the conversations they repeatedly entertain.

The content they consume.

The people they spend time around.

The thoughts they continuously allow to grow inside their minds.

Because they understand a simple truth:

What consistently enters your mind eventually affects your behavior.

And behavior shapes outcomes.

Which is why protecting your mindset is not selfish.

It is necessary.

A vision requires belief before results appear.

It requires confidence before proof exists.

It requires persistence during seasons when progress is not yet visible.

Those things become much harder when negativity constantly surrounds you.

Your future needs focused energy.

Not endless emotional battles with every opinion that disagrees with your path.

Protect your peace.

Protect your confidence.

Protect your perspective.

And most importantly, protect your vision.

Because some of the greatest achievements in history were once ideas that other people doubted.

The difference is that someone believed strongly enough to continue building anyway.

Be that person.

Stay focused.

Stay disciplined.

Keep moving forward.

And do not allow someone else's limitations to become the boundaries of your future.

WEALTH LESSON

Focused people progress faster because less energy is wasted on negativity and unnecessary emotional distractions.

AFFIRMATION

"I protect my vision, my peace, and my future intentionally."

TODAY'S POWER MOVE

Distance yourself from one negative influence that weakens your mindset.

DAY 139

You Deserve To Believe In Yourself Again

POWER QUOTE

"Failure should teach you, not permanently define you."

REFLECTION

Life has a way of testing belief.

Not only belief in the future.

Belief in yourself.

There are seasons where people begin questioning everything because too many things went wrong.

The relationship ended.

The opportunity disappeared.

The plan failed.

The money ran out.

The dream took longer than expected.

And after enough disappointments, something subtle begins happening.

People stop trusting themselves.

They stop believing in their ability to succeed.

Not because they are incapable.

Because repeated setbacks convinced them that failure says something permanent about who they are.

But failure is not identity.

Failure is experience.

A failed relationship does not mean you are unlovable.

A failed business does not mean you are incapable.

A rejected opportunity does not mean you are unworthy.

A mistake does not mean you are broken.

It means you are human.

Every person who has ever accomplished something meaningful has experienced disappointment.

Every leader has made mistakes.

Every entrepreneur has experienced setbacks.

Every successful person has encountered moments where things did not unfold according to plan.

The difference is not that they avoided failure.

The difference is that they refused to become it.

They learned from it.

Adapted because of it.

Grew through it.

But they never allowed temporary outcomes to become permanent labels.

Unfortunately, many people do.

One painful season becomes proof that they are not good enough.

One rejection becomes proof that they should stop trying.

One mistake becomes proof that they are destined to repeat it forever.

This is where growth requires a different perspective.

Your past experiences are part of your story.

They are not the definition of your identity.

The person you are becoming should not be limited by the person you were during your worst moment.

You are allowed to learn.

Allowed to heal.

Allowed to mature.

Allowed to become wiser than the version of yourself that made previous mistakes.

Growth requires giving yourself permission to evolve.

To stop carrying old labels that no longer fit.

To stop introducing yourself internally through your failures.

To stop measuring your future through the lens of your past disappointments.

Because confidence is rebuilt the same way it was lost.

One experience at a time.

One promise kept.

One lesson applied.

One decision made differently.

One act of courage repeated consistently.

Over time, self-belief returns.

Not because life becomes perfect.

Because you begin gathering evidence that you are stronger, wiser, and more capable than you once believed.

Do not allow failure to have the final word.

Do not allow disappointment to become your identity.

Do not allow your worst chapter to become the title of your story.

You are more than your mistakes.

More than your setbacks.

More than your losses.

Your future is still being written.

And some of the strongest people in the world are simply individuals who decided that failure would become a lesson rather than a life sentence.

WEALTH LESSON

Self-belief influences resilience, opportunity-seeking behavior, and long-term growth.

AFFIRMATION

"I choose to believe in myself again despite past disappointments."

TODAY'S POWER MOVE

Write down one strength you still possess regardless of past failures.

DAY 140

Keep Becoming The Person You Need

POWER QUOTE

"The future you desire requires intentional growth from the current you."

REFLECTION

Many people focus heavily on the future they want.

A healthier life.

A stronger relationship.

Greater financial stability.

More peace.

More success.

More freedom.

These goals are valuable.

But there is an important question many people forget to ask:

Who do I need to become to sustain the future I desire?

Because every level of life requires something different from you.

The person capable of managing greater opportunities is often different from the person who first dreamed about them.

The person capable of maintaining peace is often different from the person who once lived in constant chaos.

The person capable of building wealth is often different from the person who once made decisions purely from emotion.

Growth is not only about changing circumstances.

It is about changing capacity.

Your ability to think differently.

Respond differently.

Lead differently.

Handle pressure differently.

Make decisions differently.

Which is why transformation requires more than wishful thinking.

It requires evolution.

Many people want different results while remaining committed to the same habits.

The same emotional patterns.

The same behaviors.

The same mindsets.

But a different future often requires a different approach.

Stronger discipline.

Healthier routines.

Greater self-awareness.

Higher standards.

More emotional maturity.

Deeper healing.

Not because who you are today is inadequate.

But because growth naturally expands what you are capable of carrying.

The responsibilities attached to your future may require skills you are still developing.

The opportunities attached to your future may require confidence you are still building.

The peace attached to your future may require healing you are still working through.

And that is okay.

Growth is not proof that something is wrong with you.

Growth is proof that you are becoming.

Too many people become discouraged when they realize how much work remains.

They focus on the distance still ahead.

The habits they still need to improve.

The areas where they still need growth.

But progress should not be measured only by how far you have left to go.

It should also be measured by how far you have already come.

The awareness you now possess.

The lessons you have learned.

The boundaries you have established.

The habits you have improved.

The strength you have developed.

All of these things matter.

The process of becoming is already changing your life, even when the results are not fully visible yet.

Every intentional choice is shaping identity.

Every lesson is expanding capacity.

Every challenge is creating growth.

Keep evolving.

Keep learning.

Keep rebuilding.

Keep becoming.

Because the future you desire is not only waiting for different circumstances.

It is waiting for a stronger, wiser, healthier version of you to arrive as well.

And every day you choose growth, you move one step closer to becoming that person.

WEALTH LESSON

Long-term success requires continuous emotional growth, discipline, and intentional evolution.

AFFIRMATION

"I continue becoming stronger, wiser, and more disciplined every day."

TODAY'S POWER MOVE

Identify one quality your future self needs and intentionally practice it today.

DAY 141

Stop Doubting The Process

POWER QUOTE

"Growth often feels uncomfortable before it becomes visible."

REFLECTION

One of the most difficult parts of personal growth is waiting.

Waiting for results.

Waiting for clarity.

Waiting for confidence.

Waiting for visible evidence that all your effort is actually working.

Most people begin a new journey with excitement.

They imagine rapid progress.

Quick breakthroughs.

Immediate change.

But real transformation rarely follows that timeline.

Growth is often much slower than people expect.

And much deeper.

Healing takes time because wounds are not repaired overnight.

Discipline takes time because habits are built through repetition.

Confidence takes time because trust must be earned through consistent action.

Financial stability takes time because lasting wealth is built gradually.

The challenge is that people often become discouraged during the middle.

The beginning feels exciting.

The destination feels inspiring.

But the middle feels uncertain.

It is the place where effort continues but results are not always obvious.

Where work is happening, yet evidence seems limited.

This is where many people start questioning themselves.

"Is this even working?"

"Am I making progress?"

"Should I just give up?"

These questions are common because growth often develops internally before it appears externally.

A seed does not become a tree the moment it is planted.

For a long period, important work happens beneath the surface.

Roots expand.

Foundations strengthen.

Systems develop.

None of it is visible.

Yet all of it is necessary.

Without strong roots, visible growth cannot be sustained.

The same principle applies to life.

Some of the most important progress happens where nobody can see it.

The mindset becoming healthier.

The emotional reactions becoming calmer.

The habits becoming stronger.

Self-awareness becoming deeper.

Discipline is becoming more consistent.

These changes may not receive applause.

They may not create immediate recognition.

But they matter.

In many ways, they matter more than the visible results people often chase.

Because internal growth creates the foundation for external growth.

That is why patience is so important.

Not passive waiting.

Active patience.

The willingness to continue showing up while the process unfolds.

The willingness to keep building even when progress feels invisible.

The willingness to trust that meaningful change is occurring, even when proof has not fully appeared yet.

Do not confuse quiet growth with no growth.

Do not mistake delayed results for failure.

Do not abandon the process simply because transformation is taking longer than expected.

Some of the strongest foundations in life are built slowly.

Some of the greatest transformations happen privately.

Some of the most powerful breakthroughs are preceded by long periods of unseen development.

Keep going.

Keep learning.

Keep rebuilding.

Keep planting seeds that support your future.

Because growth is still happening.

Even when you cannot fully see it yet.

And one day, what feels invisible now may become the very foundation that makes your transformation impossible to ignore.

WEALTH LESSON

Long-term success requires patience because meaningful growth compounds slowly over time.

AFFIRMATION

"I trust the process even when progress feels invisible."

TODAY'S POWER MOVE

Continue working toward one goal today without obsessing over immediate results.

DAY 142

Emotional Discipline Creates Stability

POWER QUOTE

"A calm mind protects the future better than emotional chaos."

REFLECTION

Every person experiences emotions.

Fear.

Anger.

Frustration.

Excitement.

Disappointment.

Anxiety.

Joy.

Emotions are a natural part of being human.

The problem is not having emotions.

The problem begins when emotions become the primary decision-maker.

Many people lose opportunities not because they lacked ability, but because they reacted impulsively.

A moment of anger damaged a relationship.

A moment of fear prevented action.

A moment of insecurity created self-sabotage.

A moment of panic led to a poor financial decision.

Temporary emotions created consequences that lasted far longer than the feelings themselves.

That is why emotional discipline matters so deeply.

Emotional discipline is not emotional suppression.

It is not pretending emotions do not exist.

It is not becoming cold, detached, or unfeeling.

True emotional discipline is emotional wisdom.

The ability to recognize what you are feeling without immediately surrendering control to it.

It is learning how to pause before reacting.

Reflect before responding.

Think before deciding.

This ability becomes one of the most valuable skills a person can develop.

Because life will always contain emotional moments.

Stressful conversations.

Unexpected setbacks.

Financial uncertainty.

Disappointments.

Criticism.

Pressure.

The people who navigate these moments well are rarely those who never feel emotion.

They are often the people who learned how to manage it.

A calm mind creates space for better decisions.

Better communication.

Better planning.

Better problem-solving.

Better leadership.

When emotions are running high, perspective often becomes narrow.

People focus only on immediate discomfort.

Immediate relief.

Immediate reaction.

But emotional wisdom expands perspective.

It allows people to consider long-term consequences.

Long-term goals.

Long-term values.

Which is why emotionally disciplined individuals often experience greater stability.

They are less likely to make decisions they later regret.

Less likely to allow temporary frustration to destroy meaningful opportunities.

Less likely to abandon important goals during difficult seasons.

Their emotions still matter.

They simply do not allow emotions to become the sole authority over their lives.

This creates protection.

Protection for relationships.

Protection for finances.

Protection for peace.

Protection for the future they are working to build.

Every time you pause before reacting, you strengthen emotional discipline.

Every time you choose reflection over impulse, you strengthen emotional discipline.

Every time you respond intentionally instead of emotionally, you strengthen emotional discipline.

Over time, these moments compound.

They create wisdom.

Maturity.

Stability.

And a stronger foundation for every area of life.

Because success is not only about what you know.

It is also about how well you manage yourself when life becomes difficult.

And few skills protect a person's future more than the ability to remain calm, thoughtful, and intentional when emotions are demanding immediate action.

WEALTH LESSON

Emotional regulation improves financial and personal stability because intentional decisions outperform impulsive reactions.

AFFIRMATION

"I respond with wisdom, peace, and emotional maturity."

TODAY'S POWER MOVE

Pause before reacting emotionally to anything stressful today.

DAY 143

You Are Allowed To Rest

POWER QUOTE

"Rest is not failure. Rest is preparation."

REFLECTION

Many ambitious people struggle with something they rarely talk about.

They feel guilty when they rest.

The moment they slow down, a voice inside them starts asking questions.

"Shouldn't I be doing more?"

"Am I falling behind?"

"Am I wasting time?"

"Why am I not being productive right now?"

Over time, rest begins to feel uncomfortable.

Not because rest is wrong.

Because they have unknowingly connected their worth to constant output.

The problem is that human beings were never designed to operate without recovery.

Everything in life follows a rhythm.

Work and rest.

Effort and recovery.

Growth and restoration.

Even nature operates in seasons.

Yet many people expect themselves to perform at maximum capacity every day without interruption.

Eventually, that approach creates consequences.

Mental fatigue increases.

Creativity decreases.

Patience weakens.

Focus declines.

Emotional stability becomes harder to maintain.

What once looked like dedication slowly becomes exhaustion.

That is why burnout is so dangerous.

Burnout often disguises itself as commitment.

People tell themselves they are being disciplined.

Being productive.

Being ambitious.

Meanwhile, they are running on empty.

The irony is that constant exhaustion rarely improves performance.

It often weakens it.

A tired mind makes poorer decisions.

A tired body struggles to perform consistently.

A tired spirit finds it difficult to stay inspired.

That is why intentional rest is not laziness.

It is maintenance.

Just as a vehicle requires fuel, your mind and body require restoration.

Rest allows perspective to return.

Energy to recover.

Creativity to recharge.

Emotions to settle.

Clarity to reappear.

Many breakthroughs happen after rest.

Not because the person stopped caring.

Because they finally created space to think clearly again.

The healthiest form of discipline includes recovery.

It recognizes that sustainability matters.

Anyone can sprint for a short period.

But long-term growth requires endurance.

And endurance requires balance.

The goal is not to work less.

The goal is to work wisely.

To understand when effort is needed and when recovery is necessary.

To recognize that protecting your energy is part of protecting your future.

Rest should not be viewed as the opposite of productivity.

Often, it is what makes productivity possible.

So if you find yourself feeling guilty for slowing down, remember this:

Recovery is not abandoning your goals.

Recovery is preparing yourself to pursue them more effectively.

The strongest people are not those who drive themselves into the ground.

They are those who learn how to balance ambition with wisdom.

Effort with restoration.

Discipline with recovery.

Because sustainable success is not built by never stopping.

It is built by knowing when to push forward and when to replenish the strength needed to continue.

Rest is not a detour from growth.

Sometimes it is an essential part of it.

WEALTH LESSON

Rest improves long-term productivity because recovery strengthens focus, emotional regulation, and consistency.

AFFIRMATION

"I allow myself to rest without abandoning my goals."

TODAY'S POWER MOVE

Take intentional time today to restore your mind and body without guilt.

DAY 144

Discipline Is Built In Small Moments

POWER QUOTE

"Your future changes through repeated small decisions."

REFLECTION

When most people think about discipline, they imagine a dramatic turning point.

A life-changing decision.

A powerful breakthrough.

A moment where everything suddenly changes.

While those moments can be meaningful, discipline is rarely built that way.

More often, discipline is built quietly.

In ordinary moments.

Moments that seem small at the time.

Choosing to wake up when you said you would.

Following through on a commitment.

Managing your money responsibly.

Finishing a task you do not feel like doing.

Protecting your focus when distractions are competing for your attention.

These decisions rarely receive applause.

Nobody celebrates them.

Nobody creates headlines about them.

Yet they are often the moments that shape a person's future.

Because discipline is not an event.

It is a pattern.

A collection of repeated behaviors that gradually become part of your identity.

Every time you follow through, you strengthen that pattern.

Every time you honor a commitment, you strengthen that pattern.

Every time you choose responsibility over convenience, you strengthen that pattern.

The challenge is that discipline often feels unrewarding in the beginning.

The effort is immediate.

The reward is delayed.

You make the healthy choice today but do not see the full benefit tomorrow.

You save money today but do not see financial freedom next week.

You work on a skill today but do not see mastery immediately.

Because the results are delayed, many people underestimate the value of their daily actions.

They assume small choices do not matter.

But small choices matter precisely because they compound.

A single decision may not change your life.

Thousands of similar decisions can.

This is how transformation usually happens.

Not through one extraordinary action.

Through ordinary actions repeated consistently over time.

Eventually, the behaviors that once required effort become habits.

The habits become standards.

The standards become identity.

And the identity begins shaping every area of life.

Which is why discipline becomes easier for some people over time.

Not because they are more talented.

Not because they are more motivated.

Because they have practiced the behavior long enough for it to become part of who they are.

Their actions and identity have become aligned.

Do not underestimate the power of small moments.

Do not dismiss ordinary acts of discipline because they seem insignificant.

Do not abandon consistency because the rewards are taking longer than expected.

The most important changes in life often happen quietly.

One choice at a time.

One habit at a time.

One commitment at a time.

And one day, the results that seemed invisible will become impossible to ignore.

Because discipline is not built in one giant moment.

It is built in the small moments that most people overlook.

And those moments, repeated long enough, have the power to change everything.

WEALTH LESSON

Small, disciplined habits compound financially, emotionally, and mentally over time.

AFFIRMATION

"I respect the power of small, disciplined actions."

TODAY'S POWER MOVE

Follow through intentionally on every small responsibility you commit to today.

DAY 145

Stop Living In Survival Mode

POWER QUOTE

"You were created for more than constant emotional survival."

REFLECTION

There are people who have spent so much time surviving that they no longer remember what peace feels like.

They wake up stressed.

Go to sleep worried.

Carry tension everywhere they go.

Constantly preparing for the next problem.

The next disappointment.

The next setback.

After enough years of living this way, survival mode begins to feel normal.

People become accustomed to emotional exhaustion.

Accustomed to anxiety.

Accustomed to operating under pressure.

And because it becomes familiar, they begin believing this is simply how life works.

But survival mode was never meant to become a permanent identity.

It was designed as a temporary response to difficult circumstances.

A way to endure challenging seasons.

Not a way to live forever.

The problem is that prolonged survival mode changes the way people think.

When someone is focused entirely on making it through the day, long-term vision becomes difficult.

Dreams begin shrinking.

Planning becomes harder.

Hope becomes more fragile.

The future starts feeling less like a possibility and more like a burden.

People stop asking what they want from life and start asking only what they need to survive it.

That is why healing matters so deeply.

Healing is not only about recovering from pain.

It is about teaching your mind that safety is possible again.

That peace is possible again.

That stability is possible again.

It is learning how to live without constantly expecting disaster.

Learning how to trust that not every season will be as difficult as the last one.

Learning how to believe that life can contain more than survival.

This process takes time.

The mind often holds onto old patterns long after circumstances have changed.

A person may leave a difficult environment while still carrying the emotional habits it created.

This is why healing requires patience.

You are not only changing circumstances.

You are retraining perspective.

Retraining beliefs.

Retraining the way you relate to yourself and the future.

Little by little, something begins to shift.

You stop living only in reaction.

You begin living with intention.

You start making decisions based on where you want to go rather than what you are trying to avoid.

You begin creating a future instead of merely surviving the present.

This is where real transformation begins.

Not when every problem disappears.

But when you finally believe that peace deserves a place in your life too.

Your future deserves more than constant emotional survival.

It deserves clarity.

Purpose.

Stability.

Joy.

Growth.

It deserves the freedom to dream again.

To plan again.

To believe again.

And while survival may have helped you make it through difficult seasons, it does not have to define the rest of your story.

You were not created only to survive life.

You were created to live it.

And healing is often the bridge that carries you from one reality to the other.

WEALTH LESSON

Long-term wealth requires emotional stability because survival thinking often creates short-term decision-making.

AFFIRMATION

"I release survival mode and build intentionally toward peace and stability."

TODAY'S POWER MOVE

Notice one survival-based behavior and intentionally replace it with a healthier response today.

DAY 146

Stop Being Afraid To Expand

POWER QUOTE

"Your next level may require a version of you that feels unfamiliar right now."

REFLECTION

Growth sounds exciting until it begins requiring change.

Most people enjoy the idea of a better future.

More success.

More peace.

More influence.

More opportunity.

More freedom.

What they often do not anticipate is that every new level of life usually requires a new level of them.

Greater opportunities bring greater responsibility.

Greater influence brings greater visibility.

Greater success often brings greater pressure.

For that reason, growth can feel uncomfortable.

Not because something is wrong.

Because expansion requires adaptation.

Many people unknowingly resist the very growth they say they want.

They desire new opportunities but fear the responsibility attached to them.

They desire success but fear being seen.

They desire leadership but fear making mistakes publicly.

They desire change but fear leaving familiar patterns behind.

This resistance is often subtle.

It appears as procrastination.

Self-doubt.

Overthinking.

Avoidance.

Perfectionism.

Not because people lack potential, but because growth asks them to become someone different than they have been before.

A larger future requires greater capacity.

The ability to manage stress differently.

Communicate differently.

Lead differently.

Think differently.

Respond differently.

As a result personal development is not optional for lasting success.

You cannot continuously operate with yesterday's habits while expecting tomorrow's opportunities.

The future often requires emotional strength that is still being developed.

Patience that is still being refined.
Wisdom that is still being learned.
Discipline that is still being practiced.
And that is okay.
Growth is not a sign that you are inadequate.
Growth is evidence that you are expanding.
Just as muscles strengthen through resistance, character often strengthens through responsibility.
The pressure you feel may not be a signal to retreat.
It may be a signal that your capacity is increasing.
Every challenge is teaching something.
Every responsibility is developing something.
Every season is preparing something.
The person you are becoming is often being shaped long before the results become visible.
This is why courage matters.
Not the absence of fear.
The willingness to continue despite it.
The willingness to step beyond familiar limits.
To embrace new expectations.
To accept that growth will sometimes feel uncomfortable because comfort and expansion rarely exist in the same place for long.
Do not fear becoming more than you have been.
Do not fear outgrowing old versions of yourself.
Do not fear the responsibility attached to the future you desire.
The growth you are experiencing today may be preparing you for opportunities you cannot yet see.
Keep developing.
Keep learning.
Keep stretching beyond what feels familiar.
Because every meaningful future requires expansion.
And every season of expansion is helping you become someone capable of carrying what once felt impossible.
The life you desire is not only asking for your effort.
It is asking for your evolution.
And that evolution is already underway.

WEALTH LESSON

Expansion requires emotional maturity because larger opportunities create larger responsibilities.

AFFIRMATION

"I welcome growth, expansion, and the responsibility attached to it."

TODAY'S POWER MOVE

Do something today that stretches you beyond your current comfort zone.

DAY 147

Protect Your Inner Peace

POWER QUOTE

"Peace is one of the highest forms of wealth."

REFLECTION

Many people spend years pursuing success while neglecting the very thing that allows success to be enjoyed.

Inner peace.

They focus on earning more.

Achieving more.

Building more.

Accomplishing more.

Yet despite reaching goals, they remain emotionally exhausted.

Constantly stressed.

Constantly overwhelmed.

Constantly carrying tension into every area of life.

This happens because external success and internal peace are not the same thing.

A person can achieve impressive things while still feeling emotionally drained.

They can accumulate wealth while lacking calm.

They can gain recognition while losing themselves in the process.

That is why protecting your inner world matters so deeply.

Peace influences far more than emotions.

It affects how you think.

How you communicate.

How you make decisions.

How you handle pressure.

How you respond when life becomes difficult.

A peaceful mind operates differently than a chaotic one.

When people are emotionally overwhelmed, everything feels urgent.

Small problems feel larger.

Minor setbacks feel catastrophic.

Simple decisions feel exhausting.

But when peace is present, perspective improves.

Clarity improves.

Patience improves.

Wisdom improves.

This does not mean peaceful people never face challenges.

It means they are not controlled by every challenge they face.

They remain grounded.

Steady.

Intentional.

Because they have learned that protecting their emotional environment is part of protecting their future.

Many people are careful about what enters their homes.

Careful about what enters their bank accounts.

Careful about what enters their bodies.

Yet they are careless about what enters their minds.

Every conversation.

Every opinion.

Every conflict.

Every source of negativity.

Given unlimited access.

Over time, that emotional clutter begins creating internal chaos.

Which is why boundaries matter.

Not every conversation deserves your energy.

Not every argument deserves your attention.

Not every person's opinion deserves influence over your self-worth.

Not every environment deserves access to your peace.

Protecting your peace is not avoidance.

It is wisdom.

It is recognizing that your mental and emotional health directly affects the quality of your life.

The healthiest people understand this.

They become intentional about what they consume.

Who they spend time around.

What they allow to occupy their thoughts.

What they repeatedly give emotional energy to.

Because they understand a powerful truth:

Your inner world eventually influences your outer world.

The quality of your thoughts affects the quality of your decisions.

The quality of your decisions affects the quality of your future.

Peace is not something that happens accidentally.

It is something that must be protected intentionally.

One boundary at a time.

One decision at a time.

One habit at a time.

So continue building your goals.

Continue pursuing growth.

Continue working toward the future you desire.

But do not neglect the condition of your inner world while doing it.

Because a peaceful mind is not a luxury.

It is one of the greatest assets you can possess.

And often, the most meaningful success is not simply creating a life that looks good from the outside.

It is creating a life that feels healthy, stable, and peaceful from within.

WEALTH LESSON

Mental peace improves emotional regulation, productivity, and long-term financial discipline.

AFFIRMATION

"I protect my peace because my emotional health matters deeply."

TODAY'S POWER MOVE

Distance yourself from one unnecessary source of emotional chaos today.

DAY 148

You Are Still Becoming

POWER QUOTE

"Growth does not stop simply because life became difficult."

REFLECTION

One of the quickest ways people become discouraged is by comparing their current reality to an unrealistic expectation of where they believe they should be.

They tell themselves:

"I should be further ahead by now."

"I should be more disciplined by now."

"I should be fully healed by now."

"I should have everything figured out by now."

And when reality fails to match those expectations, frustration begins to grow.

They overlook progress.

Ignore growth.

Discount lessons learned.

All because they are focused on a version of themselves that does not yet exist.

The truth is that becoming is a lifelong process.

There is no point where a person graduates from growth.

No season where learning completely ends.

No moment where every emotional wound is healed, every habit is perfected, and every challenge disappears forever.

Life continues inviting people to grow.

To adapt.

To learn.

To evolve.

This is not evidence that you are behind.

It is evidence that you are human.

Every stage of life presents new opportunities for development.

New lessons.

New responsibilities.

New areas requiring greater maturity.

The person you are today is not supposed to know everything the future version of you will know.

That wisdom is earned through experience.

The discipline you desire is built through repetition.

The confidence you desire is built through evidence.

The healing you desire is built through intentional work over time.

Growth unfolds in layers.

As one area improves, another area often reveals itself.

As one lesson is learned, another lesson appears.

This can sometimes feel frustrating.

But it is also beautiful.

Because it means life continues offering opportunities to become more than you were before.

Too many people shame themselves for still having work to do.

They criticize themselves for not being perfect.

For not always responding correctly.

For not always feeling strong.

For not always having clarity.

But perfection was never the goal.

The goal is progress.

The goal is greater awareness than yesterday.

Greater wisdom than yesterday.

Greater intentionality than yesterday.

Growth should not be measured only by what remains unfinished.

It should also be measured by what has already changed.

The boundaries you now maintain.

The habits you have strengthened.

The lessons you have learned.

The emotional patterns you have outgrown.

The decisions you now make differently.

All of these things matter.

All of these things are evidence of transformation.

So be patient with yourself.

You are not failing because you are still growing.

You are growing because growth is part of being alive.

You are still becoming.

Still learning.

Still healing.

Still evolving.

And that process is not something to be ashamed of.

It is something to be grateful for.

Because every lesson learned, every habit strengthened, and every challenge navigated is helping shape the person you are becoming.

And that person is stronger, wiser, and more capable than the version of you who first began the journey.

Keep going.

The process is working, even if it is not finished yet.

WEALTH LESSON

Long-term growth requires patience because meaningful transformation happens gradually over time.

AFFIRMATION

"I honor the process of becoming who I am meant to be."

TODAY'S POWER MOVE

Acknowledge one area where you have emotionally or mentally grown over the past year.

DAY 149

Scarcity Cannot Build Peacefully

POWER QUOTE

"A fearful mindset struggles to create a peaceful future."

REFLECTION

Money influences far more than bank accounts.

It influences emotions.

Decisions.

Relationships.

Confidence.

Stress levels.

And the way people view the future.

For that reason, a person's relationship with money often matters just as much as the amount of money they possess.

Many people carry financial fears they do not fully recognize.

Some grew up watching financial instability.

Some experienced periods of lack.

Some faced unexpected setbacks that created lasting anxiety.

Over time, these experiences can shape the way people think about money.

Even when circumstances improve, old fears often remain.

A person may have enough resources but still feel unsafe.

Still panic.

Still expect disaster.

Still struggle to trust that stability is possible.

This is the hidden impact of scarcity thinking.

Scarcity is not only a financial condition.

It is often a mental and emotional condition.

It teaches people to focus on what might go wrong.

To expect loss.

To react from fear instead of preparation.

As a result, behavior begins changing.

People avoid looking at their finances because the numbers create anxiety.

They overspend emotionally because temporary comfort feels easier than facing stress.

They delay planning because uncertainty feels overwhelming.

They constantly worry about the future while doing little to prepare for it.

Ironically, these fear-based behaviors often create the very instability people are trying to avoid.

Fear rarely builds peace.

Panic rarely builds stability.

Reaction rarely builds wealth.

Wealth is usually built differently.

Through preparation.

Through patience.

Through intentional decisions repeated over time.

A financially healthy person is not necessarily someone who never worries.

It is often someone who has learned how to respond wisely when worry appears.

Someone who plans instead of panics.

Someone who prepares instead of avoids.

Someone who focuses on what can be controlled rather than becoming consumed by what cannot.

That is why healing your relationship with money is so important.

Money should not be a constant source of emotional fear.

It should become a tool.

A tool that helps create security.

Opportunity.

Freedom.

And stability.

The goal is not to worship money.

Nor is it to fear it.

The goal is to develop a healthier relationship with it.

One built on awareness rather than avoidance.

Planning rather than panic.

Stewardship rather than stress.

As that relationship improves, something powerful begins to happen.

Financial decisions become clearer.

Long-term thinking becomes easier.

Confidence begins to grow.

Peace begins to return.

Because a calm and intentional mind builds differently than a fearful one.

And the future is often shaped not only by how much money you earn, but by the mindset you bring to managing it.

Heal the fear.

Strengthen the habits.

Develop the discipline.

And allow money to become a tool that supports your future rather than a source of constant emotional burden.

Because true financial stability begins long before it appears in a bank account.

It begins in the way you think.

WEALTH LESSON

Financial peace grows when fear-based reactions are replaced with intentional planning and emotional discipline.

AFFIRMATION

"I replace scarcity thinking with wisdom, preparation, and peace."

TODAY'S POWER MOVE

Notice one fear-based financial habit today and intentionally challenge it.

DAY 150

You Are Rewriting Your Story

POWER QUOTE

"Your past may explain you, but it does not have to imprison your future."

REFLECTION

Many people unknowingly live according to stories that were written during some of the most painful seasons of their lives.

Stories shaped by rejection.

Disappointment.

Failure.

Fear.

Survival.

Stories that quietly influence how they see themselves and what they believe is possible for their future.

Over time, these stories become identities.

A person who was repeatedly rejected may begin believing they are unworthy.

A person who experienced financial hardship may begin believing stability is impossible.

A person who spent years in survival mode may begin believing peace is unrealistic.

The experience ends, but the identity remains.

This is one of the reasons growth can feel so challenging.

Because transformation is not only about changing behavior.

It is about changing the story behind the behavior.

Many people continue living from old identities long after they have outgrown them.

They make decisions through the lens of old fears.

View opportunities through the lens of old disappointments.

Approach relationships through the lens of old wounds.

Without realizing it, they allow yesterday's experiences to shape tomorrow's possibilities.

But healing creates something powerful:

Choice.

The opportunity to decide which parts of your past will guide you and which parts you will leave behind.

You are not required to remain loyal to identities that were created during your most painful chapters.

You are allowed to become someone new.

Someone healthier.

Someone stronger.

Someone more disciplined.

Someone more confident.

Someone more emotionally free.

This does not mean pretending the past never happened.

It means refusing to let the past have the final word.

Every intentional decision becomes part of a new story.

Every healthy boundary.

Every disciplined habit.

Every courageous conversation.

Every healed response.

Every act of self-respect.

These moments may seem small individually.

Yet together they begin creating evidence of a different identity.

An identity no longer controlled by old fears.

An identity no longer trapped by old limitations.

An identity aligned with the future rather than imprisoned by the past.

This process takes time.

Most meaningful transformations do.

The old story was not built in a day.

The new story will not be either.

But every intentional choice helps strengthen it.

Every lesson learned helps reinforce it.

Every step forward helps bring it to life.

One day, you may look back and realize something remarkable happened.

The life that once felt impossible became familiar.

The confidence you once admired in others became part of who you are.

The peace you once hoped for became your reality.

The future you once doubted became the life you were living.

Not because of one dramatic moment.

But because of countless small decisions that slowly transformed the way you saw yourself.

Your history is part of your story.

But it is not the entire story.

The pen is still in your hands.

And every day you choose growth, healing, discipline, and intentionality, you are writing a new chapter.

One that is no longer defined by what happened to you.

But by who you chose to become.

WEALTH LESSON

Identity transformation improves financial and emotional outcomes because behavior changes when self-perception changes.

AFFIRMATION

"I intentionally rewrite my story through healing, discipline, and growth."

TODAY'S POWER MOVE

Write down one old belief about yourself that you are no longer willing to carry into your future.

DAY 151

The Life You Want Requires Focus

POWER QUOTE

"Distraction steals energy from the future you are trying to build."

REFLECTION

Many people assume they need more talent, more resources, or more opportunities to change their lives.

Often, what they need most is greater focus.

Potential is rarely the problem.

Attention is.

There are countless intelligent, capable, and gifted individuals who struggle to create meaningful progress because their energy is constantly divided.

Their attention is pulled in every direction.

Notifications.

Social media.

Comparison.

Drama.

Unnecessary conflicts.

Endless distractions competing for space in their minds.

As a result, they remain busy but not productive.

Occupied but not advancing.

Exhausted but not fulfilled.

A distracted life makes it difficult to build momentum.

Momentum requires consistency.

Consistency requires focus.

And focus requires intentionality.

This is why attention is one of the most valuable resources a person possesses.

Whatever consistently receives your attention eventually begins shaping your life.

The ideas you consume.

The conversations you entertain.

The problems you repeatedly focus on.

The habits you reinforce daily.

All of these things influence your future.

Attention directs energy.

And energy creates results.

People who build meaningful lives understand this principle.

They become selective.

Not because they are antisocial.

Not because they are uninterested in others.

But because they understand that every distraction carries a cost.

Every unnecessary argument costs emotional energy.

Every hour lost to comparison costs mental clarity.

Every habit of constant reaction steals time from intentional creation.
Focused people think differently.
They ask different questions.
Instead of asking, "What has my attention?"
They ask, "What deserves my attention?"
That distinction changes everything.
Not every opportunity deserves a yes.
Not every conversation deserves engagement.
Not every opinion deserves consideration.
Not every distraction deserves access to your mind.
People who achieve meaningful progress often become excellent protectors of their attention.
They establish boundaries.
Create routines.
Limit unnecessary noise.
Reduce sources of distraction.
And little by little, their energy becomes concentrated rather than scattered.
This concentration creates momentum.
Momentum creates progress.
And progress creates confidence.
The goal is not perfection.
The goal is awareness.
To recognize where your attention is going.
To evaluate whether it aligns with the future you are trying to build.
And to make adjustments when necessary.
Because every day your attention is shaping something.
Building something.
Strengthening something.
The question is whether it is strengthening the life you truly want.
Protect your focus.
Protect your energy.
Protect your attention.
Because your future is being built by what consistently occupies your mind.
And the people who create extraordinary lives are often not the people with the most talent.
They are the people who learned how to direct their attention toward what matters most and stay there long enough for growth to occur.
Where attention flows consistently, results eventually follow.

WEALTH LESSON

Focused execution creates stronger results because energy is directed intentionally instead of emotionally scattered.

AFFIRMATION

"I protect my focus and direct my energy toward purposeful growth."

TODAY'S POWER MOVE

Spend one uninterrupted hour today focused entirely on your future goals.

DAY 152

Stop Punishing Yourself For Being Human

POWER QUOTE

"Growth becomes difficult when self-hatred becomes your inner voice."

REFLECTION

We often believe being hard on themselves will make them stronger.

They assume constant self-criticism creates discipline.

That harsh internal pressure creates improvement.

That shame creates motivation.

So every mistake becomes evidence that they are not good enough.

Every setback becomes proof they are failing.

Every difficult season becomes another reason to criticize themselves.

At first, this approach can seem productive.

It may create temporary urgency.

Temporary pressure.

Temporary action.

But over time, constant self-criticism creates a different problem.

Exhaustion.

Because no one thrives in an environment of relentless judgment.

Not even when that environment exists inside their own mind.

Imagine trying to grow in a place where every mistake is met with ridicule.

Every weakness is attacked.

Every setback is used as proof of inadequacy.

Growth would become difficult.

Confidence would weaken.

Progress would feel heavier than necessary.

Yet many people speak to themselves this way every day.

The truth is that awareness and self-criticism are not the same thing.

Awareness says:

"I made a mistake."

Self-criticism says:

"I am the mistake."

Awareness focuses on behavior.

Self-criticism attacks identity.

One creates growth.

The other often creates shame.

And shame rarely produces lasting transformation.

Healthy growth requires accountability.

It requires honesty.

It requires taking responsibility for choices and behaviors.

But accountability works best when it is paired with compassion.

Compassion is not making excuses.

It is recognizing your humanity while continuing to pursue improvement.

It is understanding that mistakes are part of learning.

That setbacks are part of growth.

That difficult seasons are part of life.

Every person you admire has failed.

Every successful person has experienced disappointment.

Every disciplined person has had moments where they struggled.

What separates resilient people is not perfection.

It is their ability to recover.

To learn.

To adjust.

To continue moving forward without allowing mistakes to define them.

Growth becomes sustainable when people learn how to challenge themselves without destroying themselves.

To maintain high standards without losing self-respect.

To pursue excellence without demanding perfection.

You are going to make mistakes.

You are going to have difficult days.

You are going to experience moments where you fall short of your own expectations.

That does not make you weak.

It makes you human.

The goal is not to avoid every setback.

The goal is to respond to setbacks in a way that supports growth.

To learn the lesson.

Make the adjustment.

And continue building.

Because strength is not measured by how rarely you fall.

It is measured by how consistently you get back up.

And some of the strongest people in the world are not those who never struggle.

They are those who learned how to rebuild themselves without becoming their own worst enemy.

Growth requires honesty.

But it also requires grace.

And lasting transformation is often built when both exist together.

WEALTH LESSON

Healthy self-awareness improves emotional stability because growth becomes more sustainable without constant self-condemnation.

AFFIRMATION

"I correct myself with wisdom instead of destroying myself with shame."

TODAY'S POWER MOVE

Speak to yourself today with patience, accountability, and emotional compassion.

DAY 153

Your Healing Will Influence Generations

POWER QUOTE

"When one person heals, future generations benefit too."

REFLECTION

Many people think healing is a personal journey.

And it is.

But it is also much bigger than that.

The choices you make today often reach further than you realize.

They influence the people around you.

The environments you create.

The relationships you build.

And the examples you leave behind.

Every family carries patterns.

Some are healthy.

Some are not.

Patterns of communication.

Patterns of handling conflict.

Patterns surrounding money.

Patterns surrounding discipline.

Patterns surrounding emotional expression.

Many of these behaviors are passed from one generation to the next without anyone intentionally choosing them.

People simply repeat what they observed.

What they experienced.

What became familiar.

That is why unhealthy patterns can survive for decades.

Not because people want them to continue.

But because few people stop long enough to question them.

Few people pause and ask:

"Is this helping or hurting?"

"Do I want this pattern to continue?"

"What kind of example am I creating?"

Growth begins when those questions are asked honestly.

Healing begins when someone becomes willing to confront what previous generations may have ignored.

That work is not always easy.

It requires awareness.

Courage.

Responsibility.

And often a willingness to do things differently than they have always been done.

A person who learns healthier financial habits creates a different example.

A person who develops emotional regulation creates a different example.

A person who establishes healthy boundaries creates a different example.

A person who chooses discipline over dysfunction creates a different example.

These changes may seem personal.

But their influence extends outward.

The way you handle stress affects the people around you.

The way you communicate affects the people around you.

The way you approach money affects the people around you.

The way you treat yourself affects the people around you.

Every healed pattern creates the possibility for healthier environments.

Healthier relationships.

Healthier futures.

Which is why your growth matters.

Not because you are trying to become perfect.

But because every improvement creates the opportunity for something different to follow.

A different standard.

A different mindset.

A different legacy.

Many people inherit fear without realizing it.

Scarcity without realizing it.

Avoidance without realizing it.

The powerful opportunity available to you is that you do not have to pass those patterns forward unchanged.

You can become the interruption.

The turning point.

The person who decides that something healthier will begin here.

That decision may not create immediate results.

Most meaningful change does not.

But over time, the impact becomes significant.

One healthier choice influences another.

One new habit influences another.

One improved mindset influences another.

And eventually a completely different future begins taking shape.

Never underestimate the value of the work you are doing today.

Every lesson learned.

Every unhealthy pattern confronted.

Every act of growth.

Every act of healing.

Every act of discipline.

All of it matters.

Because when you change yourself intentionally, you often change far more than yourself.

You help create a legacy that future generations can build upon rather than recover from.

And that may be one of the most meaningful forms of success a person can achieve.

WEALTH LESSON

Long-term legacy is shaped not only through money, but through emotional health, discipline, and intentional living.

AFFIRMATION

"I heal intentionally so future generations can experience healthier lives."

TODAY'S POWER MOVE

Reflect today on one unhealthy pattern you are determined to break permanently.

DAY 154

Stop Letting Fear Delay Your Future

POWER QUOTE

"Fear grows stronger every time you continuously obey it."

REFLECTION

Many people think healing is a personal journey.

And it is.

But it is also much bigger than that.

The choices you make today often reach further than you realize.

They influence the people around you.

The environments you create.

The relationships you build.

And the examples you leave behind.

Every family carries patterns.

Some are healthy.

Some are not.

Patterns of communication.

Patterns of handling conflict.

Patterns surrounding money.

Patterns surrounding discipline.

Patterns surrounding emotional expression.

Many of these behaviors are passed from one generation to the next without anyone intentionally choosing them.

People simply repeat what they observed.

What they experienced.

What became familiar.

That is why unhealthy patterns can survive for decades.

Not because people want them to continue.

But because few people stop long enough to question them.

Few people pause and ask:

"Is this helping or hurting?"

"Do I want this pattern to continue?"

"What kind of example am I creating?"

Growth begins when those questions are asked honestly.

Healing begins when someone becomes willing to confront what previous generations may have ignored.

That work is not always easy.

It requires awareness.

Courage.

Responsibility.

And often a willingness to do things differently than they have always been done.

A person who learns healthier financial habits creates a different example.

A person who develops emotional regulation creates a different example.

A person who establishes healthy boundaries creates a different example.
A person who chooses discipline over dysfunction creates a different example.
These changes may seem personal.
But their influence extends outward.
The way you handle stress affects the people around you.
The way you communicate affects the people around you.
The way you approach money affects the people around you.
The way you treat yourself affects the people around you.
Every healed pattern creates the possibility for healthier environments.
Healthier relationships.
Healthier futures.
That is why your growth matters.
Not because you are trying to become perfect.
But because every improvement creates the opportunity for something different to follow.
A different standard.
A different mindset.
A different legacy.
Many people inherit fear without realizing it.
Scarcity without realizing it.
Avoidance without realizing it.
The powerful opportunity available to you is that you do not have to pass those patterns forward unchanged.
You can become the interruption.
The turning point.
The person who decides that something healthier will begin here.
That decision may not create immediate results.
Most meaningful change does not.
But over time, the impact becomes significant.
One healthier choice influences another.
One new habit influences another.
One improved mindset influences another.
And eventually a completely different future begins taking shape.
Do not underestimate the value of the quiet work you are doing today.
Every lesson learned.
Every unhealthy pattern confronted.
Every act of growth.
Every act of healing.
Every act of discipline.
All of it matters.
Because when you change yourself intentionally, you often change far more than yourself.
You help create a legacy that future generations can build upon rather than recover from.
And that may be one of the most meaningful forms of success a person can achieve.

WEALTH LESSON

Growth often requires calculated risk because comfort rarely creates major expansion long-term.

AFFIRMATION

"I move forward courageously even when uncertainty exists."

TODAY'S POWER MOVE

Take one action today that fear has been convincing you to avoid.

DAY 155

Emotional Maturity Creates Better Decisions

POWER QUOTE

"Wise people pause before reacting emotionally."

REFLECTION

Every person experiences emotions.

Frustration.

Fear.

Disappointment.

Anger.

Anxiety.

Excitement.

Joy.

The goal of maturity is not to eliminate emotions.

The goal is to learn how to manage them wisely.

Many people assume emotional maturity means becoming unemotional.

Detached.

Cold.

Unaffected.

But true emotional maturity is something entirely different.

It is the ability to feel deeply without allowing every feeling to control your behavior.

It is recognizing emotions without surrendering your decisions to them.

This distinction matters because emotions are powerful.

When unmanaged, they can create significant damage.

A moment of anger can damage a relationship.

A moment of fear can stop a person from pursuing an opportunity.

A moment of insecurity can create self-sabotage.

A moment of panic can lead to poor financial decisions.

The emotion itself is not the problem.

The reaction often is.

Which is why emotional maturity becomes such a valuable life skill.

Emotionally mature people still experience difficult feelings.

They still become frustrated.

They still feel afraid.

They still experience disappointment.

The difference is that they create space between the emotion and the response.

They pause.

Reflect.

Consider consequences.

Think beyond the immediate moment.

Instead of reacting impulsively, they respond intentionally.

That pause may seem small.

Yet it can completely change outcomes.

It can save relationships.

Protect opportunities.

Prevent unnecessary conflict.

Preserve peace.

Over time, these moments create stability.

Stability in communication.

Stability in decision-making.

Stability in finances.

Stability in relationships.

And stability in personal growth.

Many of the challenges people face are not caused by a lack of intelligence.

They are caused by emotional reactions that override wisdom.

Knowledge alone is not enough.

A person may know what the right decision is and still choose differently when emotions take control.

That is why emotional discipline is so important.

It helps align actions with values rather than temporary feelings.

It helps people remain focused during stressful seasons.

It helps them make decisions they will still respect tomorrow.

Emotional maturity does not mean becoming perfect.

It means becoming intentional.

Learning how to sit with discomfort without immediately escaping it.

Learning how to communicate without attacking.

Learning how to face fear without allowing fear to lead.

Learning how to stay grounded when life becomes difficult.

These skills are developed over time.

Through practice.

Through awareness.

Through experience.

Every moment you choose reflection over impulse, you strengthen them.

Every moment you choose wisdom over reaction, you strengthen them.

Every moment you choose growth over emotional chaos, you strengthen them.

And eventually, those choices become part of who you are.

Because emotional maturity is not measured by how little you feel.

It is measured by how wisely you handle what you feel.

And that wisdom becomes one of the strongest foundations upon which a meaningful life can be built.

WEALTH LESSON

Emotional regulation improves financial and personal outcomes because thoughtful decisions reduce unnecessary chaos.

AFFIRMATION

"I respond with emotional wisdom, calmness, and maturity."

TODAY'S POWER MOVE

Pause before reacting emotionally today and choose intentional communication instead.

DAY 156

You Do Not Need To Rush Your Growth

POWER QUOTE

"Slow growth is still meaningful growth."

REFLECTION

Every person experiences emotions.

Frustration.

Fear.

Disappointment.

Anger.

Anxiety.

Excitement.

Joy.

The goal of maturity is not to eliminate emotions.

The goal is to learn how to manage them wisely.

Many people assume emotional maturity means becoming unemotional.

Detached.

Cold.

Unaffected.

But true emotional maturity is something entirely different.

It is the ability to feel deeply without allowing every feeling to control your behavior.

It is recognizing emotions without surrendering your decisions to them.

This distinction matters because emotions are powerful.

When unmanaged, they can create significant damage.

A moment of anger can damage a relationship.

A moment of fear can stop a person from pursuing an opportunity.

A moment of insecurity can create self-sabotage.

A moment of panic can lead to poor financial decisions.

The emotion itself is not the problem.

The reaction often is.

This is why emotional maturity becomes such a valuable life skill.

Emotionally mature people still experience difficult feelings.

They still become frustrated.

They still feel afraid.

They still experience disappointment.

The difference is that they create space between the emotion and the response.

They pause.

Reflect.

Consider consequences.

Think beyond the immediate moment.

Instead of reacting impulsively, they respond intentionally.

That pause may seem small.

Yet it can completely change outcomes.

It can save relationships.

Protect opportunities.

Prevent unnecessary conflict.

Preserve peace.

Over time, these moments create stability.

Stability in communication.

Stability in decision-making.

Stability in finances.

Stability in relationships.

And stability in personal growth.

Many of the challenges people face are not caused by a lack of intelligence.

They are caused by emotional reactions that override wisdom.

Knowledge alone is not enough.

A person may know what the right decision is and still choose differently when emotions take control.

Which is why emotional discipline is so important.

It helps align actions with values rather than temporary feelings.

It helps people remain focused during stressful seasons.

It helps them make decisions they will still respect tomorrow.

Emotional maturity does not mean becoming perfect.

It means becoming intentional.

Learning how to sit with discomfort without immediately escaping it.

Learning how to communicate without attacking.

Learning how to face fear without allowing fear to lead.

Learning how to stay grounded when life becomes difficult.

These skills are developed over time.

Through practice.

Through awareness.

Through experience.

Every moment you choose reflection over impulse, you strengthen them.

Every moment you choose wisdom over reaction, you strengthen them.

Every moment you choose growth over emotional chaos, you strengthen them.

And eventually, those choices become part of who you are.

Because emotional maturity is not measured by how little you feel.

It is measured by how wisely you handle what you feel.

And that wisdom becomes one of the strongest foundations upon which a meaningful life can be built.

WEALTH LESSON

Intentional growth creates stronger long-term stability than rushed emotional decision-making.

AFFIRMATION

"I honor my growth process without comparing my timing to others."

TODAY'S POWER MOVE

Acknowledge one area where you have quietly grown over time.

DAY 157

Your Future Needs Boundaries

POWER QUOTE

"People who protect their peace protect their future too."

REFLECTION

Many people think boundaries are about keeping others out.

In reality, boundaries are often about protecting what matters most.

Your peace.

Your energy.

Your time.

Your healing.

Your future.

Without boundaries, life can quickly become overwhelming.

People begin saying yes when they want to say no.

Giving more than they can sustain.

Accepting responsibilities that were never theirs to carry.

Trying to satisfy everyone while slowly neglecting themselves.

At first, this may look generous.

Helpful.

Selfless.

But over time, something begins to happen.

Exhaustion grows.

Resentment grows.

Stress grows.

The emotional cost becomes difficult to ignore.

Because no one can continuously pour into others while ignoring their own well-being.

Eventually, emotional depletion affects everything.

Focus becomes weaker.

Discipline becomes harder.

Patience becomes shorter.

Goals become more difficult to pursue.

The person who was trying to help everyone finds themselves struggling to help themselves.

That is why boundaries are not selfish.

They are responsible.

Healthy boundaries acknowledge a simple truth:

Your energy is limited.

Your time is limited.

Your emotional capacity is limited.

And because these resources are valuable, they must be managed intentionally.

Boundaries help create that protection.

They help you recognize where your responsibilities end and someone else's begin.

They help you communicate expectations clearly.

They help prevent other people's demands from constantly determining how you spend your life.

Many people avoid boundaries because they fear disappointing others.

They fear being misunderstood.

They fear appearing unkind.

But protecting your well-being does not make you selfish.

It makes you wise.

In fact, people who lack boundaries often find themselves unable to show up fully in the areas that matter most.

Their energy becomes scattered.

Their attention becomes divided.

Their peace becomes fragile.

Boundaries help restore balance.

They create space for recovery.

Space for growth.

Space for intentional living.

Not everyone deserves unlimited access to your thoughts.

Your emotions.

Your time.

Your attention.

Access should be earned through respect, trust, and mutual care.

Healthy relationships understand this.

Healthy people respect this.

And healthy growth often depends upon this.

The goal is not to build walls around your life.

The goal is to build gates.

To become intentional about what enters and what remains outside.

To recognize that protecting your emotional environment is part of protecting your future.

Every meaningful goal requires energy.

Every season of healing requires energy.

Every season of growth requires energy.

Boundaries help preserve that energy.

They allow you to invest more fully in the life you are building rather than constantly recovering from unnecessary emotional depletion.

Protect your peace.

Protect your time.

Protect your healing.

Protect your growth.

Because boundaries are not barriers to a meaningful life.

They are often the very thing that makes a meaningful life sustainable.

WEALTH LESSON

Healthy boundaries improve focus and emotional energy, allowing stronger long-term execution and discipline.

AFFIRMATION

"I honor boundaries that protect my peace, purpose, and future."

TODAY'S POWER MOVE

Say no today to one thing that continuously drains your emotional energy.

DAY 158

The Way You See Yourself Matters

POWER QUOTE

"Identity influences behavior more than motivation alone."

REFLECTION

Every person carries a story about who they believe they are.

Whether they realize it or not, that story influences almost every decision they make.

It affects confidence.

Habits.

Relationships.

Goals.

Financial choices.

And the way they respond to challenges.

This is because people naturally behave in ways that align with their identity.

A person who sees themselves as responsible tends to make different decisions than someone who sees themselves as careless.

A person who sees themselves as resilient responds differently to setbacks than someone who sees themselves as defeated.

A person who believes growth is possible approaches life differently than someone who believes change is impossible.

Identity quietly shapes behavior.

That is why the conversations you have with yourself matter so much.

Many people spend years reinforcing harmful identities without realizing it.

They repeatedly tell themselves:

"I am lazy."

"I always mess things up."

"I am bad with money."

"I never follow through."

"I am not capable."

At first, these statements may seem harmless.

But repeated often enough, they begin shaping expectations.

And expectations begin shaping behavior.

Eventually, people start acting in alignment with the labels they have accepted.

Not because the labels are true.

Because the labels have become familiar.

The mind tends to look for evidence supporting what it already believes.

This is why changing behavior often requires changing identity first.

You cannot continuously describe yourself as incapable while expecting confident action.

You cannot constantly reinforce weakness while expecting strength.

You cannot repeatedly speak limitation over yourself while expecting expansion.

Transformation begins internally.

Long before it becomes visible externally.

This does not mean pretending to be someone you are not.

It means becoming intentional about who you are becoming.

Instead of reinforcing old limitations, begin reinforcing growth.

Not through empty affirmations.

Through honest and empowering truths.

You are capable of learning.

Capable of improving.

Capable of becoming more disciplined.

Capable of healing.

Capable of building a different future than the one you have experienced before.

As those beliefs strengthen, behavior begins changing.

Small decisions begin changing.

Standards begin changing.

Habits begin changing.

And over time, the identity becomes stronger.

This is how meaningful transformation often happens.

Not through one dramatic moment.

But through repeated alignment between belief and behavior.

Every promise you keep to yourself strengthens identity.

Every disciplined action strengthens identity.

Every healthy choice strengthens identity.

Every courageous decision strengthens identity.

Little by little, you become the person your actions repeatedly confirm.

That is why identity matters so deeply.

Because people rarely rise far beyond the version of themselves they believe they are.

Protect your self-perception.

Pay attention to your internal dialogue.

Be intentional about the story you are reinforcing.

Because the life you build externally is often influenced by the identity you cultivate internally.

And the moment your identity begins changing, your future often begins changing with it.

WEALTH LESSON

Healthy self-identity improves discipline, consistency, and long-term emotional resilience.

AFFIRMATION

"I build an identity rooted in confidence, discipline, and growth."

TODAY'S POWER MOVE

Speak positively about yourself and your future today.

DAY 159

You Are Allowed To Begin Again

POWER QUOTE

"One mistake does not erase your ability to rebuild."

REFLECTION

One of the most damaging things a person can do is confuse a mistake with their identity.

A financial mistake becomes:

"I am bad with money."

A failed relationship becomes:

"I am impossible to love."

A business setback becomes:

"I am not capable of success."

Over time, people stop viewing failure as something they experienced and start viewing it as something they are.

That shift is dangerous.

Because once failure becomes identity, growth becomes much harder.

People stop trying.

Stop believing.

Stop taking healthy risks.

Not because they lack potential, but because shame convinced them their future has already been decided.

But failure was never meant to become a permanent label.

It was meant to become a lesson.

Life has always been a process of learning.

Learning what works.

Learning what does not.

Learning how to communicate better.

Manage money better.

Build healthier relationships.

Make wiser decisions.

Nobody arrives with all of that knowledge perfectly developed.

It is gained through experience.

Which means mistakes are not evidence that you are broken.

They are often evidence that you are learning.

The problem is that shame distorts perspective.

It whispers that one bad decision defines your entire future.

That one setback cancels your potential.

That one difficult season determines the rest of your story.

None of those things are true.

The most successful people in every field have experienced failure.

They have lost opportunities.

Made poor decisions.

Faced rejection.

Experienced disappointment.

Watched plans fall apart.

The difference is not that they avoided failure.

The difference is that they refused to build their identity around it.

They learned.

Adjusted.

Recovered.

And continued moving forward.

That ability to begin again is one of the greatest strengths a person can develop.

Because life will always include moments that do not go according to plan.

The question is not whether mistakes will happen.

The question is what you will do after they happen.

Will you allow the experience to become a prison?

Or will you allow it to become a teacher?

Growth begins when people stop asking, "What does this failure say about me?"

And start asking, "What can this experience teach me?"

That shift creates possibility.

It creates movement.

It creates hope.

Because lessons can be applied.

Wisdom can be gained.

Skills can be strengthened.

And futures can be rebuilt.

You are allowed to learn from your mistakes.

Allowed to heal from them.

Allowed to outgrow them.

Allowed to become wiser because of them.

Your past decisions may explain parts of your journey, but they do not determine your destiny.

The chapter may have been painful.

The lesson may have been difficult.

The consequences may have been real.

But the story is not over.

Keep learning.

Keep rebuilding.

Keep moving forward.

Because failure is something you may experience.

It is not something you have to become.

And the future still deserves your effort, your belief, and your willingness to begin again.

WEALTH LESSON

Resilience strengthens long-term growth because people who rebuild continue creating new opportunities.

AFFIRMATION

"I allow myself to begin again stronger and wiser than before."

TODAY'S POWER MOVE

Release one past mistake that you have been emotionally carrying too heavily.

DAY 160

Discipline Protects Your Dreams

POWER QUOTE

"Dreams without discipline eventually become frustration."

REFLECTION

Most people pay close attention to what they allow into their homes.

They think carefully about security.

Cleanliness.

Organization.

Protection.

Yet many people are far less careful about what they allow into their minds.

The conversations they entertain.

The content they consume.

The environments they remain in.

The people they spend the most time around.

Over time, these influences shape emotional energy more than many realize.

And emotional energy affects everything.

The way you think.

The way you communicate.

The way you make decisions.

The way you handle challenges.

The way you view the future.

A person who is emotionally exhausted often thinks differently than a person who is emotionally healthy.

Problems feel larger.

Patience becomes shorter.

Motivation becomes weaker.

Decision-making becomes more reactive.

The issue is not intelligence.

It is depletion.

When emotional energy is constantly drained, even simple responsibilities can begin feeling overwhelming.

Which is why protecting your emotional environment matters.

Not because life should be free from difficulty.

But because unnecessary emotional chaos creates unnecessary burdens.

Many people spend years surrounded by negativity without recognizing its impact.

Constant criticism.

Constant conflict.

Constant comparison.

Constant stress.

Over time, these influences become normal.

Yet normal does not always mean healthy.

A healthy emotional environment supports growth.

It encourages clarity.

It creates space for reflection.

It allows healing to occur.

It provides the stability necessary for long-term progress.

This does not mean avoiding every difficult conversation.

Nor does it mean isolating yourself from reality.

It means becoming intentional.

Intentional about what consistently receives access to your attention.

Intentional about the voices you repeatedly listen to.

Intentional about the environments that shape your mindset.

Because every environment is influencing something.

Strengthening something.

Reinforcing something.

The question is whether it is strengthening the future you want to create.

Rest is part of this process.

So is recovery.

So is spending time in places and around people who contribute to peace rather than constant turmoil.

Many people view these things as luxuries.

In reality, they are forms of preparation.

A well-rested mind thinks more clearly.

A peaceful mind makes better decisions.

A supported mind handles challenges more effectively.

Emotional care is not weakness.

It is maintenance.

Just as physical health requires attention, emotional health requires attention too.

The strongest people are not always those who endure the most chaos.

Often, they are the people who learned how to protect their energy wisely.

Who learned when to engage and when to step back.

Who learned that peace is something worth preserving.

Your emotional environment matters.

The conversations matter.

The content matters.

The people matter.

The atmosphere you create around yourself matters.

Because the quality of your inner world eventually influences the quality of your outer life.

Protect it intentionally.

Nurture it consistently.

And remember that one of the greatest gifts you can give your future is an environment that supports the person you are becoming.

WEALTH LESSON

Discipline transforms long-term goals into reality because repeated action compounds over time.

AFFIRMATION

"I protect my future through discipline, consistency, and intentional action."

TODAY'S POWER MOVE

Dedicate focused effort today toward one long-term dream or responsibility.

DAY 161

Stop Letting Your Past Define Your Future

POWER QUOTE

"Your history may explain your pain, but it does not have to control your destiny."

REFLECTION

Pain has a way of leaving fingerprints on the mind.

A rejection creates doubt.

A heartbreak creates fear.

A financial setback creates insecurity.

A failure creates hesitation.

The experience ends, but the emotional imprint often remains.

Without realizing it, many people begin organizing their lives around old wounds.

They make decisions based on what hurt them.

Avoid risks because of past disappointments.

Lower expectations because of previous failures.

Protect themselves from pain instead of positioning themselves for growth.

Over time, something dangerous happens.

They begin identifying more with their struggles than with their potential.

More with what happened to them than with who they are capable of becoming.

The rejection becomes part of their identity.

The loss becomes part of their identity.

The hardship becomes part of their identity.

And little by little, the past begins shaping the future.

Not because it has to.

Because it was never challenged.

The truth is that your experiences matter.

They shaped you.

They taught you.

They influenced your perspective.

Ignoring that reality would be dishonest.

But allowing those experiences to permanently define you is equally dangerous.

A difficult chapter was never meant to become your entire story.

The version of you that was created during survival mode served a purpose.

That version helped you endure.

Helped you cope.

Helped you make it through difficult seasons.

But survival is not meant to become a permanent identity.

Eventually, growth requires something different.

Not just surviving.

Thriving.

Not just protecting yourself from pain.

Building a meaningful future.
Not just avoiding disappointment.
Creating possibility.
This is where healing becomes powerful.
Healing allows people to loosen their attachment to old identities.
To stop introducing themselves internally through their wounds.
To stop measuring future opportunities through past experiences.
To stop asking only, "What happened to me?"
And begin asking:
"Who do I want to become?"
That question shifts attention.
From the past to the future.
From the wound to the vision.
From survival to growth.
Because the future is not created by endlessly revisiting old pain.
It is created by intentionally building new patterns.
New habits.
New beliefs.
New standards.
New ways of thinking.
Every disciplined choice becomes evidence of growth.
Every healthy boundary becomes evidence of growth.
Every courageous step becomes evidence of growth.
Every healed response becomes evidence of growth.
Little by little, a new identity begins forming.
One that is not controlled by old wounds.
One that is not limited by old failures.
One that is not trapped by old fears.
Your past may explain parts of your journey.
But it does not own your future.
You are allowed to become more than your disappointments.
More than your heartbreak.
More than your mistakes.
More than your hardest season.
You are allowed to evolve beyond the version of yourself that was built for survival.
And as you continue growing, healing, and rebuilding, you may discover that the life you once thought was impossible becomes possible one intentional decision at a time.
Because transformation begins the moment you stop defining yourself by what happened to you and start defining yourself by who you are becoming.

WEALTH LESSON

Identity transformation improves long-term behavior because people begin making decisions aligned with growth instead of old survival patterns.

AFFIRMATION

"I refuse to let my past limit the future I am capable of building."

TODAY'S POWER MOVE

Write down one limiting belief from your past that you are intentionally releasing today.

DAY 162

Your Energy Shapes Your Life

POWER QUOTE

"The energy you carry influences the decisions you make."

REFLECTION

Most people understand the importance of protecting their physical environment.

They lock their doors.

Maintain their homes.

Pay attention to what they eat.

Protect their physical health.

Yet many people pay far less attention to their emotional environment.

The conversations they allow into their lives.

The content they consume daily.

The people they spend the most time around.

The situations they repeatedly expose themselves to.

Over time, these influences quietly shape the way they think, feel, and behave.

This matters because emotional energy affects nearly everything.

A constantly stressed mind thinks differently than a peaceful one.

An exhausted mind makes different decisions than a rested one.

A fearful mind approaches opportunities differently than a confident one.

The quality of your emotional environment often influences the quality of your choices.

And the quality of your choices influences the quality of your future.

Many people underestimate how draining certain environments can become.

Constant negativity.

Constant conflict.

Constant comparison.

Constant drama.

At first, these things may seem manageable.

But emotional exhaustion rarely appears all at once.

It accumulates.

One stressful conversation at a time.

One negative influence at a time.

One emotionally draining environment at a time.

Eventually, the mind becomes overwhelmed.

Focus weakens.

Patience decreases.

Motivation fades.

Clarity becomes harder to maintain.

This is why emotional care is not a luxury.

It is a responsibility.

Protecting your peace is not selfish.

It is preparation.

Preparation for clearer thinking.

Better decisions.

Healthier relationships.

Greater emotional stability.

A strong future requires a strong foundation.

And emotional well-being is part of that foundation.

This does not mean avoiding every challenge.

Growth often requires difficult conversations.

Hard decisions.

Uncomfortable seasons.

But there is a difference between healthy challenges and unnecessary emotional chaos.

Healthy challenges help you grow.

Unnecessary chaos drains your ability to grow.

Learning that distinction is wisdom.

It allows you to become more intentional about what receives access to your mind and energy.

The healthiest people are often not those with the easiest lives.

They are people who learned how to protect their emotional environment.

They choose relationships carefully.

They establish boundaries.

They create space for rest.

They pay attention to what they repeatedly consume.

They understand that their emotional energy is valuable.

And they treat it accordingly.

Because every environment is shaping something.

Reinforcing something.

Strengthening something.

The question is whether it is strengthening the future you want to build.

Protect your peace.

Protect your focus.

Protect your energy.

Protect your mind.

Because the person you are becoming is influenced by the environments you repeatedly allow around you.

And one of the greatest investments you can make in your future is creating an emotional environment that supports growth rather than constantly working against it.

WEALTH LESSON

Healthy emotional energy improves focus, productivity, and long-term decision-making.

AFFIRMATION

"I protect my energy because it influences the quality of my life."

TODAY'S POWER MOVE

Pay attention today to what drains your energy and what restores it.

DAY 163

You Do Not Need To Prove Your Worth

POWER QUOTE

"Your value does not decrease because someone failed to recognize it."

REFLECTION

Many people spend years trying to earn something they already possess.

Worth.

They seek it through achievement.

Through relationships.

Through recognition.

Through approval.

Through the opinions of other people.

They believe that if enough people accept them, admire them, validate them, or praise them, they will finally feel secure within themselves.

But there is a problem with building confidence that way.

Other people's opinions are constantly changing.

One day they support you.

The next day they criticize you.

One day they celebrate your success.

The next day they question your decisions.

If your self-worth depends entirely on external approval, your emotional stability will always be vulnerable to external circumstances.

You will spend your life chasing validation instead of developing confidence.

This is why so many people become emotionally exhausted.

They are constantly performing.

Constantly proving.

Constantly trying to earn acceptance.

Trying to convince others that they are enough.

Trying to gain approval from people who may never fully understand them.

Over time, this creates pressure.

Because no amount of validation can permanently solve an internal belief problem.

If someone secretly believes they are not enough, external praise only provides temporary relief.

Soon they need more.

More recognition.

More approval.

More reassurance.

The cycle continues.

True confidence develops differently.

It is built from within.

Not through perfection.

Not through superiority.

Not through becoming better than everyone else.

Through self-respect.

The quiet confidence that develops when your actions align with your values.

When you keep promises to yourself.

When you maintain healthy boundaries.

When you act with integrity.

When you continue growing even when nobody is watching.

These experiences create evidence.

Evidence that you can trust yourself.

Evidence that you are capable.

Evidence that your worth is not dependent upon public opinion.

Self-respect becomes a stronger foundation than validation because it remains available regardless of what others think.

There will always be people who misunderstand you.

People who disagree with you.

People who fail to recognize your value.

That reality is unavoidable.

But their inability to recognize your worth does not reduce your worth.

Many people spend years waiting for someone else to confirm what they should begin believing themselves.

That they are valuable.

Capable.

Worthy of growth.

Worthy of healing.

Worthy of peace.

The healthiest confidence emerges when people stop treating their worth like something that must be earned from everyone around them.

Instead, they begin building a relationship with themselves based on honesty, discipline, growth, and self-respect.

Little by little, their confidence becomes more stable.

Less dependent on praise.

Less vulnerable to criticism.

Less controlled by comparison.

Because it is rooted in something deeper.

Your worth is not determined by how many people approve of you.

It is not determined by how many people understand you.

It is not determined by how much recognition you receive.

Your worth is not up for public vote.

It never was.

The goal is not becoming perfect enough for everyone else.

The goal is becoming secure enough within yourself that your peace no longer depends on constant approval from others.

And that kind of confidence is one of the most powerful forms of freedom a person can experience.

WEALTH LESSON

Emotional security improves decision-making because people stop making fear-based choices for validation.

AFFIRMATION

"I know my value even when external validation is absent."

TODAY'S POWER MOVE

Do something today because it aligns with your values, not because it gains approval from others.

DAY 164

Wealth Is Built Through Repetition

POWER QUOTE

"Financial freedom is usually built through repeated disciplined decisions."

REFLECTION

Many people spend their lives searching for a breakthrough.

A single opportunity.

A single investment.

A single decision that instantly changes everything.

While breakthroughs do happen, most meaningful success is built differently.

More quietly.

More gradually.

More consistently.

The greatest transformations are often the result of small actions repeated over long periods of time.

Saving a little money each month.

Learning a little more each day.

Improving one habit at a time.

Making one better decision after another.

None of these actions seem extraordinary in isolation.

In fact, they often feel insignificant.

That is why many people overlook them.

They focus on dramatic change while underestimating the power of steady progress.

But life is heavily influenced by compounding.

Compounding is the process by which small actions accumulate and create results far greater than the effort initially appears capable of producing.

A single workout rarely transforms a body.

A single deposit rarely creates wealth.

A single book rarely changes a life.

Yet repeated consistently, those actions become powerful.

The challenge is that compounding requires patience.

People naturally want immediate evidence that their efforts matter.

They want quick results.

Instant validation.

Visible progress.

But compounding operates differently.

For a long time, the results appear small.

Sometimes almost invisible.

This is where many people quit.

Not because the process is failing.

Because the results are not yet obvious.

They abandon good habits before those habits have time to produce meaningful outcomes.

They stop investing before growth has time to occur.

They stop learning before knowledge has time to compound.

They stop building before momentum has time to develop.

What they fail to realize is that some of the most important growth happens beneath the surface.

Momentum is building.

Skills are improving.

Confidence is developing.

Financial stability is increasing.

Even when the changes are difficult to measure.

This is why discipline is so valuable.

Discipline allows people to continue before the rewards become visible.

It helps them remain committed to actions that support their future, even when immediate results are limited.

The disciplined person understands something powerful:

Small decisions matter.

Not because of what they accomplish today.

Because of what they accumulate into tomorrow.

A single responsible financial decision may seem insignificant.

But hundreds of responsible financial decisions can completely change a person's future.

A single hour of learning may seem small.

But years of learning can create expertise.

A single healthy habit may feel ordinary.

But consistent habits shape identity.

This is how meaningful lives are built.

Not through constant dramatic moments.

Through repeated intentional actions that gradually create momentum.

So do not underestimate your daily choices.

Do not dismiss small progress.

Do not abandon consistency because results are taking longer than expected.

The future is often built quietly.

One habit.

One decision.

One investment.

One lesson.

One day at a time.

And one day, the results that once seemed invisible become impossible to ignore.

Because compounding may be quiet.

But its impact can be life-changing.

The people who understand this rarely chase shortcuts.

They trust the process.

Stay consistent.

And allow time to multiply the value of their disciplined efforts.

That is where extraordinary results are often born.

WEALTH LESSON

Compounding rewards disciplined consistency over long periods of time.

AFFIRMATION

"I build wealth through repeated intentional decisions."

TODAY'S POWER MOVE

Make one financially disciplined decision today that supports your long-term future.

DAY 165

Stop Overthinking Every Step

POWER QUOTE

"Overthinking often delays opportunities more than failure ever could."

REFLECTION

A lot of people believe they need complete certainty before taking action.

They want every answer.

Every detail.

Every possible outcome mapped out in advance.

They tell themselves they are being responsible.

Careful.

Prepared.

And sometimes they are.

But sometimes preparation becomes something else.

Avoidance.

Fear wearing the disguise of planning.

Because there comes a point where gathering more information no longer creates progress.

It simply delays action.

This is one of the most common traps people fall into.

They wait for perfect confidence.

Perfect timing.

Perfect clarity.

Perfect certainty.

But life rarely offers any of those things.

Most meaningful opportunities arrive with unanswered questions attached to them.

Most important decisions involve some level of uncertainty.

Most growth requires movement before confidence fully arrives.

This can feel uncomfortable.

Because action creates vulnerability.

Action creates risk.

Action creates the possibility of failure.

And the mind naturally wants to avoid those possibilities.

So people stay where they are.

Thinking.

Planning.

Analyzing.

Waiting.

Hoping clarity will appear before they move.

Yet clarity often works in the opposite direction.

Many of life's greatest lessons are learned through experience.

Not observation.

Not theory.
Experience.
You learn by doing.
You discover strengths by testing them.
You gain confidence by taking action.
You develop wisdom by navigating situations that once felt intimidating.
The person you want to become cannot be built entirely through preparation.
At some point, preparation must become participation.
This does not mean acting recklessly.
Planning still matters.
Research still matters.
Wisdom still matters.
But there is a difference between thoughtful preparation and endless hesitation.
One moves you forward.
The other keeps you standing still.
Overthinking often creates emotional paralysis.
The mind becomes trapped in possibilities.
Every risk appears larger.
Every challenge appears more threatening.
Every uncertainty becomes a reason to wait.
Eventually, years can pass while people remain emotionally stuck at the starting line.
Not because they lacked ability.
Because they waited for a level of certainty that was never going to arrive.
Growth asks something different.
It asks for courage.
The willingness to move before every fear disappears.
The willingness to act before complete confidence exists.
The willingness to trust that experience will teach what preparation alone cannot.
Every meaningful achievement begins with imperfect action.
Every skill begins with inexperience.
Every success story begins with someone deciding to move despite uncertainty.
Your future does not require perfection.
It requires participation.
It requires willingness.
It requires movement.
Because action creates feedback.
Feedback creates learning.
Learning creates growth.
And growth creates confidence.
Do not spend your life waiting for certainty that may never come.
Prepare wisely.

Think carefully.

But when the time comes, move.

Take the step.

Make the call.

Start the project.

Apply for the opportunity.

Have the conversation.

Trust the process enough to begin.

Because many of the answers you are searching for will not appear before you move.

They will appear because you moved.

And often, the clarity you want is waiting on the other side of action.

WEALTH LESSON

Execution creates momentum faster than over analysis because movement creates opportunities for growth and learning.

AFFIRMATION

"I stop overthinking and begin moving with courage and wisdom."

TODAY'S POWER MOVE

Take one action today that you have been delaying through overthinking.

DAY 166

Emotional Peace Is Productive

POWER QUOTE

"A peaceful mind creates stronger decisions."

REFLECTION

Many people have been taught that success requires constant pressure.

Constant stress.

Constant urgency.

Constant exhaustion.

They believe that if they are not overwhelmed, they are not working hard enough.

If they are not anxious, they are not ambitious enough.

If they are not exhausted, they are not productive enough.

Over time, stress becomes glorified.

Burnout becomes normalized.

Emotional chaos becomes confused with commitment.

But there is a problem with living this way.

It is difficult to build a healthy future while constantly operating from survival mode.

Stress can create temporary urgency.

It can force action in short bursts.

It can help people respond to immediate challenges.

But chronic stress comes with a cost.

It weakens focus.

Reduces patience.

Clouds judgment.

Drains emotional energy.

And eventually makes consistent discipline harder to maintain.

The mind was never designed to live in a constant state of alarm.

This is why peace matters.

Not because peace removes responsibility.

Because peace improves performance.

A peaceful mind thinks more clearly.

It evaluates situations more accurately.

It responds instead of reacts.

It creates space for wisdom to operate.

When people are emotionally grounded, they often make better decisions.

They communicate more effectively.

Handle pressure more intentionally.

And recover from setbacks more quickly.

Peace is not laziness.

Peace is stability.

It is the ability to remain centered even when circumstances become difficult.

Many of the most effective people are not constantly panicking.
They are not constantly overwhelmed.
They have simply learned how to manage their emotional state wisely.
They understand that emotional stability is an asset.
Because a calm mind builds differently than a chaotic one.
A calm mind can plan long-term.
A calm mind can solve problems thoughtfully.
A calm mind can remain disciplined when emotions fluctuate.
This does not mean life will always feel peaceful.
Challenges will come.
Unexpected setbacks will happen.
Difficult seasons are unavoidable.
But there is a difference between experiencing stress and living inside it permanently.
One is temporary.
The other becomes destructive.
The healthiest growth occurs when effort and peace work together.
When ambition is supported by emotional stability.
When discipline is supported by clarity.
When goals are pursued without sacrificing mental well-being in the process.
Many people are chasing success while neglecting the very foundation that would help them sustain it.
Their peace.
Their rest.
Their emotional health.
Yet sustainable success requires all three.
Because what you build is only valuable if you are healthy enough to enjoy it.
Protecting your peace is not avoiding responsibility.
It is preparing yourself to handle responsibility more effectively.
It is creating an internal environment where focus can thrive.
Where discipline can last.
Where wisdom can guide decisions.
And where growth becomes sustainable rather than exhausting.
Never underestimate the value of emotional stability.
The world often celebrates pressure.
But lasting success is frequently built by people who learned how to remain calm while others remained consumed by chaos.
Because peace is not the absence of ambition.
It is one of the strongest foundations ambition can stand upon.

WEALTH LESSON

Mental peace improves focus, productivity, and long-term financial discipline.

AFFIRMATION

"I allow peace to strengthen the way I think, build, and lead."

TODAY'S POWER MOVE

Protect your peace intentionally today by limiting unnecessary emotional chaos.

DAY 167

You Are Capable Of Reinvention

POWER QUOTE

"Transformation requires the courage to become unfamiliar with your past self."

REFLECTION

One of the most limiting beliefs a person can carry is the belief that they are permanently stuck.

Stuck in old habits.

Stuck in old fears.

Stuck in old patterns.

Stuck in old versions of themselves.

They begin believing that because something has been true for years, it must remain true forever.

The person who struggled financially begins believing they will always struggle.

The person who battled insecurity begins believing confidence belongs to someone else.

The person who has reacted emotionally for years begins believing emotional stability is impossible.

Over time, these beliefs become invisible prisons.

Not because they are true.

Because they go unquestioned.

People stop imagining change.

Stop expecting growth.

Stop believing transformation is available to them.

Yet one of the most powerful truths about being human is the ability to evolve.

You are not required to remain who you were five years ago.

Or even one year ago.

The person you are today is already different from previous versions of yourself.

You have learned.

Experienced.

Survived.

Adapted.

Grown.

Life itself is evidence that change is possible.

The challenge is that reinvention rarely happens all at once.

Most people imagine transformation as a dramatic moment.

A sudden breakthrough.

A complete overnight change.

But lasting reinvention is usually much quieter.

It happens through decisions.

Repeated choices.

Small adjustments made consistently over time.

A healthier response during a stressful moment.

A better financial decision.

A new boundary.

A new routine.
A new standard.
Each choice becomes evidence that change is occurring.
Little by little, the old identity begins losing its grip.
Not because the past disappears.
Because the future becomes stronger than the past.
Reinvention does not require denying your history.
It does not require pretending mistakes never happened.
Or acting as though difficult seasons did not shape you.
Your past matters.
The lessons matter.
The experiences matter.
But they do not have to become permanent limitations.
There is a difference between learning from your past and living inside it.
One creates wisdom.
The other creates stagnation.
Growth requires the courage to release identities that no longer serve your future.
To stop introducing yourself internally through old failures.
Old fears.
Old insecurities.
Old limitations.
And begin aligning yourself with who you are becoming.
This process is not always comfortable.
People become attached to familiar versions of themselves.
Even when those versions create suffering.
Because familiarity often feels safer than change.
But your future may require a different version of you.
A more disciplined version.
A more confident version.
A more emotionally healthy version.
A more intentional version.
The beautiful thing is that this transformation is available one decision at a time.
Every healthy choice strengthens it.
Every disciplined action reinforces it.
Every courageous step expands it.
And eventually, what once felt impossible begins feeling natural.
You realize you are no longer the person you used to be.
Not because of one dramatic breakthrough.
But because of hundreds of intentional choices that slowly changed your direction.
Never believe that your past has the authority to permanently define your future.
You are allowed to grow.

Allowed to heal.

Allowed to change.

Allowed to reinvent yourself.

Because transformation is not reserved for a select few.

It is available to anyone willing to choose growth repeatedly.

And every decision you make today is helping shape the person you are becoming tomorrow.

WEALTH LESSON

New behaviors create new outcomes because identity influences financial and emotional decision-making.

AFFIRMATION

"I allow myself to evolve into a stronger and healthier version of myself."

TODAY'S POWER MOVE

Identify one old habit you are intentionally leaving behind.

DAY 168

Your Future Needs Emotional Stability

POWER QUOTE

"Chaos may feel familiar, but peace builds stronger lives."

REFLECTION

Not everyone grows up learning what peace feels like.

Some people were raised in environments where stress was constant.

Conflict was normal.

Instability was expected.

Emotional unpredictability was part of everyday life.

Over time, the mind adapts to whatever it experiences repeatedly.

What begins as survival eventually starts feeling familiar.

And what feels familiar often feels normal.

This creates a difficult challenge later in life.

Because when someone has spent years adapting to chaos, peace can feel unfamiliar.

Sometimes even uncomfortable.

A quiet day feels strange.

A healthy relationship feels suspicious.

Financial stability feels temporary.

Emotional safety feels uncertain.

Not because peace is wrong.

Because chaos became familiar.

Many people do not realize how deeply these patterns influence their lives.

They continue expecting problems before they appear.

Preparing for disappointment before it arrives.

Remaining emotionally guarded even when circumstances have improved.

The difficult season may be over, but the survival habits remain.

This is why healing matters so deeply.

Healing is not only recovering from what happened.

It is learning how to live differently afterward.

Learning how to trust peace.

Learning how to accept stability.

Learning how to believe that life does not always have to feel like an emergency.

This process requires patience.

The mind often needs time to adjust to healthier environments.

Just as chaos was learned through repetition, peace is often learned through repetition too.

One healthy decision at a time.

One stable routine at a time.

One healthy boundary at a time.

One calm response at a time.

Little by little, the nervous system begins learning something new.

Safety.
The ability to exist without constant fear.
Without constant panic.
Without constantly expecting the worst.
This creates space for growth.
Because stable minds build differently.
They make clearer decisions.
They think more long-term.
They communicate more effectively.
They manage challenges with greater wisdom.
Emotional stability strengthens every area of life.
Relationships improve.
Discipline improves.
Financial decisions improve.
Confidence improves.
Not because life becomes perfect.
Because the foundation becomes healthier.
Many people spend years trying to change external circumstances while overlooking the emotional patterns shaping their responses.
Yet sustainable growth often begins internally.
By creating a healthier relationship with peace.
By allowing stability to become familiar.
By recognizing that you do not have to keep repeating patterns that were created during difficult seasons.
Your future deserves more than emotional survival.
More than constant stress.
More than endless instability.
It deserves emotional safety.
Clarity.
Balance.
And the freedom to build a life that is not constantly controlled by old patterns.
Peace is not weakness.
Peace is not complacency.
Peace is strength under control.
It is stability in motion.
And while chaos may have been part of your past, it does not have to become your future.
You can learn a different way to live.
A different way to think.
A different way to build.
One intentional choice at a time.
Because peace is not something reserved for other people.
It is something you can learn, create, and protect for yourself as well.

WEALTH LESSON

Emotional stability improves financial and personal outcomes because clarity strengthens long-term thinking.

AFFIRMATION

"I build a life rooted in peace, stability, and emotional wisdom."

TODAY'S POWER MOVE

Notice one emotionally chaotic pattern and intentionally interrupt it today.

DAY 169

Stop Minimizing Your Growth

POWER QUOTE

"Progress still matters even when perfection has not been reached yet."

REFLECTION

Many people spend their lives focused on what they have not yet accomplished.

The goals they have not reached.

The habits they have not mastered.

The healing they have not completed.

The success they have not achieved.

As a result, they become experts at noticing what is missing while overlooking what has already changed.

They see the distance remaining but ignore the distance traveled.

This creates an unfair relationship with growth.

Because no matter how much progress occurs, it never feels like enough.

The finish line keeps moving.

The expectations keep rising.

And the person never pauses long enough to acknowledge how much they have already overcome.

Yet growth deserves recognition.

Not because the journey is complete.

Because progress matters.

Think about the lessons you understand today that you did not understand years ago.

The boundaries you now maintain.

The habits you have strengthened.

The emotional reactions you have learned to manage.

The decisions you make differently.

The wisdom you have gained through experience.

None of those things happened by accident.

They required effort.

Reflection.

Discipline.

Patience.

Growth often happens so gradually that people fail to notice it.

Just as a tree does not appear taller every day, personal transformation is often difficult to recognize while it is happening.

But that does not mean it is not happening.

Every healthier choice matters.

Every responsible decision matters.

Every difficult conversation handled with maturity matters.

Every unhealthy pattern interrupted matters.

These moments may seem small individually.

Yet together they create transformation.

The problem is that comparison often blinds people to their own progress.
They compare their beginning to someone else's middle.
Their current chapter to someone else's highlight reel.
Their private struggles to someone else's public success.
And in doing so, they lose sight of their own journey.
Growth was never meant to be measured only by outcomes.
It should also be measured by development.
By awareness.
By character.
By the person you are becoming along the way.
The truth is that meaningful transformation rarely happens overnight.
It unfolds gradually.
One lesson at a time.
One habit at a time.
One decision at a time.
One season at a time.
This is why self-respect matters.
Not only respecting your future goals.
Respecting the effort that has already brought you this far.
You can acknowledge progress without becoming complacent.
You can celebrate growth while continuing to pursue improvement.
The two are not opposites.
In fact, gratitude often creates healthier motivation than constant self-criticism.
When people recognize their growth, they build confidence.
When they build confidence, they become more willing to continue.
And when they continue, transformation accelerates.
So take a moment to recognize what has changed.
The strength you have developed.
The lessons you have learned.
The challenges you have survived.
The habits you have improved.
The person you are becoming.
There may still be work ahead.
There may still be goals to reach.
There may still be areas requiring growth.
But do not become so focused on the destination that you forget to honor the journey.
Because progress deserves respect.
And sometimes one of the healthiest things a person can do is pause long enough to acknowledge that they are no longer who they used to be.
That realization alone is evidence that transformation is already taking place.

WEALTH LESSON

Acknowledging progress strengthens motivation because people build confidence through recognizing growth.

AFFIRMATION

"I honor my progress while continuing to grow intentionally."

TODAY'S POWER MOVE

Reflect on three ways you have emotionally, mentally, or financially improved recently.

DAY 170

Your Discipline Is Changing Your Life

POWER QUOTE

"The habits you repeat daily eventually become the life you live."

REFLECTION

One of the hardest parts of personal growth is that progress often feels invisible while it is happening.

People naturally want evidence.

Proof that their effort matters.

Proof that their discipline is working.

Proof that the sacrifices are creating something meaningful.

But most transformation does not announce itself immediately.

It develops quietly.

Behind the scenes.

One decision at a time.

A person chooses to wake up earlier.

Chooses to save money instead of spending impulsively.

Chooses to respond with maturity instead of reacting emotionally.

Chooses to continue working toward a goal despite feeling discouraged.

None of these moments seem life-changing on their own.

In fact, many of them feel ordinary.

Repetitive.

Unremarkable.

Yet these are often the moments that shape a future.

The challenge is that discipline rarely produces instant rewards.

The effort arrives first.

The results arrive later.

And between those two realities is where many people become discouraged.

They assume nothing is changing because they cannot yet see dramatic evidence.

They forget that growth often happens beneath the surface long before it becomes visible above it.

Just as a foundation is built before a building rises, many of life's greatest transformations begin in places that cannot immediately be seen.

Character is being strengthened.

Habits are being formed.

Confidence is being built.

Wisdom is being developed.

Identity is being reshaped.

All while the external results may still appear small.

This is why patience matters.

Not passive waiting.

Active trust.

The willingness to continue showing up even when progress feels slow.

The willingness to keep building even when recognition is absent.

The willingness to remain committed even when the outcome has not fully appeared.

Many people quit too early because they underestimate how much is happening behind the scenes.

They abandon the process before the process has had enough time to work.

They stop planting because they do not yet see a harvest.

Yet every disciplined action leaves an impact.

Every healthy decision strengthens something.

Every intentional choice moves life in a direction.

You may not notice it immediately.

But your future will.

The financial discipline you practice today creates options tomorrow.

The emotional maturity you develop today creates healthier relationships tomorrow.

The routines you establish today create stability tomorrow.

This is how meaningful lives are built.

Not through one extraordinary moment.

Through thousands of ordinary moments handled intentionally.

The truth is that consistency often feels boring while transformation is taking place.

It lacks the excitement of dramatic breakthroughs.

But it possesses something more powerful.

Reliability.

Momentum.

Compounding growth.

The ability to create results that last.

So do not become discouraged if progress feels slower than expected.

Do not assume that nothing is changing simply because everything has not changed yet.

Trust the process.

Trust the habits.

Trust the discipline.

Trust the small decisions that no one else sees.

Because every day you continue building, something is happening.

Something is strengthening.

Something is growing.

Something is preparing you for the future you desire.

And one day, the life you once hoped for may feel surprisingly familiar.

Not because it appeared overnight.

But because your consistency quietly built it one day at a time.

The results may not be visible yet.

But that does not mean the work is not working.

WEALTH LESSON

Repeated disciplined behaviors create long-term emotional stability, stronger finances, and sustainable growth.

AFFIRMATION

"I trust that my discipline is building a stronger future every day."

TODAY'S POWER MOVE

Stay committed to one healthy routine today regardless of your emotions.

DAY 171

Your Future Deserves Preparation

POWER QUOTE

"Hope without preparation eventually creates frustration."

REFLECTION

Many people spend years hoping for a better future.

They hope their finances improve.

Hope opportunities appear.

Hope life becomes more stable.

Hope things eventually work out.

Hope is valuable.

But hope alone is rarely enough.

A better future requires preparation.

The truth is that many opportunities are lost not because people lack potential, but because they are unprepared to sustain what they desire.

They want financial freedom but avoid budgeting.

They want peace but avoid creating boundaries.

They want growth but avoid discipline.

They want change but resist structure.

As a result, they become excited about the future without actively preparing for it.

Preparation is what transforms possibility into readiness.

It creates the foundation that allows growth to become sustainable.

Prepared people think differently.

When challenges arise, they are less likely to panic.

When opportunities appear, they are more likely to recognize them.

When pressure increases, they are better equipped to handle it.

Not because they are smarter than everyone else.

Because they prepared.

Preparation creates confidence.

A person who has practiced a skill feels different than someone who has not.

A person with a financial plan feels different than someone avoiding their finances.

A person who has established healthy routines approaches life differently than someone operating without structure.

Confidence often grows from readiness.

And readiness grows from preparation.

This is why preparation influences every area of life.

Budgets create financial preparedness.

Routines create mental preparedness.

Boundaries create emotional preparedness.

Learning creates professional preparedness.

Healing creates relational preparedness.

Every intentional action strengthens your ability to handle future responsibilities.

Many people view preparation as restrictive.

In reality, preparation often creates freedom.

A budget creates freedom because it reduces financial confusion.

A routine creates freedom because it reduces unnecessary chaos.

A plan creates freedom because it provides direction.

Preparation removes many of the obstacles that make progress harder than necessary.

This does not mean life becomes predictable.

Unexpected situations will always arise.

Challenges will always exist.

No amount of preparation eliminates uncertainty entirely.

But preparation increases resilience.

It allows people to respond more effectively when difficulties appear.

The strongest builders are rarely those who rely solely on inspiration.

They are the people who quietly prepare while others only hope.

They build systems.

Develop habits.

Strengthen skills.

Create structure.

And when opportunity arrives, they are ready to receive it.

The future you desire deserves more than excitement.

It deserves preparation.

More than wishes.

More than intentions.

More than temporary motivation.

Because opportunities are easier to create, recognize, and sustain when your life has systems strong enough to support them.

Every healthy routine matters.

Every disciplined decision matters.

Every lesson learned matters.

Every step of preparation matters.

You may not always see immediate results from the work you are doing today.

But preparation is never wasted.

It is creating capacity.

Building readiness.

Strengthening foundations.

And one day, when opportunity arrives, you may discover that the reason you were able to sustain it was because of the preparation no one else saw.

The future belongs not only to those who desire it.

But to those who prepare for it.

WEALTH LESSON

Preparation creates long-term stability because structure improves consistency and decision-making.

AFFIRMATION

"I prepare intentionally for the future I desire to build."

TODAY'S POWER MOVE

Create or improve one system today that supports your long-term goals.

DAY 172

Stop Feeding Fear

POWER QUOTE

"What you repeatedly feed emotionally eventually grows stronger."

REFLECTION

Fear is one of the most powerful forces in human life.

Not because it is always accurate.

But because it often feels convincing.

Fear tells people they are not ready.

Not qualified.

Not capable.

Not prepared enough.

It encourages hesitation.

Delay.

Avoidance.

And while fear can sometimes serve a useful purpose, it becomes destructive when it begins controlling the direction of a person's life.

Many people unknowingly build their future around fear.

They avoid opportunities because they fear failure.

Avoid relationships because they fear rejection.

Avoid visibility because they fear criticism.

Avoid growth because they fear uncertainty.

At first, these decisions may feel safe.

But safety and growth are not always the same thing.

Every time fear determines a major decision, its influence becomes stronger.

The mind begins collecting evidence that avoidance is the correct response.

What is avoided today becomes even harder to face tomorrow.

What feels uncomfortable today often feels impossible later.

This is how fear gradually expands its territory.

Not through force.

Through obedience.

Every avoided conversation.

Every delayed dream.

Every opportunity ignored.

Each one quietly reinforces fear's authority.

The good news is that courage grows the same way.

Not through perfection.

Not through the absence of fear.

Through action.

Many people mistakenly believe courageous people are fearless.

They imagine confidence arrives first and action follows afterward.

Life rarely works that way.

More often, action comes first.

Confidence follows later.

The entrepreneur starts before knowing every answer.

The speaker talks despite nervousness.

The leader steps forward despite uncertainty.

The person seeking change moves before feeling completely ready.

This is how courage develops.

Every action sends a new message to the mind:

"I can handle this."

"I can learn."

"I can grow."

"I can survive uncertainty."

Little by little, fear begins losing influence.

Not because it disappears completely.

Because it is no longer in charge.

This is an important distinction.

Fear may still exist.

Questions may still exist.

Doubt may still appear.

But courage means refusing to hand decision-making authority to those emotions.

It means acknowledging fear without allowing it to become your leader.

The future you desire will likely require courage.

The courage to try.

The courage to fail.

The courage to learn.

The courage to begin again.

Growth often requires stepping into situations where certainty does not yet exist.

That discomfort is not evidence you are moving in the wrong direction.

Sometimes it is evidence that you are expanding beyond your comfort zone.

Do not wait for fear to disappear before taking action.

You may wait forever.

Instead, move anyway.

Take the step.

Start the project.

Have the conversation.

Apply for the opportunity.

Trust yourself enough to begin.

Because courage is not built by thinking about action.

It is built through action itself.

And every time you choose growth over avoidance, fear loses a little more of its control.

Eventually, the thing that once felt impossible becomes manageable.

The thing that once felt intimidating becomes familiar.

The thing that once controlled you becomes something you learned how to overcome.

Fear becomes weaker when it is challenged.

Courage becomes stronger when it is practiced.

And your future is often shaped by which one you choose to follow.

WEALTH LESSON

Calculated courage creates opportunities because growth rarely happens inside comfort zones alone.

AFFIRMATION

"I refuse to let fear make my decisions for me."

TODAY'S POWER MOVE

Take one small courageous step today toward something you have been avoiding.

DAY 173

Discipline Builds Self-Trust

POWER QUOTE

"Every time you follow through, you strengthen your relationship with yourself."

REFLECTION

Countless individuals believe confidence is something you either have or you do not.

They view it as a personality trait.

A gift.

Something certain people were born with and others were not.

But confidence is often built much differently than people realize.

At its foundation, confidence is closely connected to trust.

Specifically, trust in yourself.

Think about the people you trust most.

You trust them because they are consistent.

They do what they say they will do.

Their actions align with their words.

Over time, that consistency creates credibility.

The same principle applies internally.

You build self-trust when your actions consistently support your intentions.

You weaken self-trust when they repeatedly conflict.

Many people unknowingly damage their confidence through broken promises to themselves.

They commit to goals and immediately abandon them.

Create routines and never follow them.

Set standards and repeatedly ignore them.

After enough repetition, a subtle belief begins forming:

"I cannot depend on myself."

That belief affects everything.

Confidence weakens.

Motivation decreases.

Goals feel harder to pursue.

Not because the person lacks ability.

Because trust has been damaged.

Imagine trying to build a relationship with someone who never follows through.

Eventually, trust would disappear.

The same thing happens within yourself.

This is why discipline matters so deeply.

Discipline is not only about productivity.

It is about integrity.

Personal integrity.

The ability to honor commitments even when emotions fluctuate.

Every time you follow through on a promise to yourself, something valuable happens.

You create evidence.

Evidence that you can be trusted.

Evidence that you are dependable.

Evidence that your future matters enough to deserve consistent effort.

These moments may seem small.

Waking up when you said you would.

Finishing a task you committed to.

Following a budget.

Keeping a boundary.

Completing a responsibility despite not feeling motivated.

Individually, these actions appear ordinary.

Collectively, they transform identity.

Because confidence grows from evidence.

Not wishful thinking.

Not positive words alone.

Evidence.

The mind pays attention to repeated behavior.

When it repeatedly sees follow-through, trust begins growing.

And as trust grows, confidence grows with it.

This is why self-trust influences so many areas of life.

Leadership improves when people trust themselves.

Decision-making improves when people trust themselves.

Emotional stability improves when people trust themselves.

Resilience improves when people trust themselves.

Because they are no longer constantly questioning their ability to handle challenges.

They have evidence.

Evidence created through consistent action.

The goal is not perfection.

No one follows through perfectly.

Everyone has setbacks.

Everyone experiences moments where they fall short.

The goal is consistency.

To become someone who generally keeps their word.

Someone who follows through more often than they quit.

Someone who respects their commitments enough to honor them repeatedly.

Little by little, self-doubt begins losing influence.

Not because life becomes easier.

Because trust becomes stronger.

And when trust becomes stronger, confidence naturally follows.

If you want to believe in yourself more, start by becoming someone you can rely on.

Keep the promise.

Follow through on the commitment.

Honor the responsibility.

Not because the action itself is extraordinary.

Because every act of discipline sends a message:

"I can trust myself."

And over time, that message becomes one of the strongest foundations upon which confidence can be built.

WEALTH LESSON

Consistency strengthens self-trust because repeated disciplined behavior creates confidence internally.

AFFIRMATION

"I strengthen self-trust through discipline and consistency."

TODAY'S POWER MOVE

Keep one promise to yourself today regardless of how you feel emotionally.

DAY 174

Healing Changes How You Build

POWER QUOTE

"A healed mind creates different decisions than a wounded one."

REFLECTION

Many people think healing is only about emotions.

Feeling better.

Feeling happier.

Feeling less overwhelmed.

While those things matter, healing reaches much deeper than temporary feelings.

Healing changes the way people live.

The way they think.

The way they communicate.

The way they make decisions.

The way they respond to challenges.

This is because unresolved emotional pain rarely stays isolated.

It quietly influences behavior.

A person carrying unresolved hurt may struggle to trust others.

A person carrying unresolved fear may avoid opportunities.

A person carrying unresolved shame may constantly question their worth.

A person carrying unresolved disappointment may stop believing positive change is possible.

Often, these behaviors are misunderstood.

People assume they lack discipline.

Lack motivation.

Lack ability.

But sometimes the issue is not capability.

Sometimes the issue is unhealed emotional patterns influencing present-day decisions.

This is why healing matters so deeply.

Healing is not about becoming a completely different person overnight.

It is about removing obstacles that have been quietly interfering with growth.

As healing progresses, people often begin noticing changes in unexpected places.

Communication improves.

Because reactions become more intentional.

Relationships improve.

Because trust and emotional awareness increase.

Confidence improves.

Because self-worth is no longer constantly under attack.

Financial decisions improve.

Because fear, scarcity, and emotional spending lose some of their influence.

Discipline improves.

Because energy is no longer being consumed by constant emotional survival.

The person begins responding to life differently.

Not because life became easier.

Because they became healthier.

This is one of the most powerful aspects of healing.

It creates freedom.

Freedom from patterns that once felt automatic.

Freedom from reactions that once felt unavoidable.

Freedom from beliefs that once felt permanent.

For many people, survival mode becomes so familiar that they forget another way of living is possible.

They become accustomed to constant stress.

Constant fear.

Constant emotional exhaustion.

Constant internal conflict.

Healing interrupts that cycle.

It teaches the mind and heart that stability is possible.

That peace is possible.

That healthier responses are possible.

This process takes time.

Most meaningful healing does.

Old wounds are rarely replaced by new patterns overnight.

They are replaced gradually.

Through awareness.

Reflection.

Practice.

Honesty.

And consistent effort.

Little by little, the person begins rebuilding.

Not only emotionally.

But mentally.

Relationally.

Financially.

And spiritually.

This is why healing should never be viewed as weakness.

It is some of the most important work a person can do.

Because healing is not simply recovering from the past.

It is preparing for the future.

It is creating the internal foundation necessary to build a healthier life.

A stronger life.

A more intentional life.

The goal is not merely to feel better.

The goal is to live better.

To think better.

To respond better.

To build better.

And often, that transformation begins the moment a person becomes willing to address the emotional patterns that have been quietly shaping their life all along.

Because healing is more than emotional work.

It is life reconstruction.

And the life rebuilt through healing is often stronger than the one that existed before the healing began.

WEALTH LESSON

Emotional healing improves financial and personal outcomes because healthier minds create healthier habits.

AFFIRMATION

"I allow healing to transform the way I live, think, and build."

TODAY'S POWER MOVE

Spend intentional time today reflecting on one emotional pattern you are actively healing from.

DAY 175

Protect Your Confidence

POWER QUOTE

"Confidence is fragile when it constantly depends on external approval."

REFLECTION

One of the quickest ways to lose confidence is to give everyone else authority over your identity.

To allow other people's opinions to become more powerful than your own understanding of who you are.

At first, this often happens subtly.

A criticism stays with you longer than it should.

A rejection becomes personal.

A comparison creates self-doubt.

A negative opinion begins carrying more weight than years of evidence to the contrary.

Over time, confidence weakens.

Not because ability disappeared.

Because perspective became distorted.

Many people unknowingly build their self-worth on unstable foundations.

Approval.

Recognition.

Validation.

Praise.

The problem is that all of these things depend on other people.

And people are inconsistent.

Their opinions change.

Their perceptions are limited.

Their judgments are often influenced by experiences that have nothing to do with you.

Yet countless individuals spend years allowing outside voices to shape how they view themselves.

They begin believing criticism more quickly than encouragement.

Doubt more quickly than possibility.

Fear more quickly than potential.

Eventually, they stop trusting their own judgment.

Stop believing in their own abilities.

Stop pursuing opportunities that once excited them.

This is why protecting your mindset matters.

Not every opinion deserves access to your identity.

Not every criticism deserves permanent residence in your mind.

Not every rejection deserves the power to redefine your future.

Some feedback is valuable.

Some criticism helps people grow.

Wisdom requires being open to learning.

But there is a difference between learning from feedback and surrendering your self-worth to it.

Healthy confidence understands that outside opinions are information.

Not identity.

They may provide insight.

They may reveal blind spots.

But they do not determine your value.

Confident people still experience doubt.

They still experience fear.

They still experience moments of insecurity.

The difference is that they refuse to allow those experiences to become permanent conclusions.

They continue moving.

Continue learning.

Continue building.

Even while uncertainty exists.

This is important because confidence is not the absence of doubt.

It is the decision to keep going despite doubt.

It is the willingness to trust your growth process when results are not yet obvious.

To trust your preparation when opportunities feel uncertain.

To trust your value when recognition feels limited.

Many of life's most important seasons require this type of belief.

There will be moments when support feels scarce.

Moments when others fail to understand your vision.

Moments when your progress is visible to almost no one but you.

Those moments reveal the true source of confidence.

Not applause.

Not popularity.

Not validation.

Self-belief.

The quiet conviction that you are capable of continuing.

Capable of learning.

Capable of adapting.

Capable of growing beyond your current circumstances.

Protect that belief carefully.

Because the world will always offer opinions.

Comparisons.

Criticism.

Doubt.

Your responsibility is not eliminating those things.

Your responsibility is deciding how much influence they deserve.

Listen wisely.

Learn when appropriate.

Grow when necessary.

But never allow outside voices to become louder than the truth of who you are becoming.

Because confidence is not built by convincing everyone else to believe in you.

It is built by continuing to believe in yourself long enough to become the person you are working toward.

And often, that belief becomes one of the most valuable assets a person can possess.

WEALTH LESSON

Confidence improves visibility, leadership, and long-term opportunities because self-belief influences action.

AFFIRMATION

"I protect my confidence and continue believing in my future."

TODAY'S POWER MOVE

Speak confidently about your goals today without minimizing yourself.

DAY 176

Stop Escaping Responsibility Through Distraction

POWER QUOTE

"Distraction often feels easier than discipline."

REFLECTION

Distraction is one of the most accepted forms of avoidance in modern life.

Because it often looks harmless.

A few extra minutes scrolling.

Another episode.

Another video.

Another hour spent consuming instead of creating.

By themselves, these moments may seem insignificant.

But when repeated consistently, they begin shaping a person's future.

A lot of people believe they struggle with focus.

Sometimes the deeper issue is not focus at all.

It is avoidance.

Focus requires attention.

Attention requires honesty.

And honesty often forces people to confront responsibilities they have been postponing.

Responsibilities that feel uncomfortable.

Conversations they need to have.

Goals they have neglected.

Habits they know need to change.

Decisions they have been avoiding.

Growth they know is necessary.

Distraction provides temporary relief from these realities.

For a moment, the pressure disappears.

The responsibility feels distant.

The discomfort becomes easier to ignore.

But ignored responsibilities rarely disappear.

They simply wait.

And often become heavier with time.

This is why distraction can be so deceptive.

It offers comfort in the present while quietly creating difficulty in the future.

Every hour spent escaping reality is an hour not spent improving it.

Every day spent avoiding important responsibilities is a day those responsibilities continue accumulating.

The cost is not always immediate.

That is what makes it dangerous.

People often notice the consequences only after months or years have passed.

When goals remain unfinished.

When opportunities have been missed.

When progress feels slower than it should.

Focus creates something different.

Focus forces engagement.

It requires a person to face reality honestly.

To acknowledge what needs attention.

To direct energy toward meaningful action.

This is not always comfortable.

In fact, growth rarely begins with comfort.

It begins with responsibility.

The willingness to address what matters most rather than what feels easiest.

Focused people are not necessarily more talented.

They simply become intentional about where their attention goes.

They understand that attention is a limited resource.

Every distraction consumes part of it.

Every commitment requires part of it.

Every goal depends upon it.

Because of this, they become protective of their focus.

They recognize that what repeatedly receives attention eventually influences outcomes.

A distracted life often creates distracted results.

A focused life creates momentum.

Momentum creates progress.

And progress creates transformation.

This does not mean eliminating all recreation or enjoyment.

Rest matters.

Recovery matters.

Healthy enjoyment matters.

The issue is not occasional entertainment.

The issue is allowing distraction to become a substitute for responsibility.

The issue is allowing avoidance to become a lifestyle.

Your future deserves more than occasional attention.

It deserves intentional focus.

It deserves effort directed toward what truly matters.

The dreams you carry require attention.

The goals you pursue require attention.

The person you are becoming requires attention.

Every day presents a choice.

To escape.

Or to engage.

To avoid.

Or to build.

To distract yourself from the future.

Or to invest in it.

Because meaningful transformation is rarely created through avoidance.

It is created when people become willing to face life honestly and build intentionally.

And often, the future people desire begins the moment they stop running from responsibility and start giving their full attention to what matters most.

WEALTH LESSON

Focused people execute faster because less energy is wasted on unnecessary distractions.

AFFIRMATION

"I stop escaping my responsibilities and begin building intentionally."

TODAY'S POWER MOVE

Eliminate one major distraction today and replace it with productive action.

DAY 177

Your Peace Is Worth Protecting

POWER QUOTE

"Not every environment deserves access to your emotional energy."

REFLECTION

Many people spend years chasing success while neglecting peace.

They focus on achievement.

Productivity.

Recognition.

Financial goals.

Yet overlook the emotional foundation that allows those things to be sustained.

The truth is that peace is not merely a pleasant feeling.

It is a valuable resource.

One that influences nearly every area of life.

When peace is disrupted, focus becomes more difficult.

Decision-making becomes less clear.

Patience becomes shorter.

Discipline becomes harder to maintain.

Even physical health can be affected.

This is why protecting peace is not a luxury.

It is a responsibility.

Many people underestimate how much their environment affects them.

The conversations they participate in.

The people they remain connected to.

The content they consume.

The situations they repeatedly place themselves within.

All of these things influence emotional well-being.

And emotional well-being influences behavior.

A person constantly surrounded by conflict often thinks differently than a person surrounded by stability.

A person constantly exposed to negativity often views opportunities differently than someone exposed to encouragement and growth.

The emotional environment matters.

More than many people realize.

This is why emotionally healthy people become intentional.

They pay attention to what repeatedly enters their lives.

Not because they are trying to avoid reality.

But because they understand that peace is easier to maintain than it is to constantly rebuild.

They recognize that not every conversation deserves engagement.

Not every disagreement requires a response.

Not every opinion deserves emotional influence.

And not every person should have unlimited access to their time, energy, and emotions.

This is not arrogance.

It is wisdom.

Because every commitment carries a cost.

Every interaction consumes energy.

Every environment shapes perspective.

The healthiest people learn how to invest these resources carefully.

They become selective.

Not cold.

Not disconnected.

Intentional.

They understand that protecting peace allows them to show up more fully in the areas that matter most.

Their relationships improve.

Their focus improves.

Their decision-making improves.

Their ability to pursue meaningful goals improves.

Because they are no longer spending most of their energy recovering from unnecessary emotional chaos.

Peace creates space.

Space to think clearly.

Space to heal.

Space to learn.

Space to build.

Space to become.

Many people assume peace is something that simply happens.

Often, it is something that must be protected.

Protected through boundaries.

Protected through wise decisions.

Protected through intentional environments.

Protected through emotional discipline.

The life you are building requires this protection.

Your goals require it.

Your healing requires it.

Your future requires it.

Because growth flourishes in healthy environments.

Just as a seed grows best in healthy soil, people grow best in environments that support clarity, stability, and well-being.

Protect your peace.

Not because life will never be difficult.

But because peace gives you the strength to navigate difficulty wisely.

And in a world filled with noise, pressure, and distraction, the ability to preserve your peace may become one of the greatest advantages you possess.

Because a peaceful mind builds differently.

And the future you are creating deserves an environment healthy enough to support it.

WEALTH LESSON

Mental peace improves emotional regulation, productivity, and financial discipline long-term.

AFFIRMATION

"I protect my peace because my future depends on emotional stability."

TODAY'S POWER MOVE

Distance yourself from one emotionally draining situation today.

DAY 178

Your Future Requires Maturity

POWER QUOTE

"Greater opportunities require greater emotional responsibility."

REFLECTION

Many people desire a larger life.

Larger opportunities.

Greater influence.

Greater financial success.

Greater impact.

Greater responsibility.

Yet few people stop to consider what those things actually require.

Because growth does not only increase rewards.

It often increases pressure.

Responsibility.

Visibility.

Expectations.

Complexity.

The life you desire may demand more from you than your current life does.

Not because success is punishment.

Because expansion requires capacity.

A small responsibility requires one level of maturity.

A larger responsibility often requires another.

This is why talent alone is rarely enough.

Skill matters.

Knowledge matters.

Opportunity matters.

But emotional maturity often determines whether success can be sustained.

Many people are capable of obtaining opportunities.

Far fewer are prepared to manage them well.

The challenge is that growth often exposes weaknesses.

The pressure of leadership reveals communication habits.

The pressure of responsibility reveals emotional patterns.

The pressure of success reveals character.

Under pressure, people often become more of who they already are.

This is why personal development matters before major opportunities arrive.

The future you want may require emotional strengths you are still developing.

Patience.

Discipline.

Self-control.

Resilience.

Humility.

The ability to remain calm during stressful seasons.

The ability to communicate clearly during conflict.

The ability to make wise decisions when emotions are high.

These skills are not always visible.

Yet they influence outcomes constantly.

Emotionally mature people approach challenges differently.

They do not avoid responsibility simply because it feels difficult.

They do not abandon commitments whenever emotions fluctuate.

They do not allow every setback to determine their direction.

Instead, they learn how to remain grounded.

To respond thoughtfully rather than react impulsively.

To handle pressure without allowing pressure to control them.

This does not mean they never struggle.

Everyone struggles.

Everyone experiences doubt.

Everyone experiences difficult seasons.

Maturity is not the absence of difficulty.

It is the ability to navigate difficulty wisely.

Many people focus almost entirely on external goals.

The promotion.

The business.

The income.

The recognition.

The opportunity.

But sustainable success often requires internal growth as much as external growth.

Because every new level of life asks new questions.

Can you handle more responsibility?

Can you manage greater pressure?

Can you lead effectively?

Can you remain disciplined when expectations increase?

Can you stay grounded when circumstances change?

The answers are often developed long before the opportunity arrives.

They are developed in daily choices.

Small acts of responsibility.

Small moments of discipline.

Small opportunities to practice emotional control.

This is how capacity grows.

Not overnight.

Gradually.

One lesson at a time.

One challenge at a time.

One season at a time.

Do not become discouraged by the areas where growth is still needed.

Growth itself is evidence that you are preparing for more.

Every challenge is teaching something.

Every responsibility is strengthening something.

Every season is developing something.

The person you are becoming today is preparing you for opportunities you may not yet see.

Because success is not only about reaching a new level.

It is about becoming the type of person who can sustain it.

And often, the greatest transformation is not what you achieve.

It is who you become while preparing to achieve it.

The future you desire may require a stronger version of you.

And that process of becoming is one of the most valuable parts of the journey.

WEALTH LESSON

Emotional maturity improves long-term stability because wiser decisions create stronger outcomes.

AFFIRMATION

"I continue growing emotionally stronger, wiser, and more disciplined."

TODAY'S POWER MOVE

Respond maturely today in a situation where you would normally react emotionally.

DAY 179

You Are Allowed To Outgrow Old Versions Of Yourself

POWER QUOTE

"Growth often requires separation from outdated identities."

REFLECTION

Growth can create unexpected emotions.

Not just excitement.

Sometimes guilt.

Sometimes discomfort.

Sometimes uncertainty.

Many people assume that becoming healthier should feel completely positive.

But personal growth often changes relationships, priorities, habits, and perspectives.

And change can feel unfamiliar.

Especially when a person has spent years adapting to environments that required survival rather than growth.

The version of you that existed during difficult seasons developed for a reason.

That version learned how to cope.

How to endure.

How to protect itself.

How to make it through circumstances that were not always easy.

There is nothing wrong with acknowledging that reality.

The problem comes when people feel obligated to remain emotionally loyal to patterns that no longer serve them.

They continue accepting behaviors they have outgrown.

Continue tolerating environments that damage their peace.

Continue repeating habits that no longer align with the future they want to create.

Not because those things are healthy.

Because they are familiar.

Familiarity can be powerful.

Even unhealthy patterns can feel comfortable when they have existed long enough.

This is why growth sometimes feels uncomfortable.

You are not only building something new.

You are releasing something old.

Old beliefs.

Old habits.

Old standards.

Old emotional patterns.

The person you are becoming may no longer fit comfortably inside the life you once accepted.

And that is not failure.

That is evolution.

Many people experience guilt when their standards begin changing.

They feel guilty for protecting their time.

Guilty for establishing boundaries.

Guilty for choosing peace.

Guilty for wanting healthier relationships.

Guilty for expecting more from themselves.

But growth naturally changes expectations.

The healthier you become, the more clearly you recognize what supports your well-being and what undermines it.

This awareness is not arrogance.

It is maturity.

You begin understanding that protecting your peace matters.

That discipline matters.

That emotional stability matters.

That your future deserves healthier foundations than your past may have provided.

As a result, certain things can no longer remain the same.

Not every habit belongs in your future.

Not every mindset belongs in your future.

Not every environment belongs in your future.

Growth requires honesty about that reality.

It requires the courage to choose what is healthy even when it feels unfamiliar.

The courage to disappoint old expectations in order to honor new priorities.

The courage to release patterns that once felt necessary but now feel limiting.

This does not mean rejecting your past.

Your past contains lessons.

Wisdom.

Experiences that helped shape who you are.

The goal is not to hate the person you used to be.

The goal is to appreciate that version of yourself while continuing to become more.

More aware.

More disciplined.

More peaceful.

More intentional.

Every season of life asks something different from us.

And sometimes the greatest act of self-respect is allowing yourself to grow beyond what once felt normal.

You are allowed to evolve.

Allowed to change.

Allowed to raise your standards.

Allowed to protect your peace.

Allowed to choose healthier patterns.

Because transformation is not about abandoning yourself.

It is about becoming more fully aligned with the person you are capable of becoming.

And often, the future begins improving the moment you stop feeling guilty for growing into it.

WEALTH LESSON

Growth improves outcomes because healthier habits and environments support long-term success.

AFFIRMATION

"I allow myself to evolve into a healthier and stronger version of myself."

TODAY'S POWER MOVE

Identify one old mindset or habit you are intentionally outgrowing.

DAY 180

Your Discipline Will Become Your Freedom

POWER QUOTE

"The routines you repeat today eventually create the life you live tomorrow."

REFLECTION

Many people view discipline as a burden.

A restriction.

A limitation.

Something that takes away freedom rather than creates it.

At first glance, that perspective seems reasonable.

Discipline requires saying no to certain things.

No to impulsive spending.

No to unhealthy habits.

No to distractions.

No to choices that feel good in the moment but create problems later.

Because of this, discipline can feel uncomfortable.

It asks for effort when convenience would be easier.

Patience when immediate gratification feels more appealing.

Responsibility when avoidance feels more comfortable.

Yet what many people fail to recognize is that discipline and freedom are deeply connected.

In fact, some of the greatest forms of freedom are created through disciplined choices.

Financial discipline creates options.

The ability to handle emergencies.

The ability to pursue opportunities.

The ability to make decisions without constant financial fear.

Emotional discipline creates stability.

The ability to remain grounded during stressful seasons.

The ability to communicate wisely rather than react impulsively.

The ability to protect relationships from unnecessary damage.

Mental discipline creates focus.

The ability to direct attention toward what matters most.

The ability to make progress despite distractions.

The ability to build momentum instead of constantly starting over.

All of these freedoms begin with discipline.

The challenge is that people often focus only on the short-term discomfort.

They notice the sacrifice.

The effort.

The inconvenience.

What they do not immediately see is the future being built behind those choices.

Every responsible decision creates something.

Every healthy habit creates something.

Every moment of discipline strengthens something.
At first, the changes may appear small.
Almost invisible.
A budget may not seem life-changing.
A morning routine may not seem extraordinary.
A difficult conversation handled with maturity may not feel significant.
But repeated consistently, these actions begin transforming a person's life.
Confidence grows.
Stability grows.
Resilience grows.
Opportunity grows.
Not because of one dramatic breakthrough.
Because of hundreds of disciplined decisions working together over time.
This is how many of life's greatest transformations occur.
Quietly.
Gradually.
Consistently.
The person who enjoys financial peace rarely arrives there by accident.
The person who demonstrates emotional stability rarely develops it overnight.
The person who creates a meaningful life rarely does so through occasional effort alone.
The foundation is usually discipline.
The willingness to keep building when results are still developing.
To continue showing up when motivation fluctuates.
To make choices based on values rather than temporary emotions.
Many people spend years searching for freedom while resisting the very habits that create it.
They want the outcome without the preparation.
The reward without the process.
The stability without the structure.
But lasting freedom is often earned through consistent stewardship.
Through learning how to manage responsibilities wisely.
Through learning how to think long-term.
Through learning how to choose what benefits the future rather than only what satisfies the present.
This is why discipline is not punishment.
It is preparation.
Preparation for the life you hope to build.
Preparation for opportunities you have not yet seen.
Preparation for responsibilities you may one day carry.
One day, you may look at your life and realize that many of the things you once prayed for were not created through one extraordinary moment.
They were built through ordinary decisions repeated faithfully over time.
The savings account.

The healthy relationship.

The peace of mind.

The confidence.

The stability.

The opportunities.

All quietly constructed through habits that once seemed small.

Never underestimate the value of discipline.

Because what feels difficult today may be creating freedoms that transform your life tomorrow.

And often, the freedom people admire most is simply the harvest of discipline practiced consistently for years.

WEALTH LESSON

Disciplined habits create long-term freedom because consistency compounds over time.

AFFIRMATION

"I build freedom through discipline, consistency, and intentional living."

TODAY'S POWER MOVE

Commit fully today to one disciplined routine that supports your future.

DAY 181

Stop Waiting For Your Life To Change Automatically

POWER QUOTE

"Transformation requires participation."

REFLECTION

Many people dream about change.

A better future.

Greater peace.

More confidence.

More financial stability.

Healthier relationships.

A stronger life.

The desire for change is common.

The willingness to participate in change is where transformation begins.

Because hope alone does not create a different future.

Wishing alone does not create a different future.

Wanting more is important, but wanting more and becoming different are not always the same thing.

Many people desire outcomes while resisting the process required to create them.

They want peace without confronting unresolved pain.

They want confidence without developing self-discipline.

They want financial freedom without changing financial habits.

They want growth without discomfort.

But meaningful transformation rarely works that way.

Life often changes when people become willing to change with it.

When they become willing to think differently.

Behave differently.

Respond differently.

Make decisions differently.

This is where growth becomes challenging.

Because change is not only external.

It is internal.

The future you desire may require a version of you that thinks differently than you think today.

A version of you with stronger boundaries.

Greater emotional maturity.

More discipline.

More patience.

More consistency.

More courage.

For many people, this realization feels uncomfortable.

Not because growth is wrong.

Because growth stretches identity.

It challenges familiar patterns.

Questions familiar habits.

Disrupts familiar routines.

The old version of you may feel comfortable because it is familiar.

Even when it is limiting.

Even when it is preventing progress.

This is why discomfort should not always be viewed as a warning sign.

Sometimes discomfort is evidence that growth is occurring.

The discomfort of learning.

The discomfort of discipline.

The discomfort of responsibility.

The discomfort of becoming someone new.

Every meaningful transformation contains moments like these.

The person learning healthier financial habits experiences discomfort.

The person establishing boundaries experiences discomfort.

The person developing emotional discipline experiences discomfort.

The person pursuing a larger vision experiences discomfort.

Yet those moments are often part of the process.

Because growth asks people to leave behind what is familiar in order to create something better.

This does not mean every uncomfortable situation is healthy.

Wisdom still matters.

Discernment still matters.

But many people delay their future because they automatically interpret discomfort as failure.

They assume difficulty means they should stop.

When sometimes difficulty simply means they are developing.

The strongest transformations often occur when people stop waiting for change to happen and begin participating in it intentionally.

When they take ownership of their choices.

Their habits.

Their mindset.

Their behaviors.

Their direction.

This is where real power begins.

Not in controlling every circumstance.

But in taking responsibility for the parts of life that can be influenced.

One decision at a time.

One habit at a time.

One lesson at a time.

One day at a time.

The future is not built only by what you desire.

It is built by what you repeatedly practice.

The person you become is shaped by the choices you make when no one is watching.

The routines you maintain.

The standards you uphold.

The responsibilities you accept.

This is why growth requires participation.

Because a new future requires a new version of you.

And that version is not created through wishful thinking.

It is created through intentional action repeated consistently over time.

The process may feel uncomfortable.

The progress may feel slow.

But every healthy choice is helping build someone stronger, wiser, and more capable than before.

And often, that is exactly how transformation begins.

WEALTH LESSON

Lasting financial and personal growth require intentional behavioral change over time.

AFFIRMATION

"I actively participate in creating the future I desire."

TODAY'S POWER MOVE

Identify one habit today that must change for your future to improve.

DAY 182

Emotional Awareness Creates Freedom

POWER QUOTE

"You cannot control what you refuse to acknowledge."

REFLECTION

Many people spend years trying to change their behavior without first understanding it.

They focus on the action.

The reaction.

The mistake.

The outcome.

But rarely pause long enough to ask a deeper question:

"What is driving this behavior in the first place?"

This is where self-awareness becomes powerful.

Because behavior rarely exists in isolation.

Behind many decisions are emotions.

Behind many reactions are beliefs.

Behind many habits are experiences that shaped the way a person learned to navigate life.

A person may overspend financially.

But the deeper issue may be stress.

Loneliness.

Fear.

A desire for temporary comfort.

A person may react defensively during conversations.

But the deeper issue may be insecurity.

Past rejection.

Fear of being misunderstood.

A person may procrastinate repeatedly.

But the deeper issue may be fear of failure.

Perfectionism.

Self-doubt.

Without awareness, people often focus only on the surface behavior.

They try to eliminate the symptom while ignoring the cause.

As a result, the pattern continues.

The behavior may change temporarily.

But eventually it returns because the root was never addressed.

This is why emotional awareness matters.

Awareness helps people move beyond automatic reactions.

It creates a pause between emotion and action.

A moment where reflection becomes possible.

Instead of immediately reacting, a person begins asking questions.

Why am I feeling this way?

What emotion is influencing this decision?

What fear is present right now?

What belief is shaping my response?

These questions may seem simple.

Yet they create powerful insight.

And insight creates options.

Many unhealthy patterns survive because they operate unconsciously.

People repeat them automatically.

Without reflection.

Without examination.

Without understanding.

But once a pattern becomes visible, something important happens.

Choice becomes available.

The person is no longer acting entirely on autopilot.

They can recognize the pattern.

Challenge the pattern.

Replace the pattern.

This is where freedom begins.

Not because awareness instantly solves every problem.

But because awareness creates the opportunity for change.

A person cannot change what they refuse to acknowledge.

They cannot heal what they refuse to examine.

They cannot improve what they do not understand.

This is why self-awareness requires honesty.

The willingness to look inward.

To recognize uncomfortable truths.

To examine habits without defensiveness.

To explore emotions without immediately escaping them.

This process is not always easy.

Many people spend years avoiding themselves because self-examination feels uncomfortable.

Yet discomfort often contains valuable information.

It reveals areas that need attention.

Areas that need healing.

Areas that need growth.

The strongest people are not necessarily those who never struggle.

Often, they are people who became willing to understand themselves.

Their triggers.

Their fears.

Their strengths.

Their weaknesses.

Their patterns.

This understanding creates wisdom.

And wisdom creates better decisions.

Every healthier response begins with awareness.

Every meaningful change begins with awareness.

Every new pattern begins with awareness.

Because transformation does not start the moment behavior changes.

It starts the moment a person becomes conscious of what has been shaping that behavior all along.

Awareness creates understanding.

Understanding creates choice.

And choice creates freedom.

That is why self-awareness remains one of the most powerful tools for personal growth.

Because the moment you become aware of a pattern, you gain the ability to begin changing it intentionally.

And often, that is where true transformation begins.

WEALTH LESSON

Self-awareness improves financial and emotional stability because intentional decisions replace impulsive reactions.

AFFIRMATION

"I become more emotionally aware, intentional, and self-controlled every day."

TODAY'S POWER MOVE

Pay attention today to what emotions are influencing your decisions most strongly.

DAY 183

Keep Showing Up For Yourself

POWER QUOTE

"Your future changes every time you refuse to abandon yourself."

REFLECTION

One of the most overlooked forms of healing is learning how to consistently show up for yourself.

Not only when life feels easy.

Not only when motivation is high.

Not only when progress is obvious.

But especially during the seasons when everything feels heavier.

The seasons when confidence feels fragile.

When results feel delayed.

When emotions feel overwhelming.

When the future feels uncertain.

Many people know how to support themselves when life is going well.

The real test often comes when life becomes difficult.

Because difficult seasons reveal the quality of the relationship you have with yourself.

Some people abandon themselves the moment progress slows.

They stop trying.

Stop believing.

Stop investing in their growth.

Not because they are incapable.

Because disappointment convinces them their effort no longer matters.

Others choose a different path.

They continue showing up.

Not perfectly.

Not fearlessly.

But consistently.

They continue taking small steps.

Continue honoring responsibilities.

Continue protecting their healing.

Continue building even when visible results are limited.

This choice matters more than many people realize.

Because every time you continue showing up during a difficult season, you send yourself an important message:

"I am not giving up on myself."

That message builds something powerful.

Trust.

Many people struggle with self-trust because they have repeatedly abandoned themselves during challenging moments.

They believed in themselves when things felt exciting.

But disconnected from themselves when things became difficult.

As a result, their confidence became dependent upon circumstances.
Yet lasting confidence is built differently.
It grows when you learn that your commitment is not controlled entirely by emotions.
That you can remain present even when motivation fluctuates.
That you can continue building even when progress feels slow.
That you can care for yourself even when life becomes emotionally demanding.
This is where resilience develops.
Not during easy seasons.
During difficult ones.
Resilience is not the absence of struggle.
It is the decision to continue despite struggle.
The willingness to keep moving forward while carrying uncertainty.
The willingness to remain committed while results are still developing.
The willingness to keep rebuilding after setbacks.
Every difficult season presents an opportunity.
An opportunity to strengthen your relationship with yourself.
To prove that your growth matters.
To prove that your healing matters.
To prove that your future matters.
The people who eventually create meaningful transformation are rarely people who never faced challenges.
Often, they are people who refused to abandon themselves while facing them.
They kept showing up.
Kept learning.
Kept adjusting.
Kept rebuilding.
Little by little, those choices changed who they became.
This is why consistency during difficult seasons carries so much value.
Anyone can continue when everything feels easy.
Character is often developed when continuing feels difficult.
That is when discipline becomes meaningful.
That is when resilience becomes real.
That is when self-trust begins growing.
The next time progress feels slow, remember this:
You do not need to have everything figured out.
You do not need to feel confident every day.
You do not need to move perfectly.
You simply need to keep showing up.
One choice at a time.
One responsibility at a time.
One day at a time.

Because every time you continue investing in yourself during a difficult season, you strengthen the belief that you are someone worth fighting for.

And that belief has the power to change every area of your life.

The strongest relationship you will ever build is the one you have with yourself.

Protect it.

Strengthen it.

And continue showing up for it, especially when life feels hard.

Because those are often the moments that shape your future the most.

WEALTH LESSON

Consistency during difficult seasons builds emotional resilience and long-term stability.

AFFIRMATION

"I continue showing up for myself even during difficult seasons."

TODAY'S POWER MOVE

Complete one meaningful task today even if your emotions try to convince you not to.

DAY 184

Your Standards Create Your Reality

POWER QUOTE

"What you continuously tolerate eventually becomes your normal."

REFLECTION

Every person has standards.

Some are intentional.

Some are unconscious.

But regardless of whether they are spoken aloud, standards influence nearly every area of life.

They influence what people accept.

What they reject.

What they pursue.

What they tolerate.

And ultimately, what they experience.

Many people focus heavily on goals while overlooking standards.

Yet goals determine direction.

Standards determine behavior.

A person may desire financial peace.

But if their standards around spending remain low, financial stress often continues.

A person may desire healthy relationships.

But if their standards around communication, respect, and boundaries remain low, unhealthy patterns often continue.

A person may desire emotional stability.

But if they continue tolerating habits that create chaos, peace becomes difficult to maintain.

This is why standards matter so deeply.

They shape daily choices.

And daily choices shape the future.

Many exhausting lives are not created by one major mistake.

They are created through small compromises repeated over time.

Tolerating behaviors that should be addressed.

Accepting environments that create stress.

Ignoring habits that slowly weaken growth.

Making exceptions so frequently that standards eventually disappear.

At first, these compromises seem harmless.

But over time they accumulate.

The result is often frustration.

People wonder why life feels heavier than it should.

Why peace feels difficult to maintain.

Why progress feels inconsistent.

Sometimes the answer is not found in what they want.

It is found in what they continue tolerating.

The healthiest forms of growth often begin with raising standards.

Not out of arrogance.

Out of self-respect.

A person who values their future begins protecting it differently.

They become more intentional with their time.

More intentional with their finances.

More intentional with their relationships.

More intentional with their environment.

Not because they believe they are better than others.

Because they understand that what they repeatedly allow eventually influences who they become.

This is especially important when it comes to peace.

Peace rarely survives in environments filled with constant chaos.

Confidence rarely grows in environments filled with constant negativity.

Discipline rarely flourishes in environments built around distraction.

Standards act like filters.

They help determine what receives access to your life.

What receives your attention.

What receives your energy.

What receives your commitment.

Higher standards do not make life perfect.

Challenges will still exist.

Mistakes will still happen.

Growth will still require effort.

But strong standards create stronger foundations.

And strong foundations support stronger futures.

The goal is not perfection.

The goal is alignment.

To ensure that your habits, decisions, and environment support the life you are trying to create.

Every standard you establish sends a message.

About what matters.

About what is acceptable.

About what kind of future you are building.

The person who protects their peace is communicating a standard.

The person who manages money responsibly is communicating a standard.

The person who honors commitments is communicating a standard.

The person who refuses to settle for unhealthy patterns is communicating a standard.

Little by little, those standards begin shaping identity.

And identity begins shaping outcomes.

Your future will largely be influenced by what you repeatedly accept and what you repeatedly reject.

That is why standards matter.

Because they quietly influence the quality of your relationships.

Your finances.

Your health.

Your discipline.

Your peace.

And ultimately, your life.

Raise them wisely.

Protect them consistently.

And remember that the life you desire will often require standards strong enough to support it.

WEALTH LESSON

Higher standards improve decision-making because intentional behavior creates healthier long-term outcomes.

AFFIRMATION

"I raise my standards because my future deserves excellence and peace."

TODAY'S POWER MOVE

Identify one area today where your standards need to increase.

DAY 185

Stop Comparing Your Chapter One To Someone Else's Chapter Twenty

POWER QUOTE

"Comparison steals peace from people who are still growing."

REFLECTION

Comparison has a way of making progress feel invisible.

A person can be growing.

Learning.

Healing.

Building.

Improving.

Yet the moment they compare themselves to someone who appears further ahead, their own progress suddenly feels insignificant.

This is one of the most damaging illusions comparison creates.

It convinces people to ignore how far they have come because they are focused on how far someone else appears to be.

The problem is that comparison is rarely accurate.

People compare their private struggles to someone else's public victories.

Their beginning to someone else's middle.

Their current chapter to someone else's highlight reel.

Without realizing it, they are measuring two completely different journeys as though they should look the same.

But no two lives are identical.

People begin from different places.

Face different obstacles.

Receive different opportunities.

Carry different responsibilities.

Experience different timelines.

Some people receive support early.

Others must build without much support at all.

Some encounter opportunities quickly.

Others spend years developing before opportunities appear.

Some experience visible success early.

Others experience slower growth that becomes visible much later.

None of these paths are inherently better or worse.

They are simply different.

Yet comparison often ignores these realities.

It reduces complex journeys into simple conclusions.

"They are ahead."

"I am behind."

"I should be further along."

Those thoughts create unnecessary pressure.

Pressure that often leads to discouragement.

Self-doubt.

Frustration.

And sometimes even abandoning progress altogether.

This is unfortunate because meaningful growth is rarely measured by speed alone.

A tree does not compete with the flower beside it.

A flower does not compete with the mountain behind it.

Each develops according to its own design and timeline.

Human growth works much the same way.

Your life is not supposed to look exactly like someone else's.

Your journey is not supposed to unfold exactly like theirs.

Your lessons.

Your challenges.

Your opportunities.

Your growth.

All belong to your unique path.

This does not mean avoiding ambition.

It does not mean refusing to learn from others.

Inspiration can be valuable.

Learning from successful people can be valuable.

The problem begins when inspiration becomes comparison.

When admiration becomes self-criticism.

When another person's success becomes evidence that you are failing.

Someone else's progress does not diminish your own.

Someone else's achievement does not reduce your potential.

Someone else's timeline does not determine your future.

The healthiest growth often occurs when people redirect their attention inward.

Not toward what others are building.

Toward what they are building.

Their habits.

Their healing.

Their discipline.

Their goals.

Their responsibilities.

Their future.

This creates a healthier standard of measurement.

Instead of asking:

"Am I ahead of someone else?"

They begin asking:

"Am I growing?"

"Am I becoming healthier?"

"Am I becoming wiser?"

"Am I becoming more disciplined than I was before?"

Those questions create progress.

Because growth is not always visible publicly.

Some of the most important transformations happen quietly.

In private decisions.

Private habits.

Private victories.

Private healing.

Long before anyone else notices.

Do not rush your journey because of someone else's timeline.

Do not diminish your progress because someone else's success is more visible.

Stay committed to your path.

Keep building.

Keep learning.

Keep growing.

Keep becoming.

Because meaningful progress is still meaningful progress, even when it happens more slowly than you expected.

And often, the people who create the strongest futures are not the ones who moved the fastest.

They are the ones who remained committed to their own journey long enough to see it through.

Run your own race.

Trust your own process.

And remember that your future is not competing with anyone else's timeline.

WEALTH LESSON

Comparison often creates emotional pressure that weakens confidence and intentional decision-making.

AFFIRMATION

"I trust my own journey and stop comparing my timing to others."

TODAY'S POWER MOVE

Celebrate one area where you have personally grown over the past year.

DAY 186

Your Habits Are Either Building Or Breaking You

POWER QUOTE

"Repeated behavior eventually becomes identity."

REFLECTION

Many people focus on major decisions while overlooking the power of daily habits.

They believe transformation happens during extraordinary moments.

A breakthrough.

A promotion.

A life-changing opportunity.

A major achievement.

While those moments can certainly influence a person's future, most lives are shaped much more quietly.

Through repetition.

Through routines.

Through habits practiced day after day.

Every habit creates momentum.

The question is not whether momentum exists.

The question is which direction it is moving.

Some habits create momentum toward growth.

Others create momentum toward stagnation.

Some habits strengthen discipline.

Others strengthen avoidance.

Some habits create peace.

Others create chaos.

This is why habits matter so deeply.

What you repeatedly do eventually becomes easier to do.

What becomes easier to do eventually becomes normal.

And what becomes normal eventually becomes part of your identity.

A person does not suddenly become disciplined.

They become disciplined through disciplined repetition.

One responsible choice at a time.

One completed commitment at a time.

One consistent routine at a time.

Likewise, a person does not suddenly become financially stable.

Financial stability is often built through repeated financial decisions.

Saving consistently.

Spending intentionally.

Planning wisely.

Making choices that support long-term goals rather than short-term impulses.

Over time, those actions compound.

The same principle applies emotionally.

People who consistently practice healthy boundaries often experience greater peace.
People who consistently protect their energy often experience greater stability.
People who consistently engage in self-awareness often develop greater emotional maturity.
None of these outcomes happen overnight.
They are created through repetition.
This is why habits are so powerful.
They shape behavior without demanding constant decision-making.
Once established, they begin influencing life automatically.
The challenge is that habits often feel insignificant while they are being formed.
A single workout seems small.
A single budget review seems small.
A single difficult conversation handled maturely seems small.
A single morning routine seems small.
Because the results are delayed, people underestimate the importance of the action.
But delayed does not mean unimportant.
Many of the most valuable outcomes in life are delayed.
Trust is delayed.
Wisdom is delayed.
Confidence is delayed.
Financial stability is delayed.
Strong relationships are delayed.
They are built gradually through repeated choices.
This is where patience becomes important.
Because the results people desire are often hiding inside the habits they continue practicing.
Every day you repeat a behavior, you strengthen it.
You strengthen the mindset behind it.
The identity behind it.
The future connected to it.
This is why awareness matters.
Because whether intentional or not, everyone is practicing something.
Everyone is reinforcing something.
Everyone is creating momentum somewhere.
The question is whether your habits are supporting the future you want.
Or quietly working against it.
Your daily routines may seem ordinary.
But ordinary actions repeated consistently often create extraordinary outcomes.
The future is not built only through major moments.
It is built through repeated moments.
Repeated decisions.
Repeated disciplines.
Repeated standards.

Repeated behaviors.

Day after day.

Month after month.

Year after year.

One day, you may look at your life and realize that what appeared to be small habits were actually powerful builders.

Builders of confidence.

Builders of peace.

Builders of stability.

Builders of opportunity.

Builders of identity.

Because your future is not only shaped by what you desire.

It is shaped by what you repeatedly practice.

And every habit you reinforce today is helping create the person you will become tomorrow.

WEALTH LESSON

Daily habits compound over time and eventually create emotional and financial outcomes long-term.

AFFIRMATION

"I build habits that strengthen my future instead of weakening it."

TODAY'S POWER MOVE

Choose one habit today that aligns with the future you are trying to build.

DAY 187

You Are Allowed To Slow Down And Rebuild

POWER QUOTE

"Pausing to heal is not the same as giving up."

REFLECTION

Many people have been taught to admire constant productivity.

Constant movement.

Constant achievement.

Constant effort.

As a result, they often feel guilty whenever they need rest.

Guilty for slowing down.

Guilty for stepping back.

Guilty for taking time to recover emotionally.

They begin treating exhaustion as proof of commitment.

Burnout as proof of ambition.

And pressure as proof of progress.

But growth was never designed to function that way.

Everything healthy requires periods of restoration.

Muscles recover after being challenged.

The mind recovers after intense focus.

Emotions recover after difficult seasons.

Even nature follows cycles of growth and renewal.

Yet many people attempt to push themselves endlessly without allowing space for recovery.

Eventually, the cost becomes visible.

Clarity decreases.

Patience weakens.

Motivation fades.

Joy disappears.

What once felt meaningful begins feeling heavy.

Not because the person is weak.

Because they are depleted.

This is an important distinction.

There is a difference between laziness and exhaustion.

A difference between avoidance and recovery.

A difference between giving up and taking time to rebuild.

Many hardworking people mistakenly criticize themselves during seasons when what they truly need is restoration.

They assume every pause is a setback.

Every moment of rest is lost progress.

Yet recovery is often part of progress itself.

A person who never pauses eventually loses effectiveness.

A person who never recovers eventually loses energy.

A person who never reflects eventually loses clarity.

This is why emotional recovery matters.

Sometimes people need space to process what they have experienced.

To reflect on what they have learned.

To reconnect with themselves.

To regain perspective.

To heal wounds that constant busyness has allowed them to ignore.

These moments are not wasted.

They are investments.

Investments in long-term well-being.

Investments in sustainability.

Investments in future strength.

The strongest people are rarely those who push themselves until they break.

Often, they are the people who learned how to listen to themselves wisely.

Who recognize when effort is needed.

And recognize when restoration is needed.

Who understand that discipline includes caring for their well-being rather than constantly sacrificing it.

This does not mean abandoning responsibility.

It does not mean avoiding challenges.

It means creating balance.

A healthy balance between effort and recovery.

Between building and restoring.

Between discipline and renewal.

Because sustainable growth requires both.

Many people can perform at a high level for a short period.

Far fewer know how to maintain growth over years.

The difference is often found in recovery.

The ability to rest before burnout becomes destruction.

The ability to pause before exhaustion becomes collapse.

The ability to heal before pain becomes deeper.

Life is not a sprint.

It is a long journey.

And long journeys require wisdom.

The wisdom to keep moving when movement is needed.

And the wisdom to recover when recovery is needed.

Never feel guilty for rebuilding your strength.

For protecting your peace.

For taking time to heal.

For creating space to breathe.

Because recovery is not the opposite of growth.

Recovery is often one of the ways growth becomes possible.

The strongest version of you is not created by endless pressure.

It is created by learning when to push forward and when to restore yourself so you can continue the journey well.

And that balance is one of the greatest forms of wisdom a person can develop.

WEALTH LESSON

Restoration improves long-term productivity because recovery strengthens emotional resilience and focus.

AFFIRMATION

"I allow myself to rest, heal, and rebuild intentionally."

TODAY'S POWER MOVE

Take intentional time today to emotionally and mentally recharge without guilt.

DAY 188

Your Thoughts Become Your Environment

POWER QUOTE

"The mind becomes shaped by the thoughts repeated inside it daily."

REFLECTION

Every person lives inside their own mind.

Every day.

Every hour.

Every moment.

No environment influences your life more consistently than the one created by your thoughts.

Because regardless of where you go, your mind goes with you.

This is why internal dialogue matters so deeply.

Many people pay close attention to the people they allow around them.

The environments they enter.

The conversations they participate in.

Yet they pay far less attention to the thoughts they repeatedly entertain.

Over time, those thoughts begin shaping reality.

Not because thoughts magically change circumstances.

Because thoughts influence behavior.

And behavior influences outcomes.

A mind constantly filled with fear often behaves differently than a mind filled with confidence.

A mind constantly filled with self-criticism often behaves differently than a mind built upon self-respect.

A mind constantly focused on limitations often struggles to recognize possibilities.

This is why mental discipline matters.

The thoughts you repeat most frequently become familiar.

The thoughts that become familiar begin influencing perspective.

And perspective influences decisions.

Consider the difference between two internal environments.

One constantly repeats:

"I am failing."

"I am behind."

"I will never figure this out."

"Nothing is working."

The other repeats:

"I can learn."

"I can improve."

"I can adapt."

"I can continue."

Neither person is guaranteed success.

But one is creating an internal environment far more supportive of growth.

This does not mean pretending problems do not exist.

It does not mean denying reality.

Healthy thinking is not blind optimism.

It is balanced perspective.

The ability to acknowledge challenges without surrendering to hopelessness.

The ability to recognize mistakes without destroying self-worth.

The ability to face reality while still believing improvement is possible.

Many people underestimate how exhausting negative thinking can become.

Constant self-criticism drains energy.

Constant fear drains focus.

Constant worry drains peace.

Over time, the mind becomes a difficult place to live.

This is why protecting your thoughts is an act of self-respect.

Not every thought deserves belief.

Not every fear deserves authority.

Not every insecurity deserves permanent residence in your mind.

Mental discipline involves learning how to challenge thoughts rather than automatically accepting them.

To ask questions.

To seek perspective.

To separate facts from assumptions.

To replace destructive thinking with healthier patterns.

This process takes practice.

Just as physical strength develops through repetition, mental strength develops through repetition.

Every time you choose a healthier perspective, you strengthen it.

Every time you interrupt self-defeating thinking, you weaken its influence.

Every time you direct your attention toward growth, resilience, gratitude, or possibility, you reinforce a healthier internal environment.

Little by little, the quality of your thinking begins changing.

And as your thinking changes, your decisions often change as well.

Your confidence grows.

Your peace grows.

Your resilience grows.

Not because life becomes easier.

Because your mind becomes stronger.

The environment you create internally eventually influences the life you create externally.

It affects how you respond to setbacks.

How you pursue opportunities.

How you handle pressure.

How you view yourself.

Protect that environment carefully.

Feed it wisely.

Strengthen it intentionally.

Because your mind is not simply a place where thoughts occur.

It is the foundation from which much of your life is built.

And the healthier that foundation becomes, the stronger your future can become as well.

WEALTH LESSON

Healthy thinking improves emotional discipline and long-term decision-making.

AFFIRMATION

"I create a healthy mental environment through disciplined thinking."

TODAY'S POWER MOVE

Replace one repeated negative thought today with a healthier belief.

DAY 189

Emotional Stability Is A Form Of Wealth

POWER QUOTE

"A peaceful mind is valuable."

REFLECTION

When people think about wealth, they often think about money.

Income.

Investments.

Assets.

Financial freedom.

While those things certainly matter, there is another form of wealth that many people overlook.

Inner peace.

Because a person can possess financial success while feeling emotionally exhausted.

They can achieve impressive goals while privately struggling with anxiety, overwhelm, or constant internal pressure.

They can appear successful externally while feeling unstable internally.

This is why emotional well-being deserves attention.

The quality of your inner world influences the quality of your outer life more than many people realize.

Emotional chaos rarely stays contained.

It affects decisions.

Relationships.

Productivity.

Focus.

Confidence.

And eventually, the direction of a person's life.

A constantly overwhelmed mind often struggles to think clearly.

A constantly anxious mind often struggles to make long-term decisions confidently.

A constantly stressed mind often finds it difficult to enjoy the very success it worked so hard to create.

This is why emotional stability matters.

Not because life should be free from challenges.

Because stability helps people navigate challenges more effectively.

Emotionally grounded people often approach life differently.

They pause before reacting.

They communicate more intentionally.

They make decisions with greater clarity.

They recover from setbacks more effectively.

They protect their energy more wisely.

Not because they never experience stress.

Because they have learned how to manage it.

Inner peace creates space.

Space to think.

Space to reflect.

Space to respond thoughtfully rather than impulsively.

Space to build a life based on values instead of constant emotional pressure.

This is one reason emotional regulation is so valuable.

It is not about suppressing emotions.

It is about understanding them.

Managing them.

Learning from them.

Without allowing them to control every decision.

Many people spend years pursuing external success while neglecting internal health.

They improve their income but ignore their stress.

Increase their responsibilities but ignore their emotional exhaustion.

Expand their opportunities but ignore their need for recovery and balance.

Eventually, the imbalance becomes costly.

Because success becomes difficult to sustain when peace is constantly absent.

True wealth includes more than financial resources.

It includes emotional resources as well.

Patience.

Clarity.

Resilience.

Stability.

The ability to remain grounded during uncertainty.

The ability to maintain perspective during pressure.

The ability to enjoy life rather than constantly surviving it.

This is why protecting your peace is not selfish.

It is stewardship.

Stewardship of your mind.

Your emotions.

Your energy.

Your future.

Every healthy boundary supports that peace.

Every healing decision supports that peace.

Every intentional habit supports that peace.

Little by little, those choices create a stronger internal foundation.

And strong foundations support stronger lives.

The goal is not simply to become wealthy on paper.

The goal is to build a life that feels healthy to live.

A life where success and peace can exist together.

A life where achievement does not require the destruction of your well-being.

A life where growth is supported by emotional stability rather than constant chaos.

Because money can create opportunities.

But peace helps you enjoy them.

Money can create comfort.

But peace creates contentment.

Money can improve circumstances.

But peace improves the experience of living.

That is why inner peace should never be viewed as a luxury.

It is one of the most valuable forms of wealth a person can possess.

And the people who understand that often build lives that are not only successful, but truly fulfilling.

WEALTH LESSON

Emotional stability improves financial and personal outcomes because clear thinking creates wiser decisions.

AFFIRMATION

"I value emotional peace as an important part of my success."

TODAY'S POWER MOVE

Protect your emotional peace intentionally today by reducing unnecessary stress.

DAY 190

Your Future Is Worth Fighting For

POWER QUOTE

"The life you desire deserves your continued effort."

REFLECTION

There will be moments in life when giving up feels easier than continuing.

Moments when progress seems invisible.

When effort feels unrewarded.

When motivation feels distant.

When disappointment feels heavier than hope.

These seasons are part of nearly every meaningful journey.

Yet many people mistakenly interpret them as evidence that something is wrong.

They assume difficulty means they are failing.

They assume slow progress means they are not growing.

They assume frustration means they should stop.

But difficult seasons are not always signs of failure.

Sometimes they are signs of development.

Growth often takes place long before results become visible.

Just because you cannot yet see the outcome does not mean the process is not working.

A seed spends time developing beneath the surface before anyone sees evidence of growth above it.

Personal transformation often follows a similar pattern.

There are seasons where discipline is being strengthened.

Patience is being developed.

Character is being refined.

Resilience is being built.

Even though external results may still appear limited.

This is where many people face an important decision.

Will they allow temporary discomfort to determine their future?

Or will they continue building despite the discomfort?

The people who eventually transform their lives are rarely the people who never struggled.

They are rarely the people who never doubted themselves.

They are rarely the people who always felt motivated.

More often, they are the people who continued anyway.

They continued when progress felt slow.

Continued when confidence felt weak.

Continued when circumstances felt discouraging.

Continued when results had not yet caught up with their effort.

This is the power of persistence.

Persistence is not dramatic.

It is often quiet.

Unnoticed.

Ordinary.
It looks like showing up one more day.
Making one more responsible decision.
Honoring one more commitment.
Taking one more step forward.
Again and again.
Many people underestimate how much strength is developed during difficult seasons.
The struggle itself is rarely the goal.
But the lessons gained from the struggle often become valuable assets.
The patience learned.
The wisdom gained.
The resilience developed.
The confidence built through overcoming challenges.
All of these things become part of the person you are becoming.
This is why persistence matters so deeply.
Because the future you desire is not built only during exciting seasons.
It is also built during difficult ones.
During the days when discipline must carry you further than motivation can.
During the moments when commitment becomes more important than emotion.
During the seasons when the results are not yet visible but the work continues anyway.
The truth is that most meaningful transformations take longer than people expect.
Healing takes time.
Trust takes time.
Financial stability takes time.
Character takes time.
Growth takes time.
And because these things take time, persistence becomes essential.
You do not need to move perfectly.
You do not need to have everything figured out.
You do not need to feel inspired every day.
You simply need to continue.
To keep building.
Keep learning.
Keep healing.
Keep showing up.
Because every day you remain committed is another day invested in your future.
One day, you may look back and realize that the season you almost quit was the very season that strengthened you the most.
The season that taught you resilience.
The season that developed your character.
The season that prepared you for what came next.

Do not underestimate the power of staying committed when things feel difficult.

Because persistence has a way of creating outcomes that temporary emotions could never fully see.

And often, the people who experience the greatest transformation are simply the people who refused to stop building before the breakthrough arrived.

WEALTH LESSON

Long-term success requires emotional endurance because meaningful goals often take time to fully develop.

AFFIRMATION

"I continue fighting for the future I know I am capable of building."

TODAY'S POWER MOVE

Dedicate focused effort today toward one goal that still matters deeply to you.

DAY 191

Stop Letting Temporary Feelings Control Permanent Goals

POWER QUOTE

"Your emotions deserve acknowledgment, not complete control over your future."

REFLECTION

There will be days when you do not feel your best.

Days when energy feels low.

When motivation feels distant.

When confidence feels weaker than usual.

When life feels heavier than you expected.

These experiences are part of being human.

No one feels inspired every day.

No one feels strong every day.

No one moves through life without seasons of discouragement.

The problem is not experiencing difficult emotions.

The problem begins when temporary emotions are given authority over permanent decisions.

Many people make life-changing choices during temporary moments of frustration.

They quit goals because progress feels slow.

End important commitments because emotions feel overwhelming.

Abandon dreams because fear temporarily becomes louder than hope.

Give up on themselves because disappointment clouds perspective.

Yet emotions are often temporary.

What feels unbearable today may feel manageable next week.

What feels hopeless today may look completely different in a few months.

What feels confusing today may eventually become clear.

This is why emotional maturity matters.

Emotionally mature people do not ignore their feelings.

They acknowledge them.

Respect them.

Learn from them.

But they do not automatically surrender control to them.

They understand an important truth:

Feelings provide information.

They should not always provide direction.

Fear may inform you that something feels uncertain.

It does not necessarily mean you should stop.

Frustration may reveal that progress is slower than expected.

It does not necessarily mean the effort is worthless.

Discouragement may appear during difficult seasons.

It does not necessarily mean the future is impossible.

Many of life's greatest regrets are created when temporary emotions make permanent decisions.

A person quits too early.
Walks away too soon.
Stops building before results arrive.
Not because success was impossible.
Because emotions temporarily convinced them it was.
This is why consistency becomes so valuable.
Consistency protects people from becoming controlled by emotional fluctuations.
It allows progress to continue even when motivation changes.
It creates stability during unstable seasons.
It provides direction when emotions feel uncertain.
The most successful people are not people who always feel motivated.
They are people who learned how to remain committed when motivation disappeared.
Who learned how to continue when excitement faded.
Who learned how to honor their responsibilities even during emotionally difficult seasons.
This does not mean pushing yourself without rest.
It does not mean ignoring emotional health.
Rest is important.
Recovery is important.
Reflection is important.
But there is a difference between caring for yourself and abandoning yourself.
Emotionally mature people learn how to do the first without falling into the second.
They learn how to pause without quitting.
Rest without surrendering.
Recover without losing direction.
This ability becomes a powerful advantage.
Because life will always include emotional highs and lows.
There will be seasons of confidence.
And seasons of doubt.
Seasons of excitement.
And seasons of frustration.
Seasons where progress feels obvious.
And seasons where progress feels invisible.
The people who continue growing are often the people who refuse to let those fluctuations determine their future.
They keep showing up.
Keep learning.
Keep adjusting.
Keep building.
One day at a time.
Your future deserves that kind of commitment.
Not only during easy seasons.
Not only during motivated seasons.

But during difficult seasons as well.

Because lasting transformation is rarely built through occasional effort.

It is built through continued effort.

Through consistency.

Through resilience.

Through the decision to remain committed even when emotions temporarily suggest otherwise.

Feel what you feel.

Acknowledge what you feel.

Learn from what you feel.

But do not allow a temporary emotion to make a permanent decision for your future.

Because your future deserves more than the emotions of a single moment.

It deserves the wisdom to keep moving forward anyway.

WEALTH LESSON

Long-term success requires emotional discipline because temporary emotions should not control long-term decisions.

AFFIRMATION

"I stay committed to my future even when my emotions fluctuate."

TODAY'S POWER MOVE

Complete one important responsibility today regardless of how you feel emotionally.

DAY 192

Your Peace Is More Valuable Than Constant Approval

POWER QUOTE

"People-pleasing often destroys emotional peace slowly."

REFLECTION

Many people spend years carrying responsibilities that were never truly theirs to carry.

They carry other people's expectations.

Other people's emotions.

Other people's disappointments.

Other people's opinions.

And because they fear conflict, rejection, or disapproval, they continue saying yes when they want to say no.

They continue giving when they need rest.

Continue sacrificing when they need support.

Continue remaining silent when boundaries are necessary.

At first, these choices may seem harmless.

Even noble.

After all, caring about others is important.

Supporting others is valuable.

Being compassionate matters.

But there is a difference between kindness and self-abandonment.

Many people cross that line without realizing it.

They become so focused on avoiding disappointment that they stop paying attention to their own needs.

Their own health.

Their own peace.

Their own growth.

Over time, the cost begins to appear.

Emotional exhaustion.

Resentment.

Burnout.

Loss of motivation.

Loss of confidence.

A growing sense that life feels heavier than it should.

Not because they are weak.

Because they have been carrying more than they were meant to carry.

This is why boundaries matter.

Boundaries are not walls designed to keep people out.

They are guidelines that help protect what is important.

Your energy.

Your peace.

Your time.

Your emotional well-being.

Healthy boundaries create clarity.

They help people understand what you can give and what you cannot.

What you are responsible for and what you are not.

What you will tolerate and what you will not.

Many people struggle with boundaries because they associate them with selfishness.

They fear being viewed as difficult.

Unkind.

Self-centered.

But healthy boundaries are often acts of wisdom, not selfishness.

A person who never protects their energy eventually has very little energy left to give.

A person who never protects their peace eventually struggles to maintain it.

A person who never protects their well-being eventually finds themselves depleted.

This is why courage is necessary.

Because boundaries often require disappointing people.

Not everyone will understand your decisions.

Not everyone will agree with your limits.

Not everyone will celebrate your growth.

And that is okay.

Your responsibility is not to make everyone comfortable.

Your responsibility is to live in a way that supports a healthy and sustainable life.

That may mean saying no.

It may mean stepping back from unhealthy dynamics.

It may mean creating distance from environments that consistently drain you.

It may mean choosing your healing over someone else's expectations.

None of these choices make you selfish.

They make you responsible.

Responsible for the life you have been given.

Responsible for the future you are building.

Responsible for the person you are becoming.

The truth is that peace requires protection.

It rarely survives without boundaries.

It rarely thrives where people have unlimited access to your energy, attention, and emotions.

This does not mean becoming cold or disconnected.

It means becoming intentional.

Learning where to invest your energy.

Learning what deserves your attention.

Learning what supports your growth and what repeatedly undermines it.

The healthiest people are not those who please everyone.

The healthiest people are often those who learned how to respect themselves enough to establish limits.

To communicate clearly.

To protect their well-being.

To honor their needs without guilt.

You are allowed to choose peace.

Allowed to protect your energy.

Allowed to say no.

Allowed to create space for healing.

Allowed to prioritize growth.

Because your life was never meant to be controlled entirely by the expectations of others.

And sometimes one of the most powerful forms of self-respect is learning that disappointing someone else may be necessary in order to stop disappointing yourself.

WEALTH LESSON

Healthy boundaries protect emotional energy, focus, and long-term stability.

AFFIRMATION

"I choose peace over the pressure to constantly please everyone."

TODAY'S POWER MOVE

Set one healthy boundary today without apologizing for protecting your peace.

DAY 193

Wealth Requires Long-Term Thinking

POWER QUOTE

"Short-term comfort often delays long-term freedom."

REFLECTION

One of the greatest differences between short-term living and long-term living is the way decisions are made.

Some people make decisions based primarily on how they feel in the moment.

What feels easiest.

What feels most comfortable.

What provides the fastest relief.

What delivers immediate gratification.

While those choices may create temporary satisfaction, they often create long-term challenges.

Others learn a different approach.

They begin asking a different question:

"How will this decision affect my future?"

This question changes everything.

Because many of life's most important outcomes are not determined by a single major decision.

They are determined by repeated choices made over time.

The choice to save instead of spend impulsively.

The choice to plan instead of avoid.

The choice to learn instead of remain comfortable.

The choice to follow through even when motivation is absent.

These decisions rarely feel exciting in the moment.

In fact, long-term thinking often feels less emotionally rewarding than immediate pleasure.

That is what makes it difficult.

The reward is delayed.

The benefit is not always visible right away.

The progress can feel slow.

Yet delayed rewards often create the strongest futures.

Financial stability is usually built through years of intentional decisions.

Strong relationships are usually built through years of consistent investment.

Confidence is usually built through years of keeping promises to yourself.

Peace is usually built through years of wise choices, healthy boundaries, and emotional discipline.

None of these outcomes appear overnight.

They develop gradually.

This is why patience becomes such a valuable skill.

Patience allows people to remain committed to what matters, even when immediate rewards are limited.

It allows them to choose what is beneficial rather than simply what is comfortable.

Many people struggle because temporary emotions become louder than long-term goals.

A stressful day leads to impulsive spending.

A difficult season leads to abandoning healthy routines.

A frustrating setback leads to giving up too early.
The emotion feels urgent.
The consequence feels distant.
As a result, the present moment wins.
But people who build stable lives often learn how to pause before reacting.
They learn how to separate temporary emotions from permanent goals.
They understand that what feels good today is not always what serves them tomorrow.
This awareness creates wisdom.
Because wisdom is not only knowing what is right.
It is choosing what is right even when something else feels easier.
Long-term thinking requires emotional maturity.
The ability to tolerate temporary discomfort in exchange for future benefit.
The ability to delay gratification.
The ability to trust that small, responsible decisions are creating something meaningful even when results have not yet appeared.
Every responsible decision matters.
Every disciplined choice matters.
Every moment you choose your future over a temporary impulse matters.
Those choices are not disappearing.
They are accumulating.
Building momentum.
Building stability.
Building freedom.
The life people admire is often built long before anyone notices it.
Built through preparation.
Built through consistency.
Built through decisions that seemed ordinary at the time.
One day, many people look at someone's success and assume it happened suddenly.
What they do not see are the years of long-term thinking that made it possible.
The sacrifices.
The patience.
The planning.
The discipline.
The repeated choices that prioritized the future over the moment.
Your future is being shaped the same way.
Not only by the goals you set.
But by the decisions you make each day.
Choose wisely.
Think beyond the moment.
Think beyond the emotion.
Think beyond the temporary comfort.

Because every responsible choice today is helping create the freedom, stability, and peace you may one day enjoy tomorrow.

And often, the strongest futures are built by people who learned how to value long-term rewards more than short-term relief.

WEALTH LESSON

Long-term financial stability is built through repeated disciplined decisions over time.

AFFIRMATION

"I prioritize long-term peace over temporary emotional comfort."

TODAY'S POWER MOVE

Make one decision today that benefits your future more than your temporary emotions.

DAY 194

Your Healing Will Change How You Love

POWER QUOTE

"Healed people build healthier relationships."

REFLECTION

Relationships often reveal what people have not yet healed.

Not because relationships create every wound.

But because relationships tend to expose wounds that already exist.

A person who has experienced betrayal may struggle with trust.

A person who has experienced rejection may fear abandonment.

A person who has experienced emotional instability may become hypervigilant to conflict.

A person who has experienced disappointment may build walls to avoid being hurt again.

These responses are understandable.

They often begin as forms of protection.

Ways the mind learns to survive difficult experiences.

The challenge is that survival strategies do not always create healthy relationships.

Sometimes they create distance.

Misunderstanding.

Fear.

Conflict.

Emotional exhaustion.

Many people enter relationships believing the problem exists entirely outside of them.

Yet some of the greatest relationship improvements begin internally.

They begin when people become aware of how past experiences are influencing present behavior.

How old wounds are affecting current communication.

How fear is shaping reactions.

How insecurity is influencing decisions.

How unresolved pain is creating patterns they never intended to repeat.

This awareness can be uncomfortable.

But it is also powerful.

Because once a pattern becomes visible, it can begin to change.

Healing changes the way people communicate.

Instead of reacting impulsively, they become more thoughtful.

Instead of assuming the worst, they become more curious.

Instead of allowing fear to control conversations, they learn how to express needs more clearly.

Healing changes boundaries as well.

People become better at recognizing what is healthy and what is harmful.

They stop tolerating behaviors that consistently damage their well-being.

They learn how to protect themselves without completely shutting others out.

Healing also changes emotional safety.

When people become healthier internally, they often create healthier environments externally.

Others feel safer communicating with them.

Safer being honest.

Safer addressing conflict.

Safer expressing emotions.

Not because the relationship becomes perfect.

Because the relationship becomes more stable.

One of the greatest gifts healing provides is perspective.

The ability to separate the past from the present.

To recognize that not every disagreement is rejection.

Not every mistake is abandonment.

Not every difficult conversation is danger.

This allows people to respond more appropriately to what is actually happening rather than what old wounds fear might happen.

The result is often healthier relationships.

Healthier communication.

Healthier trust.

Healthier connection.

This does not mean healing removes every challenge.

Relationships will always require effort.

Patience.

Forgiveness.

Growth.

But healing reduces the unnecessary burdens that unresolved pain often places upon them.

Many people spend years searching for healthier relationships without realizing that part of the answer involves becoming healthier themselves.

Not because they are solely responsible for every problem.

But because they are responsible for their own growth.

Their own healing.

Their own emotional maturity.

The healthier a person becomes internally, the more capacity they often have for healthy connection externally.

This is why healing is about more than personal peace.

It influences friendships.

Family relationships.

Romantic relationships.

Professional relationships.

Every area where people connect with others.

Because relationships are rarely built only on love.

They are also built on communication.

Trust.

Emotional safety.

Self-awareness.

And the ability to respond from wisdom rather than wounds.

The goal is not to become perfect.

The goal is to become healthier.

To become more aware.

More intentional.

More emotionally grounded.

Because healed people tend to build relationships differently.

Not from survival mode.

Not from fear.

Not from emotional chaos.

But from clarity.

Stability.

And a deeper understanding of both themselves and the people around them.

And often, that changes everything.

WEALTH LESSON

Emotional healing improves relationships because healthier emotional patterns create healthier communication and trust.

AFFIRMATION

"I heal intentionally so I can love and live more peacefully."

TODAY'S POWER MOVE

Reflect today on one emotional pattern you want to improve in your relationships.

DAY 195

You Are More Resilient Than You Realize

POWER QUOTE

"Surviving difficult seasons already proves your strength."

REFLECTION

Many people spend so much time focusing on what still needs to improve that they rarely stop to acknowledge how much they have already overcome.

They focus on the goals not yet reached.

The healing not yet completed.

The success not yet achieved.

The problems not yet solved.

As a result, they unintentionally overlook something important:

Their progress.

Their resilience.

Their strength.

It is easy to become consumed by what still hurts.

The disappointment that remains.

The uncertainty that still exists.

The challenges that have not yet disappeared.

But growth requires perspective.

And perspective reminds us that today's struggles are not the entire story.

There was a time when certain challenges felt impossible to survive.

Certain losses felt unbearable.

Certain setbacks felt permanent.

Certain seasons felt endless.

Yet somehow, you continued.

Not perfectly.

Not without pain.

But you continued.

That matters.

More than many people realize.

Because resilience is often built quietly.

It is not always dramatic.

It is not always visible.

It rarely announces itself.

Most of the time, resilience looks ordinary.

Getting out of bed when life feels heavy.

Continuing to try after disappointment.

Choosing hope after heartbreak.

Taking another step after a setback.

Showing up again after failure.

These moments rarely receive applause.

Yet they shape character.

They develop strength.

They reveal a person's ability to continue when circumstances become difficult.

Society often teaches strength should always feel powerful.

Confident.

Certain.

Unshakable.

Real strength often looks very different.

Sometimes strength looks like surviving a season you never expected to endure.

Sometimes strength looks like continuing to heal after being hurt.

Sometimes strength looks like rebuilding after life forced you to start over.

Sometimes strength looks like refusing to quit on yourself.

The strongest people are not necessarily those who never struggle.

Often, they are people who learned how to keep moving despite struggle.

People who carried disappointment without allowing it to destroy their future.

People who carried pain without allowing it to define their identity.

People who experienced setbacks without surrendering their ability to hope.

This is why it is important to occasionally pause and reflect.

Not only on what remains unfinished.

But on what has already been accomplished.

The lessons learned.

The habits improved.

The wounds healed.

The wisdom gained.

The obstacles survived.

All of those things are evidence.

Evidence that growth has already occurred.

Evidence that you are stronger than you once were.

Evidence that your story contains more resilience than you may currently recognize.

Too many people minimize their progress because they are focused on the next destination.

But every journey deserves acknowledgment.

Every victory deserves recognition.

Every difficult season survived deserves respect.

Not because the work is finished.

Because the work mattered.

You are not the same person you were years ago.

Life has taught you things.

Growth has changed you.

Experience has shaped you.

And even the difficult seasons have contributed to the person you are becoming.

Give yourself credit for that.

Give yourself credit for surviving.

For learning.

For adapting.

For rebuilding.

For continuing.

Because resilience is not measured by how easy life has been.

It is measured by your willingness to keep moving forward despite the challenges you have faced.

And the fact that you are still here.

Still learning.

Still growing.

Still becoming.

Is evidence that there is already far more strength within you than you sometimes realize.

Never overlook that strength.

It helped bring you this far.

And it will help carry you forward as well.

WEALTH LESSON

Resilience strengthens long-term success because emotionally strong people continue rebuilding instead of surrendering permanently.

AFFIRMATION

"I acknowledge the strength I have developed through difficult seasons."

TODAY'S POWER MOVE

Reflect on one challenge you survived that made you emotionally stronger.

DAY 196

Protect Your Focus From Comparison

POWER QUOTE

"Comparison distracts people from building their own future."

REFLECTION

One of the easiest ways to lose momentum is to become overly focused on what everyone else is doing.

Who is succeeding faster.

Who appears more accomplished.

Who seems happier.

Who has more opportunities.

Who has achieved the goals you are still pursuing.

At first, comparison may seem harmless.

Sometimes it even feels motivating.

It can inspire people to work harder.

To think bigger.

To pursue growth.

But when comparison becomes constant, its effects often become destructive.

Instead of creating inspiration, it creates pressure.

Instead of creating focus, it creates distraction.

Instead of creating confidence, it creates self-doubt.

The problem is not noticing other people's success.

The problem is becoming emotionally consumed by it.

Many people spend so much time watching someone else's journey that they neglect their own.

They monitor everyone else's progress.

Everyone else's achievements.

Everyone else's timeline.

Meanwhile, their own growth receives less attention.

Their own healing receives less attention.

Their own responsibilities receive less attention.

This creates an exhausting cycle.

Because comparison rarely provides the full picture.

You see the visible results.

The promotion.

The business.

The relationship.

The achievement.

What you often do not see are the sacrifices.

The failures.

The delays.

The struggles.

The private battles that helped create those visible outcomes.

As a result, people compare their complete reality to someone else's partial story.
And that comparison is rarely fair.
Every life follows a different path.
Different opportunities.
Different challenges.
Different resources.
Different responsibilities.
Different timelines.
Someone else's success is not evidence of your failure.
The fact that someone else is moving quickly does not mean you are moving too slowly.
The fact that someone else's journey looks different does not mean your journey is wrong.
This is why focus matters.
Because attention is a limited resource.
Every moment spent obsessing over someone else's progress is energy that cannot be invested into your own.

Energy that could be used to improve your habits.
Strengthen your mindset.
Develop your skills.
Build your future.
The strongest builders understand this principle.
They pay attention to what they can control.
Their effort.
Their discipline.
Their decisions.
Their growth.
Their purpose.
They understand that comparison cannot build a future.
Only action can.
This does not mean ignoring other people completely.
There is value in learning from others.
There is value in celebrating the success of others.
There is value in finding inspiration in what is possible.
But there is a difference between learning from someone's journey and becoming distracted by it
One creates growth.
The other creates frustration.
Your life deserves your attention.
Your goals deserve your attention.
Your healing deserves your attention.
Your future deserves your attention.
Because meaningful progress happens when energy is directed toward what you are building rather than what everyone else is building.

The person who remains focused on their own growth often makes greater progress than the person who constantly measures themselves against others.

Not because they are more talented

Because they are more focused.

They understand that every minute spent building is more valuable than every minute spent comparing.

The future you want requires that same focus.

Stay committed to your journey.

Stay committed to your growth.

Stay committed to your purpose.

And remember that someone else's timeline has very little to do with your potential.

The race was never about becoming someone else.

It was always about becoming the strongest, healthiest, and most intentional version of yourself.

That is where real progress begins.

And that is where lasting fulfillment is often found.

WEALTH LESSON

Focused people progress faster because their energy remains directed toward personal growth instead of constant comparison.

AFFIRMATION

"I focus on my own growth instead of comparing myself to others."

TODAY'S POWER MOVE

Spend less time comparing and more time building intentionally today.

DAY 197

Confidence Is Built Through Evidence

POWER QUOTE

"Every disciplined action becomes proof that you are capable."

REFLECTION

Many people spend years believing confidence is something they must wait to feel.

They read about it.

Talk about it.

Hope for it.

Wait for it.

Yet confidence is rarely something that appears suddenly.

It is usually built.

One decision at a time.

One action at a time.

One promise kept at a time.

One of the greatest misconceptions is confidence comes primarily from positive thinking.

And while healthy thinking certainly matters, confidence requires something deeper.

Evidence.

The mind pays attention to patterns.

It watches what you repeatedly do.

Not just what you repeatedly say.

If someone constantly tells themselves they are capable but repeatedly abandons commitments, the mind notices the contradiction.

If someone constantly speaks about discipline but never follows through, the mind notices that too.

Words matter.

But actions carry tremendous weight.

This is why confidence is closely connected to self-trust.

And self-trust is built through consistency.

Every time you keep a promise to yourself, you create evidence.

Evidence that you can be trusted.

Evidence that you are dependable.

Evidence that your future matters enough to deserve follow-through.

These moments often seem small.

Waking up when you said you would.

Completing a responsibility you wanted to avoid.

Following through on a commitment after motivation disappeared.

Taking action despite fear.

Maintaining a healthy habit when excuses would be easier.

Individually, these moments may not feel significant.

Collectively, they become powerful.

Because every act of follow-through strengthens your relationship with yourself.

Many people struggle with confidence because they have unknowingly practiced self-abandonment.

They make promises and break them.

Set goals and ignore them.

Create standards and repeatedly compromise them.

Over time, trust weakens.

And when trust weakens, confidence often weakens with it.

The person begins doubting themselves.

Not because they lack potential.

Because their actions have not yet provided enough evidence.

The good news is that evidence can be rebuilt.

Trust can be rebuilt.

Confidence can be rebuilt.

Not through perfection.

Through consistency.

Every time you follow through, you send yourself a message:

"I can depend on myself."

Every time you honor a commitment, you strengthen that message.

Every time you continue despite fear, discomfort, or uncertainty, you reinforce that message again.

Eventually, the evidence begins accumulating.

The mind starts recognizing a new pattern.

A pattern of reliability.

A pattern of discipline.

A pattern of resilience.

And confidence begins growing naturally.

Not because someone convinced you to believe in yourself.

Because your actions provided reasons to believe.

This is why confidence is often quieter than people expect.

It is not always loud.

Not always dramatic.

Not always visible.

Sometimes confidence simply looks like trust.

Trust that you will show up.

Trust that you will continue.

Trust that you will handle challenges when they appear.

Trust that you will not immediately abandon yourself when life becomes difficult.

That kind of confidence cannot be borrowed from someone else.

It must be built personally.

One choice at a time.

One commitment at a time.

One disciplined action at a time.

The strongest confidence is not built through pretending to be fearless.

It is built through proving to yourself repeatedly that fear does not have to control your behavior.

That discomfort does not have to stop your progress.

That setbacks do not have to define your future.

Confidence grows when actions and intentions begin aligning.

When promises become behavior.

When goals become effort.

When words become evidence.

And often, the moment you realize you can truly depend on yourself is the moment confidence begins changing everything.

Because self-belief becomes far stronger when it is supported by proof.

And that proof is created every time you keep your word to yourself.

WEALTH LESSON

Consistency strengthens confidence because repeated disciplined behavior builds self-trust over time.

AFFIRMATION

"I build confidence through disciplined action and consistency."

TODAY'S POWER MOVE

Follow through completely today on something you normally procrastinate emotionally.

DAY 198

Stop Feeding Emotional Chaos

POWER QUOTE

"Peace requires intentional protection."

REFLECTION

Most people understand the importance of protecting their physical environment.

They notice when a space becomes cluttered.

Disorganized.

Unhealthy.

Uncomfortable.

Yet far fewer people pay close attention to their emotional environment.

The conversations they absorb.

The content they consume.

The people they spend time around.

The energy they repeatedly expose themselves to.

Over time, these influences begin shaping more than many people realize.

They influence perspective.

Mood.

Focus.

Confidence.

Discipline.

And ultimately, behavior.

This is why emotional environments matter.

Because people rarely remain unaffected by what consistently surrounds them.

A person who spends every day surrounded by negativity often begins thinking differently.

A person who constantly consumes drama often begins feeling differently.

A person who repeatedly exposes themselves to chaos often struggles to maintain peace internally.

Not because they are weak.

Because environments influence people.

The mind absorbs more than it realizes.

Every conversation leaves an impression.

Every environment teaches something.

Every repeated influence reinforces something.

The question is whether those influences are strengthening your future or weakening it.

Many people unintentionally feed emotional chaos into their lives every day.

Constant conflict.

Constant outrage.

Constant comparison.

Constant criticism.

Constant overstimulation.

Eventually, the nervous system becomes accustomed to dysfunction.

Stress feels normal.

Chaos feels familiar.

Peace begins feeling unusual.

This can create a difficult cycle.

People desire calm while continuously consuming what creates turmoil.

They desire focus while continuously feeding distraction.

They desire confidence while continuously surrounding themselves with negativity.

The result is frustration.

Not because peace is impossible.

Because the environment does not support it.

This is why intentionality matters.

You must become aware of what you are repeatedly allowing into your life.

What conversations dominate your attention?

What content shapes your thinking?

What relationships influence your emotional state?

What environments consistently support or undermine your well-being?

These questions matter.

Because emotional health is not only shaped by internal work.

It is also shaped by external influences.

The healthiest people often become intentional gatekeepers.

Not controlling.

Not isolated.

Intentional.

They recognize that not everything deserves access to their attention.

Not every conversation deserves unlimited emotional investment.

Not every source of information deserves daily influence over their mindset.

They become selective because they understand the value of peace.

This does not mean avoiding reality.

Life will always contain challenges.

Difficult conversations.

Stressful moments.

Unexpected problems.

But there is a difference between facing life's challenges and voluntarily surrounding yourself with unnecessary chaos.

One develops strength.

The other often drains it.

Protecting your emotional environment is an act of wisdom.

It means creating conditions that support growth.

Conditions that support healing.

Conditions that support focus.

Conditions that support emotional stability.

The environments you choose today will influence the person you become tomorrow.

That is why awareness matters.

Pay attention to what consistently enters your mind.

Pay attention to who consistently influences your energy.

Pay attention to what repeatedly shapes your perspective.

Because emotional environments eventually become emotional outcomes.

And the healthier the environment, the easier it becomes to build a healthier life.

Protect your peace.

Protect your focus.

Protect your mind.

Not because life should be lived in fear.

But because the future you are building deserves an environment strong enough to support it.

And often, meaningful transformation begins with changing not only what you do, but also what you repeatedly allow around you.

WEALTH LESSON

Healthy emotional environments improve productivity, emotional regulation, and long-term focus.

AFFIRMATION

"I intentionally create environments that support peace and growth."

TODAY'S POWER MOVE

Remove one unnecessary source of negativity from your environment today.

DAY 199

The Person You Are Becoming Matters

POWER QUOTE

"Success is not only about what you achieve. It is about who you become while achieving it."

REFLECTION

Many people focus intensely on reaching the next level.

The next promotion.

The next income goal.

The next opportunity.

The next achievement.

The next milestone.

There is nothing wrong with ambition.

Growth often begins with a vision for something greater.

The challenge comes when people become so focused on what they want to achieve that they neglect who they are becoming in the process.

Because success is not only about reaching a destination.

It is also about developing the capacity to remain there.

Many people work hard to obtain opportunities.

Far fewer work equally hard to develop the character required to sustain them.

This is why internal growth matters.

A person may achieve financial success.

But without discipline, that success can disappear.

A person may gain influence.

But without integrity, that influence can become destructive.

A person may achieve recognition.

But without emotional maturity, that recognition can become overwhelming.

External success often magnifies what already exists internally.

Strong character becomes more visible.

Weak character becomes more visible.

Healthy habits become more important.

Unhealthy habits become more costly.

This is why personal development should never be viewed as separate from success.

It is part of success.

The version of yourself you become often determines how well you manage what you achieve.

Character matters.

Because character influences decisions when nobody is watching.

Integrity matters.

Because integrity creates trust.

Discipline matters.

Because discipline creates consistency.

Emotional maturity matters.

Because emotional maturity helps people navigate pressure wisely.
Many people dream about receiving greater opportunities.
Yet every opportunity introduces new responsibilities.
More visibility.
More expectations.
More pressure.
More complexity.
Without internal stability, those demands can become difficult to manage.
This is why growth should never be measured only by accomplishments.
It should also be measured by development.
Are you becoming wiser?
More disciplined?
More patient?
More emotionally grounded?
More responsible?
More self-aware?
These qualities often determine whether success becomes sustainable.
Because lasting success is rarely supported by talent alone.
It is supported by character.
The strongest foundations are built before the opportunity arrives.
They are built through daily choices.
The decision to act with integrity.
The decision to honor commitments.
The decision to take responsibility.
The decision to continue growing even when no immediate reward is visible.
These moments shape identity.
And identity influences outcomes.
Many people assume the goal is simply to reach the next level.
But every new level requires a new version of you.
A stronger version.
A wiser version.
A more disciplined version.
A more emotionally mature version.
The process of becoming that person is not a distraction from success.
It is preparation for success.
This is why healing matters.
Because unresolved pain can affect decision-making.
This is why self-awareness matters.
Because blind spots can create unnecessary problems.
This is why discipline matters.
Because opportunities are easier to achieve than they are to maintain.

The future you desire deserves more than ambition alone.

It deserves preparation.

The preparation of your mind.

Your character.

Your habits.

Your emotional health.

Your integrity.

Do not only focus on what you hope to gain.

Pay attention to who you are becoming.

Because one day, the opportunities you desire may arrive.

And when they do, your character will help determine what happens next.

The greatest success is not simply achieving more.

It is becoming the type of person who can manage success responsibly, wisely, and peacefully.

And often, that transformation begins long before anyone else can see it.

WEALTH LESSON

Long-term success becomes sustainable when emotional maturity and discipline grow alongside achievement.

AFFIRMATION

"I focus on becoming stronger internally while building externally."

TODAY'S POWER MOVE

Practice one quality today that reflects the person you are becoming.

DAY 200

You Are Still Building Your Story

POWER QUOTE

"A difficult chapter does not mean the story is over."

REFLECTION

There are seasons in life when discouragement feels overwhelming.

Seasons when progress feels invisible.

When healing feels slow.

When answers feel distant.

When the future feels uncertain.

During those moments, it is easy to make a dangerous mistake.

To believe that the chapter you are living in is the entire story.

Pain has a way of narrowing perspective.

A difficult season can convince people that things will always feel this way.

A setback can make people believe they are permanently behind.

A disappointment can make people question whether their future will ever improve.

But life rarely remains the same forever.

People change.

Circumstances change.

Understanding changes.

Perspective changes.

Healing happens.

Growth happens.

New opportunities appear.

What feels permanent today often becomes a memory tomorrow.

This is why hope matters.

Not blind optimism.

Not pretending difficulties do not exist.

But the willingness to believe that your current circumstances are not the final chapter of your life.

Many people who eventually built meaningful lives once experienced seasons where they felt completely lost.

They questioned themselves.

Questioned their direction.

Questioned their future.

Some experienced heartbreak.

Others experienced failure.

Others experienced uncertainty so overwhelming they could not imagine how things would improve.

Yet life continued moving.

And so did they.

One day at a time.

One lesson at a time.

One decision at a time.

Growth rarely announces itself while it is happening.

Most of the time it develops quietly.

In the way you think.

The way you respond.

The way you recover.

The way you continue despite difficulties.

This is why it is important not to judge your entire future by your current season.

A difficult chapter does not mean the story is broken.

A setback does not mean the journey is over.

A painful season does not mean a meaningful future is no longer possible.

In many cases, the seasons people would later describe as transformational were the same seasons they once believed would defeat them.

The season that taught resilience.

The season that developed patience.

The season that revealed hidden strength.

The season that forced growth they never would have chosen but ultimately benefited from.

Life has a way of producing wisdom through experiences we did not initially understand.

What feels confusing today may become clear later.

What feels painful today may eventually reveal purpose.

What feels like an ending today may actually be preparation for a beginning.

This does not mean every hardship is easy.

Some seasons are genuinely difficult.

Some wounds require time.

Some losses deserve grief.

Some challenges take patience to overcome.

But even in those moments, it is important to remember that your life is still unfolding.

You are still learning.

Still growing.

Still becoming.

The person you are today is not the final version of who you will become.

There are lessons you have not learned yet.

Strengths you have not discovered yet.

Opportunities you have not encountered yet.

Relationships you have not experienced yet.

Parts of yourself you have not fully met yet.

That is why discouragement should never be allowed to write the ending of your story.

It only sees the current page.

It cannot see the chapters still ahead.

Keep moving.

Keep learning.

Keep healing.

Keep building.

Keep believing that growth remains possible.

Because your story is not finished.

It is still being written.

And some of the most meaningful chapters may still be waiting for you just beyond the season you are currently living through.

The future is not determined solely by where you are today.

It is shaped by the choices you continue making tomorrow.

And as long as you continue showing up, there is still room for growth, healing, purpose, and possibility in the chapters ahead.

WEALTH LESSON

Resilience and persistence create long-term growth because transformation takes time and continued effort.

AFFIRMATION

"I continue building my life with hope, discipline, and intention."

TODAY'S POWER MOVE

Write down one vision you still believe is possible for your future.

DAY 201

Your Future Needs Emotional Discipline

POWER QUOTE

"A peaceful future cannot be built through constant emotional impulsiveness."

REFLECTION

Life presents every person with moments they cannot control.

Unexpected setbacks.

Disappointments.

Delays.

Criticism.

Conflict.

Stress.

No matter how disciplined, successful, or prepared someone becomes, difficult moments will still appear.

The difference is often not the challenge itself

The difference is the response.

Many people spend years reacting to life

Every inconvenience creates frustration

Every setback creates panic.

Every disappointment creates hopelessness.

Every difficult season creates the temptation to quit.

As a result, circumstances gain control over their emotions, decisions, and direction.

Life begins to feel unstable because their internal state changes with every external event.

This is why emotional discipline matters.

Not because emotions are bad.

Not because feelings should be ignored.

But because emotions are powerful influences that require wise management.

Emotional discipline is the ability to experience emotions without becoming controlled by them

The ability to feel frustration without becoming destructive

To feel fear without becoming paralyzed

To feel disappointment without abandoning your future

To feel anger without damaging important relationships.

This ability becomes one of the greatest forms of personal strength.

Because many of life's biggest problems are not created by the event itself.

They are created by the reaction to the event.

A moment of anger damages a relationship.

A moment of panic creates a poor financial decision.

A moment of fear causes someone to abandon a meaningful opportunity.

A moment of discouragement causes someone to quit too early.

The event passes.

But the consequences remain.

Emotionally mature people understand this.

They know that not every feeling requires immediate action.

Not every emotion requires an immediate response.

Sometimes the wisest thing a person can do is pause.

Take a breath.

Create space.

Think clearly before acting.

That pause is powerful.

Because it creates the opportunity for choice.

Without a pause, people often react automatically.

With a pause, people can respond intentionally

And intentional responses usually create better outcomes.

This does not mean suppressing emotions.

Suppressed emotions often create problems of their own.

The goal is not emotional avoidance.

The goal is emotional awareness.

To recognize what you are feeling.

Understand why you are feeling it.

And then choose your response carefully.

This process strengthens over time.

Every moment you practice patience instead of impulsiveness, emotional discipline grows.

Every moment you choose reflection instead of reaction, emotional discipline grows.

Every moment you remain grounded during stress, emotional discipline grows.

Little by little, a new pattern develops.

A pattern of stability.

A pattern of wisdom.

A pattern of intentional living.

This stability affects every area of life.

Relationships become healthier because communication improves.

Finances become stronger because impulsive decisions decrease.

Opportunities increase because fear loses some of its control.

Peace becomes easier to maintain because emotional chaos no longer dominates every situation.

A calm mind sees possibilities that an overwhelmed mind often misses.

A grounded person makes decisions that a panicked person often cannot.

This is why emotional discipline is not merely a personal skill.

It is a life skill.

A skill that protects relationships.

Protects opportunities.

Protects goals.

Protects peace.

Life will always present challenges.

People will disappoint you.

Plans will change.

Unexpected obstacles will appear.

You cannot control all of those things.

But you can learn how to control your response.

And often, your response becomes far more important than the event itself.

Because while circumstances influence life, your responses shape it.

The stronger your emotional discipline becomes, the more intentional your future becomes.

And that intentionality is one of the greatest advantages a person can develop.

WEALTH LESSON

Emotional regulation improves long-term stability because intentional decisions create healthier outcomes than impulsive reactions.

AFFIRMATION

"I respond with emotional wisdom, peace, and maturity."

TODAY'S POWER MOVE

Practice pausing before emotionally reacting to stressful situations today.

DAY 202

Stop Treating Yourself Like An Option

POWER QUOTE

"When you constantly neglect yourself, your confidence slowly weakens."

REFLECTION

Many people would never intentionally abandon someone they care about.

They would offer support.

Encouragement.

Patience.

Understanding.

They would make time for them.

Listen to them.

Show up when they are needed.

Yet many people struggle to offer those same things to themselves.

They prioritize everyone else's needs.

Everyone else's expectations.

Everyone else's emergencies.

Everyone else's emotions.

Meanwhile, their own well-being slowly moves to the bottom of the list.

At first, this pattern may feel responsible.

Helpful.

Selfless.

But over time, something important begins to happen.

Self-neglect quietly accumulates.

People stop paying attention to their own needs.

Their own healing.

Their own goals.

Their own peace.

Their own growth.

Day by day, they invest energy everywhere except within themselves.

The result is often emotional exhaustion.

Not because they are incapable.

Not because they are weak.

Because they have been giving without replenishing.

Supporting without restoring.

Showing up for others while failing to show up for themselves.

This is why self-respect matters.

Self-respect is not only about how you allow others to treat you.

It is also about how you treat yourself.

The promises you keep.

The boundaries you honor.

The care you provide.

The standards you maintain.

Every action sends a message.

When you continuously ignore your needs, you send yourself a message.

When you repeatedly abandon your goals, you send yourself a message.

When you consistently neglect your well-being, you send yourself a message.

Over time, those messages shape self-worth.

Because self-worth is not built only through positive thoughts.

It is reinforced through behavior.

Through actions that communicate:

"My life matters."

"My growth matters."

"My health matters."

"My future matters."

Many people wait until they are completely burned out before giving themselves permission to rest.

Wait until they are emotionally overwhelmed before giving themselves permission to heal.

Wait until they are exhausted before acknowledging their own needs.

But healthy living was never meant to operate that way.

Care should not be reserved only for emergencies.

It should be practiced consistently.

This is where discipline becomes important.

Not only discipline in work.

Discipline in self-care.

Discipline in maintaining boundaries.

Discipline in protecting peace.

Discipline in making time for what supports your growth.

Because the relationship you have with yourself influences everything else.

It influences confidence.

Relationships.

Decisions.

Resilience.

The way you handle setbacks.

The way you pursue opportunities.

The way you respond to challenges.

People who consistently show up for themselves often develop something powerful:

Self-trust.

The belief that they will not immediately abandon themselves when life becomes difficult.

That trust creates stability.

And stability creates confidence.

The truth is that your future deserves your attention.

Your healing deserves your attention.

Your goals deserve your attention.

Your peace deserves your attention.

Not because you are more important than everyone else.

But because you are important too.

You cannot continuously pour into every other area of life while neglecting the foundation that supports all of them.

Eventually, that foundation requires care.

Growth requires care.

Healing requires care.

Discipline requires care.

Self-respect grows when your actions begin reflecting the belief that your life has value.

That your future is worth investing in.

That your well-being deserves protection.

And that your growth deserves effort.

Do not wait until exhaustion forces you to pay attention to yourself.

Choose to show up for yourself now.

Choose to invest in your healing.

Choose to protect your peace.

Choose to honor your goals.

Because one of the most powerful forms of growth is learning that you deserve the same care, patience, and commitment that you so freely offer to everyone else.

WEALTH LESSON

Self-respect improves emotional stability because intentional self-care strengthens discipline and confidence.

AFFIRMATION

"I prioritize my peace, growth, and future intentionally."

TODAY'S POWER MOVE

Do something today that reflects genuine care for your future self.

DAY 203

Your Consistency Is Creating Momentum

POWER QUOTE

"Repeated effort eventually creates visible transformation."

REFLECTION

One of the greatest challenges of personal growth is remaining committed when there is little visible evidence that anything is changing.

People naturally want to see results.

They want proof that their effort matters.

Proof that their sacrifices are worth it.

Proof that their discipline is working.

When those results appear slowly, discouragement often follows.

The routine begins feeling repetitive.

The work begins feeling unnoticed.

The progress begins feeling invisible.

And many people start questioning whether they should continue.

This is where patience becomes essential.

Because some of the most valuable transformations in life happen quietly.

Long before anyone notices them.

Long before recognition arrives.

Long before the results become obvious.

A person does not become financially stable overnight.

A person does not become emotionally healthy overnight.

A person does not become disciplined overnight.

These outcomes are usually built gradually.

One decision at a time.

One habit at a time.

One day at a time.

The challenge is that people often judge progress by what they can immediately see.

If the results are not obvious, they assume nothing is happening.

But growth is not always visible.

Consider how a foundation is built.

Before the structure rises above the ground, significant work happens beneath the surface.

Preparation.

Reinforcement.

Construction.

None of it looks impressive from the outside.

Yet it is necessary.

Without the foundation, the structure cannot last.

Personal growth works in much the same way.

Many of the habits that eventually create extraordinary outcomes appear ordinary while they are being practiced.

Waking up on time.

Managing money responsibly.

Following through on commitments.

Choosing patience over impulsiveness.

Responding with maturity during difficult situations.

These actions rarely feel dramatic.

Yet they are quietly building something.

Character.

Stability.

Wisdom.

Confidence.

Self-respect.

The results may not appear immediately.

But that does not mean the work lacks value.

Many people quit because they underestimate the power of small repeated actions.

They believe progress must feel exciting.

Fast.

Visible.

Constantly rewarding.

Yet meaningful growth often feels repetitive.

Because repetition is what creates mastery.

Repetition is what creates consistency.

Repetition is what transforms behavior into identity.

The people who eventually achieve meaningful goals are not always the most talented.

Often, they are the people who remained committed long enough for the process to work.

They trusted the routine.

Trusted the preparation.

Trusted the small actions.

Even when results were delayed.

This is where faith in the process becomes important.

Not blind faith.

Earned faith.

The understanding that responsible actions create value even before visible rewards arrive.

Every disciplined morning matters.

Every healthy boundary matters.

Every wise financial decision matters.

Every emotionally mature response matters.

Not because each action changes everything instantly.

Because thousands of those actions working together eventually change everything.

Transformation compounds.

Quietly.

Gradually.

Consistently.

Until one day people notice what appears to be a sudden change.

The confidence.

The stability.

The success.

The peace.

The growth.

What they often fail to see are the years of small choices that created it.

The habits.

The routines.

The sacrifices.

The commitment.

The invisible work.

Do not become discouraged simply because the results have not fully appeared yet.

Some of the most important changes are occurring beneath the surface.

Strength is developing.

Wisdom is developing.

Discipline is developing.

Character is developing.

And those things matter.

Keep showing up.

Keep building.

Keep practicing.

Keep trusting the process.

Because delayed growth is still growth.

And often, the life you once dreamed about is being built long before you can clearly see it.

The future is rarely created through one extraordinary moment.

It is usually created through ordinary actions practiced consistently over time.

And that is why the process deserves your trust.

WEALTH LESSON

Consistency compounds over time and eventually creates emotional, financial, and personal transformation.

AFFIRMATION

"I trust that my consistency is creating meaningful change."

TODAY'S POWER MOVE

Repeat one positive habit today regardless of how small the progress feels.

DAY 204

You Do Not Need To Fear Starting Over

POWER QUOTE

"Sometimes rebuilding creates stronger foundations than what existed before."

REFLECTION

Few things feel more intimidating than starting over.
Beginning again.
Rebuilding after loss.
Creating a new direction after a chapter ends.
For many people, the idea of starting over feels uncomfortable because they associate it with failure.
They see the ending of something as proof that they did something wrong. A relationship ends.
A plan falls apart.
A business struggles.
A dream changes.
And immediately they begin questioning themselves.
They focus on what was lost.
What did not work.
What could have been.
What should have happened.
But rebuilding is not the same as failure.
In many cases, rebuilding is evidence of courage.
It takes courage to begin again when disappointment is still fresh.
It takes courage to try again after setbacks.
It takes courage to walk away from something that is no longer healthy, even when it is familiar.
The truth is that not everything is meant to remain in your life forever.
Some environments serve a purpose for a season.
Some relationships teach lessons.
Some experiences reveal strengths you did not know you possessed.
Some chapters prepare you for future chapters.
Growth often requires change.
And change sometimes requires endings.
The challenge is that endings rarely feel comfortable while they are happening.
They create uncertainty.
Questions.
Doubt.
Fear.
People naturally want stability.
They want predictable outcomes.
They want assurance that everything will work out exactly as planned.

Life does not always provide those guarantees.
Sometimes it asks people to move forward without knowing exactly what comes next.
That uncertainty can feel frightening.
Yet uncertainty also creates possibility.
Possibility for growth.
Possibility for healing.
Possibility for wisdom.
Possibility for a future that could not have existed without the change.
Many people look back on difficult transitions and realize something surprising.
The ending they once feared became the beginning they eventually needed.
The setback that felt devastating created new opportunities.
The loss that felt permanent created room for growth.

The chapter they fought hardest to keep was the very chapter they eventually outgrew.
This does not mean every ending is easy.
Some endings deserve grief.
Some transitions require time.
Some rebuilding seasons are genuinely painful.
Acknowledging that pain is important.
But pain should not be confused with failure.
Pain often accompanies growth.
Pain often accompanies change.
Pain often accompanies transformation.
The strongest lives are not built by people who avoided every setback.
They are built by people who learned how to rebuild after setbacks.
Who learned how to begin again.
Who learned how to remain hopeful when certainty disappeared.
Rebuilding creates opportunities that survival mode rarely allows.
The opportunity to make healthier choices.
To establish stronger boundaries.
To create better habits.
To pursue goals with greater wisdom.
To build a life that reflects who you are becoming rather than who you used to be.
This is why new beginnings deserve respect.
They require humility.
Patience.
Faith.
Discipline.
And courage.
The courage to believe that your future can still be meaningful even when the previous chapter ended differently than you expected.

If you find yourself rebuilding, do not automatically assume you have failed.

Ask a different question:

What foundation am I being given the opportunity to create now?

Because rebuilding is often less about replacing what was lost and more about creating something stronger.

Something healthier.

Something more aligned with the person you are becoming.

Life will include chapters that end unexpectedly.

Plans that change.

Dreams that evolve.

But as long as you continue learning, growing, and moving forward, the story is not over.

Sometimes the most powerful transformations begin the moment people stop fearing new beginnings and start embracing the possibility hidden inside them.

Because rebuilding is not failure.

Often, it is the first step toward a stronger future.

WEALTH LESSON

Resilience creates long-term opportunity because rebuilding often leads to stronger future outcomes.

AFFIRMATION

"I trust myself to rebuild stronger than before."

TODAY'S POWER MOVE

Reflect on one area of your life where rebuilding may actually create healthier long-term peace.

DAY 205

Your Mindset Shapes Your Financial Life

POWER QUOTE

"People often build externally according to what they believe internally."

REFLECTION

Few people realize financial growth begins with income.

A better job.

A larger paycheck.

A new opportunity.

Additional revenue.

While income certainly matters, financial growth often begins much earlier than people realize.

It begins in the mind.

Because before people manage money, they develop beliefs about money.

Beliefs shaped by childhood experiences.

Family conversations.

Financial struggles.

Cultural influences.

Past mistakes.

Successes.

Failures.

Over time, those beliefs become financial patterns.

And those patterns influence behavior.

This is why two people with similar incomes can experience very different financial outcomes.

The difference is not always found in how much they earn.

Sometimes it is found in how they think.

A person operating from constant scarcity often approaches money differently.

They may panic when challenges arise.

Avoid looking at financial realities.

Make decisions based on fear rather than strategy.

Or struggle to believe long-term stability is possible.

The fear feels protective.

But over time, fear can create behaviors that reinforce the very instability a person hopes to escape.

Shame can have a similar effect.

Many people carry shame from past financial mistakes.

Debt.

Poor decisions.

Lost opportunities.

Financial setbacks.

Instead of learning from those experiences, they begin identifying with them.

They convince themselves they are bad with money.

Undisciplined.

Incapable.

Unworthy of financial success.

Eventually, those beliefs begin influencing behavior.

Not because they are true.

Because they have been repeated long enough to feel true.

This is why mindset matters.

The way you think about money influences the way you manage money.

A person who believes improvement is possible often approaches challenges differently.

They become more willing to learn.

More willing to plan.

More willing to adjust.

More willing to take responsibility for growth.

This does not mean positive thinking alone creates wealth.

Thoughts do not replace action.

But thoughts influence action.

And action influences outcomes.

Financial confidence is not built by pretending problems do not exist.

It is built by developing a healthier relationship with money itself.

Learning to see money as a tool rather than a source of constant fear.

Learning to approach finances with awareness rather than avoidance.

Learning to make decisions from clarity rather than panic.

This process takes time.

Just as unhealthy financial habits are developed over years, healthier financial habits are often developed gradually as well.

One responsible decision at a time.

One budget review at a time.

One savings contribution at a time.

One lesson at a time.

The goal is not perfection.

The goal is progress.

Progress in how you think.

How you plan.

How you respond to setbacks.

How you view your ability to create stability.

Many people spend years focusing exclusively on increasing income while neglecting the beliefs driving their behavior.

Yet greater income alone does not automatically solve unhealthy financial patterns.

If fear remains unchanged, fear often follows the money.

If avoidance remains unchanged, avoidance often follows the money.

If discipline remains absent, opportunities can still be lost.

This is why financial growth is both practical and psychological.

It requires strategy.
But it also requires self-awareness.
The healthiest financial futures are often built by people who develop both.
People who learn how to manage money wisely while also managing the beliefs influencing their decisions.
Because wealth is not only built through what you earn.
It is built through what you repeatedly do.
And what you repeatedly do is often influenced by what you repeatedly believe.
Protect your mindset.
Challenge limiting beliefs.
Replace fear with preparation.
Replace avoidance with awareness.
Replace shame with responsibility and growth.
Because the way you think about money today is helping shape the financial life you will experience tomorrow.
And often, one of the most powerful financial decisions a person can make is deciding to develop a healthier relationship with money itself.

WEALTH LESSON

Financial growth improves when mindset shifts from fear and scarcity toward intentional planning and discipline.

AFFIRMATION

"I build a healthier relationship with money, discipline, and stability."

TODAY'S POWER MOVE

Notice one unhealthy belief you carry about money and intentionally challenge it today.

DAY 206

Protect Your Emotional Energy Carefully

POWER QUOTE

"Your energy influences the quality of your decisions."

REFLECTION

Many people spend years learning how to manage their time.

They organize their calendars.

Their responsibilities.

Their commitments.

Their schedules.

Their goals.

Yet one of the most valuable resources they possess often goes unprotected:

Their emotional energy.

Time and energy are not the same thing.

A person may have several free hours in a day but still lack the emotional capacity to use those hours wisely.

They may have opportunities but no motivation to pursue them.

They may have goals but no mental clarity to execute them consistently.

They may have the desire to grow while feeling emotionally too exhausted to take the next step.

This is why emotional energy deserves just as much attention as time, money, and health.

The quality of your energy often determines the quality of your decisions.

When people become emotionally depleted, everything begins to feel heavier than it really is.

Minor problems feel overwhelming.

Simple decisions become exhausting.

Responsibilities appear impossible.

Patience grows thinner.

Focus becomes weaker.

Even small setbacks can feel discouraging.

Many people immediately assume they have a discipline problem.

Sometimes they do.

But often the real issue is emotional exhaustion.

Their mind has been carrying stress for too long.

Their emotions have been overloaded for weeks or even months.

Their body is functioning, but their emotional reserves are nearly empty.

When this happens, consistency naturally becomes more difficult.

This is why protecting your emotional energy is not selfish.

It is responsible.

The environment you live in influences the energy you carry.

The conversations you repeatedly engage in shape your emotional state.

The content you consume influences your thinking.

The people you allow close to you either contribute to your peace or slowly drain it.

Every influence leaves an imprint.

Some relationships encourage growth.

Others continually create anxiety.

Some environments inspire creativity.

Others reinforce confusion and chaos.

Some conversations leave you hopeful.

Others leave you emotionally exhausted long after they end.

This does not mean avoiding every difficult circumstance.

Life will always require difficult conversations.

Unexpected challenges.

Pressure.

Responsibility.

Growth.

Those experiences are part of life.

The goal is not to eliminate difficulty.

The goal is to stop voluntarily living in unnecessary emotional chaos.

Many people never pause long enough to ask themselves one important question:

"What is repeatedly draining my emotional energy?"

Instead, they continue tolerating the same unhealthy patterns.

The same exhausting relationships.

The same destructive habits.

The same environments.

The same emotional cycles.

Then they wonder why they constantly feel overwhelmed.

Awareness changes everything.

Because once you identify what is draining you, you gain the ability to respond intentionally.

Perhaps you need stronger boundaries.

Perhaps you need healthier routines.

Perhaps you need more rest.

Perhaps you need to spend less time consuming negativity.

Perhaps you simply need to protect your peace with greater intention.

Emotionally healthy people learn that protecting their energy is not about avoiding life.

It is about stewarding themselves well enough to continue showing up at their best.

Exhaustion eventually affects behavior.

It affects patience.

It affects focus.

It affects discipline.

It affects relationships.

It affects leadership.

It affects decision-making.

The more emotionally depleted a person becomes, the more difficult it becomes to consistently operate from wisdom instead of reaction.

Peaceful energy produces different outcomes than chaotic energy.

A peaceful mind can think clearly.

Plan wisely.

Respond thoughtfully.

Lead confidently.

Solve problems patiently.

A chaotic mind often spends all of its energy simply trying to survive another day.

Your emotional energy is one of your greatest personal investments.

Protect it as intentionally as you protect your finances.

Guard it as carefully as you guard your health.

Manage it with the same discipline you would use to build wealth.

Pay close attention to what consistently restores your energy.

Pay equal attention to what repeatedly drains it.

Then make decisions that support the future you are intentionally building.

Because the strongest lives are not built by people who ignore their emotional well-being.

They are built by people who learn how to protect it.

Manage it.

Strengthen it.

And invest it wisely.

Remember that not every person, conversation, opportunity, or obligation deserves unlimited access to your emotional energy.

Your future needs that energy too.

Choose carefully where you invest it.

WEALTH LESSON

Protecting your emotional energy improves consistency, decision-making, emotional regulation, and long-term productivity.

AFFIRMATION

"I intentionally protect my emotional energy so I can show up as my strongest self each day."

TODAY'S POWER MOVE

Identify one person, habit, environment, or source of negativity that repeatedly drains your emotional energy and take one intentional step today to create a healthier boundary.

DAY 207

Your Growth Will Feel Uncomfortable Sometimes

POWER QUOTE

"Discomfort is often the doorway to transformation."

REFLECTION

One of the greatest misconceptions about personal growth is believing that progress should always feel comfortable.

Many people assume that if something feels difficult, uncertain, or unfamiliar, it must be the wrong path.

They believe discomfort is evidence they are failing.

That uncertainty means they should stop.

That fear means they are not ready.

But growth rarely works that way.

Real transformation almost always requires stepping beyond what feels familiar.

Every new level of life asks something different of you.

It asks you to think differently.

Respond differently.

Lead differently.

Believe differently.

Eventually, it asks you to become someone different.

That process can feel uncomfortable because your mind naturally prefers familiarity over uncertainty.

People often become attached to routines, identities, and emotional patterns simply because they know them.

Even unhealthy patterns can begin to feel safe when they have been repeated long enough.

Someone who has spent years doubting themselves may eventually become comfortable with self-doubt.

Someone who has lived in financial instability may begin believing struggle is simply normal.

Someone who has always avoided responsibility may feel anxious the moment greater responsibility appears.

Not because growth is harmful.

But because it is unfamiliar.

Familiarity often disguises itself as safety.

This is why people sometimes remain in unhealthy relationships.

Stay in careers they have outgrown.

Continue destructive habits.

Or settle for lives they secretly know they were created to outgrow.

The familiar feels predictable.

Growth feels uncertain.

And uncertainty can be intimidating.

Yet every meaningful transformation requires leaving behind an older version of yourself.

Growth asks you to release limiting beliefs.

To challenge old habits.

To question long-held assumptions.

To replace excuses with ownership.

To exchange fear for courage.

That process is rarely comfortable.
Think about learning any new skill.
At first it feels awkward.
Mistakes happen frequently.
Confidence feels distant.
Progress seems slow.
But with repetition, what once felt uncomfortable gradually becomes natural.
The same principle applies to your identity.
Confidence develops through confident choices.
Discipline develops through disciplined actions.
Leadership develops through accepting responsibility.
Peace develops through intentionally protecting your emotional well-being.
None of these qualities appear overnight.
They are built through repeated decisions that gradually reshape the way you think and live.
This is why temporary discomfort should never be confused with permanent failure.
Discomfort often signals that something new is developing.
Your perspective is expanding.
Your character is strengthening.
Your emotional capacity is increasing.
Your identity is evolving.
Many people quit too early because they expect growth to feel easy.
When challenges arise, they assume they are moving in the wrong direction.
Instead of pushing forward, they retreat to what feels familiar.
The familiar routine.
The familiar fear.
The familiar excuses.
The familiar limitations.
Not because those things improve their lives.
But because they require less emotional effort.
Real growth asks for courage.
It asks you to continue even when confidence has not fully arrived.
It asks you to trust the process before you can clearly see the results.
Every successful person has experienced seasons where progress felt slow.
Where uncertainty felt overwhelming.
Where the future seemed unclear.
The difference is that they refused to let temporary discomfort define their future.
They understood that meaningful growth often feels uncomfortable before it feels rewarding.
When a seed begins growing beneath the soil, nothing appears to be happening on the surface.
Yet beneath the ground, roots are quietly developing.
Strength is forming.
A foundation is being established.

Your personal growth often follows the same pattern.

Just because others cannot see your progress does not mean transformation is not taking place.

Sometimes your greatest growth happens during seasons when everything feels uncertain.

When your old identity no longer fits.

But your new identity has not fully developed.

Those seasons require patience.

They require faith.

They require consistency.

Most importantly, they require perseverance.

Instead of asking,

"Why does this feel uncomfortable?"

Ask,

"What is this season teaching me?"

That single question changes your perspective.

It transforms discomfort into opportunity.

It transforms fear into curiosity.

It transforms resistance into growth.

Remember, you were never created to remain exactly the same person forever.

You were created to learn.

To mature.

To heal.

To develop.

To expand beyond the limitations that once defined you.

The discomfort you experience today may simply be evidence that your future is requiring a stronger version of you.

Embrace the process.

Trust your growth.

And keep becoming the person your future is waiting for.

WEALTH LESSON

Long-term success belongs to people who are willing to remain committed even when growth feels unfamiliar. The ability to embrace discomfort often creates opportunities that comfort never could.

AFFIRMATION

"I welcome growth, trusting that every challenge is preparing me for the person I am becoming."

TODAY'S POWER MOVE

Identify one area of your life where discomfort has been holding you back. Take one intentional action today that moves you beyond your comfort zone and closer to the future you are working to build.

DAY 208

Stop Looking For Instant Results

POWER QUOTE

"Lasting transformation usually happens slowly."

REFLECTION

One of the greatest challenges people face during personal growth is managing expectations.

Not because growth is impossible.

Because growth is often slower than people expect.

Most people begin a new journey with excitement.

A new goal.

A new habit.

A new vision for their future.

They imagine how life will improve.

How quickly things will change.

How different they will feel once progress begins.

But after the excitement fades, reality often appears.

The work becomes repetitive.

The results arrive slowly.

The process takes longer than anticipated.

And many people begin questioning whether they should continue.

Not because growth has stopped.

Because growth is not happening as quickly as their emotions expected.

This is where patience becomes essential.

Because many of life's most valuable outcomes require time.

Healing requires time.

Trust requires time.

Confidence requires time.

Financial stability requires time.

Character requires time.

Strong foundations are rarely built overnight.

Yet modern culture often encourages unrealistic expectations.

People see finished results.

Finished businesses.

Finished success stories.

Finished transformations.

What they rarely see are the years that came before.

The failures.

The setbacks.

The sacrifices.

The repetition.

The discipline.

The countless ordinary days that made extraordinary outcomes possible.

As a result, people compare their beginning to someone else's finished chapter.

And when their own progress feels slower, discouragement follows.

This discouragement causes many people to quit too early.

They abandon healthy habits before they have time to work.

Abandon goals before momentum develops.

Abandon routines before the benefits fully appear.

Not because success was impossible.

Because patience ran out before the process finished.

The truth is that growth often happens beneath the surface first.

Long before visible results appear.

A person may be developing discipline before achieving success.

Developing emotional stability before experiencing peace.

Developing financial wisdom before accumulating wealth.

Developing confidence before opportunities arrive.

These developments may not be immediately visible.

But they are still valuable.

In fact, they are often the very things that make future success possible.

This is why consistency matters so much.

Consistency allows growth to continue even when excitement disappears.

Even when results are delayed.

Even when progress feels slow.

Every healthy choice matters.

Every disciplined action matters.

Every responsible decision matters.

Not because each action changes everything instantly.

Because each action contributes to a larger outcome.

Growth compounds.

Just as interest compounds.

Just as habits compound.

Just as wisdom compounds.

Small actions repeated consistently create results that eventually become difficult to ignore.

The challenge is that compounding often feels invisible in the beginning.

The first few days seem insignificant.

The first few weeks seem insignificant.

Sometimes even the first few months seem insignificant.

Then one day the accumulated effort becomes visible.

The results appear.

The progress becomes undeniable.

The transformation becomes noticeable.

What seemed slow suddenly reveals its value.

This is why patience should never be mistaken for passivity.

Patience is active.

It is the willingness to continue doing what matters while waiting for results to develop.

It is the decision to trust the process even when immediate rewards are limited.

It is the understanding that meaningful change is often occurring even when you cannot fully see it yet.

Do not allow temporary frustration to convince you that growth is absent.

Do not allow delayed results to convince you that effort is wasted.

The strongest lives are often built by people who simply stayed committed longer than others.

People who continued showing up.

Continued learning.

Continued improving.

Continued believing.

While others became discouraged and stopped.

Your future deserves that same commitment.

Because meaningful transformation rarely happens as quickly as emotions expect.

But when given enough time, consistency has a remarkable ability to create outcomes far greater than most people originally imagined.

Stay patient.

Stay disciplined.

Stay committed.

The growth is happening.

Even if it is still unfolding quietly.

WEALTH LESSON

Long-term success compounds slowly because repeated disciplined behavior creates lasting outcomes over time.

AFFIRMATION

"I remain patient and committed while building my future."

TODAY'S POWER MOVE

Continue one positive routine today without obsessing over immediate results.

DAY 209

You Are Becoming More Aware

POWER QUOTE

"Awareness is often the beginning of transformation."

REFLECTION

Many people want different results.

More peace.

More confidence.

More discipline.

Better relationships.

Greater financial stability.

Yet they often overlook an important reality:

Results rarely change until patterns change.

And patterns rarely change until they are recognized.

This is why self-awareness is so powerful.

You cannot change what you refuse to see.

You cannot improve what you do not acknowledge.

You cannot interrupt patterns that remain invisible.

Many unhealthy behaviors operate quietly beneath the surface.

Avoidance.

Fear.

Self-sabotage.

Negative self-talk.

Emotional spending.

Procrastination.

People often focus on the visible outcome while overlooking the pattern creating it.

They see the financial stress.

But not the emotional decisions behind it.

They see the relationship conflict.

But not the communication habits contributing to it.

They see the lack of progress.

But not the avoidance that has been delaying action.

As a result, they continue fighting symptoms while the root cause remains untouched.

Awareness changes that.

Awareness creates clarity.

It allows people to step back and observe themselves honestly.

To ask important questions.

Why do I keep repeating this behavior?

What emotion is driving this decision?

What fear is influencing this reaction?

What belief is shaping this pattern?

These questions require courage.

Because self-awareness is not always comfortable.

Sometimes it reveals habits people would rather avoid.

Blind spots they would rather ignore.

Patterns they have justified for years.

Yet discomfort is often the beginning of growth.

Because awareness creates something incredibly valuable:

Choice.

Before awareness, people often function automatically.

They react.

Repeat.

Escape.

Avoid.

Without fully understanding why.

But once awareness develops, a new possibility emerges.

The possibility of responding differently.

The possibility of interrupting the pattern.

The possibility of choosing growth over habit.

Consider someone who notices they spend money whenever they feel overwhelmed.

Before awareness, the behavior continues automatically.

Stress appears.

Spending follows.

The cycle repeats.

But once the pattern becomes visible, the person gains a choice.

They can pause.

Reflect.

Address the emotion differently.

The pattern no longer controls them in the same way because it is no longer operating in the dark.

The same principle applies to many areas of life.

A person may notice they avoid difficult conversations.

They may notice they become defensive when criticized.

They may notice they constantly seek validation.

They may notice they abandon goals whenever progress becomes slow.

Awareness does not instantly solve these issues.

But it creates the opportunity to solve them.

And opportunity is where transformation begins.

Many people underestimate how much growth comes from observation.

Not judgment.

Observation.

The goal is not to attack yourself.

The goal is to understand yourself.

To become curious about your behavior.

To learn from your patterns.

To identify what is helping you and what is holding you back.

The healthier your awareness becomes, the more intentional your decisions become.

And intentional decisions create different outcomes.

Different habits.

Different relationships.

Different results.

Different futures.

This is why self-awareness is often the first step in meaningful transformation.

Before discipline can improve, awareness must identify what needs attention.

Before healing can occur, awareness must recognize what hurts.

Before growth can happen, awareness must reveal where growth is needed.

The strongest transformations rarely begin with dramatic action.

They often begin with a moment of honesty.

A moment where someone finally sees a pattern clearly.

And once they see it, they can begin changing it.

Pay attention to your patterns.

Pay attention to your habits.

Pay attention to your emotional responses.

Not with shame.

With curiosity.

Because awareness is not the destination.

It is the doorway.

The doorway to better choices.

Better habits.

Better decisions.

And ultimately, a better future.

Because the moment you become aware of what has been controlling you is often the moment you begin reclaiming the power to change it.

WEALTH LESSON

Self-awareness improves financial and emotional discipline because intentional choices replace unconscious habits.

AFFIRMATION

"I become more self-aware, intentional, and emotionally disciplined every day."

TODAY'S POWER MOVE

Pay close attention today to one repeated emotional or behavioral pattern you want to change.

DAY 210

Your Future Is Worth The Discipline

POWER QUOTE

"The sacrifices you make today are shaping the freedom you experience tomorrow."

REFLECTION

One of the greatest misconceptions about discipline is that it exists to make life harder.

Many people view discipline as restriction.

Sacrifice.

Discomfort.

Something that removes enjoyment from life.

But discipline was never designed to punish you.

It was designed to serve you.

Because discipline is often the bridge between where you are and where you want to be.

The challenge is that discipline and comfort rarely ask for the same thing.

Comfort asks for immediate relief.

Discipline asks for long-term vision.

Comfort wants the easier choice.

Discipline wants the wiser choice.

Comfort focuses on the moment.

Discipline focuses on the future.

This is why disciplined decisions can feel difficult initially.

Saving money instead of spending it impulsively.

Having the difficult conversation instead of avoiding it.

Following through on responsibilities instead of procrastinating.

Addressing emotional wounds instead of distracting yourself from them.

None of these choices necessarily feel exciting in the moment.

In fact, they often feel inconvenient.

Yet inconvenience today frequently creates freedom tomorrow.

The opposite is also true.

Many decisions that create comfort today create consequences tomorrow.

This is why discipline requires perspective.

It asks you to think beyond the immediate feeling.

Beyond the temporary emotion.

Beyond the short-term desire.

And consider the future outcome.

Many people underestimate how much their future is shaped by ordinary decisions.

Not dramatic moments.

Ordinary moments.

The choice to budget.

The choice to exercise.

The choice to heal.

The choice to learn.

The choice to rest responsibly.

The choice to continue when motivation fades.

These moments often seem insignificant.

Yet they quietly create direction.

Every decision moves life somewhere.

Toward growth.

Or away from it.

Toward stability.

Or away from it.

Toward peace.

Or away from it.

Discipline is not about perfection.

No one makes the right decision every time.

No one executes flawlessly.

No one avoids mistakes completely.

The goal is not perfection.

The goal is alignment.

Making more choices that support the life you want than choices that undermine it.

This is where consistency becomes powerful.

Because one wise decision may not dramatically change your life.

But repeated wise decisions eventually do.

One healthy boundary may seem small.

One responsible financial choice may seem small.

One disciplined morning may seem small.

Yet those actions accumulate.

They build momentum.

They build confidence.

They build trust.

They build stability.

The process often feels slow because the rewards are delayed.

People want immediate evidence.

Immediate results.

Immediate transformation.

But meaningful transformation rarely works that way.

The strongest futures are usually built gradually.

Patiently.

Intentionally.

Over long periods of consistent effort.

Many people look at successful, peaceful, disciplined individuals and assume they possess something special.

What they often fail to see are the thousands of decisions that created that outcome.

The mornings they showed up.

The temptations they resisted.

The habits they practiced.

The responsibilities they honored.

The discipline they maintained when nobody was watching.

Those decisions mattered.

And your decisions matter too.

The future version of you is being shaped right now.

By what you repeatedly choose.

By what you repeatedly tolerate.

By what you repeatedly practice.

This is why discipline is ultimately an act of self-respect.

It is the decision to care enough about your future that you are willing to make choices that support it today.

The healed version of you deserves that effort.

The peaceful version of you deserves that effort.

The financially stable version of you deserves that effort.

The confident version of you deserves that effort.

Keep choosing what serves your future.

Even when the results are not yet visible.

Even when the process feels repetitive.

Even when comfort seems easier.

Because one day, you may realize that the life you were hoping for was quietly being built through the disciplined choices you almost overlooked.

And that is the true power of consistency.

WEALTH LESSON

Discipline creates freedom because repeated intentional decisions compound over time into stronger outcomes.

AFFIRMATION

"I stay disciplined because my future is worth the effort."

TODAY'S POWER MOVE

Choose discipline over temporary comfort in one area of your life today.

DAY 211

You Cannot Heal By Constantly Distracting Yourself

POWER QUOTE

"What you avoid emotionally often continues controlling you quietly."

REFLECTION

Too many people stay constantly distracted because silence forces them to confront emotions they have been trying to escape.

So instead of healing, they over-scroll.

Overwork.

Overeat.

Overconsume.

Anything to avoid sitting with themselves honestly.

But avoidance delays healing.

The emotions you refuse to acknowledge do not disappear.

They often reappear later through:

- anxiety,
- anger,
- emotional exhaustion,
- unhealthy relationships, or self-sabotage.

Healing requires honesty.

The willingness to sit with discomfort, understand your emotions, and rebuild intentionally instead of constantly escaping reality.

Freedom begins when honesty begins.

A disciplined life is rarely built through dramatic overnight change. Most transformation happens quietly through repeated intentional decisions.

A healthier mindset creates healthier decisions, and healthier decisions eventually create a healthier future.

People who remain committed during uncomfortable seasons usually experience the greatest long-term transformation.

Growth is rarely loud in the beginning. Most transformation happens privately before it becomes visible publicly.

WEALTH LESSON

Emotional awareness improves discipline because unaddressed emotions often influence financial and personal behavior unconsciously.

AFFIRMATION

"I confront my emotions honestly instead of constantly escaping them."

TODAY'S POWER MOVE

Spend quiet time today reflecting honestly on what emotions you may be avoiding.

DAY 212

Your Environment Influences Your Future

POWER QUOTE

"People become shaped by the environments they continuously remain inside."

REFLECTION

Many people focus heavily on changing their habits.

Their mindset.

Their routines.

Their behaviors.

While those things are important, they often overlook a powerful influence operating in the background:

Their environment.

The environments people spend time in quietly shape what feels normal.

What feels acceptable.

What feels possible.

What feels expected.

Over time, those influences begin affecting behavior.

This is why environment matters so deeply.

A person surrounded by negativity often finds it harder to remain optimistic.

A person surrounded by chaos often finds it harder to create peace.

A person surrounded by distraction often finds it harder to maintain focus.

Not because they lack ability.

Because environments influence behavior.

Humans naturally adapt to what surrounds them.

What is repeated becomes familiar.

What is familiar often becomes normal.

And what becomes normal eventually influences decisions.

This principle appears in nearly every area of life.

Spend enough time around people who constantly complain, and negativity begins feeling ordinary.

Spend enough time around people who avoid responsibility, and discipline begins feeling less important.

Spend enough time in environments that reward distraction, and focus becomes more difficult to maintain.

The opposite is also true.

Healthy environments encourage healthy choices.

Disciplined environments support disciplined behavior.

Peaceful environments make emotional stability easier to protect.

Growth-oriented environments often inspire growth.

This is why successful transformation is rarely only an internal process.

It is also an environmental process.

Many people attempt to build healthier lives while remaining immersed in influences that constantly undermine their efforts.

They want peace while surrounding themselves with chaos.

They want focus while feeding distraction.

They want healing while remaining connected to environments that continuously reopen wounds.

This creates unnecessary resistance.

Not because growth is impossible.

Because the environment is working against the goal.

That is why awareness matters.

Take an honest look at your surroundings.

What conversations dominate your attention?

What relationships influence your mindset?

What environments shape your daily behavior?

What influences repeatedly affect your emotional state?

These questions are important because environments quietly shape outcomes.

Many people think discipline is entirely about willpower.

But healthy environments often reduce the amount of willpower required.

When healthy choices are supported, consistency becomes easier.

When unhealthy influences are reduced, focus becomes stronger.

This does not mean avoiding every challenge.

Life will always contain difficult people.

Stressful situations.

Unexpected problems.

The goal is not creating a perfect environment.

The goal is becoming intentional about the environments you choose whenever possible.

Choosing influences that support your growth.

Choosing relationships that encourage accountability.

Choosing conversations that add value.

Choosing spaces that help you become the person you want to be.

Every environment is teaching something.

Every environment is reinforcing something.

The question is whether it is reinforcing the future you want.

Or reinforcing patterns you are trying to leave behind.

Your future deserves support.

Your healing deserves support.

Your discipline deserves support.

Your peace deserves support.

Do not underestimate the power of where you spend your time, who you spend it with, and what you repeatedly allow into your life.

Because environments are not neutral.

They shape habits.

They shape beliefs.

They shape expectations.

And eventually, they help shape destiny.

Protect your environment carefully.

Build it intentionally.

Because the life you are creating becomes easier to sustain when your environment is helping you grow rather than constantly pulling you backward.

And often, one of the most powerful changes a person can make is not changing themselves first, but changing what is constantly influencing them.

WEALTH LESSON

Supportive environments improve emotional regulation, focus, and long-term execution.

AFFIRMATION

"I intentionally create environments that support my growth and peace."

TODAY'S POWER MOVE

Identify one environment today that may be negatively affecting your mindset or discipline.

DAY 213

Stop Calling Yourself Lazy

POWER QUOTE

"Sometimes what people call laziness is actually emotional exhaustion or fear."

REFLECTION

Many people are far harder on themselves than they would ever be on someone else.

The moment their motivation drops, they immediately assume something is wrong.

They call themselves lazy.

Undisciplined.

Weak.

Uncommitted.

They judge themselves harshly for struggling.

Yet what many people fail to recognize is that not every difficult season is caused by a lack of discipline.

Sometimes the issue is deeper.

Sometimes people are emotionally exhausted.

Mentally overwhelmed.

Discouraged.

Burned out.

Carrying burdens they have not fully acknowledged.

And when those burdens go unaddressed, they eventually affect performance.

A person can want to move forward while simultaneously feeling emotionally depleted.

They can care deeply about their goals while lacking the energy to pursue them effectively.

They can desire growth while carrying exhaustion that makes every step feel heavier than it should.

This is why self-awareness matters.

Without self-awareness, people often misdiagnose their struggles.

Instead of asking what is really happening internally, they immediately attack themselves.

They assume discipline is the only answer.

Push harder.

Work longer.

Ignore their emotions.

Suppress their exhaustion.

Pretend everything is fine.

For a while, this approach may appear productive.

But eventually the mind and body begin demanding attention.

Because exhaustion does not disappear simply because it is ignored.

Burnout does not heal through denial.

Discouragement does not improve through self-condemnation.

People are not machines.

They are human beings.

And human beings require more than productivity.

They require rest.

Recovery.

Support.

Reflection.

Healing.

This does not mean ignoring responsibility.

It does not mean using emotions as an excuse to avoid growth.

There is an important difference between making excuses and recognizing genuine needs.

Self-awareness helps identify that difference.

Sometimes discipline is exactly what a person needs.

Sometimes they need to stop procrastinating.

Stop avoiding responsibility.

Stop delaying action.

But other times, what they need is restoration.

Space to recover.

Time to process.

An opportunity to regain clarity.

The wisdom lies in knowing which situation you are facing.

Many people become trapped in cycles of frustration because they treat every problem as a motivation problem.

When in reality, the issue may be emotional exhaustion.

Imagine trying to drive a car with an empty fuel tank.

Pushing harder on the accelerator does not solve the problem.

The vehicle needs fuel.

Likewise, constantly criticizing yourself may not solve emotional depletion.

Sometimes what is needed is replenishment.

Not punishment.

This is why healthy growth requires balance.

Discipline matters.

Responsibility matters.

Commitment matters.

But so do emotional health.

Mental clarity.

Rest.

Recovery.

Support.

The strongest people are not always those who push themselves the hardest.

Often, they are the people who learn how to recognize what they need.

The people who understand when to work.

When to rest.

When to persevere.

When to heal.

When to seek support.

When to extend themselves grace without abandoning accountability.

That balance creates sustainability.

Because the goal is not simply to achieve success.

The goal is to build a life you can sustain.

A life that supports growth without destroying your well-being.

A life that values discipline without neglecting healing.

A life that encourages effort while recognizing humanity.

The next time you find yourself struggling, pause before assuming laziness is the problem.

Ask yourself honest questions.

Am I avoiding responsibility?

Or am I carrying exhaustion?

Do I need greater discipline?

Or do I need greater restoration?

The answer may reveal something important.

Because meaningful growth is not created through constant self-condemnation.

It is created through honest self-awareness.

And often, the moment you stop attacking yourself long enough to understand yourself is the moment healthier growth can finally begin.

The strongest version of you is not built through shame.

It is built through awareness, wisdom, healing, and intentional action working together over time.

WEALTH LESSON

Mental and emotional wellness directly affect consistency, productivity, and financial growth.

AFFIRMATION

"I restore my energy and continue rebuilding myself intentionally."

TODAY'S POWER MOVE

Give yourself intentional emotional care today while still completing one meaningful responsibility.

DAY 214

You Deserve A Stable Life

POWER QUOTE

"Peace should not feel unfamiliar forever."

REFLECTION

Many people spend years trying to create a better life without realizing that their definition of "normal" was shaped by instability.

Not because they chose it.

Because it was what they experienced repeatedly.

Financial uncertainty.

Emotional unpredictability.

Relationship conflict.

Constant stress.

Constant pressure.

Constant survival.

When those experiences become familiar, the nervous system adapts to them.

Chaos begins to feel normal.

Uncertainty begins to feel expected.

Instability begins to feel familiar.

And familiarity is powerful.

People often gravitate toward what feels familiar, even when it is unhealthy.

This is one reason healing can feel uncomfortable.

Not because peace is dangerous.

Because peace may be unfamiliar.

Someone who spent years navigating conflict may feel uneasy when life becomes calm.

Someone who lived in survival mode may struggle to trust stability when it finally arrives.

Someone who experienced repeated disappointment may expect problems even during healthy seasons.

These reactions do not mean something is wrong.

They often mean old patterns are still influencing present experiences.

The mind is attempting to protect itself using lessons learned from the past.

The challenge is that not every lesson from the past is meant to guide the future.

Some lessons helped you survive.

But survival and thriving are not the same thing.

Survival focuses on getting through the day.

Thriving focuses on building a life.

A life with structure.

A life with peace.

A life with stability.

Many people secretly believe they must always be preparing for disaster.

Always waiting for something to go wrong.

Always expecting disappointment.

Always anticipating chaos.
Over time, that mindset becomes exhausting.
It consumes energy.
Weakens trust.
Limits joy.
Makes it difficult to fully appreciate healthy experiences when they appear.
Healing invites people into a different possibility.
The possibility that stability can be trusted.
That calmness can be safe.
That peace does not need to be temporary.
That healthy relationships can exist.
That financial clarity is possible.
That routines can create security rather than restriction.
This shift does not happen overnight.
The mind often needs time to adjust.
Time to recognize that life no longer requires the same level of emotional protection.
Time to learn that not every quiet season is the calm before another storm.
Time to believe that stability can be maintained.
This is why healing often involves relearning.
Relearning what safety feels like.
Relearning what trust feels like.
Relearning what consistency feels like.
Relearning what healthy relationships feel like.
These experiences may feel unfamiliar at first.
But unfamiliar does not mean wrong.
It may simply mean you are experiencing something healthier than what you knew before.
Many people work hard to create peace while secretly feeling uncomfortable when peace arrives.
Not because they dislike peace.
Because their nervous system is still adjusting to it.
This is where patience becomes important.
Allow yourself time to adapt.
Time to grow.
Time to accept that your future does not have to mirror your past.
You deserve more than constant survival.
You deserve stability.
You deserve healthy routines that support your well-being.
You deserve financial habits that create clarity instead of confusion.
You deserve relationships built on trust instead of fear.
You deserve an environment that encourages growth instead of chaos.
Most importantly, you deserve the opportunity to experience life without constantly carrying the weight of old instability.

The past may explain some of your patterns.

But it does not have to define your future.

You are allowed to build differently.

Think differently.

Live differently.

And as you continue healing, you may discover something beautiful:

The peace that once felt unfamiliar eventually begins feeling like home.

Not because life became perfect.

But because you finally learned that stability was never something reserved for other people.

It was something you deserved too.

WEALTH LESSON

Stability improves long-term growth because peaceful environments strengthen emotional regulation and decision-making.

AFFIRMATION

"I build a life rooted in stability, peace, and intentional living."

TODAY'S POWER MOVE

Create one small routine today that supports greater stability in your life.

DAY 215

The Person You Become Matters More Than Appearances

POWER QUOTE

"External success means little if internal peace is missing."

REFLECTION

Many people spend years chasing success.

More income.

More recognition.

More opportunities.

More achievements.

More milestones.

There is nothing wrong with ambition.

Ambition can inspire growth.

Create momentum.

Expand possibilities.

Encourage people to pursue their potential.

The challenge comes when success becomes entirely external.

When people become so focused on what others can see that they neglect what only they can feel.

Because a life can appear successful on the outside while feeling exhausted on the inside.

A person can accumulate achievements while carrying unresolved stress.

Build wealth while neglecting peace.

Gain attention while feeling disconnected from themselves.

Reach goals while sacrificing their well-being.

This is why internal growth matters.

External success may change circumstances.

Internal growth changes experience.

It affects how a person handles pressure.

Responds to challenges.

Navigates relationships.

Manages opportunities.

Protects peace.

Without internal development, success can become difficult to sustain.

The responsibilities increase.

The expectations increase.

The visibility increases.

Yet the emotional capacity required to manage those things may not have grown alongside them.

This often creates instability.

Not because achievement is harmful.

Because growth became one-sided.

Many people focus heavily on what they are building.

Far fewer focus on who they are becoming while they build it.

Yet character matters.
Integrity matters.
Discipline matters.
Emotional maturity matters.
Self-awareness matters.
These qualities influence every area of life.
They shape decisions.
Relationships.
Leadership.
Confidence.
And long-term fulfillment.
The strongest success is not built on achievement alone.
It is built on a foundation strong enough to support achievement.
A foundation of healthy habits.
Healthy thinking.
Healthy boundaries.
Healthy priorities.
Many people assume peace will automatically arrive after success.
After the income increases.
After the goal is achieved.
After the recognition comes.
But peace is rarely something that appears at the finish line.
It is something that must be practiced throughout the journey.
The same is true for emotional health.
Confidence.
Discipline.
Character.
These qualities are developed while pursuing success, not after success arrives.
This is why the process matters.
The person you become during the journey often matters as much as the destination itself.
If success costs your peace, something important may have been neglected.
If achievement destroys your health, something important may have been neglected.
If progress requires abandoning your values, something important may have been neglected.
Because success should improve your life.
Not consume it.
True success creates alignment.
Between achievement and well-being.
Between ambition and peace.
Between growth and stability.
This balance requires intentionality.
The intentional choice to care for your emotional health.

The intentional choice to develop character.

The intentional choice to protect your integrity.

The intentional choice to pursue goals without losing yourself in the process.

Your future deserves more than impressive accomplishments.

It deserves a healthy foundation.

A peaceful mind.

Strong relationships.

Emotional stability.

A sense of purpose that extends beyond external validation.

The goal is not simply to build a successful life.

The goal is to build a life you can enjoy living.

A life that feels as healthy privately as it appears publicly.

A life where achievement and well-being can coexist.

A life where success is measured not only by what you gain, but also by the person you become.

Because at the end of the day, accomplishments matter.

But the condition of your heart, your mind, your character, and your peace matter too.

And the healthiest form of success is the kind that allows both to grow together.

WEALTH LESSON

Internal emotional stability helps sustain external success long-term because healthy minds create healthier decisions.

AFFIRMATION

"I focus on building both external success and internal peace."

TODAY'S POWER MOVE

Reflect today on whether your current lifestyle supports emotional peace long-term.

DAY 216

Stop Waiting To Feel Ready

POWER QUOTE

"Many opportunities are missed while people wait for perfect confidence."

REFLECTION

A lot of people believe they are waiting for the right moment.

The right opportunity.

The right amount of money.

The right level of confidence.

The right circumstances.

The right version of themselves.

They tell themselves that once everything feels aligned, they will finally begin.

But for many people, that perfect moment never arrives.

There is always another reason to wait.

Another skill to learn.

Another fear to overcome.

Another uncertainty to resolve.

Without realizing it, preparation slowly becomes procrastination.

Not because preparation is unnecessary.

Preparation is valuable.

Learning matters.

Planning matters.

Growth matters.

The danger comes when preparation becomes an endless excuse to avoid action.

It is common to believe successful individuals felt completely ready before they took their first step.

In reality, most of them did not.

They started while uncertain.

While nervous.

While underprepared.

While questioning themselves.

While wondering if they were capable.

The difference was not the absence of fear.

The difference was the decision to move despite it.

Action has a way of teaching lessons that preparation alone never can.

You learn by doing.

You improve by practicing.

You develop confidence by experiencing.

No amount of thinking can fully replace experience.

Reading about leadership is different from leading.

Studying communication is different from having difficult conversations.

Planning a business is different from serving your first customer.

The first step often feels uncomfortable because it introduces uncertainty.
You no longer have the protection of theory.
Now you must interact with reality.
Reality includes mistakes.
Unexpected challenges.
Learning curves.
Moments of self-doubt.
But it also includes growth.
Wisdom.
Resilience.
Progress.
Every person who becomes skilled at something was once inexperienced.
Every expert was once a beginner.
Every confident individual once faced situations that made them uncomfortable.
Confidence was not the starting point.
It was the result of repeatedly showing up.
Each action created evidence.
Evidence that they could learn.
Evidence that they could adapt.
Evidence that they could recover from mistakes.
That evidence slowly replaced fear with self-trust.
Waiting until fear disappears often means waiting forever.
Fear naturally accompanies unfamiliar experiences.
It appears when people care about the outcome.
When they step beyond what is comfortable.
When they begin something meaningful.
The goal is not to eliminate fear before acting.
The goal is to stop allowing fear to make every important decision.
Courage is not the absence of fear.
It is the willingness to move even while fear is present.
There will always be things you cannot fully predict.
Questions you cannot completely answer.
Challenges you cannot entirely prepare for.
That is part of life.
Growth requires entering situations where certainty does not yet exist.
Because certainty is often earned through experience.
Not before it.
This does not mean acting recklessly.
Wise preparation is important.
Learning is important.
Seeking advice is important.

But eventually there comes a moment when more preparation adds very little.

What is needed then is movement.

The future you want cannot be built entirely through planning.

At some point, it requires action.

Your first attempt may not be perfect.

Your first conversation may feel awkward.

Your first presentation may include mistakes.

Your first opportunity may stretch you beyond your comfort zone.

That is not failure.

That is experience.

And experience is one of life's greatest teachers.

Do not wait until you feel like a completely different person before you begin.

Begin where you are.

With the knowledge you have.

With the resources you currently possess.

With the courage available today.

Then allow action to teach you what preparation never could.

Because confidence is rarely found sitting on the sidelines.

It is built by people who were willing to step onto the field before they felt completely ready.

Your future is not waiting for perfection.

It is waiting for your willingness to begin.

And sometimes, the most important step in your entire journey is simply deciding that today is enough to start.

WEALTH LESSON

Execution creates momentum because action produces learning, growth, and opportunity.

AFFIRMATION

"I stop waiting for perfect confidence and begin moving forward courageously."

TODAY'S POWER MOVE

Take one action today that you have been postponing out of fear or self-doubt.

DAY 217

Emotional Discipline Protects Relationships

POWER QUOTE

"Emotionally reactive behavior often creates unnecessary damage."

REFLECTION

It is easy to believe that relationships succeed or fail because of one thing alone:

Love.

While love is essential, it is rarely enough by itself.

Relationships also require emotional maturity.

Patience.

Trust.

Respect.

Communication.

Accountability.

Without these qualities, even genuine love can struggle under the weight of unhealthy patterns.

Many relationships are damaged not because people stop caring about one another, but because they do not yet know how to navigate difficult emotions in healthy ways.

A disagreement becomes an argument.

An argument becomes resentment.

Resentment becomes distance.

Distance slowly weakens connection.

Often, the original problem was not the conflict itself.

It was the way the conflict was handled.

Emotional regulation plays a significant role in healthy relationships.

Every person experiences frustration.

Disappointment.

Fear.

Jealousy.

Insecurity.

The goal is not to eliminate these emotions.

The goal is to learn how to respond to them responsibly.

Emotionally mature people understand that feelings deserve attention, but they do not have to control every reaction.

They learn to pause before speaking.

To listen before defending themselves.

To ask questions before making assumptions.

To seek understanding before assigning blame.

These habits protect relationships because they create emotional safety.

Emotional safety is the confidence that disagreements can happen without destroying trust.

That vulnerability will not be used as a weapon.

That honesty will be met with respect rather than hostility.

When people feel emotionally safe, communication becomes healthier.

Conflict becomes more productive.

Connection becomes stronger.

Healing also plays an important role.

Many people unknowingly carry unresolved experiences into their relationships.

Old rejection influences new conversations.

Past betrayal affects present trust.

Childhood instability shapes adult expectations.

Without realizing it, people sometimes respond to today's situation through yesterday's pain.

This does not make someone a bad partner.

It makes them human.

But it does highlight the importance of self-awareness.

The healthier you become internally, the more freedom you have to respond to the present instead of reacting from the past.

Healing helps people separate old wounds from current reality.

It allows them to recognize when fear is speaking louder than facts.

When insecurity is influencing communication.

When past experiences are shaping present expectations.

This awareness creates choice.

Instead of reacting automatically, people can respond intentionally.

Instead of escalating conflict, they can pursue understanding.

Instead of protecting themselves through distance, they can practice honest connection.

Healthy relationships are not built by perfect people.

They are built by people who remain willing to grow.

People who apologize when necessary.

People who accept responsibility for their actions.

People who remain teachable.

People who understand that love is strengthened by humility as much as affection.

Growth inside a relationship is not always comfortable.

It requires difficult conversations.

Honesty.

Reflection.

The courage to acknowledge personal weaknesses.

The willingness to change habits that repeatedly create harm.

These moments can feel challenging.

Yet they often become the turning points that deepen trust and strengthen connection.

A healthy relationship is not one where conflict never happens.

It is one where conflict is handled with respect, honesty, and emotional responsibility.

Where both people remain committed to understanding rather than simply winning.

Where healing becomes more important than pride.

Where growth becomes more important than being right.

As you continue growing emotionally, your relationships often change with you.

Your communication becomes calmer.

Your boundaries become healthier.

Your responses become more thoughtful.

Your capacity to love becomes steadier because it is no longer driven primarily by fear or emotional survival.

The healthiest relationships are built by people who are committed not only to loving one another, but also to becoming healthier versions of themselves.

Because the greatest gift you can consistently bring into any relationship is not perfection.

It is a growing heart, a teachable spirit, and the willingness to keep becoming someone who creates safety, trust, and peace wherever love is invited to grow.

WEALTH LESSON

Emotional regulation strengthens relationships because stability improves communication and trust.

AFFIRMATION

"I communicate and respond with emotional wisdom and maturity."

TODAY'S POWER MOVE

Practice intentional communication today instead of emotionally reactive communication.

DAY 218

Your Progress Still Counts

POWER QUOTE

"Small progress is still progress."

REFLECTION

Many people have become experts at noticing what is still missing.

The goals they have not reached.

The habits they have not mastered.

The dreams that remain unfinished.

The areas where they still need to improve.

While self-awareness is valuable, there is a danger in focusing only on what remains incomplete.

You may begin believing that nothing has changed.

That you are standing still.

That your effort has produced very little.

But that is often far from the truth.

Growth is rarely measured only by destinations.

It is also measured by direction.

The person you are today may already think differently than the person you were a year ago.

You may respond with greater patience.

Handle disappointment with more wisdom.

Set healthier boundaries.

Make better financial decisions.

Communicate more honestly.

Recover from setbacks more quickly.

These changes may not always feel dramatic.

But they matter.

Many people overlook them because they expected transformation to arrive all at once.

Life rarely works that way.

Meaningful growth usually develops gradually.

One healthier choice.

One difficult conversation.

One disciplined morning.

One wise decision.

One lesson learned.

These moments seem ordinary when viewed individually.

Yet together they reshape a person's life.

The challenge is that progress becomes difficult to recognize when perfection becomes the standard.

If every accomplishment is immediately dismissed because there is still more work to do, satisfaction becomes impossible.

No matter how much growth occurs, it never feels like enough.

This mindset quietly steals encouragement.

It causes people to overlook the evidence that they are already becoming stronger.

Wiser.

More disciplined.

More resilient.

Acknowledging progress does not mean becoming complacent.

It does not mean settling for less than your potential.

It simply means recognizing that every step forward deserves respect.

A person who once reacted with anger but now chooses patience has grown.

A person who once avoided responsibility but now follows through has grown.

A person who once lived in constant fear but now takes courageous action has grown.

A person who once struggled to believe in themselves but now continues despite doubt has grown.

These victories deserve recognition.

Not because the journey is finished.

Because the journey is moving.

There is wisdom in occasionally looking backward.

Not to live in the past.

But to appreciate the distance you have already traveled.

The obstacles you overcame.

The lessons you learned.

The habits you changed.

The strength you developed.

The healing you experienced.

These things are part of your story.

Too many people celebrate only major milestones.

The promotion.

The financial breakthrough.

The completed goal.

Yet those visible moments are often built upon hundreds of quiet victories that no one else ever sees.

The mornings you chose discipline.

The evenings you chose reflection instead of distraction.

The conversations where you responded with maturity instead of impulse.

The decisions that aligned with your values even when they were difficult.

Those moments matter.

They are the foundation beneath every meaningful achievement.

Growth is not only found in extraordinary moments.

It is found in ordinary faithfulness.

In showing up again.

In trying again.

In choosing better one more time.

This perspective creates gratitude.

Not gratitude because everything is perfect.

Gratitude because progress is real.

Your life may still contain challenges.

There may still be goals ahead.

There may still be habits to strengthen and lessons to learn.

But none of that erases the progress you have already made.

Do not allow the pursuit of perfection to blind you to the evidence of transformation.

Give yourself permission to acknowledge the healthier choices you have made.

The courage you have shown.

The wisdom you have gained.

The person you are becoming.

Because growth deserves recognition.

Not only when the journey is complete.

But every time you choose to keep moving forward.

And sometimes, the encouragement you need most comes from simply recognizing that you are no longer the person you used to be.

That quiet transformation is worth celebrating.

And it is worth continuing.

WEALTH LESSON

Recognizing progress strengthens motivation because confidence grows through evidence of growth.

AFFIRMATION

"I acknowledge and respect the progress I am making."

TODAY'S POWER MOVE

Write down three ways you have grown emotionally, mentally, or financially over the past year.

DAY 219

Your Future Needs Focused Energy

POWER QUOTE

"Scattered energy creates scattered results."

REFLECTION

Every person receives the same twenty-four hours in a day.

Yet people experience dramatically different outcomes.

The difference is not always intelligence.

Talent.

Resources.

Or opportunity.

Often, it comes down to where attention is invested.

Attention is one of the most valuable resources you possess.

Unlike money, it cannot be recovered once it has been spent.

Every hour invested in something is an hour that cannot be invested somewhere else.

This is why protecting your attention matters.

Many people lose momentum not because they lack ability, but because their focus is constantly being interrupted.

A notification appears.

A message demands a response.

A comparison steals their confidence.

A distraction delays an important task.

By the end of the day, they have been busy, yet very little of lasting value has been accomplished.

Modern life offers endless opportunities to divide your attention.

News.

Social media.

Entertainment.

Arguments.

Opinions.

Endless streams of information competing for a place in your mind.

None of these things are necessarily harmful on their own.

The problem arises when they consume more attention than your priorities.

Little by little, your focus becomes fragmented.

Instead of directing your energy toward meaningful work, you spend it reacting to whatever appears in front of you.

This constant shifting carries a cost.

It becomes harder to think deeply.

Harder to stay present.

Harder to complete difficult tasks.

Harder to build momentum.

Momentum is rarely created through occasional bursts of effort.

It grows through sustained attention.

The ability to remain engaged with what matters long enough to make meaningful progress.

Every interruption makes that process more difficult.

This is why focused people often build differently.

They understand that attention deserves protection.

They become intentional about how they begin their mornings.

What conversations they engage in.

What information they consume.

What commitments they accept.

They recognize that every "yes" given to one thing is also a "no" to something else.

So they choose carefully.

Protecting your attention does not require withdrawing from the world.

It requires becoming more deliberate within it.

Learning to distinguish between what is urgent and what is truly important.

Between what is merely interesting and what actually moves your life forward.

Between what entertains you for a moment and what strengthens you for years.

This level of intentionality creates clarity.

And clarity supports discipline.

When your attention is scattered, even simple decisions become more difficult.

When your attention is focused, priorities become easier to identify.

Effort becomes more effective.

Progress becomes more consistent.

Many people assume productivity is about doing more.

Often, it is about protecting yourself from doing less of what matters.

Removing unnecessary distractions.

Reducing constant interruptions.

Creating space to think.

To plan.

To create.

To solve problems.

To grow.

Every meaningful accomplishment requires periods of uninterrupted focus.

Every strong relationship requires undivided presence.

Every important goal requires sustained attention.

Your future is built where your attention repeatedly goes.

If your attention constantly follows distractions, your progress often slows.

If your attention consistently follows purpose, your progress gains momentum.

Ask yourself honestly:

What receives most of my attention each day?

Does it strengthen the future I want to build?

Or does it quietly pull me away from it?

The answer may reveal more about your future than your intentions alone.

Protect your attention.

Protect your time.

Protect your energy.

Because these resources are shaping your life every single day.

The people who accomplish meaningful things are rarely those who never face distractions.

They are the people who repeatedly choose what matters most.

And that choice, made consistently over time, becomes one of the greatest advantages a person can develop.

WEALTH LESSON

Focused execution improves productivity because less emotional energy is wasted on unnecessary distractions.

AFFIRMATION

"I direct my attention intentionally toward meaningful growth."

TODAY'S POWER MOVE

Spend focused uninterrupted time today working toward one important goal.

DAY 220

You Are Becoming Someone Stronger

POWER QUOTE

"Difficult seasons often build emotional strength people later depend on."

REFLECTION

When people are living through difficult seasons, they naturally focus on what is hurting.

The uncertainty.

The setbacks.

The disappointments.

The unanswered questions.

The emotional weight they carry from one day to the next.

Pain has a way of narrowing perspective.

It becomes difficult to see anything beyond the immediate struggle.

Every obstacle feels larger.

Every delay feels more significant.

Every setback feels more personal.

Yet while difficult seasons often take something from us, they also have the potential to build something within us.

Not because suffering is inherently valuable.

But because the way we respond to hardship can shape who we become.

Many of the qualities people admire most are not developed during comfortable seasons.

Patience grows when waiting becomes unavoidable.

Resilience develops when giving up seems easier than continuing.

Wisdom often comes through experience rather than convenience.

Emotional maturity is strengthened by learning how to navigate disappointment without allowing it to define your identity.

These qualities cannot always be learned from books alone.

They are often formed through life itself.

This is why difficult seasons deserve a broader perspective.

Instead of asking only, "Why is this happening to me?"

It can also be helpful to ask,

"What is this season teaching me?"

"What strengths am I developing?"

"What habits are being refined?"

"What character is being formed?"

These questions do not erase pain.

They simply allow pain to become part of growth rather than the end of hope.

Many people look back on seasons they once wanted to escape and realize those experiences changed them in meaningful ways.

They became more patient.

More compassionate.

More disciplined.

More courageous.

More grateful.

Not because the circumstances were enjoyable.

Because they chose to keep growing through them.

Growth during hardship rarely feels dramatic.

It often looks ordinary.

Getting up when you feel discouraged.

Honoring your responsibilities despite uncertainty.

Continuing to learn when progress feels slow.

Choosing integrity when compromise would be easier.

Remaining hopeful after disappointment.

These moments may seem small.

Yet they quietly strengthen your foundation.

Many people assume strength is something people are born with.

More often, strength is something people develop.

It is built decision by decision.

Challenge by challenge.

Recovery by recovery.

No one becomes resilient without facing situations that require resilience.

No one develops endurance without walking through seasons that test it.

This does not mean you should seek hardship.

But when hardship arrives, you can choose how it shapes you.

You can allow it to make you more bitter.

Or you can allow it to make you wiser.

You can allow it to convince you to quit.

Or you can allow it to deepen your commitment to becoming the person you hope to be.

The choice may not change the difficulty immediately.

But it can change the direction of your growth.

One day, the very qualities you are developing now may become the reason you are able to handle opportunities that once would have overwhelmed you.

The patience you are learning may strengthen future relationships.

The discipline you are practicing may support future success.

The resilience you are building may carry you through challenges you cannot yet see.

This is why you should never underestimate the work taking place beneath the surface.

Not every important change is immediately visible.

Some of the most valuable transformations happen quietly.

Within your character.

Within your mindset.

Within your ability to remain steady when life becomes uncertain.

If this season feels difficult, remember that difficulty does not always mean you are moving backward.

Sometimes it means you are being strengthened for what comes next.

Keep showing up.

Keep learning.

Keep growing.

Because the future you hope to build may depend upon the endurance, wisdom, and resilience that are quietly being formed within you today.

And one day, you may discover that the season you once questioned became one of the strongest foundations of the life you were preparing to build.

WEALTH LESSON

Resilience strengthens long-term growth because emotionally strong people continue rebuilding after setbacks.

AFFIRMATION

"I become stronger, wiser, and more resilient through every season."

TODAY'S POWER MOVE

Reflect on one difficult season that strengthened who you are becoming.

DAY 221

Stop Negotiating With Your Potential

POWER QUOTE

"Every time you settle for less than your potential, your future pays the price."

REFLECTION

Almost everyone has potential.

The ability to grow.

To learn.

To lead.

To create.

To build something meaningful.

Potential is one of the greatest gifts a person can possess.

Yet potential alone has never changed a life.

Only action does.

Many people spend years knowing they are capable of more while continuing to negotiate with their own growth.

They promise themselves they will begin tomorrow.

They wait for more confidence.

More motivation.

More certainty.

A better season.

A better opportunity.

Without realizing it, they slowly postpone the very life they hope to create.

This negotiation rarely sounds dramatic.

It often sounds reasonable.

"I'll start next week."

"I need a little more time."

"I'm just waiting until life settles down."

"I'll focus on it when I feel more motivated."

One excuse becomes another.

One delay becomes another month.

One month becomes another year.

Eventually, people begin wondering why their lives have not changed.

The answer is often found in the conversations they have been having with themselves.

Comfort is persuasive.

It promises relief without asking much in return.

It encourages familiar routines.

Predictable habits.

Temporary ease.

Growth, however, asks different questions.

It asks whether you are willing to become uncomfortable for something greater.

Whether you are willing to practice discipline when convenience is more appealing.

Whether you are willing to continue building even when progress feels slow.

This is why transformation requires decisions that emotions may not always enjoy.

Choosing to save money instead of spending impulsively.

Choosing to exercise when rest feels easier.

Choosing to have the difficult conversation instead of avoiding it.

Choosing to heal instead of continuing to hide behind distractions.

These choices rarely feel dramatic in the moment.

But they quietly separate the life you have from the life you are creating.

Many people overestimate the importance of talent while underestimating the importance of consistency.

Talent may create opportunity.

Consistency determines what happens next.

Potential may open the door.

Discipline is what allows you to walk through it.

Every meaningful goal eventually reaches a point where desire is no longer enough.

The excitement fades.

The novelty disappears.

Progress slows.

That is where commitment becomes more important than motivation.

Commitment says,

"I will continue even when I do not feel like it."

"I will keep my word to myself."

"I will choose my future over temporary comfort."

These decisions are rarely made once.

They are made repeatedly.

Day after day.

Moment after moment.

Choice after choice.

A lot of people believe their greatest obstacle is a lack of opportunity.

Sometimes the greater obstacle is repeatedly choosing what feels comfortable over what creates growth.

The life you want will ask something from you.

It will ask for discipline.

Patience.

Courage.

Responsibility.

Consistency.

Not because life is trying to make success difficult.

Because meaningful growth requires becoming someone capable of sustaining it.

The version of you that achieves your goals will likely think differently than you do today.

Respond differently.

Manage time differently.

Handle emotions differently.

Protect priorities differently.

That version of you is not created by wishing.

It is created by practicing.

Every disciplined decision becomes a vote for the person you are becoming.

Every healthy boundary reinforces your future.

Every difficult choice strengthens your character.

Every promise you keep to yourself builds self-trust.

Stop negotiating with the life you know you are capable of creating.

Stop waiting for perfect conditions that may never arrive.

Stop allowing temporary emotions to make permanent decisions about your future.

You already possess more potential than you may realize.

Now give that potential something it cannot create on its own:

Consistent action.

Because your future will not be determined by what you could have become.

It will be shaped by what you repeatedly chose to do.

And one day, you will look back and realize that your greatest breakthrough did not begin when you discovered your potential.

It began the moment you stopped negotiating with it and started living it instead.

WEALTH LESSON

Long-term success requires disciplined action because unrealized potential creates frustration instead of freedom.

AFFIRMATION

"I stop negotiating with my growth and commit fully to my future."

TODAY'S POWER MOVE

Do one thing today that your highest potential version of yourself would be proud of.

DAY 222

Emotional Safety Matters

POWER QUOTE

"A peaceful nervous system creates healthier decisions."

REFLECTION

Many people spend years trying to build a better future without realizing they are carrying an old definition of what life is supposed to feel like.

If you grew up surrounded by constant stress, unpredictability, criticism, or emotional instability, your mind and body may have learned to expect those experiences.

Over time, chaos begins to feel familiar.

Not because it is healthy.

Because it is known.

The human mind naturally adapts to repeated experiences.

What happens consistently becomes expected.

If conflict was common, calmness may feel unfamiliar.

If instability was normal, consistency may feel unusual.

If criticism was constant, encouragement may even feel difficult to believe.

These responses are not character flaws.

They are often learned survival strategies.

For many people, survival required staying alert.

Watching for problems.

Preparing for disappointment.

Expecting something to go wrong.

Those habits may have helped you through difficult seasons.

But what helps someone survive one chapter of life is not always what helps them flourish in the next.

Healing often begins with recognizing that your past does not have to dictate your future.

You are allowed to experience a different way of living.

A life where peace is not temporary.

Where relationships are built on trust instead of fear.

Where stability becomes more familiar than chaos.

This transition can feel surprisingly uncomfortable.

Not because peace is dangerous.

Because it is unfamiliar.

Many people unknowingly become suspicious when life is going well.

They begin waiting for something to fall apart.

They struggle to relax.

They anticipate conflict before it exists.

Their nervous system is responding to old experiences rather than present reality.

This is why healing is more than changing your thoughts.

It is also about teaching your mind and body that safety exists.

That calm conversations do not always lead to conflict.

That financial stability can last.

That healthy relationships do not require constant emotional survival.

That rest is not the same as laziness.

That quiet does not always mean something bad is about to happen.

This process requires patience.

The nervous system learns through repeated experience.

Each time you choose healthy boundaries.

Each time you remain in peaceful environments.

Each time you respond thoughtfully instead of reacting impulsively.

Each time you allow yourself to enjoy a calm season without expecting disaster.

You are reinforcing a new reality.

You are teaching yourself that stability can be trusted.

This work affects every area of life.

A calmer mind makes wiser decisions.

A regulated nervous system improves focus.

Greater emotional safety strengthens confidence.

Healthy relationships become easier to build because trust no longer feels impossible.

Discipline also becomes more sustainable.

It is difficult to remain consistent when all of your energy is being used simply to survive.

But when your mind is no longer constantly preparing for danger, that energy becomes available for growth.

For learning.

For creating.

For serving others.

For building the future you desire.

Healing is not about pretending your past never happened.

It is about refusing to let your past permanently define how you experience the present.

You can appreciate how your resilience carried you through difficult seasons while also recognizing that you no longer have to live as though every day is an emergency.

Your future deserves more than constant vigilance.

It deserves peace.

It deserves healthy relationships.

It deserves emotional stability.

It deserves environments where your mind can rest instead of constantly preparing for chaos.

Allow yourself to believe that calmness is not weakness.

Stability is not boring.

Peace is not something reserved for other people.

It is something you can learn to receive, protect, and build.

Because one of the greatest signs of healing is not simply surviving difficult circumstances.

It is finally believing that a peaceful life is safe enough to live.

WEALTH LESSON

Emotional stability improves long-term decision-making because peaceful minds think more clearly.

AFFIRMATION

"I create emotional safety, peace, and stability within my life."

TODAY'S POWER MOVE

Pay attention today to what environments make your mind feel calm versus emotionally overwhelmed.

DAY 223

Stop Letting Shame Control You

POWER QUOTE

"Shame keeps people emotionally trapped in old versions of themselves."

REFLECTION

Few emotional burdens are heavier than shame.

Unlike guilt, which says, "I made a mistake," shame whispers something far more destructive.

"I am the mistake."

That quiet belief has the power to shape an entire life.

Many people carry shame they rarely speak about.

Financial decisions they regret.

Relationships that ended painfully.

Opportunities they missed.

Words they wish they could take back.

Seasons where they felt lost, afraid, or emotionally overwhelmed.

Over time, those experiences become more than memories.

They become identities.

Instead of saying, "I struggled financially," they begin believing, "I'm bad with money."

Instead of saying, "I failed," they believe, "I'm a failure."

Instead of saying, "I made unhealthy choices," they conclude, "I'll never change."

That is the danger of shame.

It blurs the line between what happened and who you are.

But your experiences are not your identity.

They are chapters of your story.

And chapters were never meant to become the entire book.

Every human being has moments they would relive differently if they could.

No life is built without mistakes.

No person reaches maturity without regret.

No meaningful journey exists without moments of failure.

Mistakes are part of being human.

Remaining imprisoned by them does not have to be.

Healing begins when you separate your identity from your worst moments.

You can accept responsibility without accepting lifelong condemnation.

You can acknowledge poor decisions without believing you are permanently broken.

You can learn from your past without allowing it to dictate your future.

That distinction changes everything.

Because people rarely rise above the identity they believe they deserve.

If you continually see yourself as damaged beyond repair, your decisions often begin reflecting that belief.

You stop trying.

Stop believing.

Stop rebuilding.

Not because change is impossible.
Because shame convinced you it was.
But growth has always begun with a different perspective.
The understanding that your value was never determined by your lowest season.
That your future is not limited by your worst decision.
That wisdom often grows from experiences you once wished had never happened.
Every setback contains a lesson if you are willing to learn it.
Every failure carries insight if you are willing to examine it honestly.
Every difficult season has the potential to produce greater humility, compassion, resilience, and wisdom.
None of those things erase the past.
But they ensure the past is not wasted.
This does not mean pretending mistakes never happened.
Healing requires honesty.
Taking responsibility where responsibility belongs.
Making amends when possible.
Learning what needs to change.
But once the lesson has been learned, continuing to punish yourself serves no purpose.
Growth requires movement.
And shame keeps people standing still.
You are allowed to become wiser than the person who made those mistakes.
You are allowed to build healthier relationships.
Develop healthier financial habits.
Create stronger boundaries.
Make better decisions.
You are allowed to become someone your past could not yet imagine.
The strongest people are not those who never failed.
They are the people who refused to let failure become their identity.
Who chose learning over self-condemnation.
Growth over guilt.
Hope over hopelessness.
Every day you choose differently, you write a new paragraph in your story.
Every healthier decision becomes evidence that change is possible.
Every act of courage weakens the voice of shame.
Do not allow yesterday's mistakes to become tomorrow's limitations.
You are more than your hardest season.
More than your greatest regret.
More than your lowest moment.
Your past may explain part of your story.
But it never has the authority to decide how the story ends.
That choice belongs to the person you continue becoming today.

WEALTH LESSON

Healthy self-perception improves emotional resilience because shame often weakens confidence and decision-making.

AFFIRMATION

"I release shame and allow myself to grow beyond my past mistakes."

TODAY'S POWER MOVE

Forgive yourself today for one mistake you have been emotionally carrying too heavily.

DAY 224

The Way You Spend Your Time Shapes Your Future

POWER QUOTE

"Your daily routines quietly create your future life."

REFLECTION

Healing is rarely as predictable as people expect it to be.

Many begin the journey believing that once they decide to heal, every day will become a little easier than the one before.

They expect old fears to disappear.

Old habits to lose their influence.

Old pain to remain permanently in the past.

But real healing is far more human than that.

Some mornings you wake up feeling hopeful, clear, and emotionally grounded.

You notice how much stronger you've become.

You recognize your growth.

You respond to situations with wisdom that once seemed impossible.

Then, without warning, an old memory surfaces.

A familiar insecurity appears.

A difficult conversation awakens emotions you thought were gone.

In those moments, it is easy to believe that all of your progress has disappeared.

It has not.

Healing is not measured by whether difficult emotions ever return.

It is measured by your relationship with those emotions when they do.

Perhaps you no longer react as quickly.

Perhaps you recover more intentionally.

Perhaps you ask healthier questions instead of immediately criticizing yourself.

Those changes may seem small, but they represent tremendous growth.

The person you were years ago may have remained trapped inside those emotions for weeks or months.

Today, you recognize them, process them, and continue moving forward.

That is evidence that healing is working.

One of the greatest mistakes people make is expecting themselves to unlearn years of emotional conditioning in only a short period of time.

Patterns formed through childhood, relationships, disappointments, rejection, or survival do not disappear overnight.

They were repeated for years.

Healing requires replacing those old responses with healthier ones, one decision at a time.

Every time you choose honesty over avoidance, you weaken an old pattern.

Every time you communicate instead of shutting down, you strengthen a new one.

Every time you respond with patience instead of impulsiveness, you reinforce the person you are becoming.

Transformation happens through repetition.

Not perfection.

This is why patience is one of the greatest companions to healing.

Patience reminds you that growth cannot be rushed.

It allows you to appreciate progress without demanding instant perfection.

It gives you permission to become rather than expecting yourself to arrive immediately.

Many people spend so much time focusing on how much further they want to go that they completely overlook how far they have already come.

You may still have moments of fear.

But perhaps you no longer allow fear to make every decision.

You may still experience difficult emotions.

But they no longer control your entire life.

You may still face setbacks.

But now you recover instead of remaining defeated.

Those victories deserve acknowledgment.

Healing is not about becoming someone who never struggles.

It is about becoming someone who knows how to navigate struggle with greater wisdom, greater self-awareness, and greater compassion.

The strongest people are not those who never revisit painful emotions.

They are the ones who continue choosing growth every time life invites them to return to old patterns.

Do not become discouraged because the journey feels slower than expected.

The deepest transformations often happen quietly.

Long before anyone else notices them.

Sometimes even before you notice them yourself.

Trust the work you are doing.

Honor every healthier choice.

Celebrate every moment you refuse to become the person your pain once convinced you to be.

Because healing is not a destination you reach one day.

It is a lifelong commitment to becoming more emotionally free, more self-aware, and more aligned with the life you were created to live.

And every time you choose that path, even after a difficult day, you are proving that healing is already happening.

WEALTH LESSON

Daily habits compound into long-term emotional, financial, and personal outcomes.

AFFIRMATION

"I spend my time intentionally because my future matters deeply."

TODAY'S POWER MOVE

Audit how you spent your time today and identify one improvement you can make tomorrow.

DAY 225

Your Healing Deserves Patience

POWER QUOTE

"Not every emotional wound heals quickly, and that is okay."

REFLECTION

Healing rarely unfolds in the straight line people hope it will.

Many expect that once they begin working on themselves, every day will feel lighter than the last.

The anxiety will disappear.

The painful memories will stop resurfacing.

Old habits will lose their influence overnight.

But healing is rarely that predictable.

Some days you feel emotionally strong.

You respond with wisdom instead of impulse.

You notice how much calmer you have become.

You begin believing that a new chapter has truly started.

Then an unexpected conversation, a familiar place, or an old memory stirs emotions you thought were long behind you.

In those moments, it is easy to question everything.

You wonder if you've made any progress at all.

You wonder if you are simply returning to the person you used to be.

But healing is not the absence of difficult emotions.

It is the ability to meet those emotions differently than before.

The fact that sadness visits you does not mean it controls you.

The fact that fear appears does not mean it gets to make your decisions.

The fact that old wounds still ache occasionally does not mean they remain open.

Often, they are simply reminding you how far you have already come.

Consider how people recover after a physical injury.

There are days when strength returns quickly.

Other days the body feels sore again.

That temporary discomfort does not erase months of recovery.

It is simply part of the process.

Emotional healing follows a similar pattern.

There are breakthroughs.

There are quieter seasons.

There are moments when progress is obvious.

There are moments when growth is happening beneath the surface, even though you cannot yet feel it.

One of the greatest gifts you can give yourself during this journey is patience.

Not passive patience that waits without effort.

But active patience that continues showing up.

That continues practicing healthier habits.

That continues choosing honesty over avoidance.

That continues believing that change is taking place even when the evidence feels small.
Many of the emotional patterns you are changing were repeated for years.
Some developed during childhood.
Others formed through painful relationships, financial hardship, disappointment, or prolonged stress.
Those patterns became familiar through repetition.
New patterns are built the same way.
One healthier response at a time.
Every moment you pause before reacting strengthens emotional maturity.
Every honest conversation strengthens trust.
Every healthy boundary reinforces self-respect.
Every decision to care for yourself instead of abandoning yourself creates a new direction for your life.
These victories may seem ordinary.
Yet they quietly reshape your identity.
Do not measure your healing by whether difficult days still exist.
Measure it by the person you are becoming through them.
Are you more self-aware than before?
Do you recover more quickly?
Do you speak to yourself with greater compassion?
Do you recognize unhealthy patterns sooner?
Those are powerful signs of transformation.
Remember, the goal was never to become someone who never struggles.
The goal is to become someone who no longer allows struggle to define their identity or determine their future.
So be patient with yourself.
Honor the work that is taking place beneath the surface.
Trust that every intentional choice is strengthening a healthier foundation.
Because healing is not a race toward perfection.
It is the lifelong practice of becoming more emotionally free, more resilient, and more aligned with the life you were created to live.
And even on the days when progress feels slow, remember this:
You are still moving forward.
Sometimes the deepest healing is happening in ways you cannot yet see.

WEALTH LESSON

Emotional healing improves discipline and long-term stability because peaceful minds make healthier decisions.

AFFIRMATION

"I allow myself to heal patiently and intentionally."

TODAY'S POWER MOVE

Speak to yourself with compassion today instead of harsh criticism.

DAY 226

Stop Seeking Constant Validation

POWER QUOTE

"Confidence becomes unstable when it depends entirely on approval from others."

REFLECTION

Every human being appreciates encouragement.

Kind words.

Recognition.

Support.

There is nothing wrong with feeling grateful when others believe in you.

The problem begins when your confidence depends entirely on whether other people approve of you.

Because approval is unpredictable.

Some people will celebrate your growth.

Others will misunderstand it.

Some will encourage your dreams.

Others will question them.

Some will applaud your success.

Others may ignore it completely.

If your self-worth rises and falls with other people's opinions, your emotional stability will always remain fragile.

You will feel confident when people praise you.

You will question yourself when they don't.

That is an exhausting way to live.

Many people spend years trying to earn validation they were never meant to depend upon.

They constantly seek reassurance.

They compare themselves to others.

They measure their value by likes, compliments, promotions, or acceptance.

Without realizing it, they slowly hand their identity to people who were never meant to define it.

Healthy confidence grows differently.

It is built from the inside out.

It develops through integrity.

Through keeping promises to yourself.

Through living according to your values even when no one is watching.

Every time you choose discipline over convenience, you strengthen self-respect.

Every time you honor your boundaries, you reinforce your worth.

Every time you recover from disappointment without abandoning yourself, you build trust within yourself.

Confidence is not created by hearing, "You're enough," a thousand times.

It grows when your daily actions begin providing evidence that you can depend on yourself.

You become someone who follows through.

Someone who acts with honesty.

Someone who continues learning after failure.

Someone who remains faithful to their purpose even when recognition is delayed.

That kind of confidence is difficult to shake because it is no longer dependent on applause.
It is rooted in character.
Many of history's greatest achievements were accomplished long before anyone else believed they were possible.
Every meaningful vision experiences seasons where support is limited.
Where progress is invisible.
Where encouragement is scarce.
If you require universal approval before taking action, many of your greatest opportunities will remain untouched.
Sometimes you must believe in the work before anyone else sees its value.
Sometimes you must continue building quietly while the results are still hidden.
That is not arrogance.
It is conviction.
There is a difference between confidence and pride.
Pride seeks to prove its worth to others.
Confidence quietly knows its values and continues living them.
Pride depends on comparison.
Confidence depends on character.
Pride craves attention.
Confidence values alignment.
As your confidence becomes healthier, you also become freer.
Free to say no without guilt.
Free to pursue your purpose without constant explanation.
Free to accept criticism without allowing it to define your identity.
Free to celebrate others without feeling threatened by their success.
That freedom is one of the greatest gifts emotional maturity can provide.
You no longer spend your life chasing approval.
You spend it becoming the kind of person you respect.
Allow encouragement to inspire you.
Allow wise counsel to strengthen you.
But never place your identity in the hands of opinions that change with circumstances.
Your value does not increase because someone applauds you.
And it does not decrease because someone overlooks you.
Build a life that is anchored in integrity rather than recognition.
Develop confidence that comes from the promises you keep, the character you build, and the person you choose to become every day.
Because the strongest self-worth is not borrowed from other people's approval.
It is built quietly, consistently, and faithfully from within.
And once that foundation is established, you no longer need the world to constantly remind you of your value.
You already know it.

WEALTH LESSON

Emotional independence strengthens decision-making because people stop relying entirely on external approval.

AFFIRMATION

"I validate myself through discipline, self-respect, and intentional growth."

TODAY'S POWER MOVE

Make one decision today based on your values instead of other people's opinions.

DAY 227

You Are Strong Enough To Rebuild

POWER QUOTE

"Starting over does not erase your strength."

REFLECTION

Very few people build the life they dream of without first rebuilding parts of the life they already had.

Rebuilding is one of the most overlooked seasons of personal growth.

No one celebrates it.

No one applauds the quiet work.

Yet it is often during rebuilding that the strongest foundations are created.

Life has a way of interrupting the plans we thought would unfold smoothly.

A relationship ends unexpectedly.

A financial setback changes everything.

A dream takes longer than expected.

Confidence is shaken.

Peace feels distant.

In those moments, it can feel as though everything has been lost.

But rebuilding is not the same as starting from nothing.

You are not beginning with empty hands.

You are beginning with experience.

With lessons you did not have before.

With wisdom that hardship provided.

With resilience that comfort could never teach.

That changes everything.

The person rebuilding today is not the same person who first began the journey.

You know more.

You see more clearly.

You recognize unhealthy patterns more quickly.

You understand the importance of discipline, patience, and healthy boundaries in ways you may not have understood before.

Those lessons become part of the new foundation.

Many people become discouraged because rebuilding feels slower than building the first time.

This is often because they are no longer simply creating something new.

They are also removing what no longer serves them.

Old beliefs.

Old habits.

Old fears.

Old ways of thinking.

Strong foundations require careful work.

You cannot build lasting stability on ground that has never been strengthened.

Sometimes life exposes weak foundations not to punish you, but to give you the opportunity to rebuild them properly.

That process requires courage.

It is easier to quit than to rebuild.

It is easier to accept defeat than to believe something better can still be created.

Yet history is filled with people whose greatest achievements came after seasons of rebuilding.

Not because they avoided hardship.

Because they refused to allow hardship to have the final word.

Resilience is not measured by how little pain you experience.

It is measured by your willingness to continue despite it.

Every time you choose to try again, you strengthen that resilience.

Every time you learn instead of surrendering to discouragement, you strengthen that resilience.

Every time you refuse to let one difficult chapter define your entire story, you strengthen that resilience.

Rebuilding also changes perspective.

You begin valuing things you once overlooked.

Peace becomes more meaningful.

Financial stability becomes more intentional.

Healthy relationships become more precious.

Character becomes more important than appearance.

You stop chasing quick victories and begin investing in lasting ones.

This is one of the hidden gifts of rebuilding.

It teaches you to value foundations more than shortcuts.

Do not mistake a rebuilding season for a defeated season.

Some of the greatest transformations happen when life slows you down long enough to rebuild what truly matters.

Your confidence can be rebuilt.

Your finances can be rebuilt.

Your peace can be rebuilt.

Your relationships can be rebuilt.

Your future can be rebuilt.

Not overnight.

But one intentional decision at a time.

Brick by brick.

Habit by habit.

Choice by choice.

There may be days when the work feels invisible.

Days when progress feels painfully slow.

Keep building anyway.

Every healthy decision is another stone in the foundation.

Every disciplined action strengthens the structure.

Every lesson learned makes the next step wiser than the last.

One day, you may look back with gratitude for the season you once wanted to escape.

Not because it was easy.

But because it taught you how to build a life that was stronger, wiser, and more stable than the one you almost settled for.

Rebuilding is not proof that you failed.

It is proof that you still believe your future is worth the work.

And that belief is where every meaningful new beginning truly starts.

WEALTH LESSON

Resilience creates long-term opportunity because rebuilding often produces stronger future outcomes.

AFFIRMATION

"I trust myself to rebuild stronger, wiser, and healthier than before."

TODAY'S POWER MOVE

Take one small action today that supports rebuilding an important area of your life.

DAY 228

Peace Requires Intentional Choices

POWER QUOTE

"A peaceful life is built through repeated intentional decisions."

REFLECTION

Many people spend years searching for peace as though it is something they might accidentally discover one day.

They tell themselves,

"I'll have peace when life slows down."

"I'll have peace when I earn more money."

"I'll have peace when my problems disappear."

But peace rarely arrives because circumstances become perfect.

It is usually built long before life feels easy.

Peace is created through decisions.

Through boundaries that protect your emotional health.

Through discipline that keeps your life from drifting into chaos.

Through healing that frees you from carrying yesterday's pain into today's decisions.

Through preparation that reduces unnecessary stress before it becomes overwhelming.

These choices may not always seem significant.

Yet together they create a life that feels different.

We often believe peace is simply the absence of conflict.

In reality, peace is much deeper than that.

Peace is the confidence that you can remain grounded even when life becomes uncertain.

It is knowing that your emotions do not have to control every decision.

It is trusting the systems you have built, the boundaries you have established, and the character you continue developing.

This is why peaceful people often appear intentional.

They understand that emotional health requires maintenance.

Just as a home requires regular care, your inner life requires regular attention.

Neglected emotions do not disappear.

Neglected boundaries eventually become resentment.

Neglected relationships slowly lose trust.

Neglected habits quietly weaken discipline.

Peace is protected through daily stewardship.

The people who experience lasting peace are rarely those with the fewest responsibilities.

Often, they are the people who have learned how to manage those responsibilities wisely.

They become selective about what they allow into their minds.

They protect their time from unnecessary distractions.

They invest in relationships that encourage honesty, growth, and mutual respect.

They recognize that every "yes" carries a cost, so they choose carefully.

This does not mean they avoid every challenge.

Peace is not the absence of difficulty.

Life will still include disappointment.

Unexpected change.

Loss.

Pressure.

Moments that test your patience and resilience.

The difference is that a peaceful person is no longer emotionally controlled by every circumstance.

They have developed an inner stability that helps them respond thoughtfully instead of reacting impulsively.

That stability is built over time.

One healthy routine at a time.

One honest conversation at a time.

One forgiven offense.

One wise financial decision.

One protected boundary.

One intentional day after another.

Many people work tirelessly to build lives that look successful from the outside.

They pursue promotions.

Recognition.

Influence.

Achievement.

Yet they rarely pause to ask an equally important question:

"Will the life I am building actually feel peaceful when I arrive there?"

Because success without peace often becomes another form of exhaustion.

Achievement without emotional health becomes difficult to enjoy.

The healthiest future is one where accomplishment and inner stability grow together.

A life where your calendar reflects your values.

Your relationships reflect your character.

Your habits reflect your priorities.

And your inner world reflects the peace you have intentionally cultivated.

Do not wait for peace to find you.

Build it.

Protect it.

Strengthen it.

Choose it repeatedly through the decisions you make each day.

Because your future deserves more than a life that merely looks successful.

It deserves a life that feels whole.

A life where clarity replaces confusion.

Where stability replaces constant survival.

Where calmness becomes familiar instead of rare.

That kind of peace is not accidental.

It is the quiet reward of intentional living, practiced faithfully one day at a time.

WEALTH LESSON

Peace improves long-term execution because emotionally stable people think more clearly and build more intentionally.

AFFIRMATION

"I intentionally build a peaceful and emotionally healthy life."

TODAY'S POWER MOVE

Choose one decision today that protects your peace long-term.

DAY 229

Your Future Requires Courage

POWER QUOTE

"Fear loses power every time you continue moving anyway."

REFLECTION

Fear has stopped more dreams than failure ever has.

Not because fear is stronger than people's potential.

But because it is persuasive.

It quietly whispers reasons to wait.

Reasons to delay.

Reasons to stay where life feels familiar.

It tells people they need more certainty.

More confidence.

More preparation.

A little more time.

And while those excuses often sound reasonable, they usually have the same outcome.

Nothing changes.

Many people imagine courageous individuals as people who never experience fear.

But courage has never required the absence of fear.

Fear is a natural response to uncertainty.

To new opportunities.

To unfamiliar challenges.

To stepping beyond what feels comfortable.

The difference is that courageous people refuse to give fear the final vote.

They acknowledge it.

They respect it.

But they do not surrender their future to it.

Fear often disguises itself in subtle ways.

Sometimes it appears as perfectionism.

The belief that everything must be flawless before you begin.

Sometimes it appears as endless preparation.

Always learning.

Always planning.

Never starting.

Sometimes it appears as comparison.

Watching other people instead of building your own life.

Sometimes it appears as waiting for confidence that only action can create.

Without realizing it, years can pass while fear quietly remains in control.

The tragedy is not that fear exists.

The tragedy is allowing fear to make decisions that belong to your purpose.

Every meaningful life includes uncertainty.

No one receives complete guarantees before pursuing a dream.
No entrepreneur knows every challenge they will face.
No leader begins with perfect confidence.
No relationship comes with absolute certainty.
Life asks each of us to move before we can see the entire path.
That can feel uncomfortable.
But discomfort is often the price of growth.
Every courageous decision expands what you believe is possible.
The first difficult conversation makes the second one easier.
The first public step makes future visibility less intimidating.
The first financial risk teaches lessons that planning alone never could.
Every act of courage becomes evidence that fear is not as powerful as it once seemed.
That evidence matters.
Because confidence is built through experience.
Each time you move despite uncertainty, you teach yourself something valuable.
"I can handle difficult things."
"I can adapt."
"I can recover if things don't go perfectly."
That quiet confidence becomes stronger than fear over time.
This does not mean every decision will produce immediate success.
Some attempts will fail.
Some plans will need adjustment.
Some seasons will be harder than expected.
But failure often teaches far more than hesitation ever will.
People who act gain experience.
People who only wait gain more reasons to remain afraid.
Your future will always require decisions that your present comfort would rather avoid.
There will be moments when your purpose asks you to become visible.
To speak.
To lead.
To invest.
To trust.
To begin again.
Those moments will rarely arrive without fear standing nearby.
Do not mistake fear for a stop sign.
Often it is simply standing at the entrance of something that matters.
The question is not whether fear will appear.
It almost certainly will.
The question is whether you will continue allowing it to determine the direction of your life.
You were not created to spend your life negotiating with every fear that appears.
You were created to grow beyond them.

One decision at a time.

One courageous conversation.

One faithful step.

One opportunity accepted despite uncertainty.

Because courage is not a single extraordinary moment.

It is a habit.

A way of living.

A commitment to choosing purpose over comfort again and again.

And one day, you may discover that the life you once believed required extraordinary bravery was actually built through hundreds of ordinary moments where you simply refused to let fear make the decision for you.

WEALTH LESSON

Courage creates opportunities because growth often requires stepping beyond emotional comfort zones.

AFFIRMATION

"I continue moving forward even when fear tries to discourage me."

TODAY'S POWER MOVE

Do one thing today that fear has been convincing you to avoid.

DAY 230

Your Discipline Is Building Legacy

POWER QUOTE

"The habits you build today may change generations after you."

REFLECTION

Most people think of legacy as something they leave behind at the end of their lives.

A business.

A home.

An inheritance.

A name people remember.

While those things can certainly become part of a person's legacy, the greatest legacy is often much quieter.

It is found in the lives you influence every single day.

Legacy begins long before anyone writes your story.

It begins with the decisions you make when no one is watching.

The habits you practice.

The values you protect.

The character you develop.

The way you treat people.

The example you consistently live.

Every decision reaches further than you may realize.

When you choose discipline over convenience, you are teaching yourself that your future matters.

When you choose healing instead of allowing old wounds to control your behavior, you reduce the likelihood of passing those same patterns to the people you love.

When you become financially responsible, you create opportunities that may benefit your family long after today's challenges have passed.

When you develop emotional maturity, you help create relationships where trust, respect, and stability can flourish.

Growth is never entirely personal.

It always influences someone else.

Whether you realize it or not, people are learning from the way you live.

Children learn from what they observe more than what they are told.

Friends notice consistency.

Coworkers notice integrity.

Family members notice how you respond during difficult seasons.

Your example often speaks louder than your advice.

This is why your private life matters.

The habits no one applauds.

The promises you keep.

The difficult conversations you choose to have.

The discipline you maintain when there is no recognition.

Those moments are quietly shaping the kind of legacy you are creating.

Many people hope to leave behind wealth.
Wealth can certainly be a blessing.
But financial inheritance without wisdom is often temporary.
Character, discipline, emotional health, and integrity are forms of wealth that continue multiplying across generations.
A family can inherit more than money.
It can inherit healthy communication.
Resilience.
Strong work ethic.
Generosity.
Emotional security.
Wise financial habits.
These gifts often influence lives for decades.
That is why your personal growth carries so much significance.
You are not only becoming a healthier person.
You are creating healthier environments for the people who will share life with you.
Every time you choose patience instead of anger, you change the atmosphere around you.
Every time you choose honesty instead of avoidance, you strengthen trust.
Every time you choose responsibility instead of excuses, you make it easier for others to believe that change is possible.
Legacy is rarely built through one extraordinary achievement.
It is built through thousands of ordinary decisions repeated consistently over time.
One act of integrity.
One disciplined habit.
One healed relationship.
One wise financial choice.
One compassionate response.
These moments may seem small.
Yet together they become the foundation of a life that continues influencing others long after the moment has passed.
Do not underestimate the importance of the life you are building today.
Your future family may benefit from the healing you choose now.
Your future relationships may be strengthened by the emotional maturity you develop today.
Your future opportunities may exist because of the discipline you practice while no one is watching.
The seeds you plant today often become the harvest someone else enjoys tomorrow.
That is the power of legacy.
So live intentionally.
Heal completely.
Build wisely.
Lead with integrity.

Not only because your own future depends on it, but because someone else's future may one day be strengthened by the choices you are making right now.

The greatest legacy is not simply leaving people with more possessions.

It is leaving them with a better example of how to live, love, lead, and build a life of lasting purpose.

WEALTH LESSON

Long-term wealth includes emotional health, discipline, wisdom, and the environments created for future generations.

AFFIRMATION

"I build a legacy rooted in healing, discipline, peace, and intentional growth."

TODAY'S POWER MOVE

Make one decision today that your future self and future generations would benefit from long-term.

DAY 231

Your Future Requires Self-Control

POWER QUOTE

"Freedom grows when self-control becomes stronger than temporary emotion."

REFLECTION

Every person experiences impulses.

The impulse to spend money that should be saved.

The impulse to avoid a difficult conversation.

The impulse to procrastinate on an important responsibility.

The impulse to react emotionally instead of responding thoughtfully.

These moments are part of being human.

The question is not whether impulses will appear.

The question is whether they will become the foundation of your decisions.

Many people unknowingly build their lives around temporary feelings.

They spend because the purchase feels good in the moment.

They postpone important work because discomfort feels unpleasant.

They speak from anger because the emotion demands immediate expression.

For a brief moment, those choices may provide relief.

But temporary relief often creates long-term consequences.

The bill eventually arrives.

The opportunity passes.

The relationship becomes strained.

The habit becomes stronger.

This is why self-control is one of the most valuable forms of personal freedom.

Contrary to what many believe, self-control is not about restricting your life.

It is about protecting it.

It protects your peace from unnecessary chaos.

It protects your finances from impulsive decisions.

It protects your relationships from words spoken without wisdom.

It protects your future from choices that satisfy the present while harming tomorrow.

Every meaningful goal eventually requires self-control.

Financial stability requires saying no to purchases that conflict with your priorities.

Healthy relationships require choosing understanding over impulsive reactions.

Personal growth requires showing up when motivation fades.

Leadership requires responding with wisdom when emotions run high.

These decisions are rarely glamorous.

Most happen quietly.

No audience applauds when you choose patience instead of anger.

No headlines celebrate the day you decide to save instead of spend.

No one notices the moments you resist distraction so you can remain focused on your purpose.

Yet those unseen decisions quietly shape your entire life.

Many people think freedom means doing whatever they feel like doing.

Real freedom is much deeper.

Real freedom is having the ability to choose what is right, even when something else feels easier.

It is refusing to become a prisoner of every passing emotion.

Every time you practice self-control, you strengthen your ability to lead yourself.

You prove that your emotions do not have to dictate your future.

You build trust in your own character.

You begin seeing yourself as someone who can be depended upon.

That confidence grows because your actions consistently align with your values.

This does not mean you will always make the perfect decision.

Everyone has moments of weakness.

Everyone makes mistakes.

The goal is not perfection.

The goal is progress.

Every wise decision strengthens the habit of wisdom.

Every disciplined choice makes the next disciplined choice a little easier.

Over time, what once required tremendous effort begins to feel more natural.

That is how character is formed.

Not through one extraordinary act of discipline.

But through thousands of ordinary moments where you quietly choose your future over your feelings.

Your future deserves that kind of leadership.

It deserves choices made with clarity instead of impulse.

It deserves habits that create stability instead of regret.

It deserves a life directed by purpose rather than temporary emotion.

Every decision you make is casting a vote for the person you are becoming.

Choose the habits that strengthen your future.

Choose the responses that protect your peace.

Choose the discipline that creates lasting freedom.

Because a meaningful life is rarely built by people who follow every impulse.

It is built by people who repeatedly choose what matters most, even when it is not the easiest choice.

And one day, you will look back and realize that the greatest victories in your life were not won in dramatic moments.

They were won in the quiet decisions where you chose lasting purpose over temporary comfort.

WEALTH LESSON

Self-control strengthens financial stability because intentional decisions protect long-term goals.

AFFIRMATION

"I choose intentional discipline over temporary emotional impulses."

TODAY'S POWER MOVE

Pause before making emotional decisions today and ask whether they align with your long-term future.

DAY 232

Stop Calling Yourself Broken

POWER QUOTE

"Healing people are not broken people."

REFLECTION

One of the greatest lies pain can convince a person to believe is that they have been permanently damaged by what they have experienced.

After enough disappointment, people begin speaking about themselves differently.

"I'm too broken."

"I'll never change."

"I'm too far behind."

"I've made too many mistakes."

Over time, those statements stop sounding like temporary emotions.

They begin sounding like permanent identities.

That is the danger of unchallenged pain.

It quietly changes the way people see themselves.

Instead of recognizing that they experienced hardship, they begin believing hardship defines who they are.

But struggling does not make you broken.

Being hurt does not make you worthless.

Feeling overwhelmed does not make you weak.

It makes you human.

Every person carries experiences that have tested them.

Every person has moments they wish had unfolded differently.

Every life contains seasons of confusion, disappointment, grief, uncertainty, or failure.

Those experiences are part of being alive.

They are not evidence that your value has disappeared.

Too often, people confuse having wounds with being beyond healing.

Yet a wound is not a life sentence.

It is an invitation to care for what has been hurting.

Imagine breaking a bone.

No one expects it to heal by pretending the injury never happened.

Healing requires attention.

Time.

Care.

Patience.

The same is true emotionally.

Ignoring pain rarely removes it.

Shaming yourself for having it rarely strengthens you.

Real healing begins when you become honest enough to acknowledge what needs care without allowing it to define your identity.

There is tremendous courage in deciding that your pain will not have the final word.

That despite everything you have experienced, you will continue learning.

Continue growing.

Continue rebuilding.

Not because the journey is easy.

Because your future is worth the effort.

We often believe strength means never struggling.

In reality, strength is often revealed in what people choose after they struggle.

Do they remain trapped by hopelessness?

Or do they slowly begin rebuilding, one decision at a time?

The strongest people are rarely those who avoided hardship.

They are often the people who walked through it without allowing it to permanently harden their hearts.

Who learned compassion because they had experienced pain.

Who developed wisdom because they had made mistakes.

Who became resilient because life required them to stand up more than once.

Healing is not evidence that you failed.

It is evidence that you refused to give up on yourself.

Every counseling session.

Every honest conversation.

Every healthy boundary.

Every difficult apology.

Every intentional habit.

Every small decision to become healthier is proof that you are investing in the person you are becoming.

That deserves respect.

Not shame.

Do not allow your hardest season to become the lens through which you view your entire life.

You are more than the chapter where you struggled.

More than the relationship that hurt you.

More than the financial mistake you made.

More than the fear you are still learning to overcome.

Those experiences may have shaped you.

But they were never meant to imprison you.

One day, someone may find hope because they see how you rebuilt your life with honesty, humility, and perseverance.

Your healing may become permission for someone else to begin their own.

So be patient with yourself.

Speak to yourself with truth instead of condemnation.

Give your wounds the care they deserve instead of the shame they were never meant to carry.

Because your future is not waiting for a perfect version of you.

It is waiting for the version of you that chooses, day after day, to keep healing, keep growing, and keep believing that what happened to you will never have the authority to decide who you become.

That decision belongs to you.

WEALTH LESSON

Self-compassion improves emotional resilience because shame often weakens confidence and discipline.

AFFIRMATION

"I allow myself to heal without labeling myself as broken."

TODAY'S POWER MOVE

Speak to yourself today with patience, respect, and emotional compassion.

DAY 233

Discipline Creates Confidence

POWER QUOTE

"Confidence grows through repeated evidence that you can trust yourself."

REFLECTION

Society often teaches confidence is something they must possess before they begin.

They wait until they feel ready.

Certain.

Fearless.

Completely capable.

Only then, they believe, will they finally pursue their goals.

But confidence rarely works that way.

Confidence is usually the result of action, not the requirement for it.

Think about any skill you have developed in your life.

You were probably not confident the first time you tried it.

You learned through repetition.

You improved through experience.

You became more capable because you kept showing up.

Confidence grew alongside your commitment.

The same principle applies to nearly every area of life.

No one begins as an experienced leader.

A confident speaker.

A disciplined investor.

A healthy communicator.

People become those things by practicing them.

One decision at a time.

Many individuals unknowingly weaken their own confidence because they repeatedly abandon themselves.

They promise they will wake up early.

Then they ignore the alarm.

They promise they will save money.

Then they spend impulsively.

They promise they will begin healing.

Then they return to the same patterns that keep them stuck.

Over time, something subtle begins to happen.

They stop trusting their own words.

Every broken promise becomes another reason to doubt themselves.

Eventually, the greatest disappointment is no longer what other people failed to do.

It is what they have repeatedly failed to do for themselves.

This is why self-trust matters so deeply.

Confidence is built when your actions consistently reinforce your intentions.

Every time you keep a promise to yourself, you strengthen your belief that you are dependable.

Every time you finish what you started, you create evidence that you can be trusted.

Every time you continue despite fear, you prove that courage is becoming part of your identity.

These moments may seem ordinary.

But together they become the foundation of lasting confidence.

Many people search for confidence through external validation.

Compliments.

Recognition.

Approval.

Success.

While encouragement can be valuable, confidence built only on outside opinions remains fragile.

The strongest confidence is built internally.

It comes from quietly knowing that you will show up even when no one is watching.

That you will remain disciplined even when motivation disappears.

That you will honor your values even when compromise would be easier.

That confidence cannot be given to you.

It must be earned through consistency.

This does not require perfection.

You will still have difficult days.

You will still make mistakes.

You will still experience setbacks.

The goal is not flawless execution.

The goal is becoming someone who returns after falling.

Someone who keeps rebuilding.

Someone who refuses to let one bad day become a permanent identity.

Every time you begin again, you strengthen resilience.

Every time you choose responsibility over excuses, you deepen self-respect.

Every time you follow through despite discomfort, you reinforce the belief that you can rely on yourself.

That belief changes everything.

Because once you truly trust yourself, you stop depending entirely on motivation.

You stop waiting for the perfect mood.

You stop allowing fear to make every important decision.

You begin acting from commitment instead of emotion.

That is where lasting confidence is born.

Not in dramatic breakthroughs.

But in quiet faithfulness.

In the repeated decisions that no one else may ever see.

So keep your promises to yourself.

Finish what you begin.

Honor the standards you have set.

Show up, especially on the days when it feels difficult.

Because every disciplined choice is teaching you something powerful:

"I can depend on myself."

And there are few realizations more life-changing than that.

The confidence you are looking for is not waiting for you somewhere in the future.

It is being built today, every time your actions become consistent with the person you are choosing to become.

WEALTH LESSON

Consistency strengthens confidence because repeated disciplined behavior creates self-trust over time.

AFFIRMATION

"I build confidence through consistency and disciplined action."

TODAY'S POWER MOVE

Complete one responsibility today without procrastinating emotionally.

DAY 234

Your Mind Needs Protection Too

POWER QUOTE

"Your thoughts shape the emotional environment you live inside daily."

REFLECTION

Every person lives in two environments.

The world around them.

And the world inside their mind.

Most people spend significant time improving their external environment.

They organize their homes.

Plan their finances.

Build their careers.

Strengthen their relationships.

Yet many rarely pause to consider the environment they are creating within themselves.

The thoughts you repeatedly entertain become the atmosphere in which you live every day.

If that atmosphere is filled with constant criticism, fear, hopelessness, and comparison, it becomes difficult to experience confidence, peace, or clarity.

No one can thrive for long inside a mind that is constantly attacking itself.

This is why mental discipline matters.

Not because every negative thought can be eliminated.

But because every thought does not deserve to become a permanent belief.

Everyone experiences fear.

Everyone experiences doubt.

Everyone has moments when insecurity tries to shape the way they see themselves.

The difference is that emotionally healthy people learn not to accept every thought as truth.

They pause.

They question it.

They ask whether the thought is helping them grow or quietly keeping them trapped.

Many people unknowingly repeat the same limiting messages for years.

"I'm always behind."

"I'll never be disciplined."

"Nothing ever works for me."

"I'll probably fail again."

Repeated often enough, those thoughts begin influencing behavior.

A person who believes they will fail may stop trying.

A person who believes they are incapable may avoid opportunities that could change their life.

A person who constantly criticizes themselves often struggles to celebrate the progress they have already made.

Over time, thinking becomes identity.

And identity begins directing behavior.

The encouraging truth is that your mind can also become a place where healthier beliefs are strengthened.

Not through pretending problems do not exist.

But through choosing thoughts that are honest, constructive, and rooted in possibility.

Instead of asking,

"Why do I always fail?"

You begin asking,

"What can I learn from this?"

Instead of repeating,

"I'll never change,"

You remind yourself,

"Growth takes practice, and I am still becoming."

Those small shifts matter.

Because the conversations you have with yourself are often the longest conversations you will ever have.

Mental discipline also includes being intentional about what you allow into your mind.

The books you read.

The conversations you entertain.

The content you consume.

The voices you listen to most often.

Everything you repeatedly expose yourself to leaves an impression.

Just as healthy food strengthens the body, healthy influences strengthen the mind.

Likewise, constant negativity eventually affects perspective.

This does not mean avoiding reality.

Life includes hardship.

Disappointment.

Loss.

Challenge.

Mental discipline is not denying those experiences.

It is refusing to let them become the only story your mind tells.

You can acknowledge pain while still believing in hope.

Recognize difficulty while still pursuing growth.

Accept today's reality while continuing to build tomorrow's future.

That balance creates resilience.

The strongest minds are not those that never experience negative thoughts.

They are the minds that repeatedly return to truth, wisdom, and purpose.

One intentional thought at a time.

One healthy perspective at a time.

One disciplined decision after another.

Your inner world is shaping your outer world every single day.

The way you think influences the way you speak.

The way you speak influences the way you act.

The way you act becomes the habits that shape your life.

Protect your mind with the same care you would protect your future.

Because, in many ways, they are the same thing.

The life you eventually build will first be influenced by the environment you choose to cultivate within yourself. So fill your mind with thoughts that strengthen your character, expand your hope, reinforce your purpose, and remind you that becoming a healthier person always begins from the inside out.

WEALTH LESSON

Healthy thinking improves long-term emotional regulation and intentional decision-making.

AFFIRMATION

"I protect my mind and intentionally feed it healthier thoughts."

TODAY'S POWER MOVE

Notice and interrupt one unhealthy thought pattern today.

DAY 235

Stop Romanticizing Emotional Chaos

POWER QUOTE

"Peace is healthier than constantly surviving emotional instability."

REFLECTION

Not everyone grows up believing peace is normal.

For some people, life was filled with constant tension.

Arguments that never seemed to end.

Unpredictable relationships.

Financial instability.

Emotional highs followed by painful lows.

Over time, chaos became familiar.

And what becomes familiar often begins to feel normal.

This is why healing can sometimes feel surprisingly uncomfortable.

When life finally becomes calm, some people instinctively wait for something to go wrong.

They become suspicious of quiet seasons.

They mistake stability for boredom.

They search for problems that do not yet exist.

Not because they want chaos.

But because chaos is what they learned to expect.

The human mind often becomes accustomed to familiar patterns, even unhealthy ones.

If your nervous system has spent years preparing for conflict, peace can initially feel unfamiliar.

If you have lived in survival mode, slowing down may feel unsafe.

That does not mean something is wrong with peace.

It means your mind is learning a new way to live.

Healing is not only learning how to recover from pain.

It is learning how to remain present when life is finally calm.

It is allowing yourself to enjoy healthy relationships without expecting betrayal.

Managing your finances without assuming disaster is around the corner.

Experiencing quiet moments without feeling guilty for resting.

Trusting that not every season has to be a crisis.

This kind of healing takes patience.

You are teaching your mind and body that stability is not something to fear.

That calmness does not mean life has lost its purpose.

In fact, peace often creates the space where your greatest growth can happen.

When your mind is no longer consumed by constant survival, it can begin creating.

Learning.

Planning.

Building.

Loving.

Serving.

Energy that was once spent managing chaos becomes available for the future you want to build.

This is one reason emotional stability is so valuable.

A peaceful mind thinks more clearly.

A regulated heart communicates more wisely.

A steady life makes better long-term decisions.

Many of the goals people pursue—healthy relationships, financial stability, meaningful work, strong families—are easier to sustain when they are built from a place of emotional stability rather than constant emotional exhaustion.

That is why peace is not passive.

It is an active practice.

It requires protecting your boundaries.

Choosing healthy environments.

Managing your thoughts.

Being intentional about the relationships you cultivate.

Returning to healthy routines even when old patterns try to pull you backward.

Every time you choose calm over unnecessary chaos, you reinforce a new way of living.

Every time you refuse to create drama where none exists, you strengthen emotional maturity.

Every time you allow yourself to enjoy stability instead of questioning it, you teach yourself that peace is safe.

This does not mean life will never become difficult again.

Every life includes unexpected challenges.

Disappointment.

Loss.

Change.

But those experiences no longer have to define the atmosphere in which you live.

You can face difficult seasons without returning to a lifestyle of constant emotional turmoil.

That is one of the greatest gifts healing offers.

A peaceful life is not a small life.

It is not a boring life.

It is not a life lacking passion or purpose.

It is a life where your energy is no longer consumed by unnecessary chaos.

A life where clarity replaces confusion.

Where wisdom replaces impulsiveness.

Where stability becomes a foundation instead of a distant hope.

So do not mistake peace for emptiness.

Do not mistake calmness for weakness.

Allow yourself to become familiar with stability.

Allow yourself to believe that joy does not always have to be followed by disaster.

Allow yourself to experience a life that feels safe to live.

Because one of the greatest signs of healing is not simply surviving chaos.

It is finally discovering that peace can become your new normal.

WEALTH LESSON

Emotional peace improves long-term decision-making because stable minds think more clearly than overwhelmed ones.

AFFIRMATION

"I choose peace, stability, and emotional balance intentionally."

TODAY'S POWER MOVE

Create one calming habit today that supports emotional peace in your life.

DAY 236

You Are Capable Of More Discipline Than You Think

POWER QUOTE

"Your mind often quits before your potential actually ends."

REFLECTION

When life becomes difficult, your first reaction is not always your most accurate one.

A challenge appears.

A setback interrupts your plans.

A responsibility feels overwhelming.

Almost immediately, your mind begins searching for an escape.

"I can't do this."

"This is too much."

"I'm not strong enough."

Those thoughts feel convincing because they arrive during moments of discomfort.

But feelings are not always reliable measurements of your actual capacity.

Many people quit at the point where growth is only beginning.

Not because they have reached their limit.

Because they mistake discomfort for inability.

There is an important difference between the two.

Discomfort often means you are stretching.

Inability means you truly cannot continue.

Too often, people confuse the first with the second.

Think about learning any new skill.

The first workout feels exhausting.

The first presentation feels intimidating.

The first difficult conversation feels uncomfortable.

The first budget feels restrictive.

The first months of building a business feel uncertain.

Almost everything meaningful begins by challenging your current capacity.

If you stop every time something feels difficult, you never give yourself the opportunity to discover what you are actually capable of becoming.

Growth has always required expansion.

Expansion of patience.

Expansion of discipline.

Expansion of emotional resilience.

Expansion of responsibility.

Every season that asks more of you is also giving you an opportunity to become more.

That process is rarely comfortable.

But it is often necessary.

Consider how physical strength develops.

Muscles become stronger because they are challenged beyond what is easy.

They adapt to increasing resistance over time.
Character develops in much the same way.
Every time you remain disciplined when quitting would be easier, your endurance grows.
Every time you stay calm during pressure, your emotional stability grows.
Every time you honor your commitments despite discomfort, your self-respect grows.
You become stronger because you repeatedly practice strength.
This does not mean ignoring healthy limits.
Wisdom knows the difference between perseverance and burnout.
There are seasons that require rest.
Moments that require recovery.
Asking for help is not weakness.
Taking care of yourself is not failure.
But there is also a difference between genuine exhaustion and the natural discomfort that accompanies growth.
Learning that difference is part of emotional maturity.
Many people underestimate themselves because they only measure what they feel in the moment.
They overlook everything they have already overcome.
The difficult seasons they survived.
The responsibilities they learned to carry.
The fears they once believed would stop them.
If you looked honestly at your own life, you would likely discover that you have already accomplished things your younger self once considered impossible.
Not because life became easier.
Because you became stronger.
That same process is still happening today.
The challenge you face now may one day become the strength you no longer think twice about.
The responsibility that feels overwhelming today may eventually become part of your normal routine.
The discipline that seems difficult today may one day feel as natural as breathing.
That is how growth works.
It quietly expands your capacity until what once felt extraordinary becomes ordinary.
So when your first reaction tells you that you cannot continue, pause before believing it.
Give yourself the opportunity to discover whether it is fear speaking, discomfort speaking, or genuine limitation.
More often than you realize, you are capable of far more than your emotions initially suggest.
Stay with the process.
Keep practicing.
Keep growing.
Allow yourself to become stronger one decision at a time.
Because every challenge you face with courage is increasing your capacity for the life you are building.
And one day, you will look back and realize that the things you once thought would break you became the very experiences that proved just how strong you truly were.

WEALTH LESSON

Discipline compounds over time because repeated effort increases emotional resilience and consistency.

AFFIRMATION

"I am stronger, more disciplined, and more capable than my doubts suggest."

TODAY'S POWER MOVE

Push yourself slightly beyond your comfort zone today in one productive area.

DAY 237

Stop Waiting For Motivation To Save You

POWER QUOTE

"Motivation starts people. Discipline sustains them."

Motivation is a wonderful beginning.

It inspires action.

Creates excitement.

Fuels new ideas.

Makes difficult goals feel possible.

There is nothing wrong with feeling motivated.

The problem begins when people expect motivation to carry them every day.

Because it won't.

Some mornings you wake up energized.

Focused.

Ready to work.

Other mornings you feel tired.

Discouraged.

Distracted.

Emotionally drained.

That is part of being human.

If your progress depends entirely on how motivated you feel each day, your progress will constantly rise and fall with your emotions.

One productive week will be followed by another week of hesitation.

One burst of inspiration will be followed by long periods of inactivity.

Eventually, inconsistency becomes the habit.

This is where discipline changes everything.

Discipline quietly steps in when motivation walks away.

It reminds you why you started.

It helps you honor commitments even when excitement fades.

It teaches you that your future deserves more than temporary emotion.

It is easy to believe successful individuals simply possess more motivation than everyone else.

More often, they have simply developed stronger discipline.

They learned to keep showing up after the excitement disappeared.

They continued practicing when progress became slow.

They remained faithful to their responsibilities during seasons when no one was applauding them.

That consistency eventually separated them from people who relied only on inspiration.

Think about the most meaningful accomplishments in life.

A healthy marriage is not sustained by romantic feelings alone.

Financial stability is not built by saving money only when it feels convenient.

Strong character is not developed only on easy days.

Every lasting achievement requires commitment after emotion changes.

That is why discipline is one of the greatest expressions of self-respect.

It says,

"My future is important enough that I will continue even when I don't feel like it."

Every time you follow through on a commitment despite discomfort, you strengthen your character.

Every time you keep your word to yourself, you build self-trust.

Every time you remain consistent through an ordinary day, you prove that your purpose is stronger than your mood.

Those quiet decisions matter more than most people realize.

Life is not transformed by one extraordinary day of effort.

It is transformed by ordinary days repeated with extraordinary faithfulness.

The workout you almost skipped.

The budget you chose to follow.

The difficult conversation you decided to have.

The book you continued reading.

The business you kept building when growth felt invisible.

Those moments rarely feel significant while they are happening.

Yet they quietly become the foundation of the life you are creating.

There will always be seasons when enthusiasm fades.

Responsibilities increase.

Progress slows.

Results take longer than expected.

Those are the moments when discipline becomes most valuable.

Not because it removes difficulty.

But because it helps you move through difficulty without abandoning your purpose.

This does not mean ignoring your need for rest.

Wisdom knows when recovery is necessary.

Healthy discipline includes caring for your body, your mind, and your emotional well-being.

Rest is not the opposite of discipline.

It is often part of it.

The goal is not to become untouched by difficulty.

The goal is to become someone who remains committed despite struggle.

Someone who understands that feelings are temporary, but the choices made during those feelings often shape the future.

Do not wait to feel inspired before living according to your values.

Build routines that support your purpose.

Create habits that outlast your emotions.

Practice consistency until it becomes part of your identity.

Because motivation may introduce you to your future.

But discipline is what carries you there.

And one day, you will realize that the greatest changes in your life were not created by the days you felt the most inspired.

They were created by the ordinary days when you quietly chose to continue anyway.

WEALTH LESSON

Long-term success requires consistency because motivation alone fluctuates too much to sustain growth permanently.

AFFIRMATION

"I remain disciplined even when motivation changes."

TODAY'S POWER MOVE

Complete an important task today without waiting to feel emotionally inspired first.

DAY 238

You Deserve To Feel Proud Of Yourself

POWER QUOTE

"Discipline creates self-respect."

REFLECTION

One of the biggest misconceptions is self-respect is something they either have or they don't.

In reality, self-respect is built.

It grows through the relationship you develop with yourself.

Every day, you make promises.

Some are spoken aloud.

Others exist only in your mind.

"I'll wake up earlier tomorrow."

"I'll start saving money."

"I'll stop returning to unhealthy habits."

"I'll finally take care of my health."

"I'll finish what I started."

These promises may seem small.

But they matter.

Because every promise you repeatedly keep strengthens trust.

And every promise you repeatedly break weakens it.

Over time, many people unknowingly disappoint themselves more often than anyone else.

They postpone important responsibilities.

Ignore their goals.

Abandon healthy routines.

Excuse habits they know are holding them back.

Eventually, something deeper begins to happen.

They no longer doubt the goal.

They begin doubting themselves.

This quiet erosion of self-trust often becomes the real obstacle.

Not a lack of ability.

Not a lack of opportunity.

A lack of confidence that they will actually follow through.

That is why discipline is so powerful.

Discipline is not simply about productivity.

It is about integrity.

It is the daily practice of aligning your actions with your values.

Every time you follow through on what you said you would do, you send yourself a powerful message.

"My word matters."

"I can depend on myself."

"My future is worth today's effort."

Those messages gradually reshape identity.

Confidence does not grow because life becomes easier.

It grows because you repeatedly prove to yourself that you can be trusted.

That trust influences every area of life.

You approach opportunities differently because you believe you will remain committed.

You handle setbacks differently because you trust yourself to recover.

You pursue bigger goals because you have evidence that you are capable of honoring your commitments.

This is why self-respect cannot be separated from daily habits.

Every healthy routine is an act of self-respect.

Every financial decision that protects your future is an act of self-respect.

Every healthy boundary is an act of self-respect.

Every responsibility you handle instead of avoiding becomes another brick in the foundation of your character.

Many people search for confidence in achievements.

While achievement can certainly strengthen confidence, lasting self-respect is built long before the achievement arrives.

It is built in private.

On ordinary days.

When no one is watching.

When no one is applauding.

When you choose discipline simply because it reflects the kind of person you want to become.

This does not mean you will never fail.

Everyone has moments when they fall short.

The goal is not perfection.

The goal is becoming someone who returns.

Someone who keeps their commitments more often than they abandon them.

Someone who refuses to let one mistake become a permanent identity.

Each time you begin again, you strengthen self-respect.

Because resilience also keeps promises.

Remember that the relationship you have with yourself sets the foundation for every other relationship in your life.

If you cannot trust your own commitments, it becomes difficult to believe in your own potential.

But when your actions consistently reflect your values, something remarkable happens.

Your confidence becomes quieter.

Stronger.

More stable.

You stop needing constant reassurance because your life itself becomes evidence of who you are becoming.

So keep your word to yourself.

Honor the commitments that move your life forward.

Protect the future you are building through the choices you make today.

Because self-respect is not something you find.

It is something you earn.

One promise kept.

One responsibility completed.

One disciplined decision at a time.

And over the years, those quiet moments of integrity become the unshakable confidence that no outside opinion can ever take away.

WEALTH LESSON

Discipline strengthens confidence because repeated follow-through builds self-trust internally.

AFFIRMATION

"I build self-respect through consistency, discipline, and intentional living."

TODAY'S POWER MOVE

Do something today that your future self would deeply respect you for.

DAY 239

Your Healing Will Influence Your Future Decisions

POWER QUOTE

"Healed minds often build healthier futures."

REFLECTION

Many people think healing is only about feeling better.

Feeling less anxious.

Less hurt.

Less overwhelmed.

While those changes are certainly part of the journey, healing reaches much deeper than emotions alone.

Healing changes the way you live.

Every decision you make passes through your perspective.

If that perspective has been shaped by fear, insecurity, shame, or survival, those experiences quietly influence your choices long before you recognize they are doing so.

Someone who has been deeply rejected may struggle to trust healthy relationships.

Someone who has experienced financial hardship may make decisions from panic instead of wisdom.

Someone who has lived with constant criticism may hesitate to pursue opportunities because they have learned to expect failure before success.

These responses are often less about the present moment than they are about unresolved experiences from the past.

That is why healing matters so deeply.

It changes the lens through which you see life.

Instead of expecting rejection everywhere, you begin building trust carefully and wisely.

Instead of making financial decisions from fear, you begin making them from preparation and long-term vision.

Instead of reacting impulsively to every difficult emotion, you learn to pause, reflect, and respond with greater clarity.

Healing slowly changes your default response.

That transformation affects every part of life.

It changes the way you communicate.

The way you handle conflict.

The way you spend money.

The way you lead your family.

The way you pursue opportunities.

The way you care for yourself.

Many people try to change their behavior without ever addressing the beliefs that created the behavior in the first place.

They focus on the visible habit while ignoring the invisible wound.

But lasting transformation rarely happens from the outside in.

It begins from the inside out.

As your emotional health improves, your decisions naturally begin to change.

You no longer have to force every healthy behavior through constant willpower.

Many of those behaviors begin flowing from a healthier identity.

A person who truly believes they deserve peace starts protecting it.

A person who trusts their ability to rebuild becomes more willing to take healthy risks.

A person who has learned emotional security no longer needs to control every situation to feel safe.

That is why healing is not simply emotional relief.

It is reconstruction.

You are rebuilding the foundation upon which your life operates.

Like renovating a home, true transformation often begins beneath the surface.

The work is not always visible.

Sometimes it feels slow.

Sometimes it feels repetitive.

But strengthening the foundation is what allows everything built afterward to remain standing.

The healthier your foundation becomes, the healthier your future decisions become.

This process requires honesty.

It requires humility.

It requires the willingness to acknowledge old patterns without allowing them to become permanent identities.

Healing is not pretending the past never happened.

It is refusing to let the past continue directing the future.

Each healthy conversation weakens old patterns.

Each wise financial decision strengthens new ones.

Each boundary you establish teaches your heart that peace deserves protection.

Each act of discipline reminds you that your future is worth today's effort.

Little by little, your life begins changing—not because circumstances suddenly became perfect, but because the person making the decisions has changed.

Never underestimate the power of becoming emotionally healthier.

It may be the reason your relationships become stronger.

Your finances become steadier.

Your confidence becomes quieter but more secure.

Your purpose becomes clearer.

Healing is not weakness.

It is one of the bravest forms of rebuilding a person can choose.

Because when you heal, you are not simply changing how you feel.

You are changing how you live.

And the life you build from that healthier foundation can become stronger, wiser, and more peaceful than you ever imagined possible.

.

WEALTH LESSON

Emotional healing improves long-term outcomes because healthier emotional patterns create wiser decisions.

AFFIRMATION

"I allow healing to strengthen the way I think, live, and build."

TODAY'S POWER MOVE

Reflect today on one emotional pattern you are actively working to heal.

DAY 240

Your Future Is Still Possible

POWER QUOTE

"No difficult season has the authority to erase your potential."

REFLECTION

Every life contains chapters that feel heavier than expected.

Seasons where plans fall apart.

Doors close.

Progress slows.

Questions remain unanswered.

During those moments, it is easy to believe that the chapter you are living is the entire story.

Pain has a way of narrowing perspective.

It convinces people that today's struggle will last forever.

That this disappointment is permanent.

That this setback defines who they are becoming.

But one difficult chapter has never determined the ending of a meaningful life.

Some of the strongest people you will ever meet have lived through seasons where they questioned everything.

Their purpose.

Their abilities.

Their direction.

Their future.

Not because they lacked potential.

But because hardship has a way of testing even the strongest hearts.

The difference is that they refused to let a temporary season become a permanent identity.

They kept taking small steps when they could not yet see the destination.

They continued showing up when results were invisible.

They remained faithful to the work even when they could not fully understand what the season was producing.

That quiet perseverance changed everything.

Life has a way of teaching lessons that comfort rarely can.

Patience is often developed while waiting.

Resilience is strengthened while recovering.

Wisdom is gained through mistakes.

Compassion grows from understanding pain.

Character is revealed when no one else is watching.

These qualities cannot always be learned from success alone.

Sometimes they are shaped in the very seasons we wish we could escape.

This does not mean every painful experience has a purpose you will immediately understand.

Some seasons simply hurt.

Some losses leave questions that may never receive complete answers.

Acknowledging that reality is part of emotional honesty.

Hope does not require pretending pain is pleasant.

Hope simply refuses to believe that pain has the final word.

One of the greatest dangers during difficult seasons is allowing temporary emotions to make permanent conclusions.

"I'll never recover."

"Nothing will ever change."

"My best days are behind me."

Those thoughts often feel true in moments of discouragement.

But feelings are not always reliable forecasts of the future.

Think about your own life.

There were probably seasons you once believed you would never survive.

Conversations you feared.

Challenges you thought were impossible.

Losses that seemed unbearable.

Yet somehow, you kept moving.

Not perfectly.

Not without tears.

Not without setbacks.

But you continued.

And because you continued, you became someone different.

Stronger.

Wiser.

More compassionate.

More resilient.

The same possibility still exists today.

The chapter you are living now is still being written.

Every healthy decision adds another sentence.

Every courageous conversation adds another page.

Every disciplined habit becomes another paragraph in the story of the person you are becoming.

Do not allow today's difficulty to convince you that tomorrow has already been decided.

The future has a remarkable way of surprising people who continue building when hope feels fragile.

Keep investing in your character.

Keep protecting your peace.

Keep learning from your experiences.

Keep making the next wise decision, even if it feels small.

Stories are not changed only by dramatic turning points.

They are changed by the quiet choices people make when no one else notices.

One faithful step.

One honest conversation.

One act of courage.

One day of refusing to quit.

Eventually, those ordinary moments become the foundation of an extraordinary life.

So if this season feels heavy, remember that you are living a chapter, not the conclusion.

Your purpose is still unfolding.

Your growth is still happening.

Your future is still being shaped.

And the person you are becoming may one day look back on this difficult season, not as the ending of the story, but as the place where a stronger, wiser, and more resilient life quietly began.

WEALTH LESSON

Resilience strengthens long-term success because emotionally strong people continue rebuilding after setbacks.

AFFIRMATION

"I continue believing in the future I am capable of building."

TODAY'S POWER MOVE

Write down one future vision you still refuse to give up on.

DAY 241

Stop Living Like You Have Unlimited Time

POWER QUOTE

"One day, the future you keep postponing will become regret if you never begin."

REFLECTION

One of the greatest illusions people believe is that they will always have more time.

More time to heal.

More time to pursue their dreams.

More time to repair relationships.

More time to build healthier habits.

More time to become the person they know they are capable of becoming.

But life has a quiet way of moving forward whether we are intentional or not.

Days become weeks.

Weeks become months.

Months become years.

Without realizing it, people can spend an entire season preparing for a future they never actually begin.

The problem is rarely a lack of desire.

Most people genuinely want a better life.

They want greater peace.

Better health.

Financial stability.

Meaningful relationships.

A life filled with purpose.

What often stands in the way is not the dream itself.

It is the belief that the perfect moment has not yet arrived.

People wait until they feel more confident.

More prepared.

More experienced.

More certain.

They convince themselves that one day they will finally be ready.

Yet readiness is rarely something that appears before action.

More often, it is something that develops because of action.

Think about the opportunities you have embraced throughout your life.

You probably were not completely prepared for many of them.

You learned while doing.

You adapted while moving.

You grew because you were willing to begin before you had every answer.

That is how most meaningful progress happens.

Very few people ever feel completely ready to start a business.

To change careers.

To pursue healing.

To become financially disciplined.

To have the difficult conversation.

To take the first courageous step.

Growth asks for movement before certainty.

Not because uncertainty is enjoyable.

Because experience teaches lessons that preparation alone never can.

Waiting also carries a cost.

Every year spent postponing healthy habits is a year those habits could have been strengthening your future.

Every conversation avoided delays healing.

Every dream postponed delays the opportunity to learn, improve, and grow.

Every day spent waiting for perfect timing is a day that cannot be recovered.

This does not mean rushing into reckless decisions.

Wisdom still matters.

Planning still matters.

Preparation still matters.

But there is an important difference between preparing and postponing.

Preparation creates momentum.

Postponement creates excuses.

One moves you toward your future.

The other quietly keeps you where you are.

There comes a moment in every meaningful journey when you must stop asking whether you are completely ready and begin asking whether you are willing to grow.

Because growth has never belonged only to the people who felt fearless.

It belongs to the people who moved despite uncertainty.

Who accepted that progress would include mistakes.

Who understood that imperfect action often creates greater transformation than perfect intentions left untouched.

Your future will not be built all at once.

It will be built one decision at a time.

One habit.

One conversation.

One investment.

One courageous step.

The first step rarely feels dramatic.

Sometimes it feels small enough to question whether it matters.

But every meaningful life is built exactly that way.

One faithful choice after another.

Do not allow the pursuit of perfect timing to become the reason your purpose remains undiscovered.

The life you hope to build is waiting on the other side of a decision.

Not a perfect decision.

A committed one.

Start where you are.

Use what you have.

Learn as you go.

Allow today's imperfect beginning to become tomorrow's remarkable progress.

Because time will continue moving whether you act or not.

The question is whether your life will move with it.

And one day, you will be grateful that you stopped waiting for the perfect moment and realized that the best time to begin becoming the person you were meant to be was the moment you chose to start.

WEALTH LESSON

Intentional action creates momentum because waiting rarely changes life without execution.

AFFIRMATION

"I stop delaying my future and begin building intentionally today."

TODAY'S POWER MOVE

Take one action today toward a goal you have been postponing emotionally.

DAY 242

Your Healing Deserves Privacy Sometimes

POWER QUOTE

"Not every part of your growth process needs public access."

REFLECTION

We live in a world that encourages people to share almost everything.

Every milestone.

Every opinion.

Every achievement.

Every setback.

Every new beginning.

While there is nothing wrong with celebrating progress or inviting others into your journey, not every season of growth is meant to be lived publicly.

Some seasons are meant to be protected.

There are moments when silence becomes one of the healthiest choices you can make.

Not because you are hiding.

But because you are healing.

Growth often requires space.

Space to think without constant opinions.

Space to make mistakes without feeling the need to explain yourself.

Space to discover who you are becoming before inviting the world into the process.

Many people feel pressure to announce every goal before they have developed the discipline to sustain it.

They seek encouragement before they have built consistency.

They search for validation before they have established conviction.

Sometimes that external attention becomes another distraction.

Energy that could have been invested in growth is instead spent managing expectations.

Quiet seasons remove that pressure.

They allow you to focus on becoming instead of appearing.

There is a difference between performing growth and experiencing it.

Performing growth is concerned with how transformation looks to others.

Experiencing growth is concerned with who you are becoming when no one is watching.

The second creates lasting change.

Some of the most important work in life happens in private.

The conversations you have with yourself.

The habits you build.

The boundaries you establish.

The forgiveness you choose.

The discipline you practice.

No audience applauds those moments.

Yet those unseen decisions shape the quality of everything that eventually becomes visible.

A tree does not grow because people watch it.

It grows because its roots continue developing beneath the surface.

Your life works much the same way.

The stronger your foundation becomes, the less dependent you become on constant recognition.

This does not mean isolating yourself.

Healing often requires trusted relationships.

Wise mentors.

Supportive friends.

People who can encourage you with honesty and compassion.

The difference is that you become intentional about who has access to your process.

Not everyone deserves a front-row seat to your rebuilding.

Some people celebrate your growth.

Others misunderstand it.

Others may discourage it before it has had the chance to mature.

Protecting your peace sometimes means protecting your progress.

Privacy is not secrecy born from fear.

Healthy privacy is wisdom.

It recognizes that fragile things often need time to become strong before they are exposed to unnecessary pressure.

A seed spends a long time growing beneath the soil before anyone sees evidence of life.

The hidden work is not less important than the visible growth.

It makes the visible growth possible.

Your healing deserves that same patience.

Allow yourself to grow without constantly measuring your progress against other people's expectations.

Allow yourself to change without feeling obligated to explain every decision.

Allow yourself to become stronger before seeking recognition for your strength.

When the time is right, your life will naturally speak for itself.

People will notice the peace in your responses.

The wisdom in your decisions.

The stability in your relationships.

The discipline in your habits.

Those changes will not need excessive explanation.

They will be evident through the way you live.

Some of the greatest transformations in history were prepared in seasons of obscurity.

Not because obscurity was the goal.

But because preparation requires quiet.

So if this season feels slower...

If it feels hidden...

If it feels as though no one notices the work you are doing...

Do not become discouraged.

The deepest roots are always formed beneath the surface.

Protect your healing.

Protect your peace.

Protect the life you are quietly building.

Because not every meaningful transformation begins on a stage.

Many of the most extraordinary lives are first rebuilt in the quiet places where character is formed, healing takes root, and purpose grows strong enough to stand on its own.

WEALTH LESSON

Protecting emotional energy improves focus and consistency because less energy is spent performing growth externally.

AFFIRMATION

"I allow myself to heal and grow privately when necessary."

TODAY'S POWER MOVE

Spend quiet uninterrupted time today reconnecting with yourself emotionally.

DAY 243

Financial Freedom Begins With Awareness

POWER QUOTE

"You cannot improve what you refuse to honestly examine."

REFLECTION

Money is emotional for more people than they realize.

It is not just numbers on a screen.

It often carries fear.

Shame.

Stress.

Regret.

Hope.

Security.

Because of those emotions, many people avoid looking closely at their finances.

They postpone checking their bank account.

They ignore credit card balances.

They avoid creating a budget.

They put off opening bills.

Not because they are lazy.

Because facing reality feels emotionally uncomfortable.

For a brief moment, avoidance provides relief.

If you do not look at the numbers, you do not have to feel the anxiety they create.

But temporary relief comes with a hidden cost.

The bills continue growing.

The uncertainty increases.

The stress quietly follows you into other areas of life.

Avoidance never removes financial problems.

It only delays your ability to solve them.

This is why financial honesty is one of the most powerful forms of self-respect.

Honesty is not about criticizing yourself.

It is about seeing reality clearly enough to change it.

The moment you sit down and honestly examine your finances, something important happens.

The unknown becomes known.

Confusion begins giving way to clarity.

Instead of asking,

"Why am I always stressed about money?"

You begin asking,

"What is actually happening, and what can I do next?"

Those are two very different questions.

One keeps you trapped in emotion.

The other moves you toward solutions.

Financial awareness creates options.
You begin recognizing where your money is going.
Which habits are helping you.
Which habits are hurting you.
Which expenses align with your values.
Which purchases are simply emotional reactions.
Awareness is not meant to create guilt.
It is meant to create direction.
You cannot improve what you refuse to measure.
It is common to believe financial peace comes after they earn more money.
Sometimes additional income helps.
But countless people with higher incomes still experience constant financial anxiety because they never developed financial awareness.
Peace does not begin with a certain salary.
It begins with stewardship.
It begins when you become intentional with what you already have.
That may mean creating your first budget.
Tracking your spending honestly.
Building an emergency fund one small contribution at a time.
Paying down debt consistently.
Learning about investing.
Having difficult conversations about money instead of avoiding them.
These actions may feel ordinary.
Yet they quietly transform your financial future.
Every responsible decision creates momentum.
Every dollar given a purpose strengthens clarity.
Every month of consistency builds confidence.
Eventually, money becomes less frightening because you understand it better.
Clarity replaces confusion.
Preparation replaces panic.
Discipline replaces impulsiveness.
This is one of the greatest gifts financial honesty offers.
It removes the emotional fog that keeps so many people stuck.
You stop living in assumptions.
You start living with understanding.
And understanding creates confidence.
This process also requires compassion.
Financial mistakes do not make you a failure.
Many people were never taught healthy financial habits.
Others experienced hardship that forced difficult decisions.
Some are rebuilding after seasons of loss.

Honesty allows you to acknowledge your current reality without allowing shame to define your identity.

You are not your bank balance.

You are not your past financial mistakes.

You are the person making today's decisions.

And today's decisions have the power to change tomorrow.

Do not fear the truth about your finances.

The truth is where freedom begins.

Look at the numbers.

Make the plan.

Take the next wise step.

Repeat it again tomorrow.

Because financial peace is rarely built through one extraordinary decision.

It is built through hundreds of honest ones.

One budget.

One savings deposit.

One debt payment.

One intentional purchase.

One disciplined choice at a time.

The life you are building deserves that kind of honesty.

Because clarity creates confidence.

Confidence creates action.

And action, practiced consistently, creates the financial freedom that once seemed impossible.

WEALTH LESSON

Financial awareness improves decision-making because intentional planning replaces emotional avoidance.

AFFIRMATION

"I face my finances honestly and build stability intentionally."

TODAY'S POWER MOVE

Review one area of your finances today that you have been emotionally avoiding.

DAY 244

You Are Not Behind In Life

POWER QUOTE

"Different journeys unfold at different speeds."

REFLECTION

One of the quickest ways to lose peace is to measure your life against someone else's timeline.

It happens quietly.

You see someone buying a home.

Starting a business.

Getting married.

Receiving a promotion.

Growing their wealth.

And before long, a single thought begins repeating itself.

"I'm behind."

That thought can become surprisingly powerful.

It turns someone else's success into your personal disappointment.

It transforms inspiration into insecurity.

It replaces gratitude with discouragement.

Yet the conclusion itself is often based on an assumption that was never true.

Life has never followed one universal schedule.

Every person's journey unfolds differently.

Some people discover their purpose early.

Others spend years searching before they find meaningful direction.

Some build financial stability in their twenties.

Others begin rebuilding in their forties or fifties.

Some heal quickly from painful experiences.

Others require more time, support, and patience.

Different timelines do not determine different values.

They simply reflect different journeys.

The problem with comparison is that it rarely compares complete stories.

It compares your private struggles to someone else's public victories.

You see the promotion.

You do not see the years of preparation.

You see the successful business.

You do not see the failures that came before it.

You see the healthy relationship.

You do not see the personal growth that made it possible.

Comparison often removes the context that gives success its true meaning.

As a result, people begin criticizing themselves unfairly.

They rush decisions they are not prepared to make.

They pursue goals that are not truly theirs.

They measure progress by someone else's standards instead of their own values.
That kind of pressure rarely produces peace.
Real growth begins when you stop asking,
"Am I ahead of everyone else?"
And begin asking,
"Am I becoming healthier than I was yesterday?"
That is a question worth living by.
Are you more patient?
More disciplined?
More emotionally aware?
More financially intentional?
More honest with yourself?
Those changes may not always attract public attention.
But they represent genuine progress.
Remember that many of life's greatest transformations happen quietly.
A healthier mindset develops before a healthier career.
Financial discipline develops before financial freedom.
Emotional maturity develops before stronger relationships.
The visible results usually arrive after months or years of invisible growth.
Trust that process.
You are not racing against the world.
You are becoming the person your future requires.
That journey deserves patience.
It deserves grace.
It deserves consistency.
This does not mean becoming complacent.
Continue working.
Continue learning.
Continue preparing.
Continue building.
But let your motivation come from purpose, not panic.
Build because you believe in the life you are creating.
Not because you are trying to catch someone else's timeline.
The strongest builders understand something many people forget.
Life is not a competition to see who reaches milestones first.
It is an opportunity to build something meaningful that can endure.
Slow growth that creates lasting character is more valuable than rushed success that lacks a strong foundation.
Your future does not become less meaningful because it arrives differently than someone else's.
It becomes meaningful because it reflects your values, your growth, your resilience, and your willingness to keep moving forward.
So stop measuring your life by clocks that were never designed for your journey.

Measure it by your integrity.

Your discipline.

Your healing.

Your courage.

Measure it by the person you are becoming.

Because the life you are building does not need to look like anyone else's to be deeply successful.

Your story has its own timing.

Its own purpose.

Its own pace.

Honor it.

Trust it.

And keep building it—one intentional decision at a time.

WEALTH LESSON

Comparison weakens confidence because emotional pressure often leads to unhealthy decisions and discouragement.

AFFIRMATION

"I trust my own journey and stop comparing my timeline to others."

TODAY'S POWER MOVE

Acknowledge one area where you have personally grown instead of focusing on comparison.

DAY 245

Stop Feeding Negative Self-Talk

POWER QUOTE

"The way you speak to yourself shapes the way you build your life."

REFLECTION

There is one voice you will hear more than anyone else's throughout your life.

Your own.

Long after conversations end and people leave the room, your internal dialogue continues.

It speaks when you wake up.

When you face challenges.

When you make mistakes.

When you celebrate victories.

When you question yourself.

Because that voice is always present, the way you speak to yourself matters more than many people realize.

Many individuals unknowingly become their own harshest critic.

They say things to themselves they would never say to someone they love.

"I'll never succeed."

"I'm always behind."

"Nothing ever works for me."

"I'm just not disciplined enough."

"I always mess everything up."

At first, those thoughts may seem insignificant.

But repeated thoughts become repeated beliefs.

Repeated beliefs begin shaping identity.

And identity quietly influences behavior.

A person who constantly believes they are incapable often stops attempting difficult things.

A person who believes failure defines them may begin avoiding opportunities that could change their life.

Not because they lack ability.

Because their inner voice has convinced them not to trust themselves.

This is why mental discipline is so important.

Mental discipline is not pretending every situation is positive.

It is choosing honesty without becoming hopeless.

There is a difference between saying,

"I made a mistake,"

and saying,

"I am a mistake."

One statement creates an opportunity to learn.

The other attacks your identity.

Healthy self-talk does not ignore reality.

It faces reality with wisdom.

Instead of saying,

"I'll never change,"
you can honestly say,
"Change is difficult, but I can continue growing."
Instead of,
"I always fail,"
you can ask,
"What can I learn from this experience?"
Those small shifts seem simple.
Yet they completely change the direction of your thinking.
The goal is not to become someone who constantly flatters themselves.
The goal is to become someone who speaks truth with compassion.
The same way a wise mentor would.
A wise mentor does not ignore your weaknesses.
But they also do not define your future by them.
They acknowledge where growth is needed while reminding you that growth is possible.
Your inner voice should become that kind of guide.
Honest enough to correct you.
Wise enough to encourage you.
Patient enough to let you grow.
Every healthy thought strengthens healthier habits.
Every encouraging truth weakens unnecessary shame.
Every moment you choose self-awareness instead of self-condemnation creates space for real transformation.
Remember that your mind is the place where every decision begins.
The way you think influences the way you feel.
The way you feel influences the way you act.
The way you act becomes the habits that shape your future.
That is why protecting your inner dialogue is not merely positive thinking.
It is responsible stewardship of your mind.
Pay attention to the words you repeat most often.
Are they creating hope?
Or quietly reinforcing hopelessness?
Are they strengthening discipline?
Or justifying avoidance?
Are they helping you become the person you hope to be?
Or keeping you attached to someone you have already outgrown?
Choose your words carefully.
Because every sentence you repeatedly tell yourself becomes part of the environment your mind lives in.
Create an environment where growth is possible.
Where mistakes become lessons.
Where discipline becomes identity.
Where setbacks become opportunities to rebuild instead of reasons to quit.

The voice you hear most often should not become the one that limits your future.

Let it become the voice that reminds you to keep learning, keep growing, and keep believing that the person you are becoming is stronger than the fears you are leaving behind.

Over time, those healthier conversations will do more than change your thoughts.

They will quietly change your life.

WEALTH LESSON

Healthy thinking improves emotional resilience because thoughts influence discipline and long-term behavior.

AFFIRMATION

"I speak to myself with strength, wisdom, and belief."

TODAY'S POWER MOVE

Interrupt one repeated negative thought pattern today and replace it with truth.

DAY 246

The Life You Want Requires Sacrifice

POWER QUOTE

"Every meaningful future costs something in the present."

REFLECTION

Every meaningful life has a price.

Not a financial price alone.

An emotional one.

A personal one.

A daily one.

Many people dream about extraordinary futures.

They want financial freedom.

Healthy relationships.

Peace of mind.

Purposeful work.

Strong character.

Yet they often hope those outcomes can be achieved without changing the habits that created their current reality.

Growth has never worked that way.

Every meaningful destination requires leaving something behind.

Sometimes that means sacrificing temporary comfort.

Sometimes it means giving up habits that no longer serve you.

Sometimes it means choosing discipline when your emotions would rather choose convenience.

Sacrifice is not punishment.

It is the exchange between who you are today and who you are becoming tomorrow.

Every person sacrifices something.

The only question is what they choose to sacrifice.

Some sacrifice their future for temporary pleasure.

They overspend instead of saving.

Procrastinate instead of preparing.

Avoid difficult conversations instead of strengthening relationships.

Choose comfort instead of growth.

Others make a different exchange.

They sacrifice today's convenience for tomorrow's freedom.

They save when spending would feel easier.

They practice when quitting would feel more comfortable.

They heal instead of continuing unhealthy patterns.

They build quietly while others wait for perfect conditions.

Both groups make sacrifices.

Only the rewards are different.

One of the greatest misunderstandings about discipline is believing it removes freedom.

In reality, discipline often creates it.

Financial discipline creates options.

Emotional discipline creates healthier relationships.

Mental discipline creates clarity.

Physical discipline creates strength.

The temporary sacrifices you make today often become tomorrow's greatest freedoms.

The challenge is that sacrifice rarely feels rewarding in the moment.

No one feels immediate excitement while creating a budget instead of making an impulsive purchase.

Healing old wounds is rarely more comfortable than avoiding them.

Practicing consistency often feels ordinary compared to chasing quick results.

Yet the ordinary choices repeated over time create extraordinary lives.

Think about a farmer planting seeds.

The work comes long before the harvest.

There are days of preparation.

Patience.

Watering.

Waiting.

Nothing above the surface appears impressive.

But beneath the soil, something important is happening.

Roots are forming.

Growth is beginning.

Your sacrifices work the same way.

Every healthy decision plants something.

Every wise choice strengthens something.

Every act of discipline prepares you for opportunities that have not yet arrived.

Many people want the harvest without respecting the season of planting.

But lasting success is always built in the unseen moments.

The early mornings.

The careful planning.

The difficult conversations.

The quiet consistency that no one applauds.

Those are the moments that shape the future.

This does not mean your life should become joyless.

Healthy sacrifice is not about refusing every pleasure.

It is about refusing pleasures that consistently cost you the future you truly want.

It is learning to ask a simple question before making a decision:

"Will this move me closer to the life I want, or further away from it?"

That question has the power to change everything.

Because every decision is an investment.

You are either investing in tomorrow or borrowing against it.

Your habits reveal where your investment is being made.

The beautiful truth is that sacrifice becomes easier when your purpose becomes clearer.

When you remember what you are building, saying no to what distracts you becomes less difficult.

The temporary discomfort begins making sense because it serves something greater than the moment itself.

Do not fear sacrifice.

Fear remaining attached to habits that quietly steal the future you hope to create.

The life you desire is worth the effort.

It is worth the discipline.

It is worth the patience.

It is worth every quiet decision that no one else may ever notice.

Because one day, you will look around at the peace, stability, freedom, and purpose you have built and realize something remarkable.

The things you once believed you were giving up were never the greatest loss.

They were simply the price of becoming the person you were always capable of becoming.

WEALTH LESSON

Long-term freedom often requires short-term sacrifice and intentional decision-making.

AFFIRMATION

"I willingly sacrifice temporary comfort for long-term peace and freedom."

TODAY'S POWER MOVE

Choose one disciplined sacrifice today that supports your future goals.

DAY 247

You Deserve To Experience Stability

POWER QUOTE

"Peaceful living is possible even if chaos once felt normal."

REFLECTION

Not everyone learns what stability feels like while growing up.

For some, life was unpredictable from the very beginning.

Finances changed without warning.

Relationships felt uncertain.

Home never felt completely safe.

Conflict appeared without notice.

The future always felt uncertain.

When those experiences are repeated over many years, survival becomes more than a temporary response.

It becomes a lifestyle.

You learn to expect the worst.

To stay alert.

To prepare for disappointment before it arrives.

To believe that peace never lasts for long.

Those patterns are understandable.

They often develop because your mind and body are trying to protect you.

But what once protected you can eventually begin limiting you.

A life built entirely around survival leaves very little room for thriving.

When your energy is constantly spent preparing for the next crisis, it becomes difficult to dream.

To create.

To build.

To rest.

To enjoy the life you have worked so hard to create.

That is why healing is about far more than recovering from the past.

Healing teaches your mind that not every season has to be an emergency.

It teaches your heart that calmness is not something to distrust.

It teaches your nervous system that peace can be safe.

For many people, this feels unfamiliar at first.

A quiet day feels strange.

A healthy relationship feels almost suspicious.

Financial stability feels temporary.

Without realizing it, they wait for something to go wrong because uncertainty has become more familiar than security.

Healing gently challenges those expectations.

It reminds you that stability is not weakness.

It is not boredom.

It is not a lack of purpose.

It is the foundation that allows purpose to flourish.
A peaceful mind thinks more clearly.
A consistent routine creates momentum.
Healthy relationships provide emotional safety.
Financial clarity reduces unnecessary anxiety.
These things do not make life less meaningful.
They make it more sustainable.
You deserve to experience mornings that are not filled with panic.
Conversations that do not leave you emotionally exhausted.
Relationships where trust is stronger than fear.
Financial decisions made from wisdom instead of desperation.
A home that feels peaceful instead of unpredictable.
Those are not unrealistic dreams.
They are healthy foundations.
Building that kind of life requires intentional choices.
Healthy boundaries.
Consistent routines.
Wise stewardship of your finances.
Honest conversations.
The courage to leave environments that constantly pull you back into survival mode.
None of these changes happen overnight.
Years of living in survival cannot be undone in a single decision.
But every healthy habit teaches your mind a new reality.
Every peaceful response reminds your heart that chaos is no longer in charge.
Every disciplined choice strengthens the life you are creating.
Little by little, survival gives way to stability.
Fear gives way to confidence.
Reaction gives way to intention.
You begin living differently because you no longer believe that constant struggle is the only way life can feel real.
The beautiful truth is that stability does not make you less resilient.
It allows your resilience to serve a greater purpose.
Instead of using all your strength just to survive, you begin using it to build.
To love.
To lead.
To create.
To leave a legacy.
That is the life healing is inviting you toward.
Not a perfect life.
But a grounded one.
A life where peace is no longer an occasional visitor but a familiar companion.
A life where your routines strengthen you instead of draining you.

A life where your future is shaped by intention instead of constant emergency.

You were never meant to spend your entire life surviving.

You were meant to heal.

To grow.

To build.

And to discover that stability is not something reserved for other people.

It is something you can intentionally create, protect, and pass on to everyone whose life your own will one day touch.

WEALTH LESSON

Stable environments improve long-term discipline because emotional peace strengthens focus and decision-making.

AFFIRMATION

"I build a stable life rooted in peace, healing, and discipline."

TODAY'S POWER MOVE

Create one healthy routine today that supports greater stability in your life.

DAY 248

Stop Being Afraid of Responsibility

POWER QUOTE

"Growth often requires responsibilities that feel uncomfortable at first."

REFLECTION

Many people dream about success.

They imagine greater opportunities.

Financial freedom.

Leadership.

Influence.

A business that grows.

A career that expands.

A life filled with greater purpose.

Yet few people stop to ask an equally important question:

"Am I becoming the kind of person who can sustain what I am asking for?"

Success is often celebrated for what it provides.

But it also demands something in return.

More responsibility.

More decisions.

More visibility.

More people depending on you.

More opportunities that require wisdom instead of impulse.

For some people, those realities feel exciting.

For others, they feel overwhelming.

Without realizing it, they begin resisting the very future they say they want.

Not because they dislike success.

Because they fear the weight that comes with it.

This fear often appears quietly.

Someone delays launching the business because success might create expectations they feel unprepared to meet.

Someone avoids applying for a leadership position because visibility feels intimidating.

Someone stays financially comfortable instead of pursuing growth because greater income also requires greater stewardship.

On the surface, these decisions appear unrelated.

Beneath them is often the same question:

"What if I cannot handle what comes next?"

That question deserves honesty.

Because growth is not only about expanding your opportunities.

It is also about expanding your capacity.

Every new season asks something new of you.

Greater patience.

Greater discipline.

Greater emotional maturity.

Greater wisdom.

The beautiful truth is that capacity is not something you either possess or lack.

It is something you build.

Just as muscles become stronger through repeated resistance, emotional capacity grows through repeated responsibility.

Each challenge you face with integrity prepares you for a larger one.

Each commitment you honor strengthens your ability to carry greater opportunities.

Each difficult conversation handled with wisdom prepares you to lead with greater confidence.

Life rarely gives people everything they desire before they are prepared to manage it.

Preparation often comes first.

Expansion follows afterward.

This is why today's responsibilities matter so much.

The way you handle small opportunities reveals how you may handle larger ones.

The discipline you show with a modest income prepares you for greater financial stewardship.

The character you display in private prepares you for greater visibility in public.

The emotional stability you practice today becomes the foundation for tomorrow's leadership.

Nothing is wasted.

Every ordinary responsibility is training for something larger.

This does not mean you must become perfect before success arrives.

No one ever reaches complete readiness.

There will always be new lessons to learn.

New situations to navigate.

New challenges to overcome.

Growth continues at every stage of life.

But intentional preparation changes everything.

When you consistently strengthen your character, your future opportunities become less intimidating because you know you are becoming someone capable of carrying them.

Responsibility begins feeling less like pressure and more like purpose.

You stop seeing success as something to survive.

You begin seeing it as something to steward.

That shift changes everything.

Success is no longer measured only by what you accomplish.

It is measured by how faithfully you care for what has been entrusted to you.

How wisely you lead.

How humbly you serve.

How consistently you remain grounded while your opportunities continue growing.

Do not fear responsibility.

It is often evidence that life is inviting you to become more than you have been before.

Welcome the process.

Embrace the preparation.

Strengthen your character before the spotlight arrives.

Develop discipline before greater wealth arrives.

Build emotional maturity before greater influence arrives.

Because opportunities may open doors.

But character determines how long you remain in the room.

Become the person who can carry success with humility, wisdom, peace, and integrity.

Then, when greater opportunities arrive, you will not simply achieve them.

You will be prepared to sustain them.

And that is where lasting success is truly built.

WEALTH LESSON

Greater opportunities require greater emotional discipline and responsibility long-term.

AFFIRMATION

"I become emotionally and mentally prepared for greater responsibility."

TODAY'S POWER MOVE

Handle one responsibility today immediately instead of procrastinating emotionally.

DAY 249

Your Discipline Will Separate You

POWER QUOTE

"Most people quit during seasons where disciplined people continue."

REFLECTION

Almost everyone is willing to work hard when life feels exciting.

When motivation is high.

When progress is visible.

When people are encouraging them.

When the results arrive quickly.

Those seasons make discipline feel easy.

The real test begins when those things disappear.

When the excitement fades.

When progress slows.

When the work feels repetitive.

When no one notices your effort.

When the outcome is still uncertain.

Those are the moments that reveal the difference between interest and commitment.

Many people stop building during the quiet seasons.

Not because they no longer want the goal.

But because the emotional reward is no longer immediate.

The business grows slower than expected.

The debt takes longer to repay.

Healing feels less dramatic than it did at the beginning.

The healthy habits become routine instead of exciting.

Without realizing it, they begin believing that slow progress means no progress at all.

But some of the most important growth in life happens when nothing appears to be changing.

Think about a tree during the winter.

Above the ground, it seems as though very little is happening.

There are no blossoms.

No visible fruit.

No dramatic signs of growth.

Yet beneath the surface, the roots continue strengthening.

Preparing for the seasons that are still to come.

Your life often grows the same way.

The seasons that feel ordinary are frequently the seasons building extraordinary strength.

Discipline creates separation because it teaches you to continue after emotions change.

Anyone can begin with excitement.

Fewer people continue with commitment.

That difference compounds over time.

One extra workout.

One more chapter read.
One additional payment toward debt.
One difficult conversation handled with maturity.
One ordinary day where you simply choose to show up again.
Those moments seem insignificant on their own.
Together, they become the life you eventually look back and admire.
This is why consistency is so powerful.
It quietly multiplies.
Every disciplined decision makes the next one a little easier.
Every healthy habit strengthens your identity.
Every promise you keep to yourself deepens your self-respect.
Eventually, the habits that once required tremendous effort become part of who you are.
People often admire successful lives without recognizing the countless ordinary days that made them possible.
They see the harvest.
They rarely see the years of planting.
They notice the confidence.
They overlook the hundreds of moments when that person chose courage despite uncertainty.
They celebrate the financial stability.
They rarely witness the disciplined decisions that quietly built it.
Success almost always looks more dramatic from the outside than it felt while it was being created.
That is why comparison can be so misleading.
You may believe someone else's growth happened quickly simply because you only saw the finished result.
The reality is that most meaningful accomplishments are built through patient, repetitive faithfulness.
There will be days when you feel like stopping.
Days when your emotions argue that your effort no longer matters.
Those days deserve special attention.
Because the decisions you make when motivation disappears often shape your future more than the decisions you make when motivation is abundant.
Anyone can move when the path feels easy.
Character is revealed by those who continue when the road becomes difficult.
So do not underestimate the quiet seasons.
Do not dismiss the ordinary routines.
Do not abandon the habits simply because they no longer feel exciting.
Those are the very moments that create separation.
Those are the days that strengthen resilience.
Those are the choices that quietly compound into a life marked by peace, wisdom, stability, and purpose.
Keep showing up.
Keep building.
Keep honoring the commitments you have made to your future.
Because one day, you will realize that the greatest difference between where you started and where you arrived was not one extraordinary breakthrough.

It was the simple decision to continue when most people would have stopped.

And that quiet commitment will become one of the greatest strengths you ever build.

WEALTH LESSON

Consistency creates long-term advantage because repeated disciplined action compounds over time.

AFFIRMATION

"I stay disciplined even when progress feels slow or difficult."

TODAY'S POWER MOVE

Continue working on one long-term goal today regardless of emotional resistance.

DAY 250

Your Future Is Being Built Right Now

POWER QUOTE

"The habits you repeat today are quietly creating your tomorrow."

REFLECTION

When people imagine transformation, they often picture one extraordinary moment.

A breakthrough.

A life-changing opportunity.

A dramatic decision that instantly changes everything.

While those moments certainly exist, they are rarely what builds a meaningful life.

Most transformation happens quietly.

One ordinary day at a time.

The life you will live a year from now is being shaped by today's decisions.

The way you spend your morning.

The conversation you choose to have.

The money you decide to save.

The temptation you decide to resist.

The habit you repeat.

The responsibility you honor.

None of those moments seem extraordinary on their own.

Yet together they become your future.

This is why every day matters.

Not because every day will feel exciting.

But because every day offers another opportunity to reinforce the person you are becoming.

Many people underestimate small decisions because the results are delayed.

One healthy meal does not immediately transform your health.

One workout does not instantly build strength.

One budget does not create financial freedom overnight.

One difficult conversation does not heal every relationship.

Because the results are gradual, people sometimes believe the effort is insignificant.

It is not.

The greatest force behind meaningful change is not intensity.

It is consistency.

A single day of discipline is valuable.

A hundred disciplined days quietly reshape a life.

Every repeated choice becomes another vote for the identity you are building.

Each time you choose patience over anger, you strengthen emotional maturity.

Each time you save instead of spending impulsively, you strengthen financial wisdom.

Each time you return after a setback, you strengthen resilience.

These choices become habits.

Habits become character.

Character shapes your future.
This is why the ordinary day deserves your attention.
Many people spend their lives waiting for extraordinary opportunities while overlooking the extraordinary power hidden inside ordinary routines.
The way you begin your mornings.
The books you read.
The thoughts you entertain.
The people you spend time with.
The promises you keep.
These quiet moments rarely receive applause.
Yet they influence almost everything that follows.
Imagine placing one small stone on top of another every day.
One stone seems insignificant.
A week later, the pile is still small.
Months later, it has become noticeable.
Years later, it has become something impossible to ignore.
That is how growth works.
The compounding effect is often invisible until enough time has passed for the results to become undeniable.
This is why patience and discipline always work together.
Patience keeps you from becoming discouraged by slow progress.
Discipline keeps you moving while patience does its work.
Together, they create transformation that lasts.
Do not measure today's effort only by today's results.
Measure it by the direction it is taking your life.
Every healthy response matters.
Every intentional action matters.
Every difficult decision made with wisdom matters.
Even when no one else notices.
Especially then.
Remember that your future self will one day inherit everything your present self repeatedly chooses.
The habits you practice today will become the routines you rely upon tomorrow.
The character you develop today will shape the opportunities you can sustain tomorrow.
The discipline you strengthen today will create the freedom you enjoy tomorrow.
That is why today matters so deeply.
Not because it must be perfect.
But because it is another opportunity to become the person you hope to be.
You do not build an extraordinary life in one extraordinary moment.
You build it through thousands of ordinary moments lived with extraordinary intention.
One day.
One habit.
One decision.

One faithful step at a time.
And when you eventually look back on the life you created, you will discover that your greatest transformation was never built in a single breakthrough.
It was built quietly, faithfully, and consistently—one ordinary day at a time.

WEALTH LESSON

Long-term transformation happens through repeated intentional behavior over time.

AFFIRMATION

"I intentionally build my future through disciplined daily actions."

TODAY'S POWER MOVE

Make one decision today that your future self will deeply benefit from later.

DAY 251

Stop Doubting What God Placed Inside You

POWER QUOTE

"You would not carry the vision if you were incapable of becoming it."

REFLECTION

Almost every meaningful life begins with a vision.
Not a complete blueprint.
Not every answer.
Just a quiet thought that refuses to disappear.
An idea.
A dream.
A calling.
A desire to build something that does not yet exist.
Many people experience those moments.
Far fewer trust them.
Instead, they begin questioning themselves.
"Who am I to do something like that?"
"What if I fail?"
"Someone else is already doing it better."
"Maybe I'm dreaming too big."
Over time, fear becomes louder than possibility.
Comparison becomes louder than purpose.
Doubt becomes louder than conviction.
Eventually, people begin talking themselves out of the very future they once felt inspired to pursue.
But consider this.
What if the vision continues returning because it was never meant to be ignored?
Not every passing thought deserves your attention.
But some dreams remain with you year after year.
They continue resurfacing despite setbacks.
Despite fear.

Despite seasons where you almost convinced yourself to give up.

Perhaps that persistence is not accidental.

Perhaps it is an invitation.

Every meaningful accomplishment begins as something invisible.

Before a building exists, someone imagines it.

Before a business serves its first customer, someone believes it can.

Before a book changes a life, it first exists as an unwritten idea.

Every visible reality begins as an unseen possibility.

The same is true for personal growth.

The person you hope to become often appears first as a vision before it becomes your reality.

That future version of yourself already exists in seed form.

The discipline you desire.

The confidence you admire.

The wisdom you hope to develop.

The peace you long to experience.

None of those qualities appear overnight.

They begin quietly, through repeated choices that allow the vision to grow.

Fear will always argue that you should wait.

Wait until you know more.

Wait until you have more money.

Wait until you feel completely confident.

Wait until someone else believes in you first.

But growth has never depended on complete certainty.

It has always depended on willingness.

The willingness to take one step before seeing the entire path.

The willingness to learn while moving.

The willingness to become through the process rather than before it.

This does not mean every dream will unfold exactly as you imagine.

Life has a way of refining our plans.

Teaching new lessons.

Opening unexpected doors.

Closing others.

Sometimes the vision changes as you grow.

Sometimes you change because of the vision.

Either way, movement creates clarity that standing still never will.

Many people spend years waiting for proof that they are capable.

The truth is that capability often grows because people were willing to begin.

Every skill is developed.

Every leader was once inexperienced.

Every disciplined person once struggled with consistency.

Every confident person once questioned themselves.

No one begins fully prepared.

They become prepared by continuing.

Do not allow comparison to silence what has been placed within you.

Someone else's journey was never meant to become the measure of your own.

Your purpose requires your unique experiences.

Your unique perspective.

Your unique story.

No one else can become the person you are called to become.

That responsibility belongs to you.

Protect the vision.

Feed it with learning.

Strengthen it with discipline.

Support it with consistent action.

Allow it to mature instead of abandoning it at the first sign of difficulty.

Because the future you hope to build is not created by wishing.

It is created by faithfully nurturing what has already been planted within you.

One decision at a time.

One lesson at a time.

One courageous step at a time.

Years from now, you may look back and realize that the greatest turning point in your life was not the day everything became clear.

It was the day you stopped talking yourself out of your own potential.

It was the day you chose to believe that the vision inside you deserved the opportunity to become reality.

And from that single decision, an entirely different future quietly began.

WEALTH LESSON

Belief influences behavior because people act differently when they genuinely believe growth is possible for them.

AFFIRMATION

"I trust the vision placed inside me and continue building it intentionally."

TODAY'S POWER MOVE

Write down one dream you still deeply desire to pursue and reconnect with why it matters to you.

DAY 252

Emotional Intelligence Is A Form Of Power

POWER QUOTE

"People who understand themselves deeply often build stronger lives."

One of the greatest advantages a person can develop is not simply understanding the world around them.

It is understanding themselves.

Many people spend years learning about careers.

Finances.

Business.

Relationships.

Success.

Yet they rarely stop to study the one person they will spend every moment of life with.

Themselves.

Without self-awareness, people often repeat the same emotional patterns without realizing it.

They become frustrated by situations that seem to happen over and over again.

The same conflicts.

The same fears.

The same unhealthy habits.

The same emotional reactions.

They focus on changing their circumstances while overlooking the internal patterns influencing those circumstances.

That is why self-awareness matters so deeply.

It allows you to pause before reacting.

To recognize what you are feeling instead of becoming controlled by it.

To ask important questions that many people never ask themselves.

"Why did that comment affect me so strongly?"

"Why do I keep avoiding this responsibility?"

"Why does this situation make me anxious?"

"What belief is influencing my decision right now?"

Questions like these create space between emotion and action.

And in that space, wisdom begins to grow.

A common belief is that emotional intelligence means suppressing emotions.

It does not.

Emotional intelligence is not pretending you never feel anger, fear, disappointment, or sadness.

It is learning how to experience those emotions without allowing them to control your behavior.

There is a significant difference between feeling anger and speaking carelessly.

Between experiencing fear and abandoning your purpose.

Between feeling disappointed and giving up on yourself.

Emotion itself is not the problem.

The challenge is what we choose to do with it.

People who develop emotional intelligence become better communicators because they listen before reacting.

They become better leaders because they understand both themselves and others.
They become stronger decision-makers because they recognize when temporary emotions are trying to make permanent decisions.
That kind of maturity strengthens every area of life.
Relationships become healthier because conversations become more intentional.
Financial decisions become wiser because emotional spending becomes easier to recognize.
Conflict becomes more productive because understanding replaces impulsiveness.
Peace becomes more consistent because reactions are no longer controlling every circumstance.
Self-awareness also requires humility.
It takes courage to admit when your own habits are contributing to your struggles.
To acknowledge wounds that still influence your choices.
To recognize patterns that need to change.
But honesty is never meant to produce shame.
It produces freedom.
You cannot change what you refuse to acknowledge.
The moment you become aware of a pattern, you create the opportunity to choose something different.
That is where transformation begins.
Not in perfection.
But in awareness followed by intentional action.
Every day gives you another opportunity to know yourself a little better.
To notice your triggers without being ruled by them.
To recognize your strengths without becoming prideful.
To identify your weaknesses without becoming discouraged.
To grow with honesty instead of denial.
This process is lifelong.
No one ever completely finishes learning about themselves.
Each season reveals something new.
Each challenge exposes another opportunity to grow.
Each relationship teaches another lesson about patience, humility, forgiveness, or courage.
Welcome those lessons.
They are shaping the person you are becoming.
Because the greatest leadership always begins with self-leadership.
Before you can consistently influence your finances, your relationships, your purpose, or your future, you must first learn to lead your own thoughts, emotions, and decisions with wisdom.
That is the quiet work of emotional intelligence.
It is not weakness.
It is strength guided by self-awareness.
It is discipline guided by wisdom.
It is freedom created through understanding.
And over time, that self-mastery becomes one of the strongest foundations upon which you will ever build your life.

WEALTH LESSON

Emotional intelligence improves decision-making because awareness strengthens emotional regulation and discipline.

AFFIRMATION

"I grow emotionally wiser, calmer, and more self-aware every day."

TODAY'S POWER MOVE

Observe your emotional reactions closely today instead of reacting automatically.

DAY 253

Your Future Deserves Better Habits

POWER QUOTE

"The routines you repeat daily either build freedom or build regret."

REFLECTION

Every person has habits.

Some are intentional.

Others develop quietly without much thought.

The route you drive to work.

The way you begin your morning.

How you respond to stress.

How you spend your money.

How you use your free time.

These small routines may seem insignificant on any given day.

Yet over the course of months and years, they quietly shape the direction of your life.

Many people focus heavily on outcomes while paying very little attention to the habits producing those outcomes.

They want financial stability without changing financial behavior.

They want healthier relationships without improving communication.

They want greater peace while continuing patterns that constantly create emotional chaos.

The outcome cannot consistently change if the habits remain the same.

Every repeated action becomes a vote for the person you are becoming.

Every time you choose preparation over procrastination, you strengthen responsibility.

Every time you respond calmly instead of impulsively, you strengthen emotional maturity.

Every time you save instead of spending emotionally, you strengthen financial discipline.

Those choices may feel ordinary.

But ordinary choices, repeated consistently, create extraordinary results.

This is why habits eventually become identity.

People often say,

"I'm just not a disciplined person."

Yet discipline is rarely something people suddenly become.

It is something they repeatedly practice until it becomes part of who they are.

The same is true for patience.

Integrity.

Generosity.

Wisdom.

Confidence.

Character is formed through repetition.

Your habits are quietly teaching you who you are.

That is why it is so important to examine the routines you have normalized.

Ask yourself honest questions.

"Do my daily habits reflect the future I say I want?"

"Are my routines building peace or creating unnecessary stress?"

"Do my financial habits support the life I hope to live?"

"Do the ways I manage my time align with my priorities?"

Questions like these create awareness.

And awareness creates the opportunity for change.

The encouraging truth is that you do not have to change your entire life in one day.

You simply have to begin changing today's habits.

One healthier morning routine.

One intentional conversation.

One wise financial decision.

One hour spent learning instead of scrolling.

One commitment kept instead of postponed.

Small improvements rarely feel dramatic.

But they compound.

Just as unhealthy habits quietly pull life in one direction, healthy habits quietly pull it in another.

Over time, the difference becomes impossible to ignore.

Think about water slowly shaping stone.

One drop seems insignificant.

Thousands of drops reshape the landscape.

Your habits work the same way.

They are constantly shaping your character, your opportunities, your relationships, and your future.

Whether you notice it or not.

This is why discipline is an act of hope.

Every healthy habit is a declaration that tomorrow matters.

Every intentional routine is an investment in the person you are becoming.

You may not see the full results today.

But your future self will.

One day, you will look around at the peace you have built.

The confidence you have developed.

The financial stability you have created.

The emotional maturity you have gained.

And you will realize those things did not appear by accident.

They were built through countless ordinary choices that seemed small at the time.

Protect those choices.

Protect your routines.

Protect the habits that are quietly shaping your future.

Because every day, whether you realize it or not, your habits are building the life you will eventually live.

Choose habits that strengthen your character.

Choose routines that support your purpose.

Choose discipline that creates lasting freedom.

The future is never built all at once.

It is built one habit, one decision, and one intentional day at a time.

WEALTH LESSON

Healthy habits compound financially and emotionally because repeated behavior eventually shapes long-term outcomes.

AFFIRMATION

"I build habits that support peace, growth, and long-term freedom."

TODAY'S POWER MOVE

Replace one unhealthy habit today with a healthier intentional choice.

DAY 254

Stop Letting One Bad Season Define You

POWER QUOTE

"A difficult chapter is not the same as a failed life."

REFLECTION

Every person experiences seasons they never expected.

A relationship ends.

A business struggles.

Money becomes tight.

Health declines.

Plans fall apart.

Dreams are delayed.

These moments are painful.

They deserve honesty.

They deserve compassion.

But they should never become the measure of your entire identity.

One of the greatest dangers during difficult seasons is that people begin describing themselves by what they are experiencing instead of who they are becoming.

A financial struggle becomes,

"I'm a failure."

A painful breakup becomes,

"I'm unlovable."

A business setback becomes,

"I'm not capable."

One mistake becomes,

"This is who I am."

Over time, a temporary season quietly becomes a permanent identity.

That is where many people become emotionally trapped.

The season ends.

But the belief remains.

Life moves forward.

Yet they continue seeing themselves through the lens of a chapter that was never meant to define the entire story.

This is why protecting your identity matters so deeply.

You are not your worst decision.

You are not your greatest disappointment.

You are not the season that challenged you.

You are the person who is choosing what to do next.

That distinction changes everything.

A difficult season can teach you.

Strengthen you.

Refine you.

Humble you.

Prepare you.

But it does not have the authority to decide your future unless you surrender that authority yourself.

History is filled with people whose greatest contributions came after seasons of failure.

After rejection.

After loss.

After uncertainty.

What separated them was not the absence of hardship.

It was the refusal to let hardship become their identity.

Every season carries lessons.

Some teach patience.

Some teach resilience.

Some reveal unhealthy habits that need to change.

Others expose strengths you never realized you possessed.

Pain is not always the end of the story.

Sometimes it is the beginning of a wiser one.

Think about your own life.

There were probably seasons you once believed would last forever.

Moments that felt impossible to survive.

Yet here you are.

Still learning.

Still growing.

Still rebuilding.

The person you are today exists because you continued moving through those chapters instead of allowing them to become the final page.

The same possibility exists now.

Whatever season you are currently living is exactly that.

A season.

Not your identity.

Not your destiny.

Not the complete story of your life.

The beautiful thing about seasons is that they change.

Winter gives way to spring.

Storms eventually pass.

Night gives way to morning.

Life continues moving.

So do people who refuse to stop growing.

This is why hope matters.

Hope is not pretending that everything is easy.

Hope is believing that today's reality does not have to become tomorrow's conclusion.

It is choosing to continue building while the outcome is still uncertain.

It is trusting that consistent effort, healing, discipline, and wisdom will eventually produce a different harvest.

Every healthy decision you make today becomes evidence that your story is still unfolding.

Every boundary you establish.

Every habit you strengthen.

Every fear you confront.

Every lesson you apply.

These choices become new chapters.

Stronger chapters.

Wiser chapters.

Healthier chapters.

Do not allow one painful season to become the loudest voice in your life.

Let it become one of your greatest teachers instead.

Carry the wisdom.

Leave behind the shame.

Carry the lessons.

Leave behind the labels.

Carry the growth.

Leave behind the belief that your future is limited by your past.

Because your life is not measured by one chapter.

It is measured by the courage to keep writing the story after the hardest pages have been turned.

And if you continue choosing healing, discipline, and growth, one day you will look back and realize something extraordinary.

The season you once believed would define you became the very season that prepared you for the life you were always meant to build.

WEALTH LESSON

Resilience creates long-term growth because people who recover continue creating opportunities for themselves.

AFFIRMATION

"I refuse to let temporary hardship define my future permanently."

TODAY'S POWER MOVE

Speak about your future today with hope instead of hopelessness.

DAY 255

Peace Requires Discipline Too

POWER QUOTE

"Peaceful lives are often built intentionally, not accidentally."

REFLECTION

Many people say they want peace.

Peace in their finances.

Peace in their relationships.

Peace in their minds.

Peace in their daily lives.

Yet wanting peace and building peace are not always the same thing.

Peace rarely appears by accident.

It is usually the result of intentional choices repeated over time.

Just as chaos often develops through unhealthy habits, peace is strengthened through healthy ones.

Every day, your decisions are moving your life toward one of those two directions.

Sometimes chaos enters quietly.

It begins with poor boundaries.

Saying yes when you should have said no.

Ignoring problems instead of addressing them.

Allowing constant distractions to consume your attention.

Reacting emotionally instead of responding thoughtfully.

Avoiding financial responsibilities because they feel uncomfortable.

None of these choices seem dramatic on their own.

But together, they slowly create a life that feels overwhelming.

Then people wonder why peace feels so difficult to maintain.

The answer is often hidden inside the habits they have normalized.

Peace requires discipline.

It requires learning to protect your time before it becomes overcommitted.

To protect your mind before it becomes overwhelmed.

To protect your finances before stress begins controlling your decisions.

To protect your relationships by communicating honestly instead of allowing resentment to quietly grow.

Every healthy boundary is an investment in peace.

Every wise financial decision is an investment in peace.

Every emotionally mature response is an investment in peace.

The peaceful life many people admire is rarely effortless.

It is usually built by someone who has spent years making intentional choices.

Someone who learned to regulate their emotions instead of reacting to every feeling.

Someone who developed routines that created stability.

Someone who understood that protecting peace often requires saying no to what consistently steals it.

This is one of the greatest misunderstandings about peace.

Many people imagine peace as the absence of difficulty.

But life will always include challenges.

Unexpected expenses.

Disagreements.

Disappointments.

Uncertainty.

Peace is not created because life becomes perfect.

It is created because you become steadier in the middle of life's imperfections.

That steadiness grows through discipline.

Every morning you choose intentionality over distraction.

Every conversation where you listen before reacting.

Every budget you follow instead of ignoring.

Every evening you choose rest instead of constant busyness.

These quiet choices strengthen your inner stability.

Eventually, your responses begin changing.

Situations that once overwhelmed you no longer carry the same power.

Not because your circumstances always improve immediately.

Because your foundation has become stronger.

That is what discipline quietly accomplishes.

It strengthens the person responding to life.

Many people spend years searching for peace in places where it cannot be sustained.

They chase more possessions.

More attention.

More achievement.

Yet without healthy habits, even wonderful opportunities can become sources of stress.

Real peace is built from the inside out.

It grows through emotional maturity.

Financial stewardship.

Healthy boundaries.

Intentional routines.

Wise relationships.

A mind trained to return to truth instead of panic.

These practices may not always feel exciting.

They are often repetitive.

Ordinary.

Quiet.

But that is exactly how lasting peace is built.

One disciplined decision at a time.

One healthy habit at a time.

One intentional day after another.

Protect your peace as carefully as you protect your future.

Because in many ways, they are inseparable.

A peaceful mind makes wiser decisions.

A peaceful heart builds healthier relationships.

A peaceful life creates space for purpose to flourish.

Do not wait for peace to arrive someday.

Begin building it today.

With the boundaries you establish.

The habits you strengthen.

The conversations you choose.

The thoughts you cultivate.

And the discipline you practice consistently.

Because peace is not something you stumble upon.

It is something you intentionally create.

And over time, those daily choices become more than habits.

They become the foundation of a life marked by clarity, stability, wisdom, and lasting freedom.

WEALTH LESSON

Peace improves productivity and decision-making because emotionally stable minds think more clearly long-term.

AFFIRMATION

"I intentionally build a peaceful life through disciplined choices."

TODAY'S POWER MOVE

Protect your peace today by avoiding one unnecessary source of emotional chaos.

DAY 256

You Are Allowed To Change Your Life

POWER QUOTE

"Growth begins the moment you stop believing you are permanently stuck."

REFLECTION

One of the most limiting beliefs a person can carry is the belief that they can never truly change.

People quietly tell themselves,

"This is just who I am."

"I've always struggled with money."

"I'm just an emotional person."

"I've never been disciplined."

"I'll probably always be this way."

At first, these statements seem like simple observations.

Over time, they become identities.

And once people begin identifying with unhealthy patterns, they often stop believing transformation is possible.

But your current habits are not your permanent identity.

They are your current patterns.

Patterns can change.

A person who once struggled to manage money can learn financial discipline.

A person who once reacted impulsively can learn emotional regulation.

A person who once lived in fear can develop courage.

A person who once survived can eventually learn to thrive.

None of those transformations happen overnight.

But they happen.

Many people expect change to arrive through one dramatic breakthrough.

More often, change begins through quiet repetition.

One healthier decision.

One difficult conversation.

One budget followed.

One boundary established.

One morning of showing up when motivation is absent.

These moments rarely feel extraordinary while they are happening.

Yet each one weakens an old pattern and strengthens a new one.

This is why identity is so powerful.

The life you experience tomorrow is often shaped by the beliefs you choose to accept today.

If you continue believing that your past determines your future, you may never give yourself permission to grow beyond it.

But if you begin believing that growth is possible, your daily choices begin changing.

You stop asking,

"Is change possible?"

And you begin asking,

"What decision will move me one step closer to the person I want to become?"

That question creates momentum.

Transformation also requires honesty.

You cannot change what you refuse to acknowledge.

You must be willing to recognize unhealthy habits without allowing them to become permanent labels.

There is a difference between saying,

"I struggle with discipline,"

and saying,

"I am an undisciplined person."

One describes a challenge.

The other defines your identity.

Your challenges deserve your attention.

They do not deserve ownership of your future.

Growth requires effort.

Consistency.

Self-awareness.

Patience.

There will be days when old habits try to return.

Days when progress feels slow.

Days when you question whether anything is really changing.

Do not confuse slow progress with the absence of progress.

A tree does not become strong in a single season.

Its roots deepen little by little until one day its strength becomes obvious to everyone.

Your character grows the same way.

Quietly.

Faithfully.

One intentional choice at a time.

Every time you choose discipline over distraction, you become a little stronger.

Every time you choose healing over avoidance, you become a little healthier.

Every time you choose responsibility over excuses, you become a little wiser.

These moments are shaping the future version of you long before anyone else can see the results.

Do not underestimate what today's choices are building.

The person you hope to become is not created by wishing.

They are created through repeated decisions that align with your values.

So stop introducing yourself to yourself through your old patterns.

Introduce yourself through your potential.

Through your commitment.

Through your willingness to keep growing.

Because you are not trapped inside the person you used to be.

You are becoming the person your future requires.

Keep rebuilding.

Keep learning.

Keep healing.

Keep showing up.

One day, you will realize that the greatest transformation in your life did not happen because everything changed at once.

It happened because you refused to believe that yesterday's version of you had to become tomorrow's reality.

And from that decision, an entirely new life quietly began.

WEALTH LESSON

Identity transformation improves outcomes because healthier beliefs create healthier behavior.

AFFIRMATION

"I allow myself to evolve into a healthier and stronger version of myself."

TODAY'S POWER MOVE

Identify one old pattern you are intentionally committed to changing.

DAY 257

Your Future Needs Better Boundaries

POWER QUOTE

"Boundaries protect peace, focus, and emotional stability."

REFLECTION

A lot of people believe boundaries exist to keep others out.

Healthy boundaries serve a much greater purpose.

They protect what is valuable.

Your peace.

Your energy.

Your time.

Your emotional well-being.

Your ability to continue becoming the person you are called to be.

Without boundaries, life slowly begins filling with obligations that were never meant to belong to you.

You say yes when your heart knows you should say no.

You carry responsibilities that belong to someone else.

You remain in conversations that repeatedly drain your spirit.

You tolerate behaviors that quietly erode your confidence and peace.

At first, these decisions may seem generous.

Over time, they often become exhausting.

Many people become emotionally depleted not because they lack strength, but because they have never learned where healthy responsibility ends and unhealthy self-sacrifice begins.

They spend so much time taking care of everyone else's needs that they neglect their own.

Eventually, that exhaustion begins affecting every area of life.

Their patience becomes shorter.

Their focus weakens.

Their discipline becomes inconsistent.

Their relationships suffer.

Their joy slowly disappears beneath the weight of constant emotional overload.

This is why boundaries are not selfish.

They are responsible.

Imagine trying to pour water into someone else's cup while your own remains empty.

Eventually, there is nothing left to give.

Healthy boundaries make sure your own well-being is not constantly sacrificed in the name of helping everyone else.

That does not mean becoming distant or uncaring.

It means recognizing that you cannot sustainably care for others while continually abandoning yourself.

One of the greatest signs of emotional maturity is learning that love and boundaries can exist together.

You can care deeply about someone while refusing unhealthy behavior.

You can be compassionate without becoming responsible for every problem.

You can forgive someone without allowing repeated harm to continue.

You can serve others without losing yourself.

Those truths often require courage.

Because setting boundaries may disappoint people who benefited from your lack of them.

Not everyone will understand your growth.

Some people become uncomfortable when you begin protecting your time.

Others may resist when you stop accepting treatment that once felt normal.

That discomfort does not automatically mean you are doing something wrong.

Sometimes it means your life is becoming healthier.

Boundaries also protect your future.

Every unnecessary commitment consumes time that could have been invested in your purpose.

Every emotionally draining environment reduces energy that could have strengthened your family, your work, your healing, or your growth.

Protecting your peace is not only about avoiding stress.

It is about creating space for what truly matters.

The life you hope to build requires emotional capacity.

It requires clear thinking.

Intentional relationships.

Healthy routines.

Steady discipline.

Those qualities flourish in environments where peace is protected instead of constantly threatened.

Learning to establish boundaries is a process.

You may not always do it perfectly.

There will be moments when saying no feels uncomfortable.

Moments when choosing yourself feels unfamiliar.

Moments when guilt tries to convince you that protecting your well-being is selfish.

Remember this:

Boundaries are not walls built out of bitterness.

They are doors built with wisdom.

They help you decide what deserves access to your life and what no longer supports the person you are becoming.

Every healthy boundary is an investment in your future.

Every intentional decision to protect your peace strengthens your emotional resilience.

Every environment you choose carefully helps shape the quality of the life you are building.

So guard your peace with wisdom.

Protect your energy with intention.

Choose relationships that encourage growth instead of constant exhaustion.

Create routines that strengthen your well-being instead of draining it.

Because your future deserves more than a life spent constantly recovering from unnecessary emotional depletion.

It deserves stability.

Clarity.

Healthy relationships.

Purpose.

And the kind of peace that grows when you finally realize that protecting your well-being is not an act of selfishness.

It is an act of stewardship for the life you have been entrusted to build.

WEALTH LESSON

Healthy boundaries strengthen emotional regulation and focus because energy is protected more intentionally.

AFFIRMATION

"I protect my peace through clear boundaries and intentional choices."

TODAY'S POWER MOVE

Say no today to something that continuously drains your emotional energy unnecessarily.

DAY 258

Stop Waiting For Easy

POWER QUOTE

"Growth rarely feels comfortable while it is happening."

REFLECTION

We often believe life will become easier before they become more disciplined.

They wait for a season with less stress.

More motivation.

More confidence.

More certainty.

Then, they tell themselves, they will finally begin.

But meaningful transformation rarely begins after life becomes comfortable.

More often, it begins in the middle of discomfort.

Discomfort is one of the most misunderstood parts of growth.

People often assume that if something feels difficult, they must be doing something wrong.

In reality, many of life's healthiest changes feel unfamiliar before they feel natural.

The first workout challenges your body.

The first budget challenges your spending habits.

The first healthy boundary challenges old relationship patterns.

The first honest conversation challenges your fear of conflict.

The first steps toward healing often require facing emotions you have spent years trying to avoid.

None of those experiences are comfortable.

But discomfort is not always a warning.

Sometimes it is evidence that you are stretching beyond the limits that once defined you.

Think about learning to walk as a child.

Every step involved uncertainty.

Falling.

Trying again.

If discomfort had been interpreted as failure, no one would ever have learned to walk.

Growth has always required temporary awkwardness before lasting confidence.

The same principle continues throughout adulthood.

Every meaningful goal asks you to become someone you have never been before.

That requires leaving familiar patterns behind.

Familiar habits.

Familiar excuses.

Familiar fears.

Even unhealthy patterns can feel comfortable simply because they are familiar.

Healing often feels uncomfortable because it asks you to stop returning to survival patterns that once protected you.

Discipline feels uncomfortable because it replaces immediate gratification with long-term purpose.

Responsibility feels uncomfortable because it stretches your capacity.

Growth asks for change.
And change almost always feels unfamiliar before it feels rewarding.
This is why patience is so important.
Do not judge your progress only by today's emotions.
Judge it by the direction your choices are taking your life.
Every disciplined decision is expanding your capacity.
Every healthy habit is reshaping your character.
Every difficult conversation handled with wisdom is strengthening your relationships.
Every act of courage is teaching your mind that fear no longer has to make your decisions.
None of this happens instantly.
Transformation rarely announces itself with dramatic moments.
More often, it arrives quietly.
One repeated decision at a time.
One ordinary day after another.
Many people quit because they mistake discomfort for failure.
The people who experience lasting transformation usually understand something different.
They recognize that discomfort often comes before confidence.
Practice comes before mastery.
Healing comes before peace.
Discipline comes before freedom.
They keep going because they understand the process.
This does not mean ignoring exhaustion or pretending every challenge should simply be pushed through.
Wisdom still knows when to rest.
When to ask for help.
When to recover.
Healthy growth includes recovery.
But recovery is different from retreating every time something becomes uncomfortable.
One restores your strength.
The other keeps you trapped in familiar limitations.
Your future will ask more of you than your past ever did.
More responsibility.
More emotional maturity.
More patience.
More wisdom.
The discomfort you experience today may be preparing you for opportunities you cannot yet see.
So do not become discouraged simply because growth feels difficult.
Do not mistake unfamiliarity for failure.
Allow yourself to become comfortable with the process of becoming.
Because every challenge you meet with courage is quietly expanding the person you are capable of becoming.
One day, you will look back on the seasons that once stretched you and realize they were never meant to stop you.
They were preparing you.

Preparing your character.

Preparing your discipline.

Preparing your perspective.

Preparing you for a life that your former self could only imagine.

Keep going.

The discomfort you are experiencing today may be the very doorway through which your future is waiting.

WEALTH LESSON

Transformation requires emotional endurance because meaningful transformation often develops gradually through discomfort.

AFFIRMATION

"I continue growing even when the process feels difficult."

TODAY'S POWER MOVE

Push yourself through one uncomfortable but necessary task today.

DAY 259

Your Future Is Built Through Repetition

POWER QUOTE

"What you repeatedly do eventually becomes who you are."

REFLECTION

Many people think identity is something they simply have.

In reality, identity is something they continually build.

Every day, your thoughts, habits, decisions, and emotional responses are quietly reinforcing the person you are becoming.

Identity is not usually formed during life's biggest moments.

It is formed during the ordinary ones.

The way you respond to disappointment.

The way you speak to yourself after making a mistake.

The way you manage your finances when no one is watching.

The way you honor your commitments when motivation has disappeared.

These quiet moments often shape your character far more than dramatic milestones ever could.

This is why repetition matters.

Every repeated thought strengthens a belief.

Every repeated behavior strengthens a habit.

Every repeated habit strengthens an identity.

That process happens whether you are intentional about it or not.

If you repeatedly avoid difficult conversations, avoidance slowly begins feeling like part of who you are.

If you repeatedly spend money emotionally instead of intentionally, financial impulsiveness begins feeling normal.

If you repeatedly choose discipline over distraction, responsibility gradually becomes part of your character.

Your identity is constantly being shaped by what you consistently practice.

Many people hope to become peaceful without practicing peace.

They hope to become disciplined without practicing discipline.

They hope to become confident without repeatedly doing courageous things.

But lasting change rarely happens that way.

You do not become patient by wishing for patience.

You become patient by repeatedly choosing calm responses when frustration would be easier.

You do not become financially responsible through good intentions alone.

You become financially responsible through repeated decisions that align with wisdom instead of impulse.

You do not become emotionally mature through age alone.

You become emotionally mature through consistently learning to pause, reflect, and respond with intention.

Every healthy response becomes another brick in the foundation of your future.

This is why consistency is so much more powerful than intensity.

One extraordinary day can inspire you.

A thousand ordinary days of faithfulness can transform you.

People often search for dramatic breakthroughs because they are exciting.

But character is usually built through repetition.
One workout rarely changes your body.
One conversation rarely transforms a relationship.
One budget rarely creates financial freedom.
Yet those actions, repeated over months and years, become almost unrecognizable in their impact.
That is the quiet power of consistency.
It compounds.
Every day you repeat a healthy habit, you make that habit a little more natural.
Eventually, what once required tremendous effort begins feeling like part of who you are.
That is when identity has begun to change.
This process also works in reverse.
Repeated excuses become a habit.
Repeated procrastination becomes a habit.
Repeated negativity becomes a habit.
The good news is that habits are learned.
Which means they can also be replaced.
You are never required to remain the person your past trained you to be.
You can intentionally choose different thoughts.
Different routines.
Different responses.
Different priorities.
One decision at a time.
Do not become discouraged if your progress feels slow.
Identity is not rewritten in a single day.
It is rewritten every time you make a choice that aligns with the person you are becoming instead of the person you used to be.
Each disciplined action is a declaration.
Each healthy boundary is a declaration.
Each wise financial decision is a declaration.
Each act of forgiveness.
Each moment of courage.
Each commitment you keep.
They all quietly say the same thing:
"This is who I am becoming."
One day, people may notice your confidence, your peace, your discipline, or your wisdom and assume those qualities appeared naturally.
Only you will know the truth.
They were built.
One repeated choice after another.
One ordinary day after another.
One intentional habit at a time.

So pay attention to what you repeat.

Because repetition becomes habit.

Habit becomes character.

Character becomes identity.

And your identity ultimately shapes the life you build.

The future version of you is not waiting to appear someday.

That person is being formed today through the choices you consistently make.

Choose them wisely.

WEALTH LESSON

Repeated disciplined behavior compounds into long-term emotional and financial transformation.

AFFIRMATION

"I intentionally repeat behaviors that strengthen my future."

TODAY'S POWER MOVE

Practice one healthy behavior consistently throughout the day today.

DAY 260

You Are Becoming The Person You Once Needed

POWER QUOTE

"Your healing may eventually become someone else's hope."

REFLECTION

Growth can be difficult to recognize while you are living through it.

When you see yourself every day, the changes often feel small.

The healthier decisions.

The calmer responses.

The stronger boundaries.

The wiser financial choices.

The greater emotional awareness.

They happen so gradually that you may begin believing nothing is changing at all.

But sometimes the clearest evidence of growth is found by looking backward instead of forward.

Think about the version of yourself from a few years ago.

The version who questioned everything.

Who doubted their ability.

Who reacted from fear instead of wisdom.

Who felt overwhelmed by problems that now seem manageable.

Who struggled to believe life could become different.

That person was doing the best they could with the knowledge, experiences, and emotional capacity they had at the time.

Do not judge them harshly.

Honor them.

Because without that version of you continuing through difficult seasons, the person you are becoming today would not exist.

Growth rarely happens all at once.

It unfolds quietly.

You become a little more patient after learning from conflict.

A little more disciplined after honoring small commitments.

A little more financially responsible after making wiser decisions.

A little more emotionally secure after choosing healing instead of avoidance.

These changes may feel ordinary.

But together they create a completely different life.

One of the most beautiful moments in personal growth is realizing that you are slowly becoming the kind of person you once desperately needed.

The encouragement you once searched for, you now know how to offer.

The emotional stability you once longed to experience, you are beginning to cultivate.

The wisdom you once hoped someone would teach you is becoming part of the way you live.

The strength you once admired in others is quietly developing within you.

That realization is powerful.

Because healing is never only about you.

Every healthier decision you make influences the people around you.

When you become emotionally mature, your relationships become safer.

When you become financially disciplined, your family benefits from greater stability.

When you learn healthy communication, conflict becomes an opportunity for understanding instead of division.

When you establish healthy boundaries, you give others permission to value their own well-being as well.

Growth creates ripple effects that often extend far beyond your own life.

This is why your healing matters.

Not because it makes you perfect.

But because it makes you more present.

More intentional.

More compassionate.

More capable of building environments where other people can flourish.

Do not become discouraged simply because there is still more work to do.

There will always be another lesson to learn.

Another habit to strengthen.

Another area of life that invites greater wisdom.

Growth is not about arriving at perfection.

It is about continuing the journey with humility and intention.

Take time to acknowledge how far you have come.

Celebrate the victories that no one else may ever see.

The conversations you handled differently.

The impulses you resisted.

The fears you faced.

The habits you changed.

The boundaries you finally established.

Those moments matter.

They are evidence that transformation is taking place.

Your future is not being built only by the goals you achieve.

It is being built by the person you are becoming along the way.

One day, someone may look at your life and find hope because of the peace you carry.

The wisdom you share.

The consistency you model.

The resilience you demonstrate.

They may never fully know the battles you fought to become that person.

But you will.

You will remember the difficult seasons.

The quiet rebuilding.

The slow progress.

The ordinary days when you chose to keep going.

And you will realize that every one of those decisions mattered.

Because they shaped someone your younger self would have admired.

Keep becoming that person.

Keep learning.

Keep healing.

Keep rebuilding.

The world does not simply need more successful people.

It needs more people who have allowed their struggles to become wisdom, their pain to become compassion, and their growth to become a source of hope for others.

That person is already being formed within you—one intentional decision at a time.

WEALTH LESSON

Personal growth creates positive ripple effects because healthier people often build healthier environments and relationships.

AFFIRMATION

"I honor the growth that is shaping me into someone stronger and wiser."

TODAY'S POWER MOVE

Reflect today on how much you have emotionally grown compared to a previous season in your life.

DAY 261

Stop Letting Fear Control Your Identity

POWER QUOTE

"Fear should be acknowledged, not obeyed."

REFLECTION

Fear is one of the most persuasive voices a person will ever encounter.

It rarely shouts.

More often, it whispers.

"Wait a little longer."

"You're not ready yet."

"What if you fail?"

"What if people judge you?"

"What if you embarrass yourself?"

Those thoughts can seem reasonable in the moment.

But when listened to repeatedly, fear begins doing something much more dangerous than creating hesitation.

It begins shrinking your life.

Many people never discover the limits of their potential because fear convinces them to live safely instead of intentionally.

They avoid applying for the opportunity.

They never start the business.

They stay in unhealthy relationships because familiarity feels safer than change.

They silence their ideas before anyone else has the chance to hear them.

They remain in places they have already outgrown because uncertainty feels more frightening than dissatisfaction.

Eventually, fear no longer influences one decision.

It begins influencing an entire lifestyle.

The tragedy is that fear often disguises itself as wisdom.

It tells you that avoiding risk is the responsible choice.

That staying comfortable is the safest path.

That waiting for certainty is maturity.

Sometimes caution is wise.

But there is a difference between wisdom and fear.

Wisdom prepares.

Fear postpones.

Wisdom evaluates.

Fear exaggerates.

Wisdom helps you move carefully.

Fear convinces you not to move at all.

Your future will always require courage because growth always asks you to leave something familiar behind.

A familiar routine.

A familiar environment.

A familiar version of yourself.

That transition rarely feels comfortable.

The unknown has a way of exposing every insecurity you hoped had disappeared.

Yet every meaningful chapter of life begins with someone willing to take a step before having every answer.

Courage does not mean fear disappears.

Even courageous people experience uncertainty.

They question themselves.

They wonder whether they are capable.

They feel vulnerable.

The difference is not the absence of fear.

The difference is the decision that fear will no longer become the author of their choices.

Every time you move forward despite fear, something begins changing inside you.

You gather evidence that you are stronger than your doubts suggested.

You begin trusting yourself more.

Not because life suddenly becomes easier.

Because you have proven that you can continue even when uncertainty remains.

That is how confidence is built.

Not by avoiding difficult situations.

But by walking through them.

Fear also loses strength through repetition.

The first difficult conversation feels intimidating.

The tenth becomes much more manageable.

The first public presentation feels overwhelming.

The hundredth feels familiar.

The first investment into your future feels risky.

Over time, wisdom replaces panic because experience has expanded your confidence.

This is why small acts of courage matter.

Every healthy boundary.

Every responsible financial decision.

Every honest conversation.

Every opportunity you pursue despite uncertainty.

Each one weakens fear's influence over your identity.

Little by little, courage becomes more familiar than avoidance.

Remember that fear always focuses on what could go wrong.

Faith focuses on what could go right through preparation, persistence, and growth.

Neither offers guarantees.

But only one allows you to fully discover who you are capable of becoming.

Years from now, you are unlikely to regret every challenge you courageously faced.

You are far more likely to wonder what might have happened if fear had not convinced you to remain still.

Do not allow temporary uncertainty to permanently reduce your future.

Protect your dreams from unnecessary doubt.

Strengthen your character through consistent action.

Keep moving, even when your steps feel small.

Because every courageous decision expands your capacity for the next one.

One day, you will look back and realize that the life you built was not created because fear disappeared.

It was created because you stopped giving fear permission to decide who you could become.

And from that moment forward, your future was no longer written by fear.

It was written by courage, one intentional decision at a time.

WEALTH LESSON

Courage creates opportunities because growth often requires uncomfortable action before confidence fully develops.

AFFIRMATION

"I move forward courageously even when fear tries to discourage me."

TODAY'S POWER MOVE

Take one action today that fear has been convincing you to delay.

DAY 262

Your Mindset Affects Your Money

POWER QUOTE

"Financial behavior is often emotional behavior in disguise."

REFLECTION

Some people believe money problems are simply math problems.

Earn more.

Spend less.

Save consistently.

Invest wisely.

Those principles are important.

But for many people, the real struggle is not knowing what to do.

It is understanding why they do what they do.

Money is deeply connected to emotion.

A person who constantly fears not having enough may hold on to money so tightly that they never invest in opportunities that could help them grow.

Someone who carries shame about past financial mistakes may avoid looking at bank statements because facing reality feels overwhelming.

Another person may spend impulsively because buying something new briefly eases feelings of stress, loneliness, or disappointment.

On the surface, these behaviors appear financial.

Underneath them, they are often emotional.

That is why financial healing requires more than learning how to budget.

It requires learning how to understand yourself.

Your financial habits are often shaped long before your first paycheck.

The conversations you heard about money as a child.

The examples you watched growing up.

The seasons of abundance or scarcity you experienced.

The beliefs you quietly accepted about wealth, success, and security.

Without realizing it, those experiences begin influencing how you earn, spend, save, give, and invest.

Some people grow up believing money is always scarce.

Others believe wealth belongs only to certain kinds of people.

Some begin associating financial success with guilt, pressure, or fear.

Those beliefs quietly become the lens through which every financial decision is made.

That is why rebuilding your financial life begins with rebuilding your financial identity.

Ask yourself honest questions.

"What do I truly believe about money?"

"When I feel financial stress, how do I usually respond?"

"What emotions influence my spending?"

"What habits keep repeating in my financial life?"

Questions like these create awareness.

And awareness creates the opportunity for change.
Financial peace begins when you stop reacting emotionally and begin responding intentionally.
Instead of spending to escape uncomfortable feelings, you learn to process those feelings in healthier ways.
Instead of avoiding your finances because they create anxiety, you choose honesty because clarity creates confidence.
Instead of believing your past mistakes define your future, you begin making decisions that reflect the person you are becoming.
This process takes time.
Years of unhealthy financial thinking are rarely replaced overnight.
But every intentional decision weakens an old pattern and strengthens a healthier one.
Every budget becomes more than a spreadsheet.
It becomes an act of self-respect.
Every savings deposit becomes more than money set aside.
It becomes evidence that you believe your future deserves preparation.
Every wise purchase becomes a reminder that your emotions no longer have to control your financial choices.
Over time, something remarkable begins to happen.
Money stops feeling like a source of constant fear.
It becomes a tool.
A resource that allows you to care for your responsibilities, create opportunities, serve others, and build the future you envision.
That shift changes everything.
You begin making decisions from wisdom instead of panic.
From preparation instead of avoidance.
From purpose instead of impulse.
Financial freedom is not created only by increasing income.
It is strengthened by developing the emotional maturity to manage whatever resources you have been entrusted with.
That is why healing your relationship with money is one of the greatest investments you can make.
Because when your mindset changes, your behavior changes.
When your behavior changes, your habits change.
When your habits change, your financial future begins changing as well.
Do not settle for learning only how to manage money.
Learn how to understand the emotions, beliefs, and patterns that influence the way you relate to it.
Because lasting financial peace is built from the inside out.
It begins with honesty.
It grows through discipline.
It is sustained through wisdom.
And one intentional decision at a time, it transforms not only your finances, but the person you become while building them.

WEALTH LESSON

Healthy financial habits improve when emotional awareness and intentional planning increase together.

AFFIRMATION

"I build a healthier emotional and financial relationship with money."

TODAY'S POWER MOVE

Notice one emotional habit today that affects your financial behavior negatively.

DAY 263

Discipline Is A Daily Choice

POWER QUOTE

"Discipline is built one decision at a time."

REFLECTION

Many people look at disciplined individuals and assume they were simply born that way.

They believe some people naturally wake up early.

Naturally stay focused.

Naturally manage money well.

Naturally follow through on commitments.

The truth is usually much less dramatic.

Discipline is rarely a personality trait.

It is a practice.

It is built one decision at a time.

No one is born knowing how to manage distractions, delay gratification, or consistently honor long-term commitments.

Those abilities are developed through repetition.

Every time you choose responsibility over convenience, you strengthen discipline.

Every time you keep a promise to yourself, you strengthen discipline.

Every time you return after missing a day instead of giving up entirely, you strengthen discipline.

These moments may feel ordinary.

But they are quietly shaping your identity.

One of the biggest misconceptions about discipline is that it should always feel motivating.

It rarely does.

Most disciplined people are not constantly inspired.

They simply refuse to let inspiration become the requirement for action.

There will always be mornings when you would rather stay in bed.

Days when your budget feels restrictive.

Moments when distractions seem far more appealing than the work in front of you.

Discipline is not the absence of those feelings.

It is the decision that your values matter more than your temporary emotions.

That decision becomes easier the more often you practice it.

Think about learning to play an instrument.

The first few lessons feel awkward.

Simple movements require tremendous concentration.

Mistakes happen constantly.

But through repetition, what once felt difficult becomes natural.

Discipline develops in much the same way.

The first time you choose to save money instead of spending impulsively, it may feel uncomfortable.

The first week of consistently exercising may feel exhausting.

The first month of creating healthy routines may require constant effort.

Eventually, however, those behaviors begin requiring less willpower because they have become part of who you are.

This is why repetition is so powerful.

Every repeated action strengthens a pathway in your character.

The more often you practice a healthy habit, the more natural it becomes.

That is how ordinary people become disciplined people.

Not through perfection.

Through persistence.

Many people give up too early because they mistake repetition for a lack of progress.

They think,

"I'm doing the same things every day. Nothing is changing."

But repetition is not evidence that growth has stopped.

Repetition is often the process through which growth is created.

The athlete repeats the same movements.

The musician practices the same scales.

The writer returns to the blank page.

The entrepreneur solves one problem after another.

The financially disciplined person follows the same budget month after month.

From the outside, these routines may appear repetitive.

From the inside, they are quietly building excellence.

Your life is no different.

Every disciplined choice compounds.

Every intentional routine strengthens your future.

Every act of consistency becomes another layer of the person you are becoming.

Do not underestimate the value of ordinary faithfulness.

You do not need to accomplish something extraordinary every day.

You simply need to continue practicing the habits that move you toward the life you want.

That is how confidence grows.

That is how wisdom grows.

That is how financial stability grows.

That is how emotional maturity grows.

One repeated decision at a time.

So stop believing discipline is reserved for a fortunate few.

It is available to anyone willing to practice it.

Not perfectly.

But consistently.

The strongest lives are rarely built through moments of extraordinary motivation.

They are built through thousands of ordinary decisions made with extraordinary commitment.

Keep showing up.

Keep following through.

Keep honoring the promises you make to yourself.

Because every disciplined action is doing more than completing today's task.

It is quietly shaping tomorrow's identity.

And one day, people may call you naturally disciplined.

Only you will know the truth.

You simply became the person who chose to keep practicing when many others chose to stop.

WEALTH LESSON

Repeated disciplined actions compound into long-term financial and emotional freedom.

AFFIRMATION

"I strengthen discipline through intentional daily decisions."

TODAY'S POWER MOVE

Commit to following through completely on one responsibility today.

DAY 264

You Are Not Your Worst Moment

POWER QUOTE

"One painful season should never become your permanent identity."

REFLECTION

Every person has moments they wish they could erase.

A decision they regret.

A relationship that ended painfully.

A financial mistake that cost more than they expected.

A season where fear became stronger than faith.

A chapter they rarely talk about because remembering it still hurts.

These moments are part of being human.

Yet many people make one life-changing mistake after experiencing them.

They stop separating what happened from who they are.

A failure becomes,

"I am a failure."

A broken relationship becomes,

"I'm impossible to love."

A financial setback becomes,

"I'll never be good with money."

A season of emotional struggle becomes,

"This is just who I am."

Without realizing it, they allow one chapter to become the title of the entire book.

That is one of the greatest lies discouragement can tell.

Your hardest season may influence you.

It may teach you.

It may humble you.

It may leave scars that take time to heal.

But it does not have the authority to define your identity.

There is a profound difference between carrying wisdom from your past and carrying shame from it.

Wisdom says,

"I learned something valuable."

Shame says,

"I will never become anything different."

One creates growth.

The other quietly imprisons it.

Think about the people you admire most.

Very few built meaningful lives without disappointment.

Many experienced rejection before acceptance.

Failure before success.

Loss before restoration.

Uncertainty before clarity.

What made the difference was not that they avoided difficult seasons.

It was that they refused to let those seasons become permanent definitions of who they were.

Growth always begins with honesty.

You cannot heal from what you refuse to acknowledge.

If you made a mistake, own it.

If you hurt someone, seek to make it right where possible.

If your choices created consequences, learn from them.

Responsibility is an essential part of transformation.

But responsibility and self-condemnation are not the same thing.

One helps you grow.

The other keeps you trapped.

Healing requires both accountability and hope.

Accountability allows you to face reality.

Hope reminds you that reality can change.

Every new day gives you another opportunity to write a different chapter.

Every healthy habit weakens an unhealthy pattern.

Every wise financial decision begins repairing past mistakes.

Every act of forgiveness begins softening old wounds.

Every disciplined choice becomes evidence that your future is no longer controlled by yesterday.

Transformation is rarely dramatic.

It is usually quiet.

The person you become is shaped by what you repeatedly choose after disappointment.

Do you quit?

Or do you rebuild?

Do you hide?

Or do you heal?

Do you accept limiting labels?

Or do you allow your character to grow beyond them?

Those questions determine far more about your future than your past ever will.

Never forget that your worth was never determined by your worst moment.

Your value did not disappear because you struggled.

Your purpose was not canceled because life became difficult.

You are still capable of learning.

Still capable of rebuilding.

Still capable of becoming wiser, stronger, and more compassionate than you were before.

One mistake cannot erase a lifetime of potential.

One painful season cannot cancel the future that still lies ahead.

The version of you standing today is not required to remain the person who made yesterday's decisions.

You have the ability to choose again.

To grow again.

To hope again.

To build again.

And every time you make a decision that aligns with wisdom instead of shame, you take another step away from the person your pain tried to convince you that you were.

Keep walking.

Keep healing.

Keep rebuilding.

Because your lowest moment was never meant to become your permanent identity.

It was simply one chapter that prepared you to write a stronger story than you ever believed possible.

WEALTH LESSON

Resilience improves long-term outcomes because emotionally strong people continue rebuilding after setbacks.

AFFIRMATION

"I refuse to define myself by my worst moments."

TODAY'S POWER MOVE

Release one painful memory today that you have been using against yourself emotionally.

DAY 265

Peace Is Built Through Boundaries

POWER QUOTE

"Peaceful lives require intentional protection."

REFLECTION

Many people dream of living a peaceful life.

They imagine waking up with clarity.

Building healthy relationships.

Managing their finances without constant anxiety.

Pursuing their purpose with confidence.

Yet they unknowingly allow habits, environments, and relationships into their lives that quietly undermine the very peace they desire.

Peace is not only something you experience.

It is something you protect.

Every day, you make decisions about what will have access to your mind, your emotions, your time, and your energy.

Those decisions matter more than most people realize.

One unhealthy environment tolerated for too long can slowly drain your confidence.

One relationship without healthy boundaries can consume emotional energy that was meant to be invested elsewhere.

One habit of constantly saying yes when you need to say no can leave you exhausted, distracted, and disconnected from your own priorities.

Peace rarely disappears all at once.

It is usually lost one small compromise at a time.

That is why boundaries are acts of wisdom.

They are not barriers designed to push people away.

They are safeguards that protect what is valuable.

Your healing deserves protection.

Your focus deserves protection.

Your emotional well-being deserves protection.

Your future deserves protection.

Healthy people understand that not everyone should have unlimited access to their time or emotional energy.

This is not because they love people less.

It is because they understand that love without wisdom eventually becomes exhaustion.

You cannot continue pouring into everyone else while neglecting your own well-being.

Eventually, even the most generous heart becomes depleted.

Healthy boundaries allow generosity to remain sustainable.

They help you give from a place of strength instead of constant depletion.

They create space for rest without guilt.

Reflection without distraction.

Growth without unnecessary interruption.

One of the greatest signs of emotional maturity is learning that protecting your peace is not selfish.

It is responsible.

A peaceful person is often not someone with fewer problems.

They are someone who has become intentional about what they allow to shape their life.

They choose relationships that encourage growth instead of constant drama.

They establish routines that strengthen stability instead of chaos.

They recognize when certain conversations, environments, or habits consistently pull them away from the person they are becoming.

Then they make the difficult decision to protect what matters most.

This requires courage.

Not everyone will understand your boundaries.

Some people may mistake them for rejection.

Others may become uncomfortable because your growth changes familiar patterns.

That discomfort does not necessarily mean you are doing something wrong.

Sometimes it is evidence that your life is becoming healthier.

Remember that every "yes" you give is also a "no" to something else.

Every hour spent in unnecessary conflict is an hour not invested in your purpose.

Every emotionally draining environment reduces energy that could have strengthened your family, your work, your healing, or your dreams.

Protecting your peace means becoming intentional about those choices.

Ask yourself often:

"Does this relationship strengthen my life or consistently drain it?"

"Does this environment help me become the person I hope to be?"

"Does this habit create greater peace or greater chaos?"

Those questions create clarity.

And clarity leads to wiser decisions.

The life you are building deserves your full attention.

It deserves healthy routines.

Supportive relationships.

Clear priorities.

And the emotional stability that comes from living with intention instead of constant reaction.

Peace is not fragile because it is weak.

Peace is valuable because it is foundational.

It strengthens your judgment.

It sharpens your focus.

It steadies your emotions.

It allows wisdom to speak more clearly than fear.

Guard it carefully.

Protect it consistently.

Honor it daily.

Because every healthy boundary you establish today becomes another brick in the foundation of the peaceful future you are building.

And one day, you will realize that some of the greatest decisions you ever made were not only about what you chose to pursue.

They were also about what you wisely chose to stop allowing into your life.

WEALTH LESSON

Healthy boundaries improve emotional regulation because protected energy strengthens focus and discipline.

AFFIRMATION

"I protect my peace through intentional boundaries and healthy decisions."

TODAY'S POWER MOVE

Create one emotional boundary today that protects your peace long-term.

DAY 266

Your Healing Is Changing You Quietly

POWER QUOTE

"Not all transformation is immediately visible."

REFLECTION

One of the most difficult parts of personal growth is that it often happens too gradually for you to notice it.

You live with yourself every day.

You experience your own thoughts.

Your own emotions.

Your own struggles.

Because the changes happen little by little, it is easy to believe nothing is changing at all.

But healing is rarely loud.

It is usually quiet.

It happens in ordinary moments that seem insignificant while you are living them.

The first time you choose not to react impulsively.

The first time you walk away from unnecessary conflict.

The first time you create a budget and actually follow it.

The first time you say no without feeling guilty.

The first time you forgive yourself instead of repeating old shame.

Those moments may not feel life-changing.

Yet they are.

Because every healthy response weakens an unhealthy pattern.

Every intentional decision strengthens a healthier identity.

Healing does not usually announce itself with dramatic breakthroughs.

More often, it reveals itself through quieter evidence.

You recover from disappointment more quickly.

You no longer lose your peace over situations that once overwhelmed you.

You notice yourself thinking differently.

Responding differently.

Choosing differently.

You begin protecting your time instead of giving it away carelessly.

You begin protecting your finances instead of spending emotionally.

You begin protecting your peace instead of constantly chasing approval.

Those are not small victories.

They are signs that your inner world is changing.

Many people underestimate these moments because they compare themselves to the version they hope to become instead of the version they used to be.

They focus on how much farther they still have to go.

They overlook how far they have already come.

Growth deserves to be measured honestly.

Not only by what still needs to improve.

But by what has already been transformed.
Think about how unhealthy habits are formed.
Rarely through one decision.
They are built through repetition.
The same is true for healing.
Every healthy choice compounds.
Every act of self-awareness strengthens emotional maturity.
Every disciplined decision reinforces self-respect.
Every difficult conversation handled with wisdom builds healthier relationships.
Over time, those repeated choices quietly become your new normal.
One day, you respond to a situation calmly that once would have consumed you with anxiety.
You handle money with patience instead of panic.
You choose peace instead of proving yourself right.
You walk away from an unhealthy environment without questioning your worth.
In that moment, you realize something remarkable.
The person you used to be no longer controls you in the same way.
That is growth.
It is not perfection.
There will still be difficult days.
Old emotions may still appear.
You may still make mistakes.
Healing does not remove your humanity.
It strengthens your ability to respond with greater wisdom when life becomes difficult.
Do not become discouraged simply because your progress feels slow.
Some of the strongest trees spend years developing deep roots before their full height is ever seen.
No one watching from the outside realizes how much invisible work is taking place beneath the surface.
Your life often grows the same way.
The quiet decisions.
The private victories.
The unseen discipline.
The daily commitment to keep rebuilding.
These are the roots of lasting transformation.
Trust the process enough to keep showing up.
Keep choosing healthier thoughts.
Keep strengthening healthier habits.
Keep protecting your peace.
Keep rebuilding your financial life.
Keep honoring your commitments.
Because every intentional decision is becoming part of the foundation upon which your future will stand.
One day, someone may admire your confidence, your peace, your discipline, or your emotional stability.
They will see the fruit.

Only you will know about the quiet seasons when the roots were growing.

Honor those seasons.

Honor your progress.

Honor the small victories that no one else may ever notice.

Because they are not small at all.

They are the evidence that the person you once hoped to become is already beginning to emerge.

And one intentional decision at a time, that quiet transformation is becoming the life you were always capable of building.

WEALTH LESSON

Emotional healing improves long-term decision-making because healthier emotional patterns create healthier behavior.

AFFIRMATION

"I trust that healing is transforming me even when progress feels gradual."

TODAY'S POWER MOVE

Acknowledge one emotional area where you have grown healthier than before.

DAY 267

Stop Abandoning Your Goals During Hard Seasons

POWER QUOTE

"Difficult seasons require adjustment sometimes, not surrender."

REFLECTION

Every meaningful journey includes difficult seasons.

There will be days when your energy feels low.

Weeks when progress seems invisible.

Moments when disappointment makes you question whether your effort is worth continuing.

Those seasons are not evidence that something has gone wrong.

They are part of the process of becoming.

Many people begin with excitement.

They feel motivated.

Focused.

Inspired by the vision of the future they hope to create.

But eventually, life becomes difficult.

Unexpected expenses appear.

Relationships become complicated.

Work becomes exhausting.

Healing feels slower than expected.

The routines that once felt exciting begin feeling repetitive.

This is often the moment when people make a costly mistake.

They stop completely.

Not because they no longer want the future they dreamed about.

But because they confuse temporary difficulty with permanent defeat.

Growth has never required perfection.

It has always required persistence.

There is an important difference between slowing down and giving up.

Sometimes your body needs rest.

Sometimes your heart needs time to heal.

Sometimes wisdom requires adjusting your pace because life demands more of your attention in another area.

That is not failure.

Healthy people understand the difference between recovery and surrender.

Recovery prepares you to continue.

Surrender convinces you to stop.

Learning that distinction is one of the greatest forms of emotional maturity.

Imagine someone climbing a mountain.

There are moments when they stop to catch their breath.

Drink water.

Regain their strength.

No one would call that quitting.

It is preparation to continue climbing.

Life works the same way.

Some seasons require a slower pace.

They require grace.

Reflection.

Recovery.

But they still move in the direction of growth.

That is what matters.

One of the greatest dangers during difficult seasons is believing that temporary emotions accurately predict your future.

Discouragement says,

"Nothing is changing."

Exhaustion says,

"You'll never make it."

Fear says,

"You should quit now before things get worse."

Those emotions are real.

But they are not always reliable guides.

The truth is that some of your greatest growth is taking place precisely when it feels least visible.

Every time you continue showing up despite discouragement, resilience grows.

Every time you choose wisdom instead of impulsiveness, emotional maturity grows.

Every time you return after a setback instead of abandoning yourself, self-trust grows.

Those victories may not receive applause.

But they are shaping the person your future depends on.

Do not measure your life only by how quickly you move.

Measure it by whether you continue moving in the right direction.

Some days your progress will be significant.

Other days your greatest accomplishment may simply be refusing to quit.

That is still progress.

The strongest people are rarely those who never became tired.

They are the people who learned how to rest without abandoning their purpose.

Who adjusted their pace without abandoning their values.

Who honored their humanity without giving up on their future.

There is wisdom in recognizing your limits.

Resting when necessary.

Asking for help.

Taking care of your emotional health.

Those decisions do not weaken discipline.

They strengthen it by making it sustainable.

Remember that your future is not asking you to be perfect.

It is asking you to remain faithful.

Faithful to your healing.

Faithful to your growth.

Faithful to the promises you have made to yourself.

One intentional decision at a time.

So when difficult seasons arrive, do not immediately assume you are failing.

Instead, ask yourself,

"What does wisdom require of me today?"

Perhaps today's victory is taking one small step instead of ten.

Perhaps it is choosing rest instead of burnout.

Perhaps it is simply deciding that no matter how heavy this season feels, you will not abandon the life you are building.

Because difficult seasons always pass.

Character remains.

And the resilience you develop during today's struggles may become the very strength that carries you through tomorrow's opportunities.

Keep rebuilding.

Keep healing.

Keep moving forward.

Even if your pace changes.

Because temporary slowing down is never the same as permanently giving up.

And one day, you will be grateful that you chose to continue when quitting would have been easier.

WEALTH LESSON

Consistency during difficult seasons creates emotional resilience and long-term growth.

AFFIRMATION

"I continue building my future even during emotionally difficult seasons."

TODAY'S POWER MOVE

Take one small productive action today instead of emotionally shutting down completely.

DAY 268

Emotional Stability Is Strength

POWER QUOTE

"Calmness is power when life becomes chaotic."

REFLECTION

Many people misunderstand what emotional strength looks like.

They imagine strength as never feeling afraid.

Never feeling hurt.

Never becoming overwhelmed.

Always appearing confident.

Always having the perfect response.

But real emotional strength looks very different.

It is not the absence of emotion.

It is the ability to remain anchored when emotions become intense.

Anyone can remain calm when life is easy.

The real test of emotional maturity comes when life becomes difficult.

When plans change unexpectedly.

When someone disappoints you.

When finances become uncertain.

When criticism feels unfair.

When pressure begins to build.

Those moments reveal whether your emotions are leading your decisions or whether your values are.

Many people confuse emotional intensity with emotional strength.

Speaking louder is not strength.

Reacting faster is not strength.

Allowing every emotion to control every decision is not authenticity.

True strength often looks surprisingly quiet.

It pauses before responding.

It listens before speaking.

It reflects before reacting.

It chooses wisdom over impulse.

That kind of strength is rarely noticed in dramatic moments.

It is developed through daily practice.

Every time you choose to slow your reaction instead of immediately responding, you strengthen emotional regulation.

Every time you remain respectful during disagreement, you strengthen emotional maturity.

Every time you refuse to let fear dictate your financial decisions, you strengthen emotional resilience.

Every time you choose peace over proving yourself right, you strengthen your character.

These decisions may appear small.

Yet together they shape the person you become.

Emotional instability has consequences that often extend far beyond the moment.

An impulsive response can damage trust that took years to build.
An emotional financial decision can create months of unnecessary stress.
An uncontrolled reaction can close doors that patience might have opened.
That is why emotional regulation is not simply about managing feelings.
It is about protecting your future.
The ability to stay grounded during pressure influences every area of life.
It strengthens relationships because people feel emotionally safe around you.
It strengthens leadership because wise decisions are made with clarity instead of panic.
It strengthens financial stewardship because short-term emotions no longer control long-term goals.
It strengthens your peace because your circumstances no longer determine the condition of your inner world.
This does not mean suppressing emotions.
Healthy people do not ignore sadness.
They do not pretend disappointment does not exist.
They do not deny fear.
Instead, they acknowledge what they feel without allowing those emotions to become permanent decision-makers.
They ask themselves,
"What am I feeling?"
"Why am I feeling this?"
"What response aligns with the person I want to become?"
Those questions create space between emotion and action.
And in that space, wisdom begins to lead.
Emotional regulation is learned.
No one is born with complete self-control.
It develops through repeated practice.
Through self-awareness.
Through healing.
Through humility.
Through the willingness to admit when a better response is possible.
Some days you will respond well.
Other days you will realize afterward that you could have handled a situation differently.
That does not mean growth has stopped.
It means growth continues.
Every reflection becomes another opportunity to mature.
Every lesson becomes another opportunity to strengthen your character.
Do not measure strength by how loudly someone reacts.
Measure it by how steadily they remain rooted when life becomes difficult.
The strongest people are often the calmest people.
Not because they have fewer challenges.
Because they have learned not to surrender their peace every time a challenge appears.
Your future will place greater responsibility into your hands.

Greater opportunities.

Greater leadership.

Greater influence.

Those blessings will require more than talent.

They will require emotional stability.

They will require the ability to remain grounded when pressure increases.

Begin building that strength today.

One intentional response at a time.

One calm decision at a time.

One honest moment of self-awareness at a time.

Because true emotional strength is not found in never facing storms.

It is found in learning how to remain steady while walking through them.

And over time, that quiet steadiness becomes one of the greatest strengths you will ever possess.

WEALTH LESSON

Emotional stability improves decision-making because calm thinking creates healthier long-term outcomes.

AFFIRMATION

"I remain emotionally grounded, calm, and intentional during difficult moments."

TODAY'S POWER MOVE

Practice emotional calmness today during one stressful situation.

DAY 269

Stop Waiting To Become Someone Else

POWER QUOTE

"The future version of you is built through the choices you make now."

REFLECTION

Many people imagine transformation as a single life-changing moment.

They picture waking up one morning with complete confidence.

Perfect discipline.

Unshakable peace.

A completely different mindset.

As though one decision could instantly erase years of old habits, unhealthy thinking, and emotional patterns.

Real life rarely works that way.

Transformation is usually much quieter.

Much slower.

Much more ordinary.

It is built through choices that seem almost insignificant while you are making them.

One healthier response.

One disciplined morning.

One wise financial decision.

One honest conversation.

One boundary that protects your peace.

One decision to continue after disappointment instead of giving up.

None of those moments feel extraordinary by themselves.

Yet together, they become extraordinary.

Think about a sculptor standing before a block of stone.

The masterpiece is not created with one strike of the hammer.

It is shaped through thousands of careful movements.

Each one removes a little more of what does not belong.

Each one reveals a little more of what was waiting to emerge.

Personal growth happens in much the same way.

Every intentional choice removes something that no longer serves you.

Fear.

Avoidance.

Impulsiveness.

Self-doubt.

Every healthy habit reveals more of the person you are capable of becoming.

This is why patience is so important.

Many people quit because they expect visible transformation before invisible foundations have finished developing.

They become discouraged because today's effort looks too small.

But small does not mean insignificant.

Small decisions repeated consistently become powerful over time.

One day of saving money may seem unimportant.

Years of consistent saving can change a family's future.

One day of choosing calm over anger may feel unnoticed.

Years of emotional maturity can transform every relationship in your life.

One workout does not build strength.

One chapter does not build wisdom.

One prayer does not build deep faith.

One disciplined day does not completely reshape your character.

But repetition does.

Every time you repeat a healthy behavior, you strengthen the identity connected to it.

Eventually, what once required tremendous effort begins feeling natural.

Not because life became easier.

Because you became different.

This is the beautiful reality of transformation.

You are not waiting for some future version of yourself to suddenly appear.

You are creating that person today.

Every decision is either reinforcing an old identity or strengthening a new one.

Every thought you entertain.

Every habit you repeat.

Every response you choose.

They all become part of the person you are becoming.

That realization should encourage you.

Because it means your future is not determined by one dramatic breakthrough.

It is influenced by what you choose today.

Even if today's choice feels small.

Especially then.

There will be seasons when progress feels invisible.

When you wonder whether all the effort is making any difference.

Remember the seed beneath the soil.

For a long time, nothing seems to happen above the surface.

Yet beneath the ground, roots are spreading.

Strength is developing.

Life is growing where no one can see it.

When the time is right, what was happening in secret finally becomes visible.

Your growth often follows the same pattern.

The quiet discipline.

The private healing.

The repeated decisions.

The ordinary faithfulness.

They are preparing a future that cannot yet be fully seen.

Do not rush the process.

Do not despise the ordinary days.

Do not underestimate the quiet work happening inside you.

Every intentional decision is another step away from the person you used to be.

Every disciplined habit is another brick in the foundation of the life you are building.

Every act of courage is another reminder that your future is being shaped right now.

Transformation is not magic.

It is not accidental.

It is not reserved for a fortunate few.

It is the result of thousands of intentional choices made with patience, humility, and consistency.

One decision.

One habit.

One lesson.

One day at a time.

And eventually, you will look back and realize something remarkable.

The person you hoped to become did not arrive overnight.

They were quietly built through the ordinary choices you almost overlooked.

Those choices changed your identity.

And your new identity changed your life.

WEALTH LESSON

Transformation compounds gradually because repeated intentional behavior shapes identity over time.

AFFIRMATION

"I intentionally become the person my future requires."

TODAY'S POWER MOVE

Practice one habit today that aligns with the future version of yourself you want to become.

DAY 270

Your Future Is Worth Protecting

POWER QUOTE

"Every disciplined decision protects the life you are trying to build."

REFLECTION

Every meaningful achievement requires protection.

A garden is not sustained simply because seeds were planted.

It must be watered.

Nurtured.

Protected from weeds.

Protected from neglect.

Protected from anything that quietly threatens healthy growth.

Your life works much the same way.

Many people focus almost entirely on building.

Building a career.

Building financial stability.

Building healthier relationships.

Building emotional peace.

Building a stronger future.

But far fewer people think about protecting what they are building.

Yet protection is just as important as progress.

A dream can be delayed by constant distraction.

Peace can be weakened by unhealthy environments.

Discipline can slowly disappear through neglected routines.

Financial stability can be undone by repeated emotional decisions.

The future you hope to experience depends not only on the goals you pursue, but also on the things you refuse to allow into your life.

Every day, something competes for your attention.

Notifications.

Entertainment.

Comparison.

Negativity.

Conflict.

Distractions rarely announce themselves as dangerous.

Most appear harmless.

One unnecessary hour.

One unhealthy habit.

One conversation that continually drains your energy.

One decision to postpone what matters most.

By themselves, these moments may seem insignificant.

Repeated consistently, they quietly shape your future.

That is why stewardship matters.

Stewardship is recognizing that your life has been entrusted to you.

Your time is valuable.

Your attention is valuable.

Your emotional energy is valuable.

Your character is valuable.

Treating those gifts carelessly eventually affects every area of your life.

Treating them intentionally allows them to flourish.

Protect your attention.

Your attention directs your energy.

If your mind is constantly consumed by distractions, it becomes difficult to focus on what truly matters.

Protect your emotional energy.

Not every argument deserves your participation.

Not every opinion deserves your response.

Not every relationship deserves unlimited access to your heart.

Protect your routines.

The habits you repeat each day quietly become the architecture of your future.

A healthy routine is not restrictive.

It is liberating.

It frees you from constantly having to decide whether you will do what matters.

Protect your mindset.

The thoughts you repeatedly entertain eventually influence the decisions you repeatedly make.

Hope strengthens perseverance.

Gratitude strengthens contentment.

Wisdom strengthens discipline.

Fear, resentment, and constant comparison often weaken them.

Choose carefully what you allow to shape your thinking.

Protection also requires honesty.

Sometimes the greatest threat to your future is not another person.

It is an unhealthy habit you have continued to tolerate.

Procrastination.

Avoidance.

People-pleasing.

Impulsive spending.

Negative self-talk.

Comfort disguised as contentment.

Growth requires the courage to recognize these patterns without allowing them to define you.

Every unhealthy habit you replace creates more room for the life you truly want.

Remember that every meaningful goal has an unseen cost.

Success requires saying no to distractions.

Peace requires saying no to unnecessary chaos.

Financial stability requires saying no to impulsive choices.
Healthy relationships require saying no to destructive communication.
Purpose requires saying no to many opportunities so you can fully commit to the right ones.
These decisions are not losses.
They are investments.
Each one protects something far more valuable than what you temporarily give up.
Imagine your future as a home under construction.
Every disciplined decision lays another brick.
Every healed response strengthens another wall.
Every healthy boundary reinforces the foundation.
Every wise financial choice adds another layer of stability.
Now imagine allowing neglect to slowly damage that structure.
Ignoring small cracks.
Overlooking weak foundations.
Allowing unnecessary damage because it feels easier than making repairs.
Eventually, what was once strong becomes unstable.
The same principle applies to your life.
Protect what you are building while it is still being built.
Do not wait until peace has been lost to value it.
Do not wait until your time has been wasted to protect it.
Do not wait until unhealthy habits have become deeply rooted before deciding to change them.
Your future deserves intentional care today.
The person you are becoming deserves an environment where healing can continue.
Where discipline can grow.
Where purpose can flourish.
Where peace can remain.
Because one day, you will live inside the future you are creating now.
And the quality of that future will be shaped not only by what you chose to pursue—
but by what you faithfully chose to protect.
One intentional decision at a time.

WEALTH LESSON

Protecting healthy routines and emotional stability strengthens long-term consistency and growth.

AFFIRMATION

"I intentionally protect the future I am working hard to build."

TODAY'S POWER MOVE

Protect one important habit, goal, or emotional boundary intentionally today.

DAY 271

Stop Making Decisions From Fear

POWER QUOTE

"Fear-based decisions often create unstable outcomes."

REFLECTION

Fear is one of the most powerful emotions a person can experience.

It has the ability to influence the way you think.

The way you feel.

The way you interpret situations.

And ultimately, the decisions you make.

By itself, fear is not the enemy.

Fear is a normal human response.

It exists to alert you to possible danger and encourage caution when caution is necessary.

The problem begins when fear stops becoming a signal and starts becoming a leader.

When every important decision is filtered through fear, life gradually becomes smaller.

Opportunities are ignored because they feel uncertain.

Dreams are postponed because failure seems possible.

Conversations are avoided because rejection feels painful.

Healthy boundaries are never established because disappointing someone feels uncomfortable.

Without realizing it, fear begins writing a story that was never meant to belong to you.

Many people assume fear always tells the truth.

It does not.

Fear often speaks in possibilities, not certainties.

"What if you fail?"

"What if people judge you?"

"What if everything falls apart?"

Those questions can feel convincing.

But notice something important.

Fear almost never asks,

"What if you succeed?"

"What if this opportunity changes your life?"

"What if this difficult conversation strengthens your relationship?"

"What if the person you are becoming is waiting on the other side of this decision?"

Fear has a natural tendency to magnify risk while minimizing possibility.

That is why emotional awareness matters so deeply.

You must learn to recognize the difference between a feeling and a fact.

Feeling afraid does not mean you are incapable.

Feeling uncertain does not mean you are making the wrong decision.

Feeling uncomfortable does not mean growth is impossible.

Sometimes those feelings simply mean you are standing at the edge of something unfamiliar.

And unfamiliar does not automatically mean unsafe.

Think about every meaningful achievement in your life.

There was likely uncertainty before it happened.

The first day at a new job.

The first presentation you gave.

The first investment you made in your future.

The first difficult conversation that ultimately strengthened a relationship.

At one point, each of those moments probably felt intimidating.

If fear had been allowed to make the decision, many of those experiences would never have happened.

This is why courage is so valuable.

Courage is not the absence of fear.

It is the decision that your values will carry more authority than your emotions.

It is acknowledging your fear without surrendering your future to it.

That kind of courage develops through practice.

Every time you choose action over avoidance, courage grows.

Every time you keep a promise despite uncertainty, confidence grows.

Every time you remain faithful during uncomfortable seasons, resilience grows.

Little by little, fear begins losing the influence it once had over your identity.

This does not mean fear disappears completely.

Even the wisest and strongest people experience fear.

The difference is that they have learned to ask better questions.

Instead of asking,

"How do I avoid every uncomfortable feeling?"

They ask,

"What response aligns with the person I am becoming?"

That question changes everything.

It shifts your attention from temporary emotion to lasting purpose.

It reminds you that your future should not be governed by the loudest feeling of the moment.

It should be shaped by wisdom, character, and intentional choices.

There will always be reasons to stay where you are.

Fear will gladly provide them.

But growth always asks for movement.

Not reckless movement.

Not impulsive movement.

Intentional movement.

Movement guided by preparation, wisdom, and courage.

Your future deserves decisions made from clarity rather than panic.

Your relationships deserve responses made from maturity rather than fear.

Your finances deserve stewardship rather than avoidance.

Your purpose deserves faithfulness rather than hesitation.

Every courageous decision you make becomes evidence that fear no longer has the final word.

Every intentional step weakens its control over your life.

One day, you will look back and realize that the greatest turning points in your life were not the moments when fear disappeared.

They were the moments when you chose to move forward anyway.

Because your future was never meant to be written by fear.

It was meant to be built through courage, wisdom, and one intentional decision after another.

WEALTH LESSON

Emotionally regulated thinking improves financial and personal outcomes because intentional decisions create healthier long-term results.

AFFIRMATION

"I refuse to let fear control the direction of my future."

TODAY'S POWER MOVE

Pause before making emotionally fearful decisions today and ask yourself what wisdom would choose instead.

DAY 272

Your Peace Is More Valuable Than Proving Yourself

POWER QUOTE

"You do not need to emotionally exhaust yourself trying to prove your worth."

REFLECTION

From an early age, many people learn to measure their value through the opinions of others.

Good grades earn praise.

Achievement earns recognition.

Being agreeable earns acceptance.

Helping everyone earns appreciation.

Over time, a quiet belief can begin forming beneath the surface:

"My worth depends on how other people see me."

That belief is exhausting.

Because the opinions of people constantly change.

One person applauds you.

Another criticizes you.

One relationship makes you feel valued.

Another leaves you questioning yourself.

If your identity depends entirely on external validation, your peace will rise and fall with every opinion around you.

Many people spend years trying to earn something that cannot create lasting security.

Approval.

Recognition.

Acceptance.

They overextend themselves to avoid disappointing others.

They hide parts of themselves to fit into environments where they were never meant to belong.

They constantly perform, hoping that if they accomplish enough, achieve enough, or please enough people, they will finally feel secure.

But no amount of external praise can permanently fill an internal void.

Eventually, the applause fades.

The compliments stop.

The expectations grow.

And the person who built their identity on approval is left wondering who they are when no one is watching.

That is why healthy confidence must be built from within.

Not through arrogance.

Not through believing you no longer need people.

But through developing a quiet confidence that is rooted in character rather than applause.

Real confidence grows every time you keep a promise to yourself.

Every time you choose integrity when no one else notices.

Every time you protect your peace instead of chasing approval.

Every time you remain faithful to your values even when they are unpopular.

Those moments create something far more valuable than temporary praise.

They create self-respect.

Self-respect is different from self-esteem.

Self-esteem often rises and falls with circumstances.

Self-respect grows from living in alignment with your principles.

It is the quiet confidence that comes from knowing your actions reflect the person you are becoming.

People who possess deep emotional security do not stop caring about others.

They simply stop allowing every opinion to determine their identity.

They welcome encouragement without becoming dependent on it.

They accept constructive feedback without allowing criticism to define them.

They celebrate success without needing constant recognition.

Their foundation has moved.

It is no longer built on performance.

It is built on purpose.

This shift changes every area of life.

Relationships become healthier because you stop seeking love through constant self-sacrifice.

Work becomes more meaningful because you pursue excellence instead of approval.

Leadership becomes more authentic because you are guided by conviction rather than popularity.

Peace becomes more consistent because your emotional stability is no longer controlled by changing opinions.

This kind of confidence does not develop overnight.

It grows quietly.

Every boundary you establish strengthens it.

Every unhealthy comparison you refuse weakens insecurity.

Every act of discipline reminds you that your value is not determined by someone else's opinion.

You begin discovering something beautiful.

You do not need to earn your worth through endless performance.

You simply need to live in a way that honors the life you have been given.

There will always be people who misunderstand you.

Some will overlook your efforts.

Others may never fully appreciate your growth.

Do not allow that to become the measure of your identity.

The people who matter most will value your character more than your performance.

And even when recognition is absent, your integrity remains.

Your discipline remains.

Your healing remains.

Your purpose remains.

Those are foundations that cannot be taken away by changing opinions.

Stop building your identity on applause.

Build it on honesty.

Build it on discipline.

Build it on healing.

Build it on the quiet confidence that comes from becoming the person you respect when you look in the mirror.

Because lasting peace is not found in finally convincing everyone else of your value.

It is found in no longer needing to.

The strongest confidence is not the confidence that receives the loudest applause.

It is the confidence that remains steady even when the room is silent.

And that quiet confidence will carry you farther than external validation ever could.

WEALTH LESSON

Emotional security improves long-term stability because decisions become less dependent on approval from others.

AFFIRMATION

"I release the pressure to constantly prove my worth to others."

TODAY'S POWER MOVE

Do something today because it aligns with your values, not because it earns approval.

DAY 273

Healing Requires Accountability Too

POWER QUOTE

"Growth becomes difficult when people refuse to confront their own patterns honestly."

REFLECTION

Healing begins with honesty.

Not only the honesty to acknowledge what hurt you.

But also the honesty to recognize what needs to change within you.

A common belief is healing is only about processing pain.

Learning to forgive.

Understanding past experiences.

Those things are essential.

But healing also asks deeper questions.

"What habits am I repeating that continue creating the same outcomes?"

"What emotional patterns keep pulling me back into unhealthy cycles?"

"What behaviors no longer align with the person I want to become?"

Those questions require courage.

Because it is often easier to identify what others have done than to examine our own choices.

There are moments when life wounds us in ways we never deserved.

Those experiences deserve compassion.

They deserve patience.

They deserve healing.

But there are also moments when our own responses begin prolonging the pain.

Avoidance.

Procrastination.

Defensiveness.

People-pleasing.

Emotional impulsiveness.

Refusing to set boundaries.

Holding on to resentment.

These patterns may have developed for understandable reasons.

Yet understanding them does not mean we should continue living by them.

That is where accountability becomes one of the greatest acts of self-respect.

Many people misunderstand accountability.

They confuse it with self-condemnation.

They believe admitting unhealthy behavior means attacking their own worth.

It does not.

Accountability is not saying,

"I am a bad person."

It is saying,

"This behavior is no longer helping me build the life I want."

Those are two very different statements.
One creates shame.
The other creates growth.
Healthy accountability is rooted in hope.
It believes that change is possible.
It recognizes that your past explains some of your patterns, but it does not excuse remaining trapped in them forever.
The beautiful truth is that awareness creates choice.
The moment you recognize an unhealthy habit, you gain the opportunity to replace it.
You may not change everything immediately.
But you can begin.
One response at a time.
One decision at a time.
One habit at a time.
This is how real transformation unfolds.
Not through denial.
Through honesty.
Imagine trying to repair a home while refusing to acknowledge where the damage exists.
No matter how beautiful the decorations become, the foundation remains weak.
Healing works the same way.
You cannot strengthen what you refuse to examine.
But the moment you are willing to face the cracks with humility, restoration becomes possible.
This process requires grace.
You will not respond perfectly every time.
There will be days when old habits return.
Moments when familiar emotions tempt you to react in familiar ways.
Do not mistake those moments for failure.
Use them as opportunities to learn.
Ask yourself,
"What can this moment teach me?"
"What healthier response can I choose next time?"
Growth is not built by never making mistakes again.
It is built by becoming increasingly willing to learn from them.
Every honest conversation with yourself strengthens self-awareness.
Every unhealthy habit you replace strengthens your character.
Every difficult truth you accept without shame strengthens your future.
Little by little, accountability stops feeling like criticism.
It begins feeling like freedom.
Because every unhealthy pattern you release creates more space for peace.
More room for discipline.
More capacity for healthy relationships.

More opportunity to become the person you were created to be.

Remember that healing is not simply returning to who you were before life became difficult.

It is becoming someone wiser because of what you have lived through.

Someone more intentional.

More emotionally mature.

More disciplined.

More compassionate.

That version of you is not created by avoiding difficult truths.

It is created by facing them with courage.

So be gentle with yourself.

But also be honest.

Extend yourself grace.

But do not stop growing.

Offer yourself compassion.

But do not stop changing.

Because accountability is not the opposite of healing.

It is one of the greatest expressions of it.

And every time you choose honesty over avoidance, you take another step toward the peaceful, disciplined, and resilient life your future deserves.

WEALTH LESSON

Self-awareness improves long-term growth because healthier outcomes require healthier behaviors.

AFFIRMATION

"I take accountability for the habits and patterns I need to change."

TODAY'S POWER MOVE

Reflect honestly today on one behavior that no longer aligns with your future goals.

DAY 274

Your Discipline Will Outlive Motivation

POWER QUOTE

"Feelings fluctuate. Discipline sustains progress."

REFLECTION

Motivation is a beautiful beginning.

It inspires new goals.

It creates excitement.

It fills people with hope that life can become different.

Many dreams begin with a moment of inspiration.

A powerful conversation.

A meaningful book.

A life-changing realization.

A decision to finally stop living the way you have always lived.

Those moments matter.

They create momentum.

But motivation was never designed to carry you for the rest of the journey.

It comes and goes.

Some mornings you wake up energized.

Other mornings you feel tired.

Distracted.

Discouraged.

Uncertain.

If your progress depends entirely on how motivated you feel each day, your growth will always rise and fall with your emotions.

That is why discipline is so valuable.

Discipline continues after excitement fades.

It keeps showing up when no one is watching.

It honors commitments when results are still invisible.

It chooses responsibility even when comfort feels more appealing.

This is the difference between people who admire change and people who experience it.

The first group waits until they feel inspired.

The second group learns how to continue whether inspiration is present or not.

Think about the people who achieve lasting success in any area of life.

Athletes do not train only when they feel excited.

Writers do not create only when inspiration arrives.

Financially disciplined people do not save money only when it feels easy.

Healthy relationships are not strengthened only on the days when love feels effortless.

They are strengthened through consistent choices made over time.

Life rewards faithfulness far more often than it rewards temporary enthusiasm.

There will be seasons when progress feels slow.

Days when your efforts seem unnoticed.

Weeks when you question whether anything is changing.

Those are often the moments that shape your character the most.

Because discipline asks a powerful question:

"Will you continue even when today's emotions tell you not to?"

Every time you answer yes, something inside you changes.

You begin building self-trust.

You prove that your values matter more than your temporary feelings.

You strengthen resilience.

Little by little, you stop relying on emotional momentum and start relying on intentional commitment.

That is where lasting transformation begins.

This does not mean ignoring your emotions.

Emotions are important.

They provide valuable information about your experiences.

But emotions make poor leaders.

Some days they encourage you.

Other days they discourage you.

If you allow them to determine every decision, your direction will constantly change.

Discipline gives your life stability.

It allows your principles to guide you when your emotions fluctuate.

Imagine building a house.

The foundation is poured before anyone admires the finished structure.

It is repetitive work.

Often unnoticed.

But without it, nothing lasting can stand.

Discipline is the foundation of the life you hope to build.

The routines no one applauds.

The early mornings.

The wise financial decisions.

The difficult conversations.

The quiet acts of integrity.

The repeated choice to continue.

These ordinary moments quietly support extraordinary futures.

Remember that motivation may start the journey.

Discipline finishes it.

Motivation says,

"I'm excited to begin."

Discipline says,

"I'm committed to continue."

Motivation is emotional.

Discipline is intentional.

Motivation is temporary.

Discipline becomes part of your identity.

That is why consistency changes lives.

Every day you keep your word to yourself, you become a little stronger.

Every day you continue despite slow progress, you become a little wiser.

Every day you honor your commitments instead of your changing emotions, you become a little more dependable.

Eventually, those small decisions become the person you are known to be.

Not because you were always motivated.

Because you learned how to remain faithful when motivation disappeared.

So do not become discouraged when inspiration fades.

Expect it.

Prepare for it.

And decide in advance that your future will not be determined by your feelings alone.

It will be built through the habits you continue practicing, the promises you continue keeping, and the discipline you continue choosing.

Because one day, you will look back and realize that the greatest breakthroughs in your life did not happen on the days you felt the most inspired.

They happened because you kept going on the days you did not.

And that quiet consistency became the foundation of everything you eventually built.

WEALTH LESSON

Long-term success requires repeated consistent effort because motivation alone is emotionally unreliable.

AFFIRMATION

"I remain disciplined even when motivation fluctuates."

TODAY'S POWER MOVE

Complete one important responsibility today without waiting to feel inspired first.

DAY 275

You Deserve A Life That Feels Peaceful

POWER QUOTE

"Success without peace eventually feels emotionally empty."

REFLECTION

Many people spend their lives chasing success.

A higher income.

A bigger business.

A respected career.

More influence.

More recognition.

These goals are not wrong.

Achievement can create opportunities, provide security, and allow you to serve others in meaningful ways.

The problem begins when external success becomes more important than internal health.

It is possible to build a successful career while quietly losing your peace.

To accumulate wealth while living with constant anxiety.

To receive admiration from thousands of people while feeling disconnected from yourself.

To achieve everything you once dreamed of and still feel emotionally exhausted.

That is why success must be defined carefully.

Success is not only what people can see.

It is also what you experience when no one else is watching.

Can you rest without guilt?

Can you enjoy what you have built?

Can you be fully present with the people you love?

Can you face challenges without constantly living in panic?

Can you go to bed with peace instead of carrying the weight of endless striving?

Those questions often reveal more about true success than titles, income, or recognition ever could.

Many people assume peace is something that comes after achievement.

"Once I reach this goal, then I'll finally relax."

"Once I earn more money, then I'll have peace."

"Once my business succeeds, then I'll enjoy life."

But peace that is postponed is often peace that never arrives.

Because every new achievement creates another goal.

Another expectation.

Another responsibility.

If you never learn how to protect your emotional well-being during the journey, success alone will not suddenly teach you how.

Peace is not the reward at the end of the road.

It is meant to become part of the way you travel.

That requires intention.

It requires boundaries that protect your time.

Habits that protect your health.

Relationships that encourage honesty instead of performance.

Moments of stillness that remind you your worth is greater than your productivity.

It also requires emotional maturity.

The ability to recognize when ambition is becoming unhealthy.

When comparison is stealing your joy.

When constant busyness is replacing meaningful living.

When your pursuit of success is quietly costing you the very life you hoped success would create.

Healthy ambition and emotional health are not enemies.

They strengthen each other.

A peaceful mind makes wiser financial decisions.

A healthy emotional life creates stronger leadership.

Clear thinking improves problem-solving.

Healthy relationships provide support during difficult seasons.

Rest allows your mind to perform at its best.

These are not distractions from success.

They are part of what makes success sustainable.

Imagine building a beautiful home on an unstable foundation.

From the outside, everything appears impressive.

But hidden cracks continue growing beneath the surface.

Eventually, the structure begins to suffer.

Life works the same way.

Your internal world is the foundation beneath every visible achievement.

If that foundation is neglected, external success becomes increasingly difficult to enjoy.

That is why emotional health deserves your attention.

Not because it guarantees an easy life.

But because it strengthens your ability to live wisely through every season.

Continue pursuing your goals.

Work hard.

Develop your gifts.

Build wealth.

Create opportunities.

Leave a legacy.

But do not sacrifice the very things that make those achievements meaningful.

Protect your peace.

Protect your character.

Protect your relationships.

Protect your health.

Protect your joy.

Because one day, your greatest accomplishment will not simply be the success people admired from a distance.

It will be the life you were able to enjoy because your heart remained healthy while your responsibilities continued to grow.

The most successful life is not the one that only looks impressive.

It is the one that feels whole.

Where purpose and peace walk together.

Where ambition is guided by wisdom.

Where achievement is strengthened by integrity.

Where discipline is balanced by rest.

And where the person you become is just as beautiful as the life you build.

That is the kind of success worth pursuing.

The kind that not only changes your circumstances—

but allows you to experience them with clarity, gratitude, and lasting peace.

WEALTH LESSON

Peace improves decision-making because emotionally stable minds think more clearly long-term.

AFFIRMATION

"I intentionally build a life rooted in peace and emotional stability."

TODAY'S POWER MOVE

Protect your peace today by reducing one unnecessary source of stress or emotional chaos.

DAY 276

Your Future Is Bigger Than Your Current Fear

POWER QUOTE

"Fear should never become bigger than your vision."

REFLECTION

Every meaningful dream eventually asks the same question:

"Will you move forward even when you are afraid?"

That question comes to every person.

Not because fear is unusual.

But because growth always requires stepping into places you have never been before.

The first time you pursue a new opportunity.

The first time you start a business.

The first time you apply for a position that feels beyond your qualifications.

The first time you set a healthy boundary.

The first time you choose healing over familiar pain.

None of those moments feel completely comfortable.

They were never meant to.

Growth introduces uncertainty because it invites you beyond the limits of what is familiar.

Many people spend years waiting for fear to disappear before taking action.

They tell themselves,

"When I feel more confident, I'll begin."

"When I'm completely ready, I'll move."

"When I know I can't fail, I'll take the chance."

Unfortunately, that day rarely arrives.

Confidence is rarely the starting point.

More often, confidence is the result of courageous action repeated over time.

Fear is not proof that you are incapable.

It is often proof that something important is standing in front of you.

Think about every meaningful accomplishment in your life.

Before you experienced it, there was uncertainty.

Before success came preparation.

Before clarity came questions.

Before confidence came repeated acts of courage.

No one develops strength without first carrying something heavy.

No one develops resilience without first facing adversity.

No one develops courage without first experiencing fear.

This is why courage is not the absence of fear.

Courage is choosing to let purpose become louder than hesitation.

Fear says,

"Stay where it feels safe."

Purpose says,

Fear says,

"You might fail."

Purpose says,

"You might grow."

Fear focuses on everything that could go wrong.

Purpose reminds you of everything that becomes possible if you remain faithful.

Many opportunities are not lost because people lack ability.

They are lost because fear quietly convinces capable people to remain still.

Fear creates convincing arguments.

It magnifies uncertainty.

It exaggerates risk.

It whispers that waiting is wiser than acting.

Sometimes waiting is wise.

Preparation matters.

Planning matters.

Wisdom matters.

But there comes a moment when preparation must become action.

Otherwise, preparation quietly becomes another form of procrastination.

One of the greatest tragedies is not failure.

It is reaching the end of a season wondering what might have happened if fear had not made your decisions.

Every courageous step expands your capacity.

The first difficult conversation strengthens your communication.

The first wise investment strengthens your financial confidence.

The first healthy boundary strengthens your self-respect.

The first opportunity you pursue despite uncertainty strengthens your belief in yourself.

Little by little, courage becomes a habit.

Not because fear disappears.

Because you stop allowing it to determine your direction.

Remember that your future will always require a version of you that your present self is still becoming.

More mature.

More disciplined.

More resilient.

More emotionally grounded.

You cannot become that person while remaining inside every familiar comfort zone.

Growth always asks for movement.

Sometimes small movement.

Sometimes uncomfortable movement.

But always intentional movement.

Do not wait until every question has an answer.

Do not wait until every doubt disappears.

Do not wait until fear gives you permission.

Your future has never depended on the absence of uncertainty.

It has always depended on your willingness to continue despite it.

Every courageous decision becomes another piece of evidence that your life is no longer controlled by hesitation.

Every intentional action weakens fear's influence over your identity.

One day, you will look back and realize that the moments that changed your life were not the moments when fear vanished.

They were the moments when your vision became greater than your hesitation.

When your purpose became stronger than your comfort.

When your commitment became louder than your excuses.

And because you chose courage one decision at a time, you slowly became the person your future had been waiting for all along.

WEALTH LESSON

Real growth demands calculated courage because opportunities rarely appear inside comfort zones alone.

AFFIRMATION

"I choose courage and growth over fear and limitation."

TODAY'S POWER MOVE

Take one small courageous action today toward a goal that matters deeply to you.

DAY 277

Stop Ignoring Your Emotional Needs

POWER QUOTE

"You cannot continuously neglect yourself and still expect peace internally."

REFLECTION

Many people become experts at caring for everyone except themselves.

They encourage others.

Support others.

Sacrifice for others.

Show up whenever someone needs them.

Yet when it comes to their own well-being, they quietly disappear.

They ignore exhaustion.

They dismiss stress.

They minimize emotional pain.

They convince themselves that everyone else's needs matter more than their own.

At first, this may look like kindness.

Over time, it often becomes self-neglect.

You cannot continuously give away your emotional energy without eventually feeling depleted.

Just as a body requires food to remain healthy, your emotional life requires care to remain strong.

Ignoring that reality does not make you stronger.

It simply delays the moment when exhaustion demands your attention.

Many people wait until they are completely burned out before asking themselves an important question:

"When was the last time I cared for myself with the same compassion I offer everyone else?"

That question matters.

Because sustainable growth is impossible without sustainable care.

You were never designed to live in a constant state of emotional depletion.

You were created to work.

To serve.

To build.

To love.

But you were also created to rest.

To recover.

To reflect.

To heal.

Ignoring those needs does not increase your capacity.

It slowly reduces it.

Think about the areas of life that suffer when emotional exhaustion goes unaddressed.

Your patience becomes shorter.

Your focus weakens.

Small problems begin feeling overwhelming.

Your discipline becomes inconsistent.

Your relationships become strained because you have little emotional energy left to give.

Even your physical health may begin reflecting the weight your mind has been carrying.

This is why caring for yourself is not selfish.

It is stewardship.

Stewardship means recognizing that your life has been entrusted to you.

Your body deserves care.

Your mind deserves peace.

Your heart deserves healing.

Your future deserves a version of you that is healthy enough to enjoy the life you are building.

Self-care is often misunderstood.

It is not simply about temporary comfort.

Real self-care sometimes means going to bed earlier instead of staying busy.

Creating a budget instead of avoiding your finances.

Saying no to commitments you cannot responsibly carry.

Having difficult conversations instead of allowing resentment to grow.

Asking for help when you need it.

Choosing rest before burnout chooses it for you.

These decisions are not acts of weakness.

They are acts of wisdom.

Healthy people understand that they cannot continually neglect themselves while expecting to remain emotionally available for others.

The strongest support you can offer the people you love comes from becoming emotionally healthy yourself.

When you are rested, you lead more wisely.

When you are emotionally grounded, you communicate more patiently.

When you protect your peace, you become more present.

When you honor your own well-being, you create healthier relationships because you are giving from abundance instead of depletion.

This requires boundaries.

Not every request requires your yes.

Not every problem requires your involvement.

Not every expectation deserves your emotional energy.

Learning these distinctions allows generosity to remain sustainable.

It allows love to remain joyful instead of becoming burdensome.

Remember that your worth is not measured by how exhausted you become while trying to help everyone else.

Your worth was never dependent on constant performance.

It is reflected in the wisdom with which you care for the life you have been given.

You deserve rest.

You deserve emotional honesty.

You deserve environments that strengthen your peace instead of continually draining it.

You deserve relationships where care flows both ways.

You deserve the opportunity to become the healthiest version of yourself—not only for your own sake, but for everyone whose life will be touched by your growth.

Do not wait until your mind forces you to slow down.

Choose intentional care today.

Protect your energy.

Honor your limits.

Strengthen your routines.

Prioritize your healing.

Because the future you are building will require a healthy heart, a clear mind, and a peaceful spirit.

And those things are not created by constantly abandoning yourself.

They are created by learning that caring for yourself is not stepping away from your purpose.

It is preparing yourself to fulfill it faithfully for years to come.

WEALTH LESSON

Emotional wellness improves productivity and consistency because regulated minds perform better long-term.

AFFIRMATION

"I honor my emotional needs and care for myself intentionally."

TODAY'S POWER MOVE

Do one intentional thing today that supports your emotional well-being.

DAY 278

Your Growth Is Not Always Visible Immediately

POWER QUOTE

"Some of the deepest transformation happens quietly."

REFLECTION

One of the greatest challenges of personal growth is that its most important work often happens where no one can see it.

You cannot always measure healing.

You cannot always see confidence developing.

You cannot always recognize emotional maturity while it is taking shape.

Because transformation usually begins internally long before it becomes visible externally.

Many people become discouraged during this stage.

They work hard.

They stay disciplined.

They continue healing.

Yet when they look at their circumstances, they wonder whether anything is really changing.

That is often because they are looking for visible results while invisible foundations are still being built.

Think about a seed planted beneath the ground.

For a long time, nothing appears to happen.

The soil looks unchanged.

There is no visible evidence that life is developing.

Yet beneath the surface, roots are spreading.

Strength is forming.

The foundation is becoming strong enough to support future growth.

If someone judged the seed too early, they might conclude that nothing was happening.

They would be completely wrong.

Growth was already taking place.

It simply had not become visible yet.

Your life often follows the same pattern.

The first signs of transformation are usually internal.

You begin thinking differently.

You respond more calmly.

You become less controlled by old fears.

You recognize unhealthy patterns more quickly.

You recover from disappointment faster than you once did.

These changes may not receive applause.

But they are preparing everything that comes next.

Many people quit during this invisible season because they assume slow progress means no progress.

It does not.

Some of the strongest changes in your life are happening in places that cannot yet be measured.

Character is growing.

Wisdom is deepening.

Discipline is becoming more consistent.

Peace is becoming more stable.

These are the roots that will eventually support everything else you hope to build.

Imagine building a skyscraper.

Before anyone notices the height of the building, countless hours are spent strengthening the foundation.

No one celebrates the concrete beneath the ground.

Yet without it, the structure could never rise safely.

The same principle applies to your life.

Your internal world is the foundation beneath every visible achievement.

The healthier your foundation becomes, the more responsibility your future can safely carry.

This is why patience matters.

Patience is not passive waiting.

It is faithful commitment while the results are still developing.

It is continuing to water the seed before the harvest appears.

It is continuing to practice discipline before confidence feels natural.

It is continuing to choose healing before complete peace arrives.

Patience understands that meaningful transformation cannot be rushed.

Every intentional decision matters.

Every healthy habit matters.

Every difficult conversation handled with wisdom matters.

Every emotionally mature response matters.

Every time you return after disappointment instead of giving up, you strengthen something inside yourself that success alone could never create.

Do not become so focused on what has not happened yet that you overlook what is already changing within you.

Perhaps your circumstances have not fully caught up.

But your thinking has changed.

Your boundaries have changed.

Your priorities have changed.

Your resilience has changed.

Those are not small victories.

They are the beginning of a different future.

One day, people may look at your life and admire your confidence.

Your discipline.

Your peace.

Your wisdom.

They will see the visible results.

Only you will remember the quiet seasons when no one noticed the work taking place beneath the surface.

The mornings you kept showing up.

The nights you chose healing instead of avoidance.

The repeated decisions that felt ordinary at the time.

Those unseen moments built everything.

So be patient with yourself.

Honor the process.

Celebrate the quiet victories.

Trust the work that is happening inside you, even when it has not yet become obvious to everyone else.

Because the strongest transformation is rarely the fastest.

It is the transformation that develops deep enough to last.

And one day, what has been quietly growing beneath the surface will become visible—not because it happened overnight, but because you faithfully continued building when very little seemed to be changing.

That quiet perseverance will become one of the greatest strengths of your life.

WEALTH LESSON

Compounding creates long-term results because repeated intentional behavior grows gradually over time.

AFFIRMATION

"I trust the quiet growth happening inside me."

TODAY'S POWER MOVE

Reflect today on one internal area where you know you are growing stronger.

DAY 279

Stop Feeding Scarcity Thinking

POWER QUOTE

"A fearful mindset struggles to build peacefully."

REFLECTION

Some people believe scarcity is only about a lack of money.

In reality, scarcity often begins in the mind long before it appears in a bank account.

Scarcity thinking is a way of seeing the world through constant fear.

It quietly whispers,

"There will never be enough."

"Something bad is about to happen."

"If I make one mistake, everything will fall apart."

"I have to hold on tightly because I may never have another opportunity."

When those beliefs become deeply rooted, they begin influencing every area of life.

Not only finances.

Relationships become driven by insecurity.

Decisions become driven by panic.

Opportunities become viewed as risks instead of possibilities.

Even moments of stability become difficult to enjoy because the mind is constantly preparing for disaster.

This is why healing your relationship with scarcity is so important.

Many people unknowingly carry scarcity because of experiences that shaped them long before adulthood.

Growing up in financial instability.

Living through unexpected hardship.

Watching people struggle with money.

Experiencing seasons where survival required constant vigilance.

Those experiences matter.

They often teach the nervous system to expect uncertainty.

To stay alert.

To prepare for loss.

While those responses may have once been understandable, they do not have to become permanent ways of living.

Healing begins when you recognize that yesterday's survival strategies are not always necessary for tomorrow's future.

That awareness changes everything.

Instead of reacting automatically, you begin responding intentionally.

Instead of making decisions from fear, you begin making them from wisdom.

Instead of asking,

"What if everything goes wrong?"

You begin asking,

"What decision creates the strongest future?"

That shift transforms the way you approach life.

Scarcity often creates short-term thinking.

People spend impulsively because tomorrow feels uncertain.

Or they refuse healthy opportunities because risk feels unbearable.

Or they avoid looking at their finances because honesty feels emotionally overwhelming.

These reactions provide temporary emotional relief.

But they rarely create long-term stability.

An abundant mindset does not ignore reality.

It does not pretend challenges do not exist.

It simply refuses to let fear become the foundation of every decision.

It understands that preparation is wiser than panic.

Planning is stronger than avoidance.

Consistency is more powerful than emotional reactions.

A person with a healthy financial mindset begins asking different questions.

"How can I prepare instead of worrying?"

"How can I build instead of merely survive?"

"What habits today will strengthen my future?"

These questions shift attention away from fear and toward stewardship.

They remind you that your future is shaped more by repeated intentional choices than by momentary emotions.

This transformation takes time.

Scarcity thinking is rarely replaced overnight.

Every time you create and follow a budget, you weaken fear.

Every time you save consistently instead of spending impulsively, you strengthen trust.

Every time you make a thoughtful financial decision instead of reacting emotionally, you reinforce a healthier identity.

Little by little, your relationship with money begins to change.

More importantly, your relationship with yourself begins to change.

You start believing that you are capable of building stability.

Capable of preparing wisely.

Capable of creating a future that is not controlled by constant anxiety.

That belief changes behavior.

And behavior changes outcomes.

Remember that abundance is not measured only by how much money you have.

It is reflected in how peacefully you are able to manage what you have been entrusted with.

A fearful mind can feel poor even with great wealth.

A wise and disciplined mind can build lasting security one intentional decision at a time.

Your future deserves more than survival.

It deserves stability.

Clarity.

Preparation.

Peace.

So refuse to let fear become your financial advisor.

Replace panic with planning.

Replace avoidance with honesty.

Replace scarcity with stewardship.

Because the strongest financial future is not built by people who never experienced fear.

It is built by people who learned to stop allowing fear to make their decisions.

And one intentional choice after another, they transformed not only their finances—but the mindset that shaped them.

WEALTH LESSON

Healthy financial thinking improves decision-making because intentional planning replaces emotional panic.

AFFIRMATION

"I release scarcity thinking and build my future with peace and intention."

TODAY'S POWER MOVE

Challenge one fear-based financial thought today with a healthier perspective.

DAY 280

You Are Building More Than Success

POWER QUOTE

"You are not only building wealth. You are building identity."

REFLECTION

Many people define success by what can be seen.

A successful career.

A growing business.

Financial freedom.

Recognition.

Influence.

Achievement.

These goals have value.

They create opportunities.

They provide security.

They allow people to make a meaningful impact on the lives of others.

But external success tells only part of the story.

The more important question is this:

Who are you becoming while pursuing it?

It is possible to accumulate wealth while neglecting your peace.

To gain influence while losing your integrity.

To build an impressive career while quietly sacrificing your emotional health.

To become successful in the eyes of the world while feeling disconnected from yourself.

That is why real transformation always begins on the inside.

Your external life is eventually shaped by your internal life.

The way you think determines the way you decide.

The way you manage your emotions influences the way you lead.

The way you handle disappointment shapes the way you persevere.

The habits you repeat become the character you carry into every opportunity.

This is why identity matters more than many people realize.

You are not simply building a career.

You are building a person.

Every disciplined morning shapes that person.

Every difficult conversation handled with maturity shapes that person.

Every wise financial decision shapes that person.

Every act of integrity, every healthy boundary, every commitment you keep—even when no one else notices—is shaping that person.

Those moments may never appear on a résumé.

But they become the foundation beneath everything you accomplish.

Many people spend years asking,

"How can I become more successful?"

A more powerful question is,

"Who must I become to sustain the success I desire?"

Because opportunities often grow faster than character if we are not intentional.

Responsibility increases.

Pressure increases.

Expectations increase.

Without emotional maturity, discipline, and wisdom, those same opportunities can become overwhelming.

That is why success is not only something you pursue.

It is something you prepare yourself to carry.

Preparation happens quietly.

You strengthen discipline before greater responsibility arrives.

You develop emotional regulation before leadership requires it.

You build financial wisdom before greater resources are entrusted to you.

You establish healthy values before success begins testing them.

This kind of growth is rarely dramatic.

It happens in ordinary moments.

When you choose patience instead of frustration.

When you choose honesty instead of convenience.

When you choose purpose instead of comparison.

When you choose consistency instead of waiting for motivation.

These repeated choices slowly transform your identity.

One day, people may notice your confidence.

Your peace.

Your wisdom.

Your resilience.

They may admire the success they can see.

What they will not see are the countless private decisions that created it.

The mornings you chose discipline.

The evenings you chose reflection.

The conversations that required humility.

The habits that strengthened your character.

The quiet seasons when growth was happening long before results became visible.

Those unseen moments matter.

Because they shaped someone capable of carrying the life they prayed for.

Do not become so focused on building success that you neglect becoming the kind of person who can enjoy it.

Protect your peace as intentionally as you protect your goals.

Strengthen your character as faithfully as you strengthen your skills.

Develop emotional health with the same commitment you give to professional growth.

Because the greatest achievement is not simply reaching the destination.

It is arriving there with your integrity intact.

Your relationships healthy.

Your mind peaceful.

Your heart whole.

Your future deserves more than visible success.

It deserves a version of you who is disciplined enough to remain consistent, emotionally mature enough to remain steady, wise enough to remain humble, and intentional enough to continue growing long after the goals have been achieved.

Because in the end, your greatest accomplishment will never be only what you built.

It will be the person you became while building it.

And that person will shape every success that follows.

WEALTH LESSON

Lasting success becomes sustainable when emotional growth develops alongside external achievement.

AFFIRMATION

"I intentionally build both external success and internal strength."

TODAY'S POWER MOVE

Focus today on strengthening one internal quality that your future self will need.

DAY 281

Your Life Changes When Your Standards Change

POWER QUOTE

"What you tolerate repeatedly eventually becomes your lifestyle."

REFLECTION

Every person has standards.

Some are intentional.

Others develop quietly through repeated habits and repeated compromises.

Your standards determine what you tolerate.

What you protect.

What you pursue.

And ultimately, the quality of the life you build.

Many people dream about extraordinary futures.

Financial freedom.

Healthy relationships.

Emotional peace.

Purposeful work.

A meaningful legacy.

Yet they continue accepting habits that lead in the opposite direction.

They tolerate constant distractions.

Unhealthy relationships.

Poor financial decisions.

Negative self-talk.

A lack of discipline.

Over time, those compromises become normal.

Eventually, people stop questioning them altogether.

That is why standards matter so deeply.

Your future is rarely determined by what you hope for.

It is determined by what you consistently accept.

Every time you lower your standards, you lower the quality of the life you are creating.

Every time you raise them, you strengthen the future you are building.

High standards are often misunderstood.

They are not about perfection.

They are not about becoming critical of yourself or others.

Healthy standards are expressions of self-respect.

They are quiet decisions that say,

"I will not continue living in ways that constantly move me away from the life I want."

That decision changes everything.

You begin protecting your time because you recognize it cannot be replaced.

You become more intentional with your finances because you understand every dollar reflects a decision about your future.

You become more careful about the relationships you maintain because you realize your environment shapes your character.
You stop accepting emotional chaos as normal because peace has become one of your priorities.
Higher standards are visible in ordinary moments.
They appear when you keep your word even when no one is watching.
When you arrive prepared instead of making excuses.
When you choose honesty over convenience.
When you leave environments that repeatedly damage your well-being.
When you refuse to negotiate with habits you know are undermining your future.
Those decisions rarely receive applause.
But they quietly transform your life.
Many people wait for confidence before raising their standards.
In reality, raising your standards is often what builds confidence.
Every time you refuse to settle for less than your values require, you strengthen your self-respect.
Every disciplined decision reminds you that your future matters.
Every healthy boundary reinforces the belief that your peace is worth protecting.
Every wise financial choice demonstrates that you are preparing for tomorrow instead of merely reacting to today.
Little by little, your identity begins changing.
Not because your circumstances changed first.
Because your expectations of yourself became healthier.
This also requires courage.
When you raise your standards, some people may become uncomfortable.
Not because your standards are unreasonable.
But because your growth no longer agrees with patterns that once felt normal.
You may need to leave conversations that continually drain your peace.
Walk away from habits that no longer align with your values.
Protect your attention from distractions that once consumed your time.
Those choices are not punishments.
They are investments.
Every healthy standard creates space for a healthier future.
Remember that standards are not measured by what you say you value.
They are measured by what you repeatedly practice.
Your calendar reflects your standards.
Your spending reflects your standards.
Your relationships reflect your standards.
Your daily routines reflect your standards.
If you want a different future, begin by strengthening the standards that shape your everyday life.
Ask yourself honestly:
"What have I been tolerating that no longer serves the person I want to become?"
"What standard do I need to raise today?"

Perhaps it is the way you manage your time.

Perhaps it is the way you speak to yourself.

Perhaps it is your commitment to discipline.

Perhaps it is the boundaries you have been afraid to establish.

Whatever the answer, remember this:

Your future will rarely rise above the standards you consistently maintain.

The life you dream about requires a version of you who is willing to protect what matters.

Protect your peace.

Protect your discipline.

Protect your integrity.

Protect your emotional health.

Protect your purpose.

Because every standard you faithfully uphold becomes another layer of the foundation beneath your future.

And one day, the life you have built will not simply be the result of what you hoped for.

It will be the result of the standards you refused to compromise along the way.

WEALTH LESSON

Higher standards improve long-term outcomes because intentional living strengthens discipline and stability.

AFFIRMATION

"I raise my standards because my future deserves excellence and peace."

TODAY'S POWER MOVE

Identify one area today where you need to stop tolerating less than what aligns with your future.

DAY 282

Stop Running From Difficult Conversations

POWER QUOTE

"Avoidance delays healing and clarity."

REFLECTION

Healthy relationships are not built by avoiding difficult conversations.

They are built by having them with wisdom.

Many people fear confrontation.

Not because they do not care.

But because conflict feels emotionally uncomfortable.

They worry about disappointing someone.

Creating tension.

Being misunderstood.

Losing the relationship altogether.

So instead of speaking honestly, they remain silent.

They suppress their emotions.

They ignore their needs.

They convince themselves that avoiding the conversation is the same as protecting the relationship.

For a while, it may feel easier.

The tension is delayed.

The disagreement is postponed.

The discomfort is avoided.

But silence rarely solves what honesty is meant to address.

Unspoken frustrations quietly become resentment.

Unexpressed needs become loneliness.

Unclear expectations become confusion.

The conversation you avoid today often becomes the conflict you face later.

That is why emotional maturity requires courage.

Not the courage to win every disagreement.

The courage to communicate with honesty, respect, and humility.

Healthy communication begins with one important realization:

The goal of a difficult conversation is not to defeat another person.

It is to better understand one another.

When relationships become competitions, trust weakens.

When relationships become conversations, trust has the opportunity to grow.

This requires a different approach.

Instead of reacting impulsively, pause first.

Instead of assuming motives, ask thoughtful questions.

Instead of attacking character, address the behavior.

Instead of speaking only to be heard, listen to understand.

These small shifts change the entire tone of a conversation.

Emotionally mature people recognize that honesty and kindness are not opposites.
They belong together.
Truth without compassion often creates defensiveness.
Compassion without truth often creates avoidance.
Healthy relationships need both.
There will be moments when difficult conversations are unavoidable.
A boundary must be established.
A misunderstanding needs clarification.
An apology needs to be offered.
A hurt needs to be acknowledged.
Those moments are uncomfortable.
But discomfort is not always a sign that something is wrong.
Sometimes discomfort is simply the price of deeper trust.
Think about the strongest relationships in your life.
They probably were not built because conflict never occurred.
They were strengthened because both people became willing to address conflict with respect instead of avoidance.
Trust grows when people know they can speak honestly without fear of being punished for their vulnerability.
That kind of emotional safety is not created accidentally.
It is built through repeated moments of honesty.
Communication also requires responsibility.
Before entering a difficult conversation, ask yourself:
"Am I trying to understand or only to be understood?"
"Am I speaking from wisdom or from wounded emotion?"
"Am I seeking resolution or simply releasing frustration?"
Those questions create space for maturity.
They remind you that healthy communication begins with self-awareness.
Not every conversation will end perfectly.
Some people may still disagree.
Some relationships may not change.
Some individuals may choose not to receive what you communicate with humility.
Their response is not always within your control.
Your responsibility is to communicate with integrity.
To speak truthfully.
To listen respectfully.
To remain grounded in your values rather than being controlled by temporary emotions.
This is how emotional maturity grows.
One courageous conversation at a time.
One honest apology at a time.
One healthy boundary at a time.
One respectful disagreement at a time.

Over time, you begin realizing that communication is not simply about exchanging words.

It is about building trust.

Protecting connection.

Creating clarity.

And allowing relationships to become healthier because truth is no longer being hidden behind fear.

Your future deserves relationships where honesty is welcomed instead of avoided.

Where difficult conversations become opportunities for understanding instead of reasons for division.

Where peace is built through communication, not silence.

Because lasting peace is not created by pretending everything is fine.

It is created when people care enough to speak honestly, listen humbly, and grow together through the conversations that matter most.

That is the kind of courage that strengthens relationships.

And it is the kind of courage that strengthens you.

WEALTH LESSON

Healthy communication improves relationships and emotional stability because unresolved issues create long-term stress.

AFFIRMATION

"I communicate honestly, calmly, and intentionally."

TODAY'S POWER MOVE

Address one conversation or emotional issue today that you have been avoiding unnecessarily.

DAY 283

Your Future Needs Financial Discipline

POWER QUOTE

"Money grows differently in disciplined hands."

REFLECTION

Many people imagine financial freedom as one life-changing event.

A promotion.

A successful business.

A winning investment.

A sudden opportunity that changes everything overnight.

While those moments can certainly accelerate progress, they are rarely what creates lasting wealth.

Financial freedom is usually built much more quietly.

One wise decision at a time.

One disciplined habit at a time.

One intentional choice repeated consistently over years.

This is why financial success has as much to do with behavior as it does with income.

Two people can earn the same salary and build completely different futures.

One spends impulsively whenever emotions become overwhelming.

The other plans intentionally, saves consistently, and thinks beyond today's desires.

Over time, their habits create entirely different outcomes.

Money magnifies behavior.

It does not automatically improve it.

If financial decisions are driven by fear, wealth often becomes difficult to sustain.

If they are driven by wisdom, patience, and discipline, stability becomes much more attainable.

That is why your relationship with money matters just as much as the amount of money you earn.

Many financial setbacks are not caused by a lack of intelligence.

They are caused by emotional decision-making.

Stress leads to emotional spending.

Anxiety leads to avoidance.

Comparison leads to unnecessary purchases.

Impatience leads people to chase shortcuts instead of building steadily.

These responses may provide temporary emotional relief.

But they often create greater financial pressure later.

Financial discipline asks a different question.

Instead of asking,

"What do I want right now?"

It asks,

"What decision will strengthen my future?"

That question changes everything.

It shifts your attention from temporary satisfaction to long-term stewardship.

Every dollar becomes a decision.

Every purchase becomes a reflection of your priorities.
Every budget becomes a plan for the life you hope to create.
This does not mean you can never enjoy your money.
Healthy stewardship is not built on fear or guilt.
It is built on intentionality.
Spend with wisdom.
Save with consistency.
Invest with patience.
Give with generosity.
Prepare with discipline.
Those habits create freedom because they replace reaction with purpose.
Think about how a tree grows.
No one notices the roots developing beneath the soil.
Day after day, growth seems almost invisible.
Then, years later, people admire the strength of the tree.
Wealth often develops the same way.
The emergency fund that grows little by little.
The investments that quietly compound.
The debts that gradually disappear through consistent payments.
The financial knowledge gained one lesson at a time.
None of these moments feel dramatic.
Yet together, they build extraordinary stability.
This is why patience is one of the greatest financial strengths you can develop.
The culture around us often celebrates quick success.
But lasting wealth is usually built slowly.
Quietly.
Intentionally.
It rewards consistency far more than excitement.
Every budget you follow strengthens your discipline.
Every unnecessary expense you avoid strengthens your future.
Every investment you make with wisdom plants another seed for tomorrow.
Every financial goal you faithfully pursue becomes evidence that you are learning to think beyond the present moment.
Remember that wealth is more than a number in an account.
True financial freedom includes peace.
The confidence that comes from preparation.
The ability to respond to challenges without panic.
The opportunity to give generously without fear.
The freedom to make decisions based on purpose instead of constant financial pressure.
That kind of wealth begins long before large balances appear.
It begins with daily choices.

The quiet choices no one applauds.

The moments when you choose discipline over impulse.

Planning over avoidance.

Patience over instant gratification.

Those are the decisions that shape financial futures.

One day, people may notice the stability you have built.

They may admire your success.

What they will not see are the thousands of ordinary financial decisions that made it possible.

The budgets.

The sacrifices.

The consistent habits.

The disciplined thinking.

Those unseen moments created everything.

So do not underestimate today's choices simply because they seem small.

Every intentional financial decision is another investment in the life you hope to build.

And over time, those quiet decisions become more than healthy habits.

They become the foundation of a future marked by peace, stewardship, and lasting financial freedom.

WEALTH LESSON

Long-term wealth is strengthened through consistent disciplined financial behavior over time.

AFFIRMATION

"I build financial freedom through discipline and intentional decisions."

TODAY'S POWER MOVE

Make one financially responsible decision today that supports your future goals.

DAY 284

Stop Letting Temporary Emotions Destroy Long-Term Goals

POWER QUOTE

"Emotions are temporary. Consequences often last much longer."

REFLECTION

Emotions are powerful.

They can inspire you to take courageous action.

They can deepen relationships.

They can help you recognize what matters most.

But emotions were never designed to become the leaders of your life.

They were meant to become valuable messengers.

Many of the biggest regrets people carry were not created because they lacked intelligence.

They were created because they made permanent decisions during temporary emotional moments.

A harsh word spoken in anger.

An impulsive purchase made during stress.

A relationship abandoned because disappointment felt overwhelming.

A dream given up because discouragement became louder than hope.

In those moments, emotions were real.

But they were never meant to have the final word.

One of the greatest signs of emotional maturity is learning the difference between feeling something and following it.

Feeling frustrated does not mean you should quit.

Feeling anxious does not mean you are incapable.

Feeling discouraged does not mean your progress has stopped.

Feeling uncertain does not mean your future has disappeared.

Emotions deserve acknowledgment.

They do not deserve unquestioned authority.

This is where emotional regulation becomes one of the most valuable skills you can develop.

Emotional regulation is not pretending everything is fine.

It is not suppressing sadness.

It is not ignoring fear.

Healthy people allow themselves to feel honestly.

They recognize disappointment.

They acknowledge grief.

They admit frustration.

But before making important decisions, they create space.

They pause.

They breathe.

They reflect.

They ask,

"Is this emotion telling me the truth, or is it simply telling me how this moment feels?"

That question creates wisdom.
Because emotions often describe the present.
Wisdom considers the future.
Think about financial decisions.
Stress may tempt you to spend for temporary comfort.
Fear may tempt you to avoid looking at your bank account.
Impatience may tempt you to chase risky shortcuts.
Those emotional impulses feel convincing in the moment.
Yet disciplined thinking asks a different question:
"What decision will strengthen my life six months from now?"
The same principle applies to relationships.
A painful disagreement may tempt you to walk away.
Pride may tempt you to remain silent instead of apologizing.
Loneliness may tempt you to settle for relationships that continually damage your peace.
Emotional maturity creates enough distance between feeling and action to make wiser decisions.
This ability is not developed overnight.
It grows through repeated practice.
Every time you pause before reacting, you strengthen self-control.
Every time you choose patience over impulsiveness, you strengthen wisdom.
Every time you return to your values instead of surrendering to temporary emotions, you strengthen your character.
Those small victories become your identity over time.
Imagine a ship crossing the ocean.
Storms are unavoidable.
The waves rise.
The wind shifts.
The weather changes without warning.
If the captain allowed every wave to determine the direction of the ship, the journey would never reach its destination.
Instead, the captain acknowledges the storm while remaining committed to the course.
Life works the same way.
Your emotions are like changing weather.
Some days the skies are clear.
Other days the waves are high.
Neither should determine the destination.
Your values should.
Your purpose should.
Your vision for the future should.
There will always be moments when quitting feels easier than continuing.
Moments when reacting feels easier than responding wisely.
Moments when temporary relief seems more attractive than long-term growth.

Those are the moments that quietly shape your future.

Not because they are dramatic.

Because they reveal who is leading your life.

Your emotions.

Or your principles.

The strongest people are not those who never experience fear, sadness, anger, or disappointment.

They are the people who have learned how to experience those emotions without becoming controlled by them.

They have learned that feelings are temporary.

Character is lasting.

So honor your emotions.

Listen to what they may be revealing.

But do not surrender your future to every passing feeling.

Pause before reacting.

Reflect before deciding.

Choose wisdom over impulse.

Choose purpose over panic.

Choose discipline over temporary relief.

Because every time you refuse to let a temporary emotion make a permanent decision, you strengthen the person your future depends upon.

And one intentional decision at a time, you become someone who is no longer driven by changing emotions—but guided by lasting wisdom.

WEALTH LESSON

Emotional discipline improves long-term outcomes because intentional behavior creates healthier results than impulsive reactions.

AFFIRMATION

"I refuse to let temporary emotions sabotage my future."

TODAY'S POWER MOVE

Pause before reacting emotionally today and ask whether your decision aligns with your long-term goals.

DAY 285

You Deserve Rest Without Guilt

POWER QUOTE

"Rest is part of sustainable growth."

REFLECTION

Many ambitious people carry a quiet belief they rarely say out loud.

"If I slow down, I'll fall behind."

So they keep pushing.

Working longer.

Sleeping less.

Ignoring exhaustion.

Silencing the signals their mind and body are trying to communicate.

At first, this relentless pace may even feel productive.

More hours.

More effort.

More activity.

But eventually, something begins to change.

Focus becomes harder.

Patience becomes shorter.

Creativity becomes weaker.

Small problems begin feeling overwhelming.

The very qualities that once made you effective slowly begin to disappear.

Not because you became less capable.

Because you became depleted.

This is why rest is not a luxury.

It is a responsibility.

Rest is often misunderstood.

Some people confuse it with laziness.

Others believe it is only something you earn after reaching every goal.

But intentional rest is neither avoidance nor complacency.

It is restoration.

It is creating space for your mind, body, and emotions to recover so they can continue carrying the responsibilities of tomorrow.

Think about an athlete preparing for competition.

The strongest athletes do not train without stopping.

They understand that muscles grow during recovery as much as they do during exercise.

Without recovery, strength eventually declines.

Performance suffers.

Injuries become more likely.

Life follows a similar pattern.

You cannot continually demand more from yourself while giving yourself nothing in return.

The healthiest growth is sustainable growth.

That requires rhythm.

There are seasons to work diligently.

Seasons to learn.

Seasons to build.

But there must also be moments to breathe.

To reflect.

To recover.

To reconnect with what matters most.

Without those moments, achievement can quietly become exhaustion disguised as success.

Many people wear burnout like a badge of honor.

They believe being constantly busy proves commitment.

Yet constant busyness is not always the same as meaningful progress.

Sometimes it is simply constant motion.

Wisdom asks a different question.

"Am I building a life I can sustain?"

That question matters because your future depends on more than effort.

It depends on endurance.

Endurance is not created by never resting.

It is created by learning when to work with excellence and when to recover with intention.

Rest protects your clarity.

When your mind is constantly overloaded, wise decisions become more difficult.

Small challenges begin feeling larger than they truly are.

Simple solutions become harder to recognize.

A rested mind sees possibilities that an exhausted mind often misses.

Rest also protects your discipline.

Many people think discipline means pushing yourself without limits.

Real discipline includes knowing when restoration is necessary.

Ignoring your limits is not strength.

Understanding them is wisdom.

Rest protects your relationships.

When you are emotionally exhausted, patience becomes harder.

Listening becomes harder.

Being fully present becomes harder.

The people you love deserve more than the leftovers of your energy.

They deserve your presence.

And you deserve relationships that are strengthened by a healthy, restored version of yourself.

Most importantly, rest protects your peace.

It reminds you that your worth is not measured by constant productivity.

You are more than your accomplishments.

More than your schedule.

More than your performance.

Your value does not increase because you work yourself into exhaustion.

It is reflected in the wisdom with which you steward the life you have been given.

This does not mean walking away from what still requires your attention.

It means approaching responsibility with sustainability.

Work with intention.

Rest with intention.

Build with intention.

Recover with intention.

That rhythm allows you to continue growing year after year instead of burning brightly for a season before collapsing under unnecessary pressure.

Remember that some of your greatest breakthroughs will not happen while you are rushing.

They will happen when your mind becomes quiet enough to think clearly.

When your heart becomes calm enough to listen.

When your body becomes restored enough to continue faithfully.

Do not feel guilty for honoring the limits that make long-term growth possible.

The strongest people are rarely those who never stop.

They are the people who understand that endurance requires restoration.

Because the goal is not simply to build something impressive.

The goal is to build something lasting.

And lasting success is created by people who know when to work hard, when to recover well, and how to faithfully return to the work with renewed strength.

Rest is not a detour from your purpose.

When practiced wisely, it becomes one of the disciplines that protects it.

WEALTH LESSON

Restoration improves productivity because emotionally regulated minds perform better long-term.

AFFIRMATION

"I allow myself to rest and restore without guilt."

TODAY'S POWER MOVE

Take intentional time today to recharge emotionally and mentally.

DAY 286

Your Confidence Will Grow Through Action

POWER QUOTE

"Confidence is built by doing difficult things consistently."

REFLECTION

Some people believe confidence is something you must have before you begin.

They imagine confident people waking up every morning completely certain.

Never doubting themselves.

Never questioning their ability.

Never feeling afraid.

The truth is far less glamorous.

Most confident people were once uncertain people who kept moving anyway.

Confidence is rarely the starting point.

It is usually the result.

It grows through evidence.

Evidence that you can handle difficult conversations.

Evidence that you can recover from setbacks.

Evidence that you can remain disciplined even when motivation fades.

Evidence that you can face uncertainty without abandoning yourself.

That evidence is created through action.

This is why waiting to feel completely confident before taking the next step often keeps people trapped.

They wait to apply for the opportunity.

Wait to start the business.

Wait to have the conversation.

Wait to invest in themselves.

Wait to pursue the dream.

They believe confidence will arrive first.

But confidence is built after the decision to act.

Imagine learning to ride a bicycle.

No amount of thinking creates confidence.

No amount of reading creates balance.

Eventually, you must climb onto the bicycle.

You wobble.

You make mistakes.

You may even fall.

But every attempt teaches your mind something new.

"I survived."

"I learned."

"I improved."

Little by little, uncertainty is replaced with self-trust.

Life works the same way.

Every courageous action becomes another piece of evidence that you are more capable than you once believed.

The first difficult presentation.

The first healthy boundary.

The first financial investment.

The first business you launch.

The first apology you offer.

The first time you continue despite fear.

Each experience quietly whispers,

"You are becoming someone who follows through."

That message is powerful.

Because confidence is deeply connected to self-trust.

Self-trust develops when your actions consistently support your values.

Every promise you keep to yourself strengthens that trust.

Every commitment you honor reminds you that you are dependable.

Every challenge you face instead of avoiding teaches your mind that discomfort is survivable.

Many people unknowingly weaken their confidence by repeatedly abandoning themselves.

They make commitments they never keep.

They allow fear to decide for them.

They avoid opportunities because failure feels uncomfortable.

Over time, their mind begins expecting retreat instead of resilience.

But the opposite is also true.

Every time you choose courage instead of comfort, your mind gathers new evidence.

"I finished what I started."

"I handled that conversation."

"I stayed disciplined."

"I recovered after disappointment."

"I kept going."

Those moments may seem ordinary.

Yet they become the building blocks of lasting confidence.

Confidence is not pretending fear does not exist.

It is knowing that fear no longer has the authority to decide your future.

It is walking forward while your hands still shake.

Speaking even when your voice feels uncertain.

Trying again after failure.

Continuing after rejection.

Showing up after disappointment.

That is real confidence.

It is quiet.

Steady.

Earned.

Not because life became easier.

Because you became stronger.

There will always be new challenges.

Greater responsibilities.

Larger opportunities.

Each one will introduce a new level of uncertainty.

Do not interpret that uncertainty as evidence that you are unprepared.

See it as an invitation to grow again.

The confident person you admire today is still encountering situations that stretch them.

The difference is that they have learned to trust themselves through the process.

You can develop that same trust.

One action at a time.

One promise kept at a time.

One courageous decision at a time.

Stop waiting for certainty before you begin.

Begin, and allow certainty to grow through experience.

Because your future is not waiting for a fearless version of you.

It is waiting for a faithful one.

A person who continues despite doubt.

Who honors commitments despite discomfort.

Who chooses discipline despite changing emotions.

Who keeps taking the next step even when the outcome is not fully visible.

One day, people will call you confident.

They will see your calmness.

Your courage.

Your resilience.

What they will not see are the hundreds of moments when you chose action before you felt ready.

Those moments created the evidence.

The evidence created self-trust.

And self-trust quietly became the confidence that now carries you forward.

That is how lasting confidence is built.

Not before action.

But because of it.

WEALTH LESSON

Repeated courageous action strengthens self-trust because confidence grows through evidence and experience.

AFFIRMATION

"I build confidence through courageous and disciplined action."

TODAY'S POWER MOVE

Take one action today that stretches your confidence beyond your comfort zone.

DAY 287

Stop Romanticizing Procrastination

POWER QUOTE

"Delayed action delays transformation."

REFLECTION

Many people think procrastination is simply waiting for a better time.

A better mood.

More confidence.

More motivation.

More certainty.

But procrastination often disguises itself as preparation.

People tell themselves they are still researching.

Still thinking.

Still planning.

Still getting ready.

Meanwhile, days become weeks.

Weeks become months.

And opportunities quietly pass by.

The danger of procrastination is not only the time it steals.

It is the identity it creates.

Every promise you repeatedly postpone slowly teaches your mind that your future is negotiable.

You begin trusting your excuses more than your commitments.

You start believing tomorrow will always be a better day to begin.

But tomorrow has a way of becoming another tomorrow.

Then another.

Until years have passed and the life you imagined remains exactly where it started.

Most people do not procrastinate because they are lazy.

They procrastinate because action feels emotionally uncomfortable.

Taking the first step creates uncertainty.

Responsibility.

The possibility of failure.

The possibility of rejection.

The possibility of discovering that the journey will be harder than expected.

Waiting temporarily protects you from those uncomfortable emotions.

But it also protects you from growth.

This is why procrastination is so deceptive.

It offers emotional comfort today while quietly stealing tomorrow.

Every meaningful goal eventually reaches a moment where preparation is no longer enough.

The entrepreneur eventually has to launch.

The writer eventually has to publish.

The investor eventually has to invest.

The student eventually has to begin studying.
The person seeking healing eventually has to face the conversations and habits they have been avoiding.
Action is the bridge between intention and transformation.
Without action, even the best plans remain dreams.
Most people assume they need confidence before they begin.
More often, confidence grows because they began.
Every completed task becomes evidence.
Every promise you keep strengthens self-trust.
Every difficult step reminds your mind that discomfort is survivable.
That evidence compounds.
Over time, action becomes easier because your identity begins changing.
You stop seeing yourself as someone who always delays.
You begin seeing yourself as someone who follows through.
That shift changes everything.
Because identity influences behavior.
When you believe you are dependable, you naturally begin making decisions that reinforce that belief.
Momentum replaces hesitation.
Discipline replaces excuses.
Progress replaces endless preparation.
There will never be a perfect moment to begin.
There will always be another reason to wait.
Another fear to overcome.
Another uncertainty to solve.
If you spend your life waiting for perfect emotional certainty, you may spend your life waiting.
Your future is built by the actions you take today, not the intentions you postpone until tomorrow.
Ask yourself honestly:
"What have I been delaying that I already know I need to begin?"
Perhaps it is your financial plan.
Your business.
Your healing.
A difficult conversation.
A healthy habit.
A dream you keep pushing further into the future because waiting feels safer than trying.
Whatever it is, remember this:
Your future is not waiting for perfect timing.
It is waiting for faithful action.
One decision.
One completed task.
One uncomfortable step at a time.
Stop romanticizing procrastination as preparation.
Preparation has value.

But eventually, preparation must become movement.

Because the life you want will never be built by what you intended to do.

It will always be built by what you consistently chose to do.

And years from now, your greatest breakthroughs will not come from the plans you made.

They will come from the moments you finally stopped waiting and started building.

WEALTH LESSON

Intentional execution improves productivity because preparation reduces unnecessary emotional stress.

AFFIRMATION

"I stop procrastinating and begin acting intentionally."

TODAY'S POWER MOVE

Complete one task today that you have been unnecessarily delaying.

DAY 288

Healing Will Change The Way You Think

POWER QUOTE

"A healed perspective creates different decisions."

REFLECTION

Many people think healing is simply about feeling better.

Feeling less anxious.

Feeling less angry.

Feeling less hurt.

While emotional relief is certainly part of healing, it is not the full picture.

Real healing changes far more than your emotions.

It changes your perspective.

Your habits.

Your communication.

Your relationships.

The way you make decisions.

The way you respond under pressure.

The way you see yourself.

The way you see the future.

Healing is not simply the absence of pain.

It is the presence of healthier patterns.

One of the first signs that healing is taking place is not that life becomes easier.

It is that you begin responding differently to the same situations that once controlled you.

The comment that once ruined your entire day no longer has the same power.

The disappointment that once made you quit now strengthens your resolve.

The conflict that once led to emotional reactions now invites thoughtful communication.

The financial setback that once caused panic now leads to intentional planning.

Your circumstances may not immediately change.

But you begin changing within your circumstances.

That is transformation.

Healing creates awareness.

You begin recognizing patterns you once accepted without question.

You notice the conversations that continually drain your energy.

You recognize the habits that quietly sabotage your progress.

You identify emotional triggers that once controlled your reactions without your awareness.

Awareness creates choice.

And choice creates freedom.

Instead of reacting from habit, you begin responding from awareness.

You pause before speaking.

You think before spending.

You reflect before assuming.

You establish boundaries instead of carrying resentment.

You choose peace instead of proving yourself right.

Those changes may appear small.

But together, they create an entirely different life.

Many unhealthy behaviors begin as survival strategies.

Perhaps avoiding conflict once protected you.

Perhaps constantly pleasing others helped you feel accepted.

Perhaps emotional spending temporarily distracted you from pain.

Perhaps overworking became your way of proving your worth.

Those strategies may have helped you survive a difficult season.

But healing gently asks an important question:

"Is this behavior still helping me build the future I want?"

Sometimes the answer is no.

That realization is not an invitation to shame yourself.

It is an invitation to grow.

Real healing does not ask you to become someone else overnight.

It asks you to become more intentional one decision at a time.

One healthier conversation.

One wiser financial choice.

One calmer response.

One stronger boundary.

One honest reflection.

Over time, those decisions begin replacing old survival patterns with healthier ways of living.

This is why healing and discipline belong together.

Healing gives you awareness.

Discipline helps you practice what awareness reveals.

One without the other often leaves transformation incomplete.

Awareness without action creates frustration.

Action without awareness often repeats old patterns.

Together, they create lasting change.

As healing continues, something beautiful begins happening.

You stop needing constant chaos to feel alive.

You stop confusing peace with boredom.

You stop chasing validation from people who cannot provide lasting security.

You stop abandoning yourself whenever life becomes uncomfortable.

Instead, you begin trusting yourself.

Protecting your peace.

Choosing healthier environments.

Building relationships rooted in honesty instead of fear.

Planning for the future instead of merely surviving the present.

Little by little, emotional freedom replaces emotional survival.

This is one of the greatest gifts healing offers.

Not a perfect life.

But a healthier way of living it.

There will still be difficult seasons.

Disappointments.

Unexpected challenges.

Moments that stretch your patience and your faith.

Healing does not remove every storm.

It changes how you walk through them.

You become steadier.

More thoughtful.

More resilient.

More emotionally grounded.

More intentional than you were before.

And those changes influence every area of your life.

Your relationships become healthier.

Your financial decisions become wiser.

Your communication becomes calmer.

Your confidence becomes quieter but stronger.

Your peace becomes more consistent because it is no longer dependent upon perfect circumstances.

Never underestimate what quiet healing is accomplishing inside you.

Every healthy response is evidence of growth.

Every intentional decision is evidence of maturity.

Every old pattern you refuse to repeat is evidence that your future is no longer being controlled by your past.

Because healing changes more than how you feel.

It changes how you live.

And the life you build from that place will reflect not only what you have overcome—

but who you have become in the process.

That is the kind of transformation that lasts.

WEALTH LESSON

Emotional healing improves decision-making because regulated minds create healthier long-term outcomes.

AFFIRMATION

"I allow healing to transform the way I think and live."

TODAY'S POWER MOVE

Reflect today on one emotional response that healing has already improved within you.

DAY 289

Your Future Requires Emotional Stability

POWER QUOTE

"A calm mind handles life differently than a chaotic one."

REFLECTION

People often underestimate how much emotional stability influences success.

They assume success is determined only by intelligence.

Talent.

Education.

Opportunity.

But the ability to remain emotionally grounded during pressure often separates those who thrive from those who continually sabotage their own progress.

Life will always introduce uncertainty.

Unexpected expenses.

Relationship challenges.

Professional setbacks.

Difficult conversations.

Moments where plans do not unfold the way you expected.

The question is not whether pressure will come.

The question is how you will respond when it does.

Emotional instability often causes people to react before they think.

A stressful day leads to impulsive spending.

A disagreement leads to harsh words.

A setback leads to giving up too quickly.

A moment of fear leads to abandoning opportunities that could have changed their future.

These reactions rarely come from a lack of ability.

They often come from a lack of emotional regulation.

Emotional regulation is not pretending difficult emotions do not exist.

It is learning how to experience them without allowing them to make your decisions.

There is a significant difference between feeling overwhelmed and allowing overwhelm to control your behavior.

The first is part of being human.

The second is something you can learn to manage.

One of the greatest signs of maturity is developing the ability to pause before responding.

To create space between emotion and action.

That pause may only last a few seconds.

Yet it often determines whether you build trust or destroy it.

Whether you strengthen a relationship or damage it.

Whether you make a wise financial decision or an impulsive one.

Whether you continue moving toward your goals or retreat because the moment feels uncomfortable.

A peaceful mind is not an empty mind.

It is a trained mind.

A mind that has learned not to panic every time life becomes uncertain.

A mind that understands difficult emotions are temporary, but many decisions have lasting consequences.

That kind of stability affects every area of life.

You communicate more thoughtfully because you are no longer reacting from every emotional trigger.

You lead more effectively because pressure no longer immediately creates panic.

You manage money more wisely because temporary stress no longer controls every purchase.

You build healthier relationships because people experience consistency instead of unpredictability.

Over time, emotional stability becomes one of your greatest strengths.

Not because life becomes easier.

But because you become steadier.

This is why emotional health deserves daily attention.

Protect your peace.

Pay attention to what continually drains your energy.

Practice slowing down before making important decisions.

Develop routines that help you remain grounded during difficult seasons.

The goal is not to become emotionless.

The goal is to become emotionally resilient.

Resilient people still experience disappointment.

They still experience fear.

They still experience frustration.

The difference is that they no longer allow every emotion to determine the direction of their lives.

They have learned to respond with wisdom instead of reacting from impulse.

That is a skill that compounds over time.

Every calm response strengthens your character.

Every thoughtful decision strengthens your future.

Every difficult season handled with maturity prepares you for greater responsibility.

Remember that opportunities often bring pressure with them.

Leadership creates pressure.

Financial growth creates pressure.

Influence creates pressure.

Healthy relationships require emotional responsibility.

If you want to sustain greater opportunities, you must develop the emotional capacity to carry them well.

That is why emotional stability is more than a personal strength.

It is one of the greatest investments you can make in your future.

Because the life you are building will not only require talent and ambition.

It will require a steady mind, a disciplined heart, and the wisdom to remain grounded when everything around you feels uncertain.

That kind of strength is quiet.

But it is the kind of strength that lasts.

WEALTH LESSON

Emotional stability strengthens long-term growth because clear thinking creates wiser decisions.

AFFIRMATION

"I build emotional stability through peace, healing, and self-awareness."

TODAY'S POWER MOVE

Practice emotional calmness today during a stressful or frustrating moment.

DAY 290

Your Story Is Still Being Written

POWER QUOTE

"You are not finished becoming who you are capable of becoming."

REFLECTION

Too many people make the mistake of believing one difficult season defines the rest of their life.

A financial setback.

A failed relationship.

A business that didn't work.

A season of anxiety.

A period where motivation disappeared.

These moments can feel overwhelming while you are living through them.

They can convince you that nothing will ever change.

That you have fallen too far behind.

That the best version of your life has already passed.

But difficult seasons are chapters.

They are not your identity.

Every person's story includes moments they never would have chosen.

Moments of disappointment.

Confusion.

Loss.

Failure.

The difference is that some people allow those moments to become permanent conclusions, while others allow them to become turning points.

Your current circumstances are not the final sentence of your story.

They are simply the page you are reading today.

Life has a remarkable way of changing when people refuse to stop growing.

New opportunities appear.

New relationships form.

New skills develop.

New perspectives emerge.

The person you are becoming tomorrow will not think exactly like the person you are today.

That is the beauty of growth.

You are allowed to evolve.

You are allowed to outgrow old fears.

You are allowed to become wiser than your past mistakes.

You are allowed to rebuild after seasons that once felt impossible to survive.

Do not underestimate what consistent, intentional choices can accomplish over time.

One healthy habit.

One difficult conversation.

One wise financial decision.

One act of courage.

One day of refusing to give up.

Those moments may seem insignificant on their own, but together they create a completely different future.

Some of the strongest, wisest, and most compassionate people are those who once felt completely lost.

Not because they avoided hardship.

But because they kept moving through it.

They allowed adversity to teach them instead of define them.

They chose growth instead of surrender.

Remember that your life is still unfolding.

There are experiences you have not yet lived.

People you have not yet met.

Dreams you have not yet pursued.

Strengths you have not yet discovered.

Do not allow one painful season to convince you that nothing better is ahead.

Keep learning.

Keep rebuilding.

Keep believing that change is possible.

Because your future is not determined by your hardest chapter.

It is shaped by your willingness to keep writing the chapters that come after it.

WEALTH LESSON

Persistence creates long-term transformation because continued effort allows growth and opportunity to develop over time.

AFFIRMATION

"I continue believing in the future I am capable of building."

TODAY'S POWER MOVE

Write down one vision for your future that you still deeply believe is possible.

DAY 291

Stop Ignoring What Needs To Change

POWER QUOTE

"Evolution requires honesty about what is no longer working."

REFLECTION

Some of the greatest obstacles to growth are not the problems people cannot see.

They are the ones they recognize but continue tolerating.

The unhealthy habit they promise to change "next week."

The relationship that continually drains their peace.

The financial decisions they avoid confronting.

The emotional patterns they know are holding them back.

Awareness without action eventually becomes another form of avoidance.

Many people spend years hoping life will improve while continuing the same behaviors that created their frustration.

Not because they lack intelligence.

But because change often feels uncomfortable.

The familiar can feel safer than the unknown, even when the familiar is unhealthy.

This is why transformation requires more than good intentions.

It requires the courage to stop negotiating with the habits that are quietly stealing your future.

Growth begins when you become honest enough to ask difficult questions.

"What have I been excusing that I should be changing?"

"What pattern keeps showing up in my life because I refuse to address it?"

"What am I tolerating simply because it has become familiar?"

Those questions are uncomfortable.

But they create clarity.

And clarity creates the opportunity for change.

Honesty is one of the greatest gifts you can give yourself.

Not the kind of honesty that tears you down.

The kind that sets you free.

Honesty says,

"This habit is no longer serving me."

"This environment is preventing my growth."

"This mindset is keeping me stuck."

There is no shame in recognizing where you need to grow.

In fact, recognizing it is the beginning of wisdom.

The strongest people are rarely those who pretend everything is fine.

They are the people who are willing to face reality without allowing it to define them.

Once you identify what needs to change, responsibility becomes your greatest ally.

Every healthier decision weakens an old pattern.

Every boundary strengthens your self-respect.

Every intentional financial choice creates greater stability.

Every difficult conversation handled with maturity creates healthier relationships.

Small decisions repeated consistently begin replacing old cycles with new ones.

Do not underestimate how quickly your life can begin changing once you stop protecting the very things that are hurting you.

You deserve more than living the same chapter over and over again.

You deserve growth.

You deserve peace.

You deserve relationships, habits, and environments that support the person you are becoming.

The life you want is not built by avoiding uncomfortable truths.

It is built by facing them with courage, responding with wisdom, and choosing—one intentional decision at a time—to stop settling for the patterns that no longer belong in your future.

WEALTH LESSON

Self-awareness improves outcomes because intentional growth requires recognizing unhealthy patterns honestly.

AFFIRMATION

"I face the truth honestly and commit to healthier change."

TODAY'S POWER MOVE

Identify one pattern today that you know must change for your future to improve.

DAY 292

Your Peace Is Worth More Than Chaos

POWER QUOTE

"Protecting your peace is one of the highest forms of self-respect."

REFLECTION

Some people spend so much of their lives surrounded by conflict that peace begins to feel unfamiliar.

They become accustomed to constant stress.

Constant urgency.

Constant uncertainty.

Over time, the nervous system starts expecting chaos.

When life finally becomes calm, it can even feel uncomfortable.

Not because peace is wrong.

Because chaos became familiar.

But familiarity is not the same as health.

Many people remain in unhealthy environments simply because they recognize them.

They confuse emotional intensity with connection.

They mistake unpredictability for excitement.

They believe something must always be wrong because that has been their normal for so long.

Yet emotional chaos comes at a high cost.

It quietly steals your attention.

It drains your energy.

It weakens your confidence.

It makes wise decisions more difficult because your mind is constantly responding to immediate stress instead of thinking about the future.

Living in survival mode may help you endure a difficult season.

It is not how you were meant to build a meaningful life.

Peace is often misunderstood.

Some people think peaceful living means a life without ambition.

Without challenges.

Without responsibility.

True peace is something entirely different.

It is the ability to remain steady while responsibilities continue growing.

It is having a mind that can think clearly under pressure instead of immediately reacting.

It is creating relationships where trust replaces constant emotional tension.

It is building financial stability without living in continual fear.

It is going to sleep knowing your mind is not carrying battles that never belonged to you in the first place.

Peace does not make you weaker.

It allows you to become stronger.

A peaceful mind solves problems more effectively.

A peaceful heart builds healthier relationships.

A peaceful life creates space for creativity, wisdom, and intentional growth.

That kind of peace does not happen by accident.

It is protected through daily decisions.

Choosing environments that support your well-being.

Creating healthy routines.

Establishing boundaries with people who continually disturb your emotional health.

Learning when to step away instead of engaging in unnecessary conflict.

Choosing conversations that build understanding instead of feeding drama.

Little by little, those decisions reshape what feels normal.

Eventually, peace no longer feels unfamiliar.

It feels like home.

Remember that the future you are building deserves more than surviving one crisis after another.

It deserves stability.

Clarity.

Healthy relationships.

Wise decisions.

And the freedom to grow without constantly carrying unnecessary emotional weight.

Do not settle for chaos simply because it is familiar.

Allow yourself to believe that a calm, healthy, and intentional life is possible.

Because one of the greatest signs of healing is not learning how to survive chaos.

It is learning that you no longer have to live inside it.

WEALTH LESSON

Mental peace improves decision-making because emotionally regulated minds think more clearly long-term.

AFFIRMATION

"I intentionally protect the peace I am working hard to build."

TODAY'S POWER MOVE

Remove one unnecessary source of emotional stress from your life today.

DAY 293

Stop Waiting For Someone To Save You

POWER QUOTE

"At some point, healing requires personal responsibility."

REFLECTION

Support can change your life.

Encouragement can strengthen your confidence.

Wise mentors can help you avoid unnecessary mistakes.

Healthy relationships can remind you that you do not have to face every challenge alone.

Those gifts matter.

No one was designed to navigate life completely isolated.

We all need people who believe in us.

People who tell us the truth.

People who encourage us when we feel discouraged.

But there comes a point where your future can no longer depend entirely on someone else's participation.

No mentor can develop your discipline for you.

No friend can heal your emotional wounds for you.

No partner can consistently make the decisions that belong to you.

Other people can support your journey.

They cannot walk it in your place.

This realization can feel intimidating at first.

It means accepting responsibility.

It means recognizing that while many things have happened to you, the decisions you make from this point forward still belong to you.

That responsibility is not meant to create fear.

It is meant to create freedom.

Because if your future is determined only by other people's choices, then your hope will always be limited by what they decide.

But if your daily choices still have the power to influence your future, then every new day becomes another opportunity to rebuild.

You may not be able to rewrite your past.

But you can influence the direction of your future.

One decision at a time.

One habit at a time.

One conversation at a time.

One act of courage at a time.

Growth begins when you stop waiting for someone else to rescue the life that has been entrusted to you.

That does not mean refusing help.

It means refusing to surrender your responsibility.

Some people spend years waiting for perfect circumstances before they begin changing.

They wait for more support.

More resources.

More confidence.

More certainty.

While those things are valuable, lasting transformation eventually requires personal ownership.

Ownership sounds like this:

"I may not control everything that happened to me, but I can control how I respond today."

"I cannot change yesterday, but I can make a wiser decision now."

"I cannot force others to change, but I can continue becoming the person I am called to be."

That mindset is empowering because it shifts your attention away from what you cannot control and back toward what you can.

Every healthy habit becomes your decision.

Every financial improvement becomes your decision.

Every boundary you establish becomes your decision.

Every step toward healing becomes your decision.

Those choices may seem small.

But over time, they quietly reshape your entire life.

Never underestimate the power of taking ownership of your future.

History is filled with people who rebuilt their lives not because everything became easy, but because they stopped believing their circumstances had the final word.

They learned.

Adapted.

Recovered.

Continued.

You have that same opportunity.

Accept encouragement when it comes.

Receive wisdom with gratitude.

Allow people to walk beside you.

But never forget that your greatest progress will come through the decisions only you can make.

Because every day you choose growth over excuses, responsibility over blame, and action over delay, you become stronger than you were the day before.

Your future is not waiting for someone else to build it.

It is waiting for you to keep showing up.

One intentional decision.

One faithful step.

One day at a time.

WEALTH LESSON

Personal responsibility strengthens growth because intentional action creates long-term transformation.

AFFIRMATION

"I take responsibility for building the future I desire."

TODAY'S POWER MOVE

Take ownership today over one area of your life you have been avoiding emotionally.

DAY 294

Discipline Is An Act Of Self-Respect

POWER QUOTE

"Every disciplined decision communicates what you believe you deserve."

REFLECTION

Discipline is often misunderstood.

Many people think discipline is about restriction.

Deprivation.

Constant pressure.

Or forcing yourself to live without joy.

But true discipline is not punishment.

It is one of the highest forms of self-respect.

Every disciplined decision communicates something important to yourself:

"My future is worth protecting."

When you wake up and honor your commitments, you are protecting your future.

When you create and follow a budget, you are protecting your future.

When you choose rest instead of burnout, you are protecting your future.

When you establish healthy boundaries instead of constantly overextending yourself, you are protecting your future.

Discipline is not about making life harder.

It is about making life healthier.

Many of the freedoms people desire are actually built through discipline.

Financial freedom comes from managing money with wisdom.

Physical health comes from consistent habits.

Strong relationships grow through intentional communication and trust.

Peace of mind develops when your daily choices support the life you are trying to create.

Without discipline, life often becomes reactive.

Bills are ignored until they become emergencies.

Difficult conversations are avoided until relationships become strained.

Responsibilities are postponed until stress begins to accumulate.

The cost of avoiding discipline is rarely immediate.

It appears gradually.

One neglected habit at a time.

One postponed responsibility at a time.

One small compromise repeated until it becomes a lifestyle.

That is why discipline is an investment.

You accept temporary discomfort today to create greater freedom tomorrow.

You save money instead of spending impulsively because you value long-term stability more than short-term satisfaction.

You prepare instead of procrastinating because you understand that preparation reduces unnecessary stress.

You continue showing up even when motivation fades because you know consistency produces results that emotions alone never could.

Over time, these choices begin changing the way you see yourself.

You become someone who follows through.

Someone who keeps promises.

Someone who can be trusted—not only by others, but by yourself.

That kind of self-respect cannot be purchased.

It is earned through repeated acts of integrity.

Every time you choose what is right over what is easy, you strengthen your character.

Every time you protect your peace instead of reacting impulsively, you strengthen your emotional maturity.

Every time you continue building when no one is watching, you strengthen your future.

This is why discipline is not the enemy of freedom.

It is the path to it.

The structure you create today becomes the stability you enjoy tomorrow.

The habits you practice today become the opportunities you experience later.

The sacrifices you make today become the blessings you are able to sustain in the future.

Do not view discipline as something that limits your life.

See it for what it truly is.

A daily expression of believing your future is valuable enough to prepare for.

Because every intentional choice you make today is another declaration that the life you hope to build is worth the effort required to create it.

And those quiet decisions, practiced faithfully over time, become the foundation of a life marked by peace, wisdom, freedom, and lasting fulfillment.

WEALTH LESSON

Discipline improves long-term stability because intentional routines strengthen emotional and financial outcomes.

AFFIRMATION

"I respect myself enough to remain disciplined and intentional."

TODAY'S POWER MOVE

Follow through completely on one important commitment today.

DAY 295

Your Healing Will Affect Every Area Of Your Life

POWER QUOTE

"Healing changes more than emotions. It changes behavior."

REFLECTION

Unhealed pain has a way of influencing areas of life that many people never expect.

It is not always obvious.

Sometimes it hides beneath everyday decisions.

It affects the way you communicate with people you care about.

The way you respond when life becomes stressful.

The way you view money.

The way you trust others.

The way you see yourself.

Many people assume they are simply making poor decisions, when in reality they are responding from wounds that have never been fully addressed.

A person who fears abandonment may struggle to establish healthy boundaries.

Someone who grew up in financial instability may constantly worry, even during seasons of security.

A person who has experienced repeated disappointment may avoid opportunities because expecting failure feels safer than risking hope.

These responses are understandable.

But they do not have to become permanent.

Healing begins when you recognize that your past may explain certain patterns, but it does not have to determine your future.

Awareness gives you the opportunity to choose differently.

Instead of moving on autopilot, you begin choosing your response with intention.

You learn to pause before speaking.

You become more thoughtful before making financial decisions.

You stop assuming that every disagreement is a threat.

You begin asking questions instead of immediately becoming defensive.

Little by little, your responses begin changing.

And as your responses change, your life begins changing with them.

Healing is not simply about feeling less emotional.

It is about becoming more emotionally available.

More patient.

More self-aware.

More intentional.

You stop allowing old wounds to speak for the person you are becoming.

You begin creating new patterns that reflect wisdom instead of survival.

That transformation rarely happens overnight.

It is built through countless ordinary decisions.

Choosing forgiveness instead of carrying bitterness.

Choosing responsibility instead of blame.

Choosing honesty instead of avoidance.

Choosing peace instead of constant emotional conflict.

These decisions reshape your character one day at a time.

The healthier you become internally, the healthier your external life often becomes.

Relationships become more secure because trust replaces fear.

Financial habits improve because planning replaces panic.

Communication becomes calmer because understanding replaces defensiveness.

Opportunities become easier to embrace because hope becomes stronger than self-doubt.

This is why healing is one of the greatest investments you can make.

It reaches places that success alone never can.

It strengthens the foundation beneath every relationship you build, every opportunity you pursue, and every responsibility you carry.

Never believe that healing is a sign of weakness.

It takes far more courage to confront your wounds than to continue hiding from them.

It takes strength to examine unhealthy patterns honestly.

It takes humility to admit that change is necessary.

And it takes perseverance to practice healthier responses until they become your new normal.

That is what healing truly is.

Not pretending the past never happened.

Not forgetting every painful experience.

But refusing to allow yesterday's wounds to keep writing tomorrow's story.

Because every step you take toward emotional health becomes a step toward a wiser, steadier, and more peaceful future.

And that future is built not only by what you accomplish, but by the person you become along the way.

WEALTH LESSON

Emotional healing improves long-term outcomes because healthier emotional patterns create wiser decisions.

AFFIRMATION

"I allow healing to improve every area of my life."

TODAY'S POWER MOVE

Reflect today on one emotional area where healing has already improved your behavior.

DAY 296

Stop Living Entirely In Survival Mode

POWER QUOTE

"You deserve more than constantly surviving emotionally."

REFLECTION

Some people spend so many years surviving that they forget what it feels like to truly live.

Their days become focused on simply making it through.

Getting through the week.

Getting through the bills.

Getting through the next crisis.

Getting through another difficult conversation.

When survival becomes your normal, your mind naturally shifts toward immediate needs instead of long-term possibilities.

Planning feels unnecessary because every ounce of energy is spent responding to today's problems.

Dreams begin shrinking.

Hope becomes quieter.

Peace starts feeling unfamiliar because your nervous system has learned to expect another storm.

That is one of the hidden costs of survival mode.

It convinces you that stability is unrealistic.

That life will always feel exhausting.

That something must always be wrong.

But surviving and living are not the same thing.

Survival keeps you alive.

Healing teaches you how to build a life worth enjoying.

One of the first signs of healing is that your mind slowly begins believing in the possibility of peace again.

You begin making decisions for the future instead of only reacting to the present.

You start saving money instead of constantly recovering from emergencies.

You establish routines that create consistency.

You allow yourself to imagine goals that once felt impossible because your energy is no longer consumed by constant crisis management.

This transition can feel uncomfortable.

When chaos has been familiar for years, calmness may initially feel unfamiliar.

You may even find yourself waiting for something to go wrong because that is what your mind has learned to expect.

Be patient with yourself during that process.

Your nervous system is learning something new.

It is learning that safety can exist.

That healthy relationships can exist.

That financial stability can exist.

That quiet evenings, healthy routines, and emotional consistency are not signs that life has become boring.

They are signs that life is becoming healthier.

Healing teaches you that peace is something to protect, not something to fear.

It reminds you that you do not have to remain in constant survival mode to prove your strength.

Real strength is creating a life where your mind has room to breathe.

Where your relationships create security instead of confusion.

Where your finances are guided by planning instead of panic.

Where your days are shaped by purpose instead of constant emergency.

That life is built gradually.

One healthy habit at a time.

One wise decision at a time.

One peaceful boundary at a time.

The more consistently you choose those small decisions, the more unfamiliar chaos begins to feel.

Eventually, your definition of normal changes.

You stop expecting constant instability.

You begin expecting growth.

You stop chasing emotional intensity.

You begin protecting emotional stability.

You stop surviving every day.

You begin living intentionally.

Never believe that peace is something reserved for other people.

It is something you can build.

Not overnight.

But through the choices you make every day.

Because your future deserves more than simply getting through life.

It deserves a life where you can grow, create, love, rest, and move forward with confidence instead of constant fear.

That is the life healing is preparing you to build.

WEALTH LESSON

Emotional stability improves long-term planning because survival thinking often creates reactive decision-making.

AFFIRMATION

"I release survival mode and intentionally build a peaceful future."

TODAY'S POWER MOVE

Notice one survival-based habit today and replace it with a healthier intentional response.

DAY 297

You Become Stronger Every Time You Continue

POWER QUOTE

"Resilience is built through repeated moments of refusing to quit."

REFLECTION

Strength is often misunderstood.

Many people picture strength as being fearless.

Never struggling.

Never crying.

Never feeling discouraged.

But some of the strongest people you will ever meet have experienced deep disappointment, uncertainty, and pain.

Their strength is not found in avoiding hardship.

It is found in refusing to let hardship have the final word.

Sometimes strength is simply getting out of bed when everything inside you wants to stay there.

Sometimes strength is choosing to keep your integrity after being treated unfairly.

Sometimes strength is rebuilding after something you loved came to an end.

Sometimes strength is quietly honoring your commitments when no one notices your effort.

These moments rarely receive recognition.

Yet they are the moments that shape your character.

Difficult seasons have a way of revealing what comfort often hides.

They expose your habits.

Your beliefs.

Your priorities.

Your willingness to continue when the excitement has disappeared.

While no one enjoys hardship, adversity often develops qualities that comfort alone cannot produce.

Patience grows when progress takes longer than expected.

Resilience grows when you choose to stand up after falling.

Wisdom grows when painful experiences teach lessons that success never could.

Compassion grows when you remember what it felt like to struggle.

That is why difficult seasons should never be wasted.

They may not be enjoyable, but they can become deeply meaningful if you allow them to shape you instead of harden you.

There will be moments when your progress feels invisible.

When your prayers seem unanswered.

When your efforts appear unnoticed.

Those are often the moments when your foundation is being strengthened.

Just as a tree develops its deepest roots during difficult weather, your character is often strengthened during seasons that test your perseverance.

Growth is not always dramatic.

Sometimes it looks like choosing not to quit today.

Sometimes it looks like making one wise decision after another while trusting that those small decisions are preparing you for something greater.

Never underestimate the quiet power of consistency during difficult times.

Every healthy habit you maintain while life feels hard strengthens your future.

Every responsible decision you make while emotions tell you to give up builds resilience.

Every act of faithfulness becomes evidence that your circumstances do not have complete control over who you are becoming.

Strength is not measured by how loudly you overcome obstacles.

It is often measured by how faithfully you continue despite them.

One day, you may look back on this season and realize that what once felt like a setback was actually preparing you for responsibilities you were not yet ready to carry.

The patience you developed.

The wisdom you gained.

The emotional endurance you built.

Those gifts will remain with you long after the difficult season has passed.

Keep moving forward.

Keep rebuilding.

Keep choosing what is right, even when it is difficult.

Because true strength is not found in a life without challenges.

It is found in the person you become by refusing to let those challenges stop your growth.

And that quiet strength, built one faithful decision at a time, is the kind that lasts for a lifetime.

WEALTH LESSON

Resilience strengthens long-term success because emotionally strong people continue rebuilding instead of surrendering permanently.

AFFIRMATION

"I continue growing stronger through every difficult season."

TODAY'S POWER MOVE

Complete one meaningful task today even if your emotions feel heavy or discouraged.

DAY 298

Your Future Needs Better Thinking

POWER QUOTE

"The quality of your thoughts eventually affects the quality of your life."

REFLECTION

People spend every moment of every day listening to one voice more than any other.

Their own.

The conversations you have with yourself quietly shape the way you see your life.

The way you approach challenges.

The way you interpret failure.

The way you view your future.

If your mind is constantly repeating,

"I'm not good enough."

"I'll probably fail."

"Nothing will ever change."

those thoughts eventually begin influencing your behavior.

Not because they are always true.

But because repeated thoughts slowly become deeply held beliefs.

Beliefs influence expectations.

Expectations influence decisions.

And decisions shape the direction of your life.

This is why guarding your thoughts is so important.

Your mind is like a garden.

Whatever you consistently plant will eventually grow.

If you continually feed your mind fear, comparison, resentment, and hopelessness, those thoughts begin producing corresponding emotions and behaviors.

You hesitate when opportunities appear.

You doubt yourself before you've even tried.

You expect disappointment before anything has gone wrong.

Over time, those patterns become self-fulfilling.

The opposite is also true.

When you intentionally cultivate thoughts rooted in truth, discipline, hope, and resilience, your perspective begins to change.

You start looking for solutions instead of only seeing obstacles.

You become more willing to learn because mistakes no longer define your worth.

You begin believing that growth is possible because you have stopped convincing yourself that change is impossible.

Healthy thinking is not pretending life is easy.

It is choosing to interpret life's challenges through wisdom rather than fear.

There will always be reasons to doubt yourself.

Reasons to compare your journey with someone else's.

Reasons to focus on everything that has not happened yet.

But you also have the ability to choose a different conversation.

One that asks,

"What can I learn from this?"

"What is within my control today?"

"How can I respond in a way that moves my life forward?"

Those questions create possibility.

They move your attention away from helplessness and toward responsibility.

Your thoughts influence your habits.

Your habits influence your character.

And your character influences the future you build.

This is why mental discipline deserves daily practice.

Pay attention to the words you repeatedly speak over your life.

Challenge beliefs that keep you trapped in fear.

Replace constant self-condemnation with honest self-reflection.

Encourage yourself with the same patience and grace you would offer someone you genuinely care about.

You cannot always control the first thought that enters your mind.

But you can decide which thoughts you continue believing.

That choice becomes more powerful than many people realize.

Because every healthy thought you nurture becomes another brick in the foundation of a healthier life.

Little by little, your confidence grows.

Your perspective expands.

Your resilience deepens.

Not because your circumstances immediately changed, but because your thinking did.

Protect your mind.

Feed it with truth.

Challenge what weakens you.

Strengthen what builds you.

Because the conversations you have with yourself today will quietly influence the person you become tomorrow.

Choose conversations that help build a future worth living.

WEALTH LESSON

Healthy thinking improves emotional regulation because thoughts influence behavior and long-term decision-making.

AFFIRMATION

"I intentionally create healthier thoughts that support my future."

TODAY'S POWER MOVE

Interrupt one repeated negative thought pattern today and replace it with a healthier belief.

DAY 299

Stop Quitting On Yourself Too Early

POWER QUOTE

"Many breakthroughs happen after people feel like giving up."

REFLECTION

Growth has a way of testing your commitment before it reveals the results of your effort.

This is why so many people quit too soon.

Not because they lack potential.

But because they mistake slow progress for no progress.

They expect change to happen quickly.

When it doesn't, discouragement quietly begins replacing determination.

They wonder if the work is worth it.

If the sacrifices matter.

If they should simply give up and accept where they are.

But meaningful transformation rarely follows the timeline we prefer.

Think about a builder constructing a home.

For weeks, sometimes months, much of the work happens where no one can see it.

The foundation is poured.

The framework is strengthened.

The structure is carefully prepared.

Someone passing by might assume very little is happening.

Yet those unseen stages determine whether the house will remain standing for decades.

Your life develops in much the same way.

Some of your most important growth is taking place beneath the surface.

Every disciplined habit is strengthening your foundation.

Every difficult decision handled with wisdom is shaping your character.

Every setback you refuse to surrender to is increasing your resilience.

Those changes may not be obvious to the people around you.

Sometimes they are not even obvious to you.

But they are happening.

Progress is often measured in small improvements rather than dramatic breakthroughs.

One healthier financial decision.

One stronger boundary.

One difficult conversation handled with maturity.

One day where you chose consistency instead of excuses.

Those moments seem ordinary while they are happening.

Over time, they become extraordinary because they compound.

Many people become discouraged because they compare their beginning to someone else's middle.

They see another person's success without seeing the years of quiet effort that came before it.

Comparison creates unnecessary pressure because it ignores the invisible work behind visible results.

Your journey has its own pace.

Your responsibility is not to match someone else's timeline.

It is to remain faithful to your own process.

Patience is one of the greatest forms of discipline.

It allows you to continue planting seeds long before the harvest appears.

It reminds you that meaningful things often require time.

Trust takes time.

Wisdom takes time.

Strong relationships take time.

Financial stability takes time.

Character takes time.

The greatest achievements in life are rarely built in a single moment.

They are built through hundreds of ordinary days where someone simply refused to stop.

When discouragement comes, do not ask yourself,

"Why isn't everything different yet?"

Instead ask,

"Am I becoming stronger than I was yesterday?"

Growth is not only about changing your circumstances.

It is about becoming the kind of person who can sustain the future you are building.

That process cannot be rushed.

So keep showing up.

Keep honoring your commitments.

Keep making the next wise decision.

Even when the results seem small.

Even when no one notices.

Even when progress feels slower than you hoped.

Because one day you will look back and realize that the season you almost gave up in was the very season that prepared you for everything that came afterward.

Do not abandon the process simply because it feels quiet.

Some of life's greatest transformations happen long before anyone can see them.

Stay faithful.

Stay patient.

Keep building.

The results will come in their time, but the person you become while waiting will be the greatest reward of all.

WEALTH LESSON

Persistence creates long-term opportunity because repeated effort compounds over time into meaningful results.

AFFIRMATION

"I refuse to give up on the future I am building."

TODAY'S POWER MOVE

Continue working today on one long-term goal even if progress feels slow.

DAY 300

You Are Becoming Someone Powerful

POWER QUOTE

"The strongest version of you is being built through discipline, healing, and consistency."

REFLECTION

Transformation is rarely announced with a single dramatic moment.

More often, it happens so quietly that you do not realize how much you have changed until you look back.

One day you notice that something which once overwhelmed you no longer has the same power.

A conversation that once would have turned into an argument is now handled with patience.

A setback that once would have made you quit now becomes a lesson instead of a defeat.

A temptation that once controlled your decisions no longer feels impossible to resist.

Those moments may seem small.

In reality, they are evidence that your identity is changing.

Transformation is built through ordinary decisions repeated consistently.

Every time you choose peace instead of unnecessary conflict, you strengthen emotional stability.

Every time you choose discipline instead of avoidance, you strengthen your character.

Every time you choose healing instead of repeating unhealthy patterns, you loosen the grip your past once had on your future.

Every time you choose courage instead of fear, you expand what you believe is possible.

These decisions may not attract attention.

They may not receive applause.

But they are shaping the person you are becoming.

Identity is not created by what you say you want.

It is created by what you repeatedly practice.

The person who values integrity becomes someone who tells the truth even when it is difficult.

The person who values peace becomes someone who protects healthy boundaries.

The person who values financial stability becomes someone who consistently manages resources with wisdom.

Your daily choices are quietly answering the question:

"Who am I becoming?"

This is why your routines matter.

Not because every day feels extraordinary.

But because ordinary days are where extraordinary lives are built.

Morning by morning.

Decision by decision.

Habit by habit.

Many people overlook their own progress because they are focused only on the destination.

They celebrate major milestones but ignore the hundreds of smaller victories that made those milestones possible.

Learning to pause before reacting.

Keeping a promise to yourself.

Choosing responsibility over excuses.

Walking away from an unhealthy environment.
Managing your money with greater wisdom.
Speaking to yourself with greater compassion.
These are victories.
And they deserve to be recognized.
Transformation becomes sustainable when you learn to value progress instead of perfection.
Perfection creates pressure.
Progress creates momentum.
As long as you continue moving in the right direction, you are becoming someone stronger than you were yesterday.
There will still be difficult days.
Moments when old habits try to return.
Seasons when growth feels slower than you hoped.
Do not mistake those moments for failure.
Growth is not a straight line.
It is a lifelong process of learning, adjusting, and continuing.
The important question is not whether you are perfect.
It is whether you are becoming more intentional than you were before.
Take a moment to appreciate how far you have already come.
Think about the challenges you have survived.
The lessons you have learned.
The habits you have changed.
The strength you have developed.
The person you are today did not exist a year ago.
Neither will the person you become a year from now if you continue showing up with purpose.
Never underestimate the quiet work happening inside you.
Every intentional choice is shaping your future.
Every healthy habit is reinforcing your identity.
Every act of discipline is preparing you for greater responsibility.
You are becoming someone who thinks more wisely, lives more intentionally, and responds with greater maturity than before.
That transformation may be quiet.
But it is real.
And one day, you will realize that the life you hoped to build was created through thousands of ordinary decisions that slowly transformed you into the person capable of living it.

WEALTH LESSON

Long-term success becomes sustainable when emotional growth develops alongside discipline and intentional living.

AFFIRMATION

"I continue becoming the strongest, healthiest, and most disciplined version of myself."

TODAY'S POWER MOVE

Reflect today on how much stronger and wiser you have become compared to who you once were.

DAY 301

Stop Shrinking Yourself To Fit Small Environments

POWER QUOTE

"You were not created to spend your life minimizing your potential."

REFLECTION

Many people never reach their full potential because they spend too much of their lives trying to fit into places they have already outgrown.

They lower their standards.

Hide their ambitions.

Downplay their abilities.

Remain silent about their dreams.

Not because they lack potential.

But because they fear becoming different from the people around them.

Acceptance is a powerful human desire.

Most people want to belong.

To be understood.

To feel connected.

There is nothing wrong with that.

The problem begins when belonging requires you to become less than who you were created to be.

Sometimes growth changes your conversations.

Sometimes it changes your priorities.

Sometimes it changes the environments where you feel at home.

Not because you have become better than anyone else.

But because you have become different.

Growth has a way of creating distance between the person you were and the person you are becoming.

That transition can feel lonely.

People who were comfortable with the old version of you may not always understand the new one.

Some may question your decisions.

Others may become uncomfortable with your boundaries.

Some may even discourage your growth because your progress reminds them of changes they have been avoiding themselves.

Do not mistake their discomfort for a reason to stop growing.

Not every environment is designed to support your next season.

Some places are meant to prepare you.

Others are meant to challenge you.

And some are meant to be left behind with gratitude.

Real transformation requires the courage to outgrow what no longer aligns with your future.

That may mean changing habits.

Changing routines.

Changing friendships.

Changing the way you speak to yourself.

Growth often requires letting go before you can fully embrace what comes next.

Remember that becoming your healthiest self is not an act of selfishness.

It is an act of stewardship.

The more emotionally healthy you become, the more you have to offer the people around you.

The more disciplined you become, the more faithfully you can serve your purpose.

The more peaceful you become, the more stability you bring into every room you enter.

You do not honor your potential by making yourself smaller.

You honor it by developing it.

By learning.

By growing.

By becoming someone who uses their gifts with humility, wisdom, and courage.

Not everyone will understand the person you are becoming.

That is okay.

Your responsibility is not to make everyone comfortable.

Your responsibility is to become the person your future requires.

Do not apologize for healing.

Do not apologize for raising your standards.

Do not apologize for protecting your peace.

Do not apologize for believing you are capable of more.

The people who truly care about you will celebrate your growth, even if it challenges them.

Those who cannot celebrate it may simply no longer belong in the next chapter of your journey.

Keep becoming.

Keep expanding.

Keep honoring the vision that has been placed inside you.

Because your future deserves the fullest expression of your character, your purpose, and your potential.

Never shrink your life just to fit inside someone else's comfort zone.

The world does not need a smaller version of you.

It needs the strongest, healthiest, wisest, and most authentic version you are willing to become.

WEALTH LESSON

Growth creates opportunity because expanding your mindset and identity increases your emotional and financial capacity.

AFFIRMATION

"I refuse to minimize my potential to fit environments that limit my growth."

TODAY'S POWER MOVE

Take one action today that reflects confidence in your full potential instead of fear of being seen.

DAY 302

Your Healing Will Influence Your Leadership

POWER QUOTE

"People lead differently when they heal differently."

REFLECTION

Leadership begins long before someone receives a title.

It begins with the way you lead yourself.

The way you manage your emotions.

The way you respond under pressure.

The way you treat people when no one is watching.

Countless individuals believe leadership is primarily about influence.

In reality, influence is often a reflection of character.

People may follow your position for a season.

But they trust your character over time.

This is why emotional health matters so deeply for anyone entrusted with responsibility.

Unhealed leaders often carry unresolved pain into the environments they create.

Fear becomes control.

Insecurity becomes micromanagement.

Stress becomes impatience.

Unresolved wounds become criticism, defensiveness, or emotional unpredictability.

The people around them may never know where those behaviors originated.

But they experience the consequences.

Leadership always creates ripple effects.

The emotional habits you practice privately eventually become the culture you build publicly.

That truth should not create shame.

It should create responsibility.

The healthiest leaders understand that personal growth is not separate from professional growth.

The way you speak to people matters.

The way you respond to mistakes matters.

The way you handle disappointment matters.

The way you manage conflict matters.

Every interaction teaches people what it feels like to work with you, trust you, and grow under your leadership.

Healed leaders build differently.

They create environments where people feel respected instead of intimidated.

They communicate with honesty instead of manipulation.

They correct without humiliating.

They listen before assuming.

They remain steady during difficult moments because they have learned how to regulate themselves before attempting to lead others.

This does not mean they are perfect.

Every leader makes mistakes.

Every leader faces pressure.

Every leader encounters moments of uncertainty.

The difference is that emotionally healthy leaders are willing to acknowledge those moments, learn from them, and continue growing.

They understand that humility strengthens leadership rather than weakening it.

One of the greatest gifts you can give the people you lead is consistency.

When people know they can trust your character, they feel safe enough to contribute their best work.

When they know your decisions are guided by wisdom instead of impulse, confidence grows.

When they know they can speak honestly without fear of unnecessary retaliation, relationships become stronger.

That kind of leadership cannot be manufactured.

It is cultivated through years of intentional personal growth.

Long before you lead an organization, a business, or a family, you are leading yourself.

Every disciplined habit is preparing you.

Every difficult conversation handled with maturity is preparing you.

Every unhealthy pattern you choose to confront is preparing you.

The leader you become tomorrow is being shaped by the choices you make today.

So invest in your emotional health with the same commitment you invest in your knowledge and skills.

Learn to remain calm when pressure increases.

Choose integrity when compromise feels easier.

Treat people with dignity even when disagreements arise.

Lead from conviction instead of insecurity.

Because success may give you influence, but emotional maturity determines how you use it.

And the greatest leaders are remembered not only for what they accomplished, but for the kind of people they helped others become.

That is the kind of leadership that leaves a lasting legacy.

WEALTH LESSON

Emotional intelligence strengthens leadership because regulated people create healthier decisions and environments.

AFFIRMATION

"I lead with emotional wisdom, maturity, and intentionality."

TODAY'S POWER MOVE

Practice calm and emotionally intentional leadership in one interaction today.

DAY 303

Stop Making Peace With Mediocrity

POWER QUOTE

"Comfort can quietly become the enemy of growth."

REFLECTION

Mediocrity rarely begins with one major decision.

It usually develops through small compromises that seem harmless in the moment.

Choosing comfort instead of growth.

Postponing responsibilities until tomorrow.

Accepting standards you know are beneath your potential.

Ignoring the habits that quietly shape your future.

None of these choices appear significant by themselves.

But repeated often enough, they become a lifestyle.

The danger is that people slowly adjust to less than they are capable of becoming.

They stop expecting more from themselves.

They stop pursuing excellence.

They settle into routines that feel familiar rather than meaningful.

Over time, comfort becomes a substitute for purpose.

This is why complacency is so deceptive.

It rarely announces itself.

It quietly whispers,

"You've done enough."

"Tomorrow will be fine."

"This is probably good enough."

Those thoughts feel harmless.

Yet they slowly reduce your expectations of what your life can become.

Growth requires a different mindset.

It asks you to remain teachable even after achieving success.

To continue improving when no one is demanding it.

To hold yourself to a standard that is rooted in purpose rather than convenience.

Excellence is not perfection.

It is the decision to give your best with what you have today.

It is choosing intentionality over carelessness.

Preparation over procrastination.

Progress over excuses.

The people who build extraordinary lives are rarely extraordinary because of one defining moment.

They become extraordinary because they consistently refuse to settle for habits that keep them average.

They keep learning.

They keep refining.

They keep asking,

"How can I become better than I was yesterday?"

That question creates lifelong growth.

Do not confuse contentment with complacency.

You can be grateful for where you are while still believing there is more to learn, more to build, and more to contribute.

Healthy ambition is not driven by comparison.

It is driven by stewardship.

It recognizes that your gifts, your opportunities, and your potential have been entrusted to you for a purpose.

Honoring those gifts requires effort.

It requires discipline on days when motivation is absent.

It requires courage when fear suggests staying where you are.

It requires humility to admit there is always another lesson to learn.

Every day presents a choice.

You can reinforce habits that keep you comfortable, or you can practice habits that move you toward the person you are capable of becoming.

Those choices accumulate.

Your standards accumulate.

Your routines accumulate.

Your character accumulates.

Eventually, the life you live becomes the natural result of what you repeatedly practiced.

Do not allow temporary comfort to quietly steal a lifetime of potential.

Continue raising your standards.

Continue stretching your abilities.

Continue choosing growth, even when it feels inconvenient.

Because you were never created merely to exist.

You were created to learn, to serve, to build, to lead, and to leave every season wiser than the one before.

A meaningful life is not built by settling for what is easy.

It is built by faithfully becoming everything you are capable of becoming, one intentional decision at a time.

WEALTH LESSON

Intentional growth creates long-term opportunity because disciplined people continue expanding their capacity consistently.

AFFIRMATION

"I refuse to settle for mediocrity when growth is possible."

TODAY'S POWER MOVE

Challenge yourself today to exceed the bare minimum in one important area of your life.

DAY 304

Your Thoughts Are Training Your Identity

POWER QUOTE

"The mind becomes shaped by what it repeatedly hears."

REFLECTION

Every thought you repeat consistently becomes emotional instruction Every day, your mind is listening to the story you tell yourself.

That story shapes more than your emotions.

It shapes your expectations.

Your decisions.

Your confidence.

Your willingness to keep trying when life becomes difficult.

Many people underestimate the influence of their internal dialogue because no one else can hear it.

Yet those quiet conversations become some of the loudest influences in a person's life.

If you repeatedly tell yourself that you are incapable, your actions eventually begin reflecting that belief.

If you constantly expect failure, you may stop pursuing opportunities before they even begin.

If shame becomes the voice you listen to most, it becomes difficult to believe that lasting change is possible.

Thoughts that are repeated long enough often become beliefs.

Beliefs shape identity.

And identity influences behavior.

This is why the way you speak to yourself matters so deeply.

There is a difference between honest self-evaluation and constant self-condemnation.

Honest self-evaluation says,

"I made a mistake, but I can learn from it."

Self-condemnation says,

"I am the mistake."

One creates growth.

The other creates hopelessness.

Healthy thinking does not mean pretending life is perfect.

It means refusing to let temporary emotions become permanent conclusions.

It means choosing truth instead of fear.

Wisdom instead of panic.

Hope instead of defeat.

Your mind becomes stronger when you intentionally challenge thoughts that are not serving your future.

When fear says,

"You'll never succeed,"

ask yourself,

"What evidence supports that, and what evidence contradicts it?"

When insecurity says,

"You're not capable,"

remember the challenges you have already overcome.

When shame reminds you of your worst moments, remind yourself that growth has always been possible because people are capable of learning, changing, and rebuilding.

The goal is not to eliminate every negative thought.

The goal is to stop allowing those thoughts to become the foundation of your identity.

Pay attention to what you feed your mind.

The books you read.

The conversations you entertain.

The voices you repeatedly listen to.

The words you speak over your own life.

All of these things quietly shape the environment inside you.

Just as a healthy body depends upon proper nutrition, a healthy mind depends upon healthy input.

Protecting your mind is not avoidance.

It is stewardship.

It is recognizing that your thoughts eventually influence your actions, and your actions shape your future.

Choose thoughts that encourage responsibility instead of excuses.

Choose thoughts that build resilience instead of helplessness.

Choose thoughts that remind you growth is possible, even when progress feels slow.

Little by little, those choices begin changing the way you see yourself.

You become less controlled by fear.

Less influenced by shame.

Less discouraged by temporary setbacks.

Instead, you become someone who thinks with greater clarity, responds with greater wisdom, and continues moving forward with greater confidence.

Because the life you build tomorrow will first be shaped by the conversations you allow to take place within your mind today.

Protect those conversations carefully.

They are quietly shaping the person you are becoming.

WEALTH LESSON

Healthy thinking improves emotional regulation because thoughts influence behavior and decision-making.

AFFIRMATION

"I intentionally train my mind toward growth, discipline, and peace."

TODAY'S POWER MOVE

Replace one repeated negative thought today with a healthier and more empowering belief.

DAY 305

Stop Avoiding Responsibility For Your Future

POWER QUOTE

"Your future changes when your excuses stop leading your decisions."

REFLECTION

Excuses have a way of making us feel better without making our lives better.

They offer temporary relief.

They help us avoid uncomfortable emotions.

They allow us to explain why we are not taking action.

For a moment, that can feel comforting.

But comfort without progress eventually becomes frustration.

Many people know exactly what needs to change.

They know they should manage their finances more intentionally.

Establish healthier boundaries.

Take better care of their health.

Have the difficult conversation.

Begin the business.

Return to the goals they abandoned.

The challenge is rarely a lack of knowledge.

It is the discomfort that comes with change.

Growth asks you to leave what is familiar.

To take responsibility instead of waiting for perfect circumstances.

To act before every fear has disappeared.

That is why excuses can become so dangerous.

They quietly convince you that waiting is wiser than beginning.

That tomorrow will somehow be easier than today.

That one more delay will not make a difference.

Yet every postponed decision becomes another day your future remains on hold.

Responsibility creates a different mindset.

Instead of asking,

"Why is this happening to me?"

it begins asking,

"What can I do from here?"

That question changes everything.

It shifts your attention away from blame and back toward influence.

You may not control everything that has happened in your life.

You cannot rewrite yesterday.

You cannot control every person's choices.

You cannot prevent every disappointment.

But you can choose how you respond today.

You can choose your next habit.

Your next conversation.
Your next financial decision.
Your next act of discipline.
Those choices belong to you.
That realization is not a burden.
It is one of the greatest sources of freedom.
Because if your future can still be influenced by your decisions, then hope is never completely lost.
Every responsible choice becomes a vote for the person you are becoming.
Every time you keep your word to yourself, you strengthen self-respect.
Every time you stop making excuses and start making progress, you build confidence.
Not because life suddenly became easier.
Because you became more intentional.
Taking responsibility does not mean carrying unnecessary guilt.
It does not mean blaming yourself for every hardship you have experienced.
It means accepting ownership of what belongs to you today.
Your growth.
Your healing.
Your habits.
Your attitude.
Your willingness to continue learning.
That kind of ownership is empowering because it reminds you that change is possible.
You are not powerless.
You are not trapped.
You are not defined by the decisions you made years ago.
Every new day offers another opportunity to choose differently.
Do not allow excuses to quietly become the story you tell yourself.
Choose responsibility instead.
Not because it is always comfortable.
But because it is the path that leads to growth.
The life you desire will not be built by perfect circumstances.
It will be built by the daily decisions you make when you stop waiting for life to change and begin taking ownership of the part only you can control.
That is where transformation truly begins.

WEALTH LESSON

Personal responsibility strengthens long-term growth because intentional action creates opportunity and stability.

AFFIRMATION

"I take full responsibility for building the future I desire."

TODAY'S POWER MOVE

Identify one excuse today that has been delaying your growth and intentionally challenge it.

DAY 306

Emotional Peace Is A Form Of Wealth

POWER QUOTE

"A peaceful mind is one of life's greatest luxuries."

REFLECTION

Many people spend years pursuing success while quietly neglecting the condition of their inner life.

They achieve promotions.

Build businesses.

Earn more money.

Reach impressive milestones.

Yet beneath those accomplishments, they remain overwhelmed, anxious, exhausted, or emotionally disconnected.

Success without peace eventually becomes another burden to carry.

This is why emotional well-being deserves as much attention as external achievement.

A healthy inner life influences every area of your future.

It affects the quality of your decisions.

The patience you bring into relationships.

The way you respond under pressure.

The consistency of your discipline.

Even your physical health can be influenced by the amount of stress your mind carries every day.

Peace is not something that happens when life finally becomes perfect.

It is something that is cultivated long before circumstances are ideal.

It is developed through healthy boundaries.

Intentional routines.

Honest conversations.

Rest when it is needed.

The courage to let go of what continually steals your joy.

A peaceful person is not someone who has escaped every challenge.

They are someone who has learned not to allow every challenge to control them.

When unexpected problems arise, they pause before reacting.

When conflict appears, they seek understanding before assuming the worst.

When pressure increases, they focus on what they can control instead of becoming consumed by what they cannot.

That steadiness creates strength.

People often mistake peace for passivity.

In reality, peace requires tremendous discipline.

It requires choosing forgiveness over resentment.

Wisdom over impulse.

Perspective over panic.

These choices are rarely easy.

But they become easier as you continue practicing them.

The beautiful thing about peace is that it changes the atmosphere around you.

Your relationships become healthier because people experience consistency instead of unpredictability.

Your work improves because your mind has room to think clearly.

Your leadership becomes stronger because you respond with wisdom rather than emotion alone.

Even difficult seasons become more manageable because you are no longer fighting every battle inside your own mind.

Ask yourself honestly:

"Am I building a life that only looks successful, or one that also feels healthy to live?"

That question is worth revisiting often.

There is little value in gaining achievements if you lose yourself in the process.

The goal is not simply to accomplish more.

The goal is to become someone who can enjoy what they have built with gratitude, balance, and emotional stability.

Protect your peace with the same commitment you protect your goals.

Invest in your emotional health with the same intention you invest in your career.

Create a life where success and well-being grow together instead of competing with one another.

Because one of the greatest forms of wealth is waking up each day with a clear mind, a steady heart, and the ability to build your future without sacrificing the health of your soul.

That is the kind of success that endures long after achievements alone have faded.

WEALTH LESSON

Mental peace improves emotional regulation because calm thinking creates healthier long-term decisions.

AFFIRMATION

"I value emotional peace as part of the wealth I am building."

TODAY'S POWER MOVE

Protect your emotional peace intentionally today by reducing unnecessary emotional noise.

DAY 307

Stop Letting Failure Define Your Identity

POWER QUOTE

"Failure is an experience, not a permanent identity."

REFLECTION

Failure is one of the experiences people fear most.

They fear making the wrong decision.

Losing money.

A relationship ending.

A business not succeeding.

Missing an opportunity they can never get back.

These experiences are painful.

But they are also part of being human.

No one builds a meaningful life without making mistakes along the way.

The danger is not failure itself.

The danger is allowing failure to become your identity.

There is a profound difference between saying,

"I failed,"

and believing,

"I am a failure."

One describes an event.

The other becomes a belief.

When people begin identifying with their setbacks, they often stop expecting anything better from themselves.

They become afraid to try again because they assume the outcome will always be the same.

Little by little, fear replaces hope.

Avoidance replaces courage.

And potential remains buried beneath disappointment.

But failure has another purpose if you allow it.

It can become a teacher instead of a prison.

Every mistake carries a lesson.

Every setback reveals something that can be improved.

Every disappointment has the potential to produce greater wisdom if you are willing to learn from it.

The people you admire have almost certainly experienced failure.

Many of them experienced it repeatedly.

What made the difference was not that they avoided mistakes.

It was that they refused to let those mistakes define the rest of their lives.

They adjusted.

Learned.

Improved.

Tried again.

Growth is rarely a straight path.

It includes wrong turns.

Unexpected delays.

Moments of uncertainty.

Seasons where nothing seems to work the way you hoped.

Those experiences are frustrating.

But they are often preparing you with knowledge that success alone could never teach.

Failure has a way of exposing weaknesses that comfort hides.

It reveals where more patience is needed.

Where greater discipline is required.

Where humility must grow.

Those lessons become valuable only if you continue moving forward.

Do not waste your failures by carrying them as permanent labels.

Carry them as valuable lessons instead.

Remember that one financial mistake does not determine your financial future.

One broken relationship does not determine your ability to love or be loved.

One business that did not succeed does not mean you are incapable of building another.

One difficult season does not erase everything that is still possible for your life.

Your future is shaped far more by your response to failure than by the failure itself.

Will you allow it to convince you to stop?

Or will you allow it to make you wiser?

Every time you choose to stand up after disappointment, you become more resilient.

Every lesson you apply makes your foundation stronger.

Every decision to continue reminds you that setbacks are temporary, but growth can last a lifetime.

Do not measure your life by the moments where you stumbled.

Measure it by the courage you showed in getting back up.

Because failure is never the final chapter for someone who is still willing to learn, rebuild, and keep moving forward.

The story is not over simply because one chapter was difficult.

Keep writing.

Your best pages may still be ahead.

WEALTH LESSON

Resilience improves long-term outcomes because emotionally strong people continue rebuilding after setbacks.

AFFIRMATION

"I learn from failure without allowing it to define who I am."

TODAY'S POWER MOVE

Reflect today on one lesson a past failure taught you that strengthened your future.

DAY 308

Your Discipline Is Building Freedom

POWER QUOTE

"The habits you repeat today are creating tomorrow's freedom."

REFLECTION

Discipline often asks you to choose what is beneficial over what is immediately comfortable.

That is why it can feel so difficult in the beginning.

Saving money instead of spending it.

Preparing when you would rather procrastinate.

Keeping your commitments when motivation has disappeared.

Walking away from temporary pleasure because you value lasting peace.

These choices rarely provide instant rewards.

In fact, they often require sacrifice before they produce visible results.

This is where many people become discouraged.

They expect discipline to change their lives overnight.

When it doesn't, they assume their effort is not working.

But discipline has always worked quietly.

Its greatest results are usually invisible long before they become obvious.

One workout may not change your health immediately.

A single wise financial decision may not create wealth.

A single difficult conversation may not completely restore a relationship.

Yet each of those decisions becomes part of something much greater.

They accumulate.

One responsible choice strengthens the next.

One healthy habit makes another easier to maintain.

One day of consistency becomes a week.

A week becomes a month.

Months become years.

Eventually, the life you once hoped for begins looking like your daily reality.

That is the power of compounding.

It rewards faithfulness more than intensity.

Many people search for dramatic breakthroughs while overlooking the quiet disciplines that create lasting change.

They want extraordinary outcomes built on ordinary effort.

But the strongest foundations are almost always built one brick at a time.

Every time you honor your budget, you are building financial stability.

Every time you protect your peace, you are strengthening emotional resilience.

Every time you keep a promise to yourself, you are increasing self-trust.

Every time you choose preparation over procrastination, you are investing in opportunities that have not yet arrived.

Those moments matter more than they appear.

Discipline is an act of believing in a future you cannot fully see yet.

It is choosing today's responsibility because you trust tomorrow's reward.

That requires patience.

It requires vision.

It requires the willingness to continue even when no one notices your effort.

Remember that some of the most valuable things in life grow slowly.

Trust.

Wisdom.

Character.

Healthy relationships.

Financial security.

None of them are built in a single day.

They are the result of countless decisions made with consistency over time.

Do not become discouraged because your progress feels gradual.

Gradual growth is often the strongest growth because it is built upon habits that can be sustained.

The person who quietly remains faithful to small responsibilities eventually becomes capable of carrying greater ones.

Keep choosing discipline, even when it feels inconvenient.

Keep making the next wise decision, even when the results seem distant.

One day you will realize that the freedom, confidence, stability, and peace you were searching for did not arrive through one extraordinary moment.

They were created through hundreds of ordinary decisions that you were willing to make long before anyone else could see the difference.

That is the quiet power of discipline.

And it has the ability to change an entire life.

WEALTH LESSON

Long-term freedom is built through repeated disciplined choices over time.

AFFIRMATION

"I build freedom through discipline and intentional consistency."

TODAY'S POWER MOVE

Make one disciplined decision today that benefits your long-term future instead of temporary comfort.

DAY 309

Stop Ignoring Your Intuition

POWER QUOTE

"Your inner wisdom often recognizes what your fear tries to deny."

REFLECTION

Many people have ignored warning signs they recognized long before they could fully explain them.

Something felt wrong.

A relationship seemed unhealthy.

A business opportunity felt rushed.

An environment created constant tension.

Yet they convinced themselves they were overreacting.

Sometimes that happened because they feared being alone.

Sometimes because they wanted something to work so badly that they overlooked what their heart was trying to tell them.

Sometimes because they had spent so many years doubting themselves that trusting their own judgment felt unfamiliar.

Learning to trust yourself is an important part of emotional maturity.

That does not mean acting on every emotion.

Emotions can be influenced by fear, stress, exhaustion, or past experiences.

Wisdom requires learning the difference between a temporary emotional reaction and a consistent inner awareness that continues asking you to pay attention.

Healthy intuition is often quiet.

It notices patterns before it reaches conclusions.

It pays attention to repeated behaviors instead of isolated moments.

It recognizes when your values and your environment no longer align.

As you continue healing, this awareness becomes clearer.

Old wounds often make it difficult to recognize what is truly healthy.

Someone who has become accustomed to instability may mistake chaos for passion.

Someone who has experienced repeated rejection may ignore disrespect because it feels familiar.

Someone who has lived in survival mode may overlook opportunities for peace because calmness feels unfamiliar.

Healing begins changing that.

The healthier you become emotionally, the more clearly you begin recognizing what supports your well-being and what quietly undermines it.

You stop explaining away behaviors that consistently violate your values.

You become more willing to walk away from situations that continually steal your peace.

You begin trusting the wisdom that comes from observation instead of only reacting to emotion.

Self-trust is built the same way confidence is built.

One honest decision at a time.

Every boundary you honor tells your mind,

"My well-being matters."

Every time you listen to healthy convictions instead of fear, you strengthen your ability to trust yourself again.

Every wise choice becomes evidence that your judgment is becoming stronger.

This does not mean you will never make mistakes.

No one does.

But you no longer need to live in constant fear of your own decisions.

You can gather information.

Seek wise counsel.

Pray.

Reflect carefully.

Then move forward with confidence instead of endlessly second-guessing yourself.

The goal is not perfection.

The goal is developing a life where your decisions are guided by wisdom, emotional health, and integrity rather than insecurity or fear.

Pay attention to the patterns your life keeps revealing.

Notice what consistently brings peace.

Notice what repeatedly creates confusion.

Notice the environments where you become healthier and the ones where you slowly lose yourself.

Those observations are valuable.

They help shape the future you are building.

As your healing deepens, so will your discernment.

And the more you learn to trust the healthy wisdom you have developed, the more confidently you will walk toward the life that truly aligns with who you are becoming.

That kind of self-trust is not built overnight.

It is earned through a life of honest reflection, intentional growth, and the courage to listen when wisdom quietly points you in a better direction.

WEALTH LESSON

Self-awareness improves decision-making because emotionally aware people recognize unhealthy patterns more clearly.

AFFIRMATION

"I trust my inner wisdom and emotional awareness."

TODAY'S POWER MOVE

Pay close attention today to what situations or environments genuinely feel aligned or misaligned internally.

DAY 310

You Are Still Becoming

POWER QUOTE

"Growth is not a destination. It is a continuous process."

REFLECTION

Many people carry an invisible burden.

They believe they should already have everything figured out.

They think they should already know exactly what their future looks like.

Already have complete emotional maturity.

Already have financial security.

Already have every answer.

When reality looks different, they become discouraged.

They compare themselves to people whose journeys they only partially understand.

They criticize themselves for still learning.

They mistake being in process for being behind.

But growth has never worked that way.

No one reaches a point where there is nothing left to learn.

Wisdom continues to grow.

Character continues to deepen.

Perspective continues to expand.

The healthiest people never stop becoming students of life.

Every season teaches something different.

One season teaches patience.

Another teaches courage.

Another teaches humility.

Another teaches perseverance.

If you remain willing to learn, every chapter has something valuable to offer.

The goal is not to arrive at perfection.

The goal is to become a little wiser than you were yesterday.

A little more disciplined.

A little more emotionally aware.

A little more intentional with your choices.

That kind of progress compounds over time.

Think about a tree.

It does not become fully grown in a single season.

Its roots deepen year after year.

Its branches expand gradually.

Storms strengthen it.

Seasons shape it.

Growth is steady, not rushed.

Your life follows a similar pattern.

The experiences you are living today are developing parts of you that may not fully reveal their purpose until years from now.

Be patient with your own process.

Do not confuse unfinished with unsuccessful.

You are allowed to still be learning.

You are allowed to change your perspective as you gain new understanding.

You are allowed to outgrow habits that once felt normal.

You are allowed to become someone different from who you were five years ago.

That is not inconsistency.

That is maturity.

One of the greatest signs of growth is becoming less interested in proving that you know everything and more interested in continuing to learn.

Curiosity keeps you teachable.

Humility keeps you growing.

Self-awareness keeps you honest.

Together, they create a foundation for lifelong transformation.

Celebrate how far you have come without believing you have reached the end of the journey.

There is still wisdom to gain.

Relationships to strengthen.

Skills to develop.

Habits to refine.

Dreams to pursue.

The fact that you are still growing is not evidence that you are failing.

It is evidence that you are alive, learning, and moving forward.

So release the pressure to have every answer today.

Focus instead on making today's decisions with integrity, wisdom, and purpose.

Keep learning.

Keep adjusting.

Keep becoming.

Because the person you are meant to become is not created in one perfect moment.

They are shaped over a lifetime of choosing growth, embracing change, and remaining faithful to the process, one day at a time.

WEALTH LESSON

Long-term growth requires patience because meaningful transformation develops gradually over time.

AFFIRMATION

"I honor the process of becoming who I am meant to be."

TODAY'S POWER MOVE

Reflect today on one area where you know you are becoming healthier, wiser, or stronger than before.

DAY 311

Stop Looking For Validation In Places That Drain You

POWER QUOTE

"Not every environment is capable of recognizing your value."

REFLECTION

Many people remain in environments that slowly diminish who they are becoming.

Not because those places help them grow.

But because leaving feels unfamiliar.

Sometimes it is a relationship where they constantly seek approval but rarely receive encouragement.

Sometimes it is a workplace where their contributions are overlooked.

Sometimes it is a circle of friends where growth is quietly criticized instead of celebrated.

Over time, constantly living in those environments begins affecting the way people see themselves.

They question their abilities.

Lower their standards.

Silence their ambitions.

Not because they have less potential, but because they have spent too long in places that cannot recognize it.

One of the greatest acts of self-respect is recognizing when an environment no longer supports the person you are becoming.

That does not mean every difficult relationship should end.

Nor does it mean you should avoid every uncomfortable situation.

Growth often requires difficult conversations, patience, and grace.

But there is a difference between a challenging environment that encourages growth and one that continually drains your confidence, your peace, and your sense of purpose.

Healthy environments challenge you without diminishing you.

They encourage honesty without humiliation.

They celebrate your progress instead of competing with it.

They make room for your growth rather than expecting you to remain the same.

As you continue healing, your standards begin changing.

You become less willing to tolerate constant disrespect.

Less willing to chase validation from emotionally unavailable people.

Less willing to sacrifice your well-being simply to keep others comfortable.

That is not selfishness.

It is wisdom.

Your emotional energy is valuable.

Where you invest it matters.

The people you spend the most time with influence your thinking, your expectations, and your habits more than you may realize.

That is why choosing your environment carefully is one of the most important decisions you can make.

Ask yourself honestly:

"Do the places where I spend my time help me become healthier, wiser, and more intentional?"

"Do the people around me encourage growth, or do they quietly reward me for staying the same?"

The answers to those questions can reveal more about your future than you might expect.

Sometimes the greatest breakthrough is not adding something new.

It is having the courage to leave behind what has quietly been limiting you.

Not every chapter is meant to last forever.

Some relationships serve a purpose for a season.

Some environments prepare you for the next stage of your life.

And some places must eventually be released so that new growth has room to flourish.

Choose environments that strengthen your character.

Choose relationships built on mutual respect.

Choose conversations that inspire wisdom rather than constant negativity.

Choose spaces where your healing is protected instead of repeatedly challenged.

Because the people and places you continually return to will quietly influence the person you eventually become.

Surround yourself with what calls you higher, not what continually pulls you backward.

Your future deserves an environment where your growth is not merely tolerated—
it is encouraged.

WEALTH LESSON

Healthy environments improve emotional stability because supportive spaces strengthen confidence and discipline.

AFFIRMATION

"I stop seeking validation from environments that weaken my peace and confidence."

TODAY'S POWER MOVE

Distance yourself today from one environment or interaction that repeatedly drains your emotional energy.

DAY 312

Your Future Requires Financial Awareness

POWER QUOTE

"Wealth grows where awareness and discipline exist together."

REFLECTION

Financial freedom is not built through luck.

It is built through awareness.

Most people do not wake up one morning financially secure because of a single decision.

They arrive there because of hundreds of intentional choices made over many years.

Choosing to understand where their money goes.

Choosing to spend less than they earn.

Choosing to prepare instead of hoping everything works out.

Financial peace begins with honesty.

Many people avoid looking at their finances because the numbers create anxiety.

They postpone opening bank statements.

Avoid creating a budget.

Ignore debt.

Tell themselves they will deal with it later.

For a moment, avoidance feels easier.

But avoiding a problem has never been the same as solving it.

What you refuse to measure becomes difficult to improve.

The moment you begin paying attention, you begin taking back control.

You start recognizing patterns that were once invisible.

Small purchases that quietly became expensive habits.

Subscriptions you no longer use.

Emotional spending that temporarily relieved stress but delayed long-term goals.

Opportunities to save that were hidden beneath unconscious routines.

Awareness gives you options.

Instead of wondering where your money disappeared, you begin telling it where to go.

That shift changes everything.

Money becomes a tool instead of a source of constant uncertainty.

Planning replaces panic.

Purpose replaces impulse.

Confidence replaces confusion.

Building financial stability does not require perfection.

It requires consistency.

One budget created with intention.

One unnecessary expense avoided.

One emergency fund contribution.

One wise investment.

One responsible financial decision made today instead of postponed until tomorrow.

Those decisions may seem insignificant by themselves.

Over time, they create momentum.

Just as unhealthy financial habits compound, healthy financial habits compound as well.

Small savings become meaningful reserves.

Wise investments grow through patience.

Responsible choices create opportunities that once seemed impossible.

The greatest financial transformations often begin with ordinary decisions repeated faithfully.

There will always be unexpected expenses.

Economic uncertainty.

Moments that test your discipline.

Financial wisdom is not about avoiding every challenge.

It is about building habits that help you respond wisely when challenges appear.

Remember that wealth is not measured only by income.

It is also reflected in stewardship.

Someone who manages a small amount faithfully is developing habits that prepare them to manage more.

Every dollar you save intentionally is a vote for your future.

Every plan you create is an act of believing tomorrow matters.

Every disciplined decision strengthens the financial foundation you are building.

Do not allow temporary discomfort to prevent long-term stability.

Face your finances with honesty.

Approach them with patience.

Improve them with consistency.

Because financial peace is rarely created through dramatic breakthroughs.

It is built through ordinary acts of wisdom repeated over time.

And one day, you will look back and realize that the freedom you were hoping for began the moment you decided to stop avoiding your finances and start leading them with purpose.

WEALTH LESSON

Financial awareness improves stability because intentional planning strengthens long-term decision-making.

AFFIRMATION

"I manage my finances intentionally and build long-term stability."

TODAY'S POWER MOVE

Review one financial habit today and identify how it could improve long-term freedom.

DAY 313

Stop Punishing Yourself For Growing Slowly

POWER QUOTE

"Slow progress is still meaningful progress."

REFLECTION

One of the greatest reasons people give up is because they expected growth to happen faster than it naturally does.

They imagined healing would only take a few weeks.

That discipline would become easy after a few days.

That confidence would appear the moment they decided to change.

When reality unfolds more slowly, discouragement begins whispering that nothing is happening.

But some of the most valuable things in life cannot be rushed.

A seed does not become a tree overnight.

A foundation is not built in a single afternoon.

Trust is not earned through one conversation.

Likewise, lasting transformation develops through time, patience, and repeated faithfulness.

Healing is often so gradual that you do not recognize it while it is happening.

You notice it months later when something that once triggered you no longer controls your emotions.

You notice it when you respond with patience instead of anger.

When you make a wise financial decision that the old version of you would have avoided.

When you protect your peace without feeling guilty.

These quiet moments are evidence that growth has been taking place all along.

The same is true of discipline.

Very few people wake up one day suddenly becoming highly disciplined.

Discipline is built every time you honor a commitment when no one is watching.

Every early morning.

Every difficult decision.

Every promise you keep to yourself.

Each choice may seem ordinary.

Together, they reshape your character.

Confidence follows the same pattern.

It grows as you accumulate evidence that you can trust yourself.

Not because you never struggle.

But because you continue showing up despite the struggle.

That is why comparing your progress to someone else's journey is so discouraging.

You can see another person's success.

You cannot see the years of quiet work that prepared them for it.

Everyone has invisible seasons.

Seasons of learning.

Failure.

Practice.

Waiting.
The visible results are often only the final chapter of a much longer story.
Be patient with your own process.
Do not rush what requires time to become strong.
Roots grow before fruit appears.
Character develops before influence expands.
Wisdom matures before leadership flourishes.
The strongest people are rarely those who grew the fastest.
They are often the ones who refused to stop growing.
They kept learning after making mistakes.
They kept believing when progress was difficult to measure.
They kept planting seeds during seasons when there was nothing visible to harvest.
That kind of patience is powerful.
It allows you to remain faithful without demanding immediate rewards.
Remember that transformation is not measured only by what other people can see.
Some of the greatest victories happen where no applause exists.
Inside your thoughts.
Your habits.
Your responses.
Your daily decisions.
Those unseen victories eventually become visible realities.
So do not become discouraged because your growth still feels incomplete.
Every healthy choice is moving you forward.
Every lesson is preparing you.
Every season is shaping you.
Trust the process enough to keep showing up.
Because one day you will realize that what felt like slow progress was actually steady progress.
And steady progress has a way of creating the strongest foundations.
Keep growing.
Keep learning.
Keep building.
The life you are working toward is often taking shape long before you are able to fully see it.

WEALTH LESSON

Long-term transformation compounds slowly because repeated intentional behavior creates lasting change over time.

AFFIRMATION

"I remain patient and compassionate with my growth process."

TODAY'S POWER MOVE

Acknowledge one area today where you have grown more than you give yourself credit for.

DAY 314

Your Focus Determines Your Momentum

POWER QUOTE

"Where attention goes consistently, growth usually follows."

REFLECTION

One of the greatest challenges of modern life is not a lack of opportunity.

It is a lack of focus.

Every day, your attention is competing with countless distractions.

Notifications.

Social media.

Comparison.

Breaking news.

Entertainment.

Endless opinions.

Without realizing it, many people spend more time reacting to what is happening around them than intentionally building the life they actually want.

Attention is one of your most valuable resources.

Once a day has passed, you cannot recover the hours that were scattered across unnecessary distractions.

That is why focused people often make steady progress while others remain busy without moving forward.

They understand that where attention goes, energy follows.

And where energy consistently flows, results eventually appear.

Distraction does not always look dramatic.

Sometimes it looks like checking your phone every few minutes.

Constantly comparing your progress with someone else's.

Saying yes to commitments that leave no room for your priorities.

Allowing emotional drama to consume your mental space.

Each interruption may seem small.

But together, they quietly weaken your ability to think deeply, create consistently, and follow through on what matters most.

Focus is not simply about concentrating harder.

It is about choosing what deserves your attention.

Every time you protect your schedule, you strengthen your focus.

Every time you say no to unnecessary distractions, you create space for meaningful work.

Every time you return your attention to your priorities instead of temporary noise, you reinforce the habits that build lasting success.

Your routines deserve protection.

Your goals deserve uninterrupted effort.

Your peace deserves freedom from constant mental clutter.

That does not mean you must eliminate every distraction from your life.

It means you become intentional about what is allowed to shape your thinking.

The most productive people are not always the busiest.

They are often the most focused.

They know that consistent progress comes from giving their best attention to what truly matters instead of dividing it among everything that demands immediate attention.

Ask yourself honestly:

"What has been receiving my attention that no longer deserves it?"

"What important work have I been postponing because I keep allowing myself to be distracted?"

Those questions reveal where your energy is being invested.

Small adjustments can create remarkable results.

A dedicated hour without interruptions.

A phone set aside while you work.

A morning routine that begins with purpose instead of endless scrolling.

A quiet evening spent planning instead of reacting.

These decisions may seem ordinary.

Over time, they become the foundation of extraordinary progress.

Your future will always reflect what consistently received your attention.

Guard it wisely.

Protect your focus.

Protect your routines.

Protect your peace.

Because the life you hope to build requires more than ambition.

It requires the discipline to give your attention to what truly matters, day after day, until the results begin speaking for themselves.

WEALTH LESSON

Focused execution improves long-term results because intentional attention strengthens productivity and discipline.

AFFIRMATION

"I direct my focus intentionally toward growth, peace, and purpose."

TODAY'S POWER MOVE

Spend focused uninterrupted time today working intentionally toward one meaningful goal.

DAY 315

Emotional Maturity Will Protect Your Future

POWER QUOTE

"Emotional stability creates wiser long-term decisions."

REFLECTION

Many of life's greatest regrets are not the result of a lack of intelligence.

They are the result of moments when emotions became stronger than wisdom.

An angry response that damaged a relationship.

A fearful decision that caused someone to miss an opportunity.

A prideful attitude that prevented an apology.

An impulsive purchase that created years of financial stress.

These moments remind us that knowledge alone is not enough.

A person may know the right decision and still struggle to make it if they have not learned how to regulate their emotions.

This is why emotional maturity is one of the greatest forms of strength.

It is not the absence of emotion.

It is the ability to experience emotion without allowing it to control every decision.

Emotionally mature people still feel disappointment.

They still experience frustration.

They still face fear, grief, and uncertainty.

The difference is that they have learned to pause before reacting.

They understand that emotions are important messengers, but they are not always reliable decision-makers.

A moment of anger does not always require an immediate response.

A season of fear does not always mean danger is present.

A feeling of insecurity does not always reflect reality.

Wisdom creates space between emotion and action.

That space is where better decisions are made.

Instead of reacting impulsively, emotionally mature people ask questions.

"What am I feeling?"

"Why am I feeling this?"

"Will this decision still seem wise tomorrow?"

Those questions slow the mind enough for wisdom to catch up with emotion.

This practice changes every area of life.

Relationships become healthier because conversations become more thoughtful instead of reactive.

Finances become stronger because spending becomes intentional instead of emotional.

Leadership becomes steadier because decisions are guided by principles instead of pressure.

Even personal peace grows because life is no longer controlled by every temporary feeling.

Emotional maturity is developed through practice.

Every time you choose patience over impulse, you strengthen it.

Every time you listen before speaking, you strengthen it.

Every time you respond with wisdom instead of reacting with frustration, you strengthen it.

These moments may seem ordinary.

Yet they quietly shape the person you are becoming.

The greatest battles are often won long before anyone else notices.

They are won inside your thoughts.

Inside your responses.

Inside the decisions you make when no one else is watching.

Remember that strength is not measured by how intensely you feel.

It is measured by how wisely you respond.

Anyone can react.

Few people consistently choose reflection before action.

That choice separates temporary emotional relief from lasting growth.

Your future will place greater responsibilities into your hands.

Greater opportunities.

Greater influence.

Greater pressure.

The question is not whether those moments will come.

The question is whether you are becoming the kind of person who can carry them with wisdom, humility, and self-control.

Continue developing your emotional maturity.

Practice pausing before responding.

Choose understanding before assumption.

Choose wisdom before impulse.

Because one thoughtful decision can protect years of hard work, preserve valuable relationships, and create a future built on stability instead of regret.

That is the quiet strength of emotional maturity.

And it is one of the greatest investments you can ever make in yourself.

WEALTH LESSON

Emotional regulation improves long-term outcomes because intentional responses create healthier decisions than impulsive reactions.

AFFIRMATION

"I respond with emotional wisdom, maturity, and self-control."

TODAY'S POWER MOVE

Pause intentionally today before reacting emotionally to a stressful situation.

DAY 316

Stop Being Afraid To Outgrow People

POWER QUOTE

"Growth sometimes changes what environments feel aligned anymore."

REFLECTION

Growth changes more than your habits.

It changes your perspective.

As you become healthier emotionally, wiser in your decisions, and more intentional with your life, you may begin noticing that certain things no longer feel the same.

Conversations that once entertained you may now feel exhausting.

Habits that once seemed harmless may now feel limiting.

Environments you once accepted may begin feeling inconsistent with the life you are trying to build.

At first, this can feel confusing.

You may wonder if something is wrong with you.

In reality, something may be going right.

Growth changes your standards.

The more you heal, the less willing you become to tolerate what continually steals your peace.

The more disciplined you become, the less attractive constant distraction appears.

The more emotionally mature you become, the more you value honest communication over unnecessary conflict.

This is a natural part of becoming.

Just as a child eventually outgrows clothes that once fit perfectly, you will eventually outgrow patterns, relationships, and environments that once felt familiar.

That does not mean those seasons were meaningless.

They served a purpose.

They taught lessons.

They helped shape the person you are becoming.

But not everything that belongs to one chapter belongs to the next.

Many people remain trapped because they mistake growth for disloyalty.

They believe they must continue accepting unhealthy behaviors simply because they have known someone for a long time.

They remain committed to environments that no longer support their well-being because leaving feels uncomfortable.

But loyalty should never require you to abandon your own emotional health.

Choosing growth does not mean you stop caring about people.

It means you begin caring enough about your future to stop settling for what continually pulls you backward.

Healthy growth often creates healthier boundaries.

You become more intentional about how you spend your time.

More selective about the conversations you entertain.

More protective of your emotional energy.

Not because you think you are better than anyone else.

But because you recognize that your environment quietly influences your future.

The people around you affect your thinking.

Your thinking affects your decisions.

Your decisions shape your life.

That is why your standards matter.

As your standards rise, your choices begin changing.

You stop asking,

"What can I tolerate?"

And begin asking,

"What helps me become the person I am called to be?"

That question changes everything.

It encourages you to pursue environments that inspire wisdom instead of negativity.

Relationships built on mutual respect instead of constant emotional exhaustion.

Habits that strengthen your future instead of quietly weakening it.

Growth is not about becoming someone completely different.

It is about becoming more fully aligned with your values, your purpose, and the person you are capable of becoming.

Allow yourself to evolve.

Allow yourself to learn.

Allow yourself to outgrow what no longer serves your future.

Do not feel guilty for becoming healthier.

Do not apologize for protecting your peace.

Do not be afraid of changing when change is leading you toward greater wisdom and emotional freedom.

Because every season of growth prepares you for the next chapter of your life.

And sometimes the greatest evidence that you are truly growing is not what you are adding to your life—
it is what you have finally found the courage to leave behind.

WEALTH LESSON

Healthy environments improve emotional stability because supportive spaces strengthen long-term growth.

AFFIRMATION

"I allow myself to outgrow what no longer supports my peace or growth."

TODAY'S POWER MOVE

Identify one environment or habit today that no longer aligns with the future you want to build.

DAY 317

Your Future Deserves Better Decisions

POWER QUOTE

"Every decision either strengthens your future or weakens it."

REFLECTION

Most people assume their future will be shaped by one defining moment.

A major promotion.

A life-changing investment.

A new relationship.

A breakthrough opportunity.

While those moments can certainly influence the direction of your life, they are rarely what build it.

Most lives are shaped quietly.

One decision at a time.

One habit at a time.

One ordinary day repeated thousands of times.

The future you experience tomorrow is often the result of choices that seemed insignificant today.

The money you decide to save instead of spend.

The conversation where you choose patience instead of anger.

The extra hour you invest in learning instead of scrolling.

The boundary you establish to protect your peace.

The promise you keep to yourself when no one else is watching.

Each decision seems small on its own.

But small decisions rarely remain small.

They accumulate.

Just as one drop of water can eventually carve through solid rock, repeated choices slowly shape the direction of an entire life.

That is the power of compounding.

It is not only true of money.

It is true of character.

Health.

Relationships.

Leadership.

Emotional maturity.

Every repeated action becomes another vote for the person you are becoming.

This is why intentional living matters so deeply.

It encourages you to stop drifting through life and begin making decisions with purpose.

Instead of asking,

"What feels easiest today?"

you begin asking,

"What will serve the future I want to build?"

That single shift changes countless decisions.

You become more intentional with your finances because you understand that today's spending habits influence tomorrow's opportunities.

You become more careful with your words because you recognize that trust is built one conversation at a time.

You become more disciplined with your time because you realize that hours wasted eventually become years lost.

You become more protective of your peace because you understand that your emotional environment influences every decision you make.

Many people wait for extraordinary motivation before they begin changing.

But transformation is rarely built through extraordinary moments.

It is built through ordinary faithfulness.

Showing up when no one notices.

Making the wise decision when no one is watching.

Remaining consistent when progress feels slow.

Those are the choices that quietly transform a life.

Do not underestimate today's decisions simply because they seem ordinary.

One healthy habit practiced every day is more powerful than one dramatic effort that is never repeated.

One honest conversation can strengthen a relationship.

One wise financial choice can change the course of your future.

One disciplined response can prevent years of unnecessary regret.

Your life is being built every single day, whether you notice it or not.

The question is not whether your daily choices matter.

The question is whether those choices are leading you toward the person you hope to become.

Choose intentionally.

Choose consistently.

Choose wisely.

Because the future is not created only during life's biggest moments.

It is quietly built through the countless small decisions that shape your character, your habits, and your destiny one day at a time.

WEALTH LESSON

Repeated intentional decisions compound into long-term emotional and financial transformation.

AFFIRMATION

"I make decisions that strengthen my future intentionally."

TODAY'S POWER MOVE

Choose one intentional decision today that aligns with the future you desire.

DAY 318

Stop Waiting For Perfect Timing

POWER QUOTE

"Perfectionism often disguises itself as preparation."

REFLECTION

Many dreams remain unfinished for one simple reason.

People keep waiting for the perfect moment to begin.

They tell themselves they will start when they feel more confident.

When life becomes less busy.

When they have more money.

When they know a little more.

When fear finally disappears.

The problem is that those moments rarely arrive the way we imagine.

Life seldom becomes perfectly convenient before growth begins.

There will almost always be uncertainty.

Questions that remain unanswered.

Risks that cannot be completely eliminated.

Reasons to wait just a little longer.

If you continue waiting until every condition feels ideal, you may spend years standing at the starting line while your future quietly passes by.

The people you admire were not always confident.

They did not always have complete clarity.

Many of them started while feeling nervous.

They made mistakes.

They adjusted.

They learned as they went.

What separated them from many others was not greater certainty.

It was greater willingness to move before certainty arrived.

Action has a way of creating clarity that waiting never can.

You learn by doing.

You improve by practicing.

You gain confidence by showing up again and again.

The first speech may feel uncomfortable.

The first investment may feel intimidating.

The first business may not be perfect.

The first difficult conversation may feel awkward.

But every beginning teaches something that preparation alone never could.

Perfectionism often disguises itself as wisdom.

It sounds responsible.

It sounds careful.

But many times it is simply fear wearing a more acceptable name.

It convinces people they need one more course.
One more plan.
One more year.
One more sign.
Meanwhile, opportunities continue passing by.
Remember that progress has never required perfection.
It requires movement.
Every meaningful accomplishment in your life began with a first imperfect step.
The first day you learned to walk.
The first time you drove a car.
The first interview you attended.
The first responsibility you accepted.
None of those moments were perfect.
Yet each one helped prepare you for the next.
Growth works the same way.
You become ready by being willing.
Not by waiting.
The future belongs to people who are willing to act before they feel completely prepared.
Not recklessly.
Not without wisdom.
But with enough courage to trust that they can learn along the way.
Do not allow perfectionism to quietly become procrastination.
You do not need every answer before taking the next faithful step.
You only need enough courage to begin.
Every action teaches you something.
Every lesson makes you wiser.
Every attempt strengthens your confidence.
One day you will look back and realize that the breakthrough you were waiting for did not arrive before you started.
It arrived because you started.
So stop waiting for perfect conditions.
Stop waiting to feel fearless.
Stop waiting for complete certainty.
Take the next step with the knowledge you have today.
Trust that growth will meet you along the journey.
Because the life you dream about is rarely built by people who waited until everything was perfect.
It is built by ordinary people who chose courage over hesitation and movement over endless preparation, one decision at a time.

WEALTH LESSON

Execution creates momentum because action produces learning, opportunity, and confidence over time.

AFFIRMATION

"I stop waiting for perfect timing and begin moving intentionally."

TODAY'S POWER MOVE

Take one action today toward a goal you have been delaying unnecessarily.

DAY 319

Your Healing Is Worth Protecting

POWER QUOTE

"Protect your healing process from environments that repeatedly reopen wounds."

REFLECTION

Healing is not something that happens by accident.

It grows in environments where it is protected.

Just as a seed needs healthy soil, sunlight, and water to develop, your emotional healing needs conditions that allow it to flourish.

Peace.

Healthy boundaries.

Intentional choices.

Safe relationships.

Without those things, healing becomes much more difficult.

Many people wonder why they feel as though they are making progress one week and struggling the next.

Sometimes the answer is not a lack of effort.

Sometimes it is repeated exposure to the same environments that caused the wounds in the first place.

It is difficult to heal while continually returning to places that encourage unhealthy patterns.

A relationship that constantly dismisses your feelings.

A friendship built on criticism instead of encouragement.

An environment filled with chaos, manipulation, or constant conflict.

These situations can quietly reopen wounds that were beginning to close.

Healing requires more than good intentions.

It requires wisdom.

Wisdom recognizes that not every environment deserves unlimited access to your emotional life.

Not every relationship deserves unlimited influence over your peace.

Protecting your healing is not about avoiding discomfort.

Some conversations will still be difficult.

Some relationships can be restored through honesty, forgiveness, and mutual effort.

Growth often requires those moments.

But there is a difference between temporary discomfort that produces growth and ongoing dysfunction that repeatedly causes harm.

Emotionally healthy people learn to recognize that difference.

They become intentional about where they spend their energy.

Who they allow to shape their thinking.

What voices they continually listen to.

They understand that healing is strengthened by consistency.

Peaceful environments encourage peaceful thinking.

Healthy relationships encourage healthy communication.

Wise routines encourage emotional stability.

Little by little, those influences begin reinforcing the person they are becoming.

This is why boundaries matter so deeply.

Boundaries are not walls built to keep everyone out.

They are filters that help protect what is valuable.

Your peace is valuable.

Your emotional health is valuable.

Your future is valuable.

Protecting those things is an act of wisdom, not selfishness.

As you continue healing, your standards will naturally change.

You may become less comfortable with constant negativity.

Less willing to tolerate manipulation.

Less interested in relationships built on instability.

That is not because your heart has become harder.

It is because your discernment has become healthier.

You are learning what nourishes your growth and what quietly drains it.

Do not feel guilty for protecting the life you are working so hard to rebuild.

Healing deserves room to grow.

It deserves relationships that encourage honesty.

Conversations that inspire wisdom.

Environments where peace is cultivated instead of constantly threatened.

Remember that every healthy boundary you establish is an investment in your future.

Every wise decision about where you spend your time is shaping the person you are becoming.

Every environment you choose is either strengthening your healing or making it more difficult.

Choose wisely.

Protect your peace.

Guard your heart with wisdom.

Because the healthiest future is rarely built by accident.

It is built by people who intentionally create environments where healing, growth, and emotional stability have the opportunity to flourish every single day.

WEALTH LESSON

Healthy emotional environments improve long-term stability because peace strengthens emotional regulation and clarity.

AFFIRMATION

"I protect my healing and emotional peace intentionally."

TODAY'S POWER MOVE

Set one healthy emotional boundary today that protects your healing process.

DAY 320

You Are Capable Of Becoming More

POWER QUOTE

"Growth begins when you believe change is possible for you too."

REFLECTION

One of the greatest obstacles to transformation is not a lack of ability.

It is the belief that change is no longer possible.

When people stop believing they can grow, they slowly begin accepting things that were never meant to define them.

They accept emotional chaos as though peace is impossible.

They accept financial instability as though wisdom cannot be learned.

They accept unhealthy habits as though they are permanent parts of their identity.

Over time, those beliefs quietly become limitations.

Not because they are true.

But because they remain unchallenged.

The truth is that people are remarkably capable of change.

The mind can be renewed.

Habits can be replaced.

Character can be strengthened.

Relationships can become healthier.

Financial decisions can become wiser.

None of those changes happen overnight.

But they happen every day for people who refuse to believe their current reality is their final destination.

Transformation begins with one important decision:

Refusing to confuse your current condition with your permanent identity.

You may be struggling today.

That does not mean you will always struggle.

You may be rebuilding after failure.

That does not mean you will always be rebuilding.

You may still be healing.

That does not mean you will always carry the same wounds.

Growth becomes possible the moment you begin believing that today's version of you is not the final version of you.

That belief changes the questions you ask.

Instead of saying,

"This is just who I am,"

you begin asking,

"Who am I becoming?"

That question creates movement.

It reminds you that every decision is helping shape your future.

Every healthy habit strengthens your character.

Every wise financial choice improves your stewardship.
Every difficult conversation handled with maturity strengthens your relationships.
Every boundary you honor reinforces your self-respect.
These moments may appear insignificant.
Together, they reshape an entire life.
People often underestimate the quiet power of consistency.
They expect transformation to feel dramatic.
More often, it feels ordinary.
Choosing discipline when excuses seem easier.
Choosing forgiveness instead of bitterness.
Choosing responsibility instead of blame.
Choosing hope instead of surrender.
Those ordinary decisions become extraordinary because they are repeated.
The person you are becoming is being shaped every single day.
Not only through the victories everyone notices, but through the private decisions no one else ever sees.
The thoughts you choose to believe.
The habits you practice.
The standards you refuse to lower.
The promises you continue keeping to yourself.
Never underestimate what those quiet decisions are accomplishing.
They are building a future that is stronger than your past.
A future guided by wisdom instead of fear.
By discipline instead of impulse.
By purpose instead of survival.
Do not allow yesterday's version of yourself to convince you that tomorrow cannot be different.
You are still learning.
Still healing.
Still growing.
Still becoming.
The future version of you is not created in one extraordinary moment.
It is quietly taking shape every time you choose growth over comfort, truth over excuses, and intentional action over passive acceptance.
Keep making those choices.
Because one day you will realize that the life you once believed was impossible was built through the ordinary decisions you faithfully made, one day at a time.

WEALTH LESSON

Identity transformation improves outcomes because healthier beliefs influence healthier behavior long-term.

AFFIRMATION

"I continue evolving into a healthier, stronger, and more disciplined version of myself."

TODAY'S POWER MOVE

Reflect today on one area where you know growth is already happening within you.

DAY 321

Stop Letting Your Emotions Control Your Finances

POWER QUOTE

"Emotional spending often creates long-term stress for temporary comfort."

REFLECTION

People often believe financial problems are solved only by learning more about money.

They think the answer is another budgeting app.

Another investment strategy.

Another financial book.

While knowledge is important, many financial struggles begin long before a purchase is ever made.

They begin with emotion.

Stress encourages impulsive spending.

Loneliness seeks comfort through buying something new.

Insecurity tries to prove worth through appearances.

Overwhelm convinces people that avoiding their finances is easier than facing them.

The transaction may happen in a few seconds.

But the emotions behind it may have been building for weeks.

This is why financial growth is not only about mathematics.

It is also about self-awareness.

If you never understand why you spend the way you do, changing your budget alone may not change your behavior.

You might save money for a few weeks, only to return to old habits when life becomes emotionally difficult.

Lasting financial freedom requires learning to pause before reacting.

Before making a purchase, ask yourself:

"What am I actually trying to satisfy?"

Am I buying this because I truly need it?

Or because I am anxious?

Am I purchasing this because it aligns with my long-term goals?

Or because I want temporary relief from today's emotions?

Those questions create space between impulse and action.

That space is where financial wisdom grows.

Money was never designed to heal emotional wounds.

It cannot replace healthy relationships.

It cannot remove loneliness.

It cannot create lasting confidence.

When money becomes a coping mechanism instead of a tool, it often creates temporary comfort followed by long-term regret.

But when money is guided by purpose, it becomes something entirely different.

It becomes a tool for stability.

A resource for generosity.

A means of creating opportunities.

A way to build security for the future instead of escaping the present.
Financial discipline is built one decision at a time.
Choosing to wait before making an emotional purchase.
Choosing to follow a spending plan instead of acting on impulse.
Choosing to save for tomorrow rather than satisfying every desire today.
Those decisions strengthen more than your bank account.
They strengthen your character.
They teach patience.
They develop self-control.
They increase your confidence because you begin proving to yourself that your emotions no longer control every financial choice.
The goal is not to eliminate emotion from money.
The goal is to prevent emotion from becoming the one thing directing your financial life.
As your emotional awareness grows, your financial decisions become wiser.
As your financial decisions become wiser, your confidence grows.
And as your confidence grows, money slowly becomes less of a source of fear and more of a tool for building the life you truly desire.
Remember that lasting financial freedom is not created through one extraordinary decision.
It is created through hundreds of ordinary moments where you choose wisdom over impulse, purpose over temporary comfort, and long-term peace over short-term emotional relief.
Those quiet decisions are the ones that build a future marked by stability, freedom, and lasting peace.

WEALTH LESSON

Emotional regulation improves financial stability because intentional decisions replace impulsive spending habits.

AFFIRMATION

"I manage my finances intentionally instead of emotionally."

TODAY'S POWER MOVE

Pause before making unnecessary purchases today and ask whether they align with your long-term goals.

DAY 322

Your Future Requires Better Self-Talk

POWER QUOTE

"The way you speak to yourself shapes the way you show up in life."

REFLECTION

The most influential voice in your life is often the one no one else hears.

Your own.

Long before other people encourage you or criticize you, your mind is already having conversations with itself.

Those conversations matter.

They shape the way you interpret failure.

The way you approach opportunities.

The way you respond to setbacks.

The way you see your future.

Many people unknowingly weaken themselves through constant internal criticism.

Every mistake becomes proof they are incapable.

Every setback becomes evidence they are falling behind.

Every difficult season becomes another reason to question their worth.

Over time, those thoughts stop feeling like opinions.

They begin feeling like facts.

That is the danger of repeated negative self-talk.

Thoughts become beliefs.

Beliefs become identity.

Identity influences behavior.

Someone who constantly tells themselves they are undisciplined will eventually begin acting like someone who expects to fail.

Someone who believes they are always behind may stop taking opportunities because they assume success belongs to everyone else.

The mind naturally moves toward the identity it believes to be true.

This is why your internal dialogue deserves careful attention.

There is a difference between accountability and self-condemnation.

Accountability says,

"I made a poor decision. I need to learn from it."

Self-condemnation says,

"I am incapable of making good decisions."

One creates growth.

The other creates discouragement.

Healthy self-talk is not about pretending life is perfect.

It is not repeating empty affirmations while ignoring reality.

It is learning to speak to yourself with honesty and wisdom at the same time.

It sounds like this:

"This season is difficult, but I can continue."

"I made a mistake, but I am not defined by it."

"I still have room to grow, and that is part of becoming stronger."

Those thoughts create resilience.

They encourage responsibility without destroying hope.

Pay attention to the language you use when speaking to yourself.

Would you speak to someone you deeply love the same way you sometimes speak to yourself?

If not, it may be time to change the conversation.

Your inner voice should challenge you to grow.

It should call you to greater discipline.

It should encourage honesty.

But it should never become the loudest source of hopelessness in your life.

Growth flourishes where truth and grace work together.

Truth helps you recognize what needs to change.

Grace reminds you that change is still possible.

When those two work together, transformation becomes sustainable.

Little by little, your inner dialogue begins changing.

Instead of constantly expecting failure, you begin expecting growth.

Instead of assuming every setback defines you, you begin seeing setbacks as opportunities to learn.

Instead of criticizing yourself into exhaustion, you begin strengthening yourself through wisdom, patience, and intentional action.

Protect the conversations taking place inside your mind.

They are quietly shaping your confidence.

Your discipline.

Your resilience.

And the future you are building.

Because the strongest people are not those who never struggle with negative thoughts.

They are the people who refuse to let those thoughts become the permanent voice that defines who they are becoming.

Choose an inner voice that tells the truth, encourages growth, and reminds you that every day is another opportunity to become wiser, stronger, and more faithful than the day before.

WEALTH LESSON

Healthy thinking improves emotional resilience because thoughts influence confidence and long-term behavior.

AFFIRMATION

"I speak to myself with wisdom, strength, and emotional compassion."

TODAY'S POWER MOVE

Replace one repeated negative thought today with a healthier empowering belief.

DAY 323

Stop Avoiding The Hard Work

POWER QUOTE

"The life you desire is usually built through uncomfortable consistency."

REFLECTION

Many people admire extraordinary lives.

They admire successful businesses.

Healthy relationships.

Financial freedom.

Emotional stability.

Strong character.

What they often overlook is the ordinary discipline that quietly built those extraordinary outcomes.

Every meaningful accomplishment has a hidden story.

Years of consistent effort.

Countless unseen decisions.

Sacrifices no one applauded.

Habits practiced long before the results became visible.

This is why discipline often feels disappointing in the beginning.

It is repetitive.

It is quiet.

It rarely provides immediate rewards.

Some mornings it looks like getting out of bed when you would rather stay comfortable.

Some days it looks like honoring your budget while others spend impulsively.

Sometimes it means turning off distractions so you can finish the work you promised yourself you would complete.

Other times it means choosing healing instead of escaping into temporary comforts that only delay your growth.

None of those moments seem extraordinary.

Yet they are exactly where extraordinary lives are built.

People often imagine that success is created through one breakthrough moment.

More often, it is created through thousands of faithful decisions that no one else ever notices.

Every disciplined choice strengthens your future.

Every sacrifice made with purpose becomes an investment.

Every repetition develops character.

This is why patience matters.

The rewards of discipline are almost always delayed.

The person exercising today may not notice dramatic changes tomorrow.

The person saving consistently may not feel financially free next month.

The entrepreneur building with integrity may not see immediate success.

But something important is happening beneath the surface.

Habits are becoming identity.

Identity is becoming character.

Character is preparing them for responsibilities they could not yet carry before.
There will be seasons when discipline feels ordinary.
When progress feels slow.
When the temptation to quit becomes strong because the results seem invisible.
Those are the moments that matter most.
Anyone can remain committed when everything is exciting.
The strongest people continue when excitement has faded.
They understand that consistency carries them farther than motivation ever could.
Do not despise the ordinary work.
Do not underestimate the value of repeated faithfulness.
Every promise you keep to yourself strengthens self-respect.
Every distraction you resist strengthens your focus.
Every difficult decision you make with wisdom strengthens your character.
Those small victories are preparing you for larger opportunities.
One day, people may admire the life you have built.
They may see the confidence.
The peace.
The financial stability.
The wisdom.
What they may never fully see are the countless ordinary days that made those outcomes possible.
The mornings you chose discipline over comfort.
The evenings you continued learning instead of giving up.
The moments you protected your peace instead of returning to unhealthy patterns.
The quiet decisions no one celebrated became the foundation everyone eventually noticed.
Keep showing up.
Keep practicing.
Keep choosing what is right, even when it feels repetitive.
Because extraordinary futures are rarely created through extraordinary moments alone.
They are built through ordinary acts of discipline repeated faithfully over time.
And those quiet acts of faithfulness have the power to transform an entire life.

WEALTH LESSON

Long-term success requires repeated disciplined effort because consistency compounds over time into meaningful results.

AFFIRMATION

"I remain committed even when the process feels difficult."

TODAY'S POWER MOVE

Complete one uncomfortable but necessary task today that supports your long-term future.

DAY 324

Your Peace Deserves Protection

POWER QUOTE

"Peaceful lives are intentionally protected lives."

REFLECTION

Peace is not something that simply appears.

It is something that must be protected.

Most people assume they will experience peace once life becomes easier.

Once the workload decreases.

Once the relationship improves.

Once the finances become stable.

But peace cannot depend entirely on perfect circumstances because life will always contain challenges.

Instead, peace is built through intentional choices made every day.

It grows through healthy boundaries.

Wise routines.

Emotional self-control.

And environments that support the person you are becoming.

Without these things, even the strongest people can find themselves emotionally exhausted.

Many individuals lose their peace gradually rather than suddenly.

They say yes when they should have said no.

They continue conversations that continually leave them discouraged.

They remain in environments where negativity is constant.

They allow unnecessary stress to consume the attention that should be invested in their priorities.

None of those choices seem significant on their own.

Together, they slowly erode emotional stability.

Protecting your peace requires discernment.

Not every invitation deserves your time.

Not every disagreement deserves your energy.

Not every opinion deserves your attention.

One of the greatest forms of wisdom is learning what requires a response and what simply requires release.

Peace is strengthened every time you choose what is healthy over what is familiar.

Every healthy boundary protects your emotional well-being.

Every intentional routine creates greater stability.

Every wise decision about where you spend your time strengthens your ability to remain focused on what truly matters.

This does not mean avoiding responsibility or pretending difficult situations do not exist.

Life will always present challenges.

Relationships will sometimes require difficult conversations.

Growth will often require uncomfortable decisions.

But there is a difference between carrying necessary responsibilities and carrying unnecessary burdens.

Emotionally healthy people learn to recognize that difference.

They stop trying to solve problems that do not belong to them.

They stop seeking approval from people who are unwilling to give it.

They stop allowing chaos to become a permanent guest in their minds.

Instead, they become intentional guardians of their emotional health.

Ask yourself honestly:

"What has been stealing my peace that I continue allowing into my life?"

"What boundaries would help me become healthier, wiser, and more focused?"

Those questions are worth revisiting often.

Because your emotional environment quietly influences every area of your life.

It affects the quality of your decisions.

The strength of your relationships.

Your ability to remain disciplined.

Your capacity to lead others well.

The future you are building deserves a mind that is not constantly overwhelmed by unnecessary noise.

It deserves space to think clearly.

To heal deeply.

To grow intentionally.

Protect your peace with the same commitment you protect your goals.

Guard your attention.

Choose your environments wisely.

Surround yourself with people who encourage wisdom, honesty, and growth.

Because peace is not maintained by accident.

It is maintained through intentional choices that honor your well-being day after day.

And those choices will quietly shape the life you are building for years to come.

WEALTH LESSON

Emotional peace improves long-term stability because regulated minds think more clearly and build more intentionally.

AFFIRMATION

"I intentionally protect the peace I am creating within my life."

TODAY'S POWER MOVE

Distance yourself today from one unnecessary source of emotional chaos or stress.

DAY 325

Stop Quitting Every Time Growth Feels Slow

POWER QUOTE

"Compounding takes time before results become visible."

REFLECTION

One of the greatest reasons people abandon meaningful goals is because they mistake slow progress for no progress.

They begin a healing journey expecting immediate peace.

They start managing their finances expecting instant stability.

They commit to new habits expecting rapid transformation.

When those expectations are not met, discouragement quietly begins to grow.

The problem is not that they are failing.

The problem is that they expected growth to happen faster than it naturally does.

The most valuable forms of transformation are almost always gradual.

A tree does not become strong in one season.

A marriage is not built through one meaningful conversation.

Financial security is not created through one wise investment.

Character is not formed through one disciplined decision.

Strength is developed through repetition.

Day after day.

Choice after choice.

Season after season.

This is why patience is one of the most overlooked forms of discipline.

Patience allows you to continue planting seeds before you can see the harvest.

It reminds you that today's effort still has value even when today's results are difficult to measure.

Many of life's greatest accomplishments grow beneath the surface long before anyone else notices them.

Healing often becomes visible only after months of choosing healthier responses.

Confidence develops after countless moments of following through on your commitments.

Financial stability grows through years of intentional planning and consistent stewardship.

By the time people recognize your progress, you have usually been building it quietly for much longer than they realize.

That is the nature of compounding.

Each wise decision appears small by itself.

Saving a little more this month.

Reading another chapter.

Choosing patience during conflict.

Keeping your morning routine.

Resisting an unnecessary purchase.

None of those actions seem life-changing on a single day.

But repeated hundreds of times, they quietly reshape an entire future.

Do not allow temporary emotions to convince you that slow progress is meaningless.

Growth is not measured only by dramatic breakthroughs.

It is measured by your willingness to continue showing up when the work feels ordinary.

Some of your greatest victories are happening in ways you cannot yet fully see.

Your thinking is becoming healthier.

Your habits are becoming stronger.

Your character is becoming steadier.

Your discipline is becoming more dependable.

These changes may not receive applause today.

But they are preparing you for opportunities tomorrow.

Every day you remain faithful to the process, you are strengthening the foundation beneath your future.

One day, what now feels slow will simply look consistent.

What now feels repetitive will become your lifestyle.

What now feels difficult will become part of your character.

So keep planting.

Keep learning.

Keep rebuilding.

Keep choosing the next wise decision.

Do not rush the process that is making you stronger.

The strongest lives are rarely built through sudden transformation.

They are built through ordinary acts of faithfulness repeated long after excitement has faded.

Trust the process.

Trust the discipline.

Trust the quiet work taking place beneath the surface.

Because one day you will realize that the transformation you were hoping for was happening all along—one intentional decision at a time.

WEALTH LESSON

Consistency compounds into meaningful results because repeated disciplined behavior strengthens long-term growth.

AFFIRMATION

"I remain patient and committed to my growth process."

TODAY'S POWER MOVE

Continue one positive routine today even if visible progress feels slow.

DAY 326

Your Healing Will Influence Your Future Family

POWER QUOTE

"Healed people create healthier environments."

REFLECTION

Healing is never only about you.

Its impact extends far beyond your own life.

The way you communicate.

The way you respond under pressure.

The way you handle conflict.

The way you love, forgive, and lead.

All of these things influence the people around you every single day.

Many people think healing is simply about feeling better emotionally.

In reality, healing changes the environments you create.

Unhealed pain has a way of spreading.

A person who never learned healthy communication may unintentionally pass harmful patterns into their relationships.

Someone who lives in constant fear may unknowingly create an atmosphere of anxiety for those around them.

Unresolved anger often becomes harsh words.

Unaddressed insecurity may become control.

Emotional wounds that remain hidden still influence behavior.

Sometimes those patterns continue for generations because no one stopped long enough to heal.

That is why your personal growth matters so deeply.

Every unhealthy cycle that ends with you creates the possibility of a healthier future for someone else.

When you learn to regulate your emotions, the people around you experience greater stability.

When you learn to communicate with honesty and respect, your relationships become safer.

When you choose forgiveness over bitterness, you make room for peace instead of resentment.

These changes may seem personal, but they are never isolated.

They influence your family.

Your friendships.

Your workplace.

Your future marriage.

Your future children.

Your community.

Healthy people build healthy environments.

They create spaces where others feel heard instead of dismissed.

Where correction is offered with wisdom instead of humiliation.

Where disagreements are handled with maturity instead of emotional chaos.

Where people feel safe enough to grow because they are not constantly walking on eggshells.

This does not mean healed people are perfect.

They still make mistakes.

They still experience difficult emotions.

They still have moments when they need to apologize, reflect, and learn.

The difference is that they no longer allow those moments to define the atmosphere they create.

They take responsibility.

They continue growing.

They remain teachable.

One of the greatest gifts you can give the people around you is your commitment to becoming emotionally healthier.

Not because you will never struggle again.

But because you are choosing not to pass unnecessary pain forward.

Every conversation handled with patience matters.

Every unhealthy pattern you refuse to repeat matters.

Every wise response under pressure matters.

Those decisions are shaping more than your own future.

They are shaping the experiences of everyone whose life intersects with yours.

Never underestimate the influence of your healing.

Someone may experience greater peace because you chose emotional maturity.

Someone may feel understood because you learned to listen.

Someone may believe healthy relationships are possible because you modeled one.

Your growth creates possibilities that extend beyond what you can immediately see.

Keep doing the difficult work.

Keep learning.

Keep healing.

Keep becoming more intentional.

Because every step toward emotional health is not only transforming your own life—

it is helping create a legacy of wisdom, stability, and peace that can influence generations long after you are gone.

WEALTH LESSON

Emotional healing strengthens long-term relationships because healthier emotional patterns create healthier environments.

AFFIRMATION

"I heal intentionally so I can build healthier environments for myself and others."

TODAY'S POWER MOVE

Reflect today on one unhealthy emotional pattern you are committed to breaking permanently.

DAY 327

Stop Living Only For Survival

POWER QUOTE

"You deserve a life that includes peace, purpose, and joy too."

REFLECTION

Survival is necessary for a season.

But it was never meant to become a permanent way of living.

Many people spend so much time trying to make it through one difficult day after another that they slowly stop believing life can be anything more.

They focus on paying the next bill.

Getting through the next week.

Managing the next crisis.

Protecting themselves from the next disappointment.

Over time, survival becomes familiar.

When that happens, people often stop dreaming.

They stop planning for the future.

They stop believing stability is possible.

Not because they lack potential, but because they have spent so long responding to emergencies that they have forgotten what it feels like to build intentionally.

Survival mode changes the way a person thinks.

It narrows their vision.

Instead of asking,

"What kind of life do I want to create?"

they begin asking,

"How do I just get through today?"

While that response may be understandable during difficult seasons, it becomes limiting if it never changes.

Healing invites you into something greater.

It reminds you that life is not only about enduring hardship.

It is also about creating meaning.

Building healthy relationships.

Pursuing purpose.

Experiencing peace.

Growing into the person you were created to become.

The goal is not merely to survive.

It is to flourish.

Flourishing does not mean life becomes free of challenges.

It means your life is no longer defined by them.

You begin making decisions from hope instead of fear.

From vision instead of crisis.

From purpose instead of panic.

That shift changes everything.

You begin planning instead of only reacting.

Saving instead of constantly recovering.

Building instead of merely maintaining.

You start asking bigger questions.

"What legacy do I want to leave?"

"What kind of relationships do I want to cultivate?"

"What habits will help me become the person I hope to be five years from now?"

Those questions move your attention beyond today's struggle and toward tomorrow's possibilities.

The beautiful thing about healing is that it gradually expands your vision again.

You begin believing that peace is possible.

That stability can become normal.

That healthy love exists.

That financial wisdom can replace financial anxiety.

That purpose can replace mere survival.

Do not feel guilty for wanting more than simply making it through another day.

You were created for more than constant exhaustion.

More than endless stress.

More than emotional survival.

You were created to build a life marked by wisdom, peace, meaningful relationships, faithful stewardship, and lasting purpose.

That life will not appear all at once.

It will be built one intentional decision at a time.

Every healthy boundary.

Every wise financial choice.

Every courageous conversation.

Every disciplined habit.

Every act of healing.

These are the building blocks of a life that is no longer defined by survival but strengthened by purpose.

Keep healing.

Keep dreaming.

Keep building.

Because the future you are creating deserves more than surviving.

It deserves the opportunity to truly flourish.

WEALTH LESSON

Long-term stability improves when people shift from survival thinking toward intentional long-term living.

AFFIRMATION

"I build a life rooted in peace, purpose, and intentional growth."

TODAY'S POWER MOVE

Do one thing today that supports joy, peace, or purpose in your future life.

DAY 328

Your Confidence Will Grow Through Discipline

POWER QUOTE

"Every promise you keep to yourself strengthens self-belief."

REFLECTION

Confidence is not built by waiting until you feel fearless.

It is built by learning to trust yourself.

Many people think confidence comes from praise, success, or recognition.

Those things can certainly encourage confidence for a season.

But lasting confidence is built on something much deeper.

It is built on self-trust.

Self-trust develops every time your actions align with your intentions.

Every promise you keep to yourself becomes evidence.

Evidence that you are dependable.

Evidence that you can follow through.

Evidence that you are becoming someone who does what they say they will do.

That evidence is powerful because your mind remembers it.

Just as repeated disappointments can weaken trust in another person, repeated broken promises can weaken trust in yourself.

Every time you tell yourself you will begin tomorrow but continue postponing, your confidence quietly erodes.

Every goal you repeatedly abandon teaches your mind to expect inconsistency.

Eventually, you begin doubting yourself before you even begin.

Not because you lack ability.

But because your history has taught you not to rely on your own commitments.

The encouraging truth is that self-trust can be rebuilt.

The same way it was lost.

One decision at a time.

One kept promise at a time.

You rebuild confidence when you wake up when you said you would.

When you honor your budget.

When you complete the task you wanted to avoid.

When you continue working after motivation fades.

When you choose healing over unhealthy coping habits.

These moments may seem small.

Yet every one of them sends a message to your mind:

"I can depend on myself."

That message changes the way you approach future challenges.

You stop relying only on emotion.

You begin relying on character.

You know that even when fear appears, you have continued before.

Even when motivation disappeared, you still showed up.

Even when the process became difficult, you did not abandon yourself.

Those experiences become the foundation of genuine confidence.

This is why discipline is so valuable.

It is not simply about accomplishing more.

It is about becoming someone you can trust.

Each disciplined action strengthens your identity.

Each consistent habit reinforces the belief that your future matters enough to deserve today's effort.

Over time, confidence begins to feel less like an emotion and more like a quiet certainty.

Not because life has become easier.

But because you have developed evidence that you can face difficult things without giving up.

Remember that confidence is rarely created through one extraordinary achievement.

It is created through hundreds of ordinary moments when you choose integrity over excuses, action over hesitation, and consistency over comfort.

Protect your self-trust.

Keep the promises you make to yourself.

Honor the commitments that move your life forward.

Because every act of faithfulness strengthens the bridge between who you are today and who you are becoming.

And once you become someone who trusts yourself, confidence is no longer built on perfect circumstances.

It is built on the quiet knowledge that you have learned to show up, remain faithful, and continue growing—one intentional decision at a time.

WEALTH LESSON

Consistency strengthens confidence because repeated disciplined behavior builds self-trust internally.

AFFIRMATION

"I build confidence through discipline, consistency, and follow-through."

TODAY'S POWER MOVE

Keep one promise to yourself today regardless of emotional resistance.

DAY 329

Stop Overcomplicating Your Growth

POWER QUOTE

"Small consistent actions often create the biggest transformation."

REFLECTION

Many people imagine transformation as one dramatic moment.

They picture a single decision that instantly changes everything.

A burst of motivation.

A breakthrough opportunity.

A life-changing event.

While moments like these can certainly inspire change, they rarely sustain it.

Lasting transformation is usually much quieter.

It is built through the ordinary choices most people overlook.

Choosing water instead of another unhealthy habit.

Following your budget when no one is watching.

Turning off distractions to finish meaningful work.

Taking a walk instead of remaining inactive.

Responding with patience instead of anger.

Getting enough rest instead of constantly running on exhaustion.

None of these decisions appear extraordinary on their own.

Yet each one strengthens the person you are becoming.

This is the power of consistency.

The greatest changes in life rarely happen because of one remarkable day.

They happen because ordinary days are lived with extraordinary faithfulness.

Many people abandon healthy habits because they underestimate their value.

They believe a single workout cannot improve their health.

One wise financial decision cannot create wealth.

One honest conversation cannot strengthen a relationship.

Individually, those thoughts are true.

Collectively, they are completely false.

One workout leads to another.

One wise financial choice becomes a habit.

One honest conversation creates trust for the next.

Small actions become repeated patterns.

Repeated patterns become character.

Character shapes destiny.

This is why you should never measure today's choices only by today's results.

Instead, ask yourself:

"If I repeat this decision for the next five years, where will it lead me?"

That question changes everything.

Suddenly, today's habits become much more important.

A small daily expense becomes thousands of dollars over time.
A few minutes of intentional learning become years of accumulated wisdom.
One act of forgiveness becomes the beginning of emotional freedom.
One disciplined morning routine becomes a life built on consistency.
Compounding works in every area of life.
Healthy habits compound.
Unhealthy habits compound.
Wise decisions compound.
Poor decisions compound.
The future is often nothing more than today's habits repeated long enough.
That realization is empowering.
It means you do not need to change your entire life today.
You simply need to make the next wise decision.
Then repeat it tomorrow.
And the day after that.
Transformation becomes much less overwhelming when you stop focusing on changing everything at once.
Instead, focus on becoming one percent wiser today.
One percent more disciplined.
One percent more intentional.
Those small improvements create remarkable change over time.
Never underestimate the value of simple faithfulness.
The routines that feel ordinary today may become the very foundation of the life you once prayed for.
Keep drinking the water.
Keep honoring the budget.
Keep protecting your peace.
Keep managing your emotions with wisdom.
Keep showing up when no one is applauding your effort.
Because extraordinary lives are rarely built through extraordinary moments alone.
They are built through simple, disciplined choices repeated with consistency until those choices quietly become the person you were always capable of becoming.

WEALTH LESSON

Small, disciplined habits compound over time into long-term emotional and financial transformation.

AFFIRMATION

"I trust the power of small consistent actions."

TODAY'S POWER MOVE

Commit to one simple healthy habit today and complete it consistently.

DAY 330

You Are Still Capable Of Greatness

POWER QUOTE

"No setback has the authority to erase your potential."

REFLECTION

Every meaningful life includes difficult seasons.

No one is exempt from disappointment.

Plans sometimes fall apart.

Relationships sometimes end.

Financial setbacks happen.

Mistakes are made.

Dreams may take longer than expected.

During those seasons, it becomes easy to believe that temporary circumstances have become permanent truths.

You begin wondering if you have missed your opportunity.

If you are capable enough.

If all your effort has been wasted.

Those thoughts are understandable.

But they are not always accurate.

A difficult season does not erase your value.

It does not cancel your purpose.

It does not remove your ability to build something meaningful in the future.

Some of the strongest people you will ever meet are not people who avoided hardship.

They are people who refused to let hardship have the final word.

They learned.

Adjusted.

Recovered.

And continued moving forward.

Resilience is rarely built during easy seasons.

It is developed when life asks you to keep believing while results remain unseen.

When you choose hope after disappointment.

When you choose discipline after failure.

When you choose faithfulness after plans have changed.

Those decisions quietly strengthen your character in ways comfort never could.

It is important to remember that your current chapter is not your entire story.

A single difficult season cannot summarize a lifetime.

One mistake does not define your identity.

One setback does not determine your destiny.

One disappointment does not erase everything that is still possible.

The future remains unwritten.

Every new day gives you another opportunity to respond with wisdom instead of surrender.

To rebuild instead of retreat.

To learn instead of becoming bitter.

Growth often looks less like dramatic breakthroughs and more like quiet perseverance.

Getting out of bed when motivation is low.

Keeping your commitments when no one notices.

Continuing to believe that your effort still matters, even when the results are slow to appear.

Those ordinary moments become extraordinary because they shape who you become.

There may be days when progress feels invisible.

Do not mistake invisible progress for the absence of growth.

Roots grow beneath the surface long before a tree becomes visible above the ground.

Character develops in much the same way.

The work happening inside you today may become the strength you depend on years from now.

Be patient with yourself.

Give yourself permission to continue learning.

Allow yourself to recover from setbacks without believing they define your future.

You are not required to have a perfect journey.

You are only asked to keep moving forward.

One wise decision.

One faithful step.

One intentional day at a time.

There is still more for you to learn.

More for you to build.

More for you to become.

Do not allow today's hardship to convince you that tomorrow holds no hope.

The chapter may be difficult, but the story is still being written.

And some of the most meaningful victories are achieved by people who simply refused to stop believing that a better future was still possible.

WEALTH LESSON

Resilience strengthens long-term growth because emotionally strong people continue rebuilding after setbacks.

AFFIRMATION

"I continue believing in the greatness I am capable of building."

TODAY'S POWER MOVE

Write down one future goal today that you still deeply believe is possible for your life.

DAY 331

Stop Giving Temporary Problems Permanent Power

POWER QUOTE

"Temporary pain should never convince you that your future is hopeless."

REFLECTION

Difficult seasons have a way of changing your perspective.

When pain lasts longer than expected, it can begin convincing you that life will always feel this way.

A setback begins feeling permanent.

A disappointment begins feeling like your identity.

A season of waiting begins feeling like the end of the story.

That is one of the greatest dangers of discouragement.

It quietly narrows your vision until all you can see is today's struggle.

But life has always been marked by change.

Seasons change.

People grow.

Healing unfolds.

Opportunities appear that once seemed impossible.

The circumstances surrounding your life today are not guaranteed to remain the same forever.

Think back to seasons you once believed you would never survive.

Moments that felt overwhelming.

Losses that seemed impossible to recover from.

Questions you thought would never be answered.

Yet somehow, you continued.

You learned.

You adapted.

You became stronger in ways you could not have imagined while you were living through those moments.

That is the quiet power of resilience.

Resilience is not pretending life is easy.

It is choosing to believe that today's pain does not have the authority to define tomorrow's possibilities.

It allows you to hold onto hope while acknowledging reality.

To keep building while progress feels slow.

To continue believing in a future you cannot fully see yet.

This is why perspective matters so deeply.

Your current chapter deserves your attention.

It does not deserve complete authority over your vision.

One difficult season cannot summarize an entire life.

One failure cannot erase years of potential.

One closed door does not mean every opportunity has disappeared.

Life often changes in ways we never could have predicted.

A conversation opens a new opportunity.

A lesson from failure prepares you for future success.

A season of healing creates wisdom that later strengthens someone else's life.
The chapters that feel most painful sometimes become the chapters that shape your greatest growth.
That does not make hardship enjoyable.
But it reminds us that hardship is not always meaningless.
When you refuse to surrender during difficult seasons, something important begins developing beneath the surface.
Patience grows.
Character deepens.
Perspective expands.
Faith becomes stronger.
These qualities often become the foundation for everything that follows.
Do not allow temporary discouragement to convince you that your future has already been decided.
It has not.
There is still room for growth.
Still room for healing.
Still room for unexpected opportunities.
Still room for joy that you cannot yet imagine.
Keep your eyes on the bigger story.
Continue making wise decisions, even when the results seem delayed.
Continue believing that your life is still unfolding.
Because emotionally strong people understand something that discouragement often forgets:
No season lasts forever.
The chapter you are living today is important, but it is not the conclusion.
Your future deserves patience instead of hopelessness.
It deserves perseverance instead of surrender.
And one day, you may look back and realize that the season you once feared would define your life became the very season that prepared you for everything that came next.

WEALTH LESSON

Emotional resilience strengthens long-term success because persistent people continue rebuilding during difficult seasons.

AFFIRMATION

"I refuse to let temporary struggles define my permanent future."

TODAY'S POWER MOVE

Focus today on one possibility for your future instead of only focusing on current frustration.

DAY 332

Your Energy Needs Boundaries Too

POWER QUOTE

"Everything deserves limits except your peace."

REFLECTION

Your emotional energy is one of your most valuable resources.

Unlike money, time, or possessions, you cannot easily replace it once it has been drained.

Yet many people give it away without realizing the cost.

They remain constantly available.

They absorb everyone else's problems.

They carry burdens that were never theirs to carry.

They continue investing in conversations, relationships, and environments that repeatedly leave them exhausted.

Over time, this becomes more than simple tiredness.

It becomes emotional depletion.

When your emotional energy is constantly consumed, it becomes more difficult to think clearly.

Your patience weakens.

Your focus declines.

Your discipline becomes harder to maintain.

Even simple decisions begin feeling overwhelming because your mind no longer has the capacity to process them well.

This is why protecting your emotional energy is not selfish.

It is responsible stewardship.

Healthy boundaries are not created to push people away.

They are created to preserve what is necessary for healthy living.

Every healthy boundary protects something valuable.

It protects your peace.

Your clarity.

Your emotional stability.

Your ability to remain present with the people and responsibilities that truly matter.

Not every problem belongs to you.

Not every conflict requires your involvement.

Not every opinion deserves your attention.

Learning to recognize that truth is part of emotional maturity.

Many people confuse constant availability with kindness.

But there is a difference between being compassionate and becoming emotionally consumed by everyone else's needs.

You cannot pour into others indefinitely while neglecting your own well-being.

Eventually, even generosity becomes difficult when your own emotional reserves have been depleted.

Healthy people understand the importance of renewal.

They make time for quiet reflection.

Rest.

Prayer or meditation.

Exercise.

Meaningful relationships.

Activities that restore rather than simply distract.

These practices are not luxuries.

They are investments in the quality of the life you are building.

Ask yourself honestly:

"What consistently restores my energy?"

"What consistently drains it?"

The answers to those questions deserve your attention.

Sometimes protecting your energy means limiting unnecessary conflict.

Sometimes it means spending less time in environments that constantly create stress.

Sometimes it means saying no without guilt so you can remain faithful to the responsibilities that matter most.

Those decisions are not acts of selfishness.

They are acts of wisdom.

Remember that the future you hope to build requires a healthy version of you.

It requires a clear mind capable of making wise decisions.

A peaceful heart capable of loving well.

A disciplined spirit capable of remaining faithful through difficult seasons.

None of those qualities can flourish if your emotional energy is continually exhausted.

Protect your peace with intention.

Guard your attention carefully.

Invest your energy where it produces growth instead of constant depletion.

Because every day you choose what receives your emotional investment, you are shaping the quality of the life you will eventually experience.

Choose wisely.

Your future deserves a mind that is clear, a heart that is healthy, and an inner life strong enough to build with purpose rather than merely survive from one exhausting day to the next.

WEALTH LESSON

Protected emotional energy improves focus, discipline, and long-term productivity.

AFFIRMATION

"I protect my energy intentionally because my peace matters deeply."

TODAY'S POWER MOVE

Pay attention today to what interactions energize you and which ones emotionally drain you.

DAY 333

Stop Waiting To Become Worthy

POWER QUOTE

"You do not need to earn the right to grow, heal, or succeed."

REFLECTION

Many people unknowingly place conditions on their own worth.

They tell themselves,

"I'll deserve peace when I become more successful."

"I'll be confident once I accomplish more."

"I'll finally be worthy of love when I become more attractive, more disciplined, or more accomplished."

Without realizing it, they postpone living.

They postpone joy.

They postpone rest.

They postpone believing they have value until they achieve a version of themselves that may never feel "good enough."

The problem with this mindset is that the finish line keeps moving.

One achievement leads to another expectation.

One promotion creates another goal.

One accomplishment becomes the new minimum.

If your worth depends entirely on what you accomplish, you may spend your entire life chasing a feeling that never fully arrives.

Growth is important.

Discipline matters.

Excellence is worth pursuing.

But these things should grow from a healthy identity, not become an attempt to earn one.

There is a difference between growing because you value yourself and striving because you believe you have no value until you prove it.

The first creates freedom.

The second creates exhaustion.

Healthy growth begins with the understanding that your value is not determined by your current level of success.

You are not more worthy because you earn more money.

You are not more deserving of peace because you reach another milestone.

You are not more valuable because other people finally recognize your accomplishments.

Those things may change your circumstances.

They do not determine your worth.

That understanding changes the way you approach growth.

You stop chasing perfection.

You begin pursuing wisdom.

You stop trying to impress everyone around you.

You begin becoming more aligned with your values.

You stop believing every mistake disqualifies you.

You begin seeing mistakes as opportunities to learn.

Ironically, people who no longer need to prove their worth often become healthier, stronger, and more disciplined than those who spend their lives trying to earn it.

Why?

Because they are no longer driven primarily by fear.

They are driven by purpose.

Their discipline becomes an act of stewardship instead of self-punishment.

Their healing becomes an act of self-respect instead of self-rejection.

Their goals become expressions of their potential rather than desperate attempts to feel enough.

Continue growing.

Continue learning.

Continue building.

But never confuse your progress with your value.

Your achievements will change throughout life.

Your circumstances will rise and fall.

Your opportunities will come and go.

Your worth should never be as unstable as those things.

Build your life on a stronger foundation.

Let discipline strengthen your character.

Let healing restore your heart.

Let wisdom guide your decisions.

Let purpose shape your direction.

Not because you are trying to become worthy of a meaningful life—

but because you recognize that your life already has value, and it deserves to be lived with intention.

That perspective changes everything.

It allows you to pursue excellence without becoming imprisoned by perfection.

It gives you permission to celebrate progress without believing you must earn the right to experience peace.

And it reminds you that the healthiest version of yourself is not the flawless one.

It is the one who continues growing with humility, discipline, gratitude, and the quiet confidence that true worth is not something you achieve—it is something you choose to honor through the way you live.

WEALTH LESSON

Healthy self-worth improves emotional stability because people make healthier decisions when they value themselves deeply.

AFFIRMATION

"I deserve growth, healing, peace, and abundance now."

TODAY'S POWER MOVE

Treat yourself today like someone whose future genuinely matters.

DAY 334

Your Future Is Built In Private

POWER QUOTE

"The habits practiced privately eventually create public results."

REFLECTION

People are often inspired by what they can see.

The successful business.

The confident speaker.

The healthy marriage.

The financial stability.

The respected leader.

What they rarely see is the private discipline that made those things possible.

They do not see the early mornings when no one was watching.

The evenings spent learning while others were distracted.

The sacrifices made long before there were visible rewards.

The difficult conversations that strengthened relationships.

The quiet prayers.

The consistent budgeting.

The moments of choosing healing over unhealthy coping habits.

Success is often celebrated publicly.

Character is almost always built privately.

That is why private discipline matters so deeply.

The person you become when no one is watching is eventually revealed in the life everyone else sees.

Public success is usually the visible result of invisible habits.

Every commitment you honor in private strengthens your integrity.

Every wise financial decision made quietly builds future stability.

Every emotional response you regulate without recognition strengthens your maturity.

Every healthy routine practiced consistently shapes your character.

These moments rarely receive applause.

Yet they are often the moments that matter most.

Many people become discouraged because no one notices their effort.

But not all valuable work is immediately visible.

A builder spends weeks laying a foundation before anyone admires the finished house.

An athlete trains for years before standing on a podium.

A tree spends years strengthening its roots before offering lasting shade.

The strongest foundations are almost always built out of sight.

Your life follows the same pattern.

The discipline you practice today is preparing you for responsibilities you may not yet see.

Every quiet act of faithfulness becomes another layer of strength beneath your future.

This is why integrity matters.

Integrity is choosing the right path even when there is no audience.

It is honoring your commitments because they reflect your character, not because someone else is keeping score.

It is remaining faithful during ordinary days when excitement has disappeared and recognition is absent.

Those ordinary days become extraordinary over time.

Ask yourself honestly:

"Who am I becoming when no one else is watching?"

"Are my private habits supporting the future I hope to build?"

Those questions often reveal more than any public achievement ever could.

Because eventually, private habits become public realities.

The discipline that nobody applauds becomes the confidence everyone notices.

The healing that happened in silence becomes the peace others admire.

The consistent choices made behind closed doors become the opportunities that seem effortless to those looking from the outside.

Do not become discouraged if your progress feels invisible today.

Continue honoring your commitments.

Continue protecting your peace.

Continue managing your time with intention.

Continue making wise decisions even when no one recognizes them.

The life you hope to build is being shaped in those quiet moments.

One day, people may celebrate the results.

But you will know the truth.

Those results were never created in a single moment of recognition.

They were built through countless ordinary decisions, faithfully repeated in private until they quietly transformed your life.

WEALTH LESSON

Private discipline compounds into long-term success because repeated intentional behavior creates visible outcomes over time.

AFFIRMATION

"I remain disciplined privately because my future is being built daily."

TODAY'S POWER MOVE

Complete one important responsibility today without needing recognition or validation from others.

DAY 335

Stop Romanticizing Being "Busy"

POWER QUOTE

"Being constantly overwhelmed is not the same as being productive."

REFLECTION

Many people mistake constant activity for meaningful progress.
Their schedules are always full.
Their phones are always ringing.
Their calendars are always crowded.
Their minds are always racing.
From the outside, it looks like productivity.
Yet internally, they often feel exhausted, disconnected, and overwhelmed.
Being busy is not the same as building.
Movement is not always the same as progress.
Sometimes people stay in constant motion because slowing down would force them to confront what they have been avoiding.
The emotional exhaustion they have ignored for months.
The relationships they know need attention.
The habits that are quietly working against them.
The goals they no longer feel connected to.
Busyness can become a distraction just as easily as laziness can.
It fills every quiet moment until there is no space left for reflection.
No space to ask difficult questions.
No space to notice when life has become driven by urgency instead of purpose.
Intentional living requires something many people overlook.
Clarity.
Clarity allows you to distinguish between what is important and what is merely urgent.
It helps you recognize that not every opportunity deserves a yes.
Not every request deserves your immediate attention.
Not every problem deserves your emotional energy.
Without clarity, it is easy to spend years climbing a ladder only to discover it was leaning against the wrong wall.
That is why rest and reflection are not signs of weakness.
They are disciplines.
Moments of stillness allow you to examine your direction before investing more energy into it.
They create room to ask:
"Why am I working so hard?"
"Does the way I spend my time reflect the life I say I want?"
"Am I building intentionally, or simply reacting to whatever demands my attention?"
Those questions require honesty.
But they also create freedom.
When your priorities become clear, your decisions become simpler.

You stop measuring success by how exhausted you feel.

Instead, you begin measuring it by whether your daily actions align with your values.

You work with greater purpose.

You protect your peace without feeling guilty.

You become more present in your relationships because your attention is no longer divided by unnecessary noise.

Ironically, peaceful productivity often produces better results than frantic activity.

A focused hour accomplishes more than a distracted day.

A rested mind makes wiser decisions than an exhausted one.

A clear purpose sustains discipline long after constant hustle has drained your energy.

Do not wear exhaustion as proof of significance.

Your value is not measured by how overwhelmed you become.

The goal is not to fill every moment.

The goal is to invest every moment wisely.

Choose direction over distraction.

Purpose over pressure.

Clarity over chaos.

Allow yourself the courage to pause long enough to make sure the life you are building is the life you truly want to live.

Because meaningful success is not created by running the fastest.

It is created by consistently moving in the right direction.

And when your life is guided by clarity instead of constant urgency, your work becomes more intentional, your relationships become healthier, and your peace becomes strong enough to sustain the future you are building.

WEALTH LESSON

Intentional productivity improves long-term performance because clarity strengthens focus and emotional regulation.

AFFIRMATION

"I build intentionally instead of glorifying emotional exhaustion."

TODAY'S POWER MOVE

Slow down today long enough to evaluate whether your actions are aligned with your real priorities.

DAY 336

Your Discipline Is Rewiring Your Identity

POWER QUOTE

"Every repeated healthy decision strengthens a new version of you."

REFLECTION

Identity is not built in a single moment.

It is built through repetition.

Every decision you make teaches your mind something about who you believe you are.

When you protect your peace, you reinforce the identity of someone who values emotional health.

When you follow your budget, you reinforce the identity of someone who manages money with wisdom.

When you keep your commitments, you strengthen the identity of someone who is dependable.

When you respond with patience instead of impulse, you become someone who is learning emotional maturity.

These moments may seem ordinary.

Yet they are quietly shaping the person you are becoming.

This is why consistency matters far more than occasional inspiration.

Motivation can help you begin.

Repetition determines who you become.

Many people focus only on outcomes.

They ask,

"When will I finally become successful?"

"When will I finally feel confident?"

"When will I finally experience peace?"

These are important questions.

But an even better question is,

"Who am I becoming through the choices I make every day?"

That question shifts your attention from chasing results to building character.

Because lasting success is not simply about achieving something.

It is about becoming someone capable of sustaining it.

A person who builds wealth without financial discipline may lose it.

A person who gains influence without emotional maturity may misuse it.

A person who reaches success without healthy habits may struggle to maintain it.

Character determines whether success becomes a blessing or a burden.

That is why every small decision matters.

Each one is casting a vote for your future identity.

Every time you choose honesty over convenience, you strengthen integrity.

Every time you continue working after motivation fades, you strengthen discipline.

Every time you choose forgiveness instead of bitterness, you strengthen emotional freedom.

Every wise decision becomes another piece of evidence that supports the person you are becoming.

Eventually, these repeated choices stop feeling like isolated actions.

They become part of your identity.

Discipline becomes natural because it has become part of who you are.

Peace becomes easier because you have practiced protecting it.

Financial wisdom becomes consistent because intentional stewardship has become your lifestyle.

This is the quiet power of repetition.

Transformation rarely announces itself while it is happening.

It develops quietly.

One habit.

One conversation.

One decision.

One ordinary day at a time.

People may only notice the change after months or years have passed.

They will admire the confidence.

The stability.

The wisdom.

The resilience.

What they may never fully see are the thousands of private decisions that made those qualities possible.

Never underestimate what your daily habits are teaching your mind.

Every repeated action is reinforcing an identity.

The question is whether it is reinforcing the identity you truly want to live.

Choose habits that align with your values.

Choose routines that strengthen your character.

Choose responses that reflect the person you hope to become.

Because your future is not only being shaped by the goals you pursue.

It is being shaped by the person you are becoming while pursuing them.

And one day, you will realize that the greatest transformation was never simply what you accomplished.

It was who you became through the faithful repetition of wise, intentional choices.

WEALTH LESSON

Repeated disciplined behavior reshapes identity because habits influence long-term emotional and financial outcomes.

AFFIRMATION

"I reinforce a healthier identity through disciplined daily actions."

TODAY'S POWER MOVE

Practice one behavior today that reflects the future version of yourself you are becoming.

DAY 337

Stop Letting Anxiety Rush Your Life

POWER QUOTE

"Peaceful decisions are often wiser than panic-driven ones."

REFLECTION

Anxiety has a way of making everything feel urgent.

It whispers that every problem must be solved immediately.

Every uncertainty must have an answer today.

Every decision must be made before you have had time to think clearly.

When anxiety takes control, even ordinary situations can begin feeling like emergencies.

That is why emotional regulation is so important.

It creates space between what you feel and how you respond.

Without that space, people often make decisions they later regret.

They rush into relationships because they fear being alone.

They abandon opportunities because uncertainty feels unbearable.

They make emotional purchases to relieve temporary stress.

They react in anger before understanding the full situation.

The problem is rarely the emotion itself.

The problem is believing every emotion requires immediate action.

Feelings are real.

But they are not always reliable guides for wise decision-making.

An anxious thought does not automatically mean danger is present.

A fearful feeling does not always mean you are making the wrong choice.

Sometimes your mind is simply responding to uncertainty, not reality.

This is why learning to slow down is an act of wisdom.

Before reacting, pause.

Give yourself permission to breathe.

Allow your emotions to settle before asking them to make important decisions.

Often, clarity arrives after the intensity has passed.

One of the healthiest questions you can ask yourself is:

"Am I responding to facts, or am I reacting to fear?"

That question interrupts impulsiveness.

It reminds you that not everything demanding your attention deserves your immediate response.

Peace is not created by eliminating every uncertainty.

It is created by developing the ability to remain steady while uncertainty exists.

Emotionally mature people understand this.

They still experience anxiety.

They still encounter stressful seasons.

They still face situations they cannot fully control.

The difference is that they refuse to let panic become their decision-maker.

Instead, they choose reflection over reaction.

Wisdom over urgency.

Patience over pressure.

This does not mean ignoring problems.

Healthy emotional regulation is not avoidance.

It is facing challenges with a clear mind instead of a frantic one.

Some situations require immediate action.

Many do not.

Learning the difference can protect your relationships, your finances, your health, and your future.

Every time you pause before reacting, you strengthen self-control.

Every time you choose thoughtful action over emotional impulse, you build confidence in your ability to handle pressure wisely.

Over time, this becomes part of your character.

You become someone who remains grounded when life feels uncertain.

Someone who thinks clearly when others panic.

Someone who makes decisions based on wisdom instead of fear.

That kind of stability is powerful.

It creates healthier relationships.

Better leadership.

Greater financial discipline.

And a deeper sense of peace that is not dependent on perfect circumstances.

Remember that your future will be shaped by many important decisions.

Do not allow anxiety to rush those decisions before wisdom has an opportunity to speak.

Slow down.

Breathe.

Reflect.

Then move forward with intention.

Because the strongest lives are rarely built through panic.

They are built by people who learned how to remain steady, think clearly, and choose wisdom even when life felt uncertain.

WEALTH LESSON

Calm thinking improves long-term outcomes because emotionally regulated decisions reduce unnecessary instability.

AFFIRMATION

"I slow down, think clearly, and make intentional decisions."

TODAY'S POWER MOVE

Pause intentionally today before making emotionally pressured decisions.

DAY 338

Your Healing Is Teaching You Strength

POWER QUOTE

"Some of the strongest people are people who rebuilt themselves quietly."

REFLECTION

Healing is one of the bravest decisions a person can make.

Not because it is easy.

But because it requires you to face what would often feel easier to avoid.

It asks you to confront painful memories instead of pretending they never happened.

To acknowledge unhealthy patterns instead of excusing them.

To take responsibility for your growth instead of waiting for life to change on its own.

That kind of courage is quiet.

It is rarely celebrated.

Yet it is the beginning of lasting transformation.

Many people think courage only appears in dramatic moments.

Standing before a crowd.

Taking a great risk.

Making a bold announcement.

Those moments certainly require courage.

But some of the greatest courage is displayed in private.

Choosing to attend counseling.

Apologizing when your pride wants to remain silent.

Forgiving someone without allowing bitterness to define your future.

Breaking a cycle that has existed for generations.

Learning healthier ways to communicate.

Remaining disciplined when returning to old habits would feel easier.

These decisions rarely make headlines.

Yet they reshape lives.

Healing is not simply about recovering from pain.

It is about becoming someone who is no longer controlled by it.

Each time you choose peace over chaos, you strengthen your emotional stability.

Each time you choose discipline over avoidance, you reinforce your character.

Each time you choose honesty over denial, you create space for real growth.

These choices may feel small in the moment.

Over time, they become the foundation of a completely different life.

There may be days when you wonder if you are making progress at all.

Healing often feels slow because so much of its work happens beneath the surface.

You may not notice the changes immediately.

Then one day, you respond calmly to something that once would have overwhelmed you.

You establish a healthy boundary without feeling guilty.

You face disappointment without abandoning yourself.

You handle conflict with wisdom instead of reacting impulsively.

In those moments, you realize something remarkable has happened.

The person you once were is no longer leading your life.

A stronger person has quietly emerged.

Not because life became easier.

But because you became healthier.

That is the quiet reward of consistent healing.

You do not simply experience different emotions.

You become a different person.

Someone who carries greater peace.

Greater wisdom.

Greater resilience.

Greater self-awareness.

The courage you practiced in private begins showing itself in every area of your life.

Your relationships become healthier.

Your decisions become wiser.

Your confidence becomes steadier because it is built on character instead of circumstance.

The work you do today may be preparing opportunities you cannot see yet.

Every difficult conversation.

Every healthy boundary.

Every disciplined decision.

Every act of forgiveness.

Every step toward emotional maturity is preparing you for a future that your past could never have sustained.

Keep choosing healing.

Keep choosing truth.

Keep choosing growth, even when it feels uncomfortable.

Because one day you will look back with gratitude and realize that the version of yourself who once felt broken, overwhelmed, or uncertain has become someone marked by wisdom, strength, and peace.

And that quiet transformation will be one of the greatest victories of your life.

WEALTH LESSON

Healing strengthens long-term stability because emotionally healthy people create healthier decisions and environments.

AFFIRMATION

"I grow stronger every time I choose healing and intentional growth."

TODAY'S POWER MOVE

Reflect today on one difficult season that taught you emotional strength or wisdom.

DAY 339

Stop Believing It Is Too Late

POWER QUOTE

"Growth is still possible as long as you are willing to begin again."

REFLECTION

One of the most discouraging lies people tell themselves is that they are too late.

Too late to change.

Too late to begin again.

Too late to heal.

Too late to build the life they once imagined.

They compare their journey to someone else's and conclude they have already missed their opportunity.

"I should have started years ago."

"Everyone else is ahead of me."

"If I haven't figured it out by now, maybe I never will."

Those thoughts can quietly steal hope.

Not because they are true.

But because they convince people to stop trying.

The truth is that transformation does not have an expiration date.

Life rarely unfolds according to the timelines we imagine.

Some people discover their purpose early.

Others discover it after years of disappointment.

Some build successful careers in their twenties.

Others begin entirely new careers in their forties, fifties, or beyond.

Some relationships begin quickly.

Others are formed after seasons of waiting and healing.

Growth is not a race.

It is a journey.

The danger of comparison is that it measures your life against someone else's chapter without knowing the full story behind either one.

You see another person's success.

You rarely see the failures they overcame.

The sacrifices they made.

The years they spent learning in private.

Your path is uniquely your own.

It will include different lessons.

Different timing.

Different opportunities.

That does not make it less valuable.

What matters is not whether your journey looks identical to someone else's.

What matters is whether you continue moving forward from where you are today.

You cannot rewrite yesterday.

But you can influence tomorrow.

Every wise decision you make today becomes the starting point for a different future.

Every healthy habit begins with one first day.

Every healed relationship begins with one honest conversation.

Every financial turnaround begins with one intentional choice.

Every meaningful life is built from the present moment forward.

Do not allow regret to become a permanent address.

Learn from your past.

Thank it for the lessons it taught you.

Then give your energy to what you can still build.

Remember that some of the strongest people are not those who never experienced delays.

They are the people who refused to let delays become defeat.

They kept learning.

Kept rebuilding.

Kept believing that their future was still worth investing in.

That kind of perseverance changes lives.

Your timeline does not determine your potential.

Your age does not determine your ability to grow.

Your past does not determine the limits of your future.

The only moment you truly have is this one.

Use it well.

Plant the seed today, even if you wish you had planted it years ago.

Begin the conversation.

Create the plan.

Take the first step.

Because the best time to begin may have been years ago.

The second-best time is now.

One day, you will look back with gratitude that you did not allow discouragement to convince you it was too late.

You chose to keep moving.

To keep growing.

To keep believing.

And that decision became the beginning of a future you once thought you had missed.

Every meaningful journey starts wherever you are willing to take the next faithful step.

Keep taking it.

WEALTH LESSON

Long-term growth remains possible because intentional consistent effort creates opportunity over time.

AFFIRMATION

"It is not too late for me to rebuild, heal, and grow."

TODAY'S POWER MOVE

Take one action today that reconnects you with a goal or dream you once abandoned emotionally.

DAY 340

Your Future Needs Consistency More Than Excitement

POWER QUOTE

"Consistency creates the results that motivation alone never sustains."

REFLECTION

Excitement is a wonderful place to begin.

It inspires new ideas.

Creates momentum.

Makes difficult goals feel possible.

But excitement was never designed to carry you all the way to transformation.

By its very nature, excitement comes and goes.

Some mornings you wake up energized and ready to conquer the day.

Other mornings, you feel tired, discouraged, or distracted.

If your progress depends entirely on how you feel, your consistency will rise and fall with your emotions.

That is why discipline is more dependable than motivation.

The people who build meaningful lives are rarely those who felt inspired every single day.

They are the people who continued showing up after the excitement faded.

They honored their commitments when no one was watching.

They stayed faithful to the process when the results were still invisible.

Anyone can remain committed when progress feels exciting.

Character is revealed when progress feels ordinary.

Think about a farmer planting seeds.

The excitement of planting may last only a day.

The harvest, however, requires months of patient care.

Watering.

Weeding.

Waiting.

Trusting that growth is taking place beneath the surface, even when nothing appears to be changing.

Life works much the same way.

Healthy habits often feel repetitive.

Saving money month after month.

Choosing healthy meals day after day.

Practicing emotional self-control in conversation after conversation.

Keeping promises to yourself even when no one else would know if you broke them.

These moments rarely feel dramatic.

Yet they are exactly where lasting transformation is built.

Every time you continue despite fluctuating emotions, you strengthen your character.

You teach yourself that your values matter more than your feelings in the moment.

You become someone who can be trusted.

Not because you are always excited.

But because you remain faithful.

That faithfulness begins creating something remarkable.

Consistency compounds.

One disciplined morning becomes a week.

One week becomes a month.

One month becomes a year.

Eventually, what once required tremendous effort becomes part of your identity.

You no longer exercise only when you feel motivated.

You exercise because it is who you have become.

You no longer manage your finances wisely only when life feels easy.

You do it because stewardship has become part of your character.

You no longer protect your peace only when it is convenient.

You protect it because you understand its value.

This is the quiet power of consistency.

It transforms isolated actions into lasting habits.

And lasting habits into lasting character.

Do not become discouraged when excitement fades.

It was never meant to be your foundation.

Let your commitments become stronger than your emotions.

Let your routines become stronger than your excuses.

Let your purpose become stronger than temporary discomfort.

The future you are building does not require perfection.

It requires faithful repetition.

One wise decision.

One disciplined habit.

One intentional day after another.

Because the lives people admire are rarely built on extraordinary moments of motivation.

They are built on ordinary moments of consistency repeated so faithfully that, over time, they create extraordinary results.

Keep showing up.

Keep honoring your commitments.

Keep choosing the next right step.

Your consistency today is quietly becoming the transformation you will one day look back and be grateful you never gave up on.

WEALTH LESSON

Consistency creates long-term success because repeated disciplined behavior compounds into meaningful results over time.

AFFIRMATION

"I remain consistent even when motivation changes."

TODAY'S POWER MOVE

Stay committed today to one important habit regardless of how motivated you feel emotionally.

DAY 341

Stop Abandoning Yourself During Difficult Seasons

POWER QUOTE

"Hard seasons require compassion and discipline, not self-destruction."

REFLECTION

Every person experiences seasons that feel heavier than expected.

Seasons where motivation disappears.

Where disappointment lingers.

Where simply getting through the day feels more difficult than anyone else realizes.

During those moments, many people become their own harshest critic.

Instead of offering themselves patience, they offer condemnation.

Instead of protecting healthy routines, they abandon them.

Instead of asking for support, they isolate themselves.

Instead of extending grace, they convince themselves they should already be stronger.

Yet difficult seasons are often when you need your own support the most.

Imagine a close friend came to you during one of the hardest chapters of their life.

They told you they were discouraged.

That progress felt slow.

That they were trying to rebuild after disappointment.

You would probably encourage them.

You would remind them that one difficult season does not define their future.

You would tell them to keep going.

To be patient.

To take the next step.

The question is:

Why are you sometimes unwilling to offer yourself the same compassion?

Self-compassion is not making excuses.

It is refusing to let temporary struggle become permanent self-rejection.

It allows you to acknowledge reality without losing hope.

To admit you are hurting while still believing healing is possible.

To recognize you are tired without convincing yourself you are defeated.

That perspective creates resilience.

Because people who continue caring for themselves during difficult seasons recover differently than those who abandon themselves.

They continue eating well, even if imperfectly.

They keep small routines alive.

They continue protecting their peace.

They allow themselves to rest without completely giving up.

They remember that rebuilding is rarely accomplished through dramatic breakthroughs.

It is built through ordinary acts of faithfulness repeated while life still feels difficult.

Sometimes the most courageous thing you can do is simply maintain the habits that keep you grounded.

Getting out of bed.

Taking a walk.

Reading a few pages.

Praying.

Reflecting.

Preparing one healthy meal.

Keeping one promise you made to yourself.

Those small actions may seem insignificant.

But they quietly remind your mind that your future is still worth investing in.

Remember that difficult seasons are chapters.

They are not identities.

You are not your exhaustion.

You are not your disappointment.

You are not your current struggle.

You are a person still growing, still learning, and still becoming.

Give yourself permission to rebuild without demanding perfection.

Offer yourself the same patience you would gladly extend to someone you deeply love.

Continue choosing structure over surrender.

Hope over hopelessness.

Grace over harsh self-condemnation.

Because healing is not measured by never having difficult days.

It is measured by your willingness to continue caring for yourself even while carrying them.

One day, you may look back on this season and realize that what felt like your weakest chapter quietly became the place where your resilience, wisdom, and self-respect grew the strongest.

Keep showing up for yourself.

Your future is worth that kind of faithfulness.

WEALTH LESSON

Emotional resilience improves long-term growth because people who continue supporting themselves recover more effectively from setbacks.

AFFIRMATION

"I continue caring for myself even during difficult seasons."

TODAY'S POWER MOVE

Do one intentional thing today that supports your emotional well-being and future growth.

DAY 342

Your Financial Habits Reflect Your Emotional Habits

POWER QUOTE

"The way you manage money often mirrors the way you manage emotions."

REFLECTION

One of the biggest misconceptions is financial growth is simply a matter of learning more about money.

Learn how to budget.

Learn how to invest.

Learn how to save.

While financial knowledge is important, knowledge alone does not always change behavior.

Many financial decisions are made emotionally long before they are made mathematically.

A person overwhelmed by anxiety may avoid looking at their bank account altogether.

Someone carrying deep insecurity may spend money trying to create an image that earns acceptance.

A person living in constant fear may panic whenever unexpected expenses appear, even when they have the resources to recover.

The numbers tell part of the story.

The emotions often explain the rest.

This is why lasting financial growth requires emotional awareness as much as financial education.

Your relationship with money is often influenced by your relationship with yourself.

If you constantly seek external validation, spending may become a way of temporarily feeling valuable.

If you struggle to trust yourself, long-term financial planning may feel impossible because every decision is driven by immediate emotions.

If uncertainty feels threatening, patience with investing or saving may become difficult.

None of these patterns mean you are incapable of building wealth.

They simply reveal areas where healing and self-awareness can strengthen your financial life.

Healthy money habits begin long before money enters your account.

They begin with learning to pause before reacting.

To ask yourself,

"What is motivating this decision?"

"Am I responding to wisdom or to emotion?"

Those questions create space between impulse and action.

That space is where financial maturity begins to grow.

Every wise financial decision strengthens more than your savings.

It strengthens your self-respect.

Every budget you follow reminds you that your future matters.

Every unnecessary purchase you resist teaches your mind that temporary feelings do not have to control permanent decisions.

Every dollar intentionally invested reinforces patience instead of impulsiveness.

Over time, these decisions become part of your identity.

You stop seeing yourself as someone who struggles with money.

You begin seeing yourself as someone who manages resources with wisdom.

That identity changes behavior.

You become less reactive.

More intentional.

More confident.

Not because you suddenly became wealthy overnight, but because your habits began reflecting the person you are becoming.

Financial freedom is rarely created by one extraordinary decision.

It is built through hundreds of ordinary choices made with consistency.

Choosing preparation instead of avoidance.

Planning instead of panicking.

Stewardship instead of impulse.

Remember that money is a tool.

It was never designed to determine your worth.

It was designed to serve your purpose.

The healthier your emotional life becomes, the easier it becomes to use money wisely instead of emotionally.

And as your financial habits become healthier, they reinforce something even greater than stability.

They reinforce the identity of someone who can be trusted with what they have, who plans with intention, and who is building a future marked by wisdom, peace, and faithful stewardship.

That is the kind of wealth that lasts—because it is built on character before it is reflected in a bank account.

WEALTH LESSON

Emotional awareness improves financial discipline because intentional behavior replaces reactive habits.

AFFIRMATION

"I build healthier emotional and financial habits intentionally."

TODAY'S POWER MOVE

Observe one emotional pattern today that may be influencing your financial decisions.

DAY 343

Stop Looking For Shortcuts To Transformation

POWER QUOTE

"Real growth is built, not rushed."

REFLECTION

Many people spend their lives searching for shortcuts.

The shortcut to wealth.

The shortcut to confidence.

The shortcut to healing.

The shortcut to success.

The desire is understandable.

Everyone would prefer a path that is easier, faster, and less uncomfortable.

The problem is that the most valuable things in life cannot be rushed.

There is no shortcut to emotional maturity.

It develops through difficult conversations, honest reflection, and learning to respond wisely under pressure.

There is no shortcut to financial stability.

It is built through budgeting, patience, intentional spending, and consistent stewardship over time.

There is no shortcut to confidence.

Confidence grows each time you keep a promise to yourself, face discomfort, and continue despite uncertainty.

There is no shortcut to self-respect.

It is earned by living in alignment with your values, even when doing so requires sacrifice.

Many people become discouraged because these changes happen more slowly than they expected.

They mistake gradual progress for failure.

They compare their private journey to someone else's public success.

Eventually, they begin believing they are falling behind.

But meaningful transformation has never been designed to happen overnight.

The strongest foundations are almost always built slowly.

Think about the construction of a skyscraper.

Before anyone admires its height, months are spent strengthening the foundation beneath the surface.

Without that unseen work, the building could never support what is eventually placed upon it.

Character develops the same way.

The daily decisions no one celebrates become the strength everyone eventually notices.

Every healthy habit strengthens your foundation.

Every wise financial decision increases stability.

Every difficult conversation handled with maturity deepens your character.

Every moment you choose discipline over comfort prepares you for responsibilities that are still ahead.

These moments may feel ordinary.

They are anything but ordinary.

They are quietly shaping your future.

Compounding is one of life's greatest principles.

A single wise decision may not seem significant.

But repeated consistently, those decisions create remarkable change.
One page read each day becomes books completed.
One workout becomes years of better health.
One dollar saved becomes financial security.
One act of forgiveness becomes emotional freedom.
One disciplined choice becomes a transformed identity.
The temptation to look for shortcuts often comes from wanting immediate results.
But immediate results rarely produce lasting character.
Lasting character is formed through faithful repetition.
That is why discipline becomes so powerful after excitement fades.
Anyone can stay committed while motivation is high.
The strongest people continue when the work becomes ordinary.
They understand that greatness is rarely built through dramatic moments.
It is built through ordinary faithfulness practiced for extraordinary lengths of time.
So resist the temptation to rush your growth.
Do not become discouraged by slow progress.
Do not compare your beginning to someone else's middle.
Trust the quiet work taking place beneath the surface.
Keep honoring your commitments.
Keep practicing healthy habits.
Keep choosing wisdom over impulse.
Keep investing in the person you are becoming.
Because the future you hope for is not built by shortcuts.
It is built by thousands of intentional decisions that slowly shape your character, strengthen your identity, and prepare you to carry the life you have been working toward.
One decision.
One habit.
One day at a time.
That is how lasting transformation is built.

WEALTH LESSON

Long-term success compounds gradually because repeated intentional behavior creates sustainable results over time.

AFFIRMATION

"I trust the process of steady disciplined growth."

TODAY'S POWER MOVE

Commit to one long-term habit today without expecting immediate results emotionally.

DAY 344

Your Peace Should Not Feel Like A Luxury

POWER QUOTE

"Peace is a necessity, not a reward reserved only for survival after exhaustion."

REFLECTION

Many people have become so familiar with stress that they mistake it for productivity.

If they are constantly rushing, they believe they must be accomplishing something important.

If they are always overwhelmed, they assume they are working hard enough.

If they finally stop, they often feel guilty rather than refreshed.

Over time, chaos becomes normal.

Peace begins to feel unfamiliar.

Some people even believe they must earn rest by first exhausting themselves.

But peace was never designed to be a reward for burnout.

It is a foundation for healthy living.

Your nervous system was not created to remain in constant survival mode.

It needs moments of stillness.

Time to recover.

Time to breathe.

Time to think without constant pressure.

Without those moments, even simple responsibilities begin feeling overwhelming.

The quality of your decisions starts to decline.

Your patience becomes shorter.

Your focus weakens.

Your emotions become more reactive.

Eventually, exhaustion begins making choices that wisdom should have made.

This is why peace is not laziness.

Peace creates clarity.

A calm mind notices opportunities that a frantic mind overlooks.

A rested heart responds more wisely than one that is constantly overwhelmed.

A peaceful life creates space for gratitude, creativity, healthy relationships, and intentional decision-making.

Some of the strongest people are not those who constantly push themselves to the point of collapse.

They are the people who understand the value of sustainable living.

They know when to work with excellence.

They know when to rest with purpose.

They recognize that long-term faithfulness requires renewal as much as effort.

Protecting your peace also means protecting your environment.

Not every conversation deserves your attention.

Not every conflict deserves your emotional energy.

Not every opportunity deserves your immediate yes.

Every unnecessary burden you carry takes energy away from the responsibilities that truly matter.

Wisdom teaches you to distinguish between what deserves your investment and what should simply be released.

Ask yourself honestly:

"Does the pace of my life reflect the peace I hope to experience?"

"Am I building a future that I will actually have the emotional capacity to enjoy?"

Those questions matter.

Because success without peace often becomes another form of exhaustion.

The life you are building should not only look meaningful from the outside.

It should also feel healthy from the inside.

Give yourself permission to pause.

To rest without guilt.

To create routines that restore instead of constantly deplete.

To choose calm over unnecessary chaos.

To protect your emotional health with the same commitment you protect your goals.

Remember that peace is not the absence of responsibility.

It is the presence of stability while carrying responsibility well.

Your future deserves more than constant pressure.

It deserves a clear mind.

A healthy heart.

A disciplined spirit.

And a life built with enough balance that you can not only achieve meaningful things—but also have the strength, joy, and peace to truly experience them.

That kind of life is not built by living in permanent exhaustion.

It is built by honoring both discipline and restoration, one intentional day at a time.

WEALTH LESSON

Mental peace improves long-term productivity because emotionally stable minds think more clearly and consistently.

AFFIRMATION

"I allow peace to become part of my daily life, not just a temporary escape."

TODAY'S POWER MOVE

Create one peaceful moment today without guilt or emotional pressure.

DAY 345

Stop Waiting For Confidence Before You Begin

POWER QUOTE

"Confidence is built through action, not endless hesitation."

REFLECTION

It is easy to believe confidence is something they must possess before they can begin.

They wait until they feel fearless.

Until they feel completely prepared.

Until every doubt disappears.

Until they finally believe in themselves enough to take the first step.

The problem is that confidence rarely arrives that way.

More often, confidence is the result of action, not the requirement for it.

Think about every skill you have developed throughout your life.

Confidence probably was not present the first time you tried.

You learned by doing.

You improved through repetition.

You became comfortable through experience.

The same principle applies to almost every meaningful area of life.

The entrepreneur launches while still having unanswered questions.

The speaker walks onto the stage with butterflies in their stomach.

The investor makes their first thoughtful investment while still learning.

The person beginning therapy attends the first session before knowing exactly what healing will look like.

None of these people waited until fear disappeared.

They simply decided that growth was more important than comfort.

That decision changed everything.

Every courageous action becomes evidence.

Evidence that you are capable.

Evidence that uncertainty does not have to stop you.

Evidence that you can survive situations your fear once convinced you would destroy you.

Your mind remembers that evidence.

It begins replacing fear with familiarity.

What once felt impossible slowly becomes normal.

This is how self-trust grows.

Not through positive thinking alone.

But through repeated experiences of following through on what matters.

Each time you keep a promise to yourself, you strengthen your identity.

Each time you continue despite discomfort, you remind yourself that your emotions do not have to control your decisions.

Eventually, courage becomes less about dramatic moments and more about daily faithfulness.

You stop waiting to feel ready.

You begin preparing while moving.

You stop demanding certainty.

You begin trusting your ability to learn along the way.

That shift changes the trajectory of your life.

Many opportunities are missed not because people lack talent, but because they believe they must become confident before taking action.

In reality, action is often what creates confidence.

Experience creates perspective.

Perspective reduces fear.

Reduced fear strengthens confidence.

Confidence encourages greater action.

And the cycle continues.

Do not allow uncertainty to convince you that you are unqualified to begin.

Every person you admire once stood exactly where you are.

Unsure.

Inexperienced.

Wondering whether they were capable.

The difference is that they took the next step anyway.

They allowed action to teach them what waiting never could.

Remember that courage is not the absence of fear.

It is the willingness to move while fear is still present.

The future you desire will always require you to step into unfamiliar territory.

Do not wait until the path feels completely comfortable.

Take the next faithful step.

Learn what it has to teach you.

Then take another.

One day, you will look back and realize that the confidence you were waiting for was quietly being built every time you chose courage over hesitation.

That is the kind of confidence that lasts.

Not because it was given to you.

But because it was earned through faithful action, one intentional step at a time.

WEALTH LESSON

Action creates confidence because experience strengthens self-trust over time.

AFFIRMATION

"I move forward courageously even when confidence feels incomplete."

TODAY'S POWER MOVE

Take one action today that you have been postponing because of self-doubt or fear.

DAY 346

Your Emotional Stability Will Protect Your Success

POWER QUOTE

"Success becomes difficult to sustain when emotional chaos controls decision-making."

REFLECTION

Many people spend years preparing themselves for success while neglecting the one thing that determines whether they can sustain it.

Their emotional health.

They pursue promotions.

Build businesses.

Increase their income.

Expand their influence.

Yet they rarely stop to ask whether they are becoming emotionally strong enough to carry the responsibilities they are working so hard to obtain.

Success magnifies whatever already exists within you.

If your life is built on wisdom, success often creates greater influence.

If it is built on emotional instability, success can magnify pressure, insecurity, and unhealthy patterns.

That is why emotional maturity is not separate from achievement.

It is one of its greatest foundations.

A calm mind sees opportunities that panic often overlooks.

An emotionally regulated person makes wiser financial decisions because they are less controlled by fear and impulse.

A healthy leader creates environments where people feel respected, valued, and safe to grow.

Strong relationships flourish when emotional maturity is stronger than emotional reactivity.

None of these qualities develop by accident.

They are built through intentional practice.

Learning to pause before reacting.

Choosing understanding before defensiveness.

Accepting correction without allowing pride to take control.

Responding to pressure with wisdom instead of panic.

These moments may appear ordinary.

Yet they prepare you for extraordinary responsibility.

Many people ask for greater opportunities.

Few ask whether their emotional character is prepared to carry them.

Responsibility tests more than your knowledge.

It tests your patience.

Your humility.

Your integrity.

Your ability to remain steady when expectations increase.

Without emotional maturity, even good opportunities can become overwhelming.

This is why healing matters.

Healing allows you to lead from peace instead of unresolved pain.

It allows you to make decisions based on wisdom instead of fear.

It helps you create stability instead of spreading unnecessary chaos.

The strongest leaders are rarely the loudest people in the room.

They are often the calmest.

The ones who remain thoughtful during conflict.

The ones who create confidence instead of confusion.

The ones who listen before speaking.

The ones who refuse to let temporary emotions determine permanent decisions.

That kind of strength is developed over time.

It grows through repeated choices that most people never notice.

Every difficult conversation handled with grace strengthens your leadership.

Every financial decision guided by patience strengthens your stewardship.

Every moment you choose peace over panic strengthens your character.

Those quiet victories prepare you for the visible opportunities that will eventually come.

Never separate personal growth from professional success.

The person you become will always influence what you are able to sustain.

Continue investing in your emotional health with the same commitment you invest in your goals.

Protect your peace.

Practice self-awareness.

Strengthen your discipline.

Remain teachable.

Because your future will ask you to carry greater influence, greater opportunity, and greater responsibility.

The greatest preparation for that future is not simply gaining more knowledge.

It is becoming the kind of person who can carry success with humility, wisdom, emotional stability, and peace.

That is the kind of success that not only reaches great heights—but remains there with integrity.

WEALTH LESSON

Emotional regulation strengthens long-term success because stable minds create wiser decisions.

AFFIRMATION

"I strengthen my emotional stability and protect my future intentionally."

TODAY'S POWER MOVE

Practice emotional calmness today during a stressful or frustrating moment.

DAY 347

Stop Comparing Your Healing Journey

POWER QUOTE

"Everyone heals, grows, and rebuilds at different speeds."

REFLECTION

Comparison has a quiet way of stealing joy from progress.

It convinces people that their growth is only valuable if it looks like someone else's.

They begin asking questions that slowly erode hope.

"Why am I not further ahead?"

"Why does healing still take so much effort?"

"Why does everyone else seem to be moving faster than I am?"

The problem with those questions is not that they come from a place of curiosity.

They often come from a place of comparison.

Comparison rarely tells the whole story.

You see someone else's confidence.

You rarely see the years they spent rebuilding after failure.

You see someone else's success.

You rarely see the sacrifices, disappointments, and private battles that shaped it.

You see someone's peace.

You rarely see the healing that made that peace possible.

Every person carries a different story.

Different experiences.

Different wounds.

Different responsibilities.

Different opportunities.

That is why healing cannot be measured against someone else's timeline.

Some people are rebuilding from childhood pain.

Others are recovering from financial hardship.

Some are learning healthy relationships for the very first time.

Others are breaking patterns that have existed in their family for generations.

Those journeys cannot be compared fairly.

Growth is deeply personal.

It deserves patience.

Not constant measurement against another person's progress.

A healthier question is not,

"Why am I not where they are?"

A healthier question is,

"Am I becoming healthier than I was yesterday?"

That question keeps your attention where it belongs.

On your own growth.

Your own healing.

Your own responsibilities.

Your own opportunities.

Real progress is often quieter than people expect.

You may still have difficult days.

But perhaps you recover more quickly than you once did.

You may still experience fear.

But now you move forward despite it.

You may still face financial challenges.

But now you respond with planning instead of panic.

Those changes matter.

They may seem small.

Yet they are evidence that transformation is taking place.

Do not dismiss your progress simply because it is gradual.

The strongest trees do not grow overnight.

The deepest roots develop slowly beneath the surface long before anyone notices the branches.

Character grows in much the same way.

The patience you are practicing today.

The discipline you continue choosing.

The healthier boundaries you are establishing.

The emotional maturity you are developing.

These things are quietly preparing you for a future that could not have been sustained by the person you used to be.

Celebrate progress without demanding perfection.

Honor your journey without comparing it to another person's.

Keep your eyes on the direction you are moving instead of the distance someone else has traveled.

Your life is not behind.

It is unfolding according to lessons that are uniquely shaping you.

Keep rebuilding.

Keep learning.

Keep showing yourself grace.

Because the goal was never to become someone else.

The goal has always been to become the healthiest, wisest, and most faithful version of yourself.

And every intentional step you take is bringing you closer to that person, one day at a time.

WEALTH LESSON

Self-compassion strengthens resilience because comparison often weakens confidence and emotional stability.

AFFIRMATION

"I honor my own healing journey without comparing it to others."

TODAY'S POWER MOVE

Acknowledge one area today where you know you have grown emotionally stronger than before.

DAY 348

Your Future Requires Better Emotional Habits

POWER QUOTE

"Emotional habits shape life outcomes more than people realize."

REFLECTION

Every day, life gives you opportunities to practice your emotional habits.

You practice them when plans suddenly change.

When someone disappoints you.

When conflict enters a relationship.

When unexpected financial pressure appears.

When fear whispers that giving up would be easier than continuing.

These moments often seem ordinary.

Yet they reveal something important.

They reveal the habits your emotions have been practicing.

Many people think character is revealed only during life's biggest moments.

In reality, character is revealed in ordinary moments repeated over time.

The way you respond to stress today influences how you will respond to greater responsibility tomorrow.

The way you handle disappointment today shapes how you will approach future setbacks.

The way you communicate during conflict becomes the foundation of your closest relationships.

Your emotional habits quietly become your emotional patterns.

Those patterns eventually become your identity.

And your identity influences nearly every decision you make.

This is why emotional discipline matters so deeply.

Every healthy response strengthens the person you are becoming.

Each time you pause before reacting, you strengthen self-control.

Each time you choose honesty instead of defensiveness, you strengthen humility.

Each time you forgive instead of holding onto resentment, you strengthen emotional freedom.

Each time you remain faithful to your values instead of following temporary emotions, you strengthen your character.

These decisions may seem small.

Together, they shape an entirely different future.

Healthier emotional habits create healthier relationships because trust grows where consistency exists.

They create healthier financial decisions because fear and impulse no longer control every choice.

They create healthier communication because understanding becomes more important than simply being right.

They create healthier environments because people feel safer around someone who responds with wisdom instead of constant emotional volatility.

One of the greatest gifts you can give yourself is the commitment to practice healthy emotional habits before life demands them.

Patience is easier to maintain when it has been practiced.

Peace is easier to protect when it has become a daily habit.

Wisdom is easier to apply when it has been cultivated through countless ordinary decisions.

Do not underestimate the influence of today's responses.

Every conversation.

Every disappointment.

Every temptation.

Every unexpected challenge.

Each one is another opportunity to strengthen your emotional foundation.

Remember that your future is not determined by one emotional reaction.

It is shaped by the patterns you consistently repeat.

Choose patterns that build the life you truly want.

Respond thoughtfully instead of impulsively.

Communicate with honesty and compassion.

Protect your peace without abandoning your values.

Continue showing up with discipline even when your emotions fluctuate.

Over time, those choices become part of who you are.

And one day, people may admire your wisdom, your calmness, your resilience, and your stability.

What they may never realize is that those qualities were not developed overnight.

They were built through thousands of ordinary moments when you quietly chose growth over reaction, discipline over impulse, and wisdom over temporary emotion.

That is how lasting transformation happens.

One healthy response.

One intentional decision.

One faithful day at a time.

WEALTH LESSON

Emotional discipline improves long-term outcomes because intentional emotional behavior strengthens decision-making.

AFFIRMATION

"I intentionally build healthier emotional habits every day."

TODAY'S POWER MOVE

Practice one healthier emotional response today instead of reacting automatically.

DAY 349

Stop Believing You Must Suffer Forever

POWER QUOTE

"Healing and peace are possible even after difficult seasons."

REFLECTION

Pain has a way of shaping expectations.

When someone has lived through enough disappointment, they may begin expecting more of it.

When life has been marked by instability, peace can begin feeling unfamiliar.

When relationships have repeatedly caused hurt, trust can seem impossible.

Over time, pain can quietly convince a person that suffering is simply who they are.

But pain is an experience.

It is not an identity.

It may describe a chapter of your life.

It does not have to define the rest of your story.

One of the greatest victories in healing is learning to separate what happened to you from who you are becoming.

Your past may explain some of your fears.

It does not have to determine your future.

Many people unknowingly remain trapped because they stop believing change is possible.

They expect every relationship to end the same way.

Every opportunity to disappoint them.

Every season to become another struggle.

Those expectations influence their decisions.

They stop taking healthy risks.

They avoid trusting people who have earned trust.

They settle for environments that no longer serve them because familiar pain feels safer than unfamiliar healing.

Hope interrupts that cycle.

Hope is not pretending life has never been difficult.

It is believing that difficulty does not have the final word.

It allows you to imagine a future that looks different from your past.

A future where peace becomes familiar.

Where healthy relationships become normal.

Where financial stability replaces constant fear.

Where emotional maturity replaces survival mode.

That future is built one decision at a time.

Every healthy boundary challenges an old pattern.

Every act of forgiveness loosens the grip of bitterness.

Every disciplined habit proves that growth is possible.

Every wise decision becomes evidence that your story is still changing.

Healing often happens so gradually that you may not notice it while it is taking place.

Then one day, you respond calmly to something that once would have overwhelmed you.

You walk away from an unhealthy environment without questioning your worth.

You experience peace in situations that once filled you with anxiety.

In those moments, you realize something beautiful has happened.

You are no longer living from the identity your pain tried to give you.

You are living from the identity your healing has been building.

Never allow your hardest season to become the standard by which you measure the rest of your life.

You are allowed to expect healthier relationships.

You are allowed to believe peace is possible.

You are allowed to build a stable future even if your past felt unstable.

Growth requires that kind of hope.

Because hopelessness keeps people standing still, while hope gives them the courage to take the next step.

Keep choosing that next step.

Keep rebuilding.

Keep believing that your life can become healthier than it has ever been before.

The pain you have experienced may always be part of your story.

But it does not have to be the chapter that defines your future.

Your identity is not found in what hurt you.

It is found in the person you are becoming through healing, wisdom, discipline, and faithful perseverance.

And that person is still being shaped, one intentional day at a time.

WEALTH LESSON

Hope strengthens resilience because people who believe growth is possible continue rebuilding intentionally.

AFFIRMATION

"I believe peace, healing, and stability are possible for my future."

TODAY'S POWER MOVE

Visualize one peaceful future you still deeply desire to create for yourself.

DAY 350

You Are Becoming Someone Different

POWER QUOTE

"Transformation happens through repeated intentional choices over time."

REFLECTION

One of the most encouraging truths about growth is that it often becomes visible only when you pause long enough to look back.

When you are living through the process, it can feel as though nothing is changing.

You still have difficult days.

You still make mistakes.

You still face uncertainty.

Because of that, it becomes easy to believe you are standing still.

But you are not the same person you were one year ago.

Think about the conversations you handle differently now.

The boundaries you are willing to establish.

The decisions you make with greater wisdom.

The habits you have strengthened.

The lessons you have learned through both success and disappointment.

Those changes did not happen overnight.

They happened quietly, one decision at a time.

Every time you responded with patience instead of anger, you were changing.

Every time you chose discipline instead of procrastination, you were changing.

Every time you protected your peace instead of entertaining unnecessary chaos, you were changing.

Every time you accepted responsibility instead of making excuses, you were changing.

Those moments may have seemed ordinary.

Together, they have been reconstructing your identity.

Transformation is rarely a single breakthrough.

It is gradual reconstruction.

Much like renovating a home, growth often happens one room at a time.

One habit is strengthened.

One unhealthy pattern is replaced.

One fear is confronted.

One relationship becomes healthier.

One financial decision becomes wiser.

Eventually, the entire structure begins to look different—not because everything changed at once, but because consistent improvements accumulated over time.

This is why reflection is so important.

If you only focus on how far you still have to go, you may overlook how far you have already come.

Take time to notice the victories that once felt impossible.

Perhaps you recover more quickly after disappointment.

Perhaps you communicate more honestly than you once did.

Perhaps you no longer tolerate environments that constantly drain your peace.

Perhaps your relationship with money has become more intentional.

These are not small changes.

They are evidence that your character is growing.

Growth does not require perfection.

It requires movement.

As long as you continue learning, healing, and adjusting, your life is moving in the right direction.

There will always be another lesson to learn.

Another habit to strengthen.

Another opportunity to mature.

That is not a sign that you are failing.

It is a sign that you are alive and continuing to grow.

Celebrate your progress without becoming complacent.

Honor your past without allowing it to define you.

Keep building with humility and intention.

Because the person you are becoming today is preparing you for opportunities you cannot yet see.

One year from now, you may look back again and realize that today's quiet decisions became tomorrow's remarkable transformation.

So do not underestimate the power of today's choices.

Protect your peace.

Strengthen your discipline.

Continue healing.

Remain teachable.

Keep showing up for the life you are building.

Because your future is not being shaped by one extraordinary moment.

It is being shaped every single day by the person you choose to become.

And little by little, decision by decision, you are becoming someone wiser, stronger, healthier, and more capable than the person who first began this journey.

That is the quiet miracle of faithful growth.

WEALTH LESSON

Repeated intentional behavior compounds into long-term emotional and financial transformation.

AFFIRMATION

"I continue evolving into the strongest and healthiest version of myself."

TODAY'S POWER MOVE

Reflect today on how much healthier, wiser, or more disciplined you have become over time.

DAY 351

Stop Letting Fear Of Failure Stop Your Growth

POWER QUOTE

"Fear of failure often creates failure through inaction."

REFLECTION

Many people remain stuck for one reason that often goes unnoticed.

They are not unwilling to grow.

They are afraid to make mistakes.

The fear of getting it wrong becomes stronger than the desire to move forward.

So they wait.

They wait until they feel more confident.

They wait until they know every answer.

They wait until the timing feels perfect.

They wait until failure no longer feels possible.

But that day rarely comes.

Growth has never required certainty.

It has always required courage.

Every meaningful accomplishment includes moments of uncertainty.

Every successful person has made decisions they later wished they had handled differently.

Every healthy relationship has required uncomfortable conversations.

Every wise investor has experienced setbacks.

Every great leader has made mistakes.

Failure is not evidence that you are incapable.

It is evidence that you are learning something new.

The person who never makes mistakes is often the person who never attempts anything that stretches them.

Growth requires movement.

And movement always carries the possibility of getting something wrong.

The goal is not to eliminate mistakes.

The goal is to become someone who learns from them.

Each setback has something to teach you.

Each disappointment can refine your perspective.

Each challenge can strengthen your character if you allow it to.

Many of life's greatest lessons cannot be learned from observation alone.

They are learned through experience.

Through trying.

Adjusting.

Trying again.

This is why resilience matters so much.

Resilient people do not believe they will never fail.

They simply refuse to believe that failure is the end of their story.

They understand that every mistake is temporary unless they stop growing from it.

Think about a child learning to walk.

No one expects perfection after the first attempt.

Falling is part of learning.

Getting back up is part of learning.

Eventually, what once seemed impossible becomes natural because they continued despite repeated failures.

Life continues teaching us in much the same way.

Every challenge is an invitation to become wiser.

Every setback is an opportunity to develop greater humility, patience, and perseverance.

The only true failure is allowing fear to convince you that you should never begin.

Do not allow perfectionism to disguise itself as wisdom.

Sometimes perfectionism is simply fear wearing a different name.

It promises protection.

Instead, it quietly steals opportunities.

Take the next step even if you do not have every answer.

Trust that experience will teach you what preparation alone never could.

Learn.

Adjust.

Grow.

Then keep moving forward.

Your future is not waiting for a flawless version of you.

It is waiting for a faithful one.

Someone willing to keep learning after mistakes.

Someone willing to keep rebuilding after disappointment.

Someone willing to keep believing that progress is still possible.

One decision.

One lesson.

One courageous step at a time.

Because every mistake you learn from becomes part of the wisdom that shapes the person you are becoming.

And over time, you will realize that your greatest growth did not happen because you avoided failure.

It happened because you refused to let failure stop you from becoming the person you were created to be.

WEALTH LESSON

Calculated action creates growth because experience teaches lessons that fear alone never will.

AFFIRMATION

"I release the fear of failure and continue moving forward courageously."

TODAY'S POWER MOVE

Take one action today that you have been delaying because of fear of making mistakes.

DAY 352

Your Future Deserves Emotional Stability

POWER QUOTE

"A peaceful mind builds differently than an overwhelmed one."

REFLECTION

Every decision you make passes through the filter of your emotional state.

When your emotions are healthy, you often think more clearly.

You communicate with greater wisdom.

You respond with patience instead of impulse.

You plan for the future instead of reacting only to the present.

When your emotions are consistently overwhelmed, however, every area of life can begin to suffer.

Pressure feels heavier than it really is.

Small disagreements become major conflicts.

Financial decisions become reactive instead of intentional.

Relationships become strained because emotions begin speaking louder than wisdom.

This is why emotional stability is not simply about feeling calm.

It is about creating a foundation strong enough to support every other area of your life.

Emotional stability allows you to pause before reacting.

To listen before defending yourself.

To consider long-term consequences before making short-term decisions.

It creates the space where wisdom has an opportunity to lead.

Many people assume emotionally strong individuals never experience fear, frustration, or disappointment.

The opposite is true.

Emotionally mature people experience the same emotions everyone else does.

The difference is that they have learned not to surrender control of their decisions to temporary feelings.

They acknowledge their emotions without allowing those emotions to become their identity.

They recognize disappointment without becoming defeated.

They experience pressure without abandoning their values.

They face uncertainty without allowing panic to determine their direction.

That kind of stability is developed one response at a time.

Every difficult conversation handled with patience strengthens emotional maturity.

Every stressful situation approached with wisdom strengthens resilience.

Every financial decision made thoughtfully instead of impulsively strengthens self-control.

These moments may seem insignificant.

Yet together they become the habits that shape your character.

Over time, emotional discipline begins influencing every part of your life.

Your relationships become healthier because people feel heard instead of attacked.

Your finances become stronger because your decisions are guided by planning rather than fear.

Your leadership becomes steadier because you remain dependable even during difficult seasons.

Your peace becomes deeper because your emotional stability no longer depends entirely on external circumstances.

This is why emotional health deserves the same attention you give your goals.

Achievement without emotional maturity often creates unnecessary stress.

Success without inner stability can become difficult to sustain.

The healthiest lives are not built by eliminating every challenge.

They are built by becoming the kind of person who can carry challenges with wisdom, patience, and self-control.

Continue strengthening your emotional habits.

Practice responding instead of reacting.

Protect your peace without withdrawing from responsibility.

Allow difficult seasons to teach you resilience instead of convincing you to give up.

Because every emotionally healthy response is shaping the person you are becoming.

And one day, you will realize that your greatest strength was never the absence of pressure.

It was your ability to remain grounded while carrying it.

That is the kind of strength that creates healthy relationships, wise decisions, lasting influence, and a future built on peace instead of panic.

One intentional response at a time.

WEALTH LESSON

Emotional regulation improves decision-making because calm thinking creates healthier long-term outcomes.

AFFIRMATION

"I strengthen my emotional stability and protect my peace intentionally."

TODAY'S POWER MOVE

Practice emotional calmness today during one stressful situation.

DAY 353

Stop Doubting Your Ability To Rebuild

POWER QUOTE

"You have survived difficult seasons before, and you can rebuild again."

REFLECTION

There are seasons in life that leave people feeling emotionally drained.

Dreams take longer than expected.

Plans fall apart.

Relationships change.

Financial pressure increases.

Confidence begins to weaken.

During those moments, it can become difficult to imagine that life will ever feel different.

Discouragement has a way of convincing people that today's reality is tomorrow's certainty.

But it is not.

One difficult season does not determine the rest of your life.

One setback does not erase your potential.

One disappointment does not cancel your purpose.

Life has always been filled with stories of rebuilding.

People rebuild confidence after years of self-doubt.

They rebuild their finances after painful mistakes.

They rebuild relationships through honesty, forgiveness, and trust.

They rediscover purpose after seasons of uncertainty.

They rebuild their identity after realizing they have outgrown the version of themselves that once lived in survival mode.

Rebuilding is not a sign that you failed.

It is a sign that you refused to stay broken.

Some of the strongest people you will ever meet are not those who avoided hardship.

They are the people who kept showing up after hardship changed everything.

They learned to begin again.

Again.

And again.

Each new beginning strengthened something inside them.

Resilience.

Humility.

Wisdom.

Patience.

Faith.

These qualities are rarely developed during easy seasons.

They are forged through perseverance when giving up would have been easier.

Take a moment to recognize how far you have already come.

You have survived days you once believed would overwhelm you.

You have carried burdens you never expected to carry.

You have learned lessons that comfort alone could never have taught you.

Even if your journey is not finished, your progress deserves to be acknowledged.

Too often, people overlook their own resilience because they focus only on how much farther they want to go.

But resilience is not measured only by reaching the destination.

It is measured by your willingness to keep moving despite the obstacles along the way.

Every time you choose hope instead of hopelessness, you rebuild.

Every time you keep a promise to yourself, you rebuild.

Every healthy boundary.

Every wise financial decision.

Every difficult conversation handled with maturity.

Every act of forgiveness.

Every moment you choose growth over giving up becomes another piece of the life you are creating.

Do not underestimate those moments.

They may feel ordinary today.

One day, they will become the foundation of the person you are proud to be.

Remember that rebuilding is rarely dramatic.

It usually happens quietly.

One decision.

One habit.

One courageous step at a time.

There may still be difficult days ahead.

But there will also be new opportunities.

New relationships.

New wisdom.

New strength.

The future is still being written.

And every day you continue choosing healing, discipline, and intentional growth, you are writing a different chapter than the one your pain tried to convince you was permanent.

Keep rebuilding.

Keep believing.

Keep moving forward.

Because the fact that you are still learning, still healing, and still willing to grow is already evidence of something powerful.

You are far stronger than the circumstances that tried to convince you to stop.

And the person you are becoming through this journey will one day become the greatest testimony that resilience is built one faithful step at a time.

WEALTH LESSON

Resilience creates opportunity because people who continue rebuilding create new possibilities for growth.

AFFIRMATION

"I trust myself to rebuild stronger and wiser than before."

TODAY'S POWER MOVE

Take one small intentional action today that supports rebuilding an important area of your life.

DAY 354

Your Habits Quietly Create Your Future

POWER QUOTE

"Your daily routines eventually become your life."

REFLECTION

Many people spend most of their energy thinking about the future they want.

A stronger career.

Healthier relationships.

Financial freedom.

Greater peace.

A life filled with purpose.

These goals are meaningful.

But goals alone do not shape the future.

Habits do.

Every day, whether you realize it or not, your routines are building tomorrow's reality.

The way you begin your morning.

The way you manage your money.

The way you respond when life becomes stressful.

The way you spend your free time.

The conversations you choose to have.

The boundaries you choose to protect.

Each decision may seem insignificant on its own.

Yet together, they create the direction of your life.

Many people wait for one extraordinary opportunity to transform everything.

In reality, transformation is usually the result of ordinary choices repeated with extraordinary consistency.

A healthy future is rarely created by one healthy meal.

It is created by years of intentional nourishment.

Financial stability is rarely created by one wise purchase.

It is built through countless thoughtful financial decisions.

Strong relationships are not sustained by one meaningful conversation.

They are strengthened through daily trust, honesty, patience, and consistency.

Everything meaningful compounds over time.

This is why habits deserve more attention than momentary emotions.

Feelings change.

Circumstances change.

Motivation rises and falls.

Healthy habits continue working long after excitement has disappeared.

Every repeated action becomes a vote for the person you are becoming.

Each time you choose discipline over distraction, you strengthen your focus.

Each time you choose planning over impulse, you strengthen your future.

Each time you protect your peace instead of entertaining unnecessary chaos, you strengthen your emotional health.

One decision may seem small.

A thousand similar decisions can change an entire life.

Ask yourself a simple question:

"What habits are quietly creating the future I will eventually live?"

That question shifts your attention away from wishing and toward intentional living.

Because the future is not built only by major milestones.

It is built by ordinary Tuesdays.

Quiet mornings.

Faithful evenings.

Small choices that no one else notices.

Those moments deserve your attention because they shape your character.

And character eventually shapes everything else.

Do not underestimate today's routines simply because today's results seem small.

Seeds are planted long before they become trees.

Bricks are laid one at a time before they become homes.

Character is strengthened one decision at a time before it becomes visible through a transformed life.

Protect the habits that move you toward the person you hope to become.

Guard your time.

Manage your resources wisely.

Practice emotional discipline.

Choose intentionality over autopilot.

Because every ordinary day is quietly becoming part of an extraordinary future.

One habit.

One decision.

One faithful step at a time.

That is how meaningful lives are built—not through occasional moments of greatness, but through consistent choices that honor the future you are creating every single day.

WEALTH LESSON

Repeated disciplined habits compound into long-term emotional and financial growth.

AFFIRMATION

"I intentionally build habits that strengthen my future daily."

TODAY'S POWER MOVE

Commit to one healthy habit today that aligns with the future you want to create.

DAY 355

Stop Carrying Every Burden Alone

POWER QUOTE

"Strength does not always mean suffering silently."

REFLECTION

Many people have learned to carry every burden by themselves.

They tell themselves they should be strong enough to handle everything alone.

They keep their struggles private.

They hide their emotions.

They convince themselves that asking for help is a sign of weakness.

Over time, this mindset becomes exhausting.

The weight they were never meant to carry alone slowly begins affecting every area of their life.

Their patience becomes shorter.

Their joy becomes harder to find.

Their relationships become more distant.

Even small responsibilities begin feeling overwhelming because emotional exhaustion has quietly accumulated beneath the surface.

Strength was never meant to mean isolation.

Real strength is the willingness to face reality with honesty.

Sometimes that means admitting you are tired.

Sometimes it means acknowledging that you are hurting.

Sometimes it means allowing trusted people to walk beside you while you rebuild.

Healing often requires connection.

Not because other people can do the work for you.

But because healthy support reminds you that you do not have to face every challenge in isolation.

Think about a tree growing during a storm.

Its strength is not found only in its trunk.

Its roots also depend on the stability of the ground surrounding them.

People are much the same.

We grow best when our lives include healthy relationships, wise counsel, and emotionally safe environments.

There is wisdom in knowing when to lean on others.

Not everyone deserves access to your most vulnerable places.

Healthy discernment still matters.

Choose people who encourage truth instead of enabling unhealthy patterns.

Choose people who challenge you to grow instead of keeping you comfortable in destructive habits.

Choose relationships where honesty is welcomed and healing is supported.

Those kinds of connections become part of the foundation that helps you remain steady during difficult seasons.

Remember that vulnerability is not weakness.

It is courage.

It takes courage to admit you need encouragement.

It takes courage to ask for help.

It takes courage to let someone see the parts of your story that are still healing.

Yet those moments often become the beginning of deeper freedom.

Healing accelerates when shame loses its power through honest conversation.

Hope grows stronger when it is shared with people who genuinely care.

Perspective expands when someone reminds you of truths you struggle to remember on your own.

Even the strongest people need rest.

They need encouragement.

They need places where they can stop performing and simply be honest.

Give yourself permission to receive those gifts.

You are not failing because you need support.

You are recognizing a reality that every healthy person eventually learns.

Life was never designed to be carried alone.

Continue taking responsibility for your own growth.

Continue doing the work that healing requires.

But do not confuse independence with isolation.

Sometimes one conversation restores hope.

Sometimes one encouraging voice strengthens your resolve.

Sometimes one trusted relationship becomes part of the reason you continue moving forward.

Your future deserves that kind of support.

Because rebuilding is not only about becoming stronger on your own.

It is also about becoming wise enough to recognize that healthy connection is one of the greatest strengths you can have.

Keep growing.

Keep healing.

And remember that allowing trusted people to walk beside you is not a sign that you are weak.

It is often a sign that you are becoming whole.

WEALTH LESSON

Healthy support systems improve emotional resilience because connected people often handle stress more effectively long-term.

AFFIRMATION

"I allow healthy support, connection, and emotional honesty into my life."

TODAY'S POWER MOVE

Reach out today to someone safe and supportive instead of carrying everything internally alone.

DAY 356

Your Discipline Is Rewriting Your Story

POWER QUOTE

"Every intentional decision changes the direction of your future."

REFLECTION

Your past has influenced your story.

But it does not have the authority to write the rest of it.

Many people spend years believing they are permanently defined by what has already happened.

The mistakes they made.

The opportunities they missed.

The relationships that ended.

The financial decisions they regret.

The pain they experienced.

Those experiences become so familiar that they begin feeling like identity instead of history.

But your life is not shaped only by where you have been.

It is shaped by the choices you continue making today.

Every intentional decision becomes another sentence in the story you are writing.

Every healthy boundary changes the direction of your relationships.

Every disciplined financial choice strengthens your future.

Every moment you choose healing instead of unhealthy coping patterns rewrites the person you are becoming.

Every act of integrity strengthens the foundation beneath your life.

Transformation does not happen because your past suddenly disappears.

It happens because your present decisions become stronger than your past patterns.

This is why today's choices carry so much significance.

One day of discipline may seem small.

One healthy conversation may seem ordinary.

One wise financial decision may appear insignificant.

Yet these moments are never isolated.

They accumulate.

Each one quietly moves your life in a new direction.

Imagine a ship crossing the ocean.

A small adjustment to its course may seem almost invisible at first.

But after hundreds of miles, that tiny change leads to an entirely different destination.

Your daily decisions work the same way.

Small changes in direction create extraordinary differences over time.

Choosing to protect your peace today influences tomorrow's relationships.

Choosing to save instead of overspend today strengthens next year's financial stability.

Choosing forgiveness instead of bitterness today creates emotional freedom that will shape future opportunities.

None of these decisions seem dramatic in the moment.

Together, they transform a life.

This is why hope is so powerful.

Hope reminds you that your story is still unfolding.

You are not trapped by yesterday's choices.

You are invited to make wiser ones today.

The person you are becoming is not determined by your worst chapter.

It is determined by the direction you continue choosing from this point forward.

Do not underestimate the influence of consistency.

Character is built one decision at a time.

Peace is protected one boundary at a time.

Wisdom is developed one lesson at a time.

Confidence is strengthened one kept promise at a time.

Eventually, you may look back and realize that your life looks remarkably different.

Not because one extraordinary moment changed everything.

But because thousands of ordinary decisions quietly reshaped your future.

So keep making the next wise choice.

Keep honoring your commitments.

Keep protecting your peace.

Keep investing in your growth.

Every intentional decision is another step away from old limitations and another step toward the life you are building.

Your story is still being written.

Write it with discipline.

Write it with courage.

Write it with hope.

Because the future version of your life will not simply be the result of what happened to you.

It will be the result of who you chose to become, one faithful decision at a time.

WEALTH LESSON

Repeated disciplined behavior compounds into long-term emotional and financial transformation.

AFFIRMATION

"I intentionally rewrite my future through discipline and growth."

TODAY'S POWER MOVE

Make one intentional decision today that supports the future story you want to create.

DAY 357

Stop Letting Temporary Emotions Decide Permanent Outcomes

POWER QUOTE

"A temporary feeling should not control a permanent decision."

REFLECTION

Emotions are powerful.

They can encourage you.

Warn you.

Inspire you.

Help you recognize what matters.

But emotions were never designed to lead every decision you make.

They were designed to inform you, not control you.

The challenge is that emotions are constantly changing.

A difficult conversation can make you want to quit.

A disappointing day can make you question your future.

Stress can tempt you to overspend.

Loneliness can tempt you to return to unhealthy relationships.

Fear can convince you to abandon opportunities before they even begin.

If every decision is made according to your emotions in the moment, your life will constantly change direction.

This is why emotional maturity is so valuable.

Emotionally mature people still experience disappointment.

They still feel anxiety.

They still become frustrated.

They still have moments when they want to give up.

The difference is not the absence of emotion.

The difference is the presence of self-control.

They have learned to pause before reacting.

They understand that not every feeling requires immediate action.

Sometimes the wisest decision is simply to wait.

To breathe.

To pray.

To reflect.

To allow emotions to settle before making choices that could shape the future.

That pause creates something powerful.

It creates space for wisdom.

Many of life's greatest regrets are not caused by emotions themselves.

They are caused by decisions made before emotions had time to settle.

Words spoken in anger.

Money spent impulsively.

Relationships abandoned during temporary discouragement.

Goals surrendered because one difficult day felt like permanent failure.

A single emotional moment should never be given the authority to determine the direction of your entire life.
Instead, ask yourself:
"Will this decision still make sense when my emotions become calmer?"
That simple question creates perspective.
It reminds you that feelings are temporary, while many decisions carry lasting consequences.
Every time you choose to respond thoughtfully instead of impulsively, you strengthen emotional discipline.
Every time you continue honoring your values despite fluctuating emotions, you strengthen your character.
Every time you refuse to let temporary discomfort determine permanent choices, you build resilience.
These moments become part of your identity.
Over time, you stop being controlled by every emotional wave that comes your way.
You become anchored.
Not because life has become easier.
But because you have become steadier.
That kind of stability influences every area of your life.
Your relationships become healthier because you communicate with greater patience.
Your finances become stronger because impulse no longer controls your spending.
Your goals become more attainable because you continue working even when motivation fades.
Your peace becomes deeper because your emotions no longer dictate every decision.
Remember that strength is not found in pretending you do not have emotions.
Strength is found in learning how to experience them honestly without allowing them to become your master.
Feel what you feel.
Acknowledge it.
Learn from it.
Then choose your response with wisdom.
Because your future deserves decisions rooted in character instead of temporary emotion.
And every time you choose thoughtful action over impulsive reaction, you become someone who can be trusted with greater responsibility, greater opportunity, and greater peace.
That is the quiet strength of emotional maturity.
One intentional response at a time.

WEALTH LESSON

Emotional regulation strengthens long-term stability because intentional decisions create healthier outcomes than impulsive reactions.

AFFIRMATION

"I pause, think clearly, and make intentional long-term decisions."

TODAY'S POWER MOVE

Before reacting emotionally today, ask yourself whether your response aligns with your future goals.

DAY 358

Your Future Needs Focused Energy

POWER QUOTE

"Distraction weakens momentum."

REFLECTION

One of the greatest threats to meaningful growth is not always a lack of ability.

Often, it is a lack of focus.

Many people begin each day with good intentions.

They want to build healthier habits.

Strengthen their finances.

Protect their peace.

Move closer to their goals.

But before long, their attention has been pulled in a dozen different directions.

One notification interrupts their work.

One comparison steals their confidence.

One unnecessary conversation drains their energy.

One distraction turns into an hour of lost time.

Individually, these moments seem insignificant.

Together, they quietly weaken consistency.

Attention is one of the most valuable resources you possess.

Whatever consistently receives your attention will eventually influence your thoughts.

Your thoughts influence your decisions.

Your decisions influence your habits.

Your habits shape your future.

That is why protecting your attention is not simply about productivity.

It is about protecting the direction of your life.

Focused people understand this principle.

They recognize that saying yes to everything usually means saying no to what matters most.

They guard their routines because routines protect momentum.

They guard their time because time cannot be replaced.

They guard their emotional energy because they understand that constant distraction leaves little capacity for meaningful work.

This does not mean they never experience interruptions.

It means they intentionally return their attention to what matters.

Again.

And again.

Every time you resist unnecessary distraction, you strengthen your ability to concentrate.

Every time you choose purposeful work over endless comparison, you reinforce your priorities.

Every time you protect your emotional energy instead of giving it away to unnecessary conflict, you strengthen your peace.

These choices compound.

A focused hour each day becomes hundreds of productive hours over a year.

A protected morning routine becomes years of steady discipline.

A habit of intentional attention becomes a life marked by meaningful progress.

Ask yourself honestly:

"What consistently receives my attention?"

"Is it moving me toward the life I want to build, or away from it?"

Those questions reveal more than many people realize.

Because your future is often created by whatever repeatedly captures your focus.

You cannot build an intentional life with scattered attention.

The life you hope to create deserves more than occasional concentration.

It deserves consistent presence.

Protect your routines.

Protect your time.

Protect your peace.

Limit unnecessary comparison.

Reduce unnecessary noise.

Create space where your mind can think clearly and your priorities can remain visible.

Remember that extraordinary lives are rarely built by people who gave equal attention to everything.

They are built by people who consistently gave their best attention to what mattered most.

Your focus is an investment.

Spend it wisely.

Because every moment you intentionally direct your attention toward growth, healing, discipline, and purpose, you are quietly shaping the person you are becoming.

And over time, that focused consistency will produce results that scattered effort never could.

One protected hour.

One intentional habit.

One focused day at a time.

WEALTH LESSON

Focused attention improves productivity because intentional energy creates stronger long-term execution.

AFFIRMATION

"I protect my focus and direct my energy intentionally."

TODAY'S POWER MOVE

Spend uninterrupted focused time today working toward one meaningful goal.

DAY 359

Stop Believing Your Growth Is Invisible

POWER QUOTE

"Small internal growth still matters deeply."

REFLECTION

One of the greatest mistakes people make is believing that growth only counts when it is obvious.

They look for dramatic breakthroughs.

Major accomplishments.

Instant results.

Visible success.

When those things do not appear immediately, they begin believing that nothing is changing.

But some of life's most meaningful transformations happen long before anyone else can see them.

Healing usually begins in private.

No one notices the moment you choose forgiveness over bitterness.

No one applauds the day you decide to establish healthier boundaries.

No one sees the quiet battle you win when you refuse to return to an unhealthy habit.

Yet those moments matter.

In fact, they often matter more than the achievements people celebrate publicly.

Character is built long before it is recognized.

Confidence grows quietly each time you keep a promise to yourself.

Emotional maturity develops every time you pause before reacting.

Discipline becomes stronger every time you choose responsibility over convenience.

These victories rarely receive applause.

Yet they are changing you from the inside out.

Think about the roots of a tree.

Before branches stretch toward the sky, the roots grow deep beneath the surface.

No one standing above the ground can see that growth taking place.

But without those hidden roots, the tree could never withstand the storms that will eventually come.

Your life develops in much the same way.

The quiet work you are doing today is strengthening the foundation you will rely on tomorrow.

Perhaps you still experience difficult emotions.

But now you recover more quickly than you once did.

Perhaps you still face fear.

But now you continue moving forward despite it.

Perhaps you still encounter conflict.

But now you communicate with greater wisdom instead of reacting impulsively.

Those are not small changes.

They are evidence that transformation is already taking place.

Do not overlook the progress that cannot yet be measured by external results.

The way you think is changing.

The way you respond is changing.

The standards you accept are changing.

The habits you practice are changing.

The person you are becoming is changing.

Eventually, those internal changes begin producing visible results.

Healthier relationships.

Greater peace.

Stronger finances.

Steadier confidence.

Clearer purpose.

But those outcomes are the fruit.

The real work happened much earlier, in the quiet decisions no one else could see.

Be patient with the process.

Continue choosing the healthier response.

Continue protecting your peace.

Continue practicing discipline when no one is watching.

Continue honoring the commitments you have made to yourself.

Remember that transformation is rarely announced.

It is revealed.

One day, people may notice your confidence, your wisdom, your stability, or your resilience.

What they may never realize is that those qualities were built through hundreds of ordinary decisions made faithfully over time.

So do not become discouraged because today's growth feels invisible.

Invisible growth is still growth.

Hidden roots are still growing.

And the quiet work you continue doing today is preparing you for a future that will one day make perfect sense when you look back.

Keep trusting the process.

Keep showing up.

Keep growing.

Because the person you are becoming is already stronger than the person you used to be—even if the world has not fully seen it yet.

WEALTH LESSON

Compounding creates transformation because repeated intentional behavior strengthens growth gradually over time.

AFFIRMATION

"I trust that my growth is happening even when progress feels gradual."

TODAY'S POWER MOVE

Acknowledge one internal area today where you know you have become healthier or stronger emotionally.

DAY 360

You Are Building A New Identity

POWER QUOTE

"The person you repeatedly practice becoming eventually becomes real."

REFLECTION

Many people spend years trying to discover who they are.

They search for purpose.

They search for confidence.

They search for clarity.

They search for identity.

While self-discovery is valuable, identity is not only something you uncover.

It is also something you build.

Every decision you make is quietly teaching your mind who you believe you are.

When you consistently keep promises to yourself, you begin seeing yourself as dependable.

When you protect your peace instead of entertaining unnecessary chaos, you begin seeing yourself as someone worthy of healthy boundaries.

When you communicate with honesty instead of avoidance, you begin seeing yourself as emotionally mature.

When you choose discipline instead of convenience, you begin seeing yourself as someone capable of long-term success.

These repeated choices become evidence.

Your mind remembers that evidence.

Over time, it begins replacing old beliefs with new ones.

Many people struggle to change because they keep trying to create new outcomes while reinforcing the same identity.

They say they want to become disciplined, but they repeatedly tell themselves they are lazy.

They want financial freedom, but they continue believing they are simply "bad with money."

They want healthier relationships, but they continue identifying themselves by past heartbreak.

Those internal beliefs quietly influence future behavior.

Identity always shapes action.

If you believe you are someone who gives up easily, you will often look for reasons to quit.

If you believe you are someone who follows through, you will begin making decisions that reinforce that belief.

That is why transformation is built from the inside out.

Every healthy habit is more than a task.

It is a vote for the person you are becoming.

Every workout says,

"I am someone who cares for my health."

Every budget you follow says,

"I am someone who manages resources wisely."

Every difficult conversation handled with maturity says,

"I am someone who values honesty over avoidance."

Every peaceful response during conflict says,

"I am someone who refuses to let temporary emotions control permanent decisions."

These messages accumulate.

One decision rarely changes your identity.

Thousands of consistent decisions do.

Eventually, what once required tremendous effort begins feeling natural.

Not because the work became easier.

But because your identity has changed.

You no longer have to force yourself to become someone different.

You have been practicing that person every day.

This is why consistency matters more than intensity.

A single extraordinary day cannot replace months of faithful habits.

But small intentional choices, repeated long enough, reshape the way you think, behave, and live.

So be patient with yourself.

Do not become discouraged if your transformation feels gradual.

Identity is not reconstructed in one dramatic moment.

It is rebuilt through ordinary decisions that quietly become extraordinary over time.

Keep protecting your peace.

Keep strengthening your discipline.

Keep practicing emotional maturity.

Keep choosing integrity even when no one is watching.

Because every intentional decision is reinforcing the person you are becoming.

And one day, you will realize that the life you once hoped for became possible because you first became the kind of person who could faithfully sustain it.

That is the quiet power of identity.

It is not only discovered.

It is built—one thought, one habit, one decision, and one faithful day at a time.

WEALTH LESSON

Repeated intentional behavior reshapes identity because habits influence long-term emotional and financial outcomes.

AFFIRMATION

"I intentionally build the identity that aligns with my future."

TODAY'S POWER MOVE

Practice one behavior today that reflects the strongest version of yourself you are becoming.

DAY 361

Stop Letting Your Past Speak Louder Than Your Future

POWER QUOTE

"Your past may explain you, but it does not have to permanently define you."

REFLECTION

One of the greatest obstacles to growth is not always what happened in the past.

Sometimes it is the belief that the past must continue defining the future.

Many people become trapped in old versions of themselves.

They replay old mistakes until shame begins feeling like identity.

They revisit painful memories until fear becomes familiar.

They remember who they used to be so often that they struggle to imagine who they are still capable of becoming.

The past becomes a prison instead of a teacher.

But your past was never meant to become the ceiling for your future.

It contains lessons.

It contains wisdom.

It contains experiences that have shaped you.

It does not have to become the final definition of who you are.

People change.

Not overnight.

Not through wishful thinking.

But through repeated intentional choices made consistently over time.

Healing changes the way you think.

Discipline changes the way you behave.

Awareness changes the way you make decisions.

Every healthy habit weakens the influence of an unhealthy pattern.

Every wise decision strengthens a healthier identity.

Every time you choose peace instead of chaos, you prove that your past no longer has complete control over your present.

This is why it is so important to stop introducing yourself to your future through yesterday's failures.

Yes, acknowledge your mistakes.

Learn from them.

Take responsibility where necessary.

But do not build your identity around chapters that were never meant to become permanent.

The person who once struggled financially can become a wise steward.

The person who once lived in fear can become courageous.

The person who once reacted impulsively can become emotionally grounded.

The person who once believed they were broken can become someone who helps others heal.

Transformation makes those stories possible.

Many people wait until they feel completely different before believing they have changed.

Real growth often works the opposite way.

You choose differently first.

Then, over time, your identity begins catching up with your choices.

Each healthy decision becomes another piece of evidence that you are no longer the person you used to be.

Eventually, those small pieces of evidence become unshakable confidence.

You begin trusting yourself.

Believing in yourself.

Living differently because your mind has accepted a new identity.

Do not allow shame to keep introducing you to an outdated version of yourself.

You are not required to carry every mistake into every new season.

You are allowed to outgrow old survival patterns.

You are allowed to release identities that no longer reflect the person you are becoming.

You are allowed to expect more from your future than what your past once suggested was possible.

The strongest transformations happen when people stop asking,

"Who was I?"

and begin asking,

"Who am I becoming?"

That question creates hope.

It creates movement.

It creates purpose.

Because every day you continue choosing healing, discipline, wisdom, and intentional growth, you are writing a different story than the one your past tried to convince you was permanent.

Keep moving forward.

Keep learning.

Keep rebuilding.

Your history may explain where you started.

But your daily decisions are determining where your life is going.

And the person waiting for you in your future is not controlled by who you used to be.

They are being built by who you choose to become, one intentional day at a time.

WEALTH LESSON

Identity growth improves long-term outcomes because healthier beliefs influence healthier decisions and behaviors.

AFFIRMATION

"I release the limitations of my past and continue building my future intentionally."

TODAY'S POWER MOVE

Write down one old belief or identity you are ready to stop carrying into your future.

DAY 362

Your Future Requires Inner Peace

POWER QUOTE

"A successful life without inner peace eventually feels emotionally empty."

REFLECTION

Many people spend their lives chasing visible success.

A larger income.

Greater recognition.

Higher status.

More influence.

Bigger accomplishments.

None of these goals are wrong.

Achievement can create opportunities to serve others, provide for your family, and make a meaningful impact.

The danger comes when external success becomes the only definition of a successful life.

A person can appear successful to the world while privately feeling exhausted, anxious, and emotionally overwhelmed.

They may have financial wealth but no peace.

Professional influence but unhealthy relationships.

Public recognition but constant inner turmoil.

That is not the kind of success most people truly long for.

Real success should improve your life, not quietly consume it.

This is why emotional health deserves the same attention as achievement.

Peace is not a luxury you earn after reaching your goals.

It is one of the foundations that allows you to pursue those goals wisely.

A peaceful mind makes better decisions because it is not constantly reacting to fear or pressure.

A peaceful heart communicates with greater patience because it is not controlled by unresolved emotions.

A peaceful life creates space for gratitude, creativity, healthy relationships, and sustainable growth.

Without inner stability, even success can become another source of stress.

Countless individuals believe they need to sacrifice their emotional well-being to accomplish something meaningful.

But lasting success is rarely built through constant burnout.

It is built through sustainable discipline.

Healthy boundaries.

Wisc priorities.

Intentional rest.

Emotional maturity.

These qualities allow you to carry responsibility without allowing responsibility to carry you.

Ask yourself honestly:

"Am I only building a successful life, or am I building a healthy one?"

That question changes everything.

Because there is little value in reaching your destination if you no longer have the emotional capacity to enjoy it.

Your goals should not require you to abandon your peace.

Your ambition should not require you to neglect your health.

Your dreams should not require you to become someone you no longer recognize.

Instead, let your success be built on a strong foundation.

Protect your emotional health as intentionally as you protect your career.

Guard your relationships as carefully as you guard your finances.

Create space for reflection as consistently as you create space for work.

The healthiest people understand that achievement and peace are not enemies.

They strengthen one another.

A peaceful person often leads more wisely.

Makes better financial decisions.

Builds healthier relationships.

Thinks more clearly under pressure.

And remains faithful during seasons when others become overwhelmed.

That kind of success lasts.

Not because life becomes free from challenges.

But because the person carrying those challenges has developed the emotional strength to handle them with wisdom.

As you continue building your future, never measure success only by what people can see.

Measure it by the person you are becoming.

By the peace you are protecting.

By the integrity you are practicing.

By the relationships you are nurturing.

By the character you are strengthening.

Because the greatest success is not simply creating a life that looks impressive from the outside.

It is creating a life that feels healthy, purposeful, and deeply fulfilling from the inside.

That is the kind of success worth building—one intentional choice at a time.

WEALTH LESSON

Emotional peace improves long-term stability because calm minds create healthier decisions and environments.

AFFIRMATION

"I intentionally build a life rooted in peace, healing, and emotional stability."

TODAY'S POWER MOVE

Protect your emotional peace today by creating space for calmness and reflection.

DAY 363

Stop Underestimating The Power Of Consistency

POWER QUOTE

"Small disciplined actions repeated long enough create extraordinary change."

REFLECTION

People are naturally drawn to dramatic moments.

The breakthrough.

The promotion.

The business launch.

The debt finally paid off.

The major milestone everyone celebrates.

Those moments are exciting.

But they are rarely where transformation actually begins.

Transformation usually begins in places that feel ordinary.

A disciplined morning when you choose consistency instead of comfort.

A quiet evening when you decide to stick to your budget instead of making an emotional purchase.

A difficult conversation where you respond with patience instead of reacting impulsively.

A small promise you keep to yourself even though no one else will ever know.

These moments rarely attract attention.

Yet they quietly shape the direction of your life.

Many people underestimate the power of repetition because repetition often feels unimpressive.

Doing the same healthy habits every day can seem boring.

Reading a few pages.

Saving a little money.

Exercising consistently.

Praying faithfully.

Protecting your peace.

Practicing gratitude.

None of these actions appear dramatic by themselves.

But repetition creates momentum.

And momentum changes lives.

Think about water flowing over stone.

One drop does not seem powerful.

Yet over timc, constant movement reshapes solid rock.

Your daily habits work the same way.

Every wise financial decision strengthens your future.

Every healthy response strengthens your emotional maturity.

Every focused hour strengthens your discipline.

Every intentional choice strengthens your identity.

Eventually, those repeated actions become part of who you are.

That is the quiet power of compounding.

The greatest changes in life usually happen so gradually that you barely notice them while they are taking place.

Then one day, you look back and realize your thinking has changed.

Your confidence has grown.

Your relationships have become healthier.

Your finances are stronger.

Your peace feels deeper.

None of those changes happened because of one extraordinary day.

They happened because ordinary days were lived with extraordinary faithfulness.

This is why consistency is so valuable.

Consistency keeps showing up when excitement disappears.

Consistency keeps investing when results are still invisible.

Consistency keeps building even when progress feels slow.

Over time, consistency becomes something greater than a habit.

It becomes character.

Do not become discouraged by routines simply because they feel repetitive.

Repetition is often the workshop where excellence is built.

The person you hope to become is not created by occasional moments of inspiration.

They are created by daily decisions repeated with intention.

Protect the habits that move you forward.

Honor the routines that strengthen your life.

Celebrate small victories instead of waiting only for dramatic breakthroughs.

Because every disciplined morning, every wise decision, every healthy response, and every focused hour is another brick in the foundation of your future.

One day, people may admire the life you have built.

They may call your success remarkable.

What they may never see are the thousands of ordinary choices that quietly made it possible.

That is how lasting transformation happens.

Not through one extraordinary moment.

But through ordinary faithfulness practiced consistently until it produces an extraordinary life.

WEALTH LESSON

Repeated intentional behavior compounds into long-term emotional, financial, and personal growth.

AFFIRMATION

"I trust the power of consistency and disciplined daily effort."

TODAY'S POWER MOVE

Repeat one healthy habit today regardless of how small the progress feels emotionally.

DAY 364

Your Growth Will Inspire Other People

POWER QUOTE

"The way you heal and rebuild may become someone else's hope."

REFLECTION

Many people underestimate the influence their life can have on someone else.

They assume their growth only affects them.

Their healing feels personal.

Their discipline feels private.

Their quiet victories seem too ordinary to matter.

But you never fully know who is watching your life.

Someone may be encouraged simply because they see you continue after disappointment.

Someone may find hope because you chose healing instead of bitterness.

Someone may believe change is possible because you refused to let your past define your future.

Influence is rarely created by perfection.

It is created by authenticity.

People connect with honesty more than image.

They are inspired by individuals who admit they struggled but refused to stop growing.

They respect people who acknowledge failure, learn from it, and continue moving forward with greater wisdom.

That kind of life gives others permission to believe they can do the same.

Think about the people who have inspired you.

Most likely, they were not people who lived flawless lives.

They were people who demonstrated resilience.

People who kept rebuilding after setbacks.

People who remained faithful when life became difficult.

People whose character spoke louder than their circumstances.

Their influence did not come from avoiding hardship.

It came from the way they responded to hardship.

Your life has the same potential.

Every healthy boundary you establish teaches others that peace is worth protecting.

Every disciplined financial decision demonstrates that stewardship is possible.

Every act of forgiveness reveals that healing is stronger than resentment.

Every time you continue after disappointment, you become living evidence that setbacks do not have to become permanent defeat.

You may never hear every story your life has impacted.

Someone may remember your encouragement years after you have forgotten the conversation.

A family member may choose healthier habits because they watched your consistency.

A friend may find courage because they witnessed your perseverance.

A future generation may inherit healthier patterns because you decided to break unhealthy cycles today.

Influence often works quietly.

Just as growth happens one decision at a time, impact often spreads one life at a time.

That is why your personal growth is never truly only about you.

As you become healthier, wiser, and more emotionally grounded, you create environments where other people can flourish as well.

Your peace influences your relationships.

Your integrity influences your workplace.

Your emotional maturity influences your family.

Your discipline influences those who are searching for an example worth following.

Continue becoming the person you are meant to be.

Not for recognition.

Not for applause.

But because every step toward healing strengthens both your life and the lives you may one day touch.

Never underestimate the value of your journey.

Your story is not powerful because it is perfect.

It is powerful because it reflects courage.

The courage to keep learning.

To keep healing.

To keep rebuilding.

To keep believing that growth is still possible.

One day, someone may look at your life and find the hope they needed to begin their own transformation.

And that quiet influence will become one of the greatest legacies you leave behind.

Keep growing.

Your journey matters far more than you can see today.

WEALTH LESSON

Personal growth creates positive ripple effects because healthier people often build healthier environments for others too.

AFFIRMATION

"I allow my healing, growth, and discipline to positively impact others."

TODAY'S POWER MOVE

Encourage or inspire someone today through your words, wisdom, or example.

DAY 365

The Life You Desire Is Built Daily

POWER QUOTE

"Success is not a destination. It is a disciplined identity practiced consistently."

REFLECTION

The life you desire will not be created by one extraordinary moment.

It will be built by the ordinary decisions you make every single day.

Every habit you practice.

Every thought you choose to believe.

Every financial decision you make.

Every emotional response you cultivate.

Every commitment you honor.

These moments may seem small when viewed individually.

Together, they become the architecture of your future.

Many people spend their lives waiting for one event that will change everything.

The perfect opportunity.

The perfect relationship.

The perfect job.

The perfect moment to finally become the person they hope to be.

But transformation rarely arrives that way.

It is built quietly through intentional living.

Every time you choose healing over self-destruction, you loosen the grip of old pain.

Every time you choose discipline over excuses, you strengthen your character.

Every time you choose peace over unnecessary chaos, you create space for wisdom to grow.

Every time you choose courage over fear, you remind yourself that your future is greater than your current uncertainty.

These decisions become the foundation beneath every meaningful achievement that follows.

The beautiful truth is that your life is always moving in the direction of your repeated choices.

Not your occasional motivation.

Not your temporary emotions.

Not your intentions alone.

Your repeated choices.

That is why consistency carries so much power.

It quietly transforms habits into character.

Character into identity.

Identity into a life that once seemed impossible.

There will still be difficult seasons.

Moments when progress feels slow.

Times when doubt whispers that your efforts are not making a difference.

When those moments come, remember that the strongest foundations are built long before anyone sees the finished structure.

Every disciplined day is another brick.

Every wise decision is another beam.

Every healed response strengthens the framework.

You are building something far greater than today's circumstances can fully reveal.

As you look back over this journey, recognize how much has already changed.

You have learned lessons that hardship could not take away.

You have developed resilience that comfort alone could never have produced.

You have strengthened your discipline through repetition.

You have become more self-aware through honest reflection.

You have continued rebuilding even when progress felt invisible.

That growth matters.

Not because you have reached perfection.

But because you have refused to stop becoming.

Remember that this journey has never been about becoming flawless.

It has always been about becoming faithful.

Faithful to your values.

Faithful to your healing.

Faithful to your discipline.

Faithful to the future you believe is still possible.

Your story is still unfolding.

There will be new lessons to learn.

New opportunities to embrace.

New challenges to overcome.

New ways to grow into the person you were created to become.

Do not fear those seasons.

Welcome them as opportunities to continue becoming stronger, wiser, and more grounded than before.

This is not the finish line.

It is another beginning.

A reminder that every new day offers another opportunity to choose wisely.

To live intentionally.

To protect your peace.

To strengthen your character.

To build a life that reflects who you are becoming rather than who you once were.

Keep healing.

Keep learning.

Keep growing.

Keep showing up with courage, humility, and discipline.

Because the greatest transformation is not found in one extraordinary achievement.

It is found in the person you become through thousands of ordinary decisions made with extraordinary faithfulness.

One day at a time.

One choice at a time.

One life intentionally built from the inside out.

And if you continue walking that path, you may one day look back with gratitude and realize that the future you once prayed for was quietly being built by the faithful decisions you chose to make every single day.

WEALTH LESSON

Lasting success is built through disciplined identity, emotional maturity, and repeated intentional choices over time.

AFFIRMATION

"I commit to building my future daily through discipline, healing, peace, and intentional growth."

TODAY'S POWER MOVE

Reflect on the person you have become throughout this journey and commit to continuing your growth intentionally moving forward.

CLOSING MESSAGE

This book is not about becoming rich overnight.

It is about becoming someone capable of sustaining greatness.

A wealthy life is built through repeated decisions. Repeated discipline. Repeated healing. Repeated execution.

The strongest people are not always the loudest. They are the most disciplined.

You do not need a new life. You need a reconstructed identity.

And every day you choose discipline over distraction, you move one step closer to freedom.

Success is not a destination. It is a discipline.

— Sashette McPherson Founder of Power Moves Global

FINAL REFLECTION

If you have made it to the end of this book, take a moment to acknowledge something important:

You stayed committed to your growth.

That matters.

Because transformation is not created through one emotional moment.

It is built through repeated:

- reflection,
- discipline,
- healing,
- awareness, and intentional decisions over time.

Throughout this journey, you were reminded that:

- your mindset affects your future,
- your emotional habits affect your financial habits,
- your discipline affects your opportunities,
- and your identity affects the life you ultimately build.

This book was never designed to make you perfect.

It was designed to help you become:

- more intentional,
- more emotionally aware,
- more disciplined,
- more peaceful, and more aligned with the future you desire.

Some pages may have challenged you.

Some pages may have healed you.

Some pages may have confronted patterns you were avoiding emotionally.

But growth often begins where honesty begins.

The goal was never perfection.

The goal was progress.

The goal was rebuilding your identity intentionally enough that your future could eventually become stronger than your fears, past pain, emotional limitations, and survival patterns.

As you continue forward from here, remember this:

You do not need to rebuild your entire life overnight.

Real transformation happens through:

- one disciplined decision,
- one healed response,
- one intentional habit,
- and one courageous choice at a time.

Keep protecting your peace.

Keep strengthening your discipline.

Keep building wealth wisely.

Keep healing intentionally.

Keep believing in the future you are capable of creating.

And most importantly: never stop making power moves.

— Sashette McPherson

ABOUT Sashette McPherson

Sashette McPherson is a financial strategist, speaker, entrepreneur, and the founder of Power Moves Global — a transformational platform focused on helping individuals rebuild their mindset, financial behaviors, emotional discipline, and long-term success.

With a background in finance and strategic analysis, Sashette combines:

- financial education,
- behavioral psychology,
- emotional intelligence,
- discipline coaching,
- and identity transformation, -to help people create healthier relationships with money, success, confidence, and personal growth.

Her work centers around the belief that many people are not only struggling financially — they are struggling with financial identity.

Through speaking, coaching, content creation, and Power Moves Global, she teaches individuals how to:

- shift from survival mode into intentional living,
- rebuild self-worth,
- strengthen discipline,
- heal emotionally,
- and create long-term wealth and peace intentionally.

Sashette is also the creator of:

- The Reset Program,
- Financial Identity Reconstruction™,
- and the Power Moves movement dedicated to helping ambitious individuals build stronger futures emotionally, mentally, and financially.

Her mission is simple:

To help people rebuild their identity so they can redefine their future.

Follow the journey:

Instagram: @therealsashette

Instagram: @powermovesglobal

Website:

Power Moves Global

About Power Moves Global

Power Moves Global is a transformational financial empowerment and personal growth company focused on helping individuals and small businesses build wealth, discipline, confidence, emotional intelligence, and long-term success.

At the center of Power Moves Global is the belief that many people do not simply struggle with money — they struggle with identity, emotional patterns, financial habits, discipline, and mindset.

Through:

coaching,

financial education,

transformational programs,

speaking,

community,

and strategic personal development, Power Moves Global helps people shift from:

survival mode → intentional living,

emotional chaos → emotional discipline,

scarcity thinking → wealth consciousness,

and inconsistency → purposeful execution.

Core areas of focus include:

Financial Identity Reconstruction™

- Wealth mindset development
- Discipline & accountability
- Emotional healing & self-awareness
- Personal growth & confidence
- Entrepreneurship & financial freedom
- Leadership & intentional living

Power Moves Global exists to empower people to:

rebuild their identity,

redefine their wealth,

and create lives rooted in peace, purpose, discipline, and long-term growth.

Learn more at:

Power Moves Global

Podcast: Power Moves Podcast

Instagram: @powermovesglobal

CONNECT WITH POWER MOVES GLOBAL

Website

Power Moves Global

YouTube

Power Moves Global-Media

Instagram

@therealsashette

@powermovesglobal

Programs & Coaching

Financial Identity Audit™

The Reset Program

Power Moves Coaching & Consulting